C++

Jesse Liberty *with*

Vishwajit Aklecha
Steve Haines
Steven Mitchell
Alexander Nickolov
Charles Pace
Meghraj Thakkar
Michael J. Tobler
Donald Xie
Steve Zagieboylo

SAMS

201 West 103rd Street
Indianapolis, Indiana 46290

Unleashed

C++ Unleashed

Copyright © 1999 by Sams

International Standard Book Number: 0-672-31239-5

Library of Congress Catalog Card Number: 97-69859

First Printing: November 1998

00 99 98   4   3   2   1

Printed in the United States of America

Trademarks

Warning and Disclaimer

EXECUTIVE EDITOR
Tracy Dunkelberger

AQUISITIONS EDITOR
Tracy Dunkelberger

DEVELOPMENT EDITOR
Sean Dixon

MANAGING EDITOR
Jodi Jensen

PROJECT EDITOR
Maureen A. McDaniel

COPY EDITOR
Alice Martina-Smith

INDEXER
Rebecca Salerno

PROOFREADER
Mona Brown

TECHNICAL EDITOR
Jay Armstrong
Poney Carpenter
Dan Clamage
Tom Collins
Russ Jacobs
Steven Mitchell
David Thompson

SOFTWARE DEVELOPMENT SPECIALIST
Dan Scherf

TEAM COORDINATOR
Michelle Newcomb

COVER DESIGNER
Aren Howell

INTERIOR DESIGNER
Gary Adair

LAYOUT TECHNICIANS
Ayanna Lacey
Heather Hiatt Miller

Contents at a Glance

Contents

About the Authors

Jesse Liberty is the founder and president of Liberty Associates, Inc. (http://www.libertyassociates.com), where he provides training, consulting, and mentoring in object-oriented software development. Liberty is the author of numerous best-selling books on object-oriented analysis and design and C++; was Distinguished Software Engineer and Architect for AT&T, Xerox, and PBS; and was Vice-President of Technology for Citibank. He lives with his family in the suburbs of Cambridge, Massachusetts. He can be reached at jliberty@libertyassociates.com.

with

Vishwajit Aklecha has worked for many years in the area of object-oriented software development and has a B.S in Mathematics and a M.S. in Computer Science. He is currently employed with Hewlett-Packard's International Software Operation in Bangalore, India. Vishwajit's interests are in distributed computing, frameworks research and development, and in teaching object technology. He is currently writing a book on frameworks and can be reached at vishwajit@technologist.com.

Steve Haines is a Windows Software Engineer at ENGAGE games online, an Internet video game company, where he focuses on the design and implementation of latency-critical Internet and communication-related technologies. He has been immersed in the world of Microsoft development technologies throughout his career, and has contributed his knowledge and experience into realizing the visions of Internet game-playing. He is currently seeking his M.S. in Computer Science, focusing on creative technologies and multimedia, at the University of Southern California. Steve has worked as a technical editor and consultant for both Macmillan Computer Publishing and Addison-Wesley Longman before venturing into the realm of writing. Writing has always been a passion of Steve's, to which he attributes his enthusiasm to his grandmother's extraordinary set of published plays, and hopes to add "lead author" to his resume in the near future.

Steven Mitchell is an electrical engineer, doing work in the areas of transportation and communications. He has developed a number of relational database applications for in-house use, and is currently involved in a project to develop a hardware/software protocol testing program. Steven has worked as lead technical editor on a number of C++ books. He is a registered Professional Engineer and makes his home in Alexandria, VA.

Alexander Nickolov is a software programmer specializing in COM/DCOM development. He has developed Internet-aware client/server applications in C++ throughout his career. Currently, Alexander Nickolov is a software consultant for GlobulCom Consulting and lives in Santa Barbara, California. He can be reached at `agnickolov@geocities.com`.

Charles Pace, also a contributing author to *CORBA Unleashed*, has over 14 years of experience in all kinds of progressive, cutting-edge software development. He has written a vast array of computer programs, from interactive educational games to large enterprise systems. Charles looks forward to enabling developers to deliver applications utilizing the next generation of software technology.

Meghraj Thakkar works as a Technical Specialist at Oracle Corporation. He has an M.S. in Computer Science and a B.S. in Electronic Engineering. He has several industry vendor certifications including Microsoft Certified Systems Engineer (MCSE), Novell Certified ECNE, Lotus Certified Notes Consultant, SCO UNIX ACE, and Oracle Certified Professional (OCP). He has taught several courses at the University of California, Irvine. He has presented two papers at the ECO '98 held in New York City, NY in March 1998. He has co-authored several books such as *Special Edition Using Oracle8*, *Oracle8 Server Unleashed*, and *Oracle Certified Professional—DBA* from Macmillan Computer Publishing. He has developed and presented several times a two-day course, "Supporting Oracle on Windows NT," to internal Oracle employees. Meghraj has been working with various Oracle products for the past seven years. He will be presenting at the Oracle Openworld in Adelaide, Australia in November 1998 and at the UKOUG in Birmingham, UK in December 1998.

Michael J. Tobler is a Senior Technical Specialist with BSI Consulting in Houston, Texas. He has more than 16 years experience working on software development projects, specializing in planning, designing, and developing multitier systems using C++ and Java. He is currently the president of the Houston Java Users Group. Michael is an advocate and practitioner of the Unified Modeling process from Rational and a proponent of patterns and pattern languages. He is a contributing author for *The Waite Group's C++ How-To*. He has also discovered that skydiving is a very addictive sport. Michael can be reached at `mtobler@ibm.net`.

Donald Xie is a Senior System Engineer and a Project Leader for electronic commerce and Internet development for a major automotive and industrial products distributor. He is also a C++ programming class instructor in Ziff-Davis University. Donald lives with his family in Perth, Australia.

Steve Zagieboylo has been in the software industry since 1980, and has been developing software in C++ since 1989. After stints with Lotus Development Corp., AT&T, and a few others in the greater Boston area, he is currently the president of ZagNet, a software consulting company (`http://www.zag.net`). He has taught advanced object-oriented programming in C++ at Harvard Extension School, and he continues to teach online C++ classes through Ziff-Davis University. Feel free to send him an email at `Unleashed@ZAG.net`.

Dedication

This book is dedicated to Robin, Rachel, and Stacey Liberty.

Acknowledgments

As is often the case, this book owes its existence, and certainly its quality, to a number of people whose names do not appear on the cover. Among them is one of the most extraordinary editors it has been my pleasure to work with: Tracy Dunkelberger of Macmillan Computer Publishing. She has restored my faith in the commitment of Sams Publishing to creating high-quality books of immediate use to programmers.

I want also to thank Sean Dixon and Maureen McDaniel of Macmillan who worked so diligently on this very difficult book, and who made it better than it was when submitted. Errors and confusion are my responsibility, but the quality of the book is to their credit and I can thank only them. I want also to thank Brad Jones and Chris Denny, who gave me my start with *Sams Teach Yourself C++ in 21 Days*, and who have fostered and protected my relationship with Sams despite my repeated tantrums.

I must also thank and acknowledge John Franklin and David and Adam Maclean of Wrox Publishing, and Robert Martin and the editors of *C++ Report*—all of whom have both nurtured my writing and given me permission to borrow liberally from past writings.

My wife Stacey and daughters Robin and Rachel continue to tolerate my insane working hours and provided the kind of support and encouragement required to see an effort like this through. I remain very grateful.

Tell Us What You Think!

As the reader of this book, *you* are our most important critic and commentator. We value your opinion and want to know what we're doing right, what we could do better, what areas you'd like to see us publish in, and any other words of wisdom you're willing to pass our way.

As the Executive Editor for the Advanced Programming and Distributed Architectures team at Macmillan Computer Publishing, I welcome your comments. You can fax, email, or write me directly to let me know what you did or didn't like about this book—as well as what we can do to make our books stronger.

Please note that I cannot help you with technical problems related to the topic of this book, and that due to the high volume of mail I receive, I might not be able to reply to every message.

When you write, please be sure to include this book's title and author, as well as your name and phone or fax number. I will carefully review your comments and share them with the author and editors who worked on the book.

Fax: 317-817-7070

Email: programming@mcp.com

Mail: Executive Editor
            Advanced Programming and Distributed Architectures
            Macmillan Computer Publishing
            201 West 103rd Street
            Indianapolis, IN 46290 USA

Introduction

C++ Unleashed is a survey of advanced topics in C++. The goal of this book is to provide a focused examination of each of these topics, covering the essential information you need to fully exploit the power of the C++ language.

Many of the topics in this book deserve a book in their own right. Because it is not possible, given the available space, to cover every aspect of some of these subjects, the chapters in this book explain only what is most necessary for you to gain a working understanding of the technologies they describe. Often, you will find that the information provided here is sufficient for your immediate needs. Even if that is not always the case, these chapters provide a useful foundation in these advanced issues that will allow you to quickly gain a more comprehensive understanding of them with further study.

What Is Covered

Part I, "Object-Oriented Programming"

We begin with a comprehensive introduction to object-oriented analysis and design. It is my view that C++ is best used to implement a well-designed object-oriented model, rather than to bang out quick-and-dirty code. The significant advantages of object-oriented programming can only be realized once you have done the necessary analysis and put the time in to design a well-conceived product. Chapter 1 will get you started on the difficult but rewarding path of object modeling. Along the way, I'll teach you the fundamentals of the Unified Modeling Language (UML)—the emerging industry standard.

In Chapter 2, you'll learn how to implement your object model in C++. This mapping, from design model to code, is essential if you want to use C++ to its fullest potential as an object-oriented programming language.

Chapter 3 continues this theme, focusing on how C++ supports inheritance and polymorphism. This detailed examination of the intricacies of polymorphism will lay the groundwork for creating high-quality commercial C++ applications.

Part II, "Implementation Issues"

In Chapter 4, we discuss advanced memory management techniques. We'll consider advanced issues with pointers and references and we'll discuss auto pointers and smart pointers. In Chapter 5, we'll discuss application frameworks and, within that context, we'll consider such advanced topics as multi-threading.

Also in Part II, we'll offer an in-depth introduction to the Standard Template Library. Chapter 6 focuses on the STL container classes and Chapter 7 follows with a discussion of STL iterators and algorithms. In Chapter 8, we move on to one of the newest features of ANSI C++—namespaces—and we consider how namespaces can help you avoid name clashes as you use third-party libraries.

In Chapter 9, we focus on runtime type identification and the new ANSI-style casting operators. Finally, in Chapter 10, we'll consider how you tune your application performance to optimize for speed or code size.

Part III, "Manipulating Data"

Part III opens Chapter 11—a discussion of advanced techniques using recursion. In Chapter 12, we discuss sorting algorithms, and in Chapter 13, we discuss object-oriented searching. This discussion is rounded out in Chapter 14 with a consideration of hashing and parsing techniques.

Part IV, "Object Persistence and Encryption"

Chapter 15 considers object persistence and demonstrates how to write your objects to disk and how to manage memory with persistent objects. Chapter 16 returns to the application frameworks and considers ODBC and MFC Database connections. Chapter 17 extends this discussion to consider object persistence using relational databases, and Chapter 18 discusses object-oriented databases. Finally, in Chapter 19, we discuss encryption including Diffie, Hellerman, Hoffman, and Caesar ciphers; public encryption and popular encryption approaches such as Pretty Good Privacy; and DES and Clipper.

Part V, "Distributed Computing Topics"

Chapter 20 considers CORBA, and Chapter 21 provides an in-depth introduction to COM. Finally, Chapter 22 examines the differences between Java and C++ and considers whether these differences are significant.

What You Need To Know Already

C++ Unleashed assumes you have read at least one good primer (such as *Sams Teach Yourself C++ in 21 Days*) and/or have been programming in C++ for at least six months. More experienced programmers will find detail on subjects they may not have considered before; less experienced programmers will find a host of new ideas, information, and best practices.

What Software You Need

All of the programs in this book can be created and run with Microsoft Visual C++ or any ANSI-compliant 32-bit compiler. While the example programs in the chapters on the MFC will only compile on a Windows machine (Windows 95 or Windows NT), just about all the other programs in the book will compile on any operating system.

You need no other software—just an editor, compiler, and linker. If you use an integrated development environment such as Visual C++, you are all set. While we've endeavored to test all the programs in this book on a number of compilers, we do know that it all works in Microsoft Visual C++, and thus we recommend that compiler if you don't already have another.

How To Read This Book

Think of this book as a series of "white papers" on advanced topics in C++. Feel free to jump around among the chapters, dipping into those areas which intrigue you. Again, remember that we made no attempt to be "comprehensive" on each topic; rather, our goal was to provide detailed introductions to these advanced topics. Each of these topics is the subject of one or more advanced books. Our goal here is to provide the *essential* information necessary for you to either start your further study or to obtain a quick and useful overview.

One good way to read this book is as Humpty Dumpty advised: begin at the beginning, proceed to the end, and then stop. As an alternative, you might want to read the first three chapters and then pick and choose among those topics which are of most interest to you.

In any case, enjoy and please let us know how we did. You can reach me, Jesse Liberty, on the Internet at jliberty@libertyassociates.com. There is support for the book at the Sams Web site (http://samspublishing.com) as well as at my own Web site (http://www.libertyassociates.com)—click the books and resources link.

Object-Oriented Programming

PART

I

IN THIS PART

Object-Oriented Analysis and Design

CHAPTER 1

C++ was created as a bridge between \object-oriented programming and C, the world's most popular programming language for commercial software development. The goal was to provide object-oriented design to a fast, commercial software development platform.

C was developed as a middle ground between high-level business applications languages such as COBOL and the pedal-to-the-metal, high-performance, but difficult-to-use Assembler language. C was to enforce "structured" programming, in which problems were "decomposed" into smaller units of repeatable activities called *procedures*.

The programs we're writing at the end of the 1990s are far more complex than those written at the beginning of the decade. Programs created in procedural languages tend to be difficult to manage, hard to maintain, and impossible to extend. Graphical user interfaces, the Internet, digital telephony, and a host of new technologies have dramatically increased the complexity of our projects at the very same time that consumer expectations for the quality of the user interface are rising.

In the face of this increasing complexity, developers took a long hard look at the state of the industry. What they found was disheartening, at best. Software was late, broken, defective, bug ridden, unreliable, and expensive. Projects routinely ran over budget and were delivered late to market. The cost of maintaining and building on these projects was prohibitive, and a tremendous amount of money was being wasted.

Object-oriented software development offers a path out of the abyss. Object-oriented programming languages build a strong link between the data structures and the methods that manipulate that data. More important, in object-oriented programming, you no longer think about data structures and manipulating functions; you think instead about objects. Things.

The world is populated by things: cars, dogs, trees, clouds, flowers. Things. Each *thing* has characteristics (fast, friendly, brown, puffy, pretty). Most things have behavior (move, bark, grow, rain, wilt). We don't think about a dog's data and how we might manipulate it—we think about a dog as a thing in the world, what it is like and what it does.

Building Models

If we are to manage complexity, we must create a model of the universe. The goal of the model is to create a meaningful abstraction of the real world. Such an abstraction should be simpler than the real world but should also accurately reflect the real world so that we can use the model to predict the behavior of things in the real world.

A child's globe is a classic model. The model isn't the thing itself; we would never confuse a child's globe with the Earth, but one maps the other well enough that we can learn about the Earth by studying the globe.

There are, of course, significant simplifications. My daughter's globe never has rain, floods, globe-quakes and so forth, but I can use her globe to predict how long it will take me to fly from my home to Indianapolis should I ever need to come in and explain myself to the Sams senior management when they ask me why my manuscript was late ("You see, I was doing great, but then I got lost in a metaphor and it took me hours to get out").

A model that is not simpler than the thing being modeled is not much use. There is a Steven Wright joke about just such a thing: "I have a map on which one inch equals one inch. I live at E5."

Object-oriented software design is about building good models. It consists of two significant pieces: a modeling language and a process.

Software Design: The Modeling Language

The *modeling language* is the least important aspect of object-oriented analysis and design; unfortunately, it tends to get the most attention. A modeling language is nothing more than a convention for how we'll *draw* our model on paper. We can easily decide that we'll draw our classes as triangles, and that we'll draw the inheritance relationship as a dotted line. If so, we might model a geranium as shown in Figure 1.1.

FIGURE 1.1.

Generalization/
specialization.

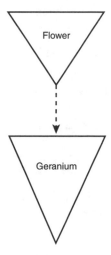

In the figure, you see that a Geranium is a special kind of Flower. If you and I agree to draw our inheritance (generalization/specialization) diagrams like this, we'll understand each other perfectly. Over time, we'll probably want to model lots of complex relationships, and so we'll develop our own complicated set of diagramming conventions and rules.

Of course, we'll need to explain our conventions to everyone else with whom we work, and each new employee or collaborator will have to learn our convention. We may interact with other companies that have their own conventions, and we'll need to allow time to negotiate a common convention and to compensate for the inevitable misunderstandings.

It would be more convenient if everyone in the industry agreed on a common modeling language. (For that matter, it would be convenient if everyone in the world agreed on a spoken language, but one thing at a time.) The *lingua franca* of software development is UML—The Unified Modeling Language. The job of the UML is to answer questions like, "How do we draw an inheritance relationship?" The geranium drawing shown in Figure 1.1 would be drawn as shown in Figure 1.2 in UML.

FIGURE 1.2.

UML drawing of specialization.

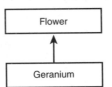

In UML, classes are drawn as rectangles, and inheritance is drawn as a line with an arrowhead. Interestingly, the arrowhead points from the more specialized class to the more general class. The direction of the arrow is counter-intuitive for most folks, but it doesn't matter much; once we all agree, the system works just fine.

The details of the UML are rather straightforward. The diagrams are not hard to use or understand, and I'll explain them as we go along in this chapter and throughout the book, rather than trying to teach the UML out of context. Although it is possible to write a whole book on the UML, the truth is that 90 percent of the time, you use only a small subset of the UML notation, and that subset is easily learned.

Software Design: The Process

The *process* of object-oriented analysis and design is far more complex and far more important than the modeling language. So of course, it is what you hear far less about.

That is because the debate about modeling languages is pretty much settled; as an industry, we've decided to use the UML. The debate about process rages on.

A *methodologist* is someone who develops or studies one or more methods. Typically, methodologists develop and publish their own methods. A *method* is a modeling language and a process. Three of the leading methodologists and their methods are Grady Booch, who developed the Booch method, Ivar Jacobson, who developed object-oriented software engineering, and James Rumbaugh, who developed Object Modeling Technology (OMT). These three men have joined together to create *Objectory*, a method and a commercial product from Rational Software, Inc. All three men are employed at Rational Software, where they are affectionately known as the *Three Amigos*.

This chapter loosely follows *Objectory*. I won't follow it rigidly because I don't believe in slavish adherence to academic theory—I'm much more interested in shipping product than in adhering to a method. Other methods have something to offer, and I tend to be eclectic, picking up bits and pieces as I go along and stitching them together into a workable framework.

The process of software design is *iterative*. That means that as we develop software, we go through the entire process repeatedly as we strive for enhanced understanding of the requirements. The design directs the implementation, but the details uncovered during implementation feed back into the design. Most important, we do not try to develop any sizable project in a single, orderly, straight line; rather, we iterate over pieces of the project, constantly improving our design and refining our implementation.

Iterative development can be distinguished from waterfall development. In waterfall development, the output from one stage becomes the input to the next, and there is no going back (see Figure 1.3). In a waterfall development process, the requirements are detailed, and the clients sign off ("Yes, this is what I want"); the requirements are then passed on to the designer, set in stone. The designer creates the design (and a wonder to behold it is) and passes it off to the programmer who implements the design. The programmer, in turn, hands the code to a QA person who tests the code and then releases it to the customer. Great in theory, disaster in practice.

FIGURE 1.3.

The waterfall method.

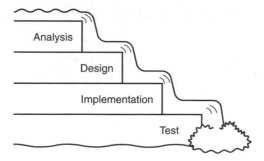

In iterative design, the visionary comes up with a concept and then we begin to work on fleshing out the requirements. As we examine the details, the vision may grow and evolve. When we have a good start on the requirements, we begin the design, knowing full well that the questions that arise during design may cause modifications back in the requirements. As we work on design, we begin prototyping and then implementing the product. The issues that arise in development feed back into design, and may even influence our understanding of the requirements. Most important, we design and implement only pieces of the full product, iterating over the design and implementation phases repeatedly.

Although the steps of the process are repeated iteratively, it is nearly impossible to describe them in such a cyclical manner. Therefore, I will describe them in sequence: vision, analysis, design, implementation, testing, rollout. Don't misunderstand me—in reality, we run through each of these steps many times during the course of the development of a single product. The iterative design process is just hard to present and understand if we cycle through each step; so I'll describe them one after the other.

Here are the steps of the iterative design process:

1. Conceptualization
2. Analysis
3. Design
4. Implementation
5. Testing
6. Rollout

Conceptualization is the "vision thing." It is the single sentence that describes the great idea. Analysis is the process of understanding the requirements. Design is the process of creating the model of your classes, from which you will generate your code. Implementation is writing it in C++; testing is making sure that you did it right, and rollout is getting it to your customers. Piece of cake. All the rest is details.

CONTROVERSIES

There are endless controversies about what happens in each stage of the iterative design process, and even about what you name those stages. Here's a secret: *it doesn't matter*. The essential steps are the same in just about every process: Find out what you need to build, design a solution, and implement that design.

Although the newsgroups and object-technology mailing lists thrive on splitting hairs, the essentials of object-oriented analysis and design are fairly straightforward. In this chapter, I'll lay out a practical approach to the process as the bedrock on which you can build the architecture of your application. In the rest of the book, we'll focus on the details of implementing your design in C++.

The goal of all this work is to produce code that meets the stated requirements and that is reliable, extensible, and maintainable. Most important, the goal is to produce high-quality code on time and on budget.

The Vision

All great software starts with a vision. One individual has an insight into a product he or she thinks would be good to build. Rarely do committees create compelling visions. The very first phase of object-oriented analysis and design is to capture this vision in a single sentence (or at most, a short paragraph). The vision becomes the guiding principal of development, and the team that comes together to implement the vision ought to refer back to it—and update it if necessary—as it goes forward.

Even if the vision statement comes out of a committee in the marketing department, one person should be designated as the "visionary." It is his or her job to be the keeper of the sacred light. As you progress, the requirements will evolve. Scheduling and time-to-market demands may modify what you try to accomplish in the first iteration of the program, but the visionary must keep an eye on the essential idea, to ensure that whatever is produced reflects the core vision with high fidelity. It is this ruthless dedication, this passionate commitment, that sees the project through to completion. If you lose sight of the vision, your product is doomed.

Requirements Analysis

The conceptualization phase, in which the vision is articulated, is very brief. It may be no longer than a flash of insight followed by the time it takes to write down what the visionary has in mind. Often, as the object-oriented expert, you join the project after the vision is already articulated.

Some companies confuse the vision statement with the requirements. A strong vision is necessary, but it is not sufficient. To move on to analysis, you must understand how the product will be used, and how it must perform. The goal of the analysis phase is to articulate and capture these requirements. The outcome of the Analysis phase is the production of a requirements document. The first section in the requirements document is the use case analysis.

Use Cases

The driving force in analysis, design, and implementation is the use cases. A *use case* is nothing more than a high-level description of how the product will be used. Use cases drive not only the analysis, they drive the design, they help you find the classes, and they are especially important in testing the product.

Creating a robust and comprehensive set of use cases may be the single most important task in analysis. It is here that you depend most heavily on your domain experts; the domain experts have the most information about the business requirements you are trying to capture.

Use cases pay little attention to user interface, and they pay no attention to the internals of the system you are building. Any system or person who interacts with the system is called an *actor*.

To summarize, here are some definitions:

- **Use case:** A description of how the software will be used.
- **Domain experts:** People with expertise in the *domain* (area) of business for which you are creating the product.
- **Actor:** Any person or system that interacts with the system you are developing.

A use case is a description of the interaction between an actor and the system itself. For purposes of use-case analysis, the system is treated as a "black box." An actor "sends a message" to the system, and something happens: Information is returned, the state of the system is changed, the spaceship changes direction, whatever.

Identify the Actors

It is important to note that not all actors are people. Systems that interact with the system you are building are also actors. Thus, if we were building an automated teller machine, the customer and the bank clerk can both be actors—as can the mortgage-tracking system. The essential characteristics of actors are as follows:

- They are external to the system
- They interact with the system

Getting started is often the hardest part of use-case analysis. Often, the best way to get going is with a "brainstorming" session. Simply write down the list of people and systems that will interact with your new system. Remember that when we discuss *people*, we really mean *roles*—the bank clerk, the manager, the customer, and so forth. One person can have more than one role.

For the ATM example just mentioned, we can expect such a list to include the following roles:

- The customer
- The bank personnel
- A back-office system
- The person who fills the ATM with money and supplies

There is no need to go beyond the obvious list at first. Generating even three or four actors may be enough to get you started on generating use cases. Each of these actors interacts with the system in different ways. We'll want to capture these interactions in our use cases.

Determine the First Use Cases

Let's start with the customer role. We might brainstorm the following use cases for a *customer*:

- Customer checks his or her balances
- Customer deposits money to his or her account
- Customer withdraws money from his or her account
- Customer transfers money between accounts
- Customer opens an account
- Customer closes an account

Should we distinguish between "Customer deposits money in his or her checking account" and "Customer deposits money in his or her savings account," or should we combine these actions (as we did in the preceding list) into "Customer deposits money to his or her account?" The answer to this question lies in whether this distinction is meaningful in the domain.

To determine whether these actions are one use case or two, you must ask whether the *mechanisms* are different (does the customer do something significantly different with these deposits) and whether the *outcomes* are different (does the system reply in a different way). The answer to both questions for the deposit issue is "no": The customer deposits money to either account in essentially the same way, and the outcome is pretty much the same; the ATM responds by incrementing the balance in the appropriate account.

Given that the actor and the system behave and respond more or less identically, regardless of whether the deposit is made to the checking or the savings account, these two use cases are actually a single use case. Later, when we flesh out use-case scenarios, we can try the two variations to see whether they make any difference at all.

As you think about each actor, you may discover additional use cases by asking these questions:

- Why is the actor using this system?

  The customer is using the system to get cash, to make a deposit, or to check an account balance.

- What outcome does the actor want from each request?

  Add cash to an account or get cash to make a purchase.

- What happened to cause the actor to use this system now?

  He or she may recently have been paid or may be on the way to make a purchase.

- What must the actor do to use the system?

  Put an ATM card into the slot in the machine.

  Aha! We need a use case for the customer logging in to the system.

- What information must the actor provide to the system?

  Enter a Personal ID number.

  Aha! We need use cases for obtaining and editing the Personal ID number.

- What information does the actor hope to get from the system?

  Balances, and so on.

You can often can find additional use cases by focusing on the attributes of the objects in the domain. The customer has a name, a PIN, and an account number; do we have use cases to manage these objects? An account has an account number, a balance, and a transaction history; have we captured these elements in the use cases?

Once we've explored the customer use cases in detail, the next step in fleshing out the list of use cases is to develop the use cases for each of the other actors. The following list shows a reasonable first set of use cases for the ATM example:

- Customer checks his or her balances
- Customer deposits money to his or her account
- Customer withdraws money from his or her account
- Customer transfers money between accounts
- Customer opens an account
- Customer closes an account
- Customer logs into his or her account

- Customer checks recent transactions
- Bank clerk logs into special management account
- Bank clerk makes an adjustment to a customer's account
- A back-office system updates a user's account based on external activity
- Changes in a user's account are reflected in a back-office system
- The ATM signals it is out of cash to dispense
- The bank technician fills the ATM with cash and supplies

Create the Domain Model

Once you have a first cut at your use cases, you can begin to flesh out your requirements document with a detailed domain model. The *domain model* is a document that captures all you know about the domain (the field of business you are working in). As part of your domain model, you create domain objects that describe all the objects mentioned in your use cases. So far, the ATM example includes these objects: customer, bank personnel, back-office systems, checking account, savings account, and so forth.

For each of these domain objects, we want to capture such essential data as the name of the object (for example, customer, account, and so on), whether or not the object is an actor, the object's principal attributes and behavior, and so forth. Many modeling tools support capturing this information in "class" descriptions. Figure 1.4 shows how this information is captured with Rational Rose.

FIGURE 1.4.

Rational Rose.

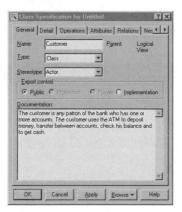

It is important to realize that what we are describing here are *not* design objects, but rather objects in the domain. This is documentation of how the world works, not documentation of how our system will work.

We can diagram the relationship among the objects in the domain of the ATM example using the UML—with exactly the same diagramming conventions we'll use later to describe the relationships among classes in the domain. This is one of the great strengths of the UML: We can use the same tools at every stage of the project.

For example, we can capture the fact that checking accounts and savings accounts are both specializations of the more general concept of a bank account by using the UML conventions for classes and generalization relationships, as shown in Figure 1.5.

FIGURE 1.5.

Specialization.

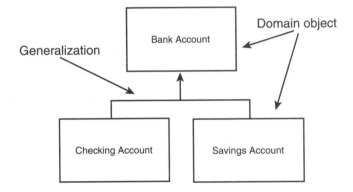

In the diagram in Figure 1.5, the boxes represent the various domain objects, and the line with an arrowhead indicates generalization. The UML specifies that this line is drawn from the *specialized* class to the more general "base" class. Thus, both Checking Account and Savings Account point up to Bank Account, indicating that each is a specialized form of Bank Account.

> **NOTE**
>
> Again, it is important to note that what we are showing at this time are relationships among objects in the domain. Later, you may decide to have a `CheckingAccount` object in your design, as well as a `BankAccount` object, and you may implement this relationship using inheritance, but these are design-time decisions. At analysis time, all we are doing is documenting our understanding of these objects in the domain.

The UML is a rich modeling language, and there are any number of relationships you can capture. The principal relationships captured in analysis, however, are generalization (or specialization), containment, and association.

1

Generalization

Generalization is often equated with "inheritance," but there is a sharp and meaningful distinction between the two. Generalization describes the relationship; inheritance is the programming implementation of generalization—it is how we manifest generalization in code.

Generalization implies that the derived object *is a* subtype of the base object. Thus, a checking account *is a* bank account. The relationship is symmetrical: Bank account *generalizes* the common behavior and attributes of checking and savings accounts.

During domain analysis, we seek to capture these relationships *as they exist in the real world.*

Containment

Often, one object is composed of many subobjects. For example, a car is composed of a steering wheel, tires, doors, radio, and so forth. A checking account is composed of a balance, a transaction history, a customer ID, and so on. We say that the checking account *has* these items; containment models the *has a* relationship. The UML illustrates the containment relationship by drawing a line with a diamond from the containing object to the contained object, as shown in Figure 1.6.

FIGURE 1.6.

Containment.

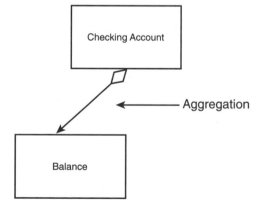

The diagram in Figure 1.6 suggests that the Checking Account "has a" Balance. You can combine these diagrams to show a fairly complex set of relationships (see Figure 1.7).

The diagram in Figure 1.7 states that a Checking Account and a Savings Account are both Bank Accounts, and that all Bank Accounts have both a Balance and a Transaction History.

FIGURE **1.7.**

Object relation-ships.

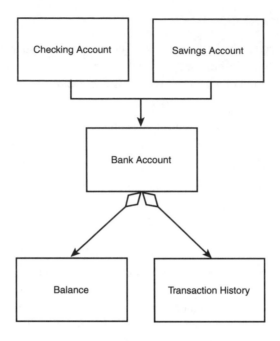

Association

The third relationship commonly captured in the domain analysis is a simple association. An association suggests that two objects know of one another and that the objects interact in some way. This definition will become much more precise in the design stage, but for analysis, we are suggesting only that Object A and Object B interact, but that neither contains the other and neither is a specialization of the other. We show this association in the UML with a simple straight line between the objects, as shown in Figure 1.8.

FIGURE **1.8.**

Association.

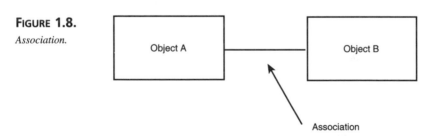

The diagram in Figure 1.8 indicates that Object A associates in some way with Object B.

Establish Scenarios

Now that we have a preliminary set of use cases and the tools with which to diagram the relationship among the objects in the domain, we are ready to formalize the use cases and give them more depth.

Each use case can be broken into a series of scenarios. A *scenario* is a description of a specific set of circumstances that distinguish among the various contingent elements of the use case. For example, the use case "Customer withdraws money from his or her account" might have the following scenarios:

- Customer requests a $300 withdrawal from checking, puts the cash in the cash slot, and the system prints a receipt.

- Customer requests a $300 withdrawal from checking, but his or her balance is $200. Customer is informed that there is not enough cash in the checking account to accomplish the withdrawal.

- Customer requests a $300 withdrawal from checking, but he or she has already withdrawn $100 today and the limit is $300 per day. Customer is informed of the problem, and he or she chooses to withdraw only $200.

- Customer requests a $300 withdrawal from checking, but there is no paper in the receipt roll. Customer is informed of the problem, and he or she chooses to proceed without a receipt.

And so forth. Each scenario explores a variation on the original use case. Often, these variations are exception conditions (not enough money in account, not enough money in machine, and so on). Sometimes, the variations explore nuances of decisions in the use case itself (for example, did the customer want to transfer money before making the withdrawal).

Not every possible scenario must be explored. We are looking for those scenarios that tease out requirements of the system or details of the interaction with the actor.

Establish Guidelines

As part of your methodology, you will want to create guidelines for documenting each scenario. You capture these guidelines in your requirements document. Typically, you'll want to ensure that each scenario includes the following:

- Preconditions—what must be true for the scenario to begin
- Triggers—what causes the scenario to begin
- What actions the actors take
- What results or changes are caused by the system

- What feedback the actors receive
- Whether there are repeating activities, and what causes them to conclude
- A description of the logical flow of the scenario
- What causes the scenario to end
- Postconditions—what must be true when the scenario is complete

In addition, you will want to name each use case, and each scenario. Thus, you might have the following situation:

Use Case:	Customer withdraws cash
Scenario:	Successful cash withdrawal from checking
Preconditions:	Customer is already logged in to system
Trigger:	Customer requests "withdrawal"
Description:	Customer chooses to withdraw cash from a checking account. There is sufficient cash in the account, there is sufficient cash and receipt paper in the ATM, and the network is up and running. The ATM asks the customer to indicate the amount of the withdrawal, and the customer asks for $300, a legal amount to withdraw at this time. The machine dispenses $300 and prints a receipt, and the customer takes the money and the receipt.
PostConditions:	Customer account is debited $300, and customer has $300 cash.

This use case can be shown with the incredibly simple diagram given in Figure 1.9.

FIGURE 1.9.

Use case diagram.

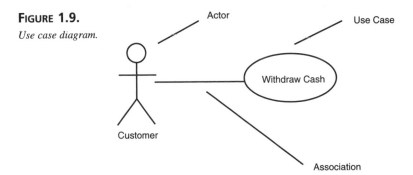

There is little information captured here except a high-level abstraction of an interaction between an actor (the customer) and the system. This diagram becomes slightly more useful when you show the interaction among use cases. I say only *slightly* more useful

because there are only two interactions possible: «uses» and «extends». The «uses» stereotype indicates that one use case is a superset of another. For example, it isn't possible to *withdraw cash* without first *logging on*. We can show this relationship with the diagram shown in Figure 1.10.

FIGURE 1.10.

The «uses» stereo-type.

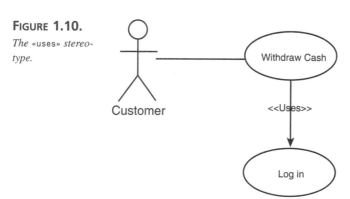

Figure 1.10 indicates that the Withdraw Cash use case "uses" the Log In use case, and thus fully implements Log In as part of Withdraw Cash.

The «extends» use case was intended to indicate conditional relationships and something akin to inheritance, but there is so much confusion in the object-modeling community about the distinction between «uses» and «extends» that many developers have simply set aside «extends», feeling that its meaning is not sufficiently well understood. Personally, I use «uses» when I would otherwise copy and paste the entire use case in place, and I use «extends» when I only *use* the use case under certain definable conditions.

Interaction Diagrams

Although the diagram of the use case itself may be of limited value, there are diagrams you can associate with the use case that can dramatically improve the documentation and understanding of the interactions. For example, we know that the Withdraw Cash scenario represents the interactions among the following domain objects: customer, checking account, and the user interface. We can document this interaction with an interaction diagram, as shown in Figure 1.11.

The interaction diagram in Figure 1.11 captures details of the scenario that may not be evident by reading the text. The objects that are interacting are *domain* objects, and the entire ATM/UI is treated as a single object, with only the specific bank account called out in any detail.

FIGURE 1.11.

UML interaction diagram.

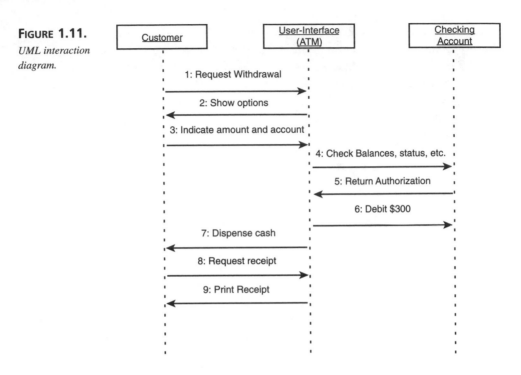

This rather simple ATM example shows only a fanciful set of interactions, but nailing down the specifics of these interactions can be a powerful tool in understanding both the problem domain and the requirements of your new system.

Create Packages

Because you generate many use cases for any problem of significant complexity, the UML allows you to group your use cases in packages.

A *package* is like a directory or a folder—it is a collection of modeling objects (classes, actors, and so forth). To manage the complexity of use cases, you can create packages aggregated by whatever characteristics make sense for your problem. Thus, you can aggregate your use cases by account type (everything affecting checking or savings), by credit or debit, by customer type, or by whatever characteristics make sense to you. More important, a single use case can appear in a number of different packages, allowing you great flexibility of design.

Application Analysis

In addition to creating use cases, the requirements document will capture your customer's assumptions, constraints, and requirements about hardware and operating

systems. Application requirements are your *particular* customer's prerequisites—those things that you would normally determine during design and implementation but that your client has decided for you.

The application requirements are often driven by the need to interface with existing (legacy) systems. In this case, understanding what the existing systems do and how they work is an essential component of your analysis.

Ideally, you'll analyze the problem, design the solution, and then decide which platform and operating system best fits your design. That scenario is as ideal as it is rare. More often, the client has a standing investment in a particular operating system or hardware platform. The client's business plan depends on your software running on the existing system, and you must capture these requirements early and design accordingly.

Systems Analysis

Some software is written to stand alone, interacting only with the end user. Often, however, you will be called on to interface to an existing system. *Systems analysis* is the process of collecting all the details of the systems with which you will interact. Will your new system be a server, providing services to the existing system, or will it be a client? Will you be able to negotiate an interface between the systems, or must you adapt to an existing standard? Will the other system be stable, or must you continually hit a moving target?

These and related questions must be answered in the analysis phase, before you begin to design your new system. In addition, you will want to try to capture the constraints and limitations implicit in interacting with the other systems. Will they slow down the responsiveness of your system? Will they put high demands on your new system, consuming resources and computing time?

Planning Documents

Once you understand what your system must do and how it must behave, it is time to take a first stab at creating a time and budget document. Often, the timeline is dictated, top-down, by the client: "You have 18 months to get this done." Ideally, you'll examine the requirements and estimate the time it will take to design and implement the solution. That is the ideal; the practical reality is that most systems come with an imposed time limit and cost limit, and the real trick is to figure out how much of the required functionality you can build in the allotted time—and at the allotted cost.

Here are a couple guidelines to keep in mind when you are creating a project budget and timeline:

- If you are given a range, the outer number is probably optimistic.
- Liberty's Law states that everything takes longer than you expect—even if you take into account Liberty's Law.

Given these realities, it is imperative that you prioritize your work. *You will not finish*—it is that simple. It is important that, when you run out of time, what you have works and is adequate for a first release. If you are building a bridge and run out of time, if you didn't get a chance to put in the bicycle path, that is too bad; but you can still open the bridge and start collecting tolls. If you run out of time and you're only half way across the river, that is not as good.

An essential thing to know about planning documents is that they are wrong. This early in the process, it is virtually impossible to offer a reliable estimate of the duration of the project. Once you have the requirements, you can get a good handle on how long the design will take, a fair estimate of how long the implementation will take, and a reasonable guesstimate of the testing time. Then you must allow yourself at least 20 to 25 percent "wiggle room," which you can tighten as you move forward and learn more.

> **NOTE**
>
> The inclusion of "wiggle room" in your planning document is not an excuse to avoid planning documents. It is merely a warning not to rely on them too much early on. As the project goes forward, you'll strengthen your understanding of how the system works, and your estimates will become increasingly precise.

Visualizations

The final piece of the requirements document is the visualization. The visualization is just a fancy name for the diagrams, pictures, screen shots, prototypes, and any other visual representations created to help you think through and design the graphical user interface of your product.

For many large projects, you may develop a full prototype to help you (and your customers) understand how the system will behave. On some teams, the prototype becomes the living requirements document; the "real" system is designed to implement the functionality demonstrated in the prototype.

Artifacts

At the end of each phase of analysis and design, you will create a series of documents or "artifacts." Table 1.1 shows some of the artifacts of the analysis phase. These documents are used by the customer to make sure that you understand what the customer needs, by end users to give feedback and guidance to the project, and by the project team to design and implement the code. Many of these documents also provide material crucial both to your documentation team and to Quality Assurance to tell them how the system *ought* to behave.

Table 1.1. Artifacts Created During the Analysis Stage of Project Development

Artifact	Description
Use case report	A document detailing the use cases, scenarios, stereotypes, preconditions, postconditions, and visualizations
Domain analysis	Document and diagrams describing the relationships among the domain objects
Analysis collaboration diagrams	Collaboration diagrams describing interactions among objects in the problem domain
Analysis activity diagrams	Activity diagrams describing interactions among objects in the problem domain
Systems analysis	Report and diagrams describing low-level and hardware systems on which the project will be built
Application analysis document	Report and diagrams describing the customer's requirements specific to this particular project
Operational constraints report	Report describing performance characteristics and constraints imposed by this client
Cost and planning document	Report with Gantt and Pert charts indicating projected scheduling, milestones, and costs

Design

Analysis focuses on understanding the problem domain, whereas design focuses on creating the solution. *Design* is the process of transforming our understanding of the requirements into a model which can be implemented in software. The result of this process is the production of a design document.

The design document is divided into two sections: Class Design and Architectural Mechanisms. The Class Design section, in turn, is divided into static design (which details the various classes and their relationships and characteristics) and dynamic design (which details how the classes interact).

The Architectural Mechanisms section of the design document provides details about how you will implement object persistence, concurrency, a distributed object system, and so forth. The rest of this chapter focuses on the class design aspect of the design document; other chapters in the rest of this book explain how to implement various architecture mechanisms.

What Are the Classes?

As a C++ programmer, you are used to creating classes. Formal design methodology requires you to separate the C++ class from the design class, though they will be intimately related. The C++ class you write in code is the implementation of the class you designed. These are isomorphic: each class in your design will correspond to a class in your code, but don't confuse one for the other. It is certainly possible to implement your design classes in another language, and the *syntax* of the class definitions might be changed.

That said, most of the time we talk about these classes without distinguishing them, because the differences are highly abstract. When you say that in your model your Cat class will have a Meow() method, understand that this means that you will put a Meow() method into your C++ class as well.

You capture the model's classes in UML diagrams and you capture the C++ classes in code which can be compiled. The distinction is meaningful yet subtle.

In any case, the biggest stumbling block for many novices is finding the initial set of classes and understanding what makes a well-designed class. One simplistic technique suggests writing out the use-case scenarios and then creating a class for every noun. Consider the following use-case scenario:

> **Customer** chooses to withdraw **cash** from **checking**. There is sufficient cash in the **account**, sufficient cash and **receipts** in the **ATM**, and the **network** is up and running. The ATM asks the customer to indicate an **amount** for the **withdrawal**, and the customer asks for $300, a legal amount to withdraw at this time. The **machine** dispenses $300 and prints a receipt, and the customer takes the **money** and the receipt.

You might pull out of this scenario the following classes:

- Customer
- Cash
- Checking
- Account
- Receipts

- ATM
- Network
- Amount
- Withdrawal
- Machine
- Money

You might then aggregate the synonyms to create this list, and then create classes for each of these nouns:

- Customer
- Cash (money, amount, withdrawal)
- Checking
- Account
- Receipts
- ATM (machine)
- Network

This is not a bad way to start as far as it goes. You might then go on to diagram the obvious relationships among some of these classes as shown in Figure 1.12.

FIGURE 1.12.

Preliminary classes.

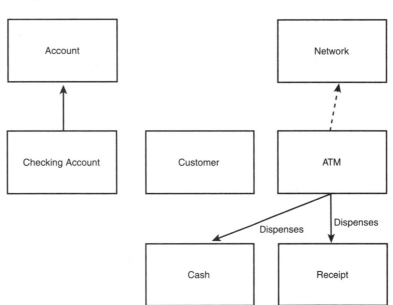

Transformations

What you began to do in the preceding section was not so much to extract the nouns from the scenario as to begin transforming objects from the domain analysis into objects in the design. That is a fine first step. Often, many of the objects in the domain will have *surrogates* in the design. An object is called a surrogate to distinguish between the actual physical receipt dispensed by an ATM and the object in your design that is merely an intellectual abstraction implemented in code.

You will likely find that *most* of the domain objects have an isomorphic representation in the design—that is, there is a one-to-one correspondence between the domain object and the design object. Other times, however, a single domain object is represented in the design by an entire series of design objects. And at times, a series of domain objects may be represented by a single design object.

In Figure 1.11, note that we have already captured the fact that `CheckingAccount` is a specialization of `Account`. We didn't set out to find the generalization relationship, but this one was self-evident, so we captured it. Similarly, we knew, from the domain analysis, that the `ATM` dispenses both `Cash` and `Receipts`, so we captured that information immediately in the design.

The relationship between `Customer` and `CheckingAccount` is less obvious. We know that there is such a relationship, but the details are not obvious, so we hold off.

Other Transformations

Once you have transformed the domain objects, you can begin to look for other useful design-time objects. A good starting place is with interfaces. Each interface between your new system and any existing (legacy) systems should be encapsulated in an interface class. If you will interact with a database of any type, this is also a good candidate for an interface class.

These interface classes offer encapsulation of the interface protocol and thus shield your code from changes in the other system. Interface classes allow you to change your own design, or to accommodate changes in the design of other systems, without breaking the rest of the code. As long as the two systems continue to support the agreed-on interface, they can move independently of one another.

Data Manipulation

Similarly, you will create classes for data manipulation. If you have to transform data from one format into another format (for example, from Fahrenheit to Celsius, or from English to Metric), you may want to encapsulate these manipulations behind a data manipulation class. You can use this technique when messaging data into required

formats for other systems or for transmission over the Internet—in short, any time you must manipulate data into a specified format, you will encapsulate the protocol behind a data manipulation class.

Views

Every "view" or "report" your system generates (or, if you generate many reports, every set of reports) is a candidate for a class. The rules behind the report—both how the information is gathered and how it is to be displayed—can be productively encapsulated inside a view class.

Devices

If your system interacts with or manipulates devices (such as printers, modems, scanners, and so forth), the specifics of the device protocol ought to be encapsulated in a class. Again, by creating classes for the interface to the device, you can plug in new devices with new protocols and not break any of the rest of your code; just create a new interface class that supports the same interface (or a derived interface), and off you go.

Static Model

Once you have established your preliminary set of classes, it is time to begin modeling their relationships and interactions. For purposes of clarity, this chapter first explains the static model and then explains the dynamic model. In the actual design process, you will move freely between the static and dynamic model, filling in details of both—and, in fact, adding new classes and sketching them in as you go.

The static model focuses on three areas of concern: responsibilities, attributes, and relationships. The most important of these—and the one you focus on first—is the set of responsibilities for each class. The most important guiding principal is this: *Each class should be responsible for one thing*.

That is not to say that each class has only one method. Far from it; many classes will have dozens of methods. But all these methods must be coherent and cohesive; that is, they must all relate to one another and contribute to the class's ability to accomplish a single area of responsibility.

In a well-designed system, each object is an instance of a well-defined and well-understood class that is responsible for one area of concern. Classes typically delegate extraneous responsibilities to other, related classes. By creating classes that have only a single area of concern, you promote the creation of highly maintainable code.

To get a handle on the responsibilities of your classes, you may find it beneficial to begin your design work with the use of CRC cards.

CRC Cards

CRC stands for Class, Responsibility, and Collaboration. A CRC card is nothing more than a 4x6 index card. This simple, low-tech device allows you to work with other people in understanding the primary responsibilities of your initial set of classes. You assemble a stack of blank 4x6 index cards and meet around a conference table for a series of CRC card sessions.

How to Conduct a CRC Session

Each CRC session should be attended, ideally, by a group of three to six people; any more becomes unwieldy. You should have a *facilitator*, whose job it is to keep the session on track and to help the participants capture what they learn. There should be at least one senior software architect, ideally someone with significant experience in object-oriented analysis and design. In addition, you will want to include at least one or two "domain experts" who understand the system requirements and who can provide expert advice in how things ought to work.

The most essential ingredient in a CRC session is the conspicuous absence of managers. This is a creative, free-wheeling session that must be unencumbered by the need to impress one's boss. The goal here is to explore, to take risks, to tease out the responsibilities of the classes and to understand how they might interact with one another.

You begin the CRC session by assembling your group around a conference table, with a small stack of 4x6 index cards. At the top of each CRC card you will write the name of a single class. Draw a line down the center of the card and write *Responsibilities* on the left and *Collaborations* on the right.

Begin by filling out cards for the most important classes you've identified. For each card, write a one-sentence or two-sentence definition on the back. You may also capture what other class this class specializes if that is obvious at the time you're working with the CRC card. Just write *Superclass:* below the class name and fill in the name of the class this class derives from.

Focus on Responsibilities

The point of the CRC session is to identify the *responsibilities* of each class. Pay little attention to the attributes, capturing only the most essential and obvious attributes as you go. The important work is to identify the responsibilities. If, in fulfilling a responsibility, the class must delegate work to another class, you capture that information under *collaborations*.

As you progress, keep an eye on your list of responsibilities. If you run out of room on your 4x6 card, it may make sense to wonder whether you're asking this class to do too much. Remember, each class should be responsible for one general area of work, and the various responsibilities listed should be cohesive and coherent—that is, they should work together to accomplish the overall responsibility of the class.

At this point, you do *not* want to focus on relationships, nor do you want to worry about the class interface or which methods will be public and which will be private. The focus is only on understanding what each class *does*.

Anthropomorphic and Use-Case Driven

The key feature of CRC cards is to make them anthropomorphic—that is, you attribute human-like qualities to each class. Here's how it works: After you have a preliminary set of classes, return to your CRC scenarios. Divide the cards around the table arbitrarily, and walk through the scenario together. For example, let's return to the following scenario:

> Customer chooses to withdraw cash from checking. There is sufficient cash in the account, sufficient cash and receipts in the ATM, and the network is up and running. The ATM asks the customer to indicate an amount for the withdrawal, and the customer asks for $300, a legal amount to withdraw at this time. The machine dispenses $300 and prints a receipt, and the customer takes the money and the receipt.

Assume we have five participants in our CRC session: Amy, the facilitator and object-oriented designer; Barry, the lead programmer; Charlie, the client; Dorris, the domain expert; and Ed, a programmer.

Amy holds up a CRC card representing `CheckingAccount` and says "I tell the customer how much money is available. He asks me to give him $300. I send a message to the dispenser telling him to give out $300 cash." Barry holds up his card and says "I'm the dispenser; I spit out $300 and send Amy a message telling her to decrement her balance by $300. Who do I tell that the machine now has $300 less? Do I keep track of that?" Charlie says, "I think we need an object to keep track of cash in the machine." Ed says, "No, the dispenser should know how much cash it has; that's part of being a dispenser." Amy disagrees: "No, someone has to coordinate the dispensing of cash. The dispenser needs to know if there is cash available and if the customer has enough in the account, and it has to count out the money and know when to close the drawer. It should delegate responsibility for keeping track of cash on hand; some kind of internal account. Whoever knows about cash on hand can also notify the back office when it is time to be refilled. Otherwise, that's asking the dispenser to do too much."

The discussion continues. By holding up cards and interacting with one another, the requirements and opportunities to delegate are teased out; each class comes alive, and its responsibilities are clarified. When the group becomes bogged down in design questions, the facilitator can make a decision and help the group move on.

Limitations of CRC Cards

Although CRC cards can be a powerful tool for getting started with design, they have inherent limitations. The first problem is that they don't scale well. In a very complex project, you can be overwhelmed with CRC cards; just keeping track of them all can be difficult.

CRC cards also don't capture the interrelationship among classes. Although it is true that collaborations are noted, the nature of the collaboration is not modeled well. Looking at the CRC cards, you can't tell whether classes aggregate one another, who creates whom, and so forth. CRC cards also don't capture attributes, so it is difficult to go from CRC cards to code. Most important, CRC cards are static; although you can act out the interactions among the classes, the CRC cards themselves do not capture this information.

In short, CRC cards are a good start, but you need to move the classes into the UML if you are to build a robust and complete model of your design. Although the transition *into* the UML is not terribly difficult, it is a one-way street. Once you move your classes into UML diagrams, there is no turning back; you set aside the CRC cards and don't come back to them. It is simply too difficult to keep the two models synchronized with one another.

Transforming CRC Cards to UML

Each CRC card can be translated directly into a class modeled with the UML. Responsibilities are translated into class methods, and whatever attributes you have captured are added as well. The class definition from the back of the card is put into the class documentation. Figure 1.13 shows the relationship between the CheckingAccount CRC card and the UML class created from that card.

Class: CheckingAccount

SuperClass: Account

Responsibilities:

> Track current balance
>
> Accept deposits and transfers in
>
> Write checks
>
> Transfer cash out
>
> Keep current day's ATM withdrawal balance

Collaborations:

> Other accounts
>
> Back-office systems
>
> Cash dispenser

FIGURE 1.13.
CRC card.

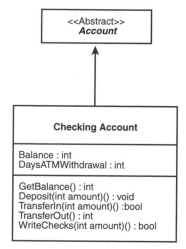

Class Relationships

After the classes are in the UML, you can begin to turn your attention to the relationships among the various classes. The principal relationships you'll model are these:

- Generalization
- Association
- Aggregation
- Composition

The Generalization relationship is implemented in C++ through public inheritance. From a design perspective, however, we focus less on the mechanism and more on the semantics: What implies.

We examined the Generalization relationship in the analysis phase, but now we turn our attention not just to the objects in the domain, but also to the objects in our design. Our efforts now are to "factor out" common functionality in related classes into base classes that can encapsulate the shared responsibilities.

When you "factor out" common functionality, you move that functionality out of the specialized classes and up into the more general class. Thus, if I notice that both my checking and my savings account need methods for transferring money in and out, I'll move the `TransferFunds()` method up into the account base class. The more you factor out of the derived classes, the more polymorphic your design will be.

One of the capabilities available in C++, which is not available in Java, is *multiple inheritance* (although Java has a similar, if limited, capability with its multiple *interfaces*).

Multiple inheritance allows a class to inherit from more than one base class, bringing in the members and methods of two or more classes.

Experience has shown that you should use multiple inheritance judiciously because it can complicate both your design and the implementation. Many problems initially solved with multiple inheritance are today solved using aggregation. That said, multiple inheritance is a powerful tool, and your design may require that a single class specializes the behavior of two or more other   classes.

Multiple Inheritance Versus Containment

Is an object the sum of its parts? Does it make sense to model a Car object as a specialization of SteeringWheel, Door, and Tire, as shown in Figure 1.14?

FIGURE 1.14.

False inheritance.

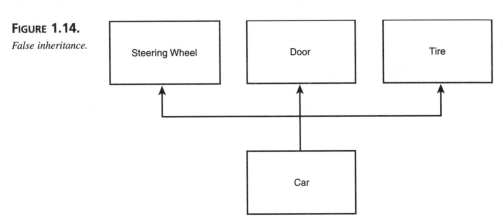

It is important to come back to the fundamentals: Public inheritance should always model generalization. The common expression for this is that inheritance should model *is-a* relationships. If you want to model the has-a relationship (for example, a car *has-a* steering wheel), you do so with aggregation, as shown in Figure 1.15.

The diagram in Figure 1.15 indicates that a car has a steering wheel, four wheels, and 2–5 doors. This is a more accurate model of the relationship between a car and its parts. Notice that the diamond in the diagram is not filled in; this is so because we are modeling this relationship as an aggregation, not as a composition. Composition implies control for the lifetime of the object. Although the car *has* tires and a door, the tires and door can exist before they are part of the car and can continue to exist after they are no longer part of the car.

Figure 1.16 models composition. This model says that the body is not only an aggregation of a head, two arms, and two legs, but that these objects (head, arms, legs) are

created when the body is created and disappear when the body disappears. That is, they have no independent existence; the body is composed of these things and their lifetimes are intertwined.

FIGURE 1.15.

Aggregation.

```
                    ┌──────────────┐
                    │     Car      │
                    │              │
                    └──────┬───────┘
              ┌────────────┼────────────┐
              1          2..5           4
       ┌──────────┐  ┌──────────┐  ┌──────────┐
       │          │  │          │  │          │
       │ Steering │  │   Door   │  │   Tire   │
       │  Wheel   │  │          │  │          │
       └──────────┘  └──────────┘  └──────────┘
```

FIGURE 1.16.

Composition.

```
                    ┌──────────────┐
                    │     Body     │
                    │              │
                    └──────┬───────┘
              ┌────────────┼────────────┐
              1            2            2
       ┌──────────┐  ┌──────────┐  ┌──────────┐
       │          │  │          │  │          │
       │   Head   │  │   Arms   │  │   Legs   │
       │          │  │          │  │          │
       └──────────┘  └──────────┘  └──────────┘
```

Discriminators and Powertypes

How might you design the classes required to reflect the various model lines of a typical car manufacturer? Suppose that you've been hired to design a system for Acme Motors, which currently manufactures five cars: the Pluto (a slow, compact car with a small engine), the Venus (a four-door sedan with a middle-sized engine), the Mars (a sport coupe with the company's biggest engine, engineered for maximum performance), the Jupiter (a minivan with the same engine as the sports coupe but designed to shift at a lower RPM and to use its power to move its greater weight), and the Earth (a station wagon with a small engine but high RPM).

You might start by creating subtypes of `Car` that reflect the various models, and then create instances of each model as they roll off the assembly line, as shown in Figure 1.17.

FIGURE 1.17.

Modeling subtypes.

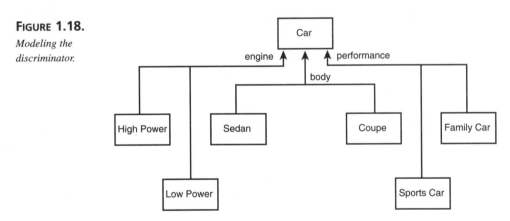

How are these models differentiated? As we saw, they are differentiated by the engine size, body type, and performance characteristics. These various discriminating characteristics can be mixed and matched to create various models. We can model this in the UML with the *discriminator* stereotype, as shown in Figure 1.18.

FIGURE 1.18.

Modeling the discriminator.

The diagram in Figure 1.18 indicates that classes can be derived from `Car` based on mixing and matching three discriminating attributes. The size of the engine dictates how powerful the car is, and the performance characteristics indicate how sporty the car is. Thus, you can have a powerful and sporty station wagon, a low-power family sedan, and so forth.

Each attribute can be implemented with a simple enumerator. Thus, the body type might be implemented with the following statement in code:

```
enum BodyType = { sedan, coupe, minivan, stationwagon };
```

It may turn out, however, that a simple value is insufficient to model a particular discriminator. For example, the performance characteristic may be rather complex. In this case, the discriminator can be modeled as a class, and the discrimination can be encapsulated in an instance of that type.

Thus, the car might model the performance characteristics in a *performance* type, which contains information about where the engine shifts and how fast it can turn. The UML stereotype for a class that encapsulates a discriminator, and that can be used to create *instances* of a class (`Car`) that are logically of different types (for example, `SportsCar` versus `LuxuryCar`) is «powertype». In this case, the `Performance` class is a powertype for car. When you instantiate `Car`, you also instantiate a `Performance` object, and you associate a given `Performance` object with a given `Car`, as shown in Figure 1.19.

FIGURE 1.19.

A discriminator as a powertype.

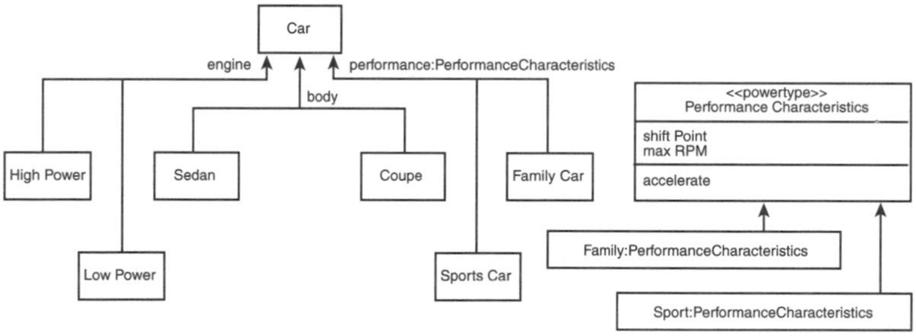

Powertypes let you create a variety of *logical* types without using inheritance. You can thus manage a large and complex set of types without the combinatorial explosion you might encounter with inheritance.

Typically, you *implement* the powertype in C++ with pointers. In this case, the `Car` class holds a pointer to an instance of `PerformanceCharacteristics` class (see Figure 1.20). I'll leave it as an exercise to the ambitious reader to convert the body and engine discriminators into powertypes.

```
Class Car : public Vehicle
{
public:
    Car();
    ~Car();
    // other public methods elided
private:
    PerformanceCharacteristics * pPerformance;
};
```

As a final note, powertypes allow you to create new *types* (not just instances) at runtime. Because each logical type is differentiated only by the attributes of the associated powertype, these attributes can be parameters to the powertype's constructor. This means that you can, at runtime, create new *types* of cars on-the-fly. That is, by passing different engine sizes and shift points to the powertype, you can effectively create new performance characteristics. By assigning those characteristics to various cars, you can effectively enlarge the set of types of cars *at runtime*.

FIGURE **1.20.**

The relationship between a Car *object and its powertype.*

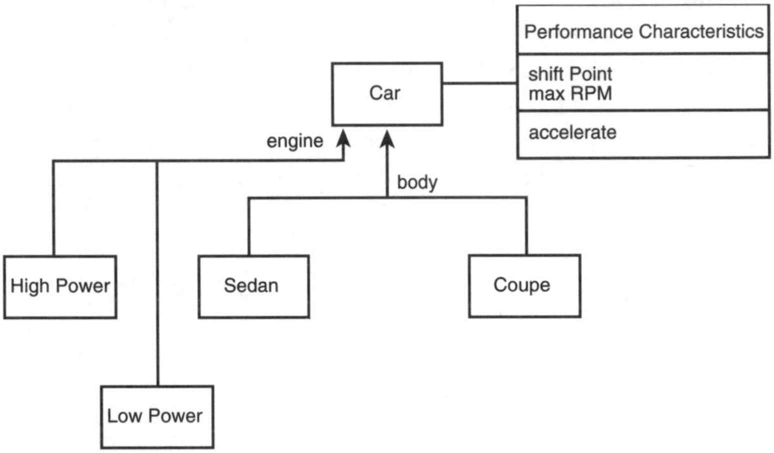

Dynamic Model

In addition to modeling the relationships among the classes, it is critical to model how they interact. For example, the CheckingAccount, ATM, and Receipt classes may interact with the Customer in fulfilling the "Withdraw Cash" use case. We return to the kinds of sequence diagrams first used in analysis, but now flesh out the details based on the methods we've developed in the classes, as shown in Figure 1.21.

This simple interaction diagram shows the interaction among a number of design classes over time. It suggests that the ATM class will delegate to the CheckingAccount class all responsibility for managing the balance, while the CheckingAccount will call on the ATM to manage display to the user.

Interaction diagrams comes in two flavors. The one in Figure 1.20 is called a *sequence diagram*. Another view on the same information is provided by the *collaboration diagram*. The sequence diagram emphasizes the sequence of events over time; the collaboration diagram emphasizes the interactions among the classes. You can generate a collaboration diagram directly from a sequence diagram; tools like Rational Rose automate this task at the press of a button (see Figure 1.22).

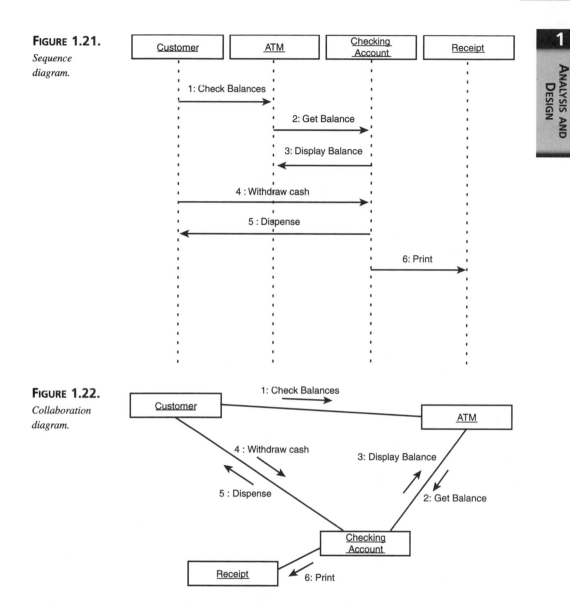

FIGURE 1.21.
Sequence diagram.

FIGURE 1.22.
Collaboration diagram.

State Transition Diagrams

As we come to understand the interactions among the objects, we have to understand the various possible *states* of each individual object. We can model the transitions among the various states in a state diagram (or state transition diagram). Figure 1.23 shows the various states of the CustomerAccount class as the customer logs into the system.

FIGURE 1.23.
*Customer account
state.*

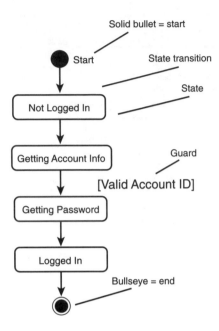

Every state diagram begins with a single start state and ends with zero or more end states. The individual states are named, and the transitions may be labeled. The guard indicates a condition that must be satisfied for an object to move from one state to another.

Super States

The customer can change his mind at any time and decide not to log in. He can do this after he swipes his card to identify his account or after he enters his password. In either case, the system must accept his request to cancel and return to the "not logged in state" (see Figure 1.24).

As you can see, in a more complicated diagram, the Canceled state quickly becomes a distraction. This is particularly annoying because canceling is an exceptional condition that should not be given prominence in the diagram. We can simplify this diagram by using a *super state*, as shown in Figure 1.25.

The diagram in Figure 1.24 provides the same information in Figure 1.23 but is much cleaner and easier to read. From the time you start logging in until the system finalizes your login, you can cancel the process. If you do cancel, you return to the state "not logged in."

FIGURE 1.24.
User may cancel.

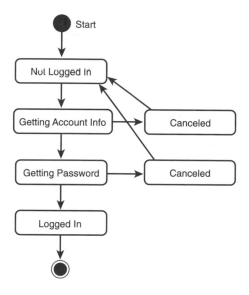

FIGURE 1.25.
Super state.

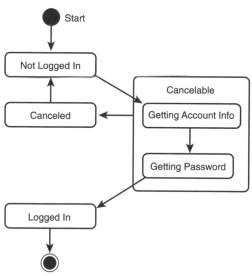

Summary

This chapter provided an introduction to the issues involved in object-oriented analysis and design. The essence of this approach is to analyze how your system will be used (use cases) and how it must perform, and then to design the classes and model their relationships and interactions.

In the old days, we sketched out a quick idea of what we wanted to accomplish and began writing code. The problem is that complex projects are never finished; and if they are finished, they are unreliable and brittle. By investing up front in understanding the requirements and modeling the design, we ensure a finished product that is correct (that is, it meets the design) and that is robust, reliable, and extensible.

Much of the rest of this book focuses on the details of Implementation. Issues relating to Testing and Rollout are beyond the scope of this book, except to mention that you want to plan your unit testing as you implement, and that you will use your requirements document as the foundation of your test plan prior to rollout.

Implementing Class Design in C++

Now you have read Chapter 1, "Object-Oriented Analysis and Design," and learned how to represent your ideas, problems, and solutions in a well-organized and understandable manner by using the Unified Modeling Language (UML). You can now show your object designs to anyone in the industry, and that person will understand exactly what you mean.

The next step is to implement your designs and turn them into a workable solution. That is the focus of this chapter: transforming the various models you have developed during analysis and design into C++ code. Specifically, this chapter discusses the transformation of the following UML diagrams into C++ code:

- Class diagrams
- Interaction diagrams (collaboration diagrams and sequence diagrams)
- State transaction diagrams
- Activity diagrams

Translating Class Diagrams into C++

Class diagrams serve two purposes: to represent the static state of classes and to exploit the relationships between those classes. In the early stages of the software development life cycle, it is important to note that the class diagram model attempts not only to define the public interface for each class but to define the associations, aggregations, and generalizations defined between the individual classes. Although defining a strong set of classes is important in building a foundation of tools to use in the final application, it is equally important to understand how each class interacts with other classes so that you can work toward providing a complete solution.

In the following sections, you learn how to transform the most common elements of a class diagram into C++ code.

Standard Classes

As described in Chapter 1, classes are represented by three partitioned rectangles, with the class's unique name specified in the top portion, attributes in the middle, and operations in the bottom. Figure 2.1 shows a class diagram.

The transformation from the class diagram in Figure 2.1 to a C++ class is a three-step process:

FIGURE 2.1.

A checking account class diagram.

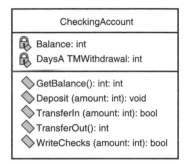

1. Give the class a name based on the name in the top rectangle of the class diagram: CheckingAccount. Remember to add a constructor and destructor for the class.

2. Add the attributes (from the middle rectangle of the diagram) to the class as private member variables. Although the variables do not necessarily have to be private, making them private promotes encapsulation. In the case of Figure 2.1, those attributes become Balance and DaysATMWithdrawal.

3. Transform the operations (in the bottom rectangle of the diagram) to public member functions. The functions become the public interface to the class. In the case of Figure 2.1, those operations become GetBalance(), Deposit(), TransferIn(), TransferOut(), and WriteChecks().

Listing 2.1 shows the complete class declaration for CheckingAccount.

LISTING 2.1. A C++ REPRESENTATION OF A UML CLASS

```
class CheckingAccount
{
public:
    // Construction / Destruction
    CheckingAccount ();
    ~CheckingAccount ();

    // Public operations
    int GetBalance ();
    void Deposit (int amount);
    BOOL TransferIn (int amount);
    int TransferOut ();
    BOOL WriteChecks (int amount);
private:
    // Private attributes
    int Balance;
    int DaysATMWithdrawal;
};
```

Template Classes

Template classes, which are also referred to as *parameterized classes*, are generic classes that cannot be used until they are instantiated. Because the data types used in a template class are not determined until the class is instantiated, you can write a generic `Stack` class once; the items pushed on the stack and popped off the stack can vary from one instantiation of the class to another. That single `Stack` class can be used for a stack of integers, floats, or any other predefined or user-defined types.

Class diagrams represent template classes in the same way as normal classes, but they have a dotted rectangle in the upper-right corner that specifies the arguments to be used in the class (see Figure 2.2).

FIGURE 2.2.

A stack *template class diagram.*

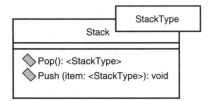

The C++ implementation of a template class corresponds to the C++ template class type. You transform Figure 2.2 into a C++ class in the same way you do a standard class—with the exception of the template class specifics:

1. Preface the class declaration with the keyword `template` and define a substitution type for the class: `<class StackType>`.

2. For each instance in which you use the variable type in question, substitute the variable type with the class name followed by the substitute type enclosed in angle brackets: `Stack<StackType>`.

Listing 2.2 shows the C++ implementation of the class diagram shown in Figure 2.2.

LISTING 2.2. A C++ TEMPLATE CLASS

```
template <class StackType>
class Stack
{
public:
    // Construction / Destruction
    Stack ();
    Stack (const Stack<StackType>& right);
    ~Stack ();

    // Assignment operator
    const Stack<StackType>& operator = (const Stack<StackType>& right);
```

```
   // Comparison operators
   int operator==(const Stack<StackType> &right) const;
   int operator!=(const Stack<StackType> &right) const;

   // Public Interface
   Stack<StackType>& Pop ();
   void Push (const Stack<StackType> &right);
};
```

Utility Classes

A *utility class* is a class that contains grouped functionality but no persistent data members (attributes). Although utility classes are not part of standard C++, some programmers like to create them; the UML therefore offers support for them. The purpose of a utility class is to take a set of functionality (such as trigonometric math functions) and group them together in a common class. There is no need to create an instance of this class because each function in the class is declared static: You simply use the functions contained in the class by fully qualifying the desired function name. For example, the trigonometric class may contain the Cosine(), Sine(), and Tangent() functions that can be called at any time by any class. The class diagram notation supports utility classes by prefacing the class name with <<Utility>>. The class diagram for the TrigMathFunctions class is shown in Figure 2.3.

FIGURE 2.3.

The
TrigMathFunctions
utility class
diagram.

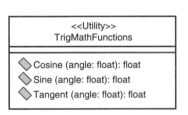

To represent a utility class in C++, each operation must be declared as static—there will only be one instance of each function for all objects of this class. Furthermore, utility classes have no constructor or destructor because there is no data to initialize or preserve. Listing 2.3 shows the C++ implementation of the TrigMathFunctions class.

LISTING 2.3. THE CLASS DECLARATION FOR A UTILITY CLASS

```
class TrigMathFunctions
{
   static float Cosine (float angle);
   static float Sine (float angle);
   static float Tangent (float angle);
};
```

Associations

Associations represent a relationship between classes. An association can be as simple as a 1:1 relationship between two classes and as complex as an N:N relationship between three or more classes. An association can be represented by a named or unnamed line between classes or by an entire association class. The following sections address each type of association and provide examples that should qualify the definitions.

1:1 Associations

An unnamed 1:1 association is a relationship between two classes (see Figure 2.4).

FIGURE 2.4.
An unnamed class association.

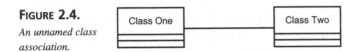

Although an unnamed association tells us that there is a relationship between two classes, it does not tell us the nature of the relationship. To define this relationship, we can place a named label above the line (see Figure 2.5).

FIGURE 2.5.
A named class association.

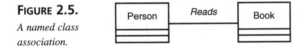

You map a 1:1 association into C++ code by defining an instance of each associated class inside the other class and providing an interface for accessing that information. Listing 2.4 contains excerpts from the class declaration for the `Person` class; Listing 2.5 contains excerpts from the declaration for the `Book` class.

LISTING 2.4. THE `Person` CLASS DECLARATION

```
#include "Book.h"

class Person
{
public:
   Person();
   ~Person();
   . . .

   //## Association: Reads
   //## Role: Person::<the_Book>
   const Book get_the_Book() const;
   void set_the_Book(const Book value);
```

2

IMPLEMENTING
CLASS DESIGN IN
C++

```cpp
private:
   Book the_Book;
};

inline const Book Person::get_the_Book() const
{
   return the_Book;
}

inline void Person::set_the_Book(const Book value)
{
   the_Book = value;
}
```

LISTING 2.5. THE Book CLASS DECLARATION

```cpp
#include "Person.h"

class Book
{
public:
   Book ();
   ~Book ();
   . . .

   //## Association: Reads
   //## Role: Book::<the_Person>
   const Person get_the_Person() const;
   void set_the_Person(const Person value);

private:
   Person the_Person;
};

inline const Person Book::get_the_Person() const
{
   return the_Person;
}

inline void Book::set_the_Person(const Person value)
{
   the_Person = value;
}
```

As you can see, the Person class has declared an instance of the Book class with the
name the_Book and provided the member functions get_the_Book() and
set_the_Book() to access the book object. Similarly, the Book class declares an instance
of the Person class with the name the_Person and provides the member functions

get_the_Person() and set_the_Person() to access the Person object. Note that the named association Reads is used only in the class diagram and is not defined in the C++ code other than as a comment.

The other type of 1:1 association involves naming the roles of the association at each end. In this way, the C++ class naming convention can easily identify the relationship between the two classes. Take an example of a Renter to an Apartment association: The Renter views the Apartment as his or her dwelling; the Apartment views the Renter as its tenant. So the named roles for the association are Tenant and Dwelling (see Figure 2.6).

FIGURE 2.6.

A named role class association.

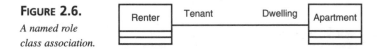

To create a C++ class from a 1:1 named role association, the two classes in question must both have a variable of the other class's type. In Listing 2.6, the Renter class has a private member variable Dwelling of type Apartment. This variable represents, to the renter, the apartment in which he or she lives (that is, his or her dwelling). Furthermore, the Renter class provides a public interface to modify its Dwelling through the two public member functions get_Dwelling() and set_Dwelling(). Similarly, the Apartment class has a private member variable Tenant of type Renter and two member functions that access the Apartment's Renter: get_Renter() and set_Renter(). Listing 2.6 shows the class declaration for the Renter class. Listing 2.7 shows the class declaration for the Apartment class.

LISTING 2.6. THE Renter CLASS DECLARATION

```
#include "Apartment.h"

class Renter
{
public:
   Renter ();
   ~Renter ();
   . . .

   //## Association: Unnamed
   //## Role: Renter::Dwelling
   const Apartment get_Dwelling() const;
   void set_Dwelling(const Apartment value);

private:
   Apartment Dwelling;
};
```

LISTING 2.7. THE Apartment CLASS DECLARATION

```
#include "Renter.h"

class Apartment
{
public:
   Apartment ();
   ~Apartment ();
   . . .

   //## Association: Unnamed
   //## Role: Apartment::Tenant
   const Renter get_Tenant() const;
   void set_Tenant(const Renter value);

private:
   Renter Tenant;
};
```

N:1 and 1:N Associations

An N:1 or 1:N association—also referred to as a one-to-many relationship, exists when one object can exist for multiple instances of the another object, but the other object can exist only once for the original object. An example of this type of association exists between a tenant and an apartment building: A tenant can have only one apartment building, but an apartment building can house multiple tenants. The class diagram notation for a one-to-many association is to place the name of the role of the association above the association line and to list the type of association below the line. Table 2.1 shows the notation for association multiplicity.

TABLE 2.1. ASSOCIATION MULTIPLICITY

Notation	Association
1	Only one
0..1	Either zero or one
0..*	Zero or more
1..*	One or more
*	Zero or more
M..N	Many to many

Figure 2.7 shows a class diagram of the association between a Tenant and an ApartmentBuilding.

FIGURE 2.7.

*A one-to-many
class association.*

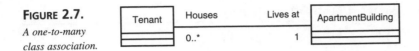

The Tenant to ApartmentBuilding association is represented in C++ in the same way as
a 1:1 association: The Tenant class has a private attribute Lives_at that is of type
ApartmentBuilding. The ApartmentBuilding to Tenant relationship, however, is more
complicated. Recall that an ApartmentBuilding can house zero or more Tenants. To
facilitate this type of association, a collection of Tenants is maintained inside the
ApartmentBuilding class. (The class declaration in Listing 2.9 uses a template class of
type UnboundedSetByValue to hold all its residents.) Listing 2.8 shows the class declaration for the Tenant class. Listing 2.9 shows the class declaration for the
ApartmentBuilding class.

LISTING 2.8. THE Tenant CLASS DECLARATION

```
// ApartmentBuilding
#include "AprtmntB.h"

class Tenant
{
public:
   Tenant ();
   ~Tenant ();
   . . .

   //## Association: Unnamed
   //## Role: Tenant::Lives at
   const ApartmentBuilding get_Lives_at() const;
   void set_Lives_at(const ApartmentBuilding value);

private:
      ApartmentBuilding Lives_at;
};
```

LISTING 2.9. THE ApartmentBuilding CLASS DECLARATION

```
// Tenant
#include "Tenant.h"

class ApartmentBuilding
{
public:
   ApartmentBuilding();
   ~ApartmentBuilding();
   . . .

   //## Association: Unnamed
```

```
//## Role: ApartmentBuilding::Houses
const UnboundedSetByValue<Tenant> get_Houses() const;
void set_Houses(const UnboundedSetByValue<Tenant> value);

private:
   UnboundedSetByValue<Tenant> Houses;
};
```

N:N Associations

An N:N association is a relationship that exists between two classes where zero or more instances of one class are associated with zero or more instances of another class. An example of this type of association is the relationship between a contractor and a company: A company can employ many contractors, and a contractor can simultaneously work for many companies (see Figure 2.8).

FIGURE 2.8.

A many-to-many class association.

The C++ implementation of this association is similar to the apartment building example in the previous section: The Company maintains a private set of Contractors named Employees, and the Contractor maintains a set of Companys he works for named Works_for. The following listings manage these collections using the template class UnboundedSetByValue. Listing 2.10 shows the class declaration for the Contractor class. Listing 2.11 shows the class declaration for the Company class.

LISTING 2.10. THE Contractor CLASS DECLARATION

```
// Company
#include "Company.h"

class Contractor
{
public:
   Contractor ();
   ~Contractor ();
   . . .

   //## Association: Unnamed
   //## Role: Contractor::Works for
   const UnboundedSetByValue<Company> get_Works_for() const;
   void set_Works_for(const UnboundedSetByValue<Company> value);

private:
   UnboundedSetByValue<Company> Works_for;
};
```

LISTING 2.11. THE Company CLASS DECLARATION

```
// Contractor
#include "Cntrctor.h"

class Company
{
public:
   Company ();
   ~Company ();
   . . .

   //## Association: Unnamed
   //## Role: Company::Employees
   const UnboundedSetByValue<Contractor> get_Employees() const;
   void set_Employees(const UnboundedSetByValue<Contractor> value);

private:
   UnboundedSetByValue<Contractor> Employees;
};
```

Aggregations

An *aggregation* implies a relationship between two classes in which one class has a more important role in the relationship than the other. The most common form of aggregation is the relationship of *composition*. In this relationship, one class actually contains the other class. An example of this relationship was presented in Chapter 1, "Object-Oriented Analysis and Design," where a BankAccount contained a Balance and a TransactionHistory.

Containment is represented in a class diagram by drawing a line between the two classes with a solid diamond on the side of the class that contains the other class (see Figure 2.9).

FIGURE 2.9.

A composition class diagram.

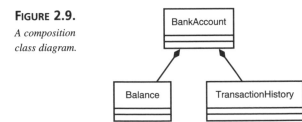

The Balance and TransactionHistory classes maintain a reference to their BankAccounts, but are contained within the BankAccount class itself; the BankAccount class creates private instances of the Balance and TransactionHistory classes.

Listing 2.12 shows the class declaration for the `BankAccount` class. The `BankAccount` class has a private member variable `the_Balance` of type `Balance` and a private member variable `the_TransactionHistory` of type `TransactionHistory`. Listing 2.13 shows the class declaration for the `Balance` class. Listing 2.14 shows the class declaration for the `TransactionHistory` class.

LISTING 2.12. THE BankAccount CLASS DECLARATION

```
// TransactionHistory
#include "TrnsctnH.h"
// Balance
#include "Balance.h"

class BankAccount
{
public:
   BankAccount ();
   ~BankAccount ();
   . . .

   //## Association: Unnamed
   //## Role: BankAccount::<the_Balance>
   const Balance get_the_Balance() const;
   void set_the_Balance(const Balance value);

   //## Association: Unnamed
   //## Role: BankAccount::<the_TransactionHistory>
   const TransactionHistory get_the_TransactionHistory() const;
   void set_the_TransactionHistory(const TransactionHistory value);

private:
   Balance the_Balance;
   TransactionHistory the_TransactionHistory;
};
```

LISTING 2.13. THE Balance CLASS DECLARATION

```
// BankAccount
#include "Bnkccunt.h"

class Balance
{
public:
   Balance ();
   ~Balance ();
   . . .
```

continues

LISTING 2.13. CONTINUED

```
   //## Association: Unnamed
   //## Role: Balance::<the_BankAccount>
   const BankAccount get_the_BankAccount() const;
   void set_the_BankAccount(const BankAccount value);

private:
   BankAccount the_BankAccount;
};
```

LISTING 2.14. THE TransactionHistory CLASS DECLARATION

```
// BankAccount
#include "Bnkccunt.h"

class TransactionHistory
{
public:
   TransactionHistory ();
   ~TransactionHistory ();
   . . .

   //## Association: Unnamed
   //## Role: TransactionHistory::<the_BankAccount>
   const BankAccount get_the_BankAccount() const;
   void set_the_BankAccount(const BankAccount value);

private:
   BankAccount the_BankAccount;
};
```

Generalization

Generalization is used to represent a general-to-specific relationship between two class-es. In C++ terms, this relationship is referred to as *inheritance*. For example, a checking account and a savings account are both more specific types of bank accounts. Generalization is represented in a class diagram by drawing an arrow from the specific class to the general class (see Figure 2.10).

In C++, generalization is represented by suffixing the class declaration of the specific class with a colon followed by the name of the general class. In Listing 2.15, the Checking class is inherited from the Account class in the statement `class Checking : public Account`. The Savings class is inherited from the Account class in the statement `class Savings : public Account`. Because the Account class has no knowledge of either the Checking or Savings class, its class declaration has been omitted. Listing 2.15 shows the class declaration for the Checking class. Listing 2.16 shows the class declaration for the Savings class.

FIGURE 2.10.

A generalization class diagram.

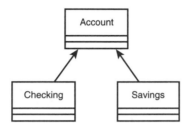

LISTING 2.15. THE Checking CLASS DECLARATION

```
// Account
#include "Account.h"

class Checking : public Account
{
    . . .
};
```

LISTING 2.16. THE Savings CLASS DECLARATION

```
// Account
#include "Account.h"

class Savings : public Account
{
    . . .
};
```

Class diagrams also support the concept of *multiple generalization*—in C++ terms, *multiple inheritance*. Multiple inheritance is represented in a class diagram by drawing arrows from the specialized class to each of its general classes. Consider the class Derived that takes the attributes of both the base class BaseA and the base class BaseB (see Figure 2.11).

FIGURE 2.11.

A multiple generalization class diagram.

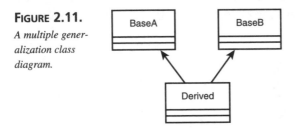

In the class diagram in Figure 2.11, the generalization arrows are drawn to both base classes. To represent multiple generalization or multiple inheritance in C++, both base classes are placed in the class declaration statement, comma delimited, *after* the colon of the derived class's declaration. The Derived class inherits from both BaseA and BaseB in the statement class Derived : public BaseA, public BaseB. Listing 2.17 shows the class declaration header for the Derived class. Because BaseA and BaseB do not have any knowledge of the Derived class, their listings have been omitted.

LISTING 2.17. THE Derived CLASS DECLARATION

```
// BaseB
#include "BaseB.h"

// BaseA
#include "BaseA.h"

class Derived : public BaseA,  public BaseB
{
    . . .
```

Translating Interaction Diagrams into C++

There are two types of interaction diagrams: collaboration diagrams and sequence diagrams. Collaboration diagrams display the interaction between objects from a logistical perspective—they show how objects are arranged with respect to one another. Sequence diagrams, on the other hand, display only the interaction without caring about the arrangement of the objects.

Both collaboration and sequence diagrams have their benefits and drawbacks. A collaboration diagram allows you to visualize the arrangement of objects as they interact, but as the number of interactions increases, the more complex and unreadable the diagram becomes. Furthermore, the model does not naturally show you the order in which interactions occur, so interactions must be numbered.

Sequence diagrams represent object interaction in a very organized fashion and note the relative order of interactions, but they eliminate the understanding that accompanies visualization.

Chapter 1 discusses the design of interaction diagrams based on the analysis of a system. After the design is complete, and the objects in an interaction diagram have been associated with classes defined in class diagrams, the implementation in C++ is fairly straightforward. There are four primary goals of a collaboration diagram:

- Identify system user interfaces
- Refine each class's public interface
- Determine which objects will interact with one another
- Understand the sequence of events that occurs given certain stimuli

First, you must incorporate into the system's user interface all allowable user interactions. *Actors* represent user interactions. The messages the actors send to system objects must be gathered from the user interface and dispatched to the system objects; actors do not typically interact directly with the system objects.

Second, you must make each message generated by an interaction diagram object correspond to the resultant object's public interface. If object A requests service X from object B, object B must have a service X operation publicly available to object A.

Third, you must allow objects that interact with one another to access each other. If object C sends a message to object D, object D must be visible to object C. This is particularly important when considering the system implementation.

Finally, you must make each message sequence that arrives at an object and is dispatched by that object represent an event that occurs within that object. If object E receives message I and dispatches message J, then the service in object E that receives message I must dispatch message J before it terminates.

Implementing Collaboration Diagrams and Sequence Diagrams in C++

Collaboration diagrams and sequence diagrams are interchangeable. As a matter of reference, modeling tools such as Rational Rose support the direct conversion from one to the other. Recall from Chapter 1 the example of a checking account ATM withdrawal transaction. The particulars of the design of both the collaboration diagram and sequence diagram have already been discussed, but they are displayed in Figures 2.12 and 2.13, respectively.

FIGURE 2.12.

The collaboration diagram for an ATM withdrawal transaction.

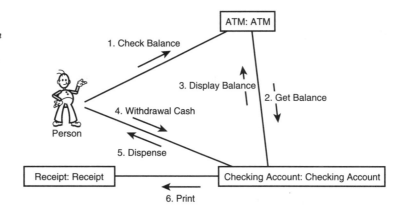

Before we start implementing classes for these diagrams, let's define the objects present in the diagrams. The objects in these diagrams are listed here:

- ATM
- CheckingAccount
- Receipt
- UserInterface

The UserInterface object is going to represent the Person's actions because the Person never directly interacts with any of the other objects.

First, let's address the system user interface. The Person in Figures 2.12 and 2.13 has three interactions with system objects:

Figure 2.13.

The sequence diagram for an ATM withdrawal transaction.

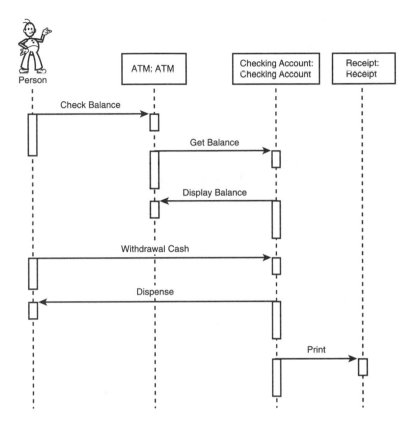

- The Person object can CheckBalances from the ATM object.
- The Person object can WithdrawCash from the CheckingAccount object.
- The Person object receives cash as the CheckingAccount object Dispenses cash to the Person.

The UserInterface object must provide the Person object with the CheckBalance and WithdrawCash options, and must provide a way to give the Person cash dispensed from the CheckingAccount. We have all been to an ATM, so the user interface to withdraw cash is familiar.

The UserInterface object can be represented by a class declaration similar to the one in Listing 2.18. This class will be expanded in the following discussion, but let's add the public interface now.

LISTING 2.18. THE `UserInterface` CLASS DECLARATION

```
class UserInterface
{
public:
    // Public Interface
    char * CheckBalance ();
    BOOL WithdrawCash ();
};
```

> **NOTE**
>
> All balances in these examples are represented as character strings. This is an implementation preference and has been done to eliminate integer limitations and floating-point rounding.

To refine each class's public interface, a corresponding member function must be added to each class that receives a message in the interaction diagram. In this example, the ATM class receives the `CheckBalance` and `DisplayBalance` messages, the `CheckingAccount` class receives the `GetBalance` and `WithdrawCash` messages, and the `Receipt` class receives the `Print` message.

Listing 2.19 shows the public interface for the ATM class, Listing 2.20 shows the public interface for the `CheckingAccount` class, and Listing 2.21 shows the public interface for the `Receipt` class.

LISTING 2.19. THE PUBLIC INTERFACE FOR THE ATM CLASS

```
class ATM
{
public:
    // Public Interface
    char * CheckBalance ();
    char * DisplayBalance ();
};
```

LISTING 2.20. THE PUBLIC INTERFACE FOR THE `CheckingAccount` CLASS

```
class CheckingAccount
{
public:
    char * GetBalance ();
    BOOL WithdrawCash ();
};
```

LISTING 2.21. THE PUBLIC INTERFACE FOR THE Receipt CLASS

```
class Receipt
{
public:
    BOOL Print ();
};
```

Now that the public interface has been extracted from the interaction diagrams and entered into the class declarations, the next step is to implement the visibility of the individual classes. In this example, the UserInterface class communicates directly with the ATM and the CheckingAccount classes. The implementation at this point is application dependent; you have several options:

- An instance of both the ATM class and the CheckingAccount class can be instantiated within the UserInterface class. Do this if the UserInterface class needs direct access to both the ATM class and the CheckingAccount class.

- Each class can be instantiated in the global system space, and a pointer to each can be passed to the UserInterface class. Do this if the class instances of the ATM class and CheckingAccount class require persistence beyond that of the UserInterface class.

- Looking ahead to the classes that must be visible from the ATM class, the CheckingAccount class object can be instantiated within the ATM class and an interface to the CheckingAccount can be provided.

There is no correct implementation decision here; it depends on the other interaction diagrams and other design constraints such as the storage mechanism for the CheckingAccount (for example, the CheckingAccounts may be stored in a database and only one instance may be visible and available inside the ATM object).

For this example, the CheckingAccount will be an object instantiated within the ATM object, and the ATM object will be instantiated within the UserInterface object. Listing 2.22 shows the UserInterface class declaration with the ATM attribute added as the private member variable the_ATM.

LISTING 2.22. THE UserInterface CLASS DECLARATION WITH THE CONTAINED ATM OBJECT

```
class UserInterface
{
public:
    // Public Interface
    char * CheckBalance ();
    BOOL WithdrawCash ();
```

continues

LISTING 2.22. CONTINUED

```
private:
    // Private Attributes
    ATM the_ATM;
};
```

Next, the ATM object interacts with only the CheckingAccount object and, as mentioned in the previous discussion, will contain an instance of the CheckingAccount object. Because it contains the CheckingAccount object, it is responsible for communicating with the CheckingAccount on behalf of the UserInterface. Listing 2.23 shows the updated ATM class declaration with the contained CheckingAccount object: the_CheckingAccount. It also has a public member function WithdrawCashFromCheckingAccount() that interacts with the CheckingAccount object for the UserInterface class.

LISTING 2.23. THE ATM CLASS DECLARATION WITH CONTAINED CheckingAccount

```
class ATM
{
public:
    // Public Interface
    char * CheckBalance ();
    char * DisplayBalance ();

    // CheckingAccount interface
    BOOL WithdrawCashFromCheckingAccount ();

private:
    // Private Attributes
    CheckingAccount the_CheckingAccount;
};
```

The CheckingAccount class does not contain any classes of its own. The Receipt class could be contained within the CheckingAccount class because there is communication with it, but it will not be because creating a Receipt object within the CheckingAccount does not follow logically. This is another implementation decision and was made because a Receipt object is not specific to a CheckingAccount object and therefore does not warrant making it part of the CheckingAccount object.

The Receipt class does not have to communicate with any class in the interaction diagram, so it has no classes visible to it.

The final step is to find each operation that receives a message and dispatches a message and implement the dispatch. The easy way to accomplish this is to follow the arrows in the interaction diagram.

The first message sent, CheckBalance, is from the UserInterface object to the ATM object. The next message sent, GetBalance, is from the ATM to the CheckingAccount object. This adds the restriction that the ATM::CheckBalace() function must call the CheckingAccount::GetBalance() function before it terminates. The implementation of the ATM::CheckBalance() function is shown in Listing 2.24.

LISTING 2.24. THE ATM CLASS IMPLEMENTATION OF CheckBalance()

```
char * ATM::CheckBalance
{
    // Perform other check balance functionality

    // Call the CheckingAccount::GetBalance function
    szBalance = the_CheckingAccount.GetBalance ();

    // Return the balance
    return szBalance;
}
```

The next message, DisplayBalance, is from the CheckingAccount object to the ATM object. The CheckingAccount object must therefore call the ATM::DisplayBalance() member function inside its GetBalance() member function. Listing 2.25 shows the implementation of the CheckingAccount::GetBalance() member function.

LISTING 2.25. THE CheckingAccount CLASS IMPLEMENTATION OF GetBalance()

```
char * CheckingAccount::GetBalance()
{
    // Look up the Balance from the database

    // Call ATM::DisplayBalance() to fire the next message
    // GetParent() returns a pointer to our parent ATM class
    GetParent()->DisplayBalance ();

    // Return the balance to the caller
    return szBalance;
}
```

The UserInterface::WithdrawCash() function is derived in a similar manner, and its implementation is displayed in Listing 2.26.

LISTING 2.26. THE `UserInterface::WithdrawCash()` FUNCTION

```
BOOL UserInterface::WithdrawCash()
{
   // Return the value that ATM::WithdrawCashFromCheckingAccount returns
   return the_ATM.WithdrawCashFromCheckingAccount();
}
```

Listing 2.27 shows the implementation of `CheckingAccount::WithdrawCash()`.
Examination of the interaction diagrams shows that this function generates two events:
`UserInterface::Dispense()` and `Receipt::Print()`. `UserInterface::Dispense()` dispenses cash from the ATM machine to the customer, and `Receipt::Print()` prints a
receipt for the customer. The assumption made in this listing is that `GetParent()` is a
function that exists in each class and that it returns a pointer to its parent. Furthermore,
the assumption is made that there is a function, `GetReceipt()`, that exists in the
`UserInterface` object that returns the system `Receipt` object. This functionality is all
developer dependent and can be implemented in any desirable (yet functional) way.

LISTING 2.27. THE `CheckingAccount::WithdrawCash()` FUNCTION

```
BOOL CheckingAccount::WithdrawCash()
{
   // Perform cash withdrawal functionality

   // Fire Dispense message to the UserInterface object
   GetParent()->GetParent()->Dispense

   // Fire the Print message to the receipt object
   GetParent()->GetParent()->GetReceipt()->Print();

   // Return result
   if (fSuccess)
      return TRUE;
   else
      return FALSE;
}
```

Translating State Transition Diagrams into C++

Interaction diagrams display the interaction between varying objects but state transition
diagrams display the changes that occur within a single object. A state transition diagram
shows all states defined inside an object and the transitions that exist between states.

State transition diagrams should be created for all objects that have the following characteristics:

- Multiple states that the object changes between
- Specific actions that must be accomplished between the states

If certain events must happen between states, state transition diagrams greatly aid the proper implementation of your designs. In a state transition diagram, the Start state represents the beginning of the transition, usually represented by the start of a member function that contains the transition. The End state represents the completion of the state transition and may or may not correspond to the end of this function. The states intermixed within the object are represented by application-dependent variables. For example, a traffic light object has three states (green, yellow, and red) that can be represented by a state integer. Although the implementation of the actual transition is application dependent, once the Start state has been initiated, the actions that must be accomplished are clearly defined and the implementation should be straightforward.

Recall the CustomerAccount class example presented in Chapter 1. Figure 2.14 shows the state transition diagram for this class.

FIGURE 2.14.

The CustomerAccount *state transition diagram.*

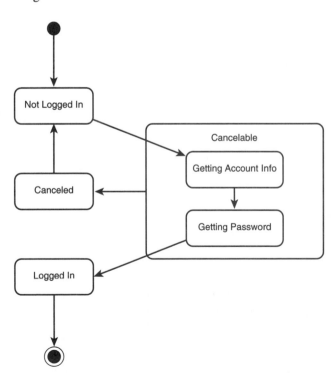

What this diagram translates to in programming terms is that the object (or, in the case of C++, the *class*) must provide an interface to allow a user to log in. More specifically, the class must somehow prompt the user for his or her account information (GettingAccountInfo()), prompt for his or her password (GettingPassword()), and change the state of the object from NotLoggedIn to LoggedIn—all the while allowing the user to cancel the operation at any point (Cancelable). These steps can be implemented in one member function or in a set of functions; the implementation is application and developer dependent. This example uses the member function LogIn to accomplish this goal.

The CustomerAccount class maintains a Boolean private member variable m_fLoggedIn that holds the customer's login status. This variable is checked by all member functions that perform any action that requires the customer to be connected (for example, GetBalance() or WithdrawCash()). The CustomerAccount class declaration is shown in Listing 2.28.

LISTING 2.28. THE CustomerAccount CLASS DECLARATION

```
class CustomerAccount
{
public:
    // Construction / Destruction
    CustomerAccount();
    ~CustomerAccount();

    // Public Interface
    BOOL LogIn();
    BOOL LogOut();
    char *GetBalance();

private:
    // Private State Data
    BOOL m_fLoggedIn=FALSE;

    // Private Data
    char *m_szBalance;
};
```

The CustomerAccount class constructor initializes the m_fLoggedIn member variable to false so that no function will try to perform an online action while offline. The destructor checks the logged-in status and logs the customer off before terminating if necessary. The LogOut() function simply sets m_fLoggedIn to false.

The LogIn function performs the actions specified in the state transition diagram: It first prompts the customer for an account number and stores it in szAccountNumber.

A real-world implementation of this object would involve more sophisticated cancellation methodologies, but to impress on you the notion that this action can be canceled, the account number is compared to Cancel before continuing. The customer is then prompted for his or her password. Again, this response is compared to Cancel. If the customer has entered both an account number and a password, the values are compared by another function ValidPassword() that probably does some database lookups and comparisons. After all of this, the state of m_fLoggedIn is changed to true. If any event is canceled, the state of m_fLoggedIn remains false and the transition does not occur. Listing 2.29 shows the implementation of the CustomerAccount class.

LISTING 2.29. THE CustomerAccount CLASS IMPLEMENTATION

```cpp
#include "CustomerAccount.h"

CustomerAccount::CustomerAccount()
{
    m_fLoggedIn = FALSE;
}

CustomerAccount::~CustomerAccount()
{
    if (m_fLoggedIn)
        LogOut();
}

BOOL CustomerAccount::LogIn()
{
    char szAccountNumber[32];
    char szPassword[32];

    // Getting Account Info
    printf ("Enter Account Number:");
    scanf ("%s",szAccountNumber);

    // Event is cancelable
    if (!strcmp (szAccountNumber, "Cancel"))
        return FALSE;

    // Getting Password
    printf ("Enter Password:");
    scanf ("%s", szPassword);

    // Event is cancelable
    if (!strcmp (szPassword, "Cancel"))
        return FALSE;
```

continues

LISTING 2.29. CONTINUED

```cpp
    // Some auxiliary function to validate the password
    if (!ValidPassword (szAccountNumber, szPassword))
       return FALSE;
    else
       // Valid password - Log the customer in
       m_fLoggedIn = TRUE;

    // Success
    return TRUE;
}

BOOL CustomerAccount::LogOut()
{
    m_fLoggedIn = FALSE;
}

char *CustomerAccount::GetBalance()
{
    // Check logged in status
    if(!m_fLoggedIn)
       return NULL;

    // Return the balance
    return m_szBalance;
}
```

Translating Activity Diagrams into C++

An activity diagram is a special type of state transition diagram that represents action states and transitions that occur at the completion of operations. Activity diagrams can be used to represent synchronous state transition diagrams in which all or most of the events in the diagram represent the completion of internally generated operations. When asynchronous events occur, use state transition diagrams to describe the model.

The implementation of activity diagrams is very similar to the implementation of state transition diagrams: The Start state represents the beginning of an operation, and the End state represents the conclusion. Because activity diagrams are synchronous, once the operation starts, all actions are clearly defined.

Consider the activity diagram in Figure 2.15.

FIGURE 2.15.

An ATM cash withdrawal activity diagram.

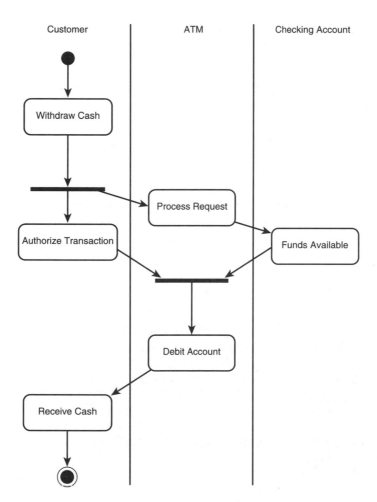

The diagram in Figure 2.15 shows three objects interacting with each other: Customer, ATM, and CheckingAccount. The diagram starts when the Customer tries to WithdrawCash. The WithdrawCash activity triggers two simultaneous activities: AuthorizeTransaction and ProcessRequest (owned by the ATM object). ProcessRequest transitions to CheckingAccount's FundsAvailable activity. Both AuthorizeTransaction and FundsAvailable transition to the ATM object's DebitAccount—the DebitAccount activity cannot occur until both preceding activities have completed. When DebitAccount completes, it transitions to ReceiveCash, and the activity diagram terminates.

When creating or reviewing an activity diagram, focus your attention on the overall procedure being implemented. Although the activity diagram in Figure 2.15 contains information that could be implemented as object interactions, the boundary of an activity diagram is limited to modeling a procedure. In this example, the procedure being modeled is a cash withdrawal transaction; the actual implementation of the object operations are superfluous to the implementation of the cash withdrawal transaction procedure.

Listings 2.30, 2.31, and 2.32 show the class declarations for the Customer, ATM, and CheckingAccount classes, respectively. The heart of the activity diagram is implemented in the two functions WithdrawCashTransaction() and ProcessRequest() in Listing 2.33.

The WithdrawCashTransaction() function first calls the operation Customer::WithdrawCash(). After this activity has completed, it calls both the Customer::AuthorizeTransaction() operation and the ProcessRequest() function. The ProcessRequest() function calls the ATM::ProcessRequest() operation, followed by the CheckingAccount::FundsAvailable() operation. The necessity of placing these operation calls in a separate function is substantiated by the dual dependency on the ATM::DebitAccount() operation. ATM::DebitAccount() function cannot start until both Customer::AuthorizeTransaction() and CheckingAccount::FundsAvailable() have completed. At this point, the last remaining steps are to call Customer::ReceiveCash() and to terminate the function.

LISTING 2.30. THE Customer CLASS DECLARATION

```
class Customer
{
public:
    // Construction / Destruction
    Customer();
    ~Customer();

    // Public Interface
    BOOL WithdrawCash();
    BOOL AuthorizeTransaction();
    void ReceiveCash();
};
```

LISTING 2.31. THE ATM CLASS DECLARATION

```
class ATM
{
public:
    // Construction / Destruction
    ATM();
    ~ATM();
```

```
    // Public Interface
    BOOL ProcessRequest();
    void DebitAccount();
};
```

LISTING 2.32. THE CheckingAccount CLASS DECLARATION

```
class CheckingAccount
{
public:
    // Construction / Destruction
    CheckingAccount();
    ~CheckingAccount();

    // Public Interface
    BOOL FundsAvailable();
}
```

LISTING 2.33. THE WithdrawCashTransaction() AND ProcessRequest() FUNCTION
IMPLEMENTATIONS

```
void WithdrawCashTransaction
{
    // Active Classes
    Customer myCustomer;
    ATM myATM;
    CheckingAccount myCheckingAccount;

    // * Start State

    // Start First Activity
    myCustomer.WithdrawCash();

    // Now that the first transaction is complete, start the next two
    if (myCustomer.AuthorizeTransaction() && ProcessRequest())
    {
        // Now that both actions have completed, continue processing
        myATM.DebitAccount();
        myCustomer.ReceiveCash();
    }

    // * End State
}

BOOL ProcessRequest ()
{
    myATM.ProcessRequest();
    return myCheckingAccount.FundsAvailable();
}
```

Summary

This chapter has discussed the implementation of some of the more popular UML design models in C++. You learned more about class diagrams, interaction diagrams (collaboration diagrams and sequence diagrams), state transaction diagrams, and activity diagrams.

The Unified Modeling Language (UML) provides some powerful tools to aid software engineers in both analysis and design. In some cases, the realization of these designs into C++ code is systematic; in other cases, it will be application dependent—but in any case, a solid foundation of the techniques used to realize these designs is imperative to the success of the project. Several tools exist to aid developers in the modeling process. The Rational Rose tool, which was used throughout this chapter, can generate C++ code for some of the diagrams and can even convert diagrams from one form to another. After reading this chapter, you should experiment with some of these automated tools to see whether they generate the C++ code you would expect them to.

Inheritance, Polymorphism, and Code Reuse

IN THIS CHAPTER

The ability to discover patterns and relationships among things in our environment is not just something humans are good at—it is something we are impelled to do. We inherited it from our ancient ancestors who used it to predict the behavior of otherwise dangerous animals. If they discovered that animals with short hair, long claws, and big teeth were known to eat the neighbors, they treated big cats with deference.

The smarter ones avoided being eaten for long enough to reproduce, and natural selection weeded out those who weren't any good at discovering patterns.

One of the principal relationships we discover at about three years of age is the *is-a* relationship. "Look Mommy, that *is a* fruit. That *is a* car." We do this long before we have the language to express it; my three-year-old pointed to a fire engine and said "big red car."

One of the great contributions of object-oriented analysis is to have found a practical use for phenomenology. Like Hegel and Kant, we must ask "What is a car? What makes a car different from a truck, from a person, from a rock?"

From one perspective, a car is the sum of its parts: steering wheel, brakes, seats, headlights. From a second perspective, equally true, a Car is a type of Vehicle. By saying that a Car is a type of Vehicle, we are using a shorthand rich in meaning.

Because a Car *is a* Vehicle, it moves and it carries things. That is the essence of being a Vehicle. Cars *inherit* the characteristics *moves* and *carries things* from their "parent" type: Vehicle. We also know that Cars *specialize* Vehicles. They are a special *kind* of Vehicle, one that meets the legal specifications for automobiles.

We model this relationship with generalization, and we implement it in C++ with inheritance.

Benefits of Inheritance

There are two great benefits to inheritance. First, we can specialize existing classes (types) and write only the code that is changed. In this way, we can reuse our existing classes (as base classes) and capitalize on the work already done. We no longer have to "copy and paste" code. Copying and pasting is particularly problematic because changes in one section of the code must be replicated in another—a dangerous and failure-prone model. Instead, by using specialization, we can make changes in the base class that automatically update all the derived classes.

The second significant benefit of inheritance is that it allows us to treat the derived objects polymorphically. *Poly* means many, *morph* means form; *polymorphism* means the ability to take many forms.

Perhaps the most common use of polymorphism is in windowing applications. The Microsoft Foundation Classes are a good example. Virtually all the onscreen "widgets" derive directly or indirectly from CWindow, which encapsulates a common interface of functionality for all onscreen objects. CWindow offers methods such as UpdateWindow(), BeginPaint(), GetWindowText(), and so forth.

Each of these methods can be overridden in any of the classes that derive from CWindow. These derived classes include CButton, CRadioButton, CListBox, and so forth. When you call UpdateWindow() on CButton, it redraws itself. When you call UpdateWindow() on CListBox, the list box also redraws itself. The details of what CButton and CListBox *do* when they update themselves are very different, but these details are encapsulated behind the UpdateWindow() interface presented by CWindow.

Object-Oriented Linked Lists

To illustrate the power of polymorphism, let's examine an object-oriented linked list. As you probably know, a linked list is a data structure designed to store an indeterminate number of objects. You can, of course, just store objects in an array, but arrays are of fixed size. If you don't know in advance how many objects you'll need, arrays are not a great choice. If you make the array too large, you waste memory; if you make it too small, you run out of room. What you want is an array that can expand; a linked list is a good starting point.

Designing the Linked List

A linked list is typically implemented as a string of *nodes*. Each node points to one object (your data) and also, potentially, to the next node in the list. If there is no next node in the list, the node points to NULL (see Figure 3.1).

FIGURE 3.1.

Linked list.

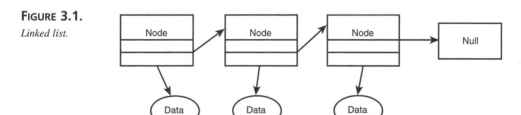

We want each node to have a specific and detailed function, so we will create three specialized types: LinkedList, TailNode, and InternalNode. The LinkedList provides the client with an entry point into the list. The TailNode acts as a sentry and marks the end of the list. Finally, the InternalNodes holds the actual data.

We'll factor out the common behavior of these three types into a base `Node` class, which supports two methods: `Insert()` and `Show()`. `Insert()` takes a data object and puts it in the list, and `Show()` displays the value of the data objects in the list. The relationship among these objects is shown in Figure 3.2.

FIGURE 3.2.

Node inheritance hierarchy.

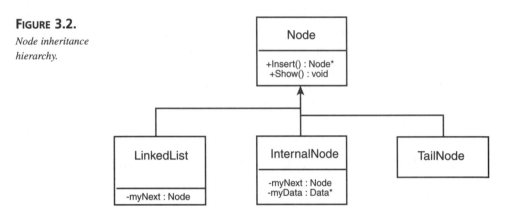

The `LinkedList` node and the `InternalNode` each has a `Node *` member variable named `myNext`. This pointer is used to find the next node in the list. This is, as you can see, a singly linked list, which means that while each node points to the next node in the list, it does not point back to the previous node.

Now all we need is something to put in the list; let's create a `Data` class. The only functionality we require of `Data` is that it have some value (we'll use an integer) and a method allowing two `Data` objects to compare themselves and decide which is "greater" so that we can put them in order. We'd also like the `Data` object to be able to display itself so that we can examine its value.

> **NOTE**
>
> In this design, we are saying that the `LinkedList` is really just a special kind of node, one responsible for presenting an interface to clients of the linked list. Does this violate the mandate that inheritance represents the *is-a* relationship? Not at all; a `LinkedList` *is* a node, a special node that marks the beginning of a list. The list itself is a virtual construct, an abstraction. The `LinkedList` object represents, essentially, a handle to the list.

Implementing the Linked List

When the `LinkedList` node is created, it immediately creates a `TailNode`:

```
LinkedList::LinkedList()
{
    nextNode = new TailNode;
}
```

Thus, an empty list consists of just these two objects: the `LinkedList` and the `TailNode`—there are no `InternalNodes` holding `Data` (see Figure 3.3).

FIGURE 3.3.

An empty list.

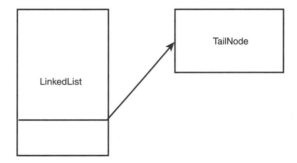

When you insert data into `LinkedList`, the `LinkedList` node hands the data to whatever its own `nextNode` pointer points to. Initially, this will be `TailNode`:

```
Node * LinkedList::Insert(Data * theData)
{
    nextNode = nextNode->Insert(theData);
    return this;
}
```

When `Insert()` is called on `TailNode`, `TailNode` knows that the object passed in is the smallest object in the list, and so `TailNode` inserts the new node into the list right before itself.

If the new object is the first object inserted, it is by definition the smallest object in the list, but any object arriving at the tail *must* be the smallest, or it would already have been inserted *by another node*, higher up in the list.

How does the `TailNode` insert the new data object? It just instantiates a new `InternalNode`. The constructor to the new `InternalNode` takes two arguments: a pointer to the data, and a pointer to whatever node created it (in this case, the `TailNode`). The new node then assigns its own data pointer to the data, and its own `nextNode` pointer to the node it was given, like this:

```
Node * TailNode::Insert(Data * theData)
{
    InternalNode * dataNode = new InternalNode(theData, this);
    return dataNode;
}
```

The new `InternalNode` points to the data and also to the `TailNode`. The `TailNode` returns to the calling object a pointer to the new node it created. In this first case, the `TailNode` returns a pointer to the new `InternalNode` to the `LinkedList`.

`LinkedList` assigns its own `nextNode` pointer to the return value from `nextNode->Insert()`. Thus, `LinkedList` is now pointing to the new `InternalNode`, as shown in Figure 3.4.

FIGURE 3.4.

After adding a node.

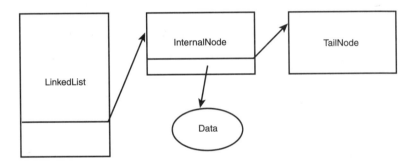

The next time through, `LinkedList` again passes the data to whatever its `nextNode` pointer is pointing to, but in this case, the pointer is pointing not to the `TailNode` but to an `InternalNode`.

When an `InternalNode` gets a `Data` object, it compares its own data with the data from the new node, like this:

```
Node * InternalNode::Insert(Data * theData)
{
    int result = myData->Compare(*theData);
```

Either the new object is smaller than the existing node or it isn't. If it is smaller, the `InternalNode` just passes the `Data` object along to whatever node its own `NextNode` data member points to. That is, the new `Data` object is passed along to the next node in the list:

```
        case kIsSmaller:
            nextNode = nextNode->Insert(theData);
            return this;
```

Each `InternalNode` in turn examines the data. If the new data is the smallest in the list, it will eventually run into the `TailNode` and be inserted as the last node in the list. On the other hand, if the new `Data` object runs into an `InternalNode` with data that is smaller than the new data, then *that* `InternalNode` inserts the new data into the list.

In this case, the `InternalNode` does just what the `TailNode` did: It creates a new `InternalNode` and tells the new `InternalNode` to point to *it* (that is, the new `InternalNode` points to the `InternalNode` that created it). This effectively inserts the new object into the list just before the current `InternalNode`. The current node then returns a pointer to the new node so that whoever called `Insert()` can now link to the new `InternalNode`.

```
case kIsSame:   // fall through
case kIsLarger: // new data comes before me
{
    InternalNode * dataNode = new InternalNode(theData, this);
    return dataNode;
}
```

NOTE

This sample code implements the design decision that objects of the same size as the current object are treated as if they were larger. You can easily rewrite this code to reject duplicates or to handle them in another way.

After the data is in the list, we ask the user for the next object. The program continues until the user signifies that he or she is done entering data. At that point, we tell the `LinkedList` to show the data. The `LinkedList` node passes this command to whatever its `NextNode` data member points to:

```
virtual void Show() { nextNode->Show(); }
```

If the list is empty, `LinkedList` points to `TailNode`. `TailNode`'s `Show()` method does nothing, so nothing is displayed. Much more common is that `LinkedList` points to an `InternalNode`. `InternalNode`'s `Show()` method is where the action is

```
virtual void Show() { myData->Show(); nextNode->Show(); }
```

Each `InternalNode` instructs its data object to print its value, and then passes the `Show()` command along to whatever node is next in the linked list. Thus, each `Data` object's `Show()` method is called in turn. Eventually, the `TailNode`'s `Show()` method is reached, and the display is completed.

When it is time to delete the list, the client has to delete only the LinkedList node. In the LinkedList destructor, we delete the next node in the list, like this:

```
~LinkedList() { delete nextNode; }
```

Each node in turn deletes the next node in the list until the TailNode is reached, at which point the deletions stop. Note that *no one* need keep track of how many nodes are in the list. Deleting LinkedList is like tipping over the first domino: Each knocks over the next as it falls until the entire list has been torn down.

Listing 3.1 shows how the whole program hangs together. I've stripped the code down to reveal just the essentials.

LISTING 3.1. OBJECT-ORIENTED LINKED LIST

```
#include <iostream.h>

enum { kSmaller, kLarger, kSame};

class Data
{
public:
    Data(int val):dataValue(val){}
    virtual ~Data(){}
    virtual int Compare(const Data &);
    virtual void Show() { cout << dataValue << endl; }
private:
    int dataValue;
};

int Data::Compare(const Data & theOtherData)
{
    if (dataValue < theOtherData.dataValue)
        return kSmaller;
    if (dataValue > theOtherData.dataValue)
        return kLarger;
    else
        return kSame;
}

class Node  // abstract data type
{
public:
    Node(){}
    virtual ~Node(){}
    virtual Node * Insert(Data * theData) = 0;
    virtual void Show() = 0;
private:
};
```

```
class InternalNode: public Node
{
public:
    InternalNode(Data * theData, Node * next);
    ~InternalNode(){ delete nextNode; delete myData; }
    virtual Node * Insert(Data * theData);
    virtual void Show() { myData->Show(); nextNode->Show(); }

private:
    Data * myData;
    Node * nextNode;
};


InternalNode::InternalNode(Data * theData, Node * next):
myData(theData),nextNode(next)
{
}

Node * InternalNode::Insert(Data * theData)
{
    int result = myData->Compare(*theData);

    switch(result)
    {
        case kSame: // fall through
        case kLarger: // new data comes before me
        {
            InternalNode * dataNode = new InternalNode(theData, this);
            return dataNode;
        }

        case kSmaller:
            nextNode = nextNode->Insert(theData);
            return this;
    }
        return this;
}

class TailNode : public Node
{
public:
    TailNode(){}
    ~TailNode(){}
    virtual Node * Insert(Data * theData);
    virtual void Show() { }

private:

};
```

continues

3

INHERITANCE, POLYMORPHISM, AND CODE REUSE

LISTING 3.1. CONTINUED

```cpp
Node * TailNode::Insert(Data * theData)
{
    InternalNode * dataNode = new InternalNode(theData, this);
    return dataNode;
}

class LinkedList : public Node
{
public:
    LinkedList();
    ~LinkedList() { delete nextNode; }
    virtual Node * Insert(Data * theData);
    virtual void Show() { nextNode->Show(); }
private:
    Node * nextNode;
};

LinkedList::LinkedList()
{
    nextNode = new TailNode;
}

Node * LinkedList::Insert(Data * theData)
{
    nextNode = nextNode->Insert(theData);
    return this;
}

int main()
{
    Data * pData;
    int val;
    LinkedList ll;

    for (;;)
    {
        cout << "What value do you want to add to the list? (0 when done):
➥";
        cin >> val;
        if (!val)
        break;
        pData = new Data(val);
        ll.Insert(pData);
    }

    cout << "\n\n";
    ll.Show();
    cout << "\n\n";
    return 0;
}
```

Each object has a single area of responsibility, and each object treats all nodes polymorphically. Yet, we can take advantage of the specialization of LinkedList, InternalNodes, and TailNode to create a very decentralized application, which enhances encapsulation and thus makes the code easier to maintain.

The most important part of this code, from the perspective of understanding polymorphism, is the point at which each Node calls nextNode->Insert(). Every node other than the TailNode knows only that it has a pointer to the next node in the list; it does not know whether that node is an InternalNode or a TailNode, but the static type makes all the difference. Examine InternalNode::Insert() and TailNode::Insert()—these functions are significantly different. The object making the call doesn't know which is being called, but the right thing happens.

In the same way, when you tell the nodes to show themselves, the right thing happens. That is, the LinkedList tells the next node to show itself, each InternalNode shows its data and then passes the command along to *its* next node; the TailNode acts as the sentry, stopping the chain.

Abstract Classes

The Data class we have been working with in the first part of this chapter is quite simple. It may be that in your application, you anticipate needing a few different, but related, data classes. It would be useful to be able to treat these objects polymorphically, allowing the linked list to manipulate Data classes without knowing or caring about the specifics of the individual derived types.

In anticipation of this, you might decide to change the Data class to be an Abstract Data Type (ADT). To do so, you would give it one or more pure virtual functions, as shown in Listing 3.2.

LISTING 3.2. DATA CLASS AS AN ABSTRACT DATA TYPE

```
class Data
{
public:
    Data(int val):myVal(val){}
    virtual ~Data(){}
    int Compare(const Data &);
    virtual void Show() = 0;
protected:
    int myVal;
};
```

The semantics of this declaration are that Data is an ADT, and that to create a concrete Data class, you must override the Show() method and provide a non-pure virtual (impure virtual?) method. The important idea is that the designer of Data is *requiring* derived classes to override the Show() method, and to provide a concrete implementation. You would do this to enforce the semantics of this object—that it is abstract and that all concrete objects derived from it will show themselves in whatever way is appropriate. You are, in essence, saying "every Data object *can* show itself, but there is no common implementation for doing so."

At this point, you can create derived classes that specialize how they display the value. For this contrived example, let's create two such classes: IntegerData, which displays the data as an integer, and GraphicData, which displays the value as a simple graph. Listing 3.3 shows these classes.

LISTING 3.3. CONCRETE DATA TYPES

```
class IntegerData : public Data
{
public:
    IntegerData(int val) : Data(val) {}
    virtual ~IntegerData() {}
    virtual void Show();
private:
};


class GraphicData : public Data
{
public:
    GraphicData(int val) : Data(val) {}
    virtual ~GraphicData() {}
    virtual void Show();
private:
};
```

Each of these classes overrides the Show() method. Here's how IntegerData does it:

```
void IntegerData::Show()
{
    cout << "The value of the integer is " << myVal << endl;
}
```

Here's how the GraphicData class overrides the Show() method:

```
void GraphicData::Show()
{
    cout << "(" << myVal << "): ";;
```

```
    for ( int i = 0; i < myVal; i++)
        cout << "*";
    cout << endl;
}
```

You can now use these classes in your source code, and decide *at runtime* which derived type to instantiate. The calling code need not know which Show() method will be called; by the power of polymorphism, the correct method is invoked, as demonstrated by Listing 3.4.

LISTING 3.4. POLYMORPHIC DATA TYPES

```
#include <iostream.h>

enum { kSmaller, kLarger, kSame};

class Data
{
public:
    Data(int val):myVal(val){}
    virtual ~Data(){}
    int Compare(const Data &);
    virtual void Show() = 0;
protected:
    int myVal;
};

class IntegerData : public Data
{
public:
    IntegerData(int val) : Data(val) {}
    virtual ~IntegerData() {}
    virtual void Show();
private:
};

void IntegerData::Show()
{
    cout << "The value of the integer is " << myVal << endl;
}

class GraphicData : public Data
{
public:
    GraphicData(int val) : Data(val) {}
    virtual ~GraphicData() {}
    virtual void Show();
private:
```

continues

LISTING 3.4. CONTINUED

```
};


void GraphicData::Show()
{
    cout << "(" << myVal << "): ";;
    for ( int i = 0; i < myVal; i++)
        cout << "*";
    cout << endl;
}


int Data::Compare(const Data & theOtherData)
{
    if (myVal < theOtherData.myVal)
        return kSmaller;
    if (myVal > theOtherData.myVal)
        return kLarger;
    else
        return kSame;
}

class Node   // abstract data type
{
public:
    Node(){}
    virtual ~Node(){}
    virtual Node * Insert(Data * theData) = 0;
    virtual void Show() = 0;
private:
};

class InternalNode: public Node
{
public:
    InternalNode(Data * theData, Node * next);
    ~InternalNode(){ delete nextNode; delete myData; }
    virtual Node * Insert(Data * theData);
    virtual void Show() { myData->Show(); nextNode->Show(); }

private:
    Data * myData;
    Node * nextNode;
};


InternalNode::InternalNode(Data * theData, Node * next):
myData(theData),nextNode(next)
{
```

```
    }

Node * InternalNode::Insert(Data * theData)
{
    int result = myData->Compare(*theData);

    switch(result)
    {
        case kSame: // fall through
        case kLarger: // new data comes before me
        {
            InternalNode * dataNode = new InternalNode(theData, this);
            return dataNode;
        }

        case kSmaller:
            nextNode = nextNode->Insert(theData);
            return this;
    }
        return this;
}

class TailNode : public Node
{
public:
    TailNode(){}
    ~TailNode(){}
    virtual Node * Insert(Data * theData);
    virtual void Show() { }

private:

};

Node * TailNode::Insert(Data * theData)
{
    InternalNode * dataNode = new InternalNode(theData, this);
    return dataNode;
}

class LinkedList : public Node
{
public:
    LinkedList();
    ~LinkedList() { delete nextNode; }
    virtual Node * Insert(Data * theData);
    virtual void Show() { nextNode->Show(); }
private:
    Node * nextNode;
};
```

continues

LISTING 3.4. CONTINUED

```
LinkedList::LinkedList()
{
    nextNode = new TailNode;
}

Node * LinkedList::Insert(Data * theData)
{
    nextNode = nextNode->Insert(theData);
    return this;
}

int main()
{
    Data * pData;
    int val;
    int whichData;
    LinkedList ll;

    for (;;)
    {
        cout << "[1] Integer, [2] Written, [0] Quit: ";
        cin >> whichData;
        if (!whichData)
        break;
        cout << "What value do you want to add to the list?  ";
        cin >> val;
        if (whichData == 1)
            pData = new IntegerData(val);
        else
            pData = new GraphicData(val);
        ll.Insert(pData);
    }

    cout << "\n\n";
    ll.Show();
    cout << "\n\n";
    return 0;
}
```

The linked list is unchanged from the earlier version in this chapter, but this time main()
asks the user which type of object he or she wants to use to store the value. Once the
user has entered the data, the call to Show() invokes the correct method. The node knows
only that it has some sort of Data object; it does not know or care whether it is an
IntegerData or a GraphicData object. Each node can have a different object, and yet the
correct method is called.

Overriding Pure Virtual Methods

Although concrete classes *must* provide an implementation to all the pure virtual functions, the abstract data type *may* provide one as well. Data is free to provide an implementation of Show(), and if it does, derived classes can invoke it by using the scope operator.

The ability to provide an implementation to pure virtual methods allows abstract data types to provide core functionality while still requiring derived classes to provide a specialized implementation. Note that the class remains abstract if the function is declared as pure virtual (=0), even if you provide an implementation. Thus, the Data class might look like this:

```cpp
class Data
{
public:
    Data(int val):myVal(val){}
    virtual ~Data(){}
    int Compare(const Data &);
    virtual void Show() = 0;
protected:
    int myVal;
};

void Data::Show()
{
    cout << "\nThis is your data. Any questions?\n";
}
```

Even though the Data class provides an implementation of Show(), the method is still pure virtual, and the class is still abstract. Derived classes that want to have instantiated objects must still override Show() and provide their own implementation. If the derived classes want to make use of Data's Show() method, they must explicitly access it with the scope operator (::)

```cpp
void GraphicData::Show()
{
    Data::Show();  // invoked using the scoping operator
    cout << "(" << myVal << "): ";;
    for ( int i = 0; i < myVal; i++)
        cout << "*";
    cout << endl;
}
```

Virtual Destructors

Not only is it common for the destructor to be virtual, it is imperative if you are going to use the class polymorphically. If, in Listing 3.4, we had not made the destructor virtual, then when the objects in the linked list were destroyed, we'd have had memory leaks in the Data objects. Remember that the Nodes do not know what *kind* of data object they're dealing with; they just delete the object as part of their own destructor:

```
~InternalNode(){ delete nextNode; delete myData; }
```

Note that myData is declared in the InternalNode class as follows:

```
Data * myData;
```

If the Data object's destructor is not virtual, then the Data part of the IntegerData is deleted, but the remainder of the derived object is not. Because IntegerData does not add any member variables in this simplified example, this won't matter much; but if IntegerData had member variables, there would be a memory leak.

Polymorphism Through Method Overloading

A second form of polymorphism does not rely on inheritance: It is accomplished by overloading a class's methods. The most common method to overload is, of course, the constructor. The constructor, like any method other than the destructor, can be over-loaded by changing either the number of parameters or their types.

Let's examine a simple class to explore the various methods you might decide to over-load. Listing 3.5 shows a simple set of classes to get us started.

LISTING 3.5. MEMBER OVERLOADING

```
#include <iostream.h>

class MyPoint
{
public:
    MyPoint (int x, int y):myX(x), myY(y) {}
    ~MyPoint(){}
    int GetX() const { return myX; }
    void SetX(int x) { myX = x; }
    int GetY() const { return myY; }
    void SetY(int y) { myY = y; }
private:
    int myX;
```

```
        int myY;
};

class MyRectangle
{
public:
    MyRectangle(MyPoint upperLeft, MyPoint lowerRight):
        myUpperLeft(upperLeft),
        myLowerRight(lowerRight)
        {}
        ~MyRectangle(){}
    int GetWidth() { return myLowerRight.GetX() - myUpperLeft.GetX(); }
    int GetHeight() { return myLowerRight.GetY() - myUpperLeft.GetY(); }

private:
    MyPoint myUpperLeft;
    MyPoint myLowerRight;
};

int main()
{
    MyPoint ul(0,0);
    MyPoint lw(20,30);
    MyRectangle myRect(ul,lw);
    cout << "This rectangle measures ";
    cout << myRect.GetWidth();
    cout << " by ";
    cout << myRect.GetHeight() << endl;
    return 0;
}
```

As you can see, a `Rectangle` class consists of a pair of points, each of which marks an opposite corner of the rectangle. The point, in turn, consists of an x and a y coordinate, as if on a grid. You create a `Rectangle` by passing in a pair of points. It is a trivial matter to overload the constructor so that you can create a `Rectangle` not by passing in a pair of points, but by passing in the x and y coordinates of the upper-left and lower-right corners of the rectangle, as shown in Listing 3.6.

LISTING 3.6. OVERLOADED CONSTRUCTOR

```
#include <iostream.h>

class Point
{
public:
    Point (int x, int y):myX(x), myY(y) {}
    ~Point(){}
```

continues

3

INHERITANCE, POLYMORPHISM, AND CODE REUSE

LISTING 3.6. CONTINUED

```cpp
    int GetX() const { return myX; }
    void SetX(int x) { myX = x; }
    int GetY() const { return myY; }
    void SetY(int y) { myY = y; }
private:
    int myX;
    int myY;
};

class Rectangle
{
public:
    Rectangle(Point upperLeft, Point lowerRight):
        myUpperLeft(upperLeft),
        myLowerRight(lowerRight)
        {}

    Rectangle(int upperLeftX, int upperLeftY, int lowerRightX, int
➥lowerRightY):
        myUpperLeft(upperLeftX,upperLeftY),
        myLowerRight(lowerRightX,lowerRightY)
        {}

        ~Rectangle(){}
    int GetWidth() { return myLowerRight.GetX() - myUpperLeft.GetX(); }
    int GetHeight() { return myLowerRight.GetY() - myUpperLeft.GetY(); }

private:
    Point myUpperLeft;
    Point myLowerRight;
};


int main()
{
    Point ul(0,0);
    Point lw(20,30);
    Rectangle myRect(ul,lw);
    Rectangle otherRect(0,5,20,30);

    cout << "myRect measures ";
    cout << myRect.GetWidth();
    cout << " by " << myRect.GetHeight() << endl;

    cout << "otherRect measures ";
    cout << otherRect.GetWidth();
    cout << " by " << otherRect.GetHeight() << endl;

    return 0;
}
```

It is important to note that the *default* constructor is *not* the constructor provided by default, but rather is any constructor that takes no parameters. It turns out that the compiler provides a default constructor for you *if you have declared no other constructors*. Because we have, in fact, explicitly declared constructors for this class, we currently have no default constructor and must provide one.

There are three other methods that the compiler provides for you if you don't declare one: the destructor, the copy constructor, and the assignment operator.

These three methods, along with the default constructor, are called the *canonical methods* of any class. It is good programming practice to explicitly declare these methods for any nontrivial class. You will find that I'll leave these out in some simple example programs in the book, but I never leave them out of commercial software.

The need for these methods becomes much clearer when the class manages memory. Let's rewrite the `Rectangle` class to keep its points on the heap, as shown in Listing 3.7.

LISTING 3.7. MEMBERS ON THE HEAP

```
class Rectangle
{
public:
    Rectangle(Point upperLeft, Point lowerRight):
        myUpperLeft ( new Point(upperLeft)),
        myLowerRight(new Point(lowerRight))
        {}

    Rectangle(int upperLeftX, int upperLeftY, int lowerRightX, int
lowerRightY):
        myUpperLeft(new Point(upperLeftX,upperLeftY)),
        myLowerRight(new Point(lowerRightX,lowerRightY))
        {}

    ~Rectangle(){ delete myUpperLeft; delete myLowerRight;}
    int GetWidth() { return myLowerRight->GetX() - myUpperLeft->GetX(); }
    int GetHeight() { return myLowerRight->GetY() - myUpperLeft->GetY(); }

private:
    Point * myUpperLeft;
    Point * myLowerRight;
};
```

I'm happy to report that *nothing* else in the program has to change; the storage mechanism of the `Point` member is entirely encapsulated within the `Rectangle` class. Note that the destructor must now delete the `Point`s, and the constructor must initialize them on the heap. Also, although I normally set pointers to `NULL` after deleting them, I don't do so in the destructor because there is no chance of the pointer being used again (the object is about to wink out of existence).

> **NOTE**
>
> I normally eschew inline methods, especially inline methods with more than one line of instruction, but for the purposes of this book, inline instructions make tighter, smaller examples that are perhaps more easily understood.

Memory Management

Once your class is managing memory, you must ensure that your copy constructor and assignment operator are making deep, not shallow, copies. The copy constructor and assignment operators provided by the compiler make bitwise, that is shallow, copies. That means they copy the pointer but not the object pointed to.

When you pass an object by value, either into a function or as a function's return value, a temporary copy of that object is made. If the object is a user-defined object (such as a `Rectangle` object from the example in the last discussion), that class's copy constructor is called to create the temporary object.

All copy constructors take one parameter: a constant reference to an object of the same class. The default copy constructor, provided by the compiler, copies each member bit by bit. Thus, if you passed a `Rectangle` into a function by value, a copy is made whose pointers point to the same memory as the original. Listing 3.8 shows a hand-written copy constructor that acts like the constructor provided by the compiler. *Do not attempt to run this code—it may crash.* The point of this exercise is to make explicit the problems with a shallow copy constructor.

LISTING 3.8. EXPLICIT SHALLOW COPY CONSTRUCTOR

```
#include <iostream.h>

class Point
{
public:
    Point (int x, int y):myX(x), myY(y) {}
    ~Point(){}
    int GetX() const { return myX; }
    void SetX(int x) { myX = x; }
    int GetY() const { return myY; }
    void SetY(int y) { myY = y; }
```

```
private:
    int myX;
    int myY;
};

class Rectangle
{
public:
    Rectangle(Point upperLeft, Point lowerRight):
        myUpperLeft ( new Point(upperLeft)),
        myLowerRight(new Point(lowerRight))
        {}

    Rectangle(int upperLeftX, int upperLeftY, int lowerRightX, int
➥lowerRightY):
        myUpperLeft(new Point(upperLeftX,upperLeftY)),
        myLowerRight(new Point(lowerRightX,lowerRightY))
        {}

    Rectangle( const Rectangle & rhs ):
        myUpperLeft(rhs.myUpperLeft),
        myLowerRight(rhs.myLowerRight)
        {
            cout << "In Rectangle's copy constructor...\n";
        }

    ~Rectangle()
        {
            cout << "\nIn destructor..." << endl;
            delete myUpperLeft;
            delete myLowerRight;
        }
    int GetWidth() { return myLowerRight->GetX() - myUpperLeft->GetX(); }
    int GetHeight() { return myLowerRight->GetY() - myUpperLeft->GetY(); }

// private:
    Point * myUpperLeft;
    Point * myLowerRight;
};

void SomeFunction( Rectangle );

int main()
{
    Point ul(0,0);
    Point lw(20,30);
    Rectangle myRect(ul,lw);

    cout << "myRect measures ";
```

continues

3
INHERITANCE,
POLYMORPHISM,
AND CODE REUSE

LISTING 3.8. CONTINUED

```cpp
    cout << myRect.GetWidth();
    cout << " by " << myRect.GetHeight() << endl;

    cout << "myRect address: " << &myRect << endl;
    cout << "myRect->myUpperLeft: " << myRect.myUpperLeft << endl;
    cout << "&myRect.myUpperLeft: " << &myRect.myUpperLeft << endl;


    SomeFunction(myRect);

    cout << "Back from SomeFunction";

    return 0;
}

void SomeFunction ( Rectangle r )
{
    cout << "r measures ";
    cout << r.GetWidth();
    cout << " by " << r.GetHeight() << endl;

    cout << "r address: " << &r << endl;
    cout << "r->myUpperLeft: " << r.myUpperLeft << endl;
    cout << "&r.myUpperLeft: " << &r.myUpperLeft << endl;

    cout << "Returning from SomeFunction!";
}
```

Here's the output from the program in Listing 3.8:

```
myRect measures 20 by 30
myRect address: 0x0012FF6C
myRect->myUpperLeft: 0x00421180
&myRect.myUpperLeft: 0x0012FF6C
In Rectangle's copy constructor…
r measures 20 by 30
r address: 0x0012FF48
r->myUpperLeft: 0x00421180
&r.myUpperLeft: 0x0012FF48
Returning from SomeFunction!
In destructor…
Back from SomeFunction
In destructor…
```

This program provides a copy constructor that mimics the simple bitwise (shallow) copy constructor provided by the compiler. Note that I have made the member variables public so that we can examine them from main(). Here's how it works: In main(), we declare a rectangle named myRect. We initialize the rectangle and report its size. We then report the address of the rectangle itself, followed by the address of the object held by myUpperLeft and then the address of that pointer.

We then pass the rectangle by value to SomeFunction(). Note that a message is printed indicating that we're passing through the copy constructor as expected. We then print out the same information for the rectangle from within SomeFunction(). The critical thing to note is that the address of the myUpperLeft Point member of r (the rectangle in SomeFunction()) is the same as the address of the myUpperLeft Point member of myRect.

When we return from SomeFunction(), the destructor is invoked as you would expect. When we then exit main(), the destructor for myRect is also called. Unfortunately, because myRect's myUpperLeft pointer points to the same object as r's, we now have a problem—r was destroyed and the Point is no longer there. Oops.

Figure 3.5 illustrates what has happened.

FIGURE 3.5.

*Two objects shar-
ing memory due to
shallow copy.*

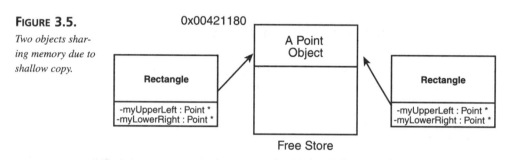

When the copy is deleted, the memory is marked as free. When the original object is deleted, you are deleting an already deleted pointer. If you are lucky, you will crash right away. Not good.

The solution to this ugly and embarrassing situation is to write a copy constructor that does not just copy the pointer, but copies the object pointed to. Figure 3.6 shows what we hope to accomplish, and Listing 3.9 demonstrates one implementation of the new copy constructor.

LISTING 3.9. DEEP COPY

```
class Rectangle
{
public:
    Rectangle(Point upperLeft, Point lowerRight):
        myUpperLeft ( new Point(upperLeft)),
```

continues

LISTING 3.9. CONTINUED

```cpp
        myLowerRight(new Point(lowerRight))
        {}

    Rectangle(int upperLeftX, int upperLeftY, int lowerRightX, int
lowerRightY):
        myUpperLeft(new Point(upperLeftX,upperLeftY)),
        myLowerRight(new Point(lowerRightX,lowerRightY))
        {}

    Rectangle( const Rectangle & rhs ):
        myUpperLeft(new Point(*myUpperLeft)),
        myLowerRight(new Point(*myLowerRight))
        {
            cout << "\nIn Rectangle's copy constructor...\n";
        }

    ~Rectangle()
    {
        cout << "\nIn destructor..." << endl;
        delete myUpperLeft; delete myLowerRight;
    }

    int GetWidth() { return myLowerRight->GetX() - myUpperLeft->GetX(); }
    int GetHeight() { return myLowerRight->GetY() - myUpperLeft->GetY(); }

// private:
    Point * myUpperLeft;
    Point * myLowerRight;
};
```

FIGURE 3.6.

Result of deep copy.

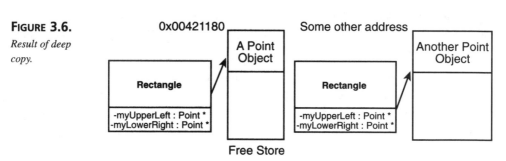

Here's the output from the revised program in Listing 3.9:

```
In Point's copy constructor
In Point's copy constructor
In Point's copy constructor
In Point's copy constructor
myRect measures 20 by 30
```

```
myRect address: 00x0012FF6C
myRect->myUpperLeft: 0x00421180
&myRect.myUpperLeft: 0x0012FF6C

In Point's copy constructor
In Point's copy constructor
In Rectangle's copy constructor…
r measures 1962613862 by 881745716
r address: 0x0012FF34
r->myUpperLeft: 0x004211E0
&r.myUpperLeft: 0x0012FF34
Returning from SomeFunction!
In destructor…
Back from SomeFunction!
In destructor…
```

We have modified the `Rectangle`'s copy constructor to create a new `Point` object. This change allocates memory for the new copy, and the output reflects this. The address of `myRect->myUpperLeft` is now different from the address of `r->myUpperLeft`, and this code does not crash.

Issues in Overloading Other Operators

Although you can overload any method, overloading operators causes the most confusion—even for experienced programmers. The trick in understanding operator overloading is that the compiler translates an operator (such as +, =, ++) into a method (such as `myClass::operator=()`).

Operators come in three flavors: unary (++, --), binary (+, -) and ternary (?). The *arity* of the operator is determined by how many terms or expressions are involved. With a unary operator, only one term is involved (for example, x++, y--). With a binary operator, two terms are involved (for example, a = b, x+y). There is only one ternary operator: the conditional operator ? (for example, x ? `true` : `false`).

You are free to overload virtually any of the built-in operators, but you cannot create new operators of your own. Therefore, although you can give your class an increment operator (++), you cannot create a squared operator. Although you can overload these operators to do anything you want, it is good programming practice for them to make sense. You *can* have the ++ operator decrement, but it would be dopey to do so.

Assignment Operator

The single most important operator to overload is the assignment operator. The same issue of deep versus shallow copies applies to the assignment operator as it does to the copy constructor. The assignment operator is a *binary* operator `--`. Two terms participate: the left side and the right side. Suppose that you write the following statement:

```
myRect = otherRect;
```

You know that the compiler turns this code into the following:

```
myRect.operator=(otherRect);
```

That is, the compiler turns the assignment into a method call on the object on the left side of the assignment operator, and passes in the object on the right side as a parameter.

Note that this assignment will invoke the compiler-created default assignment operator if you have not written your own. Again, the default assignment operator does a simple bitwise copy, and the result is a crash when the copy is destroyed. You can solve this problem by writing your own assignment operator that provides a deep copy—but watch out! There is a subtle risk!

Here is a reasonable first attempt at creating an assignment operator. It has a bug in it; see whether you can find it before reading the analysis:

```
Rectangle & Rectangle::operator=(const Rectangle & rhs)
{
    delete myUpperLeft;
    delete myLowerRight;
    myUpperLeft = new Point(*rhs.myUpperLeft);
    myLowerRight= new Point(*rhs.myLowerRight);
    return *this;
}
```

Note that this assignment operator carefully deletes the original member variables before creating new values, avoiding the obvious potential for a memory leak. There is still a problem, however. If, in your code, you write your assignment so that the object is assigned to itself, you will have a bit of a problem.

If you are passing references around, it is possible that you will end up writing something like this:

```
myFirstRect = myOtherRect;
```

In fact, under some conditions, the two names `myFirstRect` and `myOtherRect` will really point to the same object. When that happens, the member variables `myUpperLeft` and `myLowerRight` will be destroyed, and when it is time to do the copy, there will be no valid data to assign!

You protect yourself from this admittedly unlikely scenario by first checking to make sure that you've not assigned to yourself. Listing 3.10 demonstrates a working model. Again, I've temporarily provided public access to the member variables so that `main()` can prove that the addresses of the two objects are distinct.

LISTING 3.10. CHECK FOR ASSIGNMENT TO SELF

```
#include <iostream.h>

class Point
{
public:
    Point (int x, int y):myX(x), myY(y) {}
    Point (const Point & rhs):
        myX(rhs.myX),
        myY(rhs.myY)
        {
            cout << "In Point's copy constructor\n";
        }
    ~Point(){}

    int GetX() const { return myX; }
    void SetX(int x) { myX = x; }
    int GetY() const { return myY; }
    void SetY(int y) { myY = y; }
private:
    int myX;
    int myY;
};

class Rectangle
{
public:
    Rectangle(Point upperLeft, Point lowerRight):
        myUpperLeft ( new Point(upperLeft)),
        myLowerRight(new Point(lowerRight))
        {}

    Rectangle(int upperLeftX, int upperLeftY, int lowerRightX, int
➥lowerRightY):
        myUpperLeft(new Point(upperLeftX,upperLeftY)),
        myLowerRight(new Point(lowerRightX,lowerRightY))
        {}

    Rectangle( const Rectangle & rhs ):
        myUpperLeft(new Point(*myUpperLeft)),
        myLowerRight(new Point(*myLowerRight))
        {
```

continues

LISTING 3.10. CONTINUED

```cpp
                cout << "\nIn Rectangle's copy constructor...\n";
        }

    ~Rectangle()
    {
        cout << "\nIn destructor..." << endl;
        delete myUpperLeft; delete myLowerRight;
    }

    Rectangle & operator=(const Rectangle & rhs);

    int GetWidth() { return myLowerRight->GetX() - myUpperLeft->GetX(); }
    int GetHeight() { return myLowerRight->GetY() - myUpperLeft->GetY(); }

//private:
    Point * myUpperLeft;
    Point * myLowerRight;
};

Rectangle & Rectangle::operator=(const Rectangle & rhs)
{
    if ( this == &rhs )  // protect against a = a
        return *this;

    delete myUpperLeft;
    delete myLowerRight;
    myUpperLeft = new Point(*rhs.myUpperLeft);
    myLowerRight= new Point(*rhs.myLowerRight);
    return *this;
}

int main()
{
    Point ul(0,0);
    Point lw(20,30);
    Rectangle myRect(ul,lw);
    Rectangle otherRect(0,30,50,50);

    cout << "\nmyRect measures ";
    cout << myRect.GetWidth();
    cout << " by " << myRect.GetHeight() << endl;

    cout << "myRect address: " << &myRect << endl;
    cout << "myRect->myUpperLeft: " << myRect.myUpperLeft << endl;
    cout << "&myRect.myUpperLeft: " << &myRect.myUpperLeft << endl;


    cout << "\notherRect measures ";
    cout << otherRect.GetWidth();
```

```
    cout << " by " << otherRect.GetHeight() << endl;

    cout << "otherRect address: " << &otherRect << endl;
    cout << "otherRect->myUpperLeft: " << otherRect.myUpperLeft << endl;
    cout << "&otherRect.myUpperLeft: " << &otherRect.myUpperLeft << endl;


    cout << "\nAssigning myRect = otherRect...\n";
    myRect = otherRect;


    cout << "\notherRect measures ";
    cout << otherRect.GetWidth();
    cout << " by " << otherRect.GetHeight() << endl;

    cout << "otherRect address: " << &otherRect << endl;
    cout << "otherRect->myUpperLeft: " << otherRect.myUpperLeft << endl;
    cout << "&otherRect.myUpperLeft: " << &otherRect.myUpperLeft << endl;


    return 0;
}
```

Overloading the Increment Operators

The increment prefix and postfix operators have caused enormous confusion over the years, even though the implementation is straightforward when you consider the *semantics* of the two variants. The prefix operator's semantics are "increment, and then fetch." The postfix operator's semantics are "fetch, and then increment."

Consider the following statements:

```
int a=0, b=5;
a = b++;
```

After these statements are executed, a is 5 and b is 6. That is, a was assigned the value in b (5) and then the value in b was incremented. To support this, the increment operator must be prepared to return the value that was originally in b, but must also set b's value to 1 greater.

This is most easily seen with an example. First, we must decide whether the increment operator has meaning to our class. What might it mean to increment a `Rectangle`? We can, of course, assign any meaning we want—we're free to use the increment operator to return the position of the upper-left corner's coordinates:

```
Point upperLeft = myRect++;  // return the current upper left via
➥operator++
```

That is legal C++, but if you worked for me, it would be the last line of C++ you wrote in my employ. The old line about this language is true: C++ makes it harder to shoot yourself in the foot, but when you do, you blow your whole leg off.

Clearly, the increment operator (++) should be used to increment. However, it isn't obvious what it means to "increment a rectangle," and I wouldn't use the increment operator in this way. Is it meaningful to increment a Point? I'd say this is a borderline condition; you *could* decide that incrementing a Point increases both the x and y coordinate by 1, but that is (pardon me) stretching the Point. Listing 3.11 illustrates how you might provide such an increment operator.

LISTING 3.11. INCREMENT OPERATOR

```cpp
#include <iostream.h>

class Point
{
public:
    Point (int x, int y):myX(x), myY(y) {}
    Point (const Point & rhs):
        myX(rhs.myX),
        myY(rhs.myY)
        {
            cout << "In Point's copy constructor\n";
        }
    ~Point(){}

    int GetX() const { return myX; }
    void SetX(int x) { myX = x; }
    int GetY() const { return myY; }
    void SetY(int y) { myY = y; }

    const Point &      operator++();
    Point                     operator++(int);
    const Point &      operator--();
    Point                     operator--(int);

private:
    int myX;
    int myY;
};


const Point & Point::operator++()
{
    ++myX;
    ++myY;
    return *this;
}
```

```
Point   Point::operator++(int)
{
    Point temp(*this); // hold the current value
    ++myX;
    ++myY;
    return temp;
}


const Point & Point::operator--()
{
    --myX;
    --myY;
    return *this;
}

Point Point::operator--(int)
{
    Point temp(*this); // hold the current value
    --myX;
    --myY;
    return temp;
}



class Shape
{
public:
    Shape(){}
    ~Shape(){}
    virtual Shape * Clone() const { return new Shape(*this); }
};

class Rectangle : public Shape
{
public:
    Rectangle(Point upperLeft, Point lowerRight):
        myUpperLeft ( new Point(upperLeft)),
        myLowerRight(new Point(lowerRight))
        {}

    Rectangle(int upperLeftX, int upperLeftY, int lowerRightX, int
lowerRightY):
        myUpperLeft(new Point(upperLeftX,upperLeftY)),
        myLowerRight(new Point(lowerRightX,lowerRightY))
        {}

    Rectangle( const Rectangle & rhs ):
```

continues

LISTING 3.11. CONTINUED

```cpp
            myUpperLeft(new Point(*myUpperLeft)),
            myLowerRight(new Point(*myLowerRight))
            {
                cout << "\nIn Rectangle's copy constructor...\n";
            }

    Shape * Clone() const { return new Rectangle(*this); }

    ~Rectangle()
        {
                cout << "\nIn destructor..." << endl;
                delete myUpperLeft;
                delete myLowerRight;
        }

    Rectangle & operator=(const Rectangle & rhs);
    void Expand() { —(*myUpperLeft); ++(*myLowerRight); }

    int GetWidth() { return myLowerRight->GetX() - myUpperLeft->GetX(); }
    int GetHeight() { return myLowerRight->GetY() - myUpperLeft->GetY(); }
private:
    Point * myUpperLeft;
    Point * myLowerRight;
};

Rectangle & Rectangle::operator=(const Rectangle & rhs)
{
    if ( this == &rhs )   // protect against a = a
        return *this;

    delete myUpperLeft;
    delete myLowerRight;
    myUpperLeft = new Point(*rhs.myUpperLeft);
    myLowerRight= new Point(*rhs.myLowerRight);
    return *this;
}

int main()
{
    Point ul(10,10);
    Point lw(20,30);
    Rectangle myRect(ul,lw);

    cout << "\nmyRect measures ";
    cout << myRect.GetWidth();
    cout << " by " << myRect.GetHeight() << endl;

    myRect.Expand();
```

```
    cout << "\nmyRect measures ";
    cout << myRect.GetWidth();
    cout << " by " << myRect.GetHeight() << endl;


    return 0;
}
```

Note that the postfix operators capture the current state of the object in a temporary before updating their internal member variables. In this way, they can return the original state while still updating themselves.

The operators which create a temporary must, of course, return by values because you can't return a reference to an object which is going out of scope. Even when we're returning a reference to `*this`, however, we return a *constant* reference. This is so that you cannot write something like the following:

```
    Point a=7;
    a++++;
```

Because this syntax is not allowed in the built-in classes, we don't allow it here.

Virtual Copy Constructors

In addition to the constructors, destructor, copy constructors, and assignment operator, consider creating a "virtual copy constructor" for your class. Although C++ does not support the idea of virtual constructors, you often need to be able to return a copy of an object that is an exact duplicate, even when treating the object polymorphically.

The common answer to this situation is to create a *clone* method that simply returns a pointer to an object of the same type. Imagine that Rectangle derives from Shape. The Shape class might include this declaration:

```
    virtual Shape * Shape::Clone() const { return new Shape(*this); }
```

Rectangle, in turn, might override this method as follows:

```
    virtual Shape * Rectangle::Clone() const { return new
➥Rectangle(*this); }
```

Note that I return a Shape * in both cases. The new ANSI standard says that I can, in fact, return a different type in each override; so Rectangle would be free to return a Rectangle pointer. Unfortunately, few compilers have caught up with the standard as of this writing.

Multiple Inheritance

One of the capabilities available in C++, which is not available in Java, is ***multiple inheritance*** (although Java has a similar if limited capability with multiple *interfaces*). Multiple inheritance allows a class to inherit from more than one base class, bringing in the members and methods of two or more classes.

Experience has shown that multiple inheritance should be used judiciously. Often, the problem solved with multiple inheritance can be better solved with aggregation or with the use of templates. Many development systems have a hard time debugging methods of multiply inherited objects, and the entire program becomes more complex as classes become intertwined.

That said, multiple inheritance is a powerful tool, and there is no reason to set it aside. What is important is to use it when it is needed, but not as an end in itself. From the design perspective, it is important to understand what multiple inheritance models: the idea of a class sharing the characteristics and behavior of two, perhaps unrelated, other classes.

In simple multiple inheritance, the two base classes are unrelated (see Figure 3.7).

FIGURE 3.7.

Simple multiple inheritance.

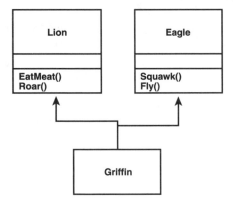

In this simple illustration, the **Griffin** class inherits from both **Lion** and **Eagle**. Thus, a **Griffin** can **EatMeat()**, **Roar()**, **Squawk()**, and **Fly()**. You implement this in C++ by listing the base classes, separated by commas. Listing 3.12 demonstrates the implementation of the classes modeled in Figure 3.7.

LISTING 3.12. IMPLEMENTING MULTIPLE INHERITANCE

```
#include <iostream.h>

class Lion
{
public:
    void EatMeat();
    void Roar();
protected:
private:
};

class Eagle
{
public:
    void Squawk();
    void Fly();
};

class Griffin : public Lion, public Eagle
{
};
```

This code is intentionally sparse—I've left out constructors, destructors, and so on to simplify the presentation and make the point. The Griffin class derives publicly both from Lion and from Eagle, therefore it specializes both these classes and implements our model that a Griffin is a Lion and also is an Eagle.

Problems in Multiple Inheritance

A problem arises when both **Lion** and **Eagle** share a common base class, for example **Animal**. Suppose that Animal has a member variable age of type int, and an accessor, GetAge(), that returns the value of the Animal's age. Figure 3.8 shows what the model looks like in UML.

Listing 3.13 shows how this model is implemented in C++. Again, I've left out all but the essential methods to illustrate the points covered in this discussion. In a real program, of course, you'd want to add constructors, destructors, and so forth.

LISTING 3.13. TWO CLASSES WITH A COMMON BASE CLASS

```
#include <iostream.h>

class Animal
{
public:
    Animal():age(1){}
    void Sleep(){}
    int GetAge() const { return age; }
```

continues

LISTING 3.13. CONTINUED

```cpp
private:
    int age;
};

class Lion : public Animal
{
public:
    void EatMeat(){}
    void Roar(){}
protected:
private:
};

class Eagle : public Animal
{
public:
    void Squawk(){}
    void Fly(){}
};

class Griffin : public Lion, public Eagle
{

};

int main()
{
    Griffin g;
    cout << g.GetAge();   // ambiguous! Won't link!
    return 0;
}
```

This common base class, **Animal**, now has a member variable that Griffin will inherit twice. When you ask for the age member variable, the compiler does not necessarily know *which* object's age you mean and will issue an error along these lines:

```
'Griffin::GetAge' is ambiguous, could be the 'GetAge' in base 'Animal' of
base 'Lion'of class 'Griffin' or the 'GetAge' in base 'Animal' of base
'Eagle' of class 'Griffin'.
```

Your compiler is trying to tell you that it doesn't know *which* Animal's age to get: the one Griffin inherits through Lion or the one Griffin inherits through Eagle. As the designer of the **Griffin** class, you must remain aware of these relationships and be prepared to solve the ambiguities they create. C++ facilitates your task by providing virtual inheritance, as demonstrated in Listing 3.14.

FIGURE 3.8.

Two classes sharing a common base class.

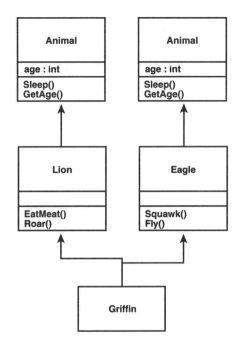

LISTING 3.14. VIRTUAL INHERITANCE

```cpp
#include <iostream.h>

class Animal
{
public:
    Animal():age(1){}
    void Sleep(){}
    int GetAge() const { return age; }
private:
    int age;
};

class Lion : virtual public Animal
{
public:
    void EatMeat(){}
    void Roar(){}
protected:
private:
};

class Eagle : virtual public Animal
```

continues

LISTING 3.14. CONTINUED

```
{
public:
    void Squawk(){}
    void Fly(){}
};

class Griffin : public Lion, public Eagle
{

};

int main()
{
    Griffin g;
    cout << g.GetAge();
    return 0;
}
```

The change here is that when the *base* classes of Griffin (that is, Lion and Eagle) derive from Animal, they do so with the key word virtual. Figure 3.9 shows this new model.

FIGURE 3.9.

Modeling virtual inheritance.

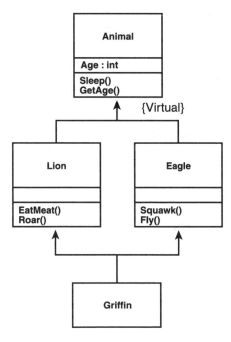

With virtual inheritance, **Griffin** inherits just one copy of the members of **Animal**, and the ambiguity is resolved. The problem with this solution is that both **Lion** and **Eagle** must know that they may be involved in a multiple inheritance relationship; the virtual keyword must be on *their* declaration of inheritance, not that of **Griffin**.

Note also that if Animal needs initialization (for example, if the age variable is passed as a parameter), then Lion and Eagle must initialize it (as usual) but Griffin *also* initializes Animal. This is very unusual, but it is the only way to resolve the ambiguity of Lion initializing to one value and Eagle initializing to another.

Listing 3.15 illustrates how you might initialize the base class in each of the virtually derived classes.

LISTING 3.15. INITIALIZING BASE CLASSES WITH VIRTUAL INHERITANCE

```
#include <iostream.h>

class Animal
{
public:
    Animal(int theAge):age(theAge){}
    void Sleep(){}
    int GetAge() const { return age; }
private:
    int age;
};

class Lion : virtual public Animal
{
public:
    Lion(int theAge, int howManyCubs):Animal(theAge),
numCubs(howManyCubs){}
    void EatMeat(){}
    void Roar(){}
protected:
private:
    int numCubs;
};

class Eagle : virtual public Animal
{
public:
    Eagle(int theAge, int theWeight):Animal(theAge), weight(theWeight){}
    void Squawk(){}
    void Fly(){}
private:
    int weight;
```

3

INHERITANCE,
POLYMORPHISM,
AND CODE REUSE

continues

LISTING 3.15. CONTINUED

```
};

class Griffin : public Lion, public Eagle
{
public:
    Griffin(int theAge, int theWeight, int howManyCubs):
        Lion(theAge, theWeight),    // initialize base class Lion
        Eagle(theAge, howManyCubs), // initilize base class Eagle
        Animal(theAge){}            // initilize virtual base class
Animal!

};

int main()
{
    int hisAge = 5;
    int hisWeight = 7;
    int litterSize = 4;
    Griffin g(hisAge, hisWeight, litterSize);
    cout << g.GetAge();
    return 0;
}
```

Multiple Inheritance Versus Containment

How do you know when to use multiple inheritance and when to avoid it? Should a car inherit from steering wheel, tire, and doors?

You could implement Car as shown here:

```
class SteeringWheel
{
};

class Door
{
};

class Tire
{
};

class Car : public SteeringWheel, public Door, public Tire
{
};
```

Although this code compiles, the model it implements is badly broken, as shown in Figure 3.10.

FIGURE 3.10.

The wrong way to model with inheritance.

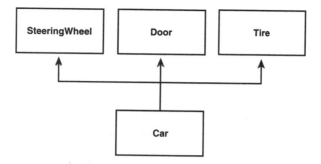

It is important to come back to the fundamentals: Public inheritance should always model specialization. The common expression for this is that inheritance should model *is-a* relationships. If you want to model the *has-a* relationship (for example, a car *has-a* steering wheel), you do so with aggregation. In C++, aggregation is implemented with member variables. That is, you give your Car class a member variable SteeringWheel:

```cpp
class SteeringWheel
{
};

class Door
{
};

class Tire
{
};

class Car
{
public:

private:
    SteeringWheel s;
    Door d[2];
    Tire t[4];
};
```

So, is a car a steering wheel, or does it *have* a steering wheel? You might argue that a car is a combination of a steering wheel, a tire, and a set of doors, but this is *not* modeled in inheritance. However, a car is not a specialization of these things—it is an aggregation of these things. A car *has* a steering wheel, it *has* doors, and it *has* tires. You diagram these relationships in the UML using the aggregation symbol shown in Figure 3.11.

FIGURE 3.11.
Modeling with aggregation.

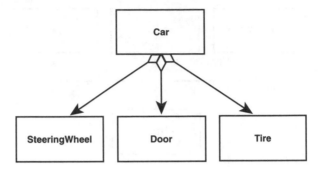

The open diamond on the `Car` class indicates that the `Car` object *has* whatever is on the other side of the connecting line. In this case, the `Car` *has* at least one steering wheel, door, and tire. We can make this drawing more precise by adding *multiplicity*—that is, by indicating how many of each object the `Car` might have (see Figure 3.12).

FIGURE 3.12.
The UML designation of multiplicity.

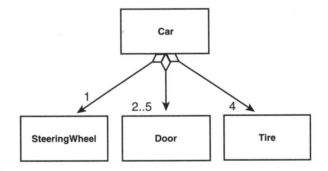

The diagram in Figure 3.12 indicates that a `Car` has exactly one `SteeringWheel` and four tires (`Vehicles` with a different number of tires are not `Cars`), and from two to five doors (coupes have two doors, hatchbacks have three, sedans have four, and minivans have five doors).

Summary

Polymorphism is a powerful tool for C++ programmers. It can be accomplished through method and operator overloading—allowing the client great flexibility in its interaction with the server object. An even more powerful implementation of polymorphism can be accomplished by overriding virtual methods in derived classes. Entire hierarchies of classes can be built, each specializing the implementation of virtual methods.

Multiple inheritance and containment provide tools for creating powerful polymorphic objects, but is important to focus less on the implementation and more on the design and semantics of your model. If you understand the design of your class, the implementation follows naturally.

Implementation Issues

PART

II

IN THIS PART

Memory Management

In my experience of teaching C++ to literally more than 10,000 students, both in person and online, I've found that the single hardest conceptual area is memory management. Even experienced C++ programmers become confused in their understanding of pointers and references. I believe that one of the principal causes of this confusion is that so many primers teach pointers mechanically ("here is how you use them") rather than conceptually ("here is what they are").

Once you understand, fully and in your core, that a pointer is *nothing more* than a variable that holds an address, the rest becomes much easier. The implications of this understanding are listed here:

- The pointer itself is a variable, and thus has an address of its own.
- The pointer contains the address of the object you care about.
- You get to the object you care about by dereferencing the pointer.
- The new operator returns an address; a pointer is a good place to keep that address.

All of this becomes somewhat more complicated when you add *references*, because they are, essentially, automatically dereferenced pointers. The tricky thing with references is that they *always* refer to the object they reference and never to themselves. Here's a good quick test of your understanding of references:

```
#include <iostream.h>

int main()
{
    int x = 7;
    int & ref = x;
    ref = 8;
    int y = 10;
    ref = y;
    cout << "x = " << x;
    cout << " y = " << y;
    cout << " ref = " << ref << endl;
    return 0;
}
```

The question is, what will this print? Stop reading here until you know the answer. Did you answer this way:

```
x = 8, y = 10, ref = 10
```

If so, you made the most common mistake (don't feel bad, it's a trick question). Refer again to this statement:

```
    ref = y;
```

This statement did *not* point ref to y—instead, it was exactly as if I had written this:

```
    x = y;
```

Thus, here is the correct answer:

```
x = 10, y = 10, ref = 10
```

Finally, pointers and references present a specific and difficult challenge in the face of exceptions. When an exception is thrown, the stack is unwound and local variables are destroyed, but pointers are not.

This chapter discusses how to manage pointers and references to ensure that your program has no memory leaks—even in the presence of unpredictable exceptions.

Memory Management and Pointers

There are two ways to allocate memory for variables in C++: on the stack and on the heap. When variables are allocated on the stack, their constructor is called at allocation and their destructor is called when the object goes out of scope. The most common way for an object to go out of scope is for the function to return as shown in Listing 4.1.

LISTING 4.1. ALLOCATING MEMORY ON THE STACK

```cpp
#include <iostream.h>

class myClass
{
public:
    myClass(int val=0):myValue(val)
    {
        cout << "In myClass constructor\n";
    }
    myClass(const myClass & rhs):myValue(rhs.myValue)
    {
        cout << "In myClass copy constructor\n";
    }
    ~myClass() { cout << "In myClass Destructor\n"; }
    int GetValue() const { return myValue; }
private:
    int myValue;
};

int someFunction(myClass c);

int main()
```

continues

LISTING 4.1. CONTINUED

```
{
    cout << "In main, ready to create object(3)...\n"<< endl;
    myClass object(3);
    cout << "In main, object's value is: " << object.GetValue() << endl;
    cout << "In main, passing object (by value) to someFunction...\n" <<
➥endl;
    someFunction(object);
    cout << "In main, returned from someFunction. Exiting...\n" << endl;
    return 0;
}

int someFunction(myClass c)
{
    cout << "In someFunction, c's value is: " << c.GetValue() << endl;
    cout << "Exiting someFunction...\n" << endl;
    return c.GetValue();
}
```

Here is the output from the program in Listing 4.1:

```
In main, ready to create object(3)…

In myClass constructor
In main, object's value is: 3
In main, passing object (by value)to someFunction…

In myClass copy constructor
In someFunction, c's value is: 3
Exiting someFunction…

In myClass Destructor
In main, returned from someFunction. Exiting…

In myClass Destructor
```

In this simple example, we create an object on the stack in main() and then pass it by value to someFunction(). Passing by value creates a copy in the scope of the someFunction() function. When that copy goes out of scope, the destructor is called. When the object in main() goes out of scope, the destructor for the original object is called.

The second way to create an object is on the heap, using the new operator, as shown in Listing 4.2. The new operator allocates an (unnamed) object on the heap and returns the address of that object, which can then be stored in a pointer.

LISTING 4.2. ALLOCATING MEMORY ON THE HEAP

```cpp
#include <iostream.h>

class myClass
{
public:
    myClass(int val=0):myValue(val) { cout << "In myClass constructor\n";
}
    myClass(const myClass & rhs):myValue(rhs.myValue)
    {
        cout << "In myClass copy constructor\n";
    }
    ~myClass() { cout << "In myClass Destructor\n"; }
    int GetValue() const { return myValue; }
private:
    int myValue;
};

int someFunction(myClass c);
int someFunction(myClass *pc);

int main()
{
    cout << "In main, ready to create object(3)..."<< endl;
    myClass * pObject = new myClass(3);
    cout << "In main, pObject's value is: " << pObject->GetValue() <<
endl;
    cout << "In main, passing pObject (by value) to someFunction..." <<
endl;
    someFunction(*pObject);
    cout << "In main, returned from someFunction(*object).";
    cout << "Calling someFunction(object)..." << endl;
    someFunction(pObject);
    cout << "In main, returned from someFunction(object). "
    cout << "Deleting pObject..." << endl;
    delete pObject;
    return 0;
}

int someFunction(myClass c)
{
    cout << "In someFunction, c's value is: " << c.GetValue() << endl;
    cout << "Exiting someFunction..." << endl;
    return c.GetValue();
}

int someFunction(myClass * c)
{
```

continues

4

LISTING 4.2. CONTINUED

```
    cout << "In someFunction(myClass *), c's value is: ";
    cout << c->GetValue() << endl;
    cout << "Exiting someFunction..." << endl;
    return c->GetValue();
}
```

Here is the output from the program in Listing 4.2:

```
In main, ready to create object(3)...
In myClass constructor
In main, pObject's value is: 3
In main, passing pObject (by value) to someFunction...
In myClass copy constructor
In someFunction, c's value is: 3
Exiting someFunction...
In myClass Destructor
In main, returned from someFunction(*object). Calling
someFunction(object)...
In someFunction(myClass *), c's value is: 3
Exiting someFunction...
In main, returned from someFunction(object). Deleting pObject...
In myClass Destructor
```

This time, we allocate the object on the heap with this call:

```
myClass * pObject = new myClass(3);
```

The constructor is called as a result. We pass the object *by value* (dereferencing the pointer) to SomeFunction() with this statement:

```
    someFunction(*pObject);
```

The copy constructor is then called. An object is now created on the stack, which is destroyed when the function returns (note the call to the destructor).

We then pass the object to the overloaded someFunction() by reference, like this:

```
    someFunction(pObject);
```

This time, the copy constructor is not called because no copy is created. The object referenced in this function is the same object as referenced in main(). When this method returns, the destructor is *not* called. At this point, we are ready to exit main() but must remember explicitly to call delete. Every call to new must be matched by a call to delete or we'll create a memory leak.

Memory Leaks

The term *memory leak* is quite popular in the industry, but it isn't often explained. Here's the idea: If you allocate memory using new and fail to reclaim that memory using delete, the memory is irretrievably lost until your program ends. It is as if the memory "leaked out" of your program.

If you make this mistake in a function that allocates a lot of memory (a few big objects or lots of small objects), and you call this function repeatedly, it is entirely possible to crash your program (or slow it down tremendously) because you will run out of available memory. C++ has no automatic memory retrieval ("garbage collection") as does Java. You must reclaim the memory yourself.

Allocating Arrays

If you allocate an array of memory, you must remember to use the special delete[] operator. If you forget to use the delete[] operator and instead call delete (with no brackets), you will deallocate only the first object, and the rest of the memory will be lost. Listing 4.3 illustrates how the delete[] operator is used.

LISTING 4.3. USING delete[]

```
#include <iostream.h>

class myClass
{
public:
    myClass(int val=0):myValue(val) { cout << "In myClass constructor\n";
➡}
    myClass(const myClass & rhs):myValue(rhs.myValue)
    {
        cout << "In myClass copy constructor\n";
    }
    ~myClass() { cout << "In myClass Destructor\n"; }
    int GetValue() const { return myValue; }
    void SetValue(int theVal) { myValue = theVal; }
private:
    int myValue;
};

void someFunction();

int main()
{
    cout << "In main, ready to call someFunction..." << endl;
```

4

MEMORY
MANAGEMENT

continues

LISTING 4.3. CONTINUED

```
        someFunction();
        cout << "In main, returned from someFunction." << endl;
        return 0;
    }

    void someFunction()
    {
        const int arraySize = 5;
        myClass * pArray = new myClass[arraySize];
        for (int i = 0; i < arraySize; i++)
            pArray[i].SetValue(i);

        for (int j = 0; j < arraySize; j++)
            cout << "pArray[" << j << "]: " << pArray[j].GetValue() << endl;


        delete [] pArray;

    }
```

Here is the output from the preceding listing:

```
In main, ready to call someFunction...
In myClass constructor
In myClass constructor
In myClass constructor
In myClass constructor
In myClass constructor
pArray[0]: 0
pArray[1]: 1
pArray[2]: 2
pArray[3]: 3
pArray[4]: 4
In myClass Destructor
In myClass Destructor
In myClass Destructor
In myClass Destructor
In myClass Destructor
In main, returned from someFunction.
```

This is another simple example that explains how memory allocation works with an array of objects on the heap. The call to new allocates five objects on the heap, which are then assigned values. This call causes each of the objects to be destroyed in turn:

```
delete [] pArray
```

For efficiency, the delete operator (without square braces) assumes that you want to delete only a single object. The delete [] operator (with square braces) tells the compiler to use the count of objects recorded when you allocate the array. The correct number of objects are then destroyed, preventing a memory leak.

Stray, Dangling, and Wild Pointers

If you delete a pointer that has already been deleted, you risk crashing your program. To ensure that this does not happen, make it a practice to set all deleted pointers to NULL. It is safe and legal to delete a null pointer, as shown in Listing 4.4.

LISTING 4.4. DELETING A NULL POINTER

```
#include <iostream.h>

class myClass
{
public:
    myClass(int val=0):myValue(val) { cout << "In myClass constructor\n";
➡}
    myClass(const myClass & rhs):myValue(rhs.myValue)
    {
        cout << "In myClass copy constructor\n";
    }
    ~myClass() { cout << "In myClass Destructor\n"; }
    int GetValue() const { return myValue; }
    void SetValue(int theVal) { myValue = theVal; }
private:
    int myValue;
};



int main()
{
    myClass * pc = new myClass(5);
    cout << "The value of the object is " << pc->GetValue() << endl;
    delete pc;
    pc = 0;
    cout << "Here is other work, passing pointers around willy nilly.\n";
    cout << "Now ready to delete again..." << endl;
    delete pc;
    cout << "No harm done" << endl;
    return 0;
}
```

The following is the output from Listing 4.4:

```
In myClass constructor
The value of the object is 5
In myClass Destructor
```

4

MEMORY
MANAGEMENT

```
Here is other work, passing pointers around willy nilly.
Now ready to delete again...
No harm done
```

Of course, this example is absurd because you would never delete the same pointer twice in a single method. The problem, of course, is that you often pass pointers into and out of methods, making copies as you go. In a complicated program, it is easy to lose track and accidentally delete an already deleted pointer. Making sure that you set deleted pointers to NULL (0) protects you from this error. It also ensures that if you try to use that pointer, you get an immediate crash rather than a subtle and difficult-to-find bug. If you are going to fail, you want to fail with a bang, not a whimper—that is, you want to fail predictably (so that you can find the bug) and you want to fail *where the bug is*, not later in the program.

const Pointers

You can use the keyword const for pointers before the type, after the type, or in both places, depending on what you are trying to accomplish.

In the following statement, pOne is a pointer to a constant integer. The value being pointed to can't be changed:

```
const int * pOne;  // pointer to a constant integer
```

In this next statement, pTwo is a constant pointer to an integer. The integer can be changed, but pTwo can't point to anything else:

```
int * const pTwo; // constant pointer to an integer
```

In this third statement, pThree is a constant pointer to a constant integer. The value being pointed to can't be changed, and pThree can't be changed to point to anything else:

```
const int * const pThree;  // constant pointer to a constant integer
```

The trick to keeping this straight is to look *to the right* of the keyword const to find out what is being declared constant. If the *type* is to the right of the keyword, the value is constant:

```
const int * p1;  // the int pointed to is constant
```

If the *variable* is to the right of the keyword const, the pointer variable itself is constant:

```
int * const p2;  // p2 is constant, it can't point to anything else
```

const Pointers and const Member Functions

When a member function is declared const, the compiler flags as an error any attempt by that function to change data in the object to which it belongs.

When you declare an object to be const, you are in effect declaring that the this pointer is a pointer to a const object. A const this pointer can be used only with const member functions.

Passing By Reference

Each time you pass an object into a function by value, a copy of the object is made. Each time you return an object from a function by value, another copy is made.

These objects are created on the stack; copying them consumes processing time and system memory. For small objects, such as the built-in integer values, this is a trivial cost.

However, with larger user-created objects, the cost is greater. The size of a user-created object on the stack is the sum of each of its member variables. These, in turn, can each be user-created objects, and passing such a massive structure by copying it onto the stack can be very expensive in performance and memory consumption.

When the temporary object is destroyed, which happens when the function returns, the object's destructor is called. If an object is returned by value, a copy of that object will be created and destroyed as well.

Passing a const Pointer

Although passing a pointer is more efficient than passing an object by value, it is also more dangerous because it exposes the object to change and defeats the protection offered in passing by value.

Passing by value is like giving a museum a photograph of your masterpiece instead of the real thing. If vandals mark it up, no harm is done to the original. Passing by reference is like sending your home address to the museum and inviting guests to come over and look at the real thing.

The solution is to pass a const pointer. Doing so prevents calling any non-const method and thus affords you the protection of passing by value while preserving the efficiency of passing by reference. Once again the guests are invited to your home, but the art is behind bulletproof glass.

Passing a constant reference can give you the same efficiency without forcing you to use the rather cumbersome syntax of dereferencing pointers. A constant reference is really a reference to a constant object (references themselves are always constant). By passing a reference to a constant object, the object cannot be changed but no copy constructor is called.

You can pass a constant reference only when you know the object will not be NULL. Remember that although it is possible to create a reference to a NULL object, doing so renders your program *invalid*. It *may* crash, it may work just fine, but it isn't legal C++ and the results are unpredictable.

Don't Return a Reference to an Object That Isn't in Scope

After C++ programmers learn to pass by reference, they have a tendency to go hog-wild. It is possible, however, to overdo it. Remember that a reference is always an alias to some other object. If you pass a reference into or out of a function, be sure to ask yourself, "What is the object I'm aliasing, and will it still exist every time it's used?"

Listing 4.5 illustrates returning a reference to a temporary object. Please note that some compilers won't let this pass, others will. In any case, this program will almost certainly crash on execution. This program is *not* valid.

LISTING 4.5. RETURNING A REFERENCE TO A TEMPORARY OBJECT

```
#include <iostream.h>

class myClass
{
public:
    myClass(int val=0):myValue(val) { cout << "In myClass constructor\n";
➡}
    myClass(const myClass & rhs):myValue(rhs.myValue)
    {
        cout << "In myClass copy constructor\n";
    }
    ~myClass() { cout << "In myClass destructor\n"; }
    int GetValue() const { return myValue; }
    void SetValue(int theVal) { myValue = theVal; }
private:
    int myValue;
};

void SomeFunction();
myClass &WorkFunction();

int main()
{
    SomeFunction();
    return 0;
}

myClass & WorkFunction()
```

```
{
    myClass mc(5);
    return mc;
}


void SomeFunction()
{
    myClass &rC = WorkFunction();
    int value = rC.GetValue();
    cout << "rC's value: " << value << endl;
}
```

Here is the output from Listing 4.5:

```
In myClass constructor
In myClass destructor
rC's value: 1245036
```

WorkFunction() creates an object on the stack and returns a reference to it, which is assigned to a local reference (rc) in SomeFunction(). Unfortunately, rc now refers to an object that has gone out of scope. Thus, the reference is invalid, and the program itself is invalid.

You might be tempted to solve this problem by having WorkFunction() create the object on the heap. Thus, when the function returns, the object will continue to exist:

```
#include <iostream.h>
class myClass
{
public:
    myClass(int val=0):myValue(val) { cout << "In myClass constructor\n";
➥}
    myClass(const myClass & rhs):myValue(rhs.myValue)
    {
        cout << "In myClass copy constructor\n";
    }
    ~myClass() { cout << "In myClass Destructor\n"; }
    int GetValue() const { return myValue; }
    void SetValue(int theVal) { myValue = theVal; }
private:
    int myValue;
};

void SomeFunction();
myClass &WorkFunction();

int main()
{
    SomeFunction();
```

```
    return 0;
}

myClass & WorkFunction()
{
    myClass * pC = new myClass(5);
    return *pC;
}

void SomeFunction()
{
    myClass &rC = WorkFunction();
    int value = rC.GetValue();
    cout << "rC's value: " << value << endl;
}
```

The following is the output:

```
In myClass constructor
rC's value: 5
```

This revised code solves the problem introduced in Listing 4.5, but at the cost of introducing a memory leak. How is the memory allocated in WorkFunction() to be recovered? You can, of course, delete it in SomeFunction(), like this:

```
#include <iostream.h>

class myClass
{
public:
    myClass(int val=0):myValue(val) { cout << "In myClass constructor\n";
➡}
    myClass(const myClass & rhs):myValue(rhs.myValue)
    {
        cout << "In myClass copy constructor\n";
    }
    ~myClass() { cout << "In myClass Destructor\n"; }
    int GetValue() const { return myValue; }
    void SetValue(int theVal) { myValue = theVal; }
private:
    int myValue;
};

void SomeFunction();
myClass &WorkFunction();

int main()
{
    SomeFunction();
    return 0;
}
```

```
myClass &WorkFunction()
{
   myClass * pC = new myClass(5);
   return *pC;
}

void SomeFunction()
{
   myClass &rC = WorkFunction();
   int value = rC.GetValue();
   cout << "rC's value: " << value << endl;
   myClass * pC = &rC; // get a pointer to the memory
   delete pC;  // oops, now rC is a reference to a null object!
}
```

The output is as follows:

```
In myClass constructor
rC's value: 5
In myClass Destructor
```

In this example, you create a pointer to the memory on the heap (by taking the address of the reference) and then you delete that object. This works; the object is deleted. The problem is that rC is now a reference to a NULL object *and that is not legal*. On many compilers, this program will compile, link, and work. Do not be deceived; your program is not valid, and it is certainly not portable.

Pointer, Pointer, Who Has the Pointer?

When your program allocates memory on the free store (the heap), a pointer is returned. It is imperative that you keep a pointer to that memory, because once the pointer is lost, the memory cannot be deleted and becomes a memory leak.

As you pass this block of memory between functions, someone will "own" the pointer. Typically, the value in the block is passed using references, and the function that created the memory is the one that deletes it. But this is a general rule, not an iron-clad one.

It is dangerous for one function to create memory and another to free it, however. Ambiguity about who owns the pointer can lead to one of two problems: forgetting to delete a pointer or deleting it twice. Either error can cause serious problems in your program. It is safer to build your functions so that they delete the memory they create.

4

MEMORY
MANAGEMENT

> **TIP**
>
> If you are writing a function that has to create memory and then pass it back to the calling function, consider changing your interface. Have the calling function allocate the memory and then pass it into your function by reference. This moves all memory management out of your program and back to the function that is prepared to delete it.

Pointers and Exceptions

Memory management of objects on the heap becomes especially problematic in the presence of exceptions. Consider the example shown in Listing 4.6.

LISTING 4.6. HEAP OBJECTS AND EXCEPTIONS

```cpp
#include <iostream.h>


class myException
{
public:
    char * errorMsg() { return "Oops."; }
};

class Point
{
public:
    Point (int x, int y):myX(x), myY(y)
    {
        cout << "Point constructor called"<< endl;
    }
    Point (const Point & rhs):
        myX(rhs.myX),
            myY(rhs.myY){ cout << "Point copy constructor called" <<
➡endl;}
        ~Point(){ cout << "Point destructor called" << endl;}
    int GetX() const { return myX; }
    void SetX(int x) { myX = x; }
    int GetY() const { return myY; }
    void SetY(int y) { myY = y; }
private:
    int myX;
    int myY;
};

class Rectangle
```

```
{
public:
    Rectangle(Point upperLeft, Point lowerRight):
        myUpperLeft ( new Point(upperLeft)),
        myLowerRight(new Point(lowerRight))
        {}

    Rectangle(Point * pUpperLeft, Point * pLowerRight):
        myUpperLeft ( new Point(*pUpperLeft)),
        myLowerRight(new Point(*pLowerRight))
        {}


    Rectangle(int upperLeftX, int upperLeftY, int lowerRightX, int
lowerRightY):
        myUpperLeft(new Point(upperLeftX,upperLeftY)),
        myLowerRight(new Point(lowerRightX,lowerRightY))
        {}

    Rectangle( const Rectangle & rhs ):
        myUpperLeft(new Point(*myUpperLeft)),
        myLowerRight(new Point(*myLowerRight))
        {}

    ~Rectangle()
    {
        cout << "In Rectangle's destructor" << endl;
        delete myUpperLeft;
        delete myLowerRight;
    }


    int GetWidth() { return myLowerRight->GetX() - myUpperLeft->GetX(); }
    int GetHeight() { return myLowerRight->GetY() - myUpperLeft->GetY(); }

    void DangerousMethod() { throw myException(); }

 private:
    Point * myUpperLeft;
    Point * myLowerRight;
};


int main()
{

    try
    {
        cout << "Begin round 1..." << endl;
```

continues

4

MEMORY
MANAGEMENT

LISTING 4.6. CONTINUED

```cpp
            Point * pUL = new Point(0,0);
            Point * pLR = new Point(20,30);
            Rectangle myRectangle(pUL, pLR);
            int w = myRectangle.GetWidth();
            int h = myRectangle.GetHeight();
            cout << "the Rectangle is " << w << " by " << h << endl;
            delete pUL;
            delete pLR;
        }
        catch ( myException & e )
        {

            cout << "caught exception: " << e.errorMsg() << "\n\n" << endl;
        }


        try
        {
            cout << "Begin round 2..." << endl;
            Point * pUL = new Point(0,0);
            Point * pLR = new Point(20,30);
            Rectangle myRectangle(pUL, pLR);
            int w = myRectangle.GetWidth();
            int h = myRectangle.GetHeight();
            cout << "the Rectangle is " << w << " by " << h << endl;
            myRectangle.DangerousMethod();
            delete pUL;
            delete pLR;
        }
        catch ( myException & e )
        {

            cout << "caught exception: " << e.errorMsg() << "\n\n" << endl;
        }


        return 0;
}
```

Here is the output produced by this code:

```
Begin round 1...
Point constructor called
Point constructor called
Point copy constructor called
Point copy constructor called
the Rectangle is 20 by 30
Point destructor called
Point destructor called
In Rectangle's destructor
```

```
Point destructor called
Point destructor called
Begin round 2…
Point constructor called
Point constructor called
Point copy constructor called
Point copy constructor called
the Rectangle is 20 by 30
In Rectangle's destructor
Point destructor called
Point destructor called
caught exception: Oops.
```

In this simple example, you create a pair of `Point` objects and then use them (creating a copy) to create a rectangle. You then delete the `Point` objects. The second time through, you call `DangerousMethod()`, which throws an exception.

Count the constructors and destructors. In round 1, there is an off-setting destructor for every call to a constructor. This is not true in round 2. Because the exception is thrown, the `delete` statements are never reached, and we have created a memory leak.

Notice that in both rounds, the `Rectangle`'s destructor *is* called. Local objects (on the stack) are destroyed when exiting an exception, but pointers are *not* deleted.

We can fix this buggy program by adding the `delete` statement to the `catch` block. Note that we have to pull the pointers out of the scope of the `try` block so that `catch` can see them, as shown in Listing 4.7.

LISTING 4.7. DELETING POINTERS IN `catch` BLOCKS

```
int main()
{
    Point * pUL = 0;
    Point * pLR  = 0;
    try
    {
        cout << "Begin round 1..." << endl;
        pUL = new Point(0,0);
        pLR = new Point(20,30);
        Rectangle myRectangle(pUL, pLR);

        int w = myRectangle.GetWidth();
        int h = myRectangle.GetHeight();
        cout << "the Rectangle is " << w << " by " << h << endl;
        delete pUL;
```

4

MEMORY
MANAGEMENT

continues

LISTING 4.7. CONTINUED

```cpp
        delete pLR;
    }
    catch ( myException & e )
    {

        cout << "caught exception: " << e.errorMsg() << "\n\n" << endl;
    }


    try
    {
        cout << "Begin round 2..." << endl;
        pUL = new Point(0,0);
        pLR = new Point(20,30);
        Rectangle myRectangle(pUL, pLR);

        int w = myRectangle.GetWidth();
        int h = myRectangle.GetHeight();
        cout << "the Rectangle is " << w << " by " << h << endl;
        myRectangle.DangerousMethod();
        delete pUL;
        delete pLR;
    }
    catch ( myException & e )
    {
        cout << "caught exception: " << e.errorMsg() << "\n\n" << endl;
        delete pUL;
        delete pLR;
    }


    return 0;
}


int main()
{

    Point * pUL = 0;
    Point * pLR  = 0;
    try
    {
        cout << "Begin round 1..." << endl;
        pUL = new Point(0,0);
        pLR = new Point(20,30);
        Rectangle myRectangle(pUL, pLR);

        int w = myRectangle.GetWidth();
        int h = myRectangle.GetHeight();
```

```
        cout << "the Rectangle is " << w << " by " << h << endl;
        delete pUL;
        delete pLR;
    }
    catch ( myException & e )
    {

        cout << "caught exception: " << e.errorMsg() << "\n\n" << endl;
    }


    try
    {
        cout << "Begin round 2..." << endl;
        pUL = new Point(0,0);
        pLR = new Point(20,30);
        Rectangle myRectangle(pUL, pLR);

        int w = myRectangle.GetWidth();
        int h = myRectangle.GetHeight();
        cout << "the Rectangle is " << w << " by " << h << endl;
        myRectangle.DangerousMethod();
        delete pUL;
        delete pLR;
    }
    catch ( myException & e )
    {
        cout << "caught exception: " << e.errorMsg() << "\n\n" << endl;
        delete pUL;
        delete pLR;
    }


    return 0;
}
```

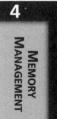

Here's the output from this revised program:

```
Begin round 1...
Point constructor called
Point constructor called
Point copy constructor called
Point copy constructor called
the Rectangle is 20 by 30
Point destructor called
Point destructor called
In Rectangle's destructor
Point destructor called
Point destructor called
Begin round 2...
Point constructor called
```

```
Point constructor called
Point copy constructor called
Point copy constructor called
the Rectangle is 20 by 30
In Rectangle's destructor
Point destructor called
Point destructor called
caught exception: Oops.


Point destructor called
Point destructor called
```

Although this revised code works, it is ugly and doesn't scale well. Copying the `deletes` into all the `catch` blocks is not a good long-term solution; it makes for code that is hard to maintain and prone to error. To *really* solve this problem, we need an object that sits on the stack but that acts like a pointer. We need a smart pointer, and the Standard Template Library offers exactly what we need: `auto_ptr`.

Using Auto Pointers

The Standard Template Library offers the `auto_ptr` class. An object of this class is intended to act like a pointer but to sit on the stack so that it is destroyed when an exception is thrown. The class works by stashing away the real pointer and deleting that pointer in its own destructor.

Listing 4.8 shows how you would rewrite the example from Listing 4.7 using `auto_ptr`.

LISTING 4.8. USING `auto_ptr`

```cpp
#include <iostream>
#include <memory>

using namespace std;

class myException
{
public:
    char * errorMsg() { return "Oops."; }
};

class Point
{
public:
    Point (int x, int y):myX(x), myY(y)
    {
        cout << "Point constructor called"<< endl;
    }
```

```
     Point (const Point & rhs):
         myX(rhs.myX),
             myY(rhs.myY){ cout << "Point copy constructor called" <<
 endl;}
         ~Point(){ cout << "Point destructor called" << endl;}
     int GetX() const { return myX; }
     void SetX(int x) { myX = x; }
     int GetY() const { return myY; }
     void SetY(int y) { myY = y; }
private:
     int myX;
     int myY;
};

class Rectangle
{
public:
     Rectangle( Point upperLeft, Point lowerRight ):
         myUpperLeft(new Point(upperLeft)),
         myLowerRight(new Point(lowerRight))
         {}

     Rectangle( auto_ptr<Point> pUpperLeft, auto_ptr<Point> pLowerRight ):
         myUpperLeft (new Point(*pUpperLeft)),
         myLowerRight(new Point(*pLowerRight))
         {}


     Rectangle(
         int upperLeftX,
         int upperLeftY,
         int lowerRightX,
         int lowerRightY ):
          myUpperLeft(new Point(upperLeftX,upperLeftY)),
          myLowerRight(new Point(lowerRightX,lowerRightY))
          {}

     Rectangle( const Rectangle & rhs ):
         myUpperLeft(new Point(*myUpperLeft)),
         myLowerRight(new Point(*myLowerRight))
         {}

     ~Rectangle(){ cout << "In Rectangle's destructor" << endl;  }


     int GetWidth() { return myLowerRight->GetX() - myUpperLeft->GetX(); }
     int GetHeight() { return myLowerRight->GetY() - myUpperLeft->GetY(); }

     void DangerousMethod() { throw myException(); }
```

4

MEMORY MANAGEMENT

continues

LISTING 4.8. CONTINUED

```cpp
private:
    auto_ptr<Point> myUpperLeft;
    auto_ptr<Point> myLowerRight;
};


int main()
{

    try
    {
        cout << "Begin round 1..." << endl;
        auto_ptr<Point> pUL(new Point(0,0));
        auto_ptr<Point> pLR(new Point(20,30));
        Rectangle myRectangle(pUL, pLR);
        int w = myRectangle.GetWidth();
        int h = myRectangle.GetHeight();
        cout << "the Rectangle is " << w << " by " << h << endl;
    }
    catch ( myException & e )
    {

        cout << "caught exception: " << e.errorMsg() << "\n\n" << endl;
    }


    try
    {
        cout << "Begin round 2..." << endl;
        auto_ptr<Point> pUL(new Point(0,0));
        auto_ptr<Point> pLR(new Point(20,30));
        Rectangle myRectangle(pUL, pLR);

        int w = myRectangle.GetWidth();
        int h = myRectangle.GetHeight();
        cout << "the Rectangle is " << w << " by " << h << endl;
        myRectangle.DangerousMethod();
    }
    catch ( myException & e )
    {
        cout << "caught exception: " << e.errorMsg() << "\n\n" << endl;
    }


    return 0;
}
```

Here's the output from the program in Listing 4.8:

```
Begin round 1…
Point constructor called
Point constructor called
Point copy constructor called
Point copy constructor called
Point destructor called
Point destructor called
the Rectangle is 20 by 30
In Rectangle's destructor
Point destructor called
Point destructor called
Begin round 2…
Point constructor called
Point constructor called
Point copy constructor called
Point copy constructor called
Point destructor called
Point destructor called
the Rectangle is 20 by 30
In Rectangle's destructor
Point destructor called
Point destructor calledcaught exception: Oops.
```

This time, the destructors are called properly *without* your having to call them at all from within main(), either in the catch statement or not! The auto_ptr manages the memory for you; you just pass in a pointer to the object and the auto_ptr does the rest.

Note that there is a subtle bug in this program; I will discuss it in a moment.

As you can see, auto_ptrs simplify memory management, and they can be used more or less like normal pointers. Consider this example:

```
int GetWidth() { return myLowerRight->GetX() - myUpperLeft->GetX(); }
```

There is no change in how we call the GetX() method: You use the points-to operator on the auto_ptr just as you would with a regular pointer.

Copying auto_ptrs

What happens when we make a copy of an auto_ptr?

There are two ways to cause a pointer to be copied. The first approach is to invoke the copy constructor:

```
Point * ptrOne = ptrTwo;
```

The second way to copy a pointer is to call the assignment operator:

```
Point * ptrOne;
ptrOne = ptrTwo;
```

4

MEMORY MANAGEMENT

In either case, the author of the `auto_ptr` template class has three choices:

- Make a shallow copy
- Make a deep copy
- Transfer ownership

If a shallow copy is made, we have the usual problem: If the copy goes out of scope, it deletes the object pointed to and the other pointer would be a wild pointer. If we make a deep copy, we bring the overhead of constructing and destroying every copy—a pretty expensive operation and inappropriate for a template class for a general library. Although this limitation caused the STL authors to choose the third path, it doesn't mean that making a deep copy is the wrong solution for you. You may want to create your own `auto_ptr` class that does a deep copy.

In any case, the Standard Template Library implementation of `auto_ptr` *transfers ownership* when a pointer is assigned. Suppose that you write the following statement:

```
auto_ptr<Point> newAutoPtr = pUL;
```

In this example, `pUL` no longer owns the `Point` object, and the `Point` object's destructor is not called when `pUL` goes out of scope. In fact, you should treat `pUL` as a pointer to `NULL`. For this reason, you must be *very* careful when passing `auto_ptrs` to functions by value.

This discussion brings us back to the program in Listing 4.8 and its subtle bug. Let's add some code to examine the `Points` we created after creating the `Rectangle`:

```cpp
int main()
{

    try
    {
        cout << "Begin round 1..." << endl;
        auto_ptr<Point> pUL(new Point(0,0));
        auto_ptr<Point> pLR(new Point(20,30));
        Rectangle myRectangle(pUL, pLR);
        int w = myRectangle.GetWidth();
        int h = myRectangle.GetHeight();
        cout << "the Rectangle is " << w << " by " << h << endl;
        cout << "the upper left point x is " << pUL->GetX() << endl;
        cout << "the lower right point x is " << pLR->GetX() << endl;
    }
    catch ( myException & e )
    {

        cout << "caught exception: " << e.errorMsg() << "\n\n" << endl;
    }
```

```
    return 0;
}
```

The output from this revised portion of the program in Listing 4.8 is shown here:

```
Begin round 1…
Point constructor called
Point constructor called
Point copy constructor called
Point copy constructor called
Point destructor called
Point destructor called
the Rectangle is 20 by 30
the upper left point x is -572662307
the lower right point x is -572662307
In Rectangle's destructor
Point destructor called
Point destructor called
```

We've simplified `main()` by removing the second `try/catch` block, and we've added two lines to print out the contents of the `Points`. They are garbage: `-572662307` (your mileage may vary). This is because we've passed the `auto_ptrs` into the `Rectangle`'s constructor by value; ownership was transferred to the internal copy made by the copy constructor. When we continue to try to use the original `auto_ptrs`, they have whatever garbage happens to be in memory.

The fix is frighteningly simple. Just pass the `auto_ptrs` by reference. All that has to change is the single member method of `Rectangle`:

```
Rectangle( auto_ptr<Point>& pUpperLeft, auto_ptr<Point>& pLowerRight ):
    myUpperLeft (new Point(*pUpperLeft)),
    myLowerRight(new Point(*pLowerRight))
    {}
```

By making this small change—the addition of two ampersands—no copy is made of the `auto_ptrs` and thus ownership is not transferred. This time the `Point` objects have valid values:

```
Begin round 1…
Point constructor called
Point constructor called
Point copy constructor called
Point copy constructor called
the Rectangle is 20 by 30
the upper left point x is 0
the lower right point x is 20
In Rectangle's destructor
Point destructor called
Point destructor called
```

```
Point destructor called
Point destructor called
```

Wait a minute! It sure *looks* like the copy constructor is being called in the following statement:

```
myUpperLeft (new Point(*pUpperLeft)),
```

Isn't that an explicit call to the copy constructor of the auto_ptr? No. Here's what happens: The auto_ptr is passed in by reference. In the initialization, it is dereferenced, returning the pointed-to object (the Point) which is then used to initialize a *new* auto_ptr—calling not the copy constructor but the constructor that takes a pointer to a Point object.

Reference Counting

In Chapter 3, "Inheritance, Polymorphism, and Code Reuse," we reviewed why it is important to write your own copy constructor and assignment operator. The goal is to ensure that you are creating *deep* copies rather than bitwise, or shallow, copies. Creating deep copies protects you from creating wild pointers, but it comes at a price.

After your deep copy is completed, you now have two objects taking up memory to hold the same information. If you are writing a String class, and you are passing strings among functions, you can end up with many copies of the same string. This is wasteful and also prone to error. It is easy to lose track of who owns the memory and thus who must delete each copy.

Reference-counted objects overcome these limitations. A reference-counted class keeps only one object in memory, but it keeps track of how many pointers are referring to it. When no one has a reference, the object deletes itself. This approach is clean, elegant, and efficient.

Writing a reference-counted object is not terribly difficult, but generalizing the class to act as a base class for all objects that might want to be reference counted does take a bit of thought. Rather than making our String class inherit from a base class ReferenceCounted, we will have the String class contain a private class declaration for a CountedString. Thus, the interface to String does not expose the reference counting; after all, the clients don't care how String manages its memory.

The internal class CountedString derives from ReferenceCounted and thus inherits all the details of managing the reference count. The CountedString class simply specializes this, adding the ability to manage a (hidden) C-style string that is the actual memory whose references are counted!

The following statement creates a string:

```
String s1("hello world");
```

When you create a string, the string's constructor initializes its internal ountedString pointer, initializing a new countedString object on the heap. The internal countedString pointer is a smart pointer so that the string doesn't have to know anything about incrementing or decrementing the references.

Thus, the string is responsible for string-like methods such as providing an index into the string. The countedString class is responsible for managing the string's memory. It inherits its reference-counting ability from its base class ReferenceCounted.

The String keeps a smart pointer to countedString, delegating responsibility for calling AddRef() and ReleaseRef() to the smart pointer:

```
class String
{
public:

    String(const char * cString = "");
    char operator[](int index) const;
    char& operator[](int index);
    // …

private:
    struct countedString : public ReferenceCounted
    {
        char * cString;

        countedString( const char * initialCString);
        countedString( const countedString & rhs);
        ~countedString();
        void initialize(const char * initialCString);

        //…

        friend class RCSmartPointer<countedString>;
    };

    RCSmartPointer<countedString> rcString;
};
```

The base class for countedString is ReferenceCounted, which is responsible for managing the reference counts and deleting the memory when it is no longer referenced:

```
class ReferenceCounted
{
public:
    void addRef();
```

```
    void removeRef();

    void markNotShareable();
    bool isShareable();
    bool isShared();

protected:
    ReferenceCounted();
    ReferenceCounted(const ReferenceCounted& rhs);
    ReferenceCounted& operator=(const ReferenceCounted& rhs);
    virtual ~ReferenceCounted();

private:
    int referenceCount;
    bool shareable;
};
```

This class keeps a reference count and a Boolean value about whether the memory can be shared. The protocol is that the object starts out shareable and can be set to nonshareable by the owning class according to its own rules.

String marks its memory nonshareable whenever it returns a nonconstant reference through the index operator. This process is known as "copy on write," in that we make a copy of the string the first time there is any chance that the memory will be overwritten. The client, of course, is oblivious to the fact that we are sharing the memory, and may want to write into only one of the copies, not all of them. Because we can't tell when the memory is overwritten, we just make a copy any time we're going to make writing possible:

```
char & String::operator[](int index)
{
    if ( rcString->isShared())
    {
        rcString->removeRef();
        rcString = new countedString(rcString->cString);
    }
    rcString->markNotShareable();
    return rcString->cString[index];
}
```

If the string is marked not shareable, it can never again be marked shareable; there is no offsetting the MarkShareable() method. We can never again know it is safe to share this memory, so we don't.

The key methods are AddRef() and RemoveRef(). Someone must call these methods each time a copy is made. We'd rather not bother String with this duty, so we create a smart pointer for reference counted objects (RCSmartPointer) which owns this responsibility:

```
template<class T>
class RCSmartPointer
{
public:
    RCSmartPointer(T* ptrToRC = 0);
    RCSmartPointer(const RCSmartPointer& rhs);
    ~RCSmartPointer();

    RCSmartPointer& operator=(const RCSmartPointer& rhs);

    T* operator->() const;
    T& operator*() const;

private:
    T * pRC;
    void initialize();
};
```

The smart pointer is initialized with a pointer to any reference-counted object—in our
case, String. It is the smart pointer's job to increment the reference count when a new
reference is added and to decrement the reference count when the pointer is deleted.
Because the smart pointer must increment the pointer for both of its constructors, it does
so through the initialize() method:

```
template<class T>
void RCSmartPointer<T>::initialize()
{
    if ( pRC == 0 )
        return;

    if ( pRC->isShareable() == false )
    {
        pRC = new T(*pRC);
    }
    pRC->addRef();
}
```

This is the essence of object-oriented design: delegation of responsibility and reuse.
Listing 4.9 shows the entire program.

LISTING 4.9. DELEGATION OF RESPONSIBILITY

```
#include <iostream.h>
#include <string.h>

template<class T>
class RCSmartPointer
{
```

continues

4

MEMORY
MANAGEMENT

LISTING 4.9. CONTINUED

```cpp
public:
    RCSmartPointer(T* ptrToRC = 0);
    RCSmartPointer(const RCSmartPointer& rhs);
    ~RCSmartPointer();

    RCSmartPointer& operator=(const RCSmartPointer& rhs);

    T* operator->() const;
    T& operator*() const;

private:
    T * pRC;
    void initialize();
};

template<class T>
void RCSmartPointer<T>::initialize()
{
    if ( pRC == 0 )
        return;

    if ( pRC->isShareable() == false )
    {
        pRC = new T(*pRC);
    }
    pRC->addRef();
}

template<class T>
RCSmartPointer<T>::RCSmartPointer(T* ptrToRC):
pRC(ptrToRC)
{
    initialize();
}

template<class T>
RCSmartPointer<T>::RCSmartPointer(const RCSmartPointer& rhs):
pRC(rhs.pRC)
{
    initialize();
}

template<class T>
RCSmartPointer<T>::~RCSmartPointer()
{
    if ( pRC )
        pRC->removeRef();
}
```

```
template<class T>
RCSmartPointer<T>& RCSmartPointer<T>::operator=(const RCSmartPointer& rhs)
{
    if ( pRC == rhs.pRC )
        return *this;

    if ( pRC )
        pRC->removeRef();

    pRC = rhs.pRC;

    return *this;
}

template<class T>
T* RCSmartPointer<T>::operator->() const
{
    return pRC;
}

template<class T>
T& RCSmartPointer<T>::operator*() const
{
    return *pRC;
}


class ReferenceCounted
{
public:
    void addRef() { ++referenceCount; }
    void removeRef() {
        if ( --referenceCount == 0 )
            delete this;
    }

    void markNotShareable() { shareable = false; }
    bool isShareable() { return shareable; }
    bool isShared() { return referenceCount > 1; }

protected:
    ReferenceCounted():referenceCount(0), shareable(true) {}
    ReferenceCounted(const ReferenceCounted& rhs):
            referenceCount(0),
            shareable(true)
            {}
    ReferenceCounted& operator=(const ReferenceCounted& rhs) { return
➥*this; }
    virtual ~ReferenceCounted(){}
```

continues

LISTING 4.9. CONTINUED

```cpp
private:
    int referenceCount;
    bool shareable;
};


class String
{
public:

    String(const char * cString = ""):rcString(new
➥countedString(cString)){}

    char operator[](int index) const { return rcString->cString[index]; }
    char& operator[](int index);
    operator char*() const { return rcString->cString; }

    void ShowCountedStringAddress() const { rcString->ShowAddress(); }

private:
    struct countedString : public ReferenceCounted
    {
        char * cString;

        countedString( const char * initialCString)
        {
            initialize(initialCString);
        }
        countedString( const countedString & rhs) {
➥initialize(rhs.cString); }
        ~countedString()
        {
            delete [] cString;
        }
        void initialize(const char * initialCString)
        {
            cString = new char[strlen(initialCString) +1];
            strcpy(cString,initialCString);
        }

        void ShowAddress() const { cout << &cString; }

        friend class RCSmartPointer<countedString>;
    };

    RCSmartPointer<countedString> rcString;
};

char & String::operator[](int index)
```

```
{
    if ( rcString->isShared())
    {
        rcString->removeRef();
        rcString = new countedString(rcString->cString);
    }
    rcString->markNotShareable();
    return rcString->cString[index];
}


int main()
{
    String s1("hello world");
    String s2 = s1;   // copy constructor
    String s3("bye");
    s3 = s2;          // assignment

    cout << "s1: " << s1 << " ";
    s1.ShowCountedStringAddress();
    cout << "\ns2: " << s2 << " ";
    s2.ShowCountedStringAddress();
    cout << "\ns3: " << s3 << " ";
    s3.ShowCountedStringAddress();


    cout << endl;
    return 0;
}
```

I added the `ShowAddress()` method to prove that the reference counting is working. Here's the output from running the program in Listing 4.9:

```
s1: hello world 0x0042118C
s2: hello world 0x0042118C
s3: hello world 0x0042118C
```

As you can see, all three strings have the same address in memory. Perfect.

Here's how it works. On the first line of `main()`, we create a `String` object. Put this in your debugger. You'll find that this innocuous line will bring you into the heart of all of these classes. Most interestingly, you'll see the reference counters invoked automatically. Here are the steps:

```
String s1("hello world");
```

We create a `String` object on the stack. Stepping in brings us to the `String` constructor:

```
String(const char * cString = ""):rcString(new countedString(cString)){}
```

In the initialization of the member variable `rcString`, we enter the new operator and then the constructor for `countedString`:

```
countedString( const char * initialCString) { initialize(initialCString); }
```

Before we enter the body of the constructor, we enter the (implicit) initialization of the base class, in which the member variable `ReferenceCount` is initialized to zero:

```
ReferenceCounted():referenceCount(0), shareable(true) {}
```

Why zero and not 1? It turns out to be easier and safer to let the derived class set this to 1. While we're here, we initialize the `ReferenceCounted` object to be shareable—the default. We then enter the body of `countedString`'s constructor, which brings us to the `initialize` member method of `countedString` (passing in the original `cString` as a parameter):

```
void initialize(const char * initialCString)
```

In the body of this initialization, a new character array is created on the heap, and its address is stored in the member variable `cString`:

```
cString = new char[strlen(initialCString) +1];
strcpy(cString,initialCString);
```

Remember that we are still initializing the `String` class's member `rcString`, which is an `RCSmartPointer`, so we enter the constructor for `RCSmartPointer`, where the internal pointer is set to point to the `ReferenceCounted` object allocated on the heap and `RCSmartPointer`'s `initialize()` method is invoked:

```
template<class T>
RCSmartPointer<T>::RCSmartPointer(T* ptrToRC):
pRC(ptrToRC)
{
    initialize();
}
```

The `initialize()` method checks to see whether the pointer was `NULL`, in which case, no action is needed. Otherwise, it checks whether the `ReferenceCounted` object is shareable. If not, new memory is allocated; otherwise, the reference counter is incremented:

```
if ( pRC->isShareable() == false )
{
    pRC = new T(*pRC);
}
pRC->addRef();
```

This causes the base class `addRef()` method to be invoked:

```
void addRef() { ++referenceCount; }
```

At the conclusion of this string of events, memory has been allocated on the heap, and this memory is managed by a reference-counted object after the reference count has been initialized. What looks like a stack-based object actually manages reference-counted memory on the heap—the best of both worlds.

WHERE'S THE COPY CONSTRUCTOR AND ASSIGNMENT OPERATOR?

In the preceding discussion, we are copying String objects, and String objects have pointers. Don't we need a copy constructor and an assignment operator? Well, we have one—the compiler-generated default. Although the default copy constructor does produce a bitwise copy, that is okay; when it copies the member rcString, the RCSmartPointer's copy constructor or assignment operator is invoked, and *it* will ensure that a deep copy is made—one that uses reference counting. String has *fully* delegated responsibility to its rcString member.

Counted Rectangles

After you have a ReferenceCounted base class, and you have the smart pointer working, you can carry this design just about anywhere. We can easily transform our Rectangle class to be a reference-counted class—and *the interface doesn't change at all*, as shown in Listing 4.10.

LISTING 4.10. REFERENCE COUNTING THE Rectangle CLASS

```
Counted Rectangles

#include <iostream>
#include <memory>
#include <string>

using namespace std;

class myException
{
public:
    char * errorMsg() { return "Oops."; }
};

template<class T>
class RCSmartPointer
{
public:
    RCSmartPointer(T* ptrToRC = 0);
```

4

MEMORY
MANAGEMENT

continues

LISTING 4.10. CONTINUED

```cpp
    RCSmartPointer(const RCSmartPointer& rhs);
    ~RCSmartPointer();

    RCSmartPointer& operator=(const RCSmartPointer& rhs);

    T* operator->() const;
    T& operator*() const;

private:
    T * pRC;
    void initialize();
};

template<class T>
void RCSmartPointer<T>::initialize()
{
    if ( pRC == 0 )
        return;

    if ( pRC->isShareable() == false )
    {
        pRC = new T(*pRC);
    }
    pRC->addRef();
}

template<class T>
RCSmartPointer<T>::RCSmartPointer(T* ptrToRC):
pRC(ptrToRC)
{
    initialize();
}

template<class T>
RCSmartPointer<T>::RCSmartPointer(const RCSmartPointer& rhs):
pRC(rhs.pRC)
{
    initialize();
}

template<class T>
RCSmartPointer<T>::~RCSmartPointer()
{
    if ( pRC )
        pRC->removeRef();
}

template<class T>
RCSmartPointer<T>& RCSmartPointer<T>::operator=(const RCSmartPointer& rhs)
```

```
{
    if ( pRC == rhs.pRC )
        return *this;

    if ( pRC )
        pRC->removeRef();

    pRC = rhs.pRC;

    return *this;
}

template<class T>
T* RCSmartPointer<T>::operator->() const
{
    return pRC;
}

template<class T>
T& RCSmartPointer<T>::operator*() const
{
    return *pRC;
}


class ReferenceCounted
{
public:
    void addRef() { ++referenceCount; }
    void removeRef() {
        if ( —referenceCount == 0 )
            delete this;
    }

    void markNotShareable() { shareable = false; }
    bool isShareable() { return shareable; }
    bool isShared() { return referenceCount > 1; }

protected:
    ReferenceCounted():referenceCount(0), shareable(true) {}
    ReferenceCounted(const ReferenceCounted& rhs):
        referenceCount(0),
        shareable(true)
        {}
    ReferenceCounted& operator=(const ReferenceCounted& rhs) { return
➥*this; }
    virtual ~ReferenceCounted(){}

private:
```

continues

4

MEMORY
MANAGEMENT

LISTING 4.10. CONTINUED

```cpp
    int referenceCount;
    bool shareable;
};


class Point
{
public:
    Point (int x, int y):myX(x), myY(y)
    {
        cout << "Point constructor called"<< endl;
    }
    Point (const Point & rhs):
        myX(rhs.myX),
            myY(rhs.myY){ cout << "Point copy constructor called" <<
endl;}
        ~Point(){ cout << "Point destructor called" << endl;}
    int GetX() const { return myX; }
    void SetX(int x) { myX = x; }
    int GetY() const { return myY; }
    void SetY(int y) { myY = y; }
private:
    int myX;
    int myY;
};

class Rectangle
{
public:
    Rectangle( Point upperLeft, Point lowerRight ):
        rcRect(new countedRect(upperLeft, lowerRight))
        {}

    Rectangle( Point * pUpperLeft, Point * pLowerRight ):
        rcRect(new countedRect(*pUpperLeft, *pLowerRight))
        {}


    Rectangle(
        int upperLeftX,
        int upperLeftY,
        int lowerRightX,
        int lowerRightY ):
        rcRect(new countedRect(new Point(upperLeftX,upperLeftY),
                new Point(lowerRightX,lowerRightY)))
        {}


    ~Rectangle(){ cout << "In Rectangle's destructor" << endl;  }
```

```
        int GetWidth()
        {
            return rcRect->myLowerRight->GetX() - rcRect->myUpperLeft->GetX();
        }
        int GetHeight()
        {
            return rcRect->myLowerRight->GetY() - rcRect->myUpperLeft->GetY();
        }

        void DangerousMethod() { throw myException(); }

    private:

        struct countedRect : public ReferenceCounted
        {
            char * cString;
            Point * myUpperLeft;
            Point * myLowerRight;

            countedRect( const Point * ul, const Point * lr) {
➡initialize(ul,lr); }
            countedRect( Point ul, Point lr ) { initialize(&ul, &lr); }
            countedRect( const countedRect & rhs)
            {
                initialize(rhs.myUpperLeft, rhs.myLowerRight);
            }
            ~countedRect()
            {
                delete myUpperLeft;
                delete myLowerRight;
            }
            void initialize(const Point * ul, const Point * lr)
            {
                myUpperLeft = new Point(*ul);
                myLowerRight = new Point(*lr);
            }


            friend class RCSmartPointer<countedRect>;
        };

        RCSmartPointer<countedRect> rcRect;


};


int main()
{
```

continues

LISTING 4.10. CONTINUED

```
    try
    {
        cout << "Begin round 1..." << endl;
        Point pUL(0,0);
        Point pLR(20,30);
        Rectangle myRectangle(pUL, pLR);
        int w = myRectangle.GetWidth();
        int h = myRectangle.GetHeight();
        cout << "the Rectangle is " << w << " by " << h << endl;
        myRectangle.DangerousMethod();
        cout << "You never get here.\n" << endl;

    }
    catch ( myException & e )
    {

        cout << "caught exception: " << e.errorMsg() << "\n\n" << endl;
    }
    return 0;
}
```

Here's the output from the program in Listing 4.10:

```
Begin round 1…
Point constructor called
Point constructor called
Point copy constructor called
Point copy constructor called
Point copy constructor called
Point copy constructor called
Point copy constructor called
Point copy constructor called
Point destructor called
Point destructor called
Point destructor called
Point destructor called
the Rectangle is 20 by 30
In Rectangle's destructor
Point destructor called
Point destructor called
Point destructor called
Point destructor called
caught exception: Oops.
```

This is a portable solution that can be used in any number of circumstances. It offers the twin benefits of using less memory and preventing memory leaks. Notice that even when the exception is thrown from DangerousMethod(), the stack is unwound and no memory is lost—the smart pointers decrement, and the allocated memory is destroyed.

Summary

The trick with memory management is to understand explicitly what memory you are allocating, and where you have a pointer to that memory. Either you must keep track of those pointers and ensure that the memory is returned when you are done with it, or you must introduce garbage collection in the form of smart pointers.

Although smart pointers have their limitations, they do help protect your code from memory leaks and are especially important in the face of exceptions. If your program is to be robust, it must be scrupulous in its efforts to manage resources and not allow memory to be lost.

4

MEMORY MANAGEMENT

How To Use Frameworks

CHAPTER 5

The great, unrealized promise of object-oriented programming is code reuse. The idea of OOP was to create classes that could serve as the foundation on which new programs could be built. Components could be plugged into a new architecture like electronics are plugged into a circuit board. By and large, however, things haven't worked out that way—with one significant exception: application framework libraries.

The vast majority of successful application framework libraries are those that facilitate the creation of applications in a windowing environment such as Windows NT or X Window. By far the most successful such library is the Microsoft Foundation Classes (MFC); this chapter focuses on the MFC as an example of what such an Application Frameworks library can provide.

> **NOTE**
>
> The MFC is large and powerful and necessarily complex. No single chapter can fully introduce all its functionality—let alone provide a comprehensive tutorial. The intent of this chapter is not to teach you how to use the MFC, but rather to dip into the MFC here and there to examine some of the universal issues common to all such application frameworks. For a detailed and comprehensive introduction of the MFC, take a look at *Professional MFC Programming*, by Mike Blaszczak (published by Wrox Press).

The Microsoft Foundation Classes

The Microsoft Foundation Class library (called *the MFC*) is an application framework that provides a structure and a set of classes with which you can build an application for Windows. The MFC provides standard user-interface implementations of windowing classes, as well as a set of utility classes to assist you in the manipulation of certain kinds of objects such as String and Time.

Getting Started

The MFC goes beyond providing a set of application-level classes and actually provides a framework within which you can use these classes. You can see the power of this approach when you use the wizards that facilitate the creation of Windows applications. Figure 5.1 shows how a new project can be created using the Application Wizard.

After you start the Application Wizard, it asks a series of questions to help you design your application within the Document/View architecture. Figure 5.2 shows the first question: Are you building a Single Document Interface (SDI) or Multi-Document Interface (MDI) application, or do you just need a simple dialog-based interface?

FIGURE 5.1.

The Application Wizard.

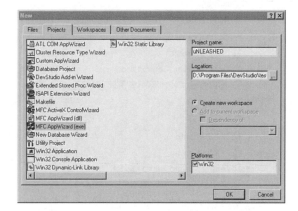

FIGURE 5.2.

What kind of view?

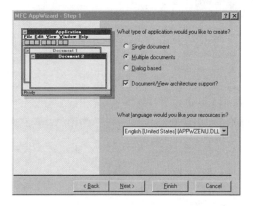

Subsequent screens of the wizard ask you to choose among various options: database support, COM support, support for Internet access, and so forth. After the Application Wizard has run, a number of classes are created that constitute the initial framework for your application (see Figure 5.3).

FIGURE 5.3.

*Classes produced
by the wizard.*

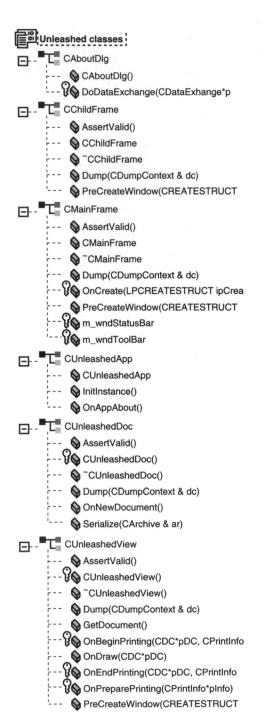

FIGURE 5.3.

*Classes produced
by the wizard.*

Note that each class contains a number of standard methods. Often, these methhods provide simple boilerplate code and then indicate where your customizing code should be added, as shown in this sample output from the Application Wizard:

```
BOOL CUnleashedDoc::OnNewDocument()
{
    if (!CDocument::OnNewDocument())
        return FALSE;

    // TODO: add reinitialization code here
    // (SDI documents will reuse this document)

    return TRUE;
}
```

At times, the code provided by the wizard is extensive; it can save you significant development time and simplify your interaction with the more complex aspects of Windows programming such as setting up COM for interprocess communication. Listing 5.1 shows the `InitInstance` method generated by the wizard.

LISTING 5.1. WIZARD GENERATED CODE

```
BOOL CUnleashedApp::InitInstance()
{
    AfxEnableControlContainer();

    // Standard initialization
    // If you are not using these features and wish to reduce the size
    //  of your final executable, you should remove from the following
    //  the specific initialization routines you do not need.

#ifdef _AFXDLL
    Enable3dControls();            // Call this when using MFC in a shared
➡DLL
#else
    Enable3dControlsStatic();      // Call this when linking to MFC
➡statically
#endif

    // Change the registry key under which our settings are stored.
    // You should modify this string to be something appropriate
    // such as the name of your company or organization.
    SetRegistryKey(_T("Local AppWizard-Generated Applications"));

    LoadStdProfileSettings();  // Load standard INI file options
➡(including MRU)

    // Register the application's document templates.  Document templates
    //  serve as the connection between documents, frame windows and
➡views.
```

```
CMultiDocTemplate* pDocTemplate;
pDocTemplate = new CMultiDocTemplate(
    IDR_UNLEASTYPE,
    RUNTIME_CLASS(CUnleashedDoc),
    RUNTIME_CLASS(CChildFrame), // custom MDI child frame
    RUNTIME_CLASS(CUnleashedView));
AddDocTemplate(pDocTemplate);

// create main MDI Frame window
CMainFrame* pMainFrame = new CMainFrame;
if (!pMainFrame->LoadFrame(IDR_MAINFRAME))
    return FALSE;
m_pMainWnd = pMainFrame;

// Parse command line for standard shell commands, DDE, file open
CCommandLineInfo cmdInfo;
ParseCommandLine(cmdInfo);

// Dispatch commands specified on the command line
if (!ProcessShellCommand(cmdInfo))
    return FALSE;

// The main window has been initialized, so show and update it.
pMainFrame->ShowWindow(m_nCmdShow);
pMainFrame->UpdateWindow();

return TRUE;
}
```

The program in Listing 5.1 is ready to run, without your adding a line of custom code. It compiles, links, and executes. The code generated by the Application Wizard provides you with the ability to create and close windows and creates a standard button bar and menu right out of the box. This framework then becomes the base to which you add your own custom behavior and user interface.

Other Wizards

In addition to the Application Wizard, the MFC provides wizards that create and manipulate classes and the methods and members of those classes, as well as wizards that hook up methods for responding to user actions such as button clicks. The MFC also provides wizards that interact with databases and that use COM. A host of new wizards is being developed even as this is written.

Gaining Perspective

The best way to approach the MFC is to distinguish between the application architecture (that is, the application, threads, managing commands, and so forth) and the document/view architecture (for example, `CWnd`, `CView`, and so forth).

Application Architecture

MFC applications consist of a single `CWinApp` class and one or more `CWinThreads`. As you might guess, `CWinApp` represents the application (or process) and the various `CWinThreads` implement multithreading. When the application starts, there is only one thread: the *primary* thread. New threads are created and destroyed, but when the application ends, it is the primary thread that ends.

Message processing—that is, responding to events—is managed by the `CCmdTarget` classes, the most important of which is `CWnd`. Window classes are and must be `CCmdTarget` derivatives because windows are the primary objects that respond to user actions such as clicks and menu choices. Threads also derive from `CCmdTarget` so that messages can be sent to the threads and the threads can respond to requests asynchronously.

The architecture of the MFC is large and complex, and this chapter does not attempt to explain it all in detail. Instead, this chapter focuses on a few mechanisms that are of value because the knowledge extends beyond the specifics of the MFC. For example, we will focus on how the MFC implements multithreading and thread safety because these issues apply when you write C++ code in *any* environment. The details may vary, but the tasks and requirements are invariable.

Multithreading

The MFC provides a set of classes for managing multithreading. Although the specifics of how the MFC implements these classes may differ from how, for example, the XOpen libraries handle multithreading, the essential tasks and objectives are universal.

The term *thread* is shorthand for *thread of execution*. The Windows operating system (and most modern operating systems) allows your application to have more than one thread of execution in a single program. It *appears* as though your program were running two or more tasks at one time, although most often what is really happening is that the computer is switching among the threads, offering the illusion of simultaneity. As a matter of fact, this is exactly how the illusion of multiprocessing is accomplished. When you run your word processing program, your Internet browser, and your spreadsheet program, the processor just switches among them.

A program represents a process, and each process may have more than one thread. The principal difference between a process and a thread is the "overhead" of each—it takes more time to switch among processes than it does to switch among threads. This is why threads are sometimes referred to as *lightweight processes*.

The thread *context* is the information the computer needs to make the switch among threads. The thread context consists of a stack (for temporary variables and the return addresses of subroutines), a kernal stack (to hold addresses for interrupt service returns), and a set of registers. In the registers, there are, among other things, the instruction pointer and the stack pointer. The instruction pointer tells the CPU where to find its next instruction (as it works its way through your source code), and the stack pointer tells the CPU where it can store or retrieve the next local variable.

The CPU is rather dumb; it just works its way through the code. The operating system (in this case, Windows) tells the CPU when to effect a thread or process switch. The operating system is said to manage *time slicing*—affording each thread its own little "slice of time" in which to execute.

> **NOTE**
>
> *Multitasking* indicates doing more than one thing at a time. An operating system can be said to be a multitasking system if it can manage more than one *process* (running program) at a time. A single process is *multithreaded* when there is more than one thread of control within the same process.

Cooperative Versus Preemptive Multithreading

Programmers familiar with Windows 3.x or with the Mac may have been exposed to a form of multithreading called *cooperative multithreading*. This primitive form of multithreading allows for more than one thread, but each thread must voluntarily release control of the processor periodically to allow other threads to run.

The problem with cooperative multithreading is that a single thread can "hog" the processor, causing all other threads to run very slowly. Worse, the thread can "hang," causing the entire application to grind to a halt.

Preemptive multithreading takes advantage of the CPU's ability to signal when it is time to switch among threads. This more sophisticated mechanism involves cooperation between the operating system (for example, Windows NT) and the CPU chip (for example, the Pentium) to ensure that each thread is allocated a preset amount of processor time (typically measured in milliseconds). The operating system rapidly switches among threads, allocating a "slice" of time based on the thread's priority.

The advantage of preemptive multithreading is that no thread can consume a disproportionate share of the system processing time—and if a thread hangs, the remaining threads can continue working.

Issues in Preemptive Multithreading

Creating programs that run in a multi*processing* environment such as Windows is fairly straightforward: You write your program as if you had uncontested access to the CPU, the disk, the database, and so forth. You leave it to the operating system to keep everything straight—you just plow ahead as though yours was the only program running.

Writing a multi*threaded* application is somewhat more complicated. Actually, it is a *lot* more complicated because suddenly your code can be interrupted at any time (which is always true). More important, more than one thread can *reenter* your code so that the same code can be running in two different threads. This can happen if functions in two different threads each call into your code.

Multithreaded applications can get dicey; if your code isn't *threadsafe*, one thread may be carefully setting up values for your database while another thread is trampling over the same values, rendering them meaningless. This is not a good thing—and can be one of the most difficult bugs to find.

For example, assume you have a function which takes a record out of a database, updates it, and writes it back. Here is the pseudocode:

```
int Updater()
{
  getARecord();
  updateIt();
  writeItBack();
}
```

Assume you also have a function, func1, in thread 1 and another function, func2, in thread 2, each of which calls Updater().

func1() is running and it calls Updater(). Updater() now begins to run in the context of thread 1 and it gets a record; but before it updates it, the thread is interrupted and thread 2 runs.

`func2()` now calls `Updater()` which runs again, this time in the context of thread 2. It gets the same record (coincidentally), updates it, and writes it back before being interrupted.

Now, thread 1 resumes, and `Updater()` resumes where it was, with the record it originally got out of the database. It will now update that record and write it back, corrupting the update achieved in thread 2.

This is one example among many where multithreading can corrupt data if your methods are not thread safe.

The short advice on multithreading is this: If you can avoid writing multithreaded code, do so. Don't use multithreading unless and until you have no choice. It makes your code more complex and far harder to maintain. It dramatically increases the likelihood of bugs—and most of the time, it decreases performance. After all, it takes time to stash away the thread context and to switch threads. Add enough threads, and the CPU spends a significant portion of its time just switching among them—and proportionally less time getting any useful work done!

Suppose that you have a program that takes a lot of data in, calculates the sum of the data, and then uses that sum in a second equation. "Aha!" you say, "Two tasks! I'll create two threads." The problem is that the second thread can't begin until the first thread is done working. Even if you could calculate them "at the same time," if you can't use the data until both are done, why not let them run in series rather than in parallel? Running the tasks together buys you nothing, and the cost of switching between the tasks may be high.

So when *do* you use multithreading? The classic scenario is one in which one task will take a long time and the second task does *not* depend on the first. Suppose that you must save data to disk and also display it onscreen. You'd hate to wait for the data to be saved before you can put it on the screen—after all, writing to disk can take a while. Why not put the "write it to disk" task into a separate thread and get on with the more important job of interacting with the user? Why not, indeed.

A Brief Case Study

I wrote an application that makes phone calls—not unlike those annoying telemarketing calls you get just as you are sitting down to dinner. The difference was that my program made calls only to people who wanted to receive them (honest!), was fully automated, and tried not to call at dinner time.

A given computer could call 72 different people at one time. After each call, the program would stash away the results of the call and, periodically, would update the database with these results. At the same time, it kept a cache of numbers to call so that it was never idle. This project cried out for multithreading.

The design of this project was somewhat complex, but for our purposes it came down to this: I ran one thread for each calling line (CCaller) for a total of 72 threads if all 72 lines were active. I also created one thread to manage the reporting functionality (CReporter) and another thread for managing the cache of calls waiting for an open line (CLocalCallQueue). Finally, there was the main thread that managed all the others and that owned the user interface (a control panel for watching the progress of the calls). Thus, this application ran 75 threads!

That's a lot of threads, but on a reasonably sophisticated machine (a Windows NT Workstation running on a Pentium PC with 128MB of RAM) it ran quite quickly and gave the illusion of all the threads running simultaneously. In addition, the application itself was not only multi*threaded*, it was multi*processed* because there were additional calling machines and there were additional components in other processes (and on other machines!) responsible for scheduling jobs and managing the database.

Let's focus on some of the kinds of issues that arise in such an environment.

Creating Threads

The first task, of course, is to create a thread. There are, in fact, two distinct ways of creating and managing threads. The first is appropriate for use with widgets (typically windows) that have to run as a thread. Imagine an object that has methods but that operates independently from all other threads. This is the first type of thread, and it derives from CWinThread.

The second type of thread is more appropriate to use when you want a function to run in its own thread. This type of thread is referred to as a *worker thread*.

Using CWinThread Objects

You create a CWinThread object just as you create any other object: You derive from CWinThread itself or from some class that in turn derives from CWinThread. When you instantiate your CWinThread-derived object, you do *not* spawn a thread; to spawn a thread, you must call CreateThread() on that object.

Creating your CWinThread object is fairly straightforward. You declare a class derived (directly or indirectly) from CWinThread and you instantiate an object of that type on the heap. You then invoke CreateThread() on that object and ensure that the method returns true (meaning that the thread was created). The code might look like this:

```
CMyClass * pThread;
pThread = new CMyClass;
```

```
if ( ! pThread->CreateThread() )
{
    MessageBox("Thread Creation Failed!\n");
    Delete pThread;
}
```

Managing Messages

One significant advantage of using messages is that the new object (pointed to by pThread) not only operates in its own thread, it can also receive messages by using ::PostThreadMessage(). In fact, the thread can receive messages even if it is not associated with any onscreen widget or window!

Given a pointer to a CWinThread object on the heap, you can send that thread a message from any other thread, as shown here:

```
pThread-PostThreadMessage(MY_MESSAGE_CONSTANT, wParam, lParam);
```

wParam and lParam are vestigial names left over from 16-bit programming. In 16-bit Windows, lParam is 32 bits but wParam is only 16 bits (w indicates a *word*—16 bits on a 16-bit operating system). Today, Windows is a true 32-bit system, and these parameters are both 32 bits (as is the int).

The first parameter is either a system-defined or a user-defined constant. The mapping between this message ID and the method that is invoked is handled by OnThreadMessage(), which in turn is defined in the message map for your CWinThread Object.

In the multithreaded application discussed earlier, each calling thread derived from CWinThread:

```
class CCaller : public CWinThread
{
public:
    bool CallCompleted(bool isConnected = true);
    bool RestoreRoute();
```

```
    // …

// board manipulation
    int             Call                ();
    void            HangUp              ();
    // …

// lifetime
    virtual BOOL    ExitInstance                ();
    virtual BOOL    InitInstance                ();
    //…

    void            MakeCalls                   ();
    void            ReceiveCalls                ();
protected:
    DECLARE_MESSAGE_MAP()
    DECLARE_DISPATCH_MAP()
    DECLARE_INTERFACE_MAP()
    IVoice*         m_pVoice1;
    //…

private:
    //…

};
```

I've left out most of this class' declaration to show only the most relevant methods. The
DECLARE_MESSAGE_MAP macro sets up the message mapping for message dispatch. In the
implementation file, we use a few more macros to tie messages to methods:

```
BEGIN_MESSAGE_MAP(CCaller, CWinThread)
    //{{AFX_MSG_MAP(CCallClientApp)
        // NOTE - the ClassWizard will add and remove mapping macros here.
        //      DO NOT EDIT what you see in these blocks of generated code!
    //}}AFX_MSG_MAP
    // Standard print setup command
    ON_THREAD_MESSAGE(WM_PLACE_CALLS,CCaller::MakeCalls)
    ON_THREAD_MESSAGE(WM_RECEIVE_CALLS,CCaller::ReceiveCalls)
    //…
END_MESSAGE_MAP()
```

Note that CCaller is shown as a class immediately derived from CWinThread in the first
line, and that two messages are being mapped. WM_PLACE_CALLS is mapped to the method
MakeCalls(), and WM_RECEIVE_CALLS is mapped to ReceiveCalls().

The declaration for these constants is in a global header file:

```
    const int WM_PLACE_CALLS =    WM_USER + 1;
    const int WM_RECEIVE_CALLS =  WM_USER + 2;
```

The details of the message-mapping macros are beyond the scope of this discussion, but you can see that it is fairly straightforward to create the CWinThread object, to set it spinning in its own thread, and then to use that object's methods either directly (from within its own thread) or indirectly (by posting messages to it).

Now other objects that have a pointer to your object can send it messages and have those messages handled in the background.

Managing Windows

The CWinThread object is designed, among other things, to manage windows (and other derived widgets) that require their own threads. Associating a window with your CWinThread object is straightforward: simply have initInstance() create the window (or widget) and retain a pointer to it. Your CWinThread object then becomes a wrapper for the window.

To facilitate this, MFC allows you to assign that window to the CWinThread object's m_pMainWnd member. This causes the message dispatch code in CWinThread to manage that window exclusively.

Note that you now have three objects to keep straight:

- The CWinThread object
- The thread itself
- The window your CWinThread object manages

Remember that creating the CWinThread object does not create the thread. You do that by calling CreateThread(). Similarly, when you destroy the thread, the CWinThread object lives on. You can change this by setting the member variable m_bAutoDelete to true (it is false by default). This setting tells Windows to destroy your CWinThread object when its thread is destroyed.

The Alternative: Worker Threads

If you simply want a method of one of your classes to operate "in the background"—that is, in its own thread—you can create a worker thread. To do this, you use AfxBeginThread(). AfxBeginThread() is actually overloaded so that you can use it for this purpose; you can also use it to manage threads with classes derived from CWinThread. Here we are concerned only with the first overload of AfxBeginThread():

```
CWinThread * AfxBeginThread()
(
    AFX_THREADPROC          pSomeThreadFunction,
    LPVOID                  pParamter,
    int                     nPriority = THREAD_PRIORITY_NORMAL,
```

```
    UINT                  nStackSize = 0,
    DWORD                 dwCreateFlags = 0,
    LPSECURITY_ATTRIBUTES lpSecurityAttributes = NULL
)
```

Because the first two parameters are the most significant, I'll discuss them last. `nPriority` is an integer value that defines the initial priority of the thread; you can set it to `THREAD_PRIORITY_HIGHEST`, `THREAD_PRIORITY_BELOW_NORMAL`, and so forth to control the relative priority of each of your threads. As shown, the default is `THREAD_PRIORITY_NORMAL`.

The fourth parameter, `nStackSize` is a `UINT`. A `UINT` is an unsigned integer; this parameter sets the initial size of the thread's stack (each thread has its own stack). The default value, zero, causes Windows to allocate the same stack size for the new thread as did the thread that spawned it.

The fifth parameter, `dwCreateFlags`, is a `DWORD` (a double word). Again, this size is vestigial; it indicates a 32-bit unsigned integer. The creation flags can be set to zero (the default) or to `CREATE_SUSPENDED`. These flags allow you to create the thread but not have it run until you call `::ResumeThread()`.

The sixth parameter is the security attributes structure. You can safely ignore this parameter and leave it at its default `NULL` setting. If you need Windows NT security, you can create and initialize your own security structure and then insert it using this parameter.

Not let's return to the first two parameters: The first parameter is the function you want to run in its own thread (we call this the *thread-controlling function*). The second parameter is a structure containing all the parameters you want to send to the controlling function.

Here's what the MFC help file has to say about the thread-controlling function:

> The controlling function defines the thread. When this function is entered, the thread starts; when it exits, the thread terminates. This function should have the following prototype:

> ```
> UINT MyControllingFunction( LPVOID pParam );
> ```

Let's be clear about terminology. Your new controlling function will be invoked by some other function, which we'll refer to as the *invoking function*. The invoking function communicates with the controlling function by the single `LPVOID` parameter. Whatever must be passed to the controlling function must be packed into that single parameter. This is not as hard as it sounds: You simply create a structure, load it with the values you want to pass in, cast it to `LPVOID`, and pass the entire structure into the controlling function using `AfxBeginThread()`.

5

**How To Use
Frameworks**

Some books suggest making the controlling function a global function; I disagree. You'll achieve better encapsulation (and thus have easier-to-maintain code) if you make the function a static member function of a particular class.

Note that you have no `this` pointer in your static member function, so you must pass in the `this` pointer as a parameter to the function. For example, you might declare your member method like this:

```
class myClass
{
public:
    static UINT    myThreadFunc(LPVOID pMe);
        // …
};
```

And you would write the implementation like this:

```
UINT myClass:: myThreadFunc (LPVOID ptheThisPointer)
{
    myClass * pmyThis = (CClientManager *) pMyThisPointer;
    ASSERT (pmyThis);
    pmyThis->SomeClassMethod();
    return 0;
}
```

You then invoke using `AfxBeginThread()`, passing in the class's `this` pointer as the second parameter:

```
AfxBeginThread(myClass:: myThreadFunc,(LPVOID) this );
```

An alternative is to make the function a *friend* of the class.

Synchronization

Now that your thread is up and running, you confront the issue of thread synchronization. The MFC provides a number of objects to help with this task: critical sections, semaphores, mutexes, and events.

Your thread can check the status of each of these objects (other than critical sections) to see whether the object is signaled or unsignaled (often called *cleared*). When a synchronization object is signaled, it indicates that your thread may have access. Until the object is signaled, your thread "waits." When a thread is waiting, it is doing nothing and is blocked.

Critical Sections

Critical sections are the simplest, easiest to use, and most limited of the synchronization objects. Your thread obeys a simple rule: When it wants to touch an area of code to be synchronized, it first asks for a lock on its `CriticalSection` object. It then blocks execution of its thread until the `CriticalSection` object can be locked. If another thread has already locked the object, your thread waits until the other thread unlocks the `CriticalSection`. The `CriticalSection` thus synchronizes access to the specified area of code. Here is how a critical section might be used to bracket code which changes a value:

```
m_CS.Lock();
s.Format("Current value: %d", m_Value);
m_Value++;
m_CS.Unlock();
```

Here the object has two variables: `m_Value` (an integer) and `m_CS` (a `CCriticalSection`). The critical section is locked, the value is incremented, and the critical section is unlocked.

Mutexes

Critical sections are great. For many purposes, they are all you need. They are fast, lightweight, and easy to use. They are, unfortunately, also limited. Their biggest limitations are that they are visible only in one process, and that you cannot wait a specified amount of time for them to unlock.

A more sophisticated synchronization device is the mutex. The word *mutex* is derived from the words *mut*ually *ex*clusive, with the implication that if two (or more) objects share a mutex, they have mutually exclusive access to whatever that mutex controls.

A mutex is very similar to a critical section: Either you own it (and can access the area of code it protects) or you do not (and you must wait). Unlike a critical section, however, a mutex can be shared across processes; your code can also specify how long to wait for the mutex to become available before you "time out." Here is how you might use a mutex to control access to code that changes a value:

```
CSingleLock theLock ( &m_myMutex );
if ( theLock.Lock(WAIT_TIME) )
{
    s.Format("Current value: %d", m_Value);
    m_Value++;
    theLock.Unlock();
}
else
{
    AfxMessageBox("Lock on Mutex failed. No increment!");
}
break;
```

Here's how a mutex works. You start by initializing a `Lock` object. If you are waiting only for one object (for example, the mutex) you can use `CSingleLock`. To wait for more than one object to become available, you use `CMultiLock`. You initialize the lock with the object you want to wait for.

When you are ready to access the protected code, you lock the `Lock` object and pass in how long you want to wait, measured in milliseconds. The default value is `INFINITE`—meaning that you want to wait until the sun goes nova and the Earth is destroyed.

Events

Event objects are useful for waiting for an event to occur. Event objects are unsignaled until some other object sets them to be signaled. Threads can wait for an event to become signaled, allowing you to say to a thread "start running when this event occurs."

Typically, you create an event in the unsignaled state and then tell one or more threads to wait for that event to become signaled. You might set such an event to notify threads when printing is complete, when a file has been downloaded, when there is a message in the queue, and so forth.

Events have a member variable, `bManualReset`, which determines what happens when you call `SetEvent()` on the `Event` object. If `bManualReset` is `false`, then all waiting threads are released when you call `SetEvent()`. If you want the event to be reset (returned to unsignaled), you must call `ResetEvent()`.

If, on the other hand, `bManualReset` is `true`, then only one waiting thread is released, and the `Event` is once again automatically reset to unsignaled.

If you have a manual reset event (`bManualReset` is `true`), you can release all the waiting threads by calling `PulseEvent()`. Doing so also automatically resets the event. Thus, `PulseEvent()` allows you to treat your manual reset event as if it were an auto-reset event.

An Example

Listing 5.1 uses a number of the synchronization devices described in the preceding sections. It is intentionally simplistic to allow you to focus on how the synchronization objects interact. This MFC application draws a simple dialog box as shown in Figure 5.4.

When you click the Start Thread 1 button in the dialog box, a worker thread is spawned. This worker thread increments and displays a value stored in the dialog box. (Normally, you would store these values in the document, but in the MFC's dialog application, there is no `Document` object.) This thread then waits a variable amount of time up to one second and repeats. Documents and views are explained in detail later in this chapter.

When you click the Start Thread 2 button in the dialog box, a second worker thread is spawned. This thread also increments and displays *the same* value stored in the dialog box. If you let these two threads run for a while, you'll see that the numbers are added to the list box out of order because the threads are competing for the same resource.

FIGURE 5.4.

A simple dialog box.

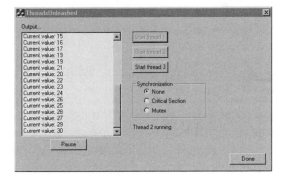

When you click the Start Thread 3 button in the dialog box, a new CWinThread-derived object is created. The dialog box then sends that new thread object a message to start work, and that thread also begins incrementing the value held in the dialog box. Now all three threads are incrementing the same value (see Figure 5.5).

FIGURE 5.5.

Adding values without synchronization.

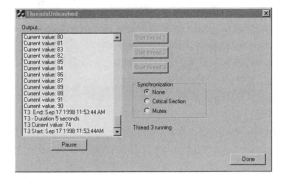

Note that the values are out of order:

```
Current value: 10
Current value: 12
Current value: 11
T3 Current value: 9
Current value: 14
Current value: 13
```

This is a direct result of three threads competing for a single value that is not under synchronization control.

5

HOW TO USE FRAMEWORKS

If you click the Critical Section radio button in the dialog box, the application accesses that value under control of a `CCriticalSection`. As you might expect, the critical section causes the numbers to be listed in order. Clicking the Mutex radio button causes these values to be accessed under the control of the `CMutex` object and sets a timeout period for access to the value. Once again, this causes the values to be listed in the correct order.

The Pause button is included to allow you to easily examine the order of the values displayed; otherwise, they scroll by very quickly.

I added a `CEvent` object that starts out unsignaled. When the dialog box is initialized, this object creates a thread that displays a message to the user, but that thread waits for the event to be signaled. As each of the three user-controlled threads is created, a counter is incremented. When all the threads are running, the event is signaled and the message is displayed, as shown in Figure 5.6.

FIGURE 5.6.

The event is signaled.

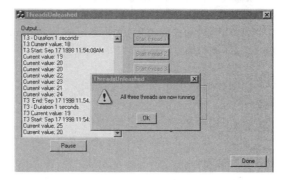

This is a silly use of the `CEvent`, but it does illustrate how it is used. The worker thread that displays this message exits when you click OK, thus terminating the thread.

A detailed examination of the code shows how these synchronization objects are used. When I created this application, I told MFC (by way of the wizard dialogs) that I wanted a dialog-based application rather than a single-document or a multi-document interface, as shown in Figure 5.7. The complete application is included on the CD-ROM that accompanies this book.

Building a dialog-based application means that I have a simpler application, but that I do not have a `CDocument` class in which I can store my state variables. The dialog example uses the `CDialog` class as a quick-and-dirty solution to the creation of the application. The constructor for `CDocument` serves to initialize these state variables:

FIGURE 5.7.

Wizard dialog.

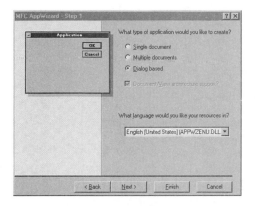

```
CThreadsUnleashedDlg::CThreadsUnleashedDlg(CWnd* pParent /*=NULL*/)
    : m_Value(0),
    m_Paused(false),
    m_MTC(0),
    m_numThreads(0),
    m_AllRunningEvent(false,true,NULL,NULL),
    CDialog(CThreadsUnleashedDlg::IDD, pParent)
{
    //{{AFX_DATA_INIT(CThreadsUnleashedDlg)
    m_RadioButtonValue = 0;
    //}}AFX_DATA_INIT
    // Note that LoadIcon does not require a subsequent DestroyIcon in
➥Win32
    m_hIcon = AfxGetApp()->LoadIcon(IDR_MAINFRAME);
}
```

In this code, m_Value is the value I'll be incrementing. m_Paused is a flag indicating that the user has clicked the Pause button; it is initialized to false. m_MTC is a pointer to a MyThreadClass object, which is created when the user clicks the Start Thread 3 button. m_NumThreads keeps count of how many user-requested threads are running, and m_AllRunningEvent is the Event object that is signaled when all three user-requested threads are running.

> **NOTE**
>
> Some code is called out in bold to draw your attention to a particularly interesting aspect or to show what we've added or changed.

The rest of this method was created by the Application Wizard.

I create my new thread in OnInitDialog(), as shown here:

```
BOOL CThreadsUnleashedDlg::OnInitDialog()
{
    CDialog::OnInitDialog();

    // … unimportant details elided…

    AfxBeginThread(ThreadsNotification,(LPVOID)this);

    return TRUE;   // return TRUE  unless you set the focus to a control
}
```

The call to AfxBeginThread(ThreadsNotification,(LPVOID)this) spawns the worker thread that is implemented in the method ThreadsNotification(). The rest of the Application Wizard code has been left out because it is boilerplate.

The ThreadsNotification() method looks like this:

```
UINT CThreadsUnleashedDlg::ThreadsNotification(LPVOID pParam)
{

    CThreadsUnleashedDlg * pThis = (CThreadsUnleashedDlg*) pParam;
    WaitForSingleObject(pThis->m_AllRunningEvent,INFINITE);

    AfxMessageBox("All three threads are now running");

    return 0;
}
```

This very simple method unpacks the parameter and casts it into a pointer to the CThreadsUnleasedDlg object that invoked this method. This approach is necessary because the worker thread function must be static; it cannot have a this pointer. We then use the this pointer to access the CEvent object passed to WaitForSingleObject(), and we tell the code to wait forever. This instruction blocks the thread and releases its time slice. When the event is signaled, this thread is released and displays its message box. The final line, return 0, causes the function to return and the thread to exit.

The dialog box is now displayed and is quiescent until a button is clicked. When the user clicks Start Thread 1, a message is sent to the dialog box which is captured in the message map:

```
    ON_BN_CLICKED(IDC_BUTTON_START_T1, OnButtonStartT1)
```

This invokes the method OnButtonStart1():

```
void CThreadsUnleashedDlg::OnButtonStartT1()
{
    CButton * pB = (CButton*)GetDlgItem(IDC_BUTTON_START_T1);
    pB->EnableWindow(false);
```

```
m_Thread1 = AfxBeginThread(ThreadFunction,(LPVOID)this);
CStatic * pStatic = ( (CStatic *) (GetDlgItem(IDC_STATIC_STATUS)));
pStatic->SetWindowText("Thread 1 running");
CountThreads();
}
```

We create a pointer to the button returned from GetDlgItem() and use that pointer to disable the button (rendering it gray, showing that it can't be pressed again).

We then create a new thread by invoking AfxBeginThread(), passing in the address of a static function that returns a UINT, and a single parameter. This is the required syntax for AfxBeginThread(). Because we want to pass in the this pointer, we just cast it to LPVOID (which translates to void **).

This action spawns a new thread and returns immediately. We then get a pointer to the CStatic object on the dialog box and update that to display Thread 1 running. Finally, we call CountThreads().

We'll explore what happens in the body of the new thread in a moment. First, let's take a quick look at CountThreads():

```
void CThreadsUnleashedDlg::CountThreads()
{
    if ( InterlockedIncrement(&m_numThreads) >= 3)
        m_AllRunningEvent.SetEvent();

}
```

The goal of this method is to increment the count of running threads; when it hits 3, it sets the AllRunningEvent event so that the notification thread can be released. Because we want to ensure that the variable m_numThreads is under synchronization control, we can take advantage of the InterlockedIncrement() method. This method takes a pointer to a long integer (4 bytes) and increments it under thread control.

> **NOTE**
>
> Under Windows NT, this approach reliably returns the newly incremented value; under Windows 95, however, it does not. Thus, the code as shown is specific to Windows NT. If you must run this code under Windows 95, increment the value and then test it separately.

The worker threads do a simple job of incrementing the m_Value member of the dialog box:

5

HOW TO USE FRAMEWORKS

```
UINT CThreadsUnleashedDlg::ThreadFunction(LPVOID pParam)
{

    CListBox * pLB = ((CListBox*)(pThis->GetDlgItem(IDC_LIST_OUTPUT)));
    CString s;
    int offset;

    srand( (unsigned)time( NULL ) );

    for ( ;; )
    {
        if ( pThis->m_Paused )
        {
            Sleep(500);
            continue;
        }

        switch ( pThis->m_RadioButtonValue )
        {

        case sNONE: // None
            s.Format("Current value: %d",pThis->m_Value);
            Sleep(rand() % 1000);
            pThis->m_Value++;
            break;

        case sCRITICAL_SECTION: // Critical Section
            pThis->m_CS.Lock();   // no timeout possible
            s.Format("Current value: %d",pThis->m_Value);
            Sleep(rand() % 1000);
            pThis->m_Value++;
            pThis->m_CS.Unlock();
            break;

        case sMUTEX: // Mutex
            CSingleLock theLock ( &(pThis->m_myMutex) );
            if ( theLock.Lock(WAIT_TIME) )
            {
                s.Format("Current value: %d",pThis->m_Value);
                Sleep(rand() % 1000);
                pThis->m_Value++;
                theLock.Unlock();
            }
            else
            {
                AfxMessageBox("Lock on Mutex failed. No increment!");
            }
            break;
        }

        offset = pLB->AddString(s);
```

```
        pLB->SetTopIndex( offset );

    }
    return 0;
}
```

The first job of this section of code is to cast the `this` pointer:

```
CThreadsUnleashedDlg * pThis = (CThreadsUnleashedDlg*) pParam;
```

Because the thread is implemented in a static member function, you must pass in a copy of the `this` pointer, which must be used (explicitly) to access the members. Because, however, this *is* a member method, it does have access to the private member variables of the class.

We immediately enter a forever loop, grabbing the value and incrementing it until the thread is destroyed. Each time through the loop, we check the value of the dialog's `m_Paused` Boolean member to see whether we should pause long enough to let the user review the progress so far:

```
if ( pThis->m_Paused )
{
    Sleep(500);
    continue;
}
```

We then look at the radio buttons. Note that we don't examine the control, but rather the member variable `m_RadioButtonValue`:

```
switch ( pThis->m_RadioButtonValue )
```

This member variable was created by the Class Wizard and is associated with the radio buttons. All the radio buttons contained in the group box are recognized as a single, mutually exclusive set of choices. To create a series of radio buttons, you mark only the first button as having the style "group" (do not mark any of the others in this way). You can then find that radio button in the Class Wizard's Member Variable tab and can create an integer "value" member variable to correspond to that button. The integer is set to the zero-based offset of the button selected; in this example, None has the value 0, Critical Section has the value 1, and Mutex has the value 2. The code to map these buttons to these values is generated by the wizard:

```
DDX_Radio(pDX, IDC_RADIO_NONE, m_RadioButtonValue);
```

While the wizard was running, I also mapped each radio button to a method, so that when the user clicks one of the radio buttons, the associated method is called:

```
ON_BN_CLICKED(IDC_RADIO_NONE, OnRadioNone)
ON_BN_CLICKED(IDC_RADIO_MUTEX, OnRadioMutex)
ON_BN_CLICKED(IDC_RADIO_CRITICAL_SECTION, OnRadioCriticalSection)
```

For example, when the user clicks the Mutex radio button (`IDC_RADIO_MUTEX`), the method `OnRadioMutex()` is invoked, as shown here:

```
void CThreadsUnleashedDlg::OnRadioMutex()
{
    UpdateData();
    CStatic * pStatic = ( (CStatic *) (GetDlgItem(IDC_STATIC_STATUS)));
    pStatic->SetWindowText("Using Mutex");

}
```

The first thing this method does is update the associated variable (`m_RadioButtonNone`) and then print a status message to the status line.

Let's return to `ThreadFunction()`; after we determine we are not paused, we switch on the value of the `m_RadioButtonValue` member, which as you now know corresponds to the radio button chosen by the user. To test the `switch` statement, I use an enumerated constant:

```
enum synch { sNONE, sCRITICAL_SECTION, sMUTEX,  sEVENT};
```

This makes the intent of the code a bit easier to decipher. If the value is `sNone` (zero), the first button None was chosen, and I simply print the value of `m_Value` and increment it. If either the Critical Section or Mutex radio button was selected, then I bracket the call to the increment function with code to manage the synchronization device.

In the case of the Critical Section radio button being selected, I lock the dialog box's critical section variable `m_CS`, print and update the value, and then unlock it:

```
        case sCRITICAL_SECTION: // Critical Section
            pThis->m_CS.Lock();  // no timeout possible
            s.Format("Current value: %d",pThis->m_Value);
            Sleep(rand() % 1000);
            pThis->m_Value++;
            pThis->m_CS.Unlock();
            break;
```

In the case of the Mutex radio button being selected, I have a bit more control. I create a `CSingleLock` object, passing in the address of the mutex. I then request a lock, specifying a timeout value. If the mutex is locked within the allotted time, I go ahead and print and update the value. If the mutex is not available within the allotted time, then I fail, print a warning message, and take no other action. This prevents the thread from hanging indefinitely, waiting for a mutex that may never become available.

When the user clicks Start Thread 3, a somewhat different sequence of events is initiated:

```
void CThreadsUnleashedDlg::OnButtonStartT3()
{
    CButton * pB = (CButton*)GetDlgItem(IDC_BUTTON_START_T3);
```

```
    pB->EnableWindow(false);
if ( ! m_MTC )
{
    m_MTC = new CMyThreadClass(this);
    BOOL bRc = m_MTC->CreateThread();
    if ( ! bRc )
    {
        CString msg("Unable to start thread!\n");
        AfxMessageBox(msg);
        // JLTODO: post quit message
    }
    m_MTC->PostThreadMessage( WM_START_WORK, 0, 0 );
    CountThreads();
}

}
```

Once again, we dim the button, but this time we check to see whether the member variable that points to our `CWinThread`-derived object is `NULL`. Assuming that it is, we are ready to create a new instance of the thread class.

While it is normally important to check whether the pointer is `NULL`, in this code we know it is not, and so the `if` statement can be rewritten using `ASSERT`.

```
    ASSERT ( ! m_MTC );
```

Because we dim the button, it isn't possible for this thread to already exist. I wrote it this way to allow for a time in the immediate future when we can create and then destroy these thread objects willy-nilly.

The goal is to instantiate an object of type `CMyThreadClass`. This class is derived from `CWinThread` and thus is able to manage a Windows thread:

```
class CMyThreadClass : public CWinThread
```

Creating the thread is a two-step process. In the first step, the thread *object* is instantiated:

```
    m_MTC = new CMyThreadClass(this);
```

In the second step, the thread itself is created:

```
    BOOL bRc = m_MTC->CreateThread();
```

Note the difference. When we create an instance using `new`, we create the object but we do not create the Windows thread. The thread is created with the call to `CreateThread()`. We talk about the object and the thread as if they were the same, but they are distinct.

After the thread is running, we want it to start work, but we do *not* want to call its `StartWork()` method directly. If we did, we would hang until that method returns (which

5

HOW TO USE FRAMEWORKS

it never does). Instead, we want to send a message asynchronously to that thread and tell it to start work. We do that using its `PostThreadMessage()` method—which returns immediately:

```
m_MTC->PostThreadMessage( WM_START_WORK, 0, 0 );
```

This statement posts a user-defined message with the value `WM_START_WORK`, to the thread. This value is also defined in our `constants.h` file as shown here:

```
const int WM_START_WORK =    WM_USER + 1;
```

When the thread detects that message, it maps it to a member method of the class by the dispatch map:

```
BEGIN_MESSAGE_MAP(CMyThreadClass, CWinThread)
    //{{AFX_MSG_MAP(CMyThreadClass)
        // NOTE - the ClassWizard will add and remove mapping macros here.
    //}}AFX_MSG_MAP
    ON_THREAD_MESSAGE(WM_START_WORK,OnStartWork)

END_MESSAGE_MAP()
```

Note that I add my own `ON_THREAD_MESSAGE` line *after* the `AFX_MSG_MAP` protected code, but before the `END_MESSAGE_MAP()` macro. Anything between these two lines can be overwritten by the wizards, but the code I've added is safe:

```
    //{{AFX_MSG_MAP(CMyThreadClass)

    //}}AFX_MSG_MAP
```

This map simply dictates that when the `WM_START_WORK` message is received, the method `OnStartWork()` is to be invoked:

```
void CMyThreadClass::OnStartWork()
{
    CStatic * pStatic = ( (CStatic *) (m_pDlg->GetDlgItem
➥(IDC_STATIC_STATUS)));
    pStatic->SetWindowText("Thread 3 running");

    CListBox * pLB = ((CListBox*)(m_pDlg->GetDlgItem(IDC_LIST_OUTPUT)));

    srand( (unsigned)time( NULL ) );
    CString s;
    CString status;
    for ( ;; )
    {
        if ( m_pDlg->IsPaused() )
        {
```

```
        Sleep(500);
        continue;
    }
    int val;

    switch ( m_pDlg->m_RadioButtonValue )
    {

    case sNONE: // None
        val = m_pDlg->GetValue();
        s.Format("T3 Current value: %d",val);
        Sleep(rand() % 1000);
        m_pDlg->SetValue(++val);
        break;

    case sCRITICAL_SECTION: // Critical Section
        m_pDlg->m_CS.Lock();  // no timeout possible
        val = m_pDlg->GetValue();
        s.Format("T3 Current value: %d",val);
        Sleep(rand() % 1000);
        m_pDlg->SetValue(++val);
        m_pDlg->m_CS.Unlock();

        break;

    case sMUTEX: // Mutex
        CSingleLock theLock ( &(m_pDlg->m_myMutex) );
        if ( theLock.Lock(WAIT_TIME) )
        {
            val = m_pDlg->GetValue();
            s.Format("T3 Current value: %d",val);
            Sleep(rand() % 1000);
            m_pDlg->SetValue(++val);
            theLock.Unlock();
        }
        else
        {
            AfxMessageBox("Lock on Mutex failed. No increment!");
        }
        break;

    }

    int offset = pLB->AddString(s);
    pLB->SetTopIndex( offset );

    }

}
```

Not surprisingly, this method is quite similar to the `ThreadFunction()` method we just examined. The significant difference is that this is *not* a static method of the dialog class, but is a simple member method of the thread class. The thread class can maintain its own state and can respond to thread messages.

To ensure proper synchronization, this thread must use the same mutex as is used by the dialog class' threads. Remember, however, that the `CMutex` can be named. To do this, we initialize the mutex in the constructor to the dialog:

```
CThreadsUnleashedDlg::CThreadsUnleashedDlg(CWnd* pParent /*=NULL*/)
    : m_Value(0),
    m_Paused(false),
    m_MTC(0),
    m_numThreads(0),
    m_AllRunningEvent(false,true,NULL,NULL),
    m_myMutex(false,"m1"),
    CDialog(CThreadsUnleashedDlg::IDD, pParent)
```

We then create another mutex as a member of the thread:

```
class CMyThreadClass : public CWinThread
{
/...
private:
    CThreadsUnleashedDlg * m_pDlg;
    CMutex m_Mutex;

};
```

Then we initialize this mutex with the same name:

```
CMyThreadClass::CMyThreadClass(CThreadsUnleashedDlg * pDlg):
m_pDlg(pDlg),
m_Mutex(false,"m1")
{

}
```

We can now modify the code in the thread object to refer to its own mutex, which is a reference to the mutex object held by the dialog:

```
        CSingleLock theLock ( &m_Mutex );
        if ( theLock.Lock(WAIT_TIME) )
        {
            //...
        }
```

Utility Classes

The MFC provides a series of utility classes, some of which we've seen in action already. These classes are added by Microsoft to the foundation classes to make programming easier—which frees you from having to do so yourself. With the advent of the Standard Template Library, many of these classes are now somewhat redundant, but to date Microsoft has simply folded the STL back into its own library.

The most important and useful utility classes are the CString class (for manipulating character strings) and the CTime classes for manipulating dates, times, and timespans.

String Manipulation Classes

Perhaps the utility class which you will use most frequently is CString. This simple string class facilitates using text strings: creating, formatting, copying, passing as parameters, and so forth.

The constructor for CString is overloaded to take no parameters (the default constructor) or to take an existing CString object (the copy constructor) or to take a number of alternatives, perhaps the most useful of which simply takes a C-style NULL-terminated string.

After your CString object exists, you can concatenate it with another CString. This code initializes s3 with the string "Hello world":

```
CString s1("Hello");
CString s2 (" world");
CString s3 = s1+s2;
```

You can use CString for sophisticated string manipulation, such as searching for substrings and the like. One of the most powerful methods is Format(), which takes a string not unlike that used by printf() and which uses the same specifiers as printf(). You've seen CString.Format() in action throughout this and other chapters.

Time Classes

Another popular set of utility classes provided by the MFC assist with manipulating time. The ANSI standard provides for a time_t data type that the MFC wraps with the CTime class. This class represents an absolute time and date within the range January 1, 1970 to January 18, 2038, inclusive. The CTime class includes utility functions to convert to and from Gregorian dates and between 12-hour and 24-hour clocks. Additional methods assist you in extracting the year, month, day, hours, minutes, and so forth from a given time value.

The CTimeSpan class provides relative time values, that is time spans. When one CTime object is subtracted from another, the result is a CTimeSpan object. You can add and subtract CTimeSpan objects from CTime objects to create new CTimeSpan objects. The range of dates you can thus manipulate is about 68 years.

We can put this class to use to measure the interval between two events. Let's modify the CMyThreadClass shown earlier, so that when it is not under synchronization control, it pauses a random interval between 1 and 5,000 milliseconds (5 seconds). We can measure the duration (in seconds) by taking the current time at the start of the work and again at the end of the work, and then measuring the difference between them:

```
CTime start, end;
CTimeSpan len;

start = CTime::GetCurrentTime();
rightNow = start.Format("T3 Start: %b %d %Y %I:%M%p");
offset = pLB->AddString(rightNow);
pLB->SetTopIndex( offset );

val = m_pDlg->GetValue();
s.Format("T3 Current value: %d",val);
Sleep(rand() % 5000);
m_pDlg->SetValue(++val);


end = CTime::GetCurrentTime();
rightNow = end.Format("T3 End: %b %d %Y %I:%M%p");
offset = pLB->AddString(rightNow);
pLB->SetTopIndex( offset );

len = end - start;
duration.Format("T3 - Duration %d seconds",len.GetSeconds());
offset = pLB->AddString(duration);
pLB->SetTopIndex( offset );
```

The CTime variable start is set to the current time before we begin working. The CTime variable end is set to the current time when we are done. The timespan len is set to the difference.

We can extract and print the current time by calling Format() on the CTime objects; we can print the duration by using the CTimeSpan member method GetSeconds().

The output from the preceding code looks like this:

```
T3Start Jul 28 1998 05:02:39PM
T3End Jul 28 1998 05:02:44PM
T3 Duration 5 seconds
T3Current value: 10
T3Start Jul 28 1998 05:02:44PM
```

```
T3End Jul 28 1998 05:02:48PM
T3 Duration 4 seconds
T3Current value: 11
T3Start:Jul 28 1998 05:02:48PM
T3End Jul 28 1998 05:02:51 PM
T3 Duration 3 seconds
T3Current value: 12
T3Start: Jul 28 1998 05:02:51PM
T3End: Jul 28 1998 05:02:55 PM
T3 Duration 4 seconds
```

Documents and Views

Of course, dialog boxes and threads are not the heart and soul of the MFC. The real reason for the existence of the MFC is to help you manage the creation and manipulation of windows—onscreen views of your data. To do this, the MFC uses documents (to manage data) and views (to manage windows and controls).

The MFC's *document/view* design pattern is a simplification of the Model/View/Controller (MVC) design pattern originally used to build user interfaces in Smalltalk-80. In MVC, you create an object that represents your data; this object is called the *model*. You then assign responsibility for viewing that data to various *views*, and decouple viewing from the responsibility for controlling or manipulating the data, which is assigned to the *controllers*.

Microsoft's variant on the MVC design pattern is the somewhat simpler Document/View pattern. In Microsoft's approach, the data (document) is still separated from the view, but the view and the controller are merged. Document/View is so intrinsic to the Microsoft Foundation Classes that it is sometimes a challenge to write programs that ignore this pattern.

It is important to note that in both the MVC and the Document/View patterns, the *model*, or *document*, is any data your program uses. Documents need not be word processing documents—they can be collections of records, tables, or amorphous data structures.

Views

The views in the MFC are represented as windows and *widgets*, or *controls*. The class CWnd is the base class for all the views, including dialog boxes, CFrameWnd (which manages the frame of a window), and CMDIChildWnd (which manages multidocument-interface windows—that is, multiple subwindows within a single frame as you might see by opening more than one document in Microsoft Word). CWnd is also the base class to CView, as well as the base to all the controls such as CButton, CListbox, and so on.

The CDocument and CView classes encapsulate the Document/View design pattern and work with the CWnd-derived classes to display the contents of the CDocument. The CView class can be extended in many powerful ways, and the MFC provides you with a family of derived classes including CScrollView (for scrolling through large documents), CEditView (for building text documents), CRichEditView (for creating documents with rich text such as FORMATTING, **bold**, *italic*, and so on), CFormView (for creating onscreen forms), CRecordView (for working with databases), and CTreeView (for creating structured views of hierarchical data).

CView is the parent class of all these derived views, and it provides a number of virtual functions for your derived class to override. The most important CView functions are probably OnInitialUpdate(), OnUpdate(), and OnDraw().

OnInitialUpdate() is called the first time the view updates itself. Every time a document changes, it notifies all the views currently attached to it. MFC calls OnInitialUpdate() the first time and calls OnUpdate() on all subsequent calls.

The default behavior for the update methods is to invalidate the window and then to invoke OnDraw(). This approach gives you tremendous flexibility in how you render your view, but also provides boilerplate code that can be used to implement default drawing functionality.

Form Views

One very popular use of the MFC is to create complex forms for gathering information from a user. There are two common methods for implementing such an application: as a simple dialog box and with the new CFormView. The CFormView combines the Document/View architecture with the ease of use of a dialog box. We'll explore the form view in some depth here, to provide a more general lesson in how such applications can be built using virtually any application framework library.

The sample program we'll implement looks like what is shown in Figure 5.8.

This application presents a form for use by a credit agency. It gathers information from the user by way of a number of flexible controls. Among the controls we'll explore are edit controls (for example, Last Name), radio buttons (for example, Spending), drop-down lists (for example, Salary Range), slider controls (for example, Credit Limit), and spin controls (for example, Member Since). We'll also explore property sheets, invoked here by selecting Profile, but which are often seen in applications as a device for gathering user preferences. As an example of a property sheet, Figure 5.9 shows the property sheet from Microsoft Word.

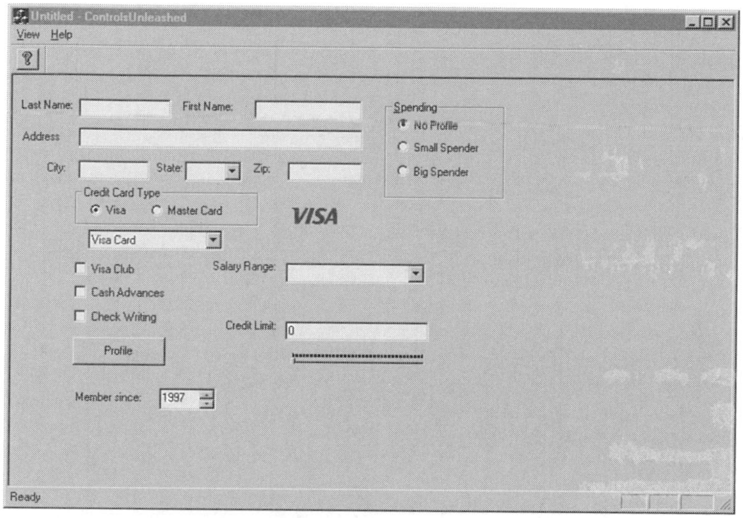

Figure 5.8.

Sample form view application.

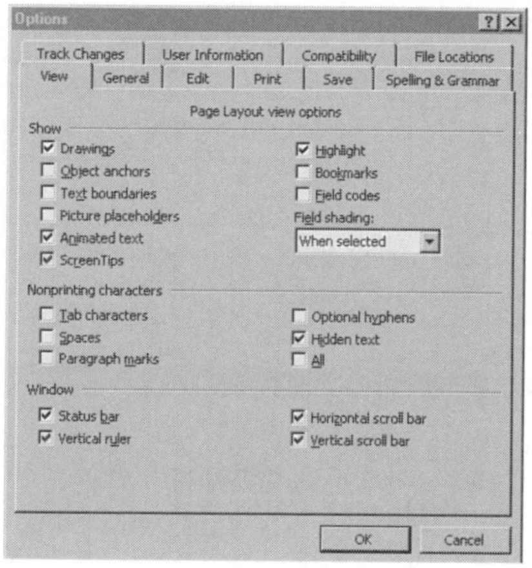

Figure 5.9.

Property sheet from Word.

As you can see, a property sheet is a way to manage a series of dialog-based forms, giving the user freedom to move among the pages as needed. The propery sheet we'll implement in this example looks like the one in Figure 5.10. This is a somewhat simpler example than the Microsoft Word property sheet, but it affords us an opportunity to examine, in detail, how property sheets are implemented.

Getting Started with Form Views

To get started, fire up a new SDI project and proceed through the wizards in the usual way. Just before we confirm the filenames, we highlight the view

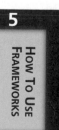

5

How To Use Frameworks

(CControlsUnleashedView) and change its type (base class) from CView to CFormView, as shown in Figure 5.11.

FIGURE 5.10.

Our example property sheet.

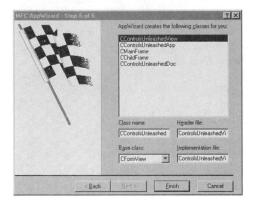

FIGURE 5.11.

Changing the view to FormView.

After the application is built, we open the resource editor and begin to build the initial form. Each of the controls should be afforded a meaningful name, and then we invoke the Class Wizard to assign variables corresponding to the value of each of the controls, as shown in Figure 5.12.

For some of the controls such as IDC_COMBOSalaryRange, we create two variables: one holds the value (m_SalaryRangeValue) and one represents the control itself (m_ComboSalaryRange).

By having a variable that holds the control itself, we can write this simple statement:

```
m_ComboSalaryRange.GetCount();
```

If we didn't have such a variable, we'd have to write this:

```
CComboBox * pBox = (CComboBox *) GetDlgItem(IDC_COMBOSalaryRange);
pBox->GetCount();
```

FIGURE 5.12.

Assigning variables for each control.

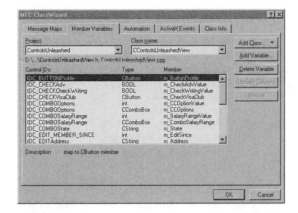

When you expect to access the control itself, using a Class Wizard–generated member variable is simpler and easier to maintain.

When all the form controls have corresponding values, the Class Wizard generates the code to ensure that these variables are updated with the values in the controls. We'll explore how this works, but note that these variables are members of the `CFormView`, not of the document. If you want to ensure that the data is stored in a central location (which is what you *will* want if more than one view will display or interact with this data), you will have to create corresponding variables in the document and manage the transfer between the view and the document manually.

Managing Data

To get the data into and out of the variables of the view, you invoke `UpdateData()`. If you pass in the parameter `false`, you initialize the controls with the data in the view. If you pass no parameter, the default value of `true` indicates that you want to update the variables with the contents of the controls.

`UpdateData()` will, eventually, invoke `DoDataExchange()` (do not invoke this method directly!), which was created by the Class Wizard (although you can create it by hand if you want). `DoDataExchange()` looks like this:

```
void CControlsUnleashedView::DoDataExchange(CDataExchange* pDX)
{
    CFormView::DoDataExchange(pDX);
    //{{AFX_DATA_MAP(CControlsUnleashedView)
    DDX_Control(pDX, IDC_COMBOSalaryRange, m_ComboSalaryRange);
    DDX_Control(pDX, IDC_SPIN_MEMBER_SINCE, m_MemberSinceControl);
    DDX_Control(pDX, IDC_STATICVISAPic, m_VisaPic);
    DDX_Control(pDX, IDC_STATICMCPic, m_MasterCardPic);
    DDX_Control(pDX, IDC_SLIDERCredit, m_CreditSlider);
    DDX_Control(pDX, IDC_RADIOVisa, m_VisaButton);
```

```
    DDX_Control(pDX, IDC_BUTTONProfile, m_ButtonProfile);
    DDX_Control(pDX, IDC_EDITCreditLimit, m_CreditLimitControl);
    DDX_Control(pDX, IDC_COMBOOptions, m_CCOptions);
    DDX_Control(pDX, IDC_CHECKVisaClub, m_CheckVisaClub);
    DDX_CBIndex(pDX, IDC_COMBOOptions, m_CCOptionValue);
    DDX_CBString(pDX, IDC_COMBOState, m_State);
    DDX_Text(pDX, IDC_EDITAddress, m_Address);
    DDX_Text(pDX, IDC_EDITCity, m_City);
    DDX_Text(pDX, IDC_EDITFirstName, m_FirstName);
    DDX_Text(pDX, IDC_EDITLastName, m_LastName);
    DDX_Radio(pDX, IDC_RADIONoProfile, m_RadioProfile);
    DDX_Radio(pDX, IDC_RADIOVisa, m_VisaButtonValue);
    DDX_Text(pDX, IDC_Zip, m_Zip);
    DDX_Check(pDX, IDC_CHECKAdv, m_CheckAdvValue);
    DDX_Check(pDX, IDC_CHECKCheckWriting, m_CheckWritingValue);
    DDX_Text(pDX, IDC_EDIT_MEMBER_SINCE, m_EditSince);
    DDV_MinMaxInt(pDX, m_EditSince, 1990, 2005);
    DDX_Text(pDX, IDC_EDITCreditLimit, m_EditCreditLimitValue);
    DDX_CBIndex(pDX, IDC_COMBOSalaryRange, m_SalaryRangeValue);
    //}}AFX_DATA_MAP
}
```

Each of these `DDX_` macros ensures that the data will be taken from the control and inserted into the variable in the right format (for example, converting from strings to `int`s as necessary). In addition, the macros provide an opportunity for automated range checking. For example, the `m_EditSince` variable is set to check the integer value entered to ensure that it is a value between 1990 and 2005. When you examine this variable in the Class Wizard, you have the opportunity to set these limits (see Figure 5.13).

FIGURE 5.13.

The Class Wizard.

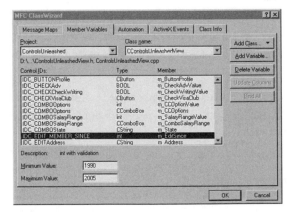

When the user attempts to leave the dialog box, if the value selected is not within the limits, the user is informed of this error and is returned to the field to make the necessary update (see Figure 5.14).

FIGURE 5.14.

Checking values.

Normally, this check is done when the user clicks the OK button, but I've modified the code to ensure that the check is done after the user leaves the field. I did this by asking the Class Wizard to create a method for the EN_KILL_FOCUS message—which is called when you tab out of the field (see Figure 5.15).

FIGURE 5.15.

Checking values when leaving fields.

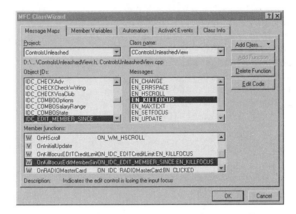

In the implementation of this method, I simply call UpdateData(), which forces the data validation:

```
void CControlsUnleashedView::OnKillfocusEditMemberSince()
{
    UpdateData();
}
```

Event-Driven Programming

The most common messages to respond to, of course, are button-push messages, which are managed in much the same way as messages generated by other controls. For example, when the Visa or Master Card buttons are clicked, we want to change the bitmap displayed and alter the check box choices available. We create an OnRADIOVisa() method to be invoked when the button is clicked:

```
void CControlsUnleashedView::OnRADIOVisa()
{
    UpdateData();

    if( m_VisaButtonValue==0 )
```

5

HOW TO USE
FRAMEWORKS

```
        {
            m_CCOptions.ResetContent();
            m_CCOptions.AddString("Visa Card");
            m_CCOptions.AddString("Visa Card Gold");
            m_CCOptions.AddString("Visa Card Platinum");
            m_CCOptions.SetCurSel(0);
             m_CheckVisaClub.EnableWindow(true);
            m_VisaPic.ShowWindow(SW_SHOW);
            m_MasterCardPic.ShowWindow(SW_HIDE);
        }
        else
        {

            m_CCOptions.ResetContent();
            m_CCOptions.AddString("Master Card Gold");
            m_CCOptions.AddString("Master Card Platinum");
            m_CCOptions.AddString("Master Card Premium");
            m_CCOptions.SetCurSel(0);
            m_CheckVisaClub.EnableWindow(false);
            m_VisaPic.ShowWindow(SW_HIDE);
            m_MasterCardPic.ShowWindow(SW_SHOW);
        }

}
```

As you can see, this method checks the value of the radio button selected and then sets the contents of the drop-down list appropriately. The method also hides the picture of Master Card and shows the picture of Visa (or vice versa).

The OnRADIOMasterCard() method simply invokes OnRADIOVisa:

```
void CControlsUnleashedView::OnRADIOMasterCard()
{
    OnRADIOVisa();
}
```

Users find it quite impressive when they select a radio button and other parts of the form respond—even though implementing this response is straightforward. We can tie other controls together as well. For example, the Credit Limit field is tied to the slider control beneath it. Moving the slider updates the credit limit field and vice versa.

We update the slider from the Credit Limit field by catching the kill focus message and setting the position of the slider based on the current contents of the edit field:

```
void CControlsUnleashedView::OnKillfocusEDITCreditLimit()
{
    UpdateData();
    m_CreditSlider.SetPos( m_EditCreditLimitValue / 1000 );
    UpdateData(false);

}
```

When the slider is moved, we can capture the horizontal scroll notification and update the edit field:

```
void CControlsUnleashedView::OnHScroll(UINT nSBCode, UINT nPos,
➥CScrollBar* pScrollBar)
{
    CSliderCtrl* p_Slider= dynamic_cast<CSliderCtrl*> (pScrollBar);
    if (!p_Slider)
        TRACE("Not really a CSliderCtrl\n");
    else
    {
        int value=p_Slider->GetPos();
        CString temp;
        temp.Format("%ld",value * 1000);
        (GetDlgItem(IDC_EDITCreditLimit))->SetWindowText(temp);
    }

        CFormView::OnHScroll(nSBCode, nPos, pScrollBar);

}
```

Notice that we must first ensure that the view is receiving this horizontal scroll notification from the slider itself. What is passed in is just a pointer to a CScrollBar. Because the CSliderCtrl class derives from CScrollBar, we can use the new ANSI dynamic_cast operator to ensure that we have a valid CSliderCtrl object before implementing the update.

Finally, we tie in the Salary combo box. Changing the salary should set a default Credit Limit, and this in turn should update the slider:

```
void CControlsUnleashedView::OnCloseupCOMBOSalaryRange()
{
    UpdateData();
    m_EditCreditLimitValue =
➥m_ComboSalaryRange.GetItemData(m_SalaryRangeValue);
    m_CreditSlider.SetPos( m_EditCreditLimitValue / 1000 );
    UpdateData(false);

}
```

This code is slightly tricky. We are setting the m_EditCreditLimitValue to the *item data* associated with the combo box. Windows did not provide this association; we did in the dialog box initialization:

```
    // associate an initial credit limit with each salary range
    for(int offset=0; offset<=m_ComboSalaryRange.GetCount(); offset++)
    {

        switch(offset)
        {
```

```
        case 0:
            crLimit=5000;
            break;
        case 1:
         crLimit=15000;
         break;
        case 2:
            crLimit=40000;
            break;
        case 3:
            crLimit=80000;
            break;
        case 4:
            crLimit=100000;
            break;
        default:
            crLimit=0;
        }
        m_ComboSalaryRange.SetItemData(offset,crLimit);
    }
```

This code associates the value 5000 with the first entry in the box, the value 15000 with the second entry, and so forth. Returning to OnCloseupCOMBOSalaryRange(), when the user chooses a Salary, we pick up the choice, use it to extract the associated item data, and then place that value in the edit box. Finally, we use the edit box's value to set the slider. This makes for a dynamic and integrated user-interface: Setting the salary sets the default credit limit.

Radio Buttons

The radio buttons within the group box are recognized by Windows as a related group. You must help Windows by ensuring that the tab order is correct. The key is that the buttons are all in sequential tab order, and that the first button has the Group style set. In addition, the first control that is not in the group box must also have its Group style set to let Windows know it has reached the end of the radio button group (see Figure 5.16).

> **NOTE**
>
> The tab order controls the order in which the user will move among the controls. You set the tab order in the resource editor by pressing Ctrl+D and then clicking each control in the order you want them invoked.

Notice that the buttons in the Credit Card Type group are sequential. Visa has its Group attribute set, and the Visa bitmap picture (`IDC_STATICMCPic`)—which is next in the tab order—has *its* group attribute set to signal that it marks the end of the radio button group.

FIGURE 5.16.

Setting the Group style.

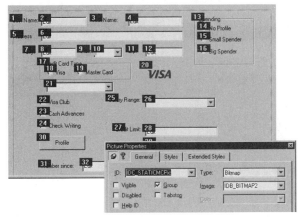

Spin Controls

The MFC allows you to marry an edit box to a spin control, as you can see with the Member Since control in Figure 5.17.

FIGURE 5.17.

Spin control.

Member since:

If you examine the dialog controls in the resource editor, you'll find they are quite distinct (see Figure 5.18).

By setting the Auto-Buddy style, you associate the spin control with the edit control immediately before it in the tab order. (Another reason to check your tab order!) You must also set Set-Buddy-Integer if you want the edit control to be manipulated by the spin control, as shown in Figure 5.19.

FIGURE 5.18.

The Resource Editor.

Member since: [Edit ▲▼]

FIGURE 5.19.

Setting buddy integer.

Member since: [Edit]

Spin Properties
▢ ? | General | Styles | Extended Styles |
Orientation:
[Vertical ▾]
Alignment:
[Right ▾]
☑ Auto buddy   ☐ Wrap
☑ Set buddy integer   ☑ Arrow keys
☑ No thousands   ☐ Hot track

Finally, you must set the range of the spin control, which is done in the view's `OnInitialUpdate()` method:

```
m_MemberSinceControl.SetRange(1990,2005);
```

Property Sheets

At this point, just about all the controls for the sample application are in place. The final step is to create the property sheet that appears when the user clicks Profile. A property sheet contains a series of related dialog boxes, each of which represents a `tabSheet` in the property sheet (see Figure 5.20).

FIGURE 5.20.

Property sheets.

This single property sheet actually consists of the container (class `CProfile : public CPropertySheet`) which contains three `CPropertyPage` derived classes: `CWorkPage`,

`CIncomePage`, and `CCreditHistoryPage`. To create these pages, you first create three separate dialog boxes.

The property pages will be sized to the largest of the pages; ideally, then, you want them to be pretty close in size to one another. The Resource editor helps the sizing problem by offering *template forms*. If you choose Insert Resource from the Resource menu and expand Dialog, you can choose from three templates: `IDD_PROPAGE_LARGE`, `IDD_PROPAGE_MEDIUM`, and `IDD_PROPAGE_SMALL`. I chose `IDD_PROPAGE_MEDIUM` three times to create each of the pages in the property sheet, as shown in Figure 5.21.

FIGURE 5.21.

Choosing a template.

The next step is to add all the controls to each property page, as shown in Figure 5.22. You do so in the normal way, using the Resource Editor.

FIGURE 5.22.

Adding the controls to the property page.

After you have positioned the controls, invoke the Class Wizard, which prompts you to create a class for your new dialog box. As an aside, I recommend that you change the filename for each of these classes to put them all in a single file. (I used `CProperty.h` and `Cproperty.cpp`.)

When all the pages are complete, it is time to create the `CPropertySheet`, which you do by right-clicking the project and invoking New Class. Name your class and have it derive from `CPropertySheet`.

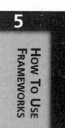

5

How To Use Frameworks

The property sheet is created dynamically on demand. When the user clicks the Profile button, the OnBUTTONProfile method (which I mapped using the Class Wizard) is invoked.

The first thing we do is to create a CProfile object (remember that CProfile derives from CPropertySheet). Next we create local instances of CCreditPage, CIncomePage, and CWorkPage and pass these as parameters to the AddPage() method of CPropertySheet. Just before adding these pages, we initialize the m_SalaryComboValue control in CIncomePage to match that of the salary combo in the controlling dialog box:

```
void CControlsUnleashedView::OnBUTTONProfile()
{
    CProfile theProfile(_T("Profile"),this);

    UpdateData();

    CCreditPage creditHistoryPage;
    CIncomePage incomePage;
    CWorkPage workPage;

    incomePage.m_SalaryComboValue = m_SalaryRangeValue;

    theProfile.AddPage(&workPage);
    theProfile.AddPage(&incomePage);
    theProfile.AddPage(&creditHistoryPage);

    // initialize dialog values here

    if ( theProfile.DoModal() == IDOK )
    {
        m_SalaryRangeValue = incomePage.m_SalaryComboValue;
        m_EditCreditLimitValue =
➥m_ComboSalaryRange.GetItemData(m_SalaryRangeValue);
        m_CreditSlider.SetPos( m_EditCreditLimitValue / 1000 );

    }

    UpdateData(false);
}
```

The property sheet is then invoked as a modal dialog box by calling the DoModal() method. If we get back IDOK (the user clicked OK), we can then take whatever action is appropriate. What is shown in the preceding code is the updating of a single control (the Salary); in a commercial application, you would probably update the document with the new data and then update all the views to reflect that new data.

Summary

You've seen that the Microsoft Foundation Class Library provides a powerful set of utilities and supporting classes to assist in building Windows applications. Each vendor may supply its own application frameworks, but the vendors share a common quality. They do the hard grunt-work of building the boiler-plate code, allowing you to focus on the semantics of your particular problem rather than the details of the particular operating system.

Because each application frameworks library is different, programmers become quite protective and defensive about their own choice. Thus, it is important you choose wisely. An ideal application framework will be a well-written, highly encapsulated, object-oriented, robust, extensible, and reliable set of classes. It will also be well supported and will evolve as the underlying operating system evolves.

Standard Template Library Container Classes

A *container* is an object that holds other objects. The Standard C++ Library provides a series of container classes that are powerful tools that help C++ developers handle common programming tasks. There are two types of Standard Template Library (STL) container classes: sequence and associative. *Sequence* containers are designed to provide sequential and random access to their members, or *elements*. *Associative* containers are optimized to access their elements by key values. As with other components of the Standard C++ Library, the STL is portable between various operating systems. All STL container classes are defined in `namespace std`.

Defining and Instantiating Templates

Before getting deep into the discussion of STL container classes, let's briefly review the concept of templates. C++ *templates* allow data types to be passed as parameters to function and class definitions. The same function or class can then be used for a variety of object types.

Defining and Instantiating Function Templates

A *function template* allows us to design a function that can be used to process different types of objects. For instance, you can specify that an argument can be an object of different types. The types of the return value can also vary depending on template parameters.

The following code snippet shows the definition of a function template:

```
template<class ClassX, class ClassY>void Square2(ClassX& x, ClassY& y)
{
    x *= x;
    y *= y;
}
```

The `Square2()` function can be used to process different types of objects, as long as those objects implement the overloading operator `*=`. For example, you can call the following function to calculate the squares of `aInt` and `aFloat`, two objects of different types:

```
Square2(int aInt, float aFloat);
```

You instantiate a function template by generating a function from the `template` function and parameters. For example, for the function template `Square2()`, consider this statement:

```
Square2(int aInt, float aFloat);
```

The preceding statement instantiates the following function:

```
Square2(int, float);
```

from

```
template<class ClassX, class ClassY>void Square2(ClassX& x, ClassY& y)
```

and the `template` parameters `ClassX` and `ClassY`.

The actual instantiation is done by the compiler based on the template you define.

Defining and Instantiating Class Templates

A *class template* provides the foundation for designing and implementing classes with
different member types. You define a class template in a way similar to the way you
design and implement a normal, nontemplate class. The difference is that members of a
class template can be parameterized. Here is an example of a template class definition:

```
template<class T>
class MyClass
{
public:
    // constructors and destructor
    MyClass();                  // default constructor
    MyClass(T& newVal);    // copy constructor
    ~MyClass();                  // destructor

    // accessors
    void SetVar(T& newVal);
    T& GetVar() const;

    // friend functions
    ostream& operator<<(ostream& os, const MyClass<T>& c);

private:
    T mVar;
};

template<class T>MyClass<T>::MyClass()
{}

template<class T>MyClass<T>::MyClass(T& newVal): mVar(newVal)
{}

template<class T>MyClass<T>::~MyClass()
{}
```

```
template<class T> void MyClass<T>::SetVar(T& newVal)
{
    mVar = newVal;
}

template<class T> T& MyClass<T>::GetVal() const
{
    return mVar;
}

template<class T> ostream& MyClass<T>::operator<<(ostream& os, const
MyClass<T>& c)
{
    os << "member variable mVar = " << c.mVar << "\n";
    return os;
}
```

Compare this to a normal class definition; the notable difference is that class members
are now type parameterized. When a member is defined outside the class definition, you
must add the following prefix to the function definition:

```
template<class T>
```

You must also parameterize `MyClass` as follows:

```
MyClass<T>
```

You instantiate a class template by generating a class definition from the template class
and parameters. The following example shows the instantiation of two classes,
`MyClass<int>` and `MyClass<string>`:

```
int    main()
{
    MyClass<int> intObj;
    intObj.SetVar(5);
    cout << "intObj.GetVar = " << intObj.GetVar() << "\n";
    cout << intObj;

    MyClass<string> strObj("This is a string");
    cout << "strObj.GetVar = " << strObj.GetVar() << "\n";
    cout << strObj;

    return 0;
}
```

Understanding Sequence Containers

The Standard Template Library sequence containers provide efficient sequential access to a list of objects. The Standard C++ Library provides three sequence containers: `vector`, `list`, and `deque`.

The Vector Container

You often use arrays to store and access a number of elements. Elements in an array are of the same type and are accessed with an index. The STL provides a container class `vector` that behaves just like an array but that is more powerful and safer to use than the standard C++ array.

A *vector* is a container optimized to provide fast access to its elements by an index. The container class `vector` is defined in the header file `<vector>` in `namespace std` (see Chapter 8, "Avoiding Name Clashes by Using Namespaces," for more information on the use of namespaces). A vector can grow itself as necessary. Suppose that you have created a vector to contain 10 elements. After you have filled the vector with 10 objects, the vector is full. If you then add another object to the vector, the vector automatically increases its capacity so that it can accommodate the 11th object. Here is how the `vector` class is defined:

```
template <class T, class A = allocator<T>> class vector
{
    // class members
};
```

The first argument (`class T`) is the type of the elements in the vector. The second argument (`class A`) is an allocator class. *Allocators* are memory managers responsible for memory allocation and deallocation of elements for the containers. By default, elements are created using the operator `new()` and are freed using the operator `delete()`. That is, the default constructor of class `T` is called to create a new element. You can define vectors that hold integers and floats as follows:

```
vector<int>     vInts;       // vector holding int elements
vector<float>   vFloats;     // vector holding float elements
```

Constructors

To use a vector, you must first create it. When a `vector` object is created, a block of memory is acquired from the operating system. The size of the block is at least large enough to hold the whole `vector` object. The exact size (called the *capacity*) of the memory block, however, may be larger than the size required to contain the vector. It is up to the implementation to decide what is the best strategy to allocate memory for vectors so that the optimal performance can be achieved.

The `vector` container provides several constructors, as shown here:

```
template <class T, class A = allocator<T>> class vector
{
public:
    // types
    typedef typename A::size_type    size_type;    // see note

    // constructors
    explicit vector(const A& = A());
    explicit vector(size_type n, const T& val = T(), const A& = A());
    vector(const vector& v);
};
```

> **NOTE**
>
> The keyword `typename` is used to state that the name that follows is a type. Although A is a type parameter, at compile time, the compiler does not know what A is. The exact meaning of `A::size_type` will not be clarified until the template class is instantiated. Therefore, the compiler does not know whether `A::size_type` is a type or a member variable. By qualifying a type name with the keyword `typename`, you indicate that the name is a type.

`A::size_type` is just a fancy name for unsigned integer. It is used to index the elements of a container. You can create vectors in different ways. For instance, the following statement creates a vector of integers with no elements:

```
vector<int> vInt1;
```

This next statement creates a vector of 100 integers, each of which is initialized using `int()`:

```
vector<int> vInt2(100);
```

You can also initialize a vector with the contents of another vector, like this:

```
vector<int> vInt3(vInt2);
```

The copy constructor of `vector` copies all elements from `vInt2` to `vInt3`. The preceding statement could be a potential performance killer if you are working with very large vectors.

Size and Capacity

A vector has a finite number of elements. The vector class provides member functions that take care of memory acquisition so that vectors can grow when required to do so. These memory acquisition functions are declared as follows:

```
template <class T, class A = allocator<T>> class vector
{
public:
    // size and capacity
    size_type    max_size() const;    // maximum number of elements
    size_type    size() const;        // number of elements in a vector
    bool         empty() const;       // size() == 0;

    size_type    capacity() const;        // size of memory allocated
    void         reserve(size_type n);    // reserve memory space for n
elements

    // increase vector size and add an element
    void         resize(size_type n, T element = T());
}
```

The member function max_size() returns the number of elements for the largest possible vector. This information is useful when you have to make sure that you can create a large vector.

Recall that a vector is allocated a block of memory that may be larger than the actual size requested when the vector is created. The capacity() function indicates the total number of elements a vector can hold within the allocated memory. If capacity() is greater than size(), you can add up to capacity()–size() elements to the vector without acquiring more memory.

You can call the member function reserve(n) to request memory space for *n* elements. The reserve() operation allocates a block of memory large enough to hold *n* elements. If the requested memory size (*n*) is less than or equal to the current capacity of the vector, no memory reallocation will take place, and the vector's capacity does not change. Otherwise, a new block of memory is allocated to accommodate the increased size, and the capacity of the vector is set to *n*.

When a vector is created, you can specify the number of elements. This number is called the *size* of the vector, which you can query by using the size() member function. The size value for the vector can be changed during the vector's life; the resize(*n*) function changes the size of the vector to *n* elements. When *n* is greater than capacity(), the compiler must allocate more memory to accommodate the vector. Listing 6.1 shows how vectors are created and resized.

LISTING 6.1. CREATING AND RESIZING VECTORS

```cpp
#include <iostream>
#include <vector>
using namespace std;

typedef vector<int>     intVector;

template<class T, class A>
void ShowVector(const vector<T, A>& v);     // display vector properties

int main()
{
    intVector     vInt1;          // define a vector of integers with no
element
    cout << "vInt1" << "\n";
    ShowVector(vInt1);

    intVector     vInt2(3);     // define a vector of integers with 3
elements
    cout << "vInt2(3)" << "\n";
    ShowVector(vInt2);

    vInt2.resize(5, 100);      // increase vInt2's size to 5
                               // and add value 100 to the end
    cout << "vInt2 after resize(5, 100)\n";
    ShowVector(vInt2);

    vInt2.reserve(10);          // reserve memory for 10 elements
    cout << "vInt2 after reserve(10)\n";
    ShowVector(vInt2);

    return 0;
}

//
// Display vector properties
//
template<class T, class A>
void ShowVector(const vector<T, A>& v)
{
    cout << "max_size() = " << v.max_size();
    cout << "\tsize() = " << v.size();
    cout << "\t" << (v.empty()? "empty": "not empty");
    cout << "\tcapacity() = " << v.capacity();
    cout << "\n\n";
}
```

The output from Listing 6.1 is given here:

```
vInt1
max_size() = 1073741823 size() = 0        empty    capacity() = 0

vInt(3)
max_size() = 1073741823 size() = 3        not empty        capacity() - 3

vInt after resize(5, 100)
max_size() = 1073741823 size() = 5        not empty        capacity() = 6

vInt after reserve(10)
max_size() = 1073741823 size() = 5        not empty        capacity() = 10
```

When an empty vector vInt1 is defined, no memory space is reserved for its potential elements by its default constructor. When vector vInt2 is defined to contain three integers, the constructor allocates just enough memory for those three elements. vInt2 is then resized to have five elements. Look at the output and notice that the compiler has increased the capacity of the vector to 6; you may have a different value for capacity() if your compiler has a different memory allocation strategy. The reserve() function is later called to allocate more memory for vInt2. This call increases vInt2's capacity to 10, but its size remains 5. The extra space for those five elements is just literally reserved for future use.

> **NOTE**
>
> The ShowVector() function is defined as a template function so that it can be used to display any type of vector. In general, if a function is to be used for different types of objects, it should be defined as a template function.

When you call the function reserve(*n*) or resize(*n*) (where *n* > capacity()) to acquire more memory for the vector, a new block of memory must be allocated. The fact that the memory allocated to a vector must be continuous implies that the newly acquired block must be right next to the previously allocated block. This may not always be possible because the memory following the initially allocated block may have already been allocated to other objects. When this situation arises, a new block of memory that is at least as big as the combined size of the original and the additional memory blocks must be allocated somewhere else. Elements of the vector, including the new element, are copied into the new memory location. And finally, the original memory block is released.

You can also use the resize() function to reduce the size of a vector. The resize() function, however, does not affect the capacity of the vector.

Element Access

A container isn't much use if you can't access its elements. The vector containers are designed to provide fast access to their elements by using an index. The following code shows the element access functions available in the vector class:

```
template <class T, class A = allocator<T>> class vector
{
public:
    // types
    typedef typename A::reference          reference;
    typedef typename A::const_reference    const_reference;

    // element access
    reference             operator[](size_type n);        // the nth
element
    const_reference     operator[](size_type n) const;

    reference              at(size_type n);               // the nth element
with
    const_reference     at(size_type n) const;            // range checking

    reference             front();    // first element
    const_reference    front() const;
    reference             back();     // last element
    const_reference    back()    const;
}
```

Note that the first lines create two typedefs: reference and const_reference. By default, reference is a reference to an object of class T, and a const_reference is const T&.

The overloaded subscripting operator [ ] provides access to elements by using subscripts—in the same way you access elements in arrays. The operator does not perform boundary checking, so programmers are responsible for making sure that the index is valid. Attempting to access elements using out-of-range subscripts yields unpredictable results. However, you can use the at() functions to check whether the index is within range and to throw an out_of_range exception so that you can use a try/catch pair to catch the exception. The out_of_range exception is defined in <stdexcept>, which is #included in <vector>. Listing 6.2 demonstrates the use of the subscripting operator and the at() member function for accessing vector elements.

LISTING 6.2. ACCESSING VECTOR MEMBERS

```
#include <iostream>
#include <vector>
using namespace std;
```

```
typedef vector<int>     intVector;

template<class T, class A>
void ShowVector(const vector<T, A>& v);

int main()
{
    intVector    vInt(3);         // define a vector of integers with 3
elements
    cout << "vInt(3)" << "\n";

    // assign a value to each element in vInt using subscripts
    for (vector<int>::size_type i = 0; i < vInt.size(); ++i)
        vInt[i] = 5 * i;

    // assign a value to an element using at() function
    try
    {
        vInt.at((intVector::size_type)4) = 50;    // out of range!
    }
    catch(out_of_range)
    {
        cout << "Index out of range" << endl;
    }
    ShowVector(vInt);

    vInt.resize(5, 100);    // increase vInt's size to 5 and
                            // add value 100 to the end
    cout << "vInt after resize(5, 100)\n";
    // now try to access the 4th element using the at() function again
    try
    {
        vInt.at((intVector::size_type)4) = 50;    // in range now
    }
    catch(out_of_range)
    {
        cout << "Index out of range" << endl;
    }
    ShowVector(vInt);

    return 0;
}

//
// Display vector properties
//
template<class T, class A>
void ShowVector(const vector<T, A>& v)
{
```

continues

LISTING 6.2. CONTINUED

```cpp
    // traverse through the vector using subscripts
    cout << "\nelements:\n";
    for (vector<T, A>::size_type i = 0; i < v.size(); ++i)
        cout << v[i] << ", ";

    cout << "\nfront() = " << v.front();
    cout << "\tback() = " << v.back();

    cout << "\n\n";
}
```

The output for Listing 6.2 is shown here:

```
vInt(3)
Index out of range

elements:
0, 5, 10,
front() = 0      back() = 10

vInt after resize(5, 100)

elements:
0, 5, 10, 100, 50,
front() = 0      back() = 50
```

You first create a vector vInt with three integer elements. Its elements can be assigned values by using the subscripting operator. When you try to use the at() function to assign a value to a nonexisting element, the try block does the range checking and throws an out_of_range exception if the position is not valid. A try/catch block is used to catch this exception twice in the listing. The exception occurs during the illegal access of a nonexisting element. After you resize the vector to five elements, the second call to the at() function works fine. The ShowVector() template function has been modified to display all elements in a vector using the subscripting operator [].

Iterators

In the preceding section, you accessed vector elements using the subscripting operator. The subscripting operator, however, may not be relevant in certain containers such as list, when accessing elements with subscripts is not efficient. The STL provides another access method: iterators. Iterators provide a standard data access model so that containers don't have to provide extensive element access operations. Each STL container uses the iterator class that is most suitable for the optimized element access operations. For example, the container class <vector> defines several member functions for facilitating the use of iterators:

```
template <class T, class A = allocator<T>> class vector
{
public:
    // types
    typedef (implementation defined)                iterator;
    typedef (implementation defined)                const_iterator;
    typedef std::reverse_iterator<iterator>         reverse_iterator;
    typedef std::reverse_iterator<const_iterator>
const_reverse_iterator;

    // iterators
    iterator           begin();        // points to the first element
    const_iterator     begin() const;
    iterator             end();        // points to the (last + 1) element
    const_iterator     end() const;

    // points to the first element of reverse sequence
    reverse_iterator         rbegin();
    const_reverse_iterator    rbegin() const;

    // points to the (last + 1) element of reverse sequence
    reverse_iterator        rend();
    const_reverse_iterator    rend()    const;
};
```

In general, iterators are not pointers. They are implemented to act like pointers. An iterator works like a pointer to an element (for example, T*) in the vector. Like other pointers, an iterator can be incremented, decremented, and dereferenced. The C++ standard requires that iterators have the increment and/or decrement operators (both prefix and postfix) that can be used to traverse through the containers. When an iterator is incremented, it points to the next element in the vector. When an iterator is decremented, it points to the previous element in the vector. An iterator can also be dereferenced to return the element it is pointing to. The dereference operator * always returns the element pointed to by the iterator.

A normal iterator allows us to traverse elements in a vector from the beginning to the end. You can also access elements in reverse order by using a reverse_iterator. Elements pointed to by an iterator can be modified. If you do not want to modify any elements in a vector, you should use a const_iterator or a const_reverse_iterator. All four of these variations are defined for the vector class in the STL. Two iterators are said to be equal if they point to the same element in the same vector. More details about iterators are provided in Chapter 7, "STL Iterators and Algorithms."

Listing 6.3 uses iterators to assign values to vector elements. The ShowVector() template function used in Listing 6.2 has been rewritten in Listing 6.3 to display vector elements using iterators.

LISTING 6.3. ACCESSING ELEMENTS WITH ITERATORS

```cpp
#include <iostream>
#include <vector>
using namespace std;

typedef vector<int>     intVector;

template<class T, class A>
void ShowVector(const vector<T, A>& v);

int main()
{
    intVector    vInt(3);          // define a vector of integers with 3
elements
    cout << "vInt(3)" << "\n";

    // assign a value to each element in vInt using an iterator
    int i = 0;
    for (intVector::iterator itor = vInt.begin(); itor != vInt.end();
++itor)
        *itor = 5 * i++;
    cout << *++itor;
    ShowVector(vInt);

    return 0;
}

//
// Display vector properties
//
template<class T, class A>
void ShowVector(const vector<T, A>& v)
{
    // traverse through the vector using an iterator
    cout << "elements displayed using an iterator:\n";
    for (vector<T, A>::const_iterator itor = v.begin(); itor != v.end();
++itor)
        cout << *itor << ", ";
    cout << "\n";

    // traverse through the vector using a reverse iterator
    cout << "elements displayed using a reverse iterator:\n";
    for (vector<T, A>::const_reverse_iterator r_itor = v.rbegin();
            r_itor < v.rend(); ++r_itor)
        cout << *r_itor << ", ";
    cout << "\n\n";
}
```

The output from Listing 6.3 is given here:

```
vInt(3)
elements displayed using an iterator:
0, 5, 10,
elements displayed using a reverse iterator:
10, 5, 0,
```

This listing demonstrates the use of iterators for element access. A nonconstant iterator is used to assign a value to each element in vector vInt. You dereference the iterator using the dereferencing operator *. The ShowVector() template function displays vector elements by using both the forward and reverse iterators. Because you do not intend to modify any elements from within the ShowVector() method, you use the const iterator on both occasions. This iterator is defined as vector<T, A>::const_iterator (or const_reverse_iterator) so that it can be used for any type of vector.

You have probably noticed the rather inconsistent styles used to traverse the vector by using forward iterators and reverse iterators. You test the forward iterator against vector::end() by using the != operator:

```
    for (vector<T, A>::const_iterator itor = v.begin(); itor != v.end();
++itor)
```

However, you use the more conventional less-than (<) operator for reverse iterators:

```
    for (vector<T, A>::const_reverse_iterator r_itor = v.rbegin();
            r_itor < v.rend(); ++r_itor)
```

This inconsistency points out a difference between forward and reverse iterators. The implementation of the < operator is not required for the forward iterators by the C++ standard, but it *is* required for reverse iterators, although STL vendors are free to implement it for both types of iterators. Although your compiler may support this operator for the forward iterator, using it will render your code less portable because the operator is not part of the C++ standard.

Modifiers

Elements can be inserted or deleted at any position in a vector. The insertion and deletion functions are called *modifiers* because they change the contents of the vector. The following modifiers are provided in the container class <vector>:

```
template <class T, class A = allocator<T>> class vector
{
public:
    // insertion and deletion

    // insert t before pos and returns an iterator pointing to the
    // newly inserted element
    iterator    insert(iterator pos, const T& t);
```

```
          // insert n copies of t before pos
          void      insert(iterator pos, size_type n, const T& t)

          // insert a range of elements before pos
          void      insert(iterator pos, const_iterator i, const_iterator j);

          void      push_back(const T& t);    // add t to the end
          void      pop_back();               // remove last element

          // remove element at position pos
          iterator  erase(iterator pos);

          // remove from the first element to the last - 1 element
          iterator  erase(iterator first, iterator last);

          // remove all elements
          void      clear();
}
```

When a new element is added to the end of the vector, one of two things may happen. If the vector's capacity is larger than its size, no memory allocation occurs; the new element is just appended to the end of the vector. If the capacity of the vector is the same as its size, a new block of memory is acquired to accommodate this new element. As was discussed with the reserve() function, acquiring a new memory block might invoke three time-consuming processes:

- Allocating a new memory block large enough to accommodate the whole vector including the newly added element
- Copying all elements to the new memory locations
- Freeing up the old memory block

On a large vector, these operations can consume a lot of CPU time and memory—a potentially expensive exercise.

The other expensive operation of the vector container is the insertion into and the deletion from the middle of a vector. When a new element is inserted in the middle of a vector, all elements after that must be moved back to give room for the new element. Similarly, when an element in the middle of a vector is removed, all the following elements must be moved up to fill in the hole. If frequent middle insertions and deletions are expected, consider using another container class, such as list (described later in this chapter). Listing 6.4 shows the insertion and deletion of elements in vectors.

LISTING 6.4. ADDING AND REMOVING ELEMENTS

```cpp
#include <iostream>
#include <vector>
using namespace std;

typedef vector<int>                  intVector;
typedef vector<int>::iterator    ivItor;

template<class T, class A>
void ShowVector(const vector<T, A>& v);

int main()
{
    intVector    vInt(5);     // define a vector of integers with 5
elements
    cout << "vInt(5)" << "\n";

    // assign a value to each element in vInt using subscripts
    for (vector<int>::size_type i = 0; i < vInt.size(); ++i)
        vInt[i] = 5 * i;

    ShowVector(vInt);

    // insert an element
    cout << "vInt after insert(vInt.begin() + 1, 50)\n";
    ivItor itor = vInt.insert(vInt.begin() + 1, 50);
    ShowVector(vInt);
    cout << "Current element is " << *itor << "\n\n";

    // insert 5 elements
    cout << "vInt after insert(vInt.end(), 5, 30)\n";
    vInt.insert(vInt.end(), 5, 30);
    ShowVector(vInt);

    // erase one element from vInt
    cout << "vInt after erase one element\n";
    vInt.erase(vInt.begin() + 3);
    ShowVector(vInt);

    // erase three elements from vInt
    cout << "vInt after erase three element\n";
    vInt.erase(vInt.begin() + 3, vInt.begin() + 6);
    ShowVector(vInt);

    // insert several elements from another vector
    intVector    vInt2(2, 0);
    cout << "vInt2" << "\n";
    ShowVector(vInt2);
```

continues

LISTING 6.4. CONTINUED

```
    cout << "vInt2 after insert from vInt\n";
    vInt2.insert(vInt2.begin() + 1, vInt.begin() + 1, vInt.begin() + 3);
    ShowVector(vInt2);

    // add an element at the end of vInt2
    cout << "vInt2 after push_back()\n";
    vInt2.push_back(100);
    ShowVector(vInt2);

    // remove an element from the end of vInt2
    cout << "vInt2 after pop_back()\n";
    vInt2.pop_back();
    ShowVector(vInt2);

    // clear vInt2
    cout << "vInt2 cleared\n";
    vInt2.clear();
    ShowVector(vInt2);

    return 0;
}

//
// Display vector properties
//
template<class T, class A>
void ShowVector(const vector<T, A>& v)
{
    cout << "size() = " << v.size() << "\tcapacity() = " << v.capacity()
<< "\n";

    // traverse through the vector using subscripts
    cout << "elements:\t";
    for (vector<T, A>::size_type i = 0; i < v.size(); ++i)
        cout << v[i] << ", ";

    cout << "\n\n";
}
```

The output from this program is as follows:

```
vInt(5)
size() = 5      capacity() = 5
elements:       0, 5, 10, 15, 20,

vInt after insert(vInt.begin() + 1, 50)
size() = 6      capacity() = 10
elements:       0, 50, 5, 10, 15, 20,
```

```
Current element is 50

vInt after insert(vInt.end(), 5, 30)
size() = 11      capacity() = 12
elements:        0, 50, 5, 10, 15, 20, 30, 30, 30, 30, 30,

vInt after erase one element
size() = 10      capacity() = 12
elements:        0, 50, 5, 15, 20, 30, 30, 30, 30, 30,

vInt after erase three element
size() = 7       capacity() = 12
elements:        0, 50, 5, 30, 30, 30, 30,

vInt2
size() = 2       capacity() = 2
elements:        0, 0,

vInt2 after insert from vInt
size() = 4       capacity() = 4
elements:        0, 50, 5, 0,

vInt2 after push_back()
size() = 5       capacity() = 8
elements:        0, 50, 5, 0, 100,

vInt2 after pop_back()
size() = 4       capacity() = 8
elements:        0, 50, 5, 0,

vInt2 cleared
size() = 0       capacity() = 8
elements:
```

You first insert an element before the second element in the vector, a potentially expensive exercise. The insert() function returns an iterator pointing to the newly added element. This resulting iterator can be dereferenced to display the new element. You then append five elements, each of which has a value of 30, to the end of vector. The end() function returns the last element plus 1, so that inserting elements before end() effectively appends them after the last element. The erase() function is then called twice; the first call removes one element (the fourth element with a value of 10) from the vector, and the second removes three elements (from the fourth to the sixth) from the vector. Then another integer vector vInt2 with two elements is defined. Two elements from vInt are inserted before the second element in vInt2. You can also add and remove elements using the push_back() and the pop_back() function, as you do with vInt2. When the entire vInt2 is cleared, the size of the vector is reduced as well. This, however, does not actually shrink the vector. Its capacity remains unchanged.

Vector Operations

The STL defines overloaded comparison operators so that two vectors of the same type
can be compared with each other. Overloaded comparison operators are often used in
standard algorithms. The comparison operators are also used by an additional vector
operation: Swap(). Swap() is used to exchange the values of each element in two vectors.
The following comparison operators are provided in the container class <vector>:

```
template <class T, class A = allocator<T>> class vector
{
public:
    // vector operations
    void swap(vector& v);      // swap elements between current vector and v

    template <class T, class A>
    void swap(const vector<T, A>&v1, const vector <T, A>&v2) {
        v1.swap(v2);
    }

    // comparison operators
    template<class T, class A>
    bool operator==(const vector<T, A>& v1, const vector<T, A>& v2);

    template<class T, class A>
    bool operator!=(const vector<T, A>& v1, const vector<T, A>& v2);

    template<class T, class A>
    bool operator<( const vector<T, A>& v1, const vector<T, A>& v2);

    template<class T, class A>
    bool operator<=(const vector<T, A>& v1, const vector<T, A>& v2);

    template<class T, class A>
    bool operator>( const vector<T, A>& v1, const vector<T, A>& v2);

    template<class T, class A>
    bool operator>=(const vector<T, A>& v1, const vector<T, A>& v2);

}
```

Two vectors v1 and v2 are equal (==) if v1.size() == v2.size() and v1[n] == v2[n]
where n has a value of between 0 and v1.size() - 1. A pseudo implementation for the
== operator is shown here:

```
template<class T, class A>
bool operator==(const vector<T, A>& v1, const vector<T, A>& v2)
{
    bool isEqual = false;

    if (v1.size() == v2.size())    {
```

```
            isEqual = true;
            for (vector<T, A>::size_type n = 0; n < v1.size(); ++n)     {
                if (v1[n] != v2[n])     {
                    isEqual = false;
                    break;
                }
            }
        }

        return isEqual;
    }
```

Vector v1 is less than vector v2 if v1 is lexicographically less than v2. The phrase "v1 is lexicographically less than v2" means that one of the following statements is true:

- The first v1[n] that is not equal to v2[n] is less than v2[n]

- All v1[n] = v2[n], where n = 0, 1, …, v1.size − 1, but v1.size() < v2.size()

The < operator can be demonstrated in the following code fragment:

```
template<class T, class A>
bool operator<(const vector<T, A>& v1, const vector<T, A>& v2)
{
    bool isLess = false;

    for (vector<T, A>::size_type n = 0; n < v2.size(); ++n)     {
        if ((n > v1.size()) || (v1[n] < v2[n]))     {
            isLess = true;
            break;
        }
    }

    return isLess;
}
```

Other operators are implemented based on == and <, as shown here:

```
template<class T, class A>
bool operator!=(const vector<T, A>& v1, const vector<T, A>& v2)
{
    return !(v1 == v2);
}

template<class T, class A>
bool operator<=(const vector<T, A>& v1, const vector<T, A>& v2)
{
    return ((v1 < v2) || (v1 == v2));
}

template<class T, class A>
bool operator>(const vector<T, A>& v1, const vector<T, A>& v2)
```

```
{
    return !(v1 <= v2);
}

template<class T, class A>
bool operator>=(const vector<T, A>& v1, const vector<T, A>& v2)
{
    return !(v1 < v2);
}
```

Now it is time to see the overloaded comparison operators in action. Listing 6.5 uses several approaches to compare vectors.

LISTING 6.5. COMPARING VECTORS

```
#include <iostream>
#include <vector>
using namespace std;

typedef vector<int>                 intVector;

template<class T, class A>
void ShowVector(const vector<T, A>& v);
template<class T, class A>
void compareVectors(const vector<T, A>& v1, const vector<T, A>& v2);

int main()
{
    intVector    vInt1(5);     // define a vector of integers with 5
elements
    cout << "vInt1(5)" << "\n";

    // assign a value to each element in vInt using subscripts
    for (vector<int>::size_type i = 0; i < vInt1.size(); ++i)    {
        vInt1[i] = 5 * i;
    }
    ShowVector(vInt1);

    intVector vInt2 = vInt1;    // define a vector vInt2 and
                                // copy elements from vInt1
    cout << "vInt2(5)" << "\n";
    ShowVector(vInt2);

    // compare vInt and vInt2
    compareVectors(vInt1, vInt2);

    // add an element at the end of vInt2
    cout << "vInt2 after push_back()\n";
    vInt2.push_back(100);
    ShowVector(vInt2);
```

```
    // compare vInt and vInt2 again
    compareVectors(vInt1, vInt2);

    // now swap vInt and vInt2
    vInt1.swap(vInt2);
    cout << "vInt1 after swap\n";
    ShowVector(vInt1);
    cout << "vInt2 after swap\n";
    ShowVector(vInt2);
    compareVectors(vInt1, vInt2);

    return 0;
}

//
// Display vector properties
//
template<class T, class A>
void ShowVector(const vector<T, A>& v)
{
    cout << "size() = " << v.size() << "\tcapacity() = " << v.capacity()
<< "\n";

    // display vector elements using subscripts
    cout << "elements:\t";
    for (vector<T, A>::size_type i = 0; i < v.size(); ++i)
        cout << v[i] << ", ";
    cout << "\n\n";
}

//
// Compare two vectors
//
template<class T, class A>
void compareVectors(const vector<T, A>& v1, const vector<T, A>& v2)
{
    if (v1 == v2)     {
        cout << "v1 == v2";
    }
    else if (v1 < v2)
    {
        cout << "v1 < v2";
    }
    else
    {
        cout << "v1 > v2";
    }
    cout << "\n\n";
}
```

The output from this program is as follows:

```
vInt1(5)
size() = 5        capacity() = 5
elements:         0, 5, 10, 15, 20,

vInt(5)
size() = 5        capacity() = 5
elements:         0, 5, 10, 15, 20,

v1 == v2

vInt2 after push_back()
size() = 6        capacity() = 10
elements:         0, 5, 10, 15, 20, 100,

v1 < v2

vInt1 after swap
size() = 6        capacity() = 10
elements:         0, 5, 10, 15, 20, 100,

vInt2 after swap
size() = 5        capacity() = 5
elements:         0, 5, 10, 15, 20,

v1 > v2
```

You first create two integer vectors vInt1 and vInt2 with identical elements by copying them from one to another. When you compare them, you find that they are equivalent— as expected. Adding a new element vInt2 makes vInt2 greater than vInt1. At last, vInt1 and vInt2 are swapped, and vInt1 becomes greater than vInt2.

One of the limitations of the vector container class is the cost of adding and removing elements in the middle of the vector. This "drawback" is largely by design because vectors occupy a continuously allocated memory block to allow fast sequential access to their elements. When frequent additions and deletions are expected, a list container is the better choice. The next section looks into the list container class.

The List Container

A list is a container designed to provide optimal frequent insertions and deletions of elements.

The list STL container class is defined in the header file <list> in the namespace std. The list class is typically implemented as a doubly-linked list, where each node has links to both the previous node and the next node in the list. The list class provides all

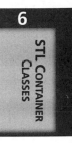

the member types and operations of the vector class, with the exceptions of subscripting capacity() and reserve().

The following code listing recaps the container members provided in the list class:

```
template <class T, class A = allocator<T>> class list
{
public:
    // types
    typedef typename A::size_type                     size_type;    // size
type

    // iterators and references types
    typedef (implementation defined)                  iterator;
    typedef (implementation defined)                  const_iterator;
    typedef std::reverse_iterator<iterator>           reverse_iterator;
    typedef std::reverse_iterator<const_iterator>
const_reverse_iterator;
    typedef typename A::reference                     reference;
    typedef typename A::const_reference               const_reference;

    // constructors
    explicit list(const A& = A());
    explicit list(size_type n, const T& val = T(), const A& = A());
    vector(const list& v);

    // size functions
    size_type    max_size() const;    // maximum number of elements
    size_type    size() const;        // number of elements in a list
    bool         empty() const;    // size() == 0;

    // increase list size and add an element
    void         resize(size_type n, T element = T());

    // element access
    reference          at(size_type n);        // the nth element with
    const_reference    at(size_type n) const;    // range checking

    reference          front();    // first element
    const_reference    front() const;
    reference          back();     // last element
    const_reference    back()    const;

    // iterators
    iterator          begin();      // points to the first element
    const_iterator    begin() const;
    iterator          end();        // points to the (last + 1) element
    const_iterator    end() const;

    // points to the first element of reverse sequence
    reverse_iterator          rbegin();
```

```
        const_reverse_iterator    rbegin() const;

        // points to the (last + 1) element of reverse sequence
        reverse_iterator            rend();
        const_reverse_iterator    rend()   const;

        // insertion and deletion

        // insert t before pos and returns an iterator pointing to the
        // newly inserted element
        iterator    insert(iterator pos, const T& t);

        // insert n copies of t before pos
        void        insert(iterator pos, size_type n, const T& t)

        // insert a range of elements before pos
        void        insert(iterator pos, const_iterator i, const_iterator j);

        // back operations
        void        push_back(const T& t);    // add t to the end
        void        pop_back();                // remove the last element

        // remove element at position pos
        iterator    erase(iterator pos);

        // remove from the first to the last - 1 elements
        iterator    erase(iterator first, iterator last);

        // remove all elements
        void        clear();

        // list operations
        void swap(list & l);    // swap elements between current list and l

        bool operator==(const list<T, A>& list1, const list<T, A>& list2);
        bool operator!=(const list<T, A>& list1, const list<T, A>& list2);
        bool operator<( const list<T, A>& list1, const list<T, A>& list2);
        bool operator<=(const list<T, A>& list1, const list<T, A>& list2);
        bool operator>( const list<T, A>& list1, const list<T, A>& list2);
        bool operator>=(const list<T, A>& list1, const list<T, A>& list2);
};
```

Memory allocation for the list container class is more dynamic than it is for the vector container class. Remember that a vector uses a continuous memory block to accommodate its elements; if an element is inserted or deleted from the middle of the vector, all the remaining memory is affected. This is less of a problem with the list container.

Because of its enhanced flexibility of memory management, the list class can provide several additional operations: splice, front operations, sort, and merge. The following sections examine these operations in detail.

Splice Operations

Splice operations reallocate elements from one list to another. The `list` container class provides three splice operations:

```
template<class T, class A = allocator<T>> class list
{
public:
    // insert all elements of x before *pos in the current list
    void splice(iterator pos, list& x);

    // insert the element *i from list x before *pos in the current list
    void splice(iterator pos, list& x, iterator i);

    // insert elements from *first to *(last - 1) from list x before *pos
    // in the current list
    void splice(iterator pos, list& x, iterator first, iterator last);
}
```

The `splice()` function removes the specified elements from list x and inserts them into the current list in the given position. This process merely performs pointer operations. The elements are not copied. Let's look at what happens behind the scenes.

Suppose that you have created two lists, ListA and ListB, as shown in Figure 6.1. After executing the `c.splice(pos, x, first, last)` operation, these two lists are allocated as shown in Figure 6.2.

FIGURE 6.1.
Two lists before a splice operation.

FIGURE 6.2.
Two lists after a splice operation.

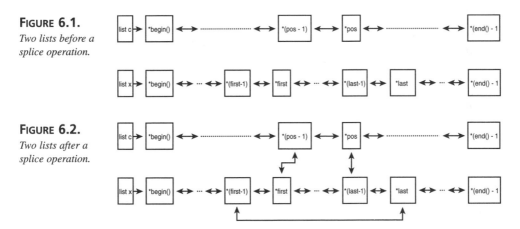

The order of the existing elements is guaranteed to be unchanged by the splice operation, and there are no memory allocations or reallocations as a result of the splice. Listing 6.6 shows the use of a splice.

LISTING 6.6. A SPLICE OPERATION EXAMPLE

```cpp
#include <iostream>
#include <list>
using namespace std;

typedef list<int>              intList;
typedef list<int>::iterator    intListItor;

template<class T, class A>
void showList(const list<T, A>& aList);

int main()
{
    // define a list of integers with 5 elements
    intList    ListA(5);
    int        j = 0;
    for (intListItor ia = ListA.begin(); ia != ListA.end(); ++ia)
        *ia = 5 * j++;
    cout << "ListA" << "\n";
    showList(ListA);

    // define a list of integers with 6 elements
    intList    ListB(6);
    j = 0;
    for (intListItor ib = ListB.begin(); ib != ListB.end(); ++ib)
        *ib = 100 * j++;
    cout << "ListB" << "\n";
    showList(ListB);

    // splice!
    cout << "Splice:\n";
    ListA.splice(++ListA.begin(), ListB, ++(++ListB.begin()), —
ListB.end());
    cout << "ListA" << "\n";
    showList(ListA);
    cout << "ListB" << "\n";
    showList(ListB);

    return 0;
}

//
// Display list elements
//
template<class T, class A>
void showList(const list<T, A>& aList)
{
    cout << "size() = " << aList.size() << ":\t";
    for (list<T, A>::const_iterator i = aList.begin(); i != aList.end();
++i)
```

```
        cout << *i << ", ";
    cout << "\n\n";
}
```

The output from this code is shown as follows:

```
ListA
size() = 5:      0, 5, 10, 15, 20,

ListB
size() = 6:      0, 100, 200, 300, 400, 500,

Splice:
ListA
size() = 7:      0, 200, 300, 400, 5, 10, 15, 20,

ListB
size() = 4:      0, 100, 500,
```

Elements in `ListA` and `ListB` are assigned values using an iterator. You then move the third and fourth elements of `ListB` into `ListA`.

The `splice()` function itself is straightforward, but there is one subtle point that is worth mentioning. Examine the following statement:

```
ListA.splice(++ListA.begin(), ListB, ++(++ListB.begin()), —ListB.end());
```

This statement says that you will splice into `ListA` part of `ListB`, beginning at the third element in `ListB` and ending at the second-to-last element of `ListB`. You have used two increment operators on `ListB.begin()` to reach the third element of `ListB`. Why can't you just use `ListB.begin + 2` instead? Because, unfortunately, the C++ standard does not require that operator + be implemented by iterator classes.

Front Operations

Unlike vectors, lists can perform the insertion and deletion of the first element efficiently. Front operations allow us to add elements to a list more efficiently because you do not have to traverse the list. This fact leads to the inclusion of two front operations—one that adds the first element and another that removes the first element:

```
template(class T, class A = allocator<T>> class list
{
public:
    void push_front(const T& t);    // add t to the beginning
    void pop_front();               // remove the first element
};
```

The use of both front operations is shown in Listing 6.7.

LISTING 6.7. FRONT OPERATIONS IN A LIST

```cpp
#include <iostream>
#include <list>
using namespace std;

typedef list<int>              intList;
typedef list<int>::iterator    intListItor;

template<class T, class A>
void showList(const list<T, A>& aList);

int main()
{
    // define a list of integers with 5 elements
    intList    ListA(5);
    int        j = 0;
    for (intListItor ia = ListA.begin(); ia != ListA.end(); ++ia)
        *ia = 5 * j++;
    cout << "ListA" << "\n";
    showList(ListA);

    // remove the first element
    ListA.pop_front();
    cout << "First element removed:\n";
    showList(ListA);

    // insert a new element at the beginning
    ListA.push_front(100);
    cout << "Insert 100 at the beginning:\n";
    showList(ListA);

    return 0;
}

//
// Display list elements
//
template<class T, class A>
void showList(const list<T, A>& aList)
{
    cout << "size() = " << aList.size() << ":\t";
    for (list<T, A>::const_iterator i = aList.begin(); i != aList.end();
++i)
        cout << *i << ", ";
    cout << "\n\n";
}
```

The output from the Listing 6.7 is shown here:

```
ListA
size() = 5:      0, 5, 10, 15, 20,

First element removed:
size() = 4:      5, 10, 15, 20,

Insert 100 at the beginning:
size() = 5:      100, 5, 10, 15, 20,
```

The first element of ListA is removed using the pop_front() function. After a new element is inserted at the front with the push_front() function, that new element becomes the first element in the list.

The front operations are stable; that is, the order and the memory locations of the existing elements in the list are not affected. The push_front() operation has to allocate memory for the new element, and the pop_front() operation must release the memory occupied by the removed element.

The sort() and merge() Operations

There are times when a list must be sorted. The list container class provides the following two sort() operations:

```
template<class T, class A = allocator<T>> class list
{
public:
    // sort algorithms
    void sort();
    template<class Compare>
    void sort(Compare);

    // reverse element order
    void reverse();

    // merge two sorted list
    void merge(list& x);
    template<class Compare>
    void merge(list& x, Compare);
};
```

The normal sort() function uses class T's comparison mechanism to sort the elements; the template sort() function uses the Compare class's comparison functions.

The reverse() function reverses the order of elements in a list, but it does not attempt to sort the list in any way.

The merge() function works rather like the following splice() operation:

```
void splice(iterator pos, list& x, iterator x.begin(), iterator x.end());
```

However, the merge() function sorts the resulting list using either the built-in or an external comparison mechanism. The two original lists must themselves be sorted before the merge() function is called. Otherwise, the resulting list may not be sorted. Listing 6.8 shows how lists can be sorted. It also demonstrates the different results of merging sorted and unsorted lists.

LISTING 6.8. MERGING AND SORTING LISTS

```cpp
#include <iostream>
#include <list>
using namespace std;

typedef list<int>              intList;
typedef list<int>::iterator    intListItor;

template<class T, class A>
void showList(const list<T, A>& aList);

int main()
{
    // define a list of integers with 5 elements
    intList    ListA(5);
    int        j = 0;
    for (intListItor ia = ListA.begin(); ia != ListA.end(); ++ia)
        *ia = 5 * j++;
    cout << "ListA" << "\n";
    showList(ListA);

    // define a list of integers with 6 elements
    intList    ListB(6);
    j = 10;
    for (intListItor ib = ListB.begin(); ib != ListB.end(); ++ib)
        *ib = 2 * j—;
    cout << "ListB" << "\n";
    showList(ListB);

    intList ListC = ListA;
    intList ListD = ListB;

    // merge without sorting first
    cout << "Merge unsorted lists:\n";
    ListA.merge(ListB);

    cout << "ListA" << "\n";
    showList(ListA);
    cout << "ListB" << "\n";
    showList(ListB);

    // reverse elements in ListA
```

```
            cout << "Reverse ListA\n";
            ListA.reverse();
            showList(ListA);

            // sort and merge
            cout << "Sort and Merge:\n";
            ListC.sort();
            ListD.sort();
            ListC.merge(ListD);

            cout << "ListC" << "\n";
            showList(ListC);
            cout << "ListD" << "\n";
            showList(ListD);

            return 0;
}

//
// Display list elements
//
template<class T, class A>
void showList(const list<T, A>& aList)
{
            cout << "size() = " << aList.size() << ":\t";
            for (list<T, A>::const_iterator i = aList.begin(); i != aList.end();
++i)
                    cout << *i << ", ";
            cout << "\n\n";
}
```

The output from Listing 6.8 is shown as follows:

```
ListA
size() = 5:       0, 5, 10, 15, 20,

ListB
size() = 6:       20, 18, 16, 14, 12, 10,

Merge unsorted lists:
ListA
size() = 11:      0, 5, 10, 15, 20, 20, 18, 16, 14, 12, 10,

ListB
size() = 0:

Reverse ListA
size() = 11:      10, 12, 14, 16, 18, 20, 20, 15, 10, 5, 0,

Sort and Merge:
ListC
```

```
size() = 11:      0, 5, 10, 10, 12, 14, 15, 16, 18, 20, 20,

ListD
size() = 0:
```

When two unsorted lists—ListA and ListB—are merged, the elements from ListB are simply appended to ListA, and the resulting ListA is unsorted. When ListA is reversed, you can see that the result is still not sorted. You then sort ListC and ListD. When you merge two sorted lists—ListC and ListD—the resulting list ListC is also sorted.

Operations to Remove Elements

Elements can be removed from lists. For instance, an Internet news-serving application may want to display a list of news items based on user profiles. When a user changes her profile, certain items may be removed from the list. The list container class provides the following four operations that remove elements from lists:

```
template<class T, class A = allocator<T>> class list
{
public:
    // remove an element from the list
    void remove(const T& t);

    template<class Predicate>
    void remove_if(Predicate p);

    // remove duplicate elements
    void unique();

    template<class Predicate>
    void unique(Predicate p);
};
```

The normal remove() function removes elements that are equal to t using the overloading T::operator==. The template remove_if() function removes elements that make the predicate p evaluate to true. The normal unique() function removes all duplicate elements from the list. Elements e_m, e_{m+1}, ..., e_n, where e_i denotes the ith element in the list, are said to be duplicated if they are in a consecutive group in the list and if e_m == e_{m+1} ==...== e_n. The template unique() function does the same thing, except that it uses predicate p instead of operator ==. Listing 6.9 shows various remove operations on lists.

LISTING 6.9. REMOVING ELEMENTS FROM LISTS

```
#include <iostream>
#include <list>
using namespace std;
```

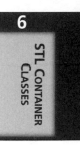

```cpp
typedef list<int>                intList;
typedef list<int>::iterator    intListItor;

template<class T, class A>
void showList(const list<T, A>& aList);

int main()
{
    // define a list of integers with 5 elements
    intList    ListA(5);
    int        j = 0;
    for (intListItor ia = ListA.begin(); ia != ListA.end(); ++ia)
        *ia = 5 * j++;
    cout << "ListA" << "\n";
    showList(ListA);

    // remove an element from ListA
    ListA.remove(5);
    cout << "5 removed from ListA:\n";
    showList(ListA);

    // define a list of integers with 6 elements
    intList    ListB(6);
    j = 10;
    for (intListItor ib = ListB.begin(); ib != ListB.end(); ++ib)
        *ib = 2 * j—;
    cout << "ListB" << "\n";
    showList(ListB);

    // splice ListA & ListB and add an element 10 at the beginning of
ListA
    cout << "splice ListA & ListB and add 10 to the beginning:\n";
    ListA.splice(++(++ListA.begin()), ListB);
    ListA.push_front(10);

    cout << "ListA" << "\n";
    showList(ListA);

    // sort ListA first
    ListA.sort();      // so that elements with same value will group
together
    cout << "ListA sorted:\n";
    showList(ListA);

    // remove duplicates from ListA
    ListA.unique();
    cout << "Duplicates in ListA removed:\n";
    showList(ListA);
```

continues

LISTING 6.9. CONTINUED

```
    return 0;
}

//
// Display list elements
//
template<class T, class A>
void showList(const list<T, A>& aList)
{
    cout << "size() = " << aList.size() << ":\t";
    for (list<T, A>::const_iterator i = aList.begin(); i != aList.end();
++i)
        cout << *i << ", ";
    cout << "\n\n";
}
```

The output from Listing 6.9 is shown here:

```
ListA
size() = 5:      0, 5, 10, 15, 20,

5 removed from ListA:
size() = 4:      0, 10, 15, 20,

ListB
size() = 6:      20, 18, 16, 14, 12, 10,

splice ListA & ListB and add 10 to the beginning:
ListA
size() = 11:     10, 0, 10, 20, 18, 16, 14, 12, 10, 15, 20,

ListA sorted:
size() = 11:     0, 10, 10, 10, 12, 14, 15, 16, 18, 20, 20,

Duplicates in ListA removed:
size() = 8:      0, 10, 12, 14, 15, 16, 18, 20,
```

When you attempt to remove any element with value 5 from integer list ListA, you remove the second element. You then insert all elements from ListB before the second element in ListA. The splice() function does not sort the resulting list. After ListA is sorted, you see that you have three elements with the value of 10 and two elements with the value of 20. The duplicate values are removed by the unique() function.

The Deque Container

A deque is like a double-ended vector—it inherits the vector container class's efficiency in sequential read and write operations. But in addition, the deque container class provides optimized front-end and back-end operations. These operations are implemented similar to the way they are in the list container class, where memory allocations are engaged only for new elements. This feature of the deque class eliminates the need to reallocate the whole container to a new memory location, as the vector class has to do. Therefore, deques are ideally suited for applications in which insertions and deletions take place at either one or both ends, and for which sequential access of elements is important. An example of such an application is a train-assembly simulator, where carriages can join the train at both ends.

The deque container class is defined in the header file <deque> in the namespace std. The deque class has all the vector member functions, plus the front operations, as shown in the following code listing:

```
template <class T, class A = allocator<T>> class deque
{
public:
    // types
    typedef typename A::size_type            size_type;    // size
type

    // iterators and references types
    typedef (implementation defined, may be T*)        iterator;
    typedef (implementation defined, may be const T*)    const_iterator;
    typedef std::reverse_iterator<iterator>        reverse_iterator;
    typedef std::reverse_iterator<const_iterator>
const_reverse_iterator;
    typedef typename A::reference            reference;
    typedef typename A::const_reference        const_reference;

    // constructors
    explicit deque(const A& = A());
    explicit deque(size_type n, const T& val = T(), const A& = A());
    vector(const deque& dq);

    // size functions
    size_type   max_size() const;   // maximum number of elements
    size_type   size() const;       // number of elements in a deque
    bool        empty() const;    // size() == 0;

    // increase deque size and add an element
    void        resize(size_type n, T element = T());

    // element access
    reference               at(size_type n);              // the nth element
```

```
with
      const_reference      at(size_type n) const;          // range checking

      reference              front();     // first element
      const_reference      front() const;
      reference               back();     // last element
      const_reference      back()     const;

      // iterators
      iterator               begin();     // points to the first element
      const_iterator       begin() const;
      iterator                end();           // points to the (last + 1) element
      const_iterator       end() const;

      // points to the first element of reverse sequence
      reverse_iterator             rbegin();
      const_reverse_iterator       rbegin() const;

      // points to the (last + 1) element of reverse sequence
      reverse_iterator             rend();
      const_reverse_iterator       rend()     const;

      // insertion and deletion

      // insert t before pos and returns an iterator pointing to the
      // newly inserted element
      iterator      insert(iterator pos, const T& t);

      // insert n copies of t before pos
      void          insert(iterator pos, size_type n, const T& t)

      // insert a range of elements before pos
      void          insert(iterator pos, const_iterator i, const_iterator j);

      // front and back operations
      void          push_front(const T& t);    // add t the beginning
      void          pop_front();                // remove the first element
      void          push_back(const T& t);    // add t to the end
      void          pop_back();                // remove the last element

      // remove element at position pos
      iterator      erase(iterator pos);

      // remove from the first element to the last - 1 element
      iterator      erase(iterator first, iterator last);

      // remove all elements
      void          clear();

      // deque operations
      void swap(deque & dq);      // swap elements between current deque and
```

dq

```
    bool operator==(const deque<T, A>& dq1, const deque<T, A>& dq2);
    bool operator!=(const deque<T, A>& dq1, const deque<T, A>& dq2);
    bool operator<( const deque<T, A>& dq1, const deque<T, A>& dq2);
    bool operator<=(const deque<T, A>& dq1, const deque<T, A>& dq2);
    bool operator>( const deque<T, A>& dq1, const deque<T, A>& dq2);
    bool operator>=(const deque<T, A>& dq1, const deque<T, A>& dq2);
};
```

Understanding Stacks

One of the most commonly used data structures in computer programming is the stack. The stack, however, is not implemented as an independent container class. Instead, it is implemented as a wrapper of a container. The template class stack is defined in the header file <stack> in the namespace std.

A *stack* is a continuously allocated block that can grow or shrink at the back end. Elements in a stack can only be accessed or removed from the back. You have seen similar characteristics in the sequence containers, notably vector and deque. In fact, any sequence container that supports the back(), push_back(), and pop_back() operations can be used to implement a stack. Most of the other container methods are not required for the stack and are therefore not exposed by the stack.

The STL stack template class is designed to contain any type of objects. The only restriction is that all elements must be of the same type.

A stack is a *LIFO* (*last in, first out*) structure. It's like an overcrowded elevator: The first person who walks in is pushed toward the wall and the last person stands right next to the door. When the elevator reaches the destination floor, the last person is the first to go out. If someone wants leave the elevator earlier, all those who stand between her and the door must make way for her, probably by going out of the elevator and then coming back in.

By convention, the open end of a stack is often called the *top* of the stack, and operations carried out to a stack are often called *push* and *pop*. The stack class inherits these conventional terms.

> **NOTE**
>
> The STL stack class is not the same as the stack mechanism used by compilers and operating systems, in which stacks can contain different types of objects. The underlying functionality, however, is very similar.

The stack's interface is simple:

```
template <class T, class Container = deque<T>>
class stack
{
public:
    typedef typename Container::value_type value_type;
    typedef typename Container::size_type size_type;
    typedef typename Container container_type;
protected:
    Container c;
public:
    explicit stack(const Container& = Container());
    bool empty() const { return c.empty(); }
    size_type size() const { return c.size(); }
    value_type& top() { return c.back(); }
    const value_type& top() const { return c.back(); }
    void push(const value_type& x) { c.push_back(x); }
    void pop() { c.pop_back(); }
};
```

T is the type of elements the stack contains. The container class can be any container that supports the back operations. The STL container class deque is used by default. The term *back operation* is carried over from the STL container classes.

As you can see, the top() function is just an interface to the container's back() function. Likewise, the push() and pop() functions are really the push_back() and pop_back() of the container. The empty() function indicates whether a stack contains no element at all. The size() function returns the number of elements a stack contains. Listing 6.10 shows some basic stack operations.

LISTING 6.10. STACK OPERATIONS

```
#include <iostream>
#include <stack>
using namespace std;

template<class T, class C>
void ShowStack(stack<T, C>& aStack);

int main()
{
    // create an integer stack
    stack<int> sInt;
    cout << "Stack sInt created:\n";
    ShowStack(sInt);

    // push elements into the stack
    for (unsigned int i = 0; i < 5; ++i)
```

```
        sInt.push(i * 2);
    cout << "sInt:\n";
    ShowStack(sInt);

    // modify the top element
    sInt.top() = 100;
    cout << "top element modified:\n";
    ShowStack(sInt);

    // get all elements
    cout << "Show all elements:\n";
    while (!sInt.empty())
    {
        cout << sInt.top() << ", ";
        sInt.pop();
    }
    cout << "\n\n";

    return 0;
}

//
// Display stack properties
//
template<class T, class C>
void ShowStack(stack<T, C>& aStack)
{
    cout << "size = " << aStack.size();
    if (!aStack.empty())
        cout << "\ttop = " << aStack.top();
    cout << "\n\n";
}
```

The output from Listing 6.10 is shown here:

```
Stack sInt created:
size = 0

sInt:
size = 5        top = 8

top element modified:
size = 5        top = 100

Show all elements:
100, 6, 4, 2, 0,
```

An empty stack sInt is created, and five elements are pushed onto it. The stack sInt automatically acquires more memory as its size increases. The last element can be accessed using the top() function. You can only modify the last element in a stack, using the `top()` function. To access an element other than the one at the top, you must remove all elements on top of that element by using the `pop()` function—in much the same way as what happens when you need to get out of a crowded elevator. You must also make sure that the stack is not empty before you access the top element, otherwise you may have a problem of stack underflow. The stack underflow effect is undefined, that is, it is implementation dependent. For example, some compilers may throw an exception, while others may ignore it silently.

We have all seen the infamous "stack overflow" error. What does it mean? In theory, a stack cannot overflow because it simply acquires more memory as required. Practically, however, available memory is always limited. When you run out of memory, you get a stack overflow or other memory-related error.

You may have noticed the rather strange `stack` constructor declaration: It can take a container as a parameter. For example, you can define and initialize a stack using the following statement:

```
stack<int> intStack(intVector);    // where intVector is defined as
                                   // vector<int> intVector;
```

This statement initializes `intStack` from `intVector`. That is, the code creates `intStack` and copies all elements from `intVector` to it.

As usual, several overloaded template comparison operators are defined for the `stack` class. These operators are generally wrappers for the corresponding container comparison operators:

```
template <class T, class Container>
bool operator==(const stack<T, Container>& x, const stack<T, Container>&
➥y);
template <class T, class Container>
bool operator< (const stack<T, Container>& x, const stack<T, Container>&
➥y);
template <class T, class Container>
bool operator!=(const stack<T, Container>& x, const stack<T, Container>&
➥y);
template <class T, class Container>
bool operator> (const stack<T, Container>& x, const stack<T, Container>&
➥y);
template <class T, class Container>
bool operator>=(const stack<T, Container>& x, const stack<T, Container>&
➥y);
template <class T, class Container>
bool operator<=(const stack<T, Container>& x, const stack<T, Container>&
➥y);
```

Understanding Queues

A *queue* is another commonly used data structure in computer programming. Elements are added to the queue at one end and taken out at the other. The classic analogy is this: A stack is like a stack of dishes at a salad bar. You add to the stack by placing a dish on top (pushing the stack down), and you take from the stack by "popping" the top dish (the one most recently added to the stack) off the top.

A queue is like a line at the theater. You enter the queue at the back, and you leave the queue at the front. This is known as a *FIFO* (first in, first out) structure; a stack is a *LIFO* (last in, first out) structure. Of course, every once in a while, you're second-to-last in a long line at the supermarket, when someone opens a new register and grabs the last person in line—turning what should be a FIFO queue into a LIFO stack, and making you grind your teeth in frustration.

Like the stack, the queue is implemented as a wrapper class to a container. The container must support front(), back(), push_back(), and pop_front() operations. Note that the characteristics of a queue rule out the vector class because there is no pop_front() operation for the vector class. The template class queue is defined in the header file <queue> in the namespace std. The interface for the template class queue looks rather familiar, as shown by the following code:

```
template <class T, class Container = deque<T> >
class queue
{
public:
    typedef typename Container::value_type value_type;
    typedef typename Container::size_type size_type;
    typedef typename Container container_type;
protected:
    Container c;
public:
    explicit queue(const Container& = Container());
    bool empty() const { return c.empty(); }
    size_type size() const { return c.size(); }
    value_type& front() { return c.front(); }
    const value_type& front() const { return c.front(); }
    value_type& back() { return c.back(); }
    const value_type& back() const { return c.back(); }
    void push(const value_type& x) { c.push_back(x); }
    void pop() { c.pop_front(); }
};
```

This code shows the similarity between the queue class and the stack template class. The more conventional push() and pop() operations are used to wrap up the container's push_back() and pop_front() operations. Listing 6.11 demonstrates basic queue operations.

LISTING 6.11. BASIC QUEUE OPERATIONS

```cpp
#include <iostream>
#include <queue>
using namespace std;

template<class T, class C>
void ShowQueue(const queue<T, C>& aQueue);

int main()
{
    // create a integer queue
    queue<int>    qInt;
    cout << "Queue qInt created:\n";
    ShowQueue(qInt);

    // push elements into the queue
    for (unsigned int i = 1; i < 5; ++i)
        qInt.push(i * 2);
    cout << "qInt:\n";
    ShowQueue(qInt);

    // modify the first and last elements
    qInt.front() = 20;
    qInt.back() = 30;
    cout << "The first and last elements modified:\n";
    ShowQueue(qInt);

    // remove first element from the queue
    qInt.pop();
    cout << "After one pop() operation\n";
    ShowQueue(qInt);

    return 0;
}


//
// Display queue elements
//
template<class T, class C>
void ShowQueue(const queue<T, C>& aQueue)
{
    cout << "size() = " << aQueue.size();
    if (!aQueue.empty())
    {
        cout << "\tfront() = " << aQueue.front();
        cout << "\tback() = " << aQueue.back();
    }
    cout << "\n\n";
}
```

The output from Listing 6.11 is shown as follows:

```
Queue qInt created:
size() = 0

qInt:
size() = 4       front() = 2      back() = 8

The first and last elements modified:
size() = 4       front() = 20     back() = 30

After one pop() operation
size() = 3       front() = 4      back() = 30
```

Elements are pushed into the queue. As can a stack, a queue can also acquire memory when its size increases. You can access the first and last elements in the queue using the front() and back() operations. After the first (top) element is removed from the queue using the pop() function, the next element becomes the new front element.

Again, overloaded comparison operators are defined to compare two queues:

```
template <class T, class Container>
bool operator==(const queue<T, Container>& x, const queue<T, Container>&
y);
template <class T, class Container>
bool operator< (const queue<T, Container>& x, const queue<T, Container>&
y);
template <class T, class Container>
bool operator!=(const queue<T, Container>& x, const queue<T, Container>&
y);
template <class T, class Container>
bool operator> (const queue<T, Container>& x, const queue<T, Container>&
y);
template <class T, class Container>
bool operator>=(const queue<T, Container>& x, const queue<T, Container>&
y);
template <class T, class Container>
bool operator<=(const queue<T, Container>& x, const queue<T, Container>&
y);
```

NOTE

As is the STL stack class, the STL queue class is not the same as the queue mechanism used by compilers and operating systems, where queues can contain different types of objects. The underlying functionality, however, is very similar.

Priority Queues

A *priority queue* is a queue whose elements are assigned a priority. The template class priority_queue is also defined in the header file <queue> in the namespace std. The element with the highest priority is the top of the queue. The interface for the template class priority_queue looks like this:

```
template <class T, class Container = vector<T>,
          class Compare = less<Container::value_type> >
class priority_queue
{
public:
typedef typename Container::value_type value_type;
typedef typename Container::size_type size_type;
typedef typename Container container_type;
protected:
Container c;
Compare comp;
public:
explicit priority_queue(const Compare& x = Compare(),
                        const Container& = Container())
: c(Container), comp(Compare)     {};
template <class InputIterator>
priority_queue(InputIterator first, InputIterator last,
               const Compare& x = Compare(), const Container& =
➥Container());
bool empty() const { return c.empty(); }
size_type size() const { return c.size(); }
const value_type& top() const { return c.front(); }
void push(const value_type& x);
void pop();
};
```

Elements of a priority queue are pushed in and popped out at one end. Any sequence that supports the front(), push_back() and pop_back() can be used as the container for priority queues. By default, the vector is used.

A priority queue must provide a way of comparing the priorities of its elements. By default, the less-than (<) operator is used. The pop() operation returns the element that has the highest priority. For elements that have equal priority, they become the top in the order in which they were initially inserted—hence a queue. For instance, assume that you have two elements A and B in a priority queue and A was inserted before B. If both A and B have a priority of five, A will become the top when there is no element that has a higher priority. When A is popped out of the queue, B becomes the top.

When an element is pushed into a priority queue, it is placed behind all elements with higher or equal priority and in front of all elements with lower priorities. How this process of placement is achieved is implementation defined.

No comparison operator is defined for priority queues.

Understanding Associative Containers

While sequence containers are designed for sequential and random access of elements using the index or an iterator, the associative containers are designed for fast random access of elements using keys. The Standard C++ Library provides four associative containers: map, multimap, set, and multiset.

You have seen that a vector is like an enhanced version of an array. It has all the characteristics of an array plus some additional features. Unfortunately, the vector also suffers from one of the significant weaknesses of arrays: It has no provision for the random access of elements using key values other than the index or iterator. Associative containers, on the other hand, provide fast random access based on key values.

The Map Container

The first associative container class is the map class. It is defined in the header file <map> in the namespace std. Before you get into the details of maps, let's recap how an array is organized and accessed. Listing 6.12 shows an array of Product objects.

LISTING 6.12. A Product LISTING

```
#include <iostream>
#include <string>
using namespace std;

class Product
{
public:
    Product(string newName = "", double newPrice = 0, int newStockLevel
➥= 0):
            mName(newName), mPrice(newPrice), mStockLevel(newStockLevel)
➥{}

    void    SetName(string newName)        {mName      = newName;
}
    void    SetName(int newStockLevel)     {mStockLevel = newStockLevel;}
    void    SetPrice(double newPrice)      {mPrice     = newPrice;    }

    string  GetName()         const        {return mName;}
    int     GetStockLevel()   const        {return mStockLevel;}
```

continues

LISTING 6.12. CONTINUED

```
    double     GetPrice()              const        {return mPrice;        }

    friend ostream& operator<<(ostream& os, Product& p)
    {
        os    << "Product: " << p.mName
            << "\tPrice: " << p.mPrice
            << "\tStock on hand: " << p.mStockLevel;
        return os;
    }

private:
    string     mName;
    int         mStockLevel;
    double     mPrice;
};

int main()
{
    Product Pen("Pen", 5.99, 58);
    Product TableLamp("Table Lamp", 28.49, 24);
    Product Speaker("Speaker", 24.95, 40);
    Product productArray[3] = {Pen, TableLamp, Speaker};

    cout << "Price list:\n";
    for (int i = 0; i < 3; ++i)     cout << productArray[i] << "\n";

    for (int j = 0; j < 3; ++j)
    {
        if (productArray[j].GetName() == "Speaker")
            cout << "\nSpeaker's price is " << productArray[j].GetPrice()
→<< "\n";
    }

    return 0;
}
```

The output from Listing 6.12 is shown here:

```
Price list:
Product: Pen          Price: 5.99    Stock on hand: 58
Product: Table Lamp   Price: 28.49   Stock on hand: 24
Product: Speaker      Price: 24.95   Stock on hand: 40

Speaker's price is 24.95
```

You can print out a nice-looking price list for all your stock using this program. But what if you want to know the price of speakers? To get this information, you will have to write some code like this:

```
    for (int j = 0; j < 3; ++j)
    {
        if (productArray[j].GetName() == "Speaker")
            cout << "Speaker's price is " << productArray[j].GetPrice() <<
➥"\n";
    }
```

This process is rather inefficient and messy. Wouldn't it be nice if you could do this:

```
    cout << "Speaker's price is " << productArray["Speaker"].GetPrice() <<
➥"\n";
```

Obviously, you can't do this with normal arrays. Fortunately, you *can* achieve this using the STL container class map. Let's modify Listing 6.12 so that it stores product listings in a map and can get the price of speakers. Listing 6.13 accomplishes this goal.

LISTING 6.13. USING map TO STORE THE Product LISTING

```
#include <iostream>
#include <string>
#include <map>
using namespace std;

class Product
{
public:
    Product():mName("New Product"), mStockLevel(0), mPrice(0)     {}
        Product(string newName, double newPrice = 0, int newStockLevel = 0):
            mName(newName), mPrice(newPrice), mStockLevel(newStockLevel)
➥{}

    void    SetName(string newName)      {mName       = newName;     }
    void    SetName(int newStockLevel)   {mStockLevel = newStockLevel;}
    void    SetPrice(double newPrice)    {mPrice      = newPrice;    }

    string   GetName()        const      {return mName;}
    int    GetStockLevel()    const       {return mStockLevel;}
    double   GetPrice()       const       {return mPrice;        }

    friend ostream& operator<<(ostream& os, Product& p)
    {
        os    << "Product: " << p.mName
           << "\tPrice: " << p.mPrice
           << "\tStock on hand: " << p.mStockLevel;
        return os;
    }

private:
```

continues

LISTING 6.13. CONTINUED

```
    string    mName;
    int        mStockLevel;
    double    mPrice;
};

int main()
{
    Product Pen("Pen", 5.99, 58);
    Product TableLamp("Table Lamp", 28.49, 24);
    Product Speaker("Speaker", 24.95, 40);

    map<string, Product> productMap;
    productMap[Pen.GetName()] = Pen;
    productMap[TableLamp.GetName()] = TableLamp;
    productMap[Speaker.GetName()] = Speaker;

    cout << "Speaker's price is " << productMap["Speaker"].GetPrice() <<
➡"\n";
    return 0;
}
```

The output from Listing 6.13 is simply this:

```
Speaker's price is 24.95
```

Listing 6.13 shows an important feature of the container class map: Elements in a map can be accessed using a key value. This implies that the container map must have a Key class. The map container must also be able to compare key values by using either the Key class's built-in comparison operator or an external comparison object. As anticipated, you find that the map container does indeed have a Key class that provides these features:

```
template<class Key, class T, class Compare = less<Key>, class A =
➡Allocator<T>>
class map
{
    // types
    typedef Compare                         key_compare;
    typedef A                               allocator_type;

    typedef typename A::deference_type    difference_type;

    typedef typename A::reference           reference;
    typedef typename A::const_reference   const_reference;
};
```

The first argument Key is the type of keys for the map; the second argument T is the type of element value. In your Product map example, the key is the product ID of type string, and the element value is of type Product. The third argument is a Compare class

that can be used to compare two key values. The fourth element A is an allocator that takes care of memory management of containers. In most cases, the default Allocator<T> should be adequate.

A map contains a sequence of key/value pairs, where each key is unique. This allows for the accurate locating of elements in a map. In addition, you must be able to sort the elements in a map according to their key values. If you don't specify a Compare class, the < comparison function will be used. You can overload the comparison operator < to compare two objects of your class. In the Product map example, the operator<(string, string) is used to compare product IDs. If you decide to order your product list by name, you can define a Compare class and provide it with the Product map. You will see more about defining a customized comparison class in Chapter 7, "STL Iterators and Algorithms."

Constructors and Destructor

The following code fragment shows the constructors and the destructor for the map container class:

```
template<class Key, class T, class Compare = less<Key>, class A =
➥Allocator<T>>
class map
{
    // constructors and destructor
    // create an empty map
    explicit map(const Compare& cmp = Compare(), const A& = A());

    // create a map and copy the first to (last - 1) elements from an
➥InputIterator
    template<class InputIterator>
    map(InputIterator first, InputIterator last,
          const Compare& cmp = Compare(), const A& = A());

    // copy constructor
    map(const map& m);

    // destructor
    ~map();

    // assignment operator
    map& operator=(const map&);
};
```

The member constructor creates a map object with an optional Compare class and/or an allocator class. (We will leave the template constructor alone for now because it involves an input iterator class; iterators are covered a little later in this chapter.) The copy constructor, destructor, and the assignment operator are standard.

Sizes

As do sequence containers, the map class provides several member functions related to the size of the map:

```
template<class Key, class T, class Compare = less<Key>, class A =
➥Allocator<T>>
class map
{
public:
    // types
    typedef typename A::size_type           size_type;

    // sizes
    size_type   size()              const;      // number of elements
    size_type max_size()            const;      // size of the largest
➥map
    bool        empty()             const    { return (size() == 0); }
};
```

All these operations are the same as their counterparts in the vector class.

Iterators

As with other standard containers, you can traverse through a map using iterators:

```
template<class Key, class T, class Compare = less<Key>, class A =
Allocator<T>>
class map
{
public:
    // types
    typedef Key                                     key_type;
    typedef T                                       mapped_type;

    typedef (implementation defined)            iterator;
    typedef (implementation defined)            const_iterator;
    typedef std::reverse_iterator<iterator>     reverse_iterator;
    typedef std::reverse_iterator<const_iterator>
➥const_reverse_iterator;

    // iterators
    iterator            begin();         // points to the first element
    const_iterator      begin() const;
    iterator            end();           // points to the (last + 1) element
    const_iterator      end() const;

    // points to the first element of reverse sequence
    reverse_iterator        rbegin();
    const_reverse_iterator    rbegin() const;
```

```
    // points to the (last + 1) element of reverse sequence
    reverse_iterator          rend();
    const_reverse_iterator    rend()   const;
};
```

Each element in a map is a `struct pair` defined in `namespace std` as follows:

```
template<class First, class Second>    struct    pair
{
    // Other struct members

    First       first;
    Second      second;
};
```

In your `Product` map example, you can change the price for any product and print a price list, as shown in Listing 6.14.

LISTING 6.14. ACCESSING MAP ELEMENTS

```
#include <iostream>
#include <string>
#include <map>
using namespace std;

class Product
{
public:
    Product():mName("New Product"), mStockLevel(0), mPrice(0)    {}
      Product(string newName, double newPrice = 0, int newStockLevel = 0):
            mName(newName), mPrice(newPrice), mStockLevel(newStockLevel)
➥{}

    void    SetName(string newName)        { mName      = newName;
➥}
    void    SetName(int newStockLevel)    { mStockLevel = newStockLevel; }
    void    SetPrice(double newPrice)     { mPrice      = newPrice;      }

    string    GetName()          const        { return mName;        }
    int       GetStockLevel()    const        { return mStockLevel; }
    double    GetPrice()         const        { return mPrice;       }

    friend ostream& operator<<(ostream& os, const Product& p)
    {
        os    << "Product: " << p.mName
           << "\tPrice: " << p.mPrice
           << "\tStock on hand: " << p.mStockLevel;
        return os;
    }
```

continues

LISTING 6.14. CONTINUED

```cpp
private:
    string      mName;
    int          mStockLevel;
    double      mPrice;
};

// template function to show all elements in a map
template<class T, class A>
void ShowMap(const map<T, A>& m);

int main()
{
    Product Pen("Pen", 5.99, 58);
    Product Lamp("Lamp", 28.49, 24);
    Product Speaker("Speaker", 24.95, 40);

    map<string, Product> productMap;
    productMap[Pen.GetName()] = Pen;
    productMap[Lamp.GetName()] = Lamp;
    productMap[Speaker.GetName()] = Speaker;

    ShowMap(productMap);
    return 0;
}

//
// Show map elements
//
template<class T, class A>
void ShowMap(const map<T, A>& m)
{
    cout << "Map elements:\n";
    for (map<T, A>::const_iterator ci = m.begin(); ci != m.end(); ++ci)
        cout << ci->first << "\t" << ci->second << "\n";

    cout << "\n\n";
}
```

The output from Listing 6.14 is shown as follows:

```
Map elements:
Lamp      Product: Lamp    Price: 28.49    Stock on hand: 24
Pen       Product: Pen     Price: 5.99     Stock on hand: 58
Speaker Product: Speaker        Price: 24.95     Stock on hand: 40
```

You have defined a default constructor for the `Product` class. This is not strictly necessary. However, it is required to construct a `productMap`, because `productMap` uses the `Product`'s default constructor to allocate memory for its elements. Three key/value pairs are assigned for elements in `productMap`. The `ShowMap()` function template is a general-purpose function that can be used to display all elements for any map. It uses an iterator to access a map's elements. Because elements in a map are a pair, you use `first` and `second` to return their key/value pair.

Element Access

The container class `map` provides several functions you can use to find elements by their key values. You can use the subscripting operator `[]` to get an element directly, or the `find()` member function to get a pointer (an iterator) to the desired element. The following code shows the access functions provided by the `map` container class:

```
template<class Key, class T, class Compare = less<Key>, class A =
➥Allocator<T>>
class map
{
public:
    // subscripting
    mapped_type& operator[](const key_type& k);

    // other operations
    // number of elements with key k, returns 0 if not found
    size_type           count(const key_type& k);

    // find element with key k, returns map::end() if not found
    iterator            find(const key_type& k);
    const_iterator     find(const key_type& k);

    // find first element with key value greater than or equal to key k
    iterator            lower_bound(const key_type& k);
    const_iterator     lower_bound(const key_type& k)      const;

    // find first element with key greater than k
    iterator            upper_bound(const key_type& k);
    const_iterator     upper_bound(const key_type& k)      const;

    // find all elements with key k
    pair(iterator, iterator)           equal_range(const key_type& k);
    pair(const_iterator, const_iterator)    equal_range(const key_type& k)
➥    const;
};
```

You have already seen that you can access an element by its key. What happens when you specify a key value that does not exist? Consider this example:

```
Product Pen("Pen", 5.99, 58);
Product TableLamp("Table Lamp", 28.49, 24);
Product Speaker("Speaker", 24.95, 40);
```

```
map<string, Product> productMap;
productMap[Pen.GetName()] = Pen;
productMap[TableLamp.GetName()] = TableLamp;
productMap[Speaker.GetName()] = Speaker;

cout << productMap["Speaker"] << "\n";    // no problem here
cout << productMap["Cup"] << "\n";         // what happens here???
```

The last statement creates a new product using the default constructor of class T—Product in this example—and inserts it into the map. If no default constructor is defined, you get a compile error.

The `find()` function, on the other hand, returns `map::end()` when the key is not found. It does not create an element.

Listing 6.15 changes the `Product` map example again to test the element access operations. Replace the `main()` function in Listing 6.14 with the code in Listing 6.15.

LISTING 6.15. ACCESSING ELEMENTS USING SUBSCRIPTS AND ITERATORS

```
int main()
{
    Product Pen("Pen", 5.99, 58);
    Product TableLamp("Table Lamp", 28.49, 24);
    Product Speaker("Speaker", 24.95, 40);

    map<string, Product> productMap;
    productMap[Pen.GetName()] = Pen;
    productMap[TableLamp.GetName()] = TableLamp;
    productMap[Speaker.GetName()] = Speaker;
    ShowMap(productMap);

    // show Speaker's price
    cout << "Speaker's price is " << productMap["Speaker"].GetPrice() <<
➥"\n";

    // change Pen's price
    productMap["Pen"].SetPrice(productMap["Pen"].GetPrice() * 1.10);
    cout << "Pen's price has been changed to " <<
➥productMap["Pen"].GetPrice()
➥ << "\n";

    // show various access functions related to Pen
    cout << "Number of Pens is " << productMap.count("Pen") << "\n";

    map<string, Product>::iterator ci = productMap.lower_bound("Pen");
    cout << "First Pen is " << ci->second << "\n";

    ci = productMap.upper_bound("Pen");
    cout << "Next to Pen is " << ci->second << "\n";
```

```
    // try to access a non-existing element
    cout << "Try Rubber: " << productMap["Rubber"] << "\n";
    ShowMap(productMap);

    // show access functions for a non-existing element
    cout << "Number of Red Pens is " << productMap.count("Red Pen") <<
➥ "\n";

    ci = productMap.lower_bound("Red Pen");
    cout << "First Red Pen is " << ci->second << "\n";

    ci = productMap.upper_bound("Red Pen");
    cout << "Next to Red Pen is " << ci->second << "\n";

    return 0;
}
```

The output from this modified code is as follows:

```
Map elements:
Pen        Product: Pen     Price: 5.99      Stock on hand: 58
Speaker Product: Speaker          Price: 24.95     Stock on hand: 40
Table Lamp         Product: Table Lamp      Price: 28.49    Stock on hand: 24

Speaker's price is 24.95
Pen's price has been changed to 6.589
Number of Pens is 1
First Pen is Product: Pen        Price: 6.589     Stock on hand: 58
Next to Pen is Product: Speaker Price: 24.95     Stock on hand: 40
Try Rubber: Product: New Product      Price: 0         Stock on hand: 0
Number of Red Pens is 0
First Red Pen is Product: Speaker      Price: 24.95     Stock on hand: 40
Next to Red Pen is Product: Speaker    Price: 24.95     Stock on hand: 40
```

You can change map elements by using the subscripting operator [ ]. For instance, the price of pens is increased by 10 percent using the Product class's SetPrice() function. You show the number of elements with key value of "Pen" by using the count() function. There is only one element here, and you know that you will never have more than one element with the same key value. The lower_bound() function finds the product pen, and the upper_bound() function gives us the element with a key value greater than "Pen". It is the speaker.

Then you try to find a product with a key value of "Rubber". It does not exist, so a new product is created using the Product class's default constructor. The count() function on a nonexisting key value returns 0, indicating that there is no product with such a key value. Note that the count() function here does not create a new element in the map. The lower_bound() function on this nonexisting key returns the element that has the next key value (in this case, the speaker). The `upper_bound()` function works the same way.

You may feel that the `lower_bound()`, `upper_bound()`, and `equal_range()` functions have rather limited use here. Remember that the container class `map` does not allow duplicate key values. You will learn more about this when you are introduced to the `multimap` class, where duplicate keys are allowed.

Insertions and Deletions

Elements can be added to or removed from a map. The `map` class provides several insertion and deletion functions:

```
template<class Key, class T, class Compare = less<Key>, class A =
➥Allocator<T>>
class map
{
public:
    // types
    typedef pair<const Key, T>    value_type;

    // insertions and deletions
    pair<iterator, bool>    insert(const value_type& val);
        // insert <Key, T> pair
    iterator    insert(iterator pos, const value_type& val);
    template<class InputIterator>
    void insert(InputIterator first, InputIterator last);

    void erase(iterator pos);
    size_type erase(const key_value* k);
    void erase(iterator first, iterator last);
    void clear();
};
```

Insertion and deletion operations work the same way as they do in vectors. Consider the following function:

```
iterator    insert(iterator pos, const value_type& val);
```

The iterator pos has no effect on where `val` is inserted because the element position is determined only after the `<Key, T>` pair is inserted.

Listing 6.16 shows how to add and remove elements from a `map` container class. Replace the `main()` function in Listing 6.14 with the code in Listing 6.16 to get the entire program.

LISTING 6.16. ADDING AND REMOVING ELEMENTS

```cpp
typedef map<string, Product>      PRODUCT_MAP;

int main()
{
    Product Pen("Pen", 5.99, 58);
    Product Lamp("Lamp", 28.49, 24);
    Product Speaker("Speaker", 24.95, 40);

    PRODUCT_MAP productMap;
    productMap[Pen.GetName()] = Pen;
    productMap[Lamp.GetName()] = Lamp;
    productMap[Speaker.GetName()] = Speaker;
    ShowMap(productMap);

    // add a new element
    cout << "Add a new element:\n";
    Product Staple("Staple", 2.99, 20);
    pair<string, Product> staplePair("Staple", Staple);
    pair<PRODUCT_MAP::iterator, bool> p = productMap.insert(staplePair);
    if (p.second)    cout << "New element added!\n";
    else             cout << "Insertion failed!\n";
    ShowMap(productMap);

    // add a new element with duplicate key Pen
    cout << "Add a new element with duplicate key Pen:\n";
    Product RedPen("Red Pen", 3.29, 12);
    pair<string, Product> RedPenPair("Pen", RedPen);
    p = productMap.insert(RedPenPair);
    if (p.second)    cout << "New element added!\n";
    else             cout << "Insertion failed!\n";
    ShowMap(productMap);

    // remove element with key "Lamp" from productMap
    cout << "remove element with key \"Lamp\" from productMap:\n";
    productMap.erase("Lamp");
    ShowMap(productMap);

    return 0;
}
```

The output from the modified code in Listing 6.16 is shown here:

```
Map elements:
Lamp    Product: Lamp   Price: 28.49    Stock on hand: 24
Pen     Product: Pen    Price: 5.99     Stock on hand: 58
Speaker Product: Speaker        Price: 24.95    Stock on hand: 40

Add a new element:
New element added!
```

```
Map elements:
Lamp     Product: Lamp     Price: 28.49     Stock on hand: 24
Pen      Product: Pen      Price: 5.99      Stock on hand: 58
Speaker Product: Speaker          Price: 24.95     Stock on hand: 40
Staple   Product: Staple Price: 2.99      Stock on hand: 20

Add a new element with duplicate key Pen:
Insertion failed!
Map elements:
Lamp     Product: Lamp     Price: 28.49     Stock on hand: 24
Pen      Product: Pen      Price: 5.99      Stock on hand: 58
Speaker Product: Speaker          Price: 24.95     Stock on hand: 40
Staple   Product: Staple Price: 2.99      Stock on hand: 20

remove element with key "Lamp" from productMap:
Map elements:
Pen      Product: Pen      Price: 5.99      Stock on hand: 58
Speaker Product: Speaker          Price: 24.95     Stock on hand: 40
Staple   Product: Staple Price: 2.99      Stock on hand: 20
```

The second value of the `pair` object returned by the `insert()` function is set to `true` if
the insertion is successful, as you see with the `staplePair`. If the key value to be added
already exists in the map, that value is set to `false`, indicating that the insertion has
failed, as you see with the `RedPenPair`.

Map Operations

The STL also provides overloaded comparison operators for comparing maps. You can
also swap the elements of two maps by using the overloaded `swap()` function. The following code fragment shows these operations, as defined by the `map` class:

```
template<class Key, class T, class Compare = less<Key>, class A =
Allocator<T>>
class map
{
public:
    // map operations
    void swap(map& m);      // swap elements between current map and m

    template<class Key, class T, class Compare, class A>
    bool operator==(const map<Key, T, Compare, A>& m1,
                    const map<Key, T, Compare, A>& m2);

    template<class Key, class T, class Compare, class A>
    bool operator!=(const map<Key, T, Compare, A>& m1,
                    const map<Key, T, Compare, A>& m2);

    template<class Key, class T, class Compare, class A>
    bool operator<( const map<Key, T, Compare, A>& m1,
                    const map<Key, T, Compare, A>& m2);
```

```
template<class Key, class T, class Compare, class A>
bool operator<=(const map<Key, T, Compare, A>& m1,
                const map<Key, T, Compare, A>& m2);

template<class Key, class T, class Compare, class A>
bool operator>( const map<Key, T, Compare, A>& m1,
                const map<Key, T, Compare, A>& m2);

template<class Key, class T, class Compare, class A>
bool operator>=(const map<Key, T, Compare, A>& m1,
                const map<Key, T, Compare, A>& m2);

};
```

The Multimap Container

A *multimap* is similar to a map except that its elements can have duplicate keys. Consequently, the `multimap` class has a similar class definition to the `map` container class, with some exceptions. It has no subscripting operators because there may be more than one element that has the same key value. The insertion operation is always okay because duplicate keys are allowed. The template class `multimap` is defined in the header file `<map>` in the `namespace std`.

Recall the syntax for the `insert()` function in class `map`:

```
pair<iterator, bool>insert(const value_type& val);
```

In the `map` class, the second element in the returning pair is used to indicate whether the insertion was successful. That second element is redundant to the `multimap` class because it is always `true`. Therefore, the `insert()` function is implemented in the `multimap` class as follows:

```
iterator insert(const value_type& val);
```

The three functions `lower_bound()`, `upper_bound()`, and `range_check()` are the primary means of accessing multimap elements with given key values. These three functions are defined by the `multimap` class as follows:

```
template<class Key, class T, class Compare = less<Key>, class A =
allocator<T>>
class multimap
{
public:
    // other class members

    // find first element with key value greater than or equal to key k
    iterator          lower_bound(const key_type& k);
    const_iterator    lower_bound(const key_type& k)    const;
```

```
    // find first element with key greater than k
    iterator            upper_bound(const key_type& k);
    const_iterator    upper_bound(const key_type& k)      const;

    // find all elements with key k
    pair(iterator, iterator)          equal_range(const key_type& k);
    pair(const_iterator, const_iterator)    equal_range(const key_type& k)
const;
};
```

The `lower_bound()` and `upper_bound()` functions were briefly discussed in the introduction to the `map` class. Now let's look at the `equal_range()` functions.

The `equal_range()` function returns a pair of iterators containing the first element with key k and the first element with a key value greater than k. The `equal_range()` function acts like a combination of the `lower_bound()` and `upper_bound()` functions in one function call. This speeds up execution time and simplifies the program to access a range of elements. Listing 6.17 shows an example using the `multimap` class.

LISTING 6.17. USING THE `multimap` CLASS

```
#include <iostream>
#include <string>
#include <map>
using namespace std;

template<class Key, class T>
void ShowMultimap(const multimap<Key, T>& m);

template<class Key, class T>
void ShowMultimapRange(const multimap<Key, T>& m, const Key& k);

int main()
{
    multimap<string, string> stateMap;
    stateMap.insert(make_pair((string)"USA", (string)"California"));
    stateMap.insert(make_pair((string)"USA", (string)"New York"));
    stateMap.insert(make_pair((string)"USA", (string)"Washington"));
    stateMap.insert(make_pair((string)"Australia", (string)"New South
➥Wales"));
    stateMap.insert(make_pair((string)"Vatican City", (string)"Vatican
➥City"));

    ShowMultimap(stateMap);
    ShowMultimapRange(stateMap, (string)"USA");

    return 0;
}
```

```
template<class Key, class T>
void ShowMultimap(const multimap<Key, T>& m)
{
    typedef multimap<Key, T>::const_iterator    Itor;

    for (Itor i = m.begin(); i != m.end(); ++i)
        cout << i->first << "\t" << i->second << "\n";
    cout << "\n";
}

template<class Key, class T>
void ShowMultimapRange(const multimap<Key, T>& m, const Key& k)
{
    typedef multimap<Key, T>::const_iterator    Itor;

    pair<Itor, Itor> p = m.equal_range(k);
    for (Itor i = p.first; i != p.second; ++i)
        cout << i->first << "\t" << i->second << "\n";
    cout << "\n";
}
```

The output from Listing 6.17 is shown here:

```
Australia       New South Wales
USA     California
USA     New York
USA     Washington
Vatican City    Vatican City

USA     California
USA     New York
USA     Washington
```

In this program, you create a multimap that holds the country/state pair. The country/state pairs are added to the multimap using the `insert()` function. The `ShowMultimap()` function is the same as the `ShowMap()` function you used earlier. The `ShowMultimapRange()` function uses the `equal_range()` function to obtain the first and last elements that have the same key value. All qualified elements are displayed using an iterator.

The Set Container

A *set* is also similar to a map. The difference is that elements in a set are not key/value pairs. Instead, an element in a set contains only a key. The template class `set` is defined in the header file `<set>` in the `namespace std`. The subscript operator `[ ]` is irrelevant here; if you know the key, you also know the value. The class `set` has member functions almost identical to those of the `map` class except that `set` contains no subscript operator

[], the value type is simply the key itself, and the value `compare` is just the `Compare` class. The following code introduces the functions available in the `set` container class:

```
template<class Key, class Compare = less<Key>, class A = Allocator<Key>>
class set
{
public:
    // other member functions

    typedef Key              value_type;     // as oppose to pair<const Key, T>
    typedef Compare     value_compare;
};
```

The Multiset Container

A *multiset* is a set that allows duplicate keys. It is also defined in the header file `<set>` in the namespace `std`. It has all the `set` member functions with one exception: The `insert()` function of the `multiset` class returns an iterator, not a `pair<iterator, bool>`; the insertion will never fail because of duplicate keys. The following code introduces the functions available in the `multiset` container class:

```
template<class Key, class Compare = less<Key>, class A = Allocator<Key>>
class multiset
{
public:
    // other member functions

    iterator insert(const value_type& v);
};
```

Considering Performance Issues

STL containers are designed to satisfy different requirements of application development. Sequence containers are best suited for the sequential and random access of elements using the subscripting operator [] and/or iterators. Associative containers, on the other hand, are optimized to provide random access of their elements by key values. In this section, you take a quick look at the performance complexity of some of the standard container operations. Table 6.1 shows some common container operations and their complexities.

TABLE 6.1. STANDARD CONTAINER OPERATION COMPLEXITY

Operation	vector	list	deque	map	multimap	set	multiset
Constructors				O(1)			
Empty container with elements				O(n)			
Destructor				O(n)			
begin(), end(), rbegin(), rend()				O(1)			
Front operation		O(1)	O(1)				
Back operation	O(1)	O(1)	O(1)				
Modifiers	O(n)	O(1)	O(n)	O(log(n))	O(log(n))	O(log(n))	O(log(n))
[]	O(1)		O(1)	O(log(n))			
at()	O(1)		O(1)				
Comparison				O(n)			

Performance of operations is often measured by the complexity of the operation; that is, the execution time compared to the number of elements involved in the operation. A constant complexity, denoted in Table 6.1 as O(1), means that the execution time does not depend on the number of elements involved. A logarithmic complexity, denoted as O(log(n)), means that the execution time is proportional to the logarithm value of the number of elements involved. A linear complexity, denoted as O(n), means that the execution time is proportional to the number of elements involved.

When the need for a standard container class arises, you must make a decision about which of the available containers is best suited for your application. You should ask two questions:

- Which containers provide the functionality required?

  For instance, if elements must be accessed by a key, any of the associative containers can be used.

- From the containers that meet the first requirement, which one is more efficient?

If elements are always to be accessed sequentially, sequence containers have the advantage over their associative counterparts. Furthermore, if frequent insertion in the middle of the element sequence is expected, the list container is the better choice.

Using the Standard C++ Library

STL container classes are part of the Standard C++ Library. They are defined in the `namespace std`. Your program must reference these classes in one of two ways.

The first way to reference the STL container classes is to use the `using namespace` directive to indicate your intention to use the Standard C++ Library. You must have the following statement in your program:

```
using namespace std;
```

This statement directs the compiler to resolve the class names and methods by looking at the `std` namespace. All your sample programs use this method.

The second method of referencing the STL classes is to explicitly qualify the class with the `std` keyword, as in this example:

```
std::vector<int> vInt;
```

You must also use `#include` to include the relevant header file in your program. For example, to use the `vector` container class, you must use the following statement:

```
#include <vector>
```

Table 6.2 summarizes the header files for each STL container class.

TABLE 6.2. STL CONTAINER CLASS HEADER FILES

Class	*Header*
vector	<vector>
list	<list>
deque	<deque>
stack	<stack>
queue	<queue>
priority_queue	<queue>
map	<map>
multimap	<map>
set	<set>
multiset	<set>

Designing Element Types

The STL container classes are designed to hold any objects. You have seen that many STL container class methods require the elements to be able to perform certain operations:

- **The element class must have a default constructor.**

  The default constructor is called when a container object is created in the following form:

  ```
  vector<MyClass> v(100);
  ```

  This statement creates a vector holding 100 `MyClass` objects created using `MyClass::MyClass()`.

- **The element class must have a copy constructor.**

  The copy constructor is called when new elements are added to the container, as in this example:

  ```
  MyClass myObject;
  vector<MyClass> v(100, myObject);      // MyClass' copy constructor is
  called
  vector<MyClass> v;
  v.push_back(myObject);      // MyClass' copy constructor is called
  ```

- **The element class must have an assignment operator** (=).

  The assignment operator is called when a new value is assigned to an element, as in this example:

  ```
  MyClass myObject;
  vector<MyClass> v(100);
  v[1] = myObject      // MyClass' assignment operator is called
  ```

When using container classes that require the comparison of their elements, you should define the overloading comparison operators. If you do not define them, you must use a specialized comparison class and explicitly specify the comparison class in the container definition. The essential comparison operators are the == and < operators. You can use these operators to implement others, including <=, >, >=, and !=, as you saw in the discussion of the container class `vector`.

After you have defined the overloaded == and < operators, you can take a free ride to derive the rest of them using the Standard C++ Library header file <utility> that provides template comparison operator implementations based on the operators == and <.

> **NOTE**
>
> Check your compiler documentation for details on how the compiler implements the STL.

Summary

The Standard Template Library provides several standard container classes that help programmers perform common data structure management functions. Standard containers are guaranteed to be implemented by compilers that conform to the C++ standard. Standard containers ensure the portability of your applications and increase your ability to reach the greatest possible number of users. For many applications, STL container classes provide sufficient functionality and reduce your coding and debugging efforts. To maximize this advantage, you must use them correctly. You must choose the container that best suits your application's requirements. In general, sequence containers provide optimized sequential and random element access with subscripts and iterators. Associative containers, on the other hand, allow for the direct access of elements by key values.

You will find that you often need to use standard containers to store customized objects. Those objects must meet a set of requirements and restrictions imposed by the chosen container. Member functions, such as the == and < comparison operators, can have a big impact on the performance of the container you choose and, ultimately, on your application. Make certain that you implement containers in the most efficient and reliable manner.

STL Iterators and Algorithms

CHAPTER 7

Iterator Classes

When we discussed STL container classes in the last chapter, we used iterators as if they were pointers to the STL container class elements, and we noted that an iterator could be dereferenced to evaluate to an element. In this chapter, we take a closer look at the iterator classes.

Iterator classes are defined in the header file `<iterator>` in `namespace std`. Iterators are an abstraction, or generalization, of pointers—that is, they implement all pointer operations. All iterator operations have the same effect as the corresponding pointer operations.

Position Within a Container

A container stores a collection of objects of the same type. How elements are stored varies among different containers. For example, elements in a vector are stored in consecutive memory blocks. A list container, on the other hand, stores its elements in any available memory space. Each standard container organizes its elements in such a way that the elements can be accessed in a specified order from the beginning of the element collection to the end of the collection. Figure 7.1 shows the element positions in a container.

FIGURE 7.1.
Elements in a container.

Typically, elements are accessed with an iterator. If an iterator points to the nth element, we can dereference it to get element n. An iterator can be incremented to point to element n + 1; an iterator can also be decremented to point to element n − 1. When an iterator evaluates to `end()`, it does not point to any element. There is no such thing as a `NULL` iterator. An iterator is said to be valid if it points to an element or if it points to the end of sequence (`end()`). An iterator is invalid if it is not initialized or if the sequence is resized.

Types of Iterators In and Out of Containers

There are five iterator categories, represented in the hierarchy shown in Figure 7.2.

Figure 7.2 does not show a class inheritance diagram. It represents the level of functionality provided by different categories of iterators. The *input iterator* and *output iterator* provide the most limited functionality. They can be used only to traverse sequences in a single pass in a forward direction. The pass is not repeatable. That is, stepping through a sequence a second time using either an input iterator or an output iterator is likely to produce a different result.

FIGURE 7.2.
Iterator hierarchy.

A *forward iterator* provides all the operations of input and output iterators and relaxes some of the restrictions imposed on input and output iterators. The most notable difference is that repeatedly stepping through the same sequence using a forward iterator produces the same results. Likewise, a *bidirectional iterator* provides all forward iterator operations. It also allows for the traversal of a sequence in reverse order.

And finally, a *random access iterator* provides all bidirectional iterator operations plus other random access-specific methods.

Table 7.1 summarizes the operations provided by iterators.

TABLE 7.1. ITERATOR OPERATIONS

Category	Input	Output	Forward	Bidirectional	Random Access
Element Access	->		->	->	->, [ ]
Read	= *i		= *i	= *i	= *i
Write		*i =	*i =	*i =	*i =
Iteration	++	++	++	++, --	, --, +, -, +=, -=
Comparison	==, !=		==, !=	==, !=	==, !=, <, <=, >, >=

Base Iterator Class

The Standard C++ Library provides a base type you can use to create your own iterator classes:

```
template<class Category, class T, class Distance = ptrdiff_t,
         class Pointer = T*, class Reference = T&>
struct iterator    {
    typedef Category     iterator_category;
    typedef T                 value_type;
    typedef Distance     diferrence_type;
```

```
    typedef Pointer          pointer;
    typedef Reference     reference;
};
```

The `Category` class must be one of the five iterator categories, which are represented with the following empty classes:

```
struct input_iterator_tag                                            {};
struct output_iterator_tag                                           {};
struct forward_iterator_tag              : public input_iterator_tag
{};
struct bidirectional_iterator_tag    {}    : public forward_iterator_tag
{};
struct random_access_iterator_tag    {}    : public
bidirectional_iterator_tag    {};
```

All these empty classes have neither member variables nor member functions—except for the default constructors and destructors, of course. They are named as `iterator tags` because they are only used as tags to represent the iterator categories; they are not actually used in any standard iterator member functions.

We can use iterator tag inheritance, on the other hand, to write generic algorithms of iterators. For example, if a function expects an input iterator, we can pass it a forward iterator; the function should execute without problem because a forward iterator must perform all input iterator operations.

Given this important use of iterator tag inheritance, you might expect that the `forward_iterator_tag` would be derived from both the `input_iterator_tag` and the `output_iterator_tag` as shown in the iterator hierarchy in Figure 7.2. The STL, however, derives the `forward_iterator_tag` only from the `input_iterator_tag`. The reason for this is that output iterators and forward iterators are used to write outputs to different types of containers.

Output iterators are often used to write values to unbounded containers such as the standard output. When we write to the standard output, we are free to output any value that has to be written. There is no need to check whether the standard output will accept our output. Although a forward iterator provides all output iterator operations, it works only on bounded containers. The forward iterator must write to an element in the container. Any attempt to step over the boundary generates either a compile-time or a runtime error. We usually cannot use a forward iterator where an output iterator is expected. Consequently, the `forward_iterator_tag` is not derived from the `output_iterator_tag`.

Practically, there is little need to write algorithms that use output iterators anyway. Output iterators do not have a value type because it is impossible to obtain a value from an output iterator; you can only write a value through it. Output iterators also do not have a distance type because it is impossible to find the distance from one output iterator to another. Finding a distance requires a comparison for equality, and output iterators do not support the operator ==. Consequently, there are few algorithms that work on output iterators. In fact, the STL iterator operations `distance()` and `advance()` are not designed to work with output iterators at all.

The next type in the iterator template class, `T`, is the type of object pointed to by the iterator. `Distance` is a signed integral type representing the distance between two iterators. By default, it is the `ptrdiff_t` type defined in `<cstddef>`. The pointer is the type of pointer that points to the iterator's `value_type`. This type is a generalized pointer type returned by the overloaded operator `->`. The reference is a reference to the iterator's `value_type`. It is returned by the overloaded dereference operator `*`.

You can derive a forward iterator from the template class iterator:

```
template <class T, class Distance = ptrdiff_t>
class forward_iterator : public iterator<forward_iterator_tag, T,
➥Distance> {
public:
    const T&    operator*() const;
    const T*    operator->()    const;
    iterator&   operator++();                 // prefix-increment
    iterator    operator++(int);       // postfix-increment

// other members
};
```

All iterators derived from the base iterator template class have a common set of attributes, including `iterator_category`, `value_type`, and so on. The STL provides a template class `iterator_traits` that characterizes iterators:

```
template<class Itor>struct iterator_traits    {
    typedef typename Itor::iterator_category    iterator_category;
    typedef typename Itor::value_type       value_type;
    typedef typename Itor::difference_type   difference_type;
    typedef typename Itor::pointer          pointer;
    typedef typename Itor::reference          reference;
};
```

The use of iterator traits is demonstrated in the iterator operation examples later in this chapter.

Input Iterators

An input iterator is an iterator that must satisfy the following set of requirements:

- **Default Constructible:** The iterator must have a default constructor so that it can be created without initializing it to any particular value. When an input iterator is created using its default destructor, it is an invalid iterator. It remains invalid until it is assigned a value.

- **Assignable:** The iterator must have a copy constructor and an overloaded assignment operator. These features allow for copying and assigning values to iterators.

- **Equality Comparable:** The iterator must have an overloaded equality operator == and an inequality operator !=. These operators allow for the comparison of two iterators.

An input iterator is an iterator that can be dereferenced when it points to an element within a sequence. The iterator can also point to the end of a sequence. When it points to the end of a sequence, the iterator actually points just past the final element in the sequence and is said to be *past the end*. A past-the-end iterator cannot be dereferenced.

An input iterator is valid if it can be dereferenced to a valid object or it is past the end. An input iterator guarantees read access to the object pointed to. For example, if `ii` is an input iterator whose `value_type` is `T`, we can access the object it points to by dereferencing it:

```
T t = *ii;     // ok
```

Because input iterators do not allow write access to the elements pointed to, the following statements contain an error:

```
T t;
*ii = t;    // error!
```

An input iterator can also be incremented to point to the next element. Both the prefix increment operator (`++ii`) and the postfix increment operator (`ii++`) must be defined. An input iterator `ii` can be incremented if `++ii` is valid. Past-the-end iterators cannot be incremented.

Output Iterators

An output iterator must be default constructible and assignable. An output iterator guarantees write access—but not read access—to the object pointed to. Consider these statements:

```
T t;
*oi = t;    // ok
t = *oi;    // error!
```

An output iterator also defines both the prefix and the postfix increment operators.

Forward Iterators

A forward iterator is like a video tape—it can be played only in one direction, but it can be played again and again. It has all the characteristics of an input iterator. That is, a forward iterator is default constructible, assignable, and equality comparable. A forward iterator can also be dereferenced and incremented. Both read and write access to the object pointed to are provided with forward iterators.

Bidirectional Iterators

A bidirectional iterator is similar to a forward iterator except that it can also be decremented.

Random Access Iterators

The random access iterator implements all the iterator operations of the bidirectional iterator, and adds methods to move from one element to another in constant time ($O(1)$). The distance between the original element and the destination element is not important. That is, the random access iterator is as quick to go from element 1 to element 37 as it is to go from element 1 to element 2.

Because random access iterators can move more than one step at a time, the addition (+ and +=) and subtraction (- and -=) operators are defined. Random access iterators also define the subscripting operator []. If `ri` is a random access iterator, `ri[n]` returns the nth element in the sequence.

In addition to being equality comparable, a random access iterator is also magnitude comparable. Therefore, it defines less-than (<), greater-than (>), less-than-or-equal-to (<=), and greater-than-or-equal-to (>=) operators. Only the less-than (<) operator is fundamental. All other operators can be derived from it.

Iterator Operations

In addition to the overloaded operators, the STL provides two functions that return the number of elements between two elements and that jump from one element to any other element in the container.

The `distance()` Function

The `distance()` function finds the distance between the current position of two iterators. That is, if the first iterator points to element 12 in a sequence, and the second iterator points to element 47 in the same sequence, the distance is 35.

```
template<class InputIterator>
```

```
iterator_traits<InputIterator>::difference_type
distance(InputIterator first, InputIterator last);
```

How do we calculate the distance between two iterators? It is an easy calculation for random access iterators because they provide subtraction operators. We can simply subtract the first iterator from the last iterator to calculate the distance:

```
template<class RandomAccessIterator>
iterator_traits<RandomAccessIterator>::difference_type
distance(RandomAccessIterator first, RandomAccessIterator last)    {
    return last - first;
}
```

Things work slightly differently for other iterators because they have no subtraction iterator defined. We must step through the sequence from the first to the last and record the number of steps:

```
template<class InputIterator>
iterator_traits<InputIterator>::difference_type
distance(InputIterator first, InputIterator last)    {
    iterator_traits<InputIterator>::difference_type n = 0;
    while (first++ != last)    ++n;
    return n;
}
```

Thanks to iterator tag inheritance, the second version of the `distance()` function works for input iterators, forward iterators, and bidirectional iterators. Because output iterators do not have a comparison operator `!=`, it is not possible to test whether two output iterators are equal. Consequently, there is no `distance()` function defined for output iterators.

The complexity—the execution time compared to the number of elements involved in the operation—of the `distance()` function depends on the category of the iterator. For random access iterators, it is constant time (`O(1)`) because the subtraction operation on random access iterators has the constant time complexity. For other iterators, the complexity is linear (`O(n)`).

The `advance()` Function

So far, we have seen how we can move iterators forward and backward by using the increment and decrement operators, respectively. We can also move random access iterators several steps at a time using the addition and subtraction functions. Other types of iterators, however, do not have the addition and subtraction functions. The STL provides the `advance()` function to move any iterator—except the output iterators—several steps at a time:

```
template<class InputIterator, class Distance>
void advance(InputIterator& ii, Distance& n);
```

In this syntax, `Distance` is a signed integral type. The distance to move, n, may evaluate to either positive or negative. If n is positive, the iterator moves forward; otherwise, the iterator moves backward. If n is zero, this function has no effect and there is no movement. n can be negative only if the iterator is either a bidirectional or a random access iterator.

There is one significant difference between different iterator categories: Only the random access iterator provides addition and subtraction operations. So the `advance()` function can be overloaded for different iterator categories:

```
template<class InputIterator, class Distance>
void advance(InputIterator& ii, Distance& n) {
    while (n--)      ++ii;
}

template<class BidirectionalIterator, class Distance>
void advance(BidirectionalIterator & bi, Distance& n) {
    if (n >= 0)     while (n--)     ++bi;
    else            while (n++)     --bi;
}

template<class RandomAccessIterator, class Distance>
void advance(RandomAccessIterator& ri, Distance& n)     {
    ri += n;
}
```

Because output iterators allow for only write access to their value types, they should move only one step at a time. The increment operator is provided for this very purpose. There is no need for an `advance()` function for output iterators.

Similar to the `distance()` function, the complexity of the `advance()` function depends on the category of the iterator. The `advance()` function has constant time complexity for random access iterators and linear complexity for other iterators.

Standard Iterator Classes

STL defines a set of iterator classes that perform some common iterating operations. These classes are described in the following sections.

The `istream_iterator` Class

The template class `istream_iterator` is defined in `<iterator>`. An istream iterator is an input iterator that performs formatted input of a given type of objects from an istream. An `istream_iterator` class can be defined as follows:

```
template <class T, class Distance = ptrdiff_t>
class istream_iterator : public input_iterator<T, Distance> {
public:
```

```
    typedef input_iterator_tag      iterator_category;
    typedef T                       value_type;
    typedef Distance                difference_type;
    typedef const T*                pointer;
    typedef const T&                reference;

    const T&              operator*() const;
    const T*              operator->()    const;
    istream_iterator&     operator++();            // pre-increment
    istream_iterator      operator++(int);         // post-increment

// other members
};
```

> **NOTE**
>
> The preceding definition is not the standard `istream_iterator` template class definition. This example serves only to illustrate important characteristics of `istream` iterators.

Listing 7.1 shows the use of an `istream` iterator to read from standard input `cin`.

LISTING 7.1. READING INPUT USING AN `istream` ITERATOR

```
#include <iostream>
#include <iterator>
using namespace std;

int main()
{
    cout << "Enter an integer: ";
    istream_iterator<int, char>    ii(cin);
    int i1 = *ii;
    cout << "i1 = " << i1 << "\n";

    cout << "Ready for another integer: ";
    int i2 = *++ii;
    cout << "i2 = " << i2 << "\n";

    return 0;
}
```

The following is the output generated by Listing 7.1:

```
Enter an integer: 6
i1 = 6
```

```
Ready for another integer: 2
i2 = 2
```

The istream iterator ii is created to accept input from standard input cin. The second template parameter is the base type of the istream. The first integer entered is assigned to i1 using the dereference operator *. The iterator should be incremented if it is to accept the next input.

The ostream_iterator Class

The template class ostream_iterator is also defined in <iterator>. An *ostream iterator* is an output iterator that performs formatted output of a given type of objects to an ostream. An ostream_iterator class may be defined as follows:

```
template <class T>
class ostream_iterator : public output_iterator {
public:
    typedef output_iterator_tag     iterator_category;
    typedef void                    value_type;
    typedef void                    difference_type;
    typedef void                    pointer;
    typedef void                    reference;

    ostream_iterator&     operator*();
    ostream_iterator&     operator++();
    ostream_iterator&     operator++(int);
    ostream_iterator&     operator=(const T&);
};
```

Listing 7.2 demonstrates the use of an ostream iterator to write integers to standard output cout.

LISTING 7.2. WRITING OUTPUT USING AN ostream ITERATOR

```
#include <iostream>
#include <iterator>
using namespace std;

int main()
{
    ostream_iterator<int, char>     oi(cout);
    *oi = 6;
    *++oi = 88;

    return 0;
}
```

The following is the output generated by Listing 7.2:

688

First we create an output iterator `oi` to output integers to standard output `cout`. In a manner similar to the way `istream_iterator` works, the second template parameter specifies the base type of `ostream`. When we assign a value `6` to its `value_type` object, it is printed to `cout`. As with `istream` iterators, an `ostream` iterator should be incremented before we attempt to output another value. In Listing 7.2, the integer `88` is printed through `oi` to the position next to `6`.

Function Objects

Containers and iterators make it possible to create, search, and modify a sequence of elements. A standard container typically defines a set of operations that can be used to manage the container and its elements. Because we often need to design specialized containers to solve problems in situations for which standard containers may not be quite suitable, we need to implement container operations. Many such operations use functions that perform generic operations such as object comparison, validation, and calculations. This section introduces some of the function objects defined in the Standard Library.

Standard function objects are defined in `<functional>` in namespace `std`. A *function object* is an object that can be called as a function. It can be any class that defines `operator()`, as shown in Listing 7.3.

LISTING 7.3. A FUNCTION OBJECT

```
#include <iostream>
using namespace std;

template<class T>
class Print    {
public:
    void operator()(T& t)    { cout << t << "\n"; }
};

int main()
{
    Print<int> DoPrint;
    for (int i = 0; i < 5; ++i)    DoPrint(i);
    return 0;
}
```

Here is the output generated by Listing 7.3:

```
0
1
2
3
4
```

A template class `Print` is defined with only one member function operator()—that simply prints a value to `cout`. As a normal class, `Print` must be instantiated so that its overloaded `operator()` can be called. In Listing 7.3, `DoPrint` is created to print integers. Listing 7.3 shows a very simple function object.

Function objects can be used by STL algorithms to perform various actions on containers. There are three different types of function objects:

- **Generators:** Function objects that take no argument. A classic example is a random number generator.

- **Unary Functions:** Function objects that take one argument. These objects may or may not return a value. The `DoPrint` function object is an example of a unary function.

- **Binary Functions:** Function objects that take two arguments. These objects may or may not return a value.

The Standard C++ Library provides two base classes to simplify the creation of function objects:

```
template<class Arg, class Result>
struct unary_function    {
    typedef Arg        argument_type;
    typedef Result     result_type;
};

template<class Arg1, class Arg2, class Result>
struct binary_function    {
    typedef Arg1        first_argument_type;
    typedef Arg2        second_argument_type;
    typedef Result     result_type;
};
```

Now we can redefine the `Print` class as follows:

```
template<class T>
class Print: public unary_function<T, void>    {
    . . .
};
```

Predicates

When the type of the return value of a unary function object is `bool`, the function is called a *unary predicate*. A binary function object that returns a `bool` value is called a *binary predicate*. The Standard C++ Library defines several common predicates in `<functional>`. These predicates are listed in Table 7.2.

TABLE 7.2. PREDICATES DEFINED IN `<functional>`

Function	Type	Description
equal_to	binary	arg1 == arg2
not_equal_to	binary	arg1 != arg2
greater	binary	arg1 > arg2
greater_equal	binary	arg1 >= arg2
less	binary	arg1 < arg2
less_equal	binary	arg1 <= arg2
logical_and	binary	arg1 && arg2
logical_or	binary	arg1 ¦¦ arg2
logical_not	unary	!arg1

The `equal_to` predicate is defined as follows:

```
template<class T>
struct equal_to : binary_function<T, T, bool>    {
    bool operator()(T& arg1, T& arg2) const    { return arg1 == arg2; }
};
```

To compare two values of type `T` using the `equal_to` predicate, you must define the overloaded comparison operator `==`. You can define the `==` operator as either a unary member function of class `T` or as an overloaded binary operator function, as shown here:

```
bool T::operator==()(T& t)          // member function of class T

template<class T>                   // generic comparison operator
bool operator==(T& arg1, T& arg2);
```

All other predicates are defined in a similar way and have similar requirements.

Arithmetic Functions

Arithmetic functions perform arithmetic operations on objects. Table 7.3 lists the functions defined by the Standard C++ Library in `<functional>`.

TABLE 7.3. ARITHMETIC FUNCTIONS DEFINED IN `<functional>`

Function	Type	Description
plus	binary	arg1 + arg2
minus	binary	arg1 - arg2
multiplies	binary	arg1 * arg2
divides	binary	arg1 / arg2
modulus	binary	arg1 % arg2
negate	unary	-arg1

Binary arithmetic functions take two arguments of one type and return a value of the same type. For instance, the `plus()` function is defined as follows:

```
template <class T>
struct plus : binary_function<T,T,T>
{
    T operator()(const T& x, const T& y) const;
};
```

The `negate()` function is defined as a unary function:

```
template <class T>
struct negate : unary_function<T,T>
{
    T operator()(const T& x) const;
};
```

Algorithm Classes

A container is a useful place to store a sequence of elements. All standard containers define operations that manipulate the containers and their elements. Implementing all these operations in your own sequences, however, can be laborious and prone to error. Because most of those operations are likely to be the same in most sequences, a set of generic algorithms can reduce the need to write your own operations for each new container. The Standard Library provides approximately 60 standard algorithms that perform the most basic and commonly used operations of containers.

Standard algorithms are defined in `<algorithm>` in namespace `std`.

Non-Mutating Sequence Operations

Non-mutating sequence operations are used to retrieve the values or positions of elements in a sequence container. A sequence is identified by a pair of iterators [first, last); first points to the first element in the sequence and last is the past-the-end iterator.

The for_each() Operation

The for_each() operation performs a unary operation on each element in a sequence.

```
template<class InputIterator, class UnaryFunction>
FunctionObject for_each(InputIterator first, InputIterator last,
➥UnaryFunction f);
```

The function f must be a unary function and perform read-only access to elements.

The find() Operation

The find() operation searches a sequence to find the first element in a sequence that is equal to a given value.

```
template<class InputIterator, class T>
InputIterator find(InputIterator first, InputIterator last, const T&
➥value);
```

If an element is found, find() returns the iterator that points to this element. Otherwise, the iterator last is returned.

The find_if() Operation

The find_if() operation searches a sequence to find the first element that, when passed to a predicate, evaluates the predicate to true.

```
template<class InputIterator, class UnaryPredicate>
InputIterator find_if(InputIterator first, InputIterator last,
UnaryPredicate pred);
```

Like find(), find_if() returns the iterator pointing to the found element; it returns the iterator last if no element is found.

The count() Operation

The count() operation counts the number of elements in a sequence that are equal to a given value.

```
template<class InputIterator, class T>
iterator_traits<InputIterator>::difference_type
count(InputIterator first, InputIterator last, const T& value);
```

Elements in the sequence are compared against the given value using the overloaded comparison operator ==. The number of qualified elements is returned.

The count_if() Operation

The `count_if()` operation counts the number of elements in a sequence that are equal to a given value. It tests the equality using an external binary predicate.

```
template<class InputIterator, class BinaryPredicate>
iterator_traits<InputIterator>::difference_type
count_if(InputIterator first, InputIterator last, BinaryPredicate pred);
```

Like `count()`, `count_if()` returns the number of qualified elements.

Listing 7.4 demonstrates the `find()` and `count()` operations.

LISTING 7.4. USING THE `find()` AND `count()` OPERATIONS

```cpp
#include <iostream>
#include <vector>
#include <iterator>
#include <functional>
#include <algorithm>
using namespace std;

const int VectorSize = 5;

template<class T>
class Print: public unary_function<T, void>
{
public:
    void operator()(T& arg1)
    {
        cout << arg1 << " ";
    }
};

template<class T>
class GreaterThanTwo: public unary_function<T, bool>
{
public:
    bool operator()(T& arg1)
    {
        return (arg1 > 2);
    }
};

template<class Container, class Iterator>
void ShowElement(Container& c, Iterator& itor);

int main()
{
```

continues

LISTING 7.4. CONTINUED

```cpp
    Print<int>     DoPrint;
    vector<int>      vInt(VectorSize);
    typedef vector<int>::iterator        Itor;

    for (int i = 0; i < VectorSize; ++i)
        vInt[i] = i;

    Itor    first = vInt.begin();
    Itor    last = vInt.end();

    cout << "for_each()\n";
    for_each(first, last, DoPrint);
    cout << "\n";

    Itor retItor = find(first, last, 2);
    cout << "find(first, last, 2) = ";
    ShowElement(vInt, retItor);
    cout << "\n";

    retItor = find(first, last, 10);
    cout << "find(first, last, 10) = ";
    ShowElement(vInt, retItor);
    cout << "\n";

    GreaterThanTwo<int>        IsGreaterThanTwo;
    retItor = find_if(first, last, IsGreaterThanTwo);
    cout << "find(first, last, IsGreaterThanTwo) = ";
    ShowElement(vInt, retItor);
    cout << "\n";

    int retSize = count(first, last, 3);
    cout << "count(first, last, 3) = " << retSize << "\n";

    retSize = count_if(first, last, IsGreaterThanTwo);
    cout << "count_if(first, last, IsGreaterThanTwo) = " << retSize <<
➥"\n";

    return 0;
}

template<class Container, class Iterator>
void ShowElement(Container& c, Iterator& itor)
{
    if (itor != c.end())
        cout << *itor;
    else
        cout << "last";
}
```

Here is the output generated by the code in Listing 7.4:

```
for_each()
0 1 2 3 4
find(first, last, 2) = 2
find(first, last, 10) = last
find(first, last, IsGreaterThanTwo) = 3
count(first, last, 3) = 1
count_if(first, last, IsGreaterThanTwo) = 2
```

A unary function object `Print` is defined to simply print its argument to standard output `cout`. We define another unary function class `GreaterThanTwo` to compare its argument against an arbitrary number 2. The type of its argument, `T`, must be able to compare with an integral type so that we can compare it to an integer.

The `ShowElement()` function template is defined to print the element pointed to by the iterator `itor` in a sequence `c`. If the iterator is a past-the-end iterator, it displays the string `last`.

In the `main()` function, a `Print` class object `DoPrint()` is defined so that we can call `DoPrint(var)` to print the value of var. A sequence [`first, last`) is created from the vector `vInt` that contains five integers 0, 1, 2, 3, and 4. The `for_each()` operation is performed to apply the `DoPrint()` function to each element of the sequence.

We can call the `find()` function to locate the first element that has a given value, as we do here to find the element with value 2. The element pointed to by the resulting iterator can be accessed by dereferencing it. We can see that element has the value of 2, as expected. Next, another call to the `find()` function finds an element with value 10. Because it cannot find such a value, it returns the pass-the-last iterator.

A `GreaterThanTwo` class object `IsGreaterThanTwo` returns `true` if its argument is greater than 2. This predicate is used by the `find_if()` operation to find the first element with a value greater than 2. This search returns the element with the value 3.

We then use the `count()` operation to find the number of elements with the value 3. The `count_if()` operation uses the predicate `IsGreaterThanTwo()` to count the number of elements with a value greater than 2; it finds two elements.

The `adjacent_find()` Operation

The `adjacent_find()` operation searches the sequence to find two adjacent elements that are equal. The Standard Library defines two overloaded `adjacent_find()` operators. The first version compares elements using the overloaded `==` operator:

```
template<class ForwardIterator>
ForwardIterator adjacent_find(ForwardIterator first, ForwardIterator
➥last);
```

The second version of `adjacent_find()` compares elements using an external binary predicate. If the predicate evaluates to `true` on two adjacent elements, they are considered to be equal:

```
template <class ForwardIterator , class…BinaryPredicate>
ForwardIterator adjacent_find(ForwardIterator first, ForwardIterator last,
                                  BinaryPredicate binary_pred);
```

Both versions return the iterator pointing to the first element in the pair if such a pair of elements is found. Otherwise, the iterator `last` is returned.

The `search_n()` Operation

The `search_n()` operation finds a given number of consecutive elements in a sequence. All those elements must be equal to a given value. The operation has two versions that differ in how they test the equality of elements:

```
template<class ForwardIterator, class Size, class T>
ForwardIterator search_n(ForwardIterator first, ForwardIterator last,
                            Size count, const T& value);

template<class ForwardIterator, class Size, class T, class
BinaryPredicate>
ForwardIterator search_n(ForwardIterator first, ForwardIterator last,
                            Size count, const T& value, BinaryPredicate
➥pred);
```

If `search_n()` finds a number of count consecutive elements in sequence [`first`, `last`), it returns the iterator pointing to the first element. Otherwise, it returns the iterator `last`.

Listing 7.5 shows the use of the `adjacent_find()` and the `search_n()` operations.

LISTING 7.5. USING THE `adjacent_find()` AND `search_n()` OPERATIONS

```
#include <iostream>
#include <vector>
#include <iterator>
#include <functional>
#include <algorithm>
using namespace std;

const int VectorSize = 10;

template<class T>
class EqualToThree: public binary_function<T, T, bool>
{
public:
    bool operator()(T& arg1, T& arg2)
```

```
        {
            return (arg1 == arg2) && (arg1 == 3);
        }
};

template<class Container, class Iterator>
void ShowElement(Container& c, Iterator& itor);

int main()
{
    vector<int>     vInt(VectorSize);
    typedef vector<int>::iterator    Itor;

    vInt[0] = 0;
    vInt[1] = 2;
    vInt[2] = 2;
    vInt[3] = 4;
    vInt[4] = 4;
    vInt[5] = 3;
    vInt[6] = 3;
    vInt[7] = 4;
    vInt[8] = 4;
    vInt[9] = 4;

    Itor    first = vInt.begin();
    Itor    last = vInt.end();
    Itor    retItor = adjacent_find(first, last);
    cout << "adjacent_find(first, last) = ";
    ShowElement(vInt, retItor);
    cout << "\n";

    EqualToThree<int>    IsEqualToThree;
    retItor = adjacent_find(first, last, IsEqualToThree);
    cout << "adjacent_find(first, last, IsEqualToThree) = ";
    ShowElement(vInt, retItor);
    cout << "\n";

    retItor = search_n(first, last, 3, 4);
    cout << "search_n(first, last, 3, 4) = ";
    ShowElement(vInt, retItor);
    cout << "\tprevious element is ";
    ShowElement(vInt, --retItor);
    cout << "\n";

    return 0;
}

template<class Container, class Iterator>
void ShowElement(Container& c, Iterator& itor)
```

continues

LISTING 7.5. CONTINUED

```
{
    if (itor != c.end())
        cout << *itor;
    else
        cout << "last";
}
```

Here is the output from the program in Listing 7.5:

```
adjacent_find(first, last) = 2
adjacent_find(first, last, IsEqualToThree) = 3
search_n(first, last, 3, 4) = 4 previous element is 3
```

The binary predicate `EqualToThree()` is defined to compare its arguments. It returns `true` only if both arguments are equal to 3. We define an integer vector `vInt` and assign its elements with test data. The element with the value 2 is returned by the `adjacent_find()` operation. An `EqualToThree` object `IsEqualToThree` is used by the predicate version of `adjacent_find()` to find consecutive elements with the value 3.

The `search_n()` operation is performed to find the first element of the second group of four; the previous element is also displayed to verify the return value.

The `find_first_of()` Operation

The `find_first_of()` operation searches a sequence to find the first occurrence of an element that is identical to any one of the elements in another sequence. There are two versions of `find_first_of()`; one uses the overloaded `==` operator and the other uses an external binary predicate to test the equality of the elements:

```
template <class InputIterator, class ForwardIterator>
InputIterator find_first_of(InputIterator first1, InputIterator last1,
                                ForwardIterator first2, ForwardIterator
►last2);

template <class InputIterator, class ForwardIterator, class
BinaryPredicate>
InputIterator find_first_of(InputIterator first1, InputIterator last1,
                                ForwardIterator first2, ForwardIterator
►last2,
                                BinaryPredicate comp);
```

If such a subsequence is found, the iterator pointing to the first element in the subsequence is returned. If the `find_first_of()` operation cannot find such a subsequence, it returns the iterator `last1`.

The `search()` Operation

There are two overloaded `search()` functions that search a sequence [first1, last1)
to find the first occurrence of a subsequence that is identical to another sequence
[first2, last2). As do the two versions of `find_first_of()`, the two versions of
`search()` use either the overloaded == operator or an external binary predicate to test
whether elements are equal.

```
template <class InputIterator, class ForwardIterator>
InputIterator search(InputIterator first1, InputIterator last1,
                     ForwardIterator first2, ForwardIterator last2);

template <class InputIterator, class ForwardIterator, class
BinaryPredicate>
InputIterator search(InputIterator first1, InputIterator last1,
                     ForwardIterator first2, ForwardIterator last2,
                     BinaryPredicate comp);
```

If such a subsequence is found, the iterator pointing to the first element in the subsequence is returned. If the `find_first_of()` operation cannot find such a subsequence, it
returns the iterator `last1`.

The `find_end()` Operation

The `find_end()` operation is perhaps misnamed. It is more like the `search()` operations
than a `find()` operation. Like `search()`, `find_end()` searches a sequence [first1,
last1) for a subsequence that is identical to another sequence [first2, last2). The
difference is that `find_end()` finds the *last* occurrence of the subsequence.

```
template<class ForwardIterator1, class ForwardIterator2>
ForwardIterator1 find_end(ForwardIterator1 first1, ForwardIterator1 last1,
                          ForwardIterator2 first2, ForwardIterator2
➥last2);

template<class ForwardIterator1, class ForwardIterator2, class
BinaryPredicate>
ForwardIterator1 find_end(ForwardIterator1 first1, ForwardIterator1 last1,
                          ForwardIterator2 first2, ForwardIterator2
➥last2,
                          BinaryPredicate pred);
```

As with the versions of `search()`, the two versions of `find_end()` differ in how they
compare elements in the sequences. Listing 7.6 shows how search functions work.

LISTING 7.6. USING OTHER SEARCH FUNCTIONS

```cpp
#include <iostream>
#include <vector>
#include <iterator>
#include <functional>
#include <algorithm>
using namespace std;

template<class Container, class Iterator>
void ShowElement(Container& c, Iterator& itor);

int main()
{
    typedef vector<int>::iterator    Itor;
    vector<int>    vInt1(10);
    vInt1[0] = 0;
    vInt1[1] = 1;
    vInt1[2] = 1;
    vInt1[3] = 2;
    vInt1[4] = 3;
    vInt1[5] = 4;
    vInt1[6] = 1;
    vInt1[7] = 2;
    vInt1[8] = 3;
    vInt1[9] = 5;

    vector<int>    vInt2(3);
    vInt2[0] = 1;
    vInt2[1] = 2;
    vInt2[2] = 3;

    Itor    first1 = vInt1.begin();
    Itor    last1  = vInt1.end();
    Itor    first2 = vInt2.begin();
    Itor    last2  = vInt2.end();

    Itor    retItor = find_first_of(first1, last1, first2, last2);
    cout << "find_first_of(first1, last1, first2, last2) = ";
    ShowElement(vInt1, retItor);
    cout << "\n";

    retItor = search(first1, last1, first2, last2);
    cout << "search(first1, last1, first2, last2) = ";
    ShowElement(vInt1, retItor);
    cout << "\n";

    retItor = find_end(first1, last1, first2, last2);
    cout << "find_end(first1, last1, first2, last2) = ";
    ShowElement(vInt1, retItor);
    cout << "\n";
```

```
    return 0;
}

template<class Container, class Iterator>
void ShowElement(Container& c, Iterator& itor)
{
    if (itor != c.end())
    {
        if (itor != c.begin())
            cout << *itor << "\tthe previous element is " << *(itor - 1);
        else
            cout << "first";
    }
    else
        cout << "last";
}
```

The following is the output generated by the code in Listing 7.6:

```
find_first_of(first1, last1, first2, last2) = 1 the previous element is 0
search(first1, last1, first2, last2) = 1          the previous element is 1
find_end(first1, last1, first2, last2) = 1        the previous element is 4
```

The ShowElement() function template is modified slightly to show not only the current element, but also the previous element so that we can see the position of the element in the sequence. The find_first_of() operation finds the second element in vector vInt1. The search() operation finds the third element as it is the first element of the first subsequence (1, 2, 3) in vInt1. The find_end() operation finds the seventh element that is the first of the last subsequence (1, 2, 3) in vInt1.

The equal() Operation

The equal() operation compares two sequences of equal size to see whether they match. The operation uses either the overloaded == operator or the binary predicate to test whether the elements are equal.

```
template<class InputIterator1, class InputIterator2>
bool equal(InputIterator1 first1, InputIterator1 last1, InputIterator2
➥first2);

template<class InputIterator1, class InputIterator2, class
BinaryPredicate>
bool equal(InputIterator1 first1, InputIterator1 last1, InputIterator2
➥first2,
            BinaryPredicate pred);
```

The second sequence starts at first2 and ends at first2 + (last1 - first1). If its size is the same as the size of the first sequence, *and* if every corresponding pair of elements are equal, equal() returns true. Otherwise, the operation returns false.

The `mismatch()` Operation

The `mismatch()` operation compares two sequences to find any mismatched elements. It compares each corresponding pair of elements and returns the first pair that does not match.

```
template<class InputIterator1, class InputIterator2>
pair<InputIterator1, InputIterator2>
mismatch(InputIterator1 first1, InputIterator1 last1, InputIterator2
➥first2);

template<class InputIterator1, class InputIterator2, class
BinaryPredicate>
pair<InputIterator1, InputIterator2>
mismatch(InputIterator1 first1, InputIterator1 last1, InputIterator2
➥first2,
          BinaryPredicate pred);
```

Like many of the other algorithms already discussed, the two versions of `mismatch()` use different methods to test the equality of elements.

Listing 7.7 demonstrates the `equal()` and `mismatch()` operations.

LISTING 7.7. MATCHING ELEMENTS USING THE `equal()` AND `mismatch()` OPERATIONS

```cpp
#include <iostream>
#include <vector>
#include <algorithm>
using namespace std;

template<class Container, class Iterator>
void ShowElement(Container& c, Iterator& itor);

int main()
{
    typedef vector<int>::iterator     Itor;
    vector<int>     vInt1(4);
    vInt1[0] = 1;
    vInt1[1] = 2;
    vInt1[2] = 3;
    vInt1[3] = 4;

    vector<int>     vInt2(3);
    vInt2[0] = 1;
    vInt2[1] = 2;
    vInt2[2] = 3;

    Itor     first1 = vInt1.begin();
    Itor     last1  = vInt1.end();
    Itor     first2 = vInt2.begin();
```

```
    if (equal(first1, last1, first2))
        cout << "vInt1 == vInt2\n";
    else
        cout << "vInt1 != vInt2\n";

    pair<Itor, Itor> pi = mismatch(first1, last1, first2);
    cout << "First mismatch element in vInt1 = ";
    ShowElement(vInt1, pi.first);
    cout << "\n";
    cout << "First mismatch element in vInt2 = ";
    ShowElement(vInt2, pi.second);
    cout << "\n";

    return 0;
}

template<class Container, class Iterator>
void ShowElement(Container& c, Iterator& itor)
{
    if (itor != c.end())
    {
        if (itor != c.begin())
            cout << *itor << "\tthe previous element is " << *(itor - 1);
        else
            cout << "first";
    }
    else
        cout << "last";
}
```

The following is the output generated by the program in Listing 7.7:

```
vInt1 != vInt2
First mismatch element in vInt1 = 4      the previous element is 3
First mismatch element in vInt2 = last
```

The integer vector vInt1 has four elements; vInt2 has three elements. Because their sizes are different, the equal() operation returns false. The mismatch() operation returns a pair of the first mismatched elements in both vectors.

Mutating Sequence Algorithms

Mutating sequence operations perform operations that change the elements in a sequence.

The fill() Operation

The fill() operation assigns a value to each element in a sequence:

```
template<class ForwardIterator, class T>
void fill(ForwardIterator first, ForwardIterator last, const T& value);
```

The `fill()` function can be defined as follows:

```
for (ForwardIterator fi = first; fi != last; ++fi)
{
    *fi = value;
}
```

Therefore, class T must be convertible to class `ForwardIterator`'s value type so that the assignment statement is valid.

The `fill_n()` Operation

The `fill_n()` operation is similar to `fill()` except that it assigns the value only to the first n elements in sequence [first, last):

```
template<class OutputIterator, class Size, class T>
void fill_n(OutputIterator first, Size n, const T& value);
```

Because the `fill()` operation performs exactly n assignments, [first, first + n) must be a valid sequence.

The `generate()` Operation

The `generate()` operation is like the `fill()` operation but it assigns the result of a generator instead of a value to each element in a sequence.

```
template<class ForwardIterator, class Generator>
void generate(ForwardIterator first, ForwardIterator last, Generator f);
```

The return value of function f must be convertible to the element type.

The `generate_n()` Operation

The `generate_n()` operation is like the `fill_n()` operation, but it assigns the result of a generator instead of a value to the first n elements in a sequence.

```
template<class OutputIterator, class Size, class Generator>
void generate(OutputIterator first, Size n, Generator f);
```

As is true with the `fill()` operation, in the `Generate()` operation the return value of function f must be convertible to the element type.

Listing 7.8 shows how sequences can be filled and generated.

LISTING 7.8. POPULATING SEQUENCES USING THE `fill()` AND `generate()` OPERATIONS

```
#include <iostream>
#include <vector>
```

```
#include <functional>
#include <algorithm>
using namespace std;

template<class T>
class Print: public unary_function<T, void>
{
public:
    void operator()(T& arg1)
    {
        cout << arg1 << " ";
    }
};

int main()
{
    Print<int>    DoPrint;

    typedef    vector<int>              VectorInt;
    typedef    VectorInt::iterator    Itor;

    VectorInt    vInt1(10);
    Itor         first1 = vInt1.begin();
    Itor         last1  = vInt1.end();

    fill(first1, last1, 5);
    cout << "vInt1 after fill(first1, last1, 5):\n";
    for_each(first1, last1, DoPrint);
    cout << "\n\n";

    generate(first1, last1, rand);
    cout << "vInt1 after generate(first1, last1, rand):\n";
    for_each(first1, last1, DoPrint);
    cout << "\n\n";

    fill_n(first1, 7, 8);
    cout << "vInt1 after fill_n(first1, 3, 8):\n";
    for_each(first1, last1, DoPrint);
    cout << "\n\n";

    generate_n(first1, 5, rand);
    cout << "vInt1 after generate_n(first1, 5, rand):\n";
    for_each(first1, last1, DoPrint);
    cout << "\n\n";

    return 0;
}
```

The following is the output generated by the program in Listing 7.8:

```
vInt1 after fill(first1, last1, 5):
5 5 5 5 5 5 5 5 5 5

vInt1 after generate(first1, last1, rand):
41 18467 6334 26500 19169 15724 11478 29358 26962 24464

vInt1 after fill_n(first1, 3, 8):
8 8 8 8 8 8 8 29358 26962 24464

vInt1 after generate_n(first1, 5, rand):
5705 28145 23281 16827 9961 8 8 29358 26962 24464
```

In Listing 7.8, we use the `for_each()` operation with a simple unary function `DoPrint` to display elements in a sequence. All elements in vector `vInt1` are assigned the value 5. The `generate()` operation uses the standard function `int rand()` to generate random integers for `vInt1` elements. The `fill_n()` and `generate_n()` operations are called to assign values to an arbitrary number of elements in `vInt1`.

The `partition()` Operation

The `partition()` operation rearranges the order of elements in a sequence so that elements that satisfy a unary predicate are placed before elements that do not.

```
template<class BidirectionalIterator, class UnaryPredicate>
BidirectionalIterator partition(BidirectionalIterator first,
                                BidirectionalIterator last,
                                UnaryPredicate pred);
```

The `partition()` operation returns an iterator pointing to the first element that does not satisfy the predicate.

The `stable_partition()` Operation

The `stable_partition()` operation partitions a sequence into two groups: one that satisfies the predicate and the other that does not. The relative order of elements in each group is preserved.

```
template<class BidirectionalIterator, class UnaryPredicate >
BidirectionalIterator stable_partition(BidirectionalIterator first,
                                       BidirectionalIterator last,
                                       UnaryPredicate pred);
```

Like `partition()`, the `stable_partition()` operation returns an iterator pointing to the first element that does not satisfy the predicate.

The `random_shuffle()` Operation

The `random_shuffle()` operation randomly rearranges the order of elements in a sequence:

7

```
template<class RandomAccessIterator>
void random_shuffle(RandomAccessIterator first, RandomAccessIterator
➥last);

template<class RandomAccessIterator, class RandomNumberGenerator>
void random_shuffle(RandomAccessIterator first, RandomAccessIterator last,
                    RandomNumberGenerator& rand);
```

The first version of the operation uses an internal random number generator to create indices for the elements. The second version uses an external random number generator that is passed as an argument.

Listing 7.9 shows the `random_shuffle()` and `partition()` operations.

LISTING 7.9. REARRANGING SEQUENCES USING THE `partition()` AND `random_shuffle()` OPERATIONS

```
#include <iostream>
#include <vector>
#include <functional>
#include <algorithm>
using namespace std;

template<class T>
class Print: public unary_function<T, void>
{
public:
    void operator()(T& arg1)
    {
        cout << arg1 << " ";
    }
};

template<class T>
class PartitionPredicate: public unary_function<T, bool>
{
public:
    bool operator()(T& arg1)
    {
        return (arg1 < 8);
    }
};

int main()
{
    Print<int>    DoPrint;

    typedef    vector<int>            VectorInt;
```

continues

LISTING 7.9. CONTINUED

```
typedef     VectorInt::iterator     Itor;

VectorInt    vInt1(10);
for (int i = 0; i < 10; i++)
    vInt1[i] = i;

Itor        first1 = vInt1.begin();
Itor        last1  = vInt1.end();

random_shuffle(first1, last1);
cout << "vInt1 after random_shuffle(first1, last1):\n";
for_each(first1, last1, DoPrint);
cout << "\n\n";

VectorInt                vInt2 = vInt1;
Itor                     first2 = vInt2.begin();
Itor                     last2  = vInt2.end();
PartitionPredicate<int>    pred;

partition(first1, last1, pred);
cout << "vInt1 after partition(first1, last1, pred):\n";
for_each(first1, last1, DoPrint);
cout << "\n\n";

stable_partition(first2, last2, pred);
cout << "vInt2 after stable_partition(first2, last2, pred):\n";
for_each(first2, last2, DoPrint);
cout << "\n\n";

return 0;
}
```

The following is the output generated by the code in Listing 7.9:

```
vInt1 after random_shuffle(first1, last1):
4 3 0 2 6 7 8 9 5 1

vInt1 after partition(first1, last1, pred):
4 3 0 2 6 7 1 5 9 8

vInt2 after stable_partition(first2, last2, pred):
4 3 0 2 6 7 5 1 8 9
```

The unary predicate function object class PartitionPredicate is defined to test whether its argument is less than 8. This function object is used by partition() operations to arrange vector elements. The random_shuffle() function is called to reorder elements in the integer vector. The resulting vector is copied to vInt2 so that we can compare the results of the partition() and stable_partition() operations. When the partition()

operation is performed on vInt1, the original order of its elements is not preserved in the partitioned sequence. On the other hand, the stable_partition() operation does not alter the element ordering in each group.

The transform() Operation

The transform() operation performs an operation on each element in a sequence and copies the result to another sequence. There are two overloaded transform() functions. The first version performs a unary operation:

```
template<class InputIterator, class OutputIterator, class UnaryOperation>
OutputIterator transform(InputIterator first, InputIterator last,
                         OutputIterator result, UnaryOperation f);
```

The second version of the function performs a binary operation on two sequences and copies the result to a third sequence:

```
template<class InputIterator1, class InputIterator2,
         class OutputIterator, class BinaryOperation>
OutputIterator transform(InputIterator1 first1, InputIterator1 last1,
                         InputIterator2 first2, OutputIterator
result,
                         BinaryOperation binary_op);
```

In both versions, elements in the original sequence(s) are not changed.

The copy() Operation

The copy() operation copies elements from one sequence to another.

```
template<class InputIterator, class OutputIterator>
OutputIterator copy(InputIterator first, InputIterator last,
OutputIterator dest);
```

Elements in sequence [first, last) are copied to the sequence starting at dest. The element *first is copied to *dest, *(first + 1) to *(dest + 1), and so on. The copy() operation returns iterator dest + (last - first), and dest must not be in the range [first, last).

The copy_backward() Operation

The copy_backward() operation copies elements from one sequence to another in reverse order:

```
template<class BidirectionalIterator, class BidirectionalIterator >
BidirectionalIterator copy_backward(BidirectionalIterator first,
                                    BidirectionalIterator last,
                                    BidirectionalIterator dest);
```

The copy_backward() operation copies elements *(last - 1) to *(dest - 1), *(last - 2) to *(dest - 2), and so on. It returns iterator dest - (last - first). Because copy() copies elements backwards from last - 1 and stores the result from dest - 1, we must use bidirectional iterators in both sequences.

The reverse() Operation

The reverse() operation reverses the order of elements in a sequence:

```
template<class BidirectionalIterator>
void reverse(BidirectionalIterator first, BidirectionalIterator last);
```

The reverse() operation swaps the first + i and the last - 1 - i elements, where 0 <= i <= (last - first) / 2.

The reverse_copy() Operation

The reverse_copy() operation copies all elements in one sequence in reverse order to a new sequence:

```
template<class BidirectionalIterator, class OutputIterator>
OutputIterator reverse_copy(BidirectionalIterator first,
               BidirectionalIterator last, OutputIterator result);
```

The original sequence is unchanged after the operation.

The rotate() Operation

The rotate() operation rotates elements in a sequence.

```
template<class ForwardIterator>
void rotate(ForwardIterator first, ForwardIterator middle, ForwardIterator
➥last);
```

After the operation, all elements are pulled towards the start of the sequence by middle - first positions. Elements moved past the first element in the sequence are pushed to the back of the sequence.

The rotate_copy() Operation

The rotate_copy() operation rotates the elements in one sequence and copies the result to a new sequence.

```
template<class ForwardIterator, class OutputIterator>
OutputIterator rotate_copy(ForwardIterator first, ForwardIterator middle,
                           ForwardIterator last, OutputIterator
➥result);
```

The original sequence is unchanged after the operation.

Listing 7.10 demonstrates some of the copy operations.

LISTING 7.10. COPYING SEQUENCE ELEMENTS USING THE COPY OPERATIONS

```cpp
#include <iostream>
#include <vector>
#include <functional>
#include <algorithm>
using namespace std;

template<class T>
class Print: public unary_function<T, void>
{
public:
    void operator()(T& arg1)
    {
        cout << arg1 << " ";
    }
};

template<class T>
class Square: public unary_function<T, T>
{
public:
    T operator()(T& arg1)
    {
        return arg1 * arg1;
    }
};

template<class Container>
void ShowElements(Container& c, char* text);

int main()
{
    typedef     vector<int>             VectorInt;
    typedef     VectorInt::iterator     Itor;

    Square<int>     Sqr;

    // create an integer vector
    VectorInt     vInt1(5);
    Itor          first1 = vInt1.begin();
    Itor          last1  = vInt1.end();
    for (int i = 0; i < 5; ++i)          vInt1[i] = 3 * i;
    ShowElements(vInt1, "vInt1 created");

    // create a vector for storing results
    VectorInt     vInt2(7);
    Itor          first2 = vInt2.begin();
    Itor          last2  = vInt2.end();
    fill(first2, last2, -1);
```

continues

7

STL ITERATORS AND ALGORITHMS

LISTING 7.10. CONTINUED

```cpp
    ShowElements(vInt2, "vInt2 created");

    // transform vInt1 to vInt2
    transform(first1, last1, first2 + 1, Sqr);
    ShowElements(vInt2, "Transformed vInt1 to vInt2");

    // copy vInt1 backwards to vInt2
    fill(first2, last2, -1);
    copy_backward(first1, last1, last2 - 1);
    ShowElements(vInt2, "vInt1 copied backwards to vInt2");

    // rotate vInt1 to vInt2
    fill(first2, last2, -1);
    rotate_copy(first1, first1 + 1, last1, first2 + 1);
    ShowElements(vInt2, "rotate_copy vInt1 to vInt2");

    // reverse vInt2
    reverse(first2, last2);
    ShowElements(vInt2, "reversed vInt2");

    return 0;
}

template<class Container>
void ShowElements(Container& c, char* text)
{
    Print<Container::value_type>    DoPrint;

    cout << text << ":\n";
    for_each(c.begin(), c.end(), DoPrint);
    cout << "\n\n";
}
```

Here is the output generated by the code in Listing 7.10:

```
vInt1 created:
0 3 6 9 12

vInt2 created:
-1 -1 -1 -1 -1 -1 -1

Transformed vInt1 to vInt2:
-1 0 9 36 81 144 -1

vInt1 copied backwards to vInt2:
-1 0 3 6 9 12 -1

rotate_copy vInt1 to vInt2:
-1 3 6 9 12 0 -1

reversed vInt2:
-1 0 12 9 6 3 -1
```

The unary function object class `Square` is defined to calculate the square of its argument value. We call the `transform()` function to calculate the square value of each element in `vInt1`. The results are copied to `vInt2`, starting from the second element. We then perform a backward copy of elements from `vInt1` to `vInt2`. Elements are copied into `vInt2` from the second `last` element.

Next, elements in `vInt1` are rotated and copied to `vInt2` from the second element. The break point is set to the second element with the value 3. It becomes the first element in the sequence, and all the following elements are moved left by one place. The initial `first` element 0 now becomes the last element.

At last, the order of elements in `vInt2` is reversed.

The `replace()` Operation

The `replace()` operation replaces with a new value all the elements in a sequence that are equal to a specific value.

```
template<class ForwardIterator, class T>
void replace(ForwardIterator first, ForwardIterator last,
             const T& old_value, const T& new_value);
```

The `replace()` operation can be implemented as follows:

```
for (ForwardIterator fi = first; fi != last; ++fi)
{
    if (*fi == old_value)     *fi = new_value;
}
```

The `replace_if()` Operation

The `replace_if()` operation is similar to the `replace()` operation. Instead of testing each element against a value, it tests whether an element causes a unary predicate to return `true`.

```
template<class ForwardIterator, class Predicate, class T>
void replace_if(ForwardIterator first, ForwardIterator last,
                Predicate pred, const T& new_ value);
```

The `replace_if()` operation can be implemented as shown here:

```
for (ForwardIterator fi = first; fi != last; ++fi)
{
    if (pred(*fi) == true)     *fi = new_value;
}
```

The `replace_copy()` Operation

The `replace_copy()` operation copies all elements from one sequence to another sequence and performs the `replace()` operation on the resulting sequence.

```
template<class InputIterator, class OutputIterator, class T>
OutputIterator replace_copy(InputIterator first, InputIterator last,
                                      OutputIterator result,
                                      const T& old_value, const T&
➥new_value);
```

The `replace_copy_if()` Operation

The `replace_copy_if()` operation copies all elements from one sequence to another sequence and performs the `replace_if()` operation on the resulting sequence.

```
template<class Iterator, class OutputIterator, class Predicate, class T>
OutputIterator replace_copy_if(Iterator first, Iterator last,
OutputIterator result,
Predicate pred, const T& new_value);
```

The `remove()` Operation

The `remove()` operation removes elements from a sequence that are equal to a specific value.

```
template<class ForwardIterator, class T>
ForwardIterator remove(ForwardIterator first, ForwardIterator last, const
T& value);
```

If n elements are removed, `remove()` returns the iterator `last` - n. The size of the sequence is unchanged. The last n elements can still be dereferenced, but they all have undefined values.

The `remove_if()` Operation

The `remove_if()` operation removes all elements in a sequence that make a unary predicate return `true`.

```
template<class ForwardIterator, class Predicate>
ForwardIterator remove_if(ForwardIterator first, ForwardIterator last,
                                  Predicate pred);
```

Like `remove()`, `remove_if()` returns the iterator `last` – n; the last n elements in the sequence contain undefined values.

The `remove_copy()` Operation

The `remove_copy()` operation copies all elements from one sequence to another sequence and performs the `remove()` operation on the resulting sequence.

```
template<class InputIterator, class OutputIterator, class T>
OutputIterator remove_copy(InputIterator first, InputIterator last,
                             OutputIterator result, const T& value);
```

The `remove_copy_if()` Operation

The `remove_copy_if()` operation copies all elements from one sequence to another sequence and performs the `remove_if()` operation on the resulting sequence.

```
template<class InputIterator, class OutputIterator, class Predicate>
OutputIterator remove_copy_if(InputIterator first, InputIterator last,
                             OutputIterator result, Predicate
➥pred);
```

The `unique()` Operation

The `unique()` operation searches a sequence for consecutive elements that have the same value and removes all but the first element. There are two versions of the `unique()` functions: One tests the elements against a value and the other checks to see whether elements cause a binary predicate to return `true`.

```
template<class ForwardIterator>
ForwardIterator unique(ForwardIterator first, ForwardIterator last);
```

```
template<class ForwardIterator, class BinaryPredicate>
ForwardIterator unique(ForwardIterator first, ForwardIterator last,
                        BinaryPredicate pred);
```

Both versions return an iterator pointing to the past-the-end element in the resulting sequence. Like the `remove()` operations, the `unique()` operation does not change the size of the sequence. If n elements are removed, the last n elements in the sequence have undefined values.

The `unique_copy()` Operation

The `unique_copy()` operation copies elements in a sequence to a new sequence and performs the `unique()` operation on the new sequence.

```
template<class InputIterator, class OutputIterator>
OutputIterator unique_copy(InputIterator first, InputIterator last,
                             OutputIterator result);
```

```
template<class InputIterator, class OutputIterator, class BinaryPredicate>
OutputIterator unique_copy(InputIterator first, InputIterator last,
                             OutputIterator result, BinaryPredicate
➥pred);
```

Both versions return an iterator pointing to the past-the-end element in the resulting sequence. If n elements are removed from the resulting sequence, the last n elements have undefined values.

The swap() Operation

The swap() operation swaps two values.

```
template<class T> void swap(T& a, T& b);
```

The iter_swap() Operation

The iter_swap() operation swaps two elements pointed to by two iterators.

```
template<class ForwardIterator1, class ForwardIterator2>
void iter_swap(ForwardIterator1 i1, ForwardIterator2 i2);
```

The iter_swap() operation can be implemented as follows:

```
swap(*i1, *i2)
```

The swap_ranges() Operation

The swap_ranges() operation swaps elements in two sequences.

```
template<class ForwardIterator1, class ForwardIterator2>
ForwardIterator2 swap_ranges(ForwardIterator1 first1, ForwardIterator1
➥last1,
                             ForwardIterator2 first2);
```

The swap_ranges() operation swaps elements in the sequence [first1, last1) and the sequence [first2, first2 + (last1 - first1)). It returns the iterator first2 + (last1 - first1). Elements in the two sequences must be convertible.

Listing 7.11 demonstrates the use of the replace(), remove(), and swap() operations.

LISTING 7.11. MANIPULATING ELEMENTS USING THE replace(), remove(), AND swap() OPERATIONS

```
#include <iostream>
#include <vector>
#include <functional>
#include <algorithm>
using namespace std;

//
// Unary function to output its argument to cout
//
template<class T>
class Print: public unary_function<T, void>
{
public:
    void operator()(T& arg1)
    {
        cout << arg1 << " ";
```

```
    }
};

//
// Unary function to test if an integer is a even number.
//
bool IsEven(int var);

//
// Display all elements in a container
//
template<class Container>
void ShowElements(Container& c, char* text);

int main()
{
    typedef     vector<int>             VectorInt;
    typedef     VectorInt::iterator     Itor;

    // create an integer vector
    VectorInt     vInt1(7);
    Itor          first1 = vInt1.begin();
    Itor          last1  = vInt1.end();
    for (int i = 0; i < 7; ++i)     vInt1[i] = 3 * i;
    ShowElements(vInt1, "vInt1 created");

    // create a second integer vector to store the results
    VectorInt     vInt2(7);
    Itor          first2 = vInt2.begin();
    Itor          last2  = vInt2.end();
    fill(first2, last2, -1);

    // replace all even numbers with value 10 in vInt1 and copy the result
➡to vInt2
    replace_copy_if(first1, last1, first2, IsEven, 10);
    ShowElements(vInt2, "replaced all even numbers with value 10");

    // remove all but the first duplicate value in vInt2
    vInt2[3] = 10;     // this creates three consecutive 10.
    ShowElements(vInt2, "vInt2 with 3 consecutive 10s");

    unique(first2, last2);
    ShowElements(vInt2, "removed duplicate values from vInt2");

    // remove all even numbers in vInt1 and copy the result to vInt2
    fill(first2, last2, -1);
    remove_copy_if(first1, last1, first2, IsEven);
    ShowElements(vInt2, "removed all even numbers");
```

continues

LISTING 7.11. CONTINUED

```
        // swap the second and third elements in vInt1 and
        // the third and fourth elements in vInt2
        ShowElements(vInt1, "Before the swap_ranges, vInt1 is");
        ShowElements(vInt2, "and vInt2 is");
        swap_ranges(first1 + 1, first1 + 3, first2 + 2);
        ShowElements(vInt1, "After the swap_ranges, vInt1 is");
        ShowElements(vInt2, "and vInt2 is");

        return 0;
}

//
// Unary function to test if an integer is an even number.
//
bool IsEven(int var)
{
        return ((var % 2) == 0);
}

//
// Display all elements in a container
//
template<class Container>
void ShowElements(Container& c, char* text)
{
        Print<Container::value_type>    DoPrint;

        cout << text << ":\n";
        for_each(c.begin(), c.end(), DoPrint);
        cout << "\n\n";
}
```

The following is the output generated by the program in Listing 7.11:

```
vInt1 created:
0 3 6 9 12 15 18

replaced all even numbers with value 10:
10 3 10 9 10 15 10

vInt2 with 3 consecutive 10s:
10 3 10 10 10 15 10

removed duplicate values from vInt2:
10 3 10 15 10 15 10

removed all even numbers:
3 9 15 -1 -1 -1 -1
```

```
Before the swap_ranges, vInt1 is:
0 3 6 9 12 15 18

and vInt2 is:
3 9 15 -1 -1 -1 -1

After the swap_ranges, vInt1 is:
0 15 -1 9 12 15 18

and vInt2 is:
3 9 3 6 -1 -1 -1
```

We call the `replace_copy_if()` function to replace all even values in `vInt1` with the value `10` and to copy the result to `vInt2`. We then assign value `10` to the fourth element in `vInt2` to create a sequence of three consecutive `10`s. The `unique()` operation removes the second and third value `10` from that minisequence. This operation should move the last two elements forward and leave the memory space originally occupied by them with undefined values. When we display `vInt2`, we can see that the fourth and the fifth elements are now `15` and `10`, just as expected. The last two elements still have the values `15` and `10` because the compiler keeps the same memory block for `vInt1`—their initial values have not been overwritten. This behavior, however, is not guaranteed, and you should never attempt to retrieve their values before they are assigned some values.

The `remove_copy_if()` operation shows that only the three valid elements—3, 9, and 15—in `vInt1` are copied to `vInt2`. Other elements in `vInt2` are not affected.

Sorting and Related Sequence Operations

All sorting and related operations have two versions. One version uses the overloaded operator < to compare elements, and the other version uses an external comparison object. This implies that all sorted sequences are ordered in ascending order. It is possible to sort a sequence in reverse order by using an external predicate, as we will see in Listing 7.12.

Sorting Operations

The STL provides a set of sorting functions that order sequences of elements according to different requirements. The following sections look at these operations.

The `sort()` Operation

The `sort()` operation sorts elements in a sequence.

```
template<class RandomAccessIterator>
void sort(RandomAccessIterator first, RandomAccessIterator last);
```

```
template<class RandomAccessIterator, class Compare>
void sort(RandomAccessIterator first, RandomAccessIterator last, Compare
➥comp);
```

After the sort() operation, elements in the sequence are ordered in ascending order. You
can sort a sequence in descending order by defining a customized compare object.
Listing 7.12 shows how.

LISTING 7.12. SORTING A SEQUENCE USING THE sort() OPERATION

```
#include <iostream>
#include <vector>
#include <functional>
#include <algorithm>
using namespace std;

//
// Unary function to output its argument to cout
//
template<class T>
class Print: public unary_function<T, void>
{
public:
    void operator()(T& arg1)
    {
        cout << arg1 << " ";
    }
};

//
// Compare function
//
bool ReverseCompare(int arg1, int arg2);

//
// Display all elements in a container
//
template<class Container>
void ShowElements(Container& c, char* text);

int main()
{
    typedef    vector<int>             VectorInt;
    typedef    VectorInt::iterator    Itor;

    // create an integer vector
    VectorInt    vInt1(7);
    Itor         first1 = vInt1.begin();
    Itor         last1  = vInt1.end();
    generate(first1, last1, rand);
```

```
    ShowElements(vInt1, "Random number sequence");

    // sort the sequence in descending order
    sort(first1, last1, ReverseCompare);
    ShowElements(vInt1, "Sorted in descending order");

    return 0;
}

//
// Compare function
//
bool ReverseCompare(int arg1, int arg2)
{
    return (arg1 > arg2);
}

//
// Display all elements in a container
//
template<class Container>
void ShowElements(Container& c, char* text)
{
    Print<Container::value_type>    DoPrint;

    cout << text << ":\n";
    for_each(c.begin(), c.end(), DoPrint);
    cout << "\n\n";
}
```

The following is the output generated by the program in Listing 7.12:

```
Random number sequence:
41 18467 6334 26500 19169 15724 11478

Sorted in descending order:
26500 19169 18467 15724 11478 6334 41
```

The sort() operation uses a binary predicate that compares two arguments and returns true if the first argument is less than the second. We define a ReverseCompare() function that returns true if the first argument is greater than the second. When the sort() operation is performed using the ReverseCompare() function, it sorts the sequence in descending order.

In this particular example, we could simply use the greater() predicate. The use of ReverseCompare(), however, demonstrates a helpful generic technique in using any customized functions in standard algorithms.

The `stable_sort()` Operation

The `stable_sort()` operation also sorts elements in a sequence. If two or more elements are equal, their relative order is preserved.

```
template<class RandomAccessIterator>
void stable_sort(RandomAccessIterator first, RandomAccessIterator last);

template<class RandomAccessIterator, class Compare>
void stable_sort(RandomAccessIterator first, RandomAccessIterator last,
➥Compare comp);
```

The `partial_sort()` Operation

The `partial_sort()` operation sorts a subset of elements with the smallest values in a sequence.

```
template<class RandomAccessIterator>
void partial_sort(RandomAccessIterator first, RandomAccessIterator middle,
                  RandomAccessIterator last);

template<class RandomAccessIterator, class Compare>
void partial_sort(RandomAccessIterator first, RandomAccessIterator middle,
                  RandomAccessIterator last, Compare comp);
```

This operation sorts the smallest `middle` - `first` elements and places them in [`first`, `middle`). The order of the rest of the elements is undefined. Listing 7.13 demonstrates a `partial_sort()` operation using a reversed compare function.

LISTING 7.13. SORTING SEQUENCES USING THE `stable()` AND `partial_sort()` OPERATIONS

```cpp
#include <iostream>
#include <vector>
#include <functional>
#include <algorithm>
using namespace std;

//
// Unary function to output its argument to cout
//
template<class T>
class Print: public unary_function<T, void>
{
public:
    void operator()(T& arg1)
    {
        cout << arg1 << " ";
    }
};

//
```

```
// Compare function
//
bool ReverseCompare(int arg1, int arg2);

//
// Display all elements in a container
//
template<class Container>
void ShowElements(Container& c, char* text);

int main()
{
    typedef     vector<int>              VectorInt;
    typedef     VectorInt::iterator      Itor;

    // create an integer vector
    VectorInt     vInt1(7);
    Itor          first1 = vInt1.begin();
    Itor          last1  = vInt1.end();
    generate(first1, last1, rand);
    ShowElements(vInt1, "Random number sequence");

    // sort the sequence in descending order
    partial_sort(first1, first1 + 3, last1, ReverseCompare);
    ShowElements(vInt1, "Partially sorted three elements in descending
➥order");

    return 0;
}

//
// Compare function
//
bool ReverseCompare(int arg1, int arg2)
{
    return (arg1 > arg2);
}

//
// Display all elements in a container
//
template<class Container>
void ShowElements(Container& c, char* text)
{
    Print<Container::value_type>     DoPrint;

    cout << text << ":\n";
    for_each(c.begin(), c.end(), DoPrint);
    cout << "\n\n";
}
```

The following is the output generated by the code in Listing 7.13:

```
Random number sequence:
41 18467 6334 26500 19169 15724 11478

Partially sorted three elements in descending order:
26500 19169 18467 41 6334 15724 11478
```

This listing is very similar to Listing 7.12. The only difference is that Listing 7.13 sorts only the three largest elements instead of the whole sequence.

The `partial_sort_copy()` Operation

The `partial_sort_copy()` operation partially sorts a sequence and copies the resulting sequence to a new sequence.

```
template<class InputIterator, class RandomAccessIterator>
RandomAccessIterator partial_sort_copy(InputIterator first, InputIterator
➥last,
                                    RandomAccessIterator result_first,
                                    RandomAccessIterator result_last);

template<class InputIterator, class RandomAccessIterator, class Compare>
RandomAccessIterator partial_sort_copy(InputIterator first, InputIterator
➥last,
                                    RandomAccessIterator result_first,
                                    RandomAccessIterator result_last,
                                    Compare comp);
```

This operation sorts the smallest n elements, where n = min(`last - first`, `result_last - result_first`), in the sequence [`first`, `last`) and copies the result to [`result_first`, `result_first + n`). It returns min(`result_first + n`, `result_last`).

The `nth_element()` Operation

The `nth_element()` operation rearranges the order of elements in a sequence so that elements that are less than or equal to the nth element are placed before the nth element. Elements in this group are sorted. Other elements are placed after the nth element and are not guaranteed to be sorted.

```
template<class RandomAccessIterator>
void nth_element(RandomAccessIterator first, RandomAccessIterator nth,
                    RandomAccessIterator last);
template<class RandomAccessIterator, class Compare>
void nth_element(RandomAccessIterator first, RandomAccessIterator nth,
                    RandomAccessIterator last, Compare comp);
```

Listing 7.14 shows an `nth_element()` operation.

LISTING 7.14. ORDERING A SEQUENCE USING THE `nth_element()` OPERATION

```cpp
#include <iostream>
#include <vector>
#include <functional>
#include <algorithm>
using namespace std;

//
// Unary function to output its argument to cout
//
template<class T>
class Print: public unary_function<T, void>
{
public:
    void operator()(T& arg1)
    {
        cout << arg1 << " ";
    }
};

//
// Compare function
//
bool ReverseCompare(int arg1, int arg2);

//
// Display all elements in a container
//
template<class Container>
void ShowElements(Container& c, char* text);

int main()
{
    typedef     vector<int>             VectorInt;
    typedef     VectorInt::iterator     Itor;

    // create an integer vector
    VectorInt   vInt1(7);
    Itor        first1 = vInt1.begin();
    Itor        last1  = vInt1.end();
    generate(first1, last1, rand);
    ShowElements(vInt1, "Random number sequence");

    // sort the sequence in descending order
    nth_element(first1, first1 + 1, last1, ReverseCompare);
    ShowElements(vInt1, "After nth_element()");

    return 0;
}
```

continues

LISTING 7.14. CONTINUED

```
//
// Compare function
//
bool ReverseCompare(int arg1, int arg2)
{
    return (arg1 > arg2);
}

//
// Display all elements in a container
//
template<class Container>
void ShowElements(Container& c, char* text)
{
    Print<Container::value_type>    DoPrint;

    cout << text << ":\n";
    for_each(c.begin(), c.end(), DoPrint);
    cout << "\n\n";
}
```

The following is the output from the code in Listing 7.14:

```
Random number sequence:
41 18467 6334 26500 19169 15724 11478

After nth_element():
26500 19169 18467 15724 11478 6334 41
```

Again, we use a reversed compare function to sort the elements in descending order. All elements that are larger than 18467 (elements 26500 and 19169) are placed in front of it and are sorted in descending order. Interestingly, elements smaller than 18467 also appear to be sorted. However, this behavior is implementation dependent.

Binary Search Operations

For all binary search operations, the sequences to be searched must be sorted before the search operations take place. The results of searching unsorted sequences are undefined.

The `lower_bound()` Operation

The `lower_bound()` operation searches a sorted sequence to find the first position in which it can insert a value without violating the sort order of the sequence.

```
template<class ForwardIterator, class T>
ForwardIterator lower_bound(ForwardIterator first, ForwardIterator last,
                            const T& value);
```

```
template<class ForwardIterator, class T, class Compare>
ForwardIterator lower_bound(ForwardIterator first, ForwardIterator last,
                            const T& value, Compare comp);
```

The operation returns the iterator `last` if it cannot find a valid insertion position.

The `upper_bound()` Operation

The `upper_bound()` operation searches a sorted sequence to find the last position from the beginning in which it can insert a value without violating the sort order of the sequence.

```
template<class ForwardIterator, class T>
ForwardIterator upper_bound(ForwardIterator first, ForwardIterator last,
                            const T& value);
```

```
template<class ForwardIterator, class T, class Compare>
ForwardIterator upper_bound(ForwardIterator first, ForwardIterator last,
                            const T& value, Compare comp);
```

Like the `lower_bound()` operation, the `upper_bound()` operation also returns the iterator `last` if it cannot find a valid insertion position.

The `equal_range()` Operation

The `equal_range()` operation finds a range in which a value can be inserted without violating the sort order of a sequence.

```
template<class ForwardIterator, class T>
pair<ForwardIterator, ForwardIterator>
equal_range(ForwardIterator first, ForwardIterator last, const T& value);
```

```
template<class ForwardIterator, class T, class Compare>
pair<ForwardIterator, ForwardIterator>
equal_range(ForwardIterator first, ForwardIterator last, const T& value,
            Compare comp);
```

This operation returns a pair of iterators pointing to the first and last positions in which the value can be inserted.

The `binary_search()` Operation

The `binary_search()` operation performs a binary search in a sorted sequence for a value.

```
template<class ForwardIterator, class T>
bool binary_search(ForwardIterator first, ForwardIterator last, const T&
➥value);
```

```
template<class ForwardIterator, class T, class Compare>
bool binary_search(ForwardIterator first, ForwardIterator last, const T&
value,
                        Compare comp);
```

This operation returns true if the value is found; it returns false if the value is not found.

The merge() Operation

The merge() operation merges two sorted sequences.

```
template<class InputIterator1, class InputIterator2, class OutputIterator>
OutputIterator merge(InputIterator1 first1, InputIterator1 last1,
                        InputIterator2 first2, InputIterator2 last2,
                        OutputIterator result);

template<class InputIterator1, class InputIterator2, class OutputIterator,
        class Compare>
OutputIterator merge(InputIterator1 first1, InputIterator1 last1,
                        InputIterator2 first2, InputIterator2 last2,
                        OutputIterator result, Compare comp);
```

If the input sequences contain equal elements, the element from the first sequence is placed in front. The operation returns the past-the-end iterator in the resulting sequence. The resulting sequence must not overlap with the input sequences. Otherwise, the result is undefined.

The inplace_merge() Operation

The inplace_merge() operation merges two consecutive sequences and puts the result back in the original sequence.

```
template<class BidirectionalIterator>
void inplace_merge(BidirectionalIterator first, BidirectionalIterator
middle,
                        BidirectionalIterator last);

template<class BidirectionalIterator, class Compare>
void inplace_merge(BidirectionalIterator first, BidirectionalIterator
middle,
                        BidirectionalIterator last, Compare comp);
```

This operation merges two sequences—[first, middle) and [middle, last)—and puts the result back in [first, last).

Listing 7.15 demonstrates several binary search operations.

LISTING 7.15. SEARCHING SEQUENCES USING BINARY SEARCH OPERATIONS

```cpp
#include <iostream>
#include <vector>
#include <functional>
#include <algorithm>
using namespace std;

//
// Unary function to output its argument to cout
//
template<class T>
class Print: public unary_function<T, void>
{
public:
    void operator()(T& arg1)
    {
        cout << arg1 << " ";
    }
};

//
// Display all elements in a container
//
template<class Container>
void ShowElements(Container& c, char* text);

int main()
{
    typedef     vector<int>             VectorInt;
    typedef     VectorInt::iterator     Itor;

    // create an integer vector
    VectorInt    vInt1(5);
    Itor         first1 = vInt1.begin();
    Itor         last1  = vInt1.end();
    vInt1[0] = 1;
    vInt1[1] = 2;
    vInt1[2] = 2;
    vInt1[3] = 4;
    vInt1[4] = 5;
    ShowElements(vInt1, "vInt1");

    // find first and last position to insert integer 2
    Itor lb = lower_bound(first1, last1, 2);
    Itor ub = upper_bound(first1, last1, 2);
    cout << "The first position to insert 2 is between " << *(lb - 1)
         << " and " << * lb << "\n";
    cout << "The last position to insert 2 is between " << *(ub - 1)
         << " and " << * ub << "\n\n";

    // find first and last position to insert integer 2 using equal_range
    pair<Itor, Itor> pi = equal_range(first1, last1, 2);
```

continues

LISTING 7.15. CONTINUED

```
    lb = pi.first;
    ub = pi.second;

    cout << "Results of equal_range:\n";
    cout << "The first position to insert 2 is between " << *(lb - 1)
        << " and " << * lb << "\n";
    cout << "The last position to insert 2 is between " << *(ub - 1)
        << " and " << * ub << "\n\n";

    // find integer 4 in vInt1
    if (binary_search(first1, last1, 4))      cout << "Found 4.\n\n";
    else                                      cout << "Can't find 4.\n\n";

    // reassign vInt1 elements
    vInt1[0] = 1;
    vInt1[1] = 4;
    vInt1[2] = 2;
    vInt1[3] = 2;
    vInt1[4] = 5;
    ShowElements(vInt1, "vInt1 reassigned");

    // inplace merge
    inplace_merge(first1, first1 + 2, last1);
    ShowElements(vInt1, "After inplace merge");

    // reassign vInt1 elements
    vInt1[0] = 1;
    vInt1[1] = 4;
    vInt1[2] = 2;
    vInt1[3] = 2;
    vInt1[4] = 5;
    ShowElements(vInt1, "vInt1 reassigned");

    // inplace merging two unsorted sequences
    inplace_merge(first1, first1 + 3, last1);
    ShowElements(vInt1, "After inplace merge on unsorted sequences");

    return 0;
}


//
// Display all elements in a container
//
template<class Container>
void ShowElements(Container& c, char* text)
{
    Print<Container::value_type>     DoPrint;

    cout << text << ":\n";
```

```
    for_each(c.begin(), c.end(), DoPrint);
    cout << "\n\n";
}
```

Here is the output from the program in Listing 7.15:

```
vInt1:
1 2 2 4 5

The first position to insert 2 is between 1 and 2
The last position to insert 2 is between 2 and 4

Results of equal_range:
The first position to insert 2 is between 1 and 2
The last position to insert 2 is between 2 and 4

Found 4.

vInt1 reassigned:
1 4 2 2 5

After inplace merge:
1 2 2 4 5

vInt1 reassigned:
1 4 2 2 5

After inplace merge on unsorted sequences:
1 4 2 2 5
```

The equal_range() operation finds both the first and the last places in which it can insert a value in one function call. This is the preferred operation to use when you need to find both places. The inplace_merge() operation requires that the two sequences be sorted before it is called. The second call to the operation shows that inplace_merge() has no effect on two unsorted sequences.

Set Operations

A *set* is a collection of objects. A *sequence* is a set in which the elements can be accessed by iterators. The Standard Library defines several set operations for sequences, as described in the following sections.

The `includes()` Operation

The includes() operation checks whether all elements in one sequence are also in other sequences.

```
template<class InputIterator1, class InputIterator2>
bool includes(InputIterator1 first1, InputIterator1 last1,
              InputIterator2 first2, InputIterator2 last2);
```

```
template<class InputIterator1, class InputIterator2, class Compare>
bool includes(InputIterator1 first1, InputIterator1 last1,
                  InputIterator2 first2, InputIterator2 last2,
                  Compare comp);
```

If every element of sequence [first2, last2) is also a member of sequence [first1, last1), the includes() operation returns true. Otherwise, the operation returns false.

The set_union() Operation

The set_union() operation combines two sorted sequences into a third sequence.

```
template<class InputIterator1, class InputIterator2, class OutputIterator>
OutputIterator set_union(InputIterator1 first1, InputIterator1 last1,
                             InputIterator2 first2, InputIterator2 last2,
                             OutputIterator result);

template<class InputIterator1, class InputIterator2,
         class OutputIterator, class Compare>
OutputIterator set_union(InputIterator1 first1, InputIterator1 last1,
                             InputIterator2 first2, InputIterator2 last2,
                             OutputIterator result, Compare comp);
```

The set_union() operation sorts the resulting sequence and returns the past-the-end iterator of the resulting sequence.

The set_intersection() Operation

The set_intersection() operation copies elements common in two sequences to a third sequence.

```
template<class InputIterator1, class InputIterator2, class OutputIterator>
OutputIterator set_intersection(InputIterator1 first1, InputIterator1
➥last1,
                                        InputIterator2 first2,
➥InputIterator2 last2,
                                        OutputIterator result);

template<class InputIterator1, class InputIterator2, class OutputIterator,
         class Compare>
OutputIterator set_intersection(InputIterator1 first1, InputIterator1
➥last1,
  InputIterator2 first2, InputIterator2 last2,
  OutputIterator result, Compare comp);
```

The set_intersection() operation sorts the resulting sequence and returns the past-the-end iterator of the resulting sequence.

The set_difference() Operation

The set_difference() operation copies elements in one sequence but not in another sequence to a third sequence.

```
template<class InputIterator1, class InputIterator2, class OutputIterator>
OutputIterator set_difference(InputIterator1 first1, InputIterator1 last1,
InputIterator2 first2, InputIterator2 last2,
OutputIterator result);

template<class InputIterator1, class InputIterator2, class OutputIterator,
         class Compare>
OutputIterator set_difference(InputIterator1 first1, InputIterator1 last1,
InputIterator2 first2, InputIterator2 last2,
OutputIterator result, Compare comp);
```

The set_difference() operation copies elements in [first1, last1) but not in
[first2, last2). The resulting sequence is a sorted sequence. The past-the-end iterator
of the resulting sequence is returned.

The set_symmetric_difference() Operation

The set_symmetric_difference() operation creates a new sequence containing elements that are not members of both of two input sequences.

```
template<class InputIterator1, class InputIterator2, class OutputIterator>
OutputIterator set_symmetric_difference(InputIterator1 first1,
➥InputIterator1 last1,
InputIterator2 first2, InputIterator2 last2,
OutputIterator result);

template<class InputIterator1, class InputIterator2, class OutputIterator,
         class Compare>
OutputIterator set_symmetric_difference(InputIterator1 first1,
➥InputIterator1 last1,
InputIterator2 first2, InputIterator2 last2,
OutputIterator result, Compare comp);
```

The set_difference() operation copies elements in [first1, last1) but not in
[first2, last2), and elements in [first2, last2) but not in [first1, last1). The
resulting sequence is a sorted sequence. The past-the-end iterator of the resulting
sequence is returned.

Listing 7.16 demonstrates Standard Library set operations.

LISTING 7.16. HANDLING SEQUENCES USING SET OPERATIONS

```
#include <iostream>
#include <vector>
#include <functional>
#include <algorithm>
using namespace std;
```

continues

LISTING 7.16. CONTINUED

```cpp
// unary function object printing its argument
template<class T>
class Print: public unary_function<T, void>
{
public:
    void operator()(T& arg1)
    {
        cout << arg1 << " ";
    }
};

int main()
{
    typedef    vector<int>              VectorInt;
    typedef    VectorInt::iterator    Itor;

    Print<int>                      DoPrint;
    int                             i = 0;

    // create first integer vector
    VectorInt    vInt1(10);
    Itor         first1 = vInt1.begin();
    Itor         last1  = vInt1.end();
    for (i = 0; i < 10; ++i)    vInt1[i] = 2 * i;

    // create second integer vector
    VectorInt    vInt2(8);
    Itor         first2 = vInt2.begin();
    Itor         last2  = vInt2.end();
    for (i = 0; i < 8; ++i)         vInt2[i] = 3 * i;

    // create third integer vector used to store set operations
    VectorInt    vInt3(20, -1);
    Itor         first3 = vInt3.begin();
    Itor         last3  = vInt3.end();

    // copy the union of vInt1 and vInt2 to vInt3
    set_union(first1, last1, first2, last2, first3);
    cout << "Union: elements in either vInt1 or vInt2:\n";
    for_each(first3, last3, DoPrint);
    cout << "\n\n";

    // randomly rearrange elements in vInt3
    random_shuffle(first3, last3);
    cout << "Random Shuffle: elements in vInt3 reordered:\n";
    for_each(first3, last3, DoPrint);
    cout << "\n\n";
```

```
    // sort vInt3
    sort(first3, last3);
    cout << "Sorted:\n";
    for_each(first3, last3, DoPrint);
    cout << "\n\n";

    // copy the intersection of vInt1 and vInt2 to vInt3
    fill(first3, last3, -1);
    set_intersection(first1, last1, first2, last2, first3);
    cout << "Intersection: elements in both vInt1 and vInt2\n";
    for_each(first3, last3, DoPrint);
    cout << "\n\n";

    // copy elements of vInt1 that are not in vInt2 to vInt3
    fill(first3, last3, -1);
    set_difference(first1, last1, first2, last2, first3);
    cout << "Difference: elements in vInt1 but not in vInt2\n";
    for_each(first3, last3, DoPrint);
    cout << "\n\n";

    // copy elements that are in vInt1 only or in vInt2 only to vInt3
    fill(first3, last3, -1);
    set_symmetric_difference(first1, last1, first2, last2, first3);
    cout << "Symmetric Difference: elements not in both vInt1 and
➥vInt2\n";
    for_each(first3, last3, DoPrint);
    cout << "\n\n";

    return 0;
}
```

The following is the output from the code in Listing 7.16:

```
Union: elements in either vInt1 or vInt2:
0 2 3 4 6 8 9 10 12 14 15 16 18 21 -1 -1 -1 -1 -1 -1

Random Shuffle: elements in vInt3 reordered:
6 -1 0 -1 15 18 12 16 -1 2 9 -1 10 -1 14 4 21 3 8 -1

Sorted:
-1 -1 -1 -1 -1 -1 0 2 3 4 6 8 9 10 12 14 15 16 18 21

Intersection: elements in both vInt1 and vInt2
0 6 12 18 -1 -1 -1 -1 -1 -1 -1 -1 -1 -1 -1 -1 -1 -1 -1 -1

Difference: elements in vInt1 but not in vInt2
2 4 8 10 14 16 -1 -1 -1 -1 -1 -1 -1 -1 -1 -1 -1 -1 -1 -1

Symmetric Difference: elements not in both vInt1 and vInt2
2 3 4 8 9 10 14 15 16 21 -1 -1 -1 -1 -1 -1 -1 -1 -1 -1
```

First, we create two integer vectors vInt1 and vInt2 and assign different values to their elements. Next, we create the third integer array that is large enough to store all the elements in vInt1 and vInt2. A set_union() operation is then performed to generate a union of vInt1 and vInt2. The result contains all elements in vInt1 and vInt2.

Heap Operations

A *heap* is a sequence in which the element with the largest value is always the first element in the sequence. Elements are pushed into and popped out of the heap only at the front of the sequence. The STL priority queue is usually implemented as a heap. The Standard Library provides two heap-to-sequence conversion operations and two heap element access operations.

The make_heap() Operation

The make_heap() operation converts a sequence to a heap.

```
template<class RandomAccessIterator>
void make_heap(RandomAccessIterator first, RandomAccessIterator last);

template<class RandomAccessIterator, class Compare>
void make_heap(RandomAccessIterator first, RandomAccessIterator last,
               Compare comp);
```

This operation converts the sequence [first, last) to the heap [first, last).

The sort_heap() Operation

The sort_heap() operation converts a heap to a sequence by sorting its elements.

```
template<class RandomAccessIterator>
void sort_heap(RandomAccessIterator first, RandomAccessIterator last);

template<class RandomAccessIterator, class Compare>
void sort_heap(RandomAccessIterator first, RandomAccessIterator last,
               Compare comp);
```

The resulting sequence is sorted.

The push_heap() Operation

The push_heap() operation adds a new element to a heap.

```
template<class RandomAccessIterator>
void push_heap(RandomAccessIterator first, RandomAccessIterator last);

template<class RandomAccessIterator, class Compare>
void push_heap(RandomAccessIterator first, RandomAccessIterator last,
               Compare comp);
```

The push_heap() operation takes a sequence [first, last). It assumes that the range [first, last - 1) is a heap and pushes the *(last - 1) element into the heap. After the operation, [first, last) becomes a heap.

The pop_heap() Operation

The pop_heap() operation removes the top element from a heap.

```
template<class RandomAccessIterator>
void pop_heap(RandomAccessIterator first, RandomAccessIterator last);

template<class RandomAccessIterator, class Compare>
void pop_heap(RandomAccessIterator first, RandomAccessIterator last,
              Compare comp);
```

The pop_heap() operation swaps the first and the last - 1 elements in the heap [first, last). The resulting sequence [first, last) is no longer a heap because the largest element is now pointed to by iterator last - 1. The pop_heap() operation then converts the sequence [first, last - 1) back to a heap. The formerly largest element can now be accessed using *(last - 1).

Listing 7.17 demonstrates heap operations.

LISTING 7.17. HEAP OPERATIONS

```
#include <iostream>
#include <vector>
#include <functional>
#include <algorithm>
using namespace std;

//
// Unary function to output its argument to cout
//
template<class T>
class Print: public unary_function<T, void>
{
public:
    void operator()(T& arg1)
    {
        cout << arg1 << " ";
    }
};

//
// Display all elements in a container
//
template<class Container>
```

continues

LISTING 7.17. CONTINUED

```cpp
void ShowElements(Container& c, char* text);

int main()
{
    typedef    vector<int>             VectorInt;
    typedef    VectorInt::iterator     Itor;

    // create an integer vector
    VectorInt    vInt1(5);
    Itor         first1 = vInt1.begin();
    Itor         last1  = vInt1.end();
    generate(first1, last1, rand);
    ShowElements(vInt1, "vInt1");

    // make vInt1 a heap
    make_heap(first1, last1);
    ShowElements(vInt1, "vInt1 is now a heap");

    // convert vInt1 to a sorted sequence
    first1 = vInt1.begin();
    last1  = vInt1.end();
    sort_heap(first1, last1);
    ShowElements(vInt1, "vInt1 is now a sorted sequence");

    // make vInt1 to a heap again so that we can test pop and push
➥operations
    first1 = vInt1.begin();
    last1  = vInt1.end();
    make_heap(first1, last1);
    ShowElements(vInt1, "vInt1 is now a heap again");

    // pop
    first1 = vInt1.begin();
    last1  = vInt1.end();
    pop_heap(first1, last1);
    cout << *(last1 - 1) << " popped, ";
    ShowElements(vInt1, "vInt1 is no longer a heap");

    // push
    first1 = vInt1.begin();
    last1  = vInt1.end();
    *(last1 - 1) = 32000;
    ShowElements(vInt1, "vInt1 is ready for a push");
    push_heap(first1, last1);
    ShowElements(vInt1, "New value pushed into vInt1");

    return 0;
}
```

```
//
// Display all elements in a container
//
template<class Container>
void ShowElements(Container& c, char* text)
{
    Print<Container::value_type>    DoPrint;

    cout << text << ":\n";
    for_each(c.begin(), c.end(), DoPrint);
    cout << "\n\n";
}
```

Here is the output from the code in Listing 7.17:

```
vInt1:
41 18467 6334 26500 19169

vInt1 is now a heap:
26500 19169 6334 18467 41

vInt1 is now a sorted sequence:
41 6334 18467 19169 26500

vInt1 is now a heap again:
26500 19169 18467 41 6334

26500 popped, vInt1 is no longer a heap:
19169 6334 18467 41 26500

vInt1 is ready for a push:
19169 6334 18467 41 32000

New value pushed into vInt1:
32000 19169 18467 41 6334
```

We convert a random sequence of numbers vInt1 to a heap using the make_heap() operation. We then convert the heap to a sorted sequence and back to a heap. The pop_heap() operation removes the first element that has the highest value from the heap and places it at the end of the sequence. Now the whole sequence [vInt1.begin(), vInt1.end()) is no longer a heap; however, the first four elements [vInt1.begin(), vInt1.end() - 1) still form a heap. When we push a large value into the heap, it becomes the new top of the heap. Note that because heap operations typically reorder the elements in a sequence, iterators previously obtained may become invalid after such operations. In this listing, therefore, we reassign the first1 and last1 iterators with the new begin() and end() values before we use them to specify a new sequence.

Minimum and Maximum Operations

The Standard Library provides functions that can be used to find the maximum or minimum value of objects.

The `min()` Operation

The `min()` operation returns the smaller of two values.

```
template<class T> const T& min(const T& a, const T& b);

template<class T, class Compare>
const T& min(const T& a, const T& b, Compare comp);
```

The `max()` Operation

The `max()` operation returns the larger of two values.

```
template<class T> const T& max(const T& a, const T& b);

template<class T, class Compare>
const T& max(const T& a, const T& b, Compare comp);
```

The `min_element()` Operation

The `min_element()` operation returns an iterator pointing to the smallest element in a sequence.

```
template<class ForwardIterator>
ForwardIterator min_element(ForwardIterator first, ForwardIterator last);

template<class ForwardIterator, class Compare>
ForwardIterator min_element(ForwardIterator first, ForwardIterator last,
                            Compare comp);
```

The `max_element()` Operation

The `max_element()` operation returns an iterator pointing to the largest element in a sequence.

```
template<class ForwardIterator>
ForwardIterator max_element(ForwardIterator first, ForwardIterator last);

template<class ForwardIterator, class Compare>
ForwardIterator max_element(ForwardIterator first, ForwardIterator last,
                            Compare comp);
```

The `lexicographical_compare()` Operation

The `lexicographical_compare()` operation compares two sequences in lexicographical order.

```
template<class InputIterator1, class InputIterator2>
bool lexicographical_compare(InputIterator1 first1, InputIterator1 last1,
                                  InputIterator2 first2, InputIterator2
↪last2);

template<class InputIterator1, class InputIterator2, class Compare>
bool lexicographical_compare(InputIterator1 first1, InputIterator1 last1,
                                  InputIterator2 first2, InputIterator2
↪last2,
                                  Compare comp);
```

This operation is better explained using the following pseudocode:

```
template<class InputIterator1, class InputIterator2>
bool lexicographical_compare(InputIterator1 first1, InputIterator1 last1,
                                  InputIterator2 first2, InputIterator2
↪last2)
{
    // traverse two sequences until one of them is exhausted
    while ((first1 != last1) && (first2 != last2))
    {
        // compare each pair of elements
        if (*first1 < *first2)    return true;
        if (*first1 > *first2)    return false;

        // *first1 == *first2, go to the next pair of elements
        ++first1;
        ++first2;
    }

    if ((first1 == last1) && (first2 != last2))
    {
        // the 1st sequence is shorter than the 2nd
        return true;
    }
    else
    {
        return false;
    }
}
```

Listing 7.18 demonstrates the `lexicographical_compare()` operation.

LISTING 7.18. COMPARING SEQUENCES USING THE `lexicographical_compare()` OPERATION

```
#include <iostream>
#include <string>
#include <algorithm>
using namespace std;
```

continues

LISTING 7.18. CONTINUED

```cpp
int main()
{
    string s1 = "abcd";
    string s2 = "abd";

    if (lexicographical_compare(s1.begin(), s1.end(), s2.begin(),
    s2.end()))
        cout << "[" << s1 << "] < [" << s2 << "]\n";
    else
        cout << "[" << s1 << "] >= [" << s2 << "]\n";

    s1 = "abcd";
    s2 = "abc";
    if (lexicographical_compare(s1.begin(), s1.end(), s2.begin(),
    s2.end()))
        cout << "[" << s1 << "] < [" << s2 << "]\n";
    else
        cout << "[" << s1 << "] >= [" << s2 << "]\n";

    s1 = "abcd";
    s2 = "abcd";
    if (lexicographical_compare(s1.begin(), s1.end(), s2.begin(),
    s2.end()))
        cout << "[" << s1 << "] < [" << s2 << "]\n";
    else
        cout << "[" << s1 << "] >= [" << s2 << "]\n";

    return 0;
}
```

The following output is generated by the program in Listing 7.18:

```
[abcd] < [abd]
[abcd] >= [abc]
[abcd] >= [abcd]
```

C++ standard strings are sequences. In Listing 7.18, we use the `lexicographical_compare()` function to compare two strings with different values.

Permutation Generators

A sequence of n elements can be ordered in n! = n * (n – 1) * (n – 2) * . . . * 2 * 1 ways. Each of these orderings is a *permutation* of the sequence. It is often useful to know the next or the previous permutation from the current ordering of the sequence. The Standard Library provides two permutation generators, which are described in the following sections.

The `next_permutation()` Operation

The `next_permutation()` operation generates the next permutation of a sequence.

```
template<class BidirectionalIterator>
bool next_permutation(BidirectionalIterator first, BidirectionalIterator
➥last);

template<class BidirectionalIterator, class Compare>
bool next_permutation(BidirectionalIterator first, BidirectionalIterator
➥last,
                            Compare comp);
```

If this operation finds the next permutation, it rearranges the sequence to the found permutation and returns `true`. Otherwise, it orders the sequence to the first permutation and returns `false`.

The `prev_permutation()` Operation

The `prev_permutation()` operation generates the previous permutation of a sequence.

```
template<class BidirectionalIterator>
bool prev_permutation(BidirectionalIterator first, BidirectionalIterator
➥last);

template<class BidirectionalIterator, class Compare>
bool prev_permutation(BidirectionalIterator first, BidirectionalIterator
➥last,
                            Compare comp);
```

If this operation finds the previous permutation, it rearranges the sequence to the found permutation and returns `true`. Otherwise, it orders the sequence to the last permutation and returns `false`.

Listing 7.19 demonstrates the use of the permutation operations.

LISTING 7.19. USING PERMUTATION OPERATIONS

```
#include <iostream>
#include <string>
#include <algorithm>
using namespace std;

int main()
{
    string s = "abdc";

    if (prev_permutation(s.begin(), s.end()))
        cout << "s = " << s << "\n";
```

continues

LISTING 7.19. CONTINUED

```
    else
        cout << "no previous permutation: s = " << s << "\n";

    if (prev_permutation(s.begin(), s.end()))
        cout << "s = " << s << "\n";
    else
        cout << "no previous permutation: s = " << s << "\n";

    if (next_permutation(s.begin(), s.end()))
        cout << "s = " << s << "\n";
    else
        cout << "no next permutation: s = " << s << "\n";

    if (next_permutation(s.begin(), s.end()))
        cout << "s = " << s << "\n";
    else
        cout << "no next permutation: s = " << s << "\n";

    return 0;
}
```

The following is the output generated by the code in Listing 7.19:

```
s = abcd
no previous permutation: s = dcba
no next permutation: s = abcd
s = abdc
```

The first `prev_permutation()` operation finds the previous permutation of sequence abdc. It happens to be the first permutation of a sequence of four letters a, b, c, and d. Because this is the first permutation of the sequence, there is no previous permutation. The next `prev_permutation()` operation rearranges the string to dcba, which is the last permutation of the sequence. This causes the first `next_permutation()` operation to fail to find its next permutation and rearranges the string to abcd, the first permutation of the sequence. The last `next_permutation()` operation finds the next permutation and reorders the string to the found permutation.

Standard Function Compositions

Function objects are often used by standard algorithms as an argument. For example, the standard algorithm `for_each()` takes a unary function object as its third argument:

```
for_each(Iterator first, Iterator last, FunctionObject f)
```

We might want to compare each element with a given value and count how many elements are greater than that value. The predicate `greater` seems to be a good candidate for the function object `f`. The only problem is that the `for_each()` algorithm needs a unary function, but the `greater` predicate is a binary function. What can we do?

We can write our own `for_each()` algorithm, or we can write our own unary `greater` predicate to compare the argument against a set value. Either approach requires us to reinvent the wheel. The Standard C++ Library provides a set of functions derived from standard functions with minor variations. They are the binder, adapter, and negater functions.

Binder Functions

A binder function can bind one of the arguments of a binary function to a constant and result in a unary function. The Standard Library provides two binder functions: `bind1st()` and `bind2nd()`. Let's look at how the `bind1st()` function is defined. The Standard Library defines a base class for the `bind1st()` function:

```
template<class BinaryOperation>
class binder1st :
public unary_function<BinaryOperation::second_argument_type,
                      BinaryOperation::result_type>
{
public:
    binder1st(const BinaryOperation & x,
              const BinaryOperation::first_argument_type& const_arg1)
    : op(x), value(const_arg1)     {}

    result_type operator()(const second_argument_type& arg2) const
    {
        return BinaryOperation(value, arg2);
    }

protected:
    BinaryOperation                              op;
    BinaryOperation::first_argument_type    value;
};
```

The `binder1st` class constructor takes two arguments: an operation class object and a constant value for the first argument. This arrangement effectively binds the new `binder1st` object to the operation class and the first argument. We can use this base class to create a binder function that compares an object to a value:

```
template<class BinaryOperation, class T>
binder1st<BinaryOperation>    bind1st(const BinaryOperation& op, const T&
➡arg1);
```

The overloaded operator `()` of the `binder1st` class can be used to perform a binary operation:

```
BinaryFunction<T>::result_type bind1st(T& arg2)
```

Listing 7.20 demonstrates the use of the `bind1st()` function to separate lowercase and uppercase characters in a string.

LISTING 7.20. USING THE `bind1st()` FUNCTION

```
#include <iostream>
#include <string>
#include <functional>
#include <algorithm>
using namespace std;

int main()
{
    string    s = "aBCdefGH";
    partition(s.begin(), s.end(), bind1st(greater<char>(), 'a'));
    cout << "s = " << s << "\n";

    return 0;
}
```

Here is the output from the code in Listing 7.20:

```
s = HBCGefda
```

We use the `bind1st()` function to bind the first argument of function `greater()` to the letter a. Because lowercase a is greater than all uppercase letters, the `bind1st(greater<char>(), 'a')` function returns `true` on letters in the string in upper-case. The `partition()` operation then moves all capital letters to the front and moves all lowercase letters to the back of the string.

The `bind2nd()` function is defined similarly to the `bind1st()` function.

Adapter Functions

Most standard algorithms use a normal function to perform certain operations on elements. However, most C++ programmers are used to defining member functions to manipulate objects. Assume that you define a list of pointers to window objects and use the `Show()` member function to display the windows:

```
class MyWindow
{
public:
    void Show();
};

list<MyWindow*> windowPtrList;
// add pointers to window objects to the list
// . . .
```

```
for_each(windowPtrList.begin(), windowPtrList.end(),MyWindow::Show);  //
►error!
```

The trouble is that the `for_each()` function expects the third argument to be `function` `f()`. `MyWindow::Show`, however, must be called through `WindowObject.Show()`. The Standard Library provides a set of member function adapters that facilitate the use of member functions in algorithms.

Member function adapter `mem_fun()` converts a member function with no arguments to a unary function with the `this` pointer. It is defined using the base class `mem_fun_t`:

```
template <class S, class T>
class mem_fun_t : public unary_function<T*, S> {
public:
    explicit mem_fun_t(S (T::*p)());
    S operator()(T* p);
};

template<class S, class T>
mem_fun_t<S, T> mem_fun(S (T::*f)())
{
    return mem_fun_t<S, T>(f);
}
```

Listing 7.21 shows the use of member function adapters to allow algorithms to call member functions.

LISTING 7.21. PASSING MEMBER FUNCTIONS TO ALGORITHMS USING MEMBER FUNCTION ADAPTERS

```
#include <iostream>
#include <list>
#include <functional>
#include <algorithm>
using namespace std;

typedef unsigned int    UINT;

class MyWindow
{
public:
    MyWindow(UINT newID = 0): mID(newID)    {}

    void Show()     const
    {
        cout << "Showing window " << mID << "\n";
    }
```

continues

LISTING 7.21. CONTINUED

```cpp
    //
    // MSVC++ 5 version
    //
    //     int Show()
    //     {
    //          cout << "Showing window " << mID << "\n";
    //          return 0;
    //     }

private:
    UINT mID;
};

int main()
{
    // create and add elements to a list of pointers to Window objects
    MyWindow*       pWin;
    list<MyWindow*>    winPtrList;

    for (UINT winID = 0; winID < 5; ++winID)
    {
        pWin = new MyWindow(winID);
        winPtrList.push_back(pWin);
    }
    pWin = 0;

    // show each window in the list
    for_each(winPtrList.begin(), winPtrList.end(),
➥mem_fun(&MyWindow::Show));

    return 0;
}
```

Here is the output from the code in Listing 7.21:

```
Showing window 0
Showing window 1
Showing window 2
Showing window 3
Showing window 4
```

A member function Show() of class MyWindow is defined to print the MyWindow object's ID. In the main() function, a list of five pointers to the MyWindow objects is created. The for_each() function is invoked to print the ID for every MyWindow object. The member function adapter mem_fun() is used to call the Show() member function. Because mem_fun() requires a member function pointer, we must pass the address of the Show() function.

> **NOTE**
>
> Because of a bug in Microsoft Visual C++ Version 5, you should use the second version of the Show() member function when compiling it using Visual C++ 5.

Pointer-to-Function Adapter Functions

A standard algorithm can use a function or a pointer to a function to manipulate elements in sequences. Listing 7.22 shows the use of a function and a pointer to a function by the for_each() algorithm.

LISTING 7.22. USING FUNCTIONS AND POINTERS TO FUNCTIONS IN ALGORITHMS

```
#include <iostream>
#include <list>
#include <functional>
#include <algorithm>
using namespace std;

typedef unsigned int    UINT;

class MyWindow
{
public:
    MyWindow(UINT newID = 0): mID(newID)    {}
    UINT GetID()    const    { return mID; }

private:
    UINT mID;
};

void ShowWindowUnary(const MyWindow& win);

int main()
{
    // create and add elements to a list of pointers to Window objects
    MyWindow*        pWin;
    list<MyWindow>   winList;
    UINT             winID;

    for (winID = 0; winID < 5; ++winID)
    {
        pWin = new MyWindow(winID);
        winList.push_back(*pWin);
    }
    pWin = 0;
```

continues

LISTING 7.22. CONTINUED

```
    // Show each window in the list - these are ok.
    cout << "ShowWindowUnary():\n";
    for_each(winList.begin(), winList.end(), ShowWindowUnary);
    cout << "\nPointer to ShowWindowUnary()\n";
    for_each(winList.begin(), winList.end(), &ShowWindowUnary);

    return 0;
}

void ShowWindowUnary(const MyWindow& win)
{
    cout << "Showing window " << win.GetID() << ".\n";
}
```

Here is the output generated by the code in Listing 7.22:

```
ShowWindowUnary():
Showing window 0.
Showing window 1.
Showing window 2.
Showing window 3.
Showing window 4.

Pointer to ShowWindowUnary():
Showing window 0.
Showing window 1.
Showing window 2.
Showing window 3.
Showing window 4.
```

We define a unary function to print the MyWindow object's mID member variable. This function is called by for_each() to print themID for each MyWindow object in winList. A pointer to this function can also be used by for_each() to perform the same operation, as demonstrated here.

Things are not quite the same for the binder functions. They cannot be used to bind a pointer to a function because they require a *copy* of the function. Consequently, the Standard Library provides two adapters to allow function pointers to be used. The first adapter is used for unary functions:

```
template <class Arg, class Result>
class pointer_to_unary_function : public unary_function<Arg, Result>
{
public:
    explicit pointer_to_unary_function(Result (* f)(Arg));
    Result operator()(Arg x) const;
};
```

```
template <class Arg, class Result>
pointer_to_unary_function<Arg, Result> ptr_fun(Result (* f)(Arg));
```

The second adapter is used for binary functions:

```
template <class Arg1, class Arg2, class Result>
class pointer_to_binary_function : public
binary_function<Arg1,Arg2,Result>
{
public:
    explicit pointer_to_binary_function(Result (* f)(Arg1, Arg2));
    Result operator()(Arg1 x, Arg2 y) const;
};

template <class Arg1, class Arg2, class Result>
pointer_to_binary_function<Arg1,Arg2,Result> ptr_fun(Result (* f)(Arg1,
➥Arg2));
```

We can then use a pointer to a function in the binder operations.

Negater Functions

In Listing 7.12, you used the ReverseCompare() function to sort a sequence in reverse order. This is a convenient but not very intuitive approach to sorting. In that example, we wanted to sort the elements in a not-less-than-or-equal-to order. The Standard Library provides two predicate negaters: one for the unary predicates and another for the binary predicates.

```
template <class Predicate>
class unary_negate : public unary_function<Predicate::argument_type,bool>
{
public:
    explicit unary_negate(const Predicate& pred);
    bool operator()(const argument_type& x) const;
};

template <class Predicate>
class binary_negate : public
binary_function<Predicate::first_argument_type,

Predicate::second_argument_type, bool>
{
public:
    explicit binary_negate(const Predicate& pred);
    bool operator()(const first_argument_type& x,
                    const second_argument_type& y) const;
};

template <class Predicate>
unary_negate<Predicate> not1(const Predicate& pred);
```

```
template <class Predicate>
binary_negate<Predicate> not2(const Predicate& pred);
```

In Listing 7.12, replace the sort(first1, last1, ReverseCompare) statement with sort(first1, last1, not2(less_equal<int>())), which does the same as the custom-made ReverseCompare() predicate.

Summary

The Standard Library provides a hierarchy of iterators that can be used to access sequences. A set of standard algorithms is defined in the Standard Library to perform common operations such as sorting and sequence traversal.

Compiler vendors often implement standard algorithms in the most efficient and reliable manner on a given operating system. The use of standard algorithms is generally preferred to handwritten functions that perform similar operations.

Avoiding Name Clashes by Using Namespaces

Name conflicts have been a source of aggravation to both C and C++ developers for years. Oddly enough, the C++ standards committee has only recently addressed this problem with the introduction of the *namespace* feature. In my opinion, the subject of name conflicts should have been addressed a long time ago.

Because the committee didn't address namespaces until recently, some vendors do not include support for namespaces in current releases of their compilers. Regardless, I recommend that you learn about namespaces now, even if your compiler does not include support for the namespace feature.

A name clash happens when a duplicate name with matching scope is found in two different translation units. The most common occurrence can be found in two different library packages. For example, a container class library will most certainly declare and implement a List class. It is not a surprise to find a List class also being used in a windowing library. Suppose that you want to maintain a list of windows for your application. Further assume that you are using the talents of the List class found in the container class library. So you declare an instance of List to hold your bevy of windows. To your dismay, you discover that the member functions you want to call are not available. What happened? Obviously—although it may not be immediately apparent—the compiler has matched your List declaration to the List container, but what you really wanted is the List found in the window library.

Namespaces are used to partition the global namespace and to eliminate, or at least reduce, name conflicts. Namespaces are similar to classes and structs. The syntax is very similar; items declared within the namespace are owned by the namespace. All items within a namespace have public visibility. Namespaces can be nested within other namespaces. Functions can be defined within the body of the namespace or defined outside of the body of the namespace. If a function is defined outside the body of the namespace, it must be qualified by the namespace's name.

This chapter discusses these items and more in greater detail. First, I want to cover some basic rules concerning name resolution, required unique names, and other precursors to namespaces.

Functions and Classes Are Resolved by Name

As it parses source code and builds a list of function and variable names, the compiler checks for name conflicts. Of course, the compiler cannot resolve all name conflicts; when the compiler cannot resolve conflicts, the linker comes into play. The compiler cannot check for name clashes across translation units; if it could, the compiler could (potentially) assume the responsibility of the linker. I am sure you have seen a variation of the following error message from your linker: `Identifier` `multiply` `defined` (`iden-tifier`, of course, being some named type). You see this linker message if you have defined the same name with the same scope in different translation units. You get a compiler error if you redefine a name within a single file having the same scope. The following example, when compiled and linked, will produce an error message by the linker:

```
// file first.cpp
int integerValue = 0 ;
int main( ) {
    int integerValue = 0 ;
    // . . .
    return 0 ;
} ;

// file second.cpp
int integerValue = 0 ;
// end of second.cpp
```

My linker announces the following diagnostic: in `second.obj`: *integerValue* already defined in `first.obj`. I suspect that your linker will give you a similar message. However, if these names are in a different scope, the compiler and linker will not complain. It is also possible to receive a warning from the compiler concerning *identifier hiding*. Oddly enough, my compiler, even at the maximum warning level, will not tell me about the hidden name in the previous example. A warning I enjoy giving to people is, "Don't trust your compiler!" Because I don't necessarily trust my compiler, I routinely use a lint program as a precursor to the compiler. If you do not own (or use) a lint program, I highly recommend that you go get one. A good lint program will warn you about many things, not just name conflicts.

In the previous example, the integer declared within `main()` does not conflict with the integer outside `main()`. I mentioned that my compiler, even at the maximum warning level, does not tell me about the potential conflict. I guess my compiler assumes that I have my own symbol table tucked away in my head! The reason the names do not clash is because they each have different scope. The `integerValue` defined within `main()` hides the `integerValue` defined outside `main()`. If you want to use the `integerValue` declared in the global namespace, you must prefix the scope resolution operator to the name. Consider this example, which assigns the value 10 to the `integerValue` outside `main()` and not to the `integerValue` declared within `main()`:

```
// file first.cpp
int integerValue = 0 ;
int main( )
{
    int integerValue = 0 ;
```

```
        ::integerValue = 10 ; //assign to global "integerValue"
        // . . .
        return 0 ;
} ;

// file second.cpp
int integerValue = 0 ;
// end of second.cpp
```

The problem with the two global integers defined outside of any functions is that they have the same name and visibility.

I use the term *visibility* to designate the scope of a defined object, whether it is a variable, a class, or a function. For example, a variable declared and defined outside any function has *file*, or *global*, scope. The visibility of this variable is from the point of its definition through the end of the file. A variable having a *block*, or *local*, scope is found within a block structure. The most common examples are variables defined within functions. The following example shows the scope of variables:

```
int globalScopeInt  = 5 ;
void f( )
{
    int localScopeInt = 10 ;
}
int main( )
{
    int localScopeInt = 15 ;
    {
        int anotherLocal = 20 ;
        int localScopeInt = 30 ;
    }
    return 0 ;
}
```

The first int definition, globalScopeInt, is visible within the functions f() and main(). The next definition is found within the function f() and is named localScopeInt. This variable has local scope, meaning that it is visible only within the block defining it. The main() function cannot access f()'s localScopeInt. When the function returns, localScopeInt goes out of scope. The third definition, also named localScopeInt, is found in the main() function. This variable has block scope. Note that main()'s localScopeInt does not conflict with f()'s localScopeInt. The next two definitions, anotherLocal and localScopeInt, both have block scope. As soon as we reach the closing brace, these two variables lose their visibility. Notice that this localScopeInt is hiding the localScopeInt defined just before the opening brace (the second localScopeInt defined in the program). When the program moves past the closing brace, the second localScopeInt defined resumes visibility. Any changes made to the localScopeInt defined within the braces does not affect the contents of the outer localScopeInt.

Names can have *internal* and *external linkage*. These two terms refer to the use or availability of a name across multiple translation units or within a single translation unit. Any name having *internal* linkage can only be referred to within the translation unit in which it is defined. For example, a variable defined to have internal linkage can be shared by functions within the same translation unit. Names having *external* linkage are available to other translation units. The following example demonstrates internal and external linkage:

```cpp
// file: first.cpp
int externalInt = 5 ;
const int j = 10 ;
int main()
{
    return 0 ;
}
```

```cpp
// file: second.cpp
extern int externalInt ;
int anExternalInt = 10 ;
const int j = 10 ;
```

The `externalInt` variable defined in `first.cpp` has external linkage. Although it is defined in `first.cpp`, `second.cpp` can also access it. The two `j`s found in both files are const, which, by default, have internal linkage. You can override the `const` default by providing an explicit declaration, as shown here:

```cpp
// file: first.cpp
extern const int j = 10 ;
```

```cpp
// file: second.cpp
extern const int j ;
#include <iostream>
int main()
{
    std::cout << "j is " << j << std::endl ;
    return 0 ;
}
```

When built, this example displays the following:

```
j is 10
```

The standards committee deprecates the following type of usage:

```cpp
static int staticInt = 10 ;
int main()
{
    //…
}
```

8

There is not much I can say about this example except that using `static` to limit the scope of an external variable to a specific translation unit is deprecated. If you are a Java programmer, you are very familiar with this terminology. *Deprecation* means that at some future (and unknown) date, the named feature will cease to exist. You should use namespaces instead of `static`.

I know; you want to be able to hide a variable from other translation units but the current translation unit requires full visibility. My recommendation is the subject of this chapter: namespaces. Simply get rid of the `static` keyword and wrap the definition within a designated namespace. This is the intent of the standards committee: Deprecate this use of `static` and replace it with a namespace. You should continue to use the `static` keyword within functions and class declarations as usual.

> **NOTE**
>
> Do not apply the `static` keyword to a variable defined at file scope. The standards committee has deprecated this type of usage. Use namespaces instead.

Creating a Namespace

If you have ever created a struct or class, creating a namespace will be a piece of cake. The syntax for a namespace declaration is similar to the syntax for a struct or class declaration: First, apply the keyword `namespace` followed by an optional namespace name, and then an opening curly brace. The namespace is concluded with a closing brace and no terminating semicolon. This is one difference between a namespace declaration and a class declaration: A class declaration concludes with a semicolon. The following code snippet is an example of a namespace declaration:

```
namespace Window {
    void move( int x, int y) ;
}
```

The name `Window` uniquely identifies the namespace. You can have many occurrences of a named namespace. These multiple occurrences can occur within a single file or across multiple translation units. The C++ standard library namespace, `std`, is a prime example of this feature. This makes sense because the standard library is a logical grouping of functionality. I discuss the namespace `std` later in this chapter.

The main concept behind namespaces is to group related items into a specified (named) area. The following is a brief example of a namespace that spans multiple header files:

```
// header1.h
```

```
namespace Window {
    void move( int x, int y) ;
}

// header2.h
namespace Window {
    void resize( int x, int y ) ;
}
```

Declaring and Defining Types

You can declare and define types and functions within namespaces. Of course, this is a design and maintenance issue. Good design dictates that you should separate interface from implementation. You should follow this principle not just with classes but also with namespaces. The following example demonstrates a cluttered and poorly defined namespace:

```
namespace Window {
    // . . . other declarations and variable definitions.
    void move( int x, int y) ; // declarations
    void resize( int x, int y ) ;
    // . . . other declarations and variable definitions.

    void move( int x, int y )
    {
        if( x < MAX_SCREEN_X  && x > 0 )
            if( y < MAX_SCREEN_Y  && y > 0 )
                platform.move( x, y ) ; // specific routine
    }

    void resize( int x, int y )
    {
        if( x < MAX_SIZE_X  && x > 0 )
            if( y < MAX_SIZE_Y  && y > 0 )
                platform.resize( x, y ) ; // specific routine
    }
    // . . . definitions continue
}
```

You can see how quickly the namespace becomes cluttered! The previous example is approximately 20 lines in length; imagine if this namespace were four times longer. The next section describes how to define functions outside a namespace; doing so helps reduce clutter in a namespace.

Defining Functions Outside a Namespace

You should define namespace functions outside the namespace body. Doing so illustrates a clear separation of the declaration of the function and its definition—and also keeps the

8

AVOIDING NAME
CLASHES

namespace body uncluttered. Separating the function definition from the namespace also allows you to put the namespace and its embodied declarations within a header file; the definitions can be placed into an implementation file. A terse example follows:

```
// file header.h
namespace Window {
    void move( int x, int y) ;
    // other declarations …
}

// file impl.cpp
void Window::move( int x, int y )
{
    // code to move the window
}
```

Adding New Members

New members can be added to a namespace only within its body. You cannot define new members using qualifier syntax. The most you can expect from this style of definition is a complaint from your compiler. The following example demonstrates this error:

```
namespace Window {
    // lots of declarations
}
//…some code
int Window::newIntegerInNamespace ; // sorry, can't do this
```

The preceding line of code is illegal. Your (conforming) compiler will issue a diagnostic reflecting the error. To correct the error—or avoid it altogether—simply move the declaration within the namespace body.

I want to point out another difference between a namespace and a class. If you define a member function within the declaration of a class, that function is implicitly inline. The compiler, of course, will have a clear conscience if it doesn't inline the function. Remember that a compiler does not have to inline a function, even if you apply the `inline` keyword. The namespace rule for inlining is different; if you define a function inside a namespace, that function will not be inlined. You may think that you can get around this limitation by applying the `inline` keyword. Unfortunately, this approach does not work.

You cannot apply an access specifier within a namespace. This is another area where namespace and class declarations diverge. All members encased within a namespace are public. The following code does not compile:

```
namespace Window {
    private:
        void move( int x, int y ) ;
}
```

Nesting Namespaces

A namespace can be nested within another namespace. The reason they can be nested is because the definition of a namespace is also declaration. As with any other namespace, you must qualify a name using the enclosing namespace. If you have nested namespaces, you must qualify each namespace in turn. For example, the following shows a named namespace nested within another named namespace:

```
namespace Window {
    namespace Pane {
        void size( int x, int y ) ;
    }
}
```

To access the function `size()` outside of `Window`, you must qualify the function with both enclosing namespace names. The following demonstrates the qualification:

```
int main( )
{
    Window::Pane::size( 10, 20 ) ;
    return 0 ;
}
```

Now that you know how to create a namespace, let's move on and explore namespace usage.

Using a Namespace

Let's take a look at an example of using a namespace and the associated use of the scope resolution operator. The syntax should be familiar to you, especially if you've been using classes. I will first declare all types and functions for use within the namespace `Window`. After I define everything required, I then define any member functions declared. These member functions are defined outside of the namespace; the names are explicitly identified using the scope resolution operator. With all that said, consider the example in Listing 8.1.

LISTING 8.1. USING A NAMESPACE

```
#include <iostream>
namespace Window {
    const int MAX_X = 30 ;
    const int MAX_Y = 40 ;
    class Pane {
        public:
```

continues

8

AVOIDING NAME
CLASHES

LISTING 8.1. CONTINUED

```
                Pane() ;
                ~Pane() ;
                void size( int x, int y ) ;
                void move( int x, int y ) ;
                void show( ) ;
            private:
                static int cnt ;
                int x ;
                int y ;
        } ;
}
int Window::Pane::cnt = 0 ;
Window::Pane::Pane() : x(0), y(0) { }
Window::Pane::~Pane() { }
void Window::Pane::size( int x, int y )
{
    if( x < Window::MAX_X  &&  x > 0 )
        Pane::x = x ;
    if( y < Window::MAX_Y  &&  y > 0 )
        Pane::y = y ;
}
void Window::Pane::move( int x, int y )
{
    if( x < Window::MAX_X  &&  x > 0 )
        Pane::x = x ;
    if( y < Window::MAX_Y  &&  y > 0 )
        Pane::y = y ;
}
void Window::Pane::show( )
{
    std::cout << "x " << Pane::x ;
    std::cout << " y " << Pane::y << std::endl ;
}

int main( )
{
    Window::Pane pane ;

    pane.move( 20, 20 ) ;
    pane.show( ) ;

    return 0 ;
}
```

If you build and run this application, the following output appears on your screen:

```
x 20 y 20
```

Take note that class `Pane` is nested inside the namespace `Window`. This is the reason you have to qualify the name `Pane` with the `Window::` qualifier.

The static variable `cnt`, which is declared in `Pane`, is defined as usual. Within the function `Pane::size()`, notice that `MAX_X` and `MAX_Y` are fully qualified. This is because `Pane` is in scope; otherwise, the compiler would issue an error diagnostic. This also holds true for the function `Pane::move()`.

Also interesting is the qualification of `Pane::x` and `Pane::y` inside both function definitions. Why is this? Well, if the function `Pane::move()` were written like this, you would have a problem:

```
void Window::Pane::move( int x, int y )
{
    if( x < Window::MAX_X  &&  x > 0 )
        x = x ;
    if( y < Window::MAX_Y  &&  y > 0 )
        y = y ;
    Platform::move( x, y ) ;
}
```

Can you spot the issue? You probably won't get much of an answer from your compiler; some won't issue any kind of diagnostic message at all. Even the trusty old lint program will let this one slide. I take that back, lint does tell us that we have a problem, but it's not at the two assignment statements:

```
x = x ;
y = y ;
```

The source of the problem is the function's arguments. Arguments x and y hide the private x and y instance variables declared within class `Pane`. Effectively, the statements assign both x and y to itself:

```
x = x ;
y = y ;
```

Go ahead, try it out yourself. Modify the `Window::Pane::move()` so that it is the same as the previous example. Simply remove the text `Pane::` from the two assignment statements. Rebuild the application and run it. Your output should be as follows:

```
x 10 y 10
```

This output reflects the fact that assignment statements are simply assigning to themselves:

```
x = x ;
y = y ;
```

The instance variables within `Pane` are not affected.

Let's rewrite the application and enhance it to support the `using` directive. The `using` directive pulls all the names from a named namespace and applies them to the current scope. This helps to cut down on excessive typing. The example is shown in Listing 8.2, rewritten with the `using` directive.

LISTING 8.2. THE `using` DIRECTIVE

```cpp
#include <iostream>

namespace Window {
    const int MAX_X = 40 ;
    const int MAX_Y = 80 ;
    class Pane {
        public:
            Pane() ;
            ~Pane() ;
            void size( int x, int y ) ;
            void move( int x, int y ) ;
            void show( ) ;
        private:
            static int cnt ;
            int x ;
            int y ;
    } ;
}
using namespace Window ;

int Pane::cnt = 0 ;
Pane::Pane() : x(10), y(10) {   }
Pane::~Pane() {   }
void Pane::size( int x, int y )
{
    if( x < MAX_X   &&   x > 0 )
        Pane::x = x ;
    if( y < MAX_Y   &&   y > 0 )
        Pane::y = y ;
}
void Pane::move( int x, int y )
{
    if( x < MAX_X   &&   x > 0 )
        x = x ;
    if( y < MAX_Y   &&   y > 0 )
        y = y ;
}
void Pane::show( )
{
    std::cout << "x " << Pane::x << " y " << Pane::y << std::endl ;
}
```

```
int main( )
{
    Pane pane ;

    pane.move( 20, 20 ) ;
    pane.show( ) ;

    return 0 ;
}
```

The output from this program is shown here:

```
x 10 y 10
```

The using directive appears after the namespace declaration:

```
using namespace Window ;
```

This statement brings all the names found in the namespace Window into the current scope. The application operates as it did before and there is less typing in this newer version. The using directive and the using declaration are discussed in the next section.

The using Keyword

The using keyword is used for both the using directive and the using declaration. The syntax of the using keyword determines whether the context is a directive or a declaration.

The using Directive

The using directive effectively exposes all names declared in a namespace to be in the current scope. You can refer to the names without qualifying them with their respective namespace names. The following example shows the using directive:

```
namespace Window {
    int value1 = 20 ;
    int value2 = 40 ;
}
. . .
Window::value1 = 10 ;

using namespace Window ;
value2 = 30 ;
```

The scope of the using directive begins at its declaration and continues on to the end of the current scope. Notice that value1 must be qualified in order to reference it. The variable value2 does not require the qualification because the directive introduces all names in a namespace into the current scope.

The using directive can be used at any level of scope. This allows you to use the directive within block scope; when that block goes out of scope, so do all the names within the namespace. The following sample shows this behavior:

```
namespace Window {
    int value1 = 20 ;
    int value2 = 40 ;
}
//. . .
void f()
{
    {
        using namespace Window ;
        value2 = 30 ;
    }
    value2 = 20 ; //error!
}
```

The last line of code in f(), value2 = 30 ; is an error because value2 is not defined. The name is accessible in the previous block because the directive pulls the name into that block. Once that block goes out of scope, so do the names in namespace Window.

Variable names declared within a local scope hide any namespace names introduced in that scope. This behavior is similar to how a local variable hides a global variable. Even if you introduce a namespace after a local variable, that local variable will hide the namespace name. The following example shows this:

```
namespace Window {
    int value1 = 20 ;
    int value2 = 40 ;
}
//. . .
void f()
{
    int value2 = 10 ;
    using namespace Window ;
    std::cout << value2 << std::endl ;
}
```

The output of this function is 10, not 40. This output confirms the fact that the value2 in namespace Window is hidden by the value2 in f(). If you need to use a name within a namespace, you must qualify the name with the namespace name.

An ambiguity can arise using a name that is both globally defined and defined within a namespace. The ambiguity surfaces only if the name is used, not just when a namespace is introduced. This is demonstrated with the following code fragment:

```
namespace Window {
    int value1 = 20 ;
```

```
}
//. . .
using namespace Window ;
int value1 = 10 ;
void f( )
{
    value1 = 10 ;
}
```

The ambiguity occurs within function `f()`. The directive effectively brings `Window::value1` into the global namespace; because there is a `value1` already globally defined, the use of `value1` in `f()` is an error. Note that if the line of code in `f()` were removed, there would not be an error.

The using Declaration

The `using` declaration is similar to the `using` directive, except that the declaration provides a finer level of control. More specifically, the `using` declaration is used to declare a specific name (from a namespace) to be in the current scope. You can then refer to the specified object by its name only. The following example demonstrates the use of the `using` declaration:

```
namespace Window {
    int value1 = 20 ;
    int value2 = 40 ;
    int value3 = 60 ;
}
//. . .
using Window::value2 ;  //bring value2 into current scope
Window::value1 = 10 ;   //value1 must be qualified
value2 = 30 ;
Window::value3 = 10 ;   //value3 must be qualified
```

The `using` declaration adds the specified name to the current scope. The declaration does not affect the other names within the namespace. In the previous example, `value2` is referenced without qualification, but `value1` and `value3` require qualification. The `using` declaration provides more control over namespace names that you bring into scope. This is in contrast with the directive which brings all names in a namespace into scope.

Once a name is brought into a scope, it is visible until the end of that scope. This behavior is just like any other declaration. A `using` declaration may be used in the global namespace or within any local scope.

It is an error to introduce a name into a local scope where a namespace name has been declared. The reverse is also true. The following example shows this:

```
namespace Window {
    int value1 = 20 ;
```

```
      int value2 = 40 ;
}
//. . .
void f()
{
   int value2 = 10 ;
   using Window::value2 ; // multiple declaration
   std::cout << value2 << std::endl ;
}
```

The second line in function f() will produce a compiler error because the name value2 is already defined. The same error occurs if the using declaration is introduced before the definition of the local value2.

Any name introduced at local scope with a using declaration hides any name outside that scope. The following code snippet demonstrates this behavior:

```
namespace Window {
   int value1 = 20 ;
   int value2 = 40 ;
}
int value2 = 10 ;
//. . .
void f()
{
   using Window::value2 ;
   std::cout << value2 << std::endl ;
}
```

The using declaration in f() hides the value2 defined in the global namespace.

As mentioned before, a using declaration gives you finer control over the names introduced from a namespace. A using directive brings all names from a namespace into the current scope. It is preferable to use a declaration over a directive because a directive effectively defeats the purpose of the namespace mechanism. A declaration is more definitive because you are explicitly identifying the names you want to introduce into a scope. A using declaration will not pollute the global namespace, as is the case with a using directive (unless, of course, you declare all names found in the namespace). Name hiding, global namespace pollution, and ambiguity is reduced to a more manageable level by using the using declaration.

The Namespace Alias

A namespace *alias* is designed to provide another name for a named namespace. An alias provides a shorthand term for you to use to refer to a namespace. This is especially true if a namespace name is very long; creating an alias can help cut down on lengthy, repetitive typing. Let's look at an example:

```
namespace the_software_company {
    int value ;
    // . . .
}
the_software_company::value = 10 ;
. . .
namespace TSC = the_software_company ;
TSC::value = 20 ;
```

A drawback, of course, is that your alias may collide with an existing name. If this is the case, the compiler will catch the conflict and you can resolve it by renaming the alias.

The Unnamed Namespace

An unnamed namespace is simply that, a namespace that does not have a name. A common use of unnamed spaces is to shield global data from potential name clashes between translation units. Every translation unit has its own, unique unnamed namespace. All names defined within the unnamed namespace (within each translation unit) can be referred to without explicit qualification. The following is an example of two unnamed namespaces found in two separate files:

```
// file: one.cpp
namespace {
    int value ;
    char p( char *p ) ;
    //. . .
}

// file: two.cpp
namespace {
    int value ;
    char p( char *p ) ;
    //. . .
}
int main( )
{
    char c = p( ptr ) ;
}
```

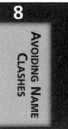

Each of the names, value and function p(), is distinct to its respective file. To refer to an (unnamed namespace) name within a translation unit, simply use the name without qualification. This usage is demonstrated in the previous example with the call to function p(). This use implies a using directive for objects referred to from an unnamed namespace. Because of this, you cannot access members of an unnamed namespace in another translation unit. The behavior of an unnamed namespace is the same as a static object having external linkage. Consider this example:

```
static int value = 10 ;
```

Remember that this use of the `static` keyword is deprecated by the standards committee. Namespaces now exist to replace code as previously shown. Another way to think of unnamed namespaces is that they are global variables with internal linkage.

The Standard Namespace `std`

The best example of namespaces is found in the C++ Standard Library. The standard library is completely encased within the namespace named `std`. All functions, classes, objects, and templates are declared within the namespace `std`.

You will, no doubt, see code such as the following:

```
#include <iostream>
using namespace std ;
```

Remember that the `using` directive pulls everything in from the named namespace. It is bad form to employ the `using` directive when using the standard library. Why? Because doing so defeats the purpose of using a namespace; the global namespace will be polluted with all the names found in the header. Keep in mind that all header files use the namespace feature, so if you include multiple standard header files, and specify the `using` directive, then everything declared in the headers will be in the global namespace. Please note that most of the examples in this book violate this rule; this action is not an intent to advocate violating the rule, but is used for brevity of the examples. You should use the `using` declaration instead, as in the following example:

```
#include <iostream>
using std::cin ;
using std::cout ;
using std::endl ;
int main( )
{
    int value = 0 ;
    cout << "So, how many eggs did you say you wanted?" << endl ;
    cin >> value ;
    cout << value << " eggs, sunny-side up!" << endl ;
    return( 0 ) ;
}
```

The following shows a sample run of the program:

```
So, how many eggs did you say you wanted?
4
4 eggs, sunny-side up!
```

As an alternative, you could fully qualify the names that you use, as in the following code sample:

```
#include <iostream>
int main( )
{
    int value = 0 ;
    std::cout << "How many eggs did you want?" << std::endl ;
    std::cin >> value ;
    std::cout << value << " eggs, sunny-side up!" << std::endl ;
    return( 0 ) ;
}
```

Sample output from this program is shown here:

```
How many eggs did you want?
4
4 eggs, sunny-side up!
```

This might be appropriate for shorter programs, but can become quite cumbersome for any significant amount of code. Imagine having to prefix `std::` for every name you use that is found in the standard library!

Summary

Global name clashes have been a problem for many years. This is no surprise because there is only one global namespace. The namespace feature is a welcome addition to the C++ standard.

Creating a namespace is a simple exercise. It is very similar to a class declaration. There are a couple of differences to note. First, a semicolon does not follow a namespace's closing brace. Second, a namespace is open, whereas a class is closed. This means that you can continue to define the namespace in other files or in separate sections of a single file.

Anything that can be declared can be inserted into a namespace. If you are designing classes for a reusable library, you should be using the namespace feature. Functions declared within a namespace should be defined outside of that namespace's body. This promotes a separation of interface from implementation and also keeps the namespace from becoming cluttered.

Namespaces can be nested. A namespace is a declaration; this fact allows you to nest namespaces. Don't forget that you must fully qualify names that are nested.

The `using` directive is used to expose all names in a namespace into the current scope. This effectively pollutes the global namespace with all names found in the named namespace. It is generally bad practice to use the `using` directive, especially with respect to the standard library. Use `using` declarations instead.

8

AVOIDING NAME CLASHES

The `using` declaration is used to expose a specific namespace name into the current scope. This allows you to refer to the object by its name only.

A namespace alias is similar in nature to a `typedef`. A namespace alias allows you to create another name for a named namespace. This can be quite useful if you are using a namespace with a long name.

Every file can contain an unnamed namespace. An unnamed namespace, as its name implies, is a namespace without a name. An unnamed namespace allows you to use the names within the namespace without qualification. It keeps the namespace names local to the translation unit. Unnamed namespaces are the same as declaring a global variable with the `static` keyword.

The C++ Standard Library is enclosed in a namespace named `std`. Avoid using the `using` directive when using the standard library; instead, use the `using` declaration.

Manipulating Object Types at Runtime

Runtime Type Information, often referred to as *RTTI*, is a special mechanism to get the runtime identification of types and expressions. Although dynamic binding is the key to manipulating object types at runtime, it is advantageous to know the exact type of an object for which you only have a pointer or reference. Often, this information allows you to perform a special-case operation more efficiently and can also prevent a base-class interface from becoming clumsy. A program can determine at runtime which of the several known derived types a base-class reference or pointer refers to. RTTI solves many special programming problems that are easier to solve if the exact type of a generic pointer is known. The RTTI mechanism consists of three elements:

- A `typeid()` operator to identify the exact type of an object type given its pointer or reference.

- A `type_info` class to find out additional type information of an object type given its pointer or reference.

- A `dynamic_cast()` operator to typecast a base-class pointer (reference) to its derived-class pointer (reference).

The `typeid()` Operator

The `typeid()` operator is a built-in C++ operator. You can use it to obtain an object's information at runtime in two ways:

- If a `typeid()` operand is a dereferenced pointer or a reference to a polymorphic type, `typeid()` returns the dynamic type of the actual object pointed or referred to. If the operand is a pointer or a nonpolymorphic type, `typeid()` returns an object that represents the static type. When `typeid()` fails to identify the type of its operand, it throws a `bad_typeid` exception. This exception is thrown when `typeid()` cannot dereference a pointer.

- The `typeid()` operator can find out whether two objects are of the same type. A call to `typeid()` returns a reference to a `const type_info`. The returned object represents additional type information of the `typeid()` operand. The returned object is used in the type comparison.

The `<typeinfo.h>` header file contains the declarations and prototypes for the following runtime-type information classes:

- `type_info`
- `bad_typeid`

The `type_info` Class

The `type_info` class provides runtime-type information about an object. Its exact definition is implementation dependent, but its declaration looks like this:

```
class type_info
{
private:
  // assigning type_info is not supported.  made private.
  type_info& operator= (const type_info&);
  type_info (const type_info&);
protected:
  type_info (const char *n): _name (n) { }

  const char *_name;
public:
  // destructor
  virtual ~type_info ();
bool operator== (const type_info& arg) const;
  bool operator!= (const type_info& arg) const;
const char* name () const
    { return _name; }
bool before (const type_info& arg) const;
};
```

The Constructor for the `type_info` Class

The `type_info` class does not provide public constructors. Hence, you cannot directly instantiate `type_info` objects in a program. `type_info` references are generated by the `typeid()` operator. For example, given an expression `expr`, the following call generates `const type_info&` for `expr`:

```
typeid(expr)
```

Because the copy constructor and assignment operator for `type_info` are private to the class, objects of this type cannot be copied.

The operator `typeid()` works like the `sizeof()` operator—it can either take an expression or a type itself. For example, given a type `T` and an object `t` of type `T`, the following applications of `typeid()` are valid:

```
typeid(T);
```

```
typeid(t);
```

The Comparison Operators

The following member operator functions provide comparisons of `type_info` references:

```
bool operator== (const type_info& arg) const;
bool operator!= (const type_info& arg) const;
```

To understand how `typeid()` and the class `type_info` are used, let's develop an example. Consider an example of the typical GUI hierarchy classes in which a class `Window` serves as the base class of the entire GUI hierarchy. Assume that `DialogBox` is a derived class that provides a function `repaintControls()`. The `repaintControls()` function is a special service that is not provided by the base class. Hence, given a `Window` pointer at runtime, it is necessary to find out whether the pointer actually points to a `DialogBox` object. We can do this by applying the `typeid()` operator to a dereferenced `Window` pointer to determine the type of the object to which the `Window` pointer is pointing. Listing 9.1 shows the code for this example.

LISTING 9.1. USING THE COMPARISON OPERATOR OF THE CLASS TYPE_INFO

```
#include <iostream.h>
#include <typeinfo.h>

class Window //polymorphic class type.
{
public:
    virtual void show() //to make Window polymorphic
    {/*...*/}
    //...
};
class DialogBox:public Window
{
public:
    virtual void show()
    {/*...*/}
    virtual void repaintControls()
    {
        //…
    }
};

void paint(Window* pw)
{
    if (typeid(*pw)==typeid(DialogBox))
    {
        cout<<"DialogBox"<<endl;
        DialogBox* pd=(DialogBox*)pw;
        pd->repaintControls();
    }
    else
    cout<<"Non-Dialog Object Type"<<endl;
}
```

```
int main()
{
    paint(new Window);
    paint(new DialogBox);
    return 0;
}
```

The program produces the following output:

```
Non-Dialog Object Type
DialogBox
```

The resultant pointer of the expression `new Window` does not point to a `DialogBox`, so the following comparison fails, and the program does not call a function unique to `DialogBox`:

```
if ( typeid(*pw)==typeid(DialogBox) )
{
    //...
}
```

Ideally, virtual functions are better choices for hierarchical types; the use of `typeid()` to replace virtual functions is certainly not an effective mechanism. This point is discussed later in this chapter.

Note that the program in Listing 9.1 uses this downcasting expression in the function `paint()`:

```
DialogBox* pd=(DialogBox*)pw;
```

Such downcasting expressions are not considered good practice in C++. C++ provides a better way to perform downcasting, as discussed later in this chapter in "The `dynamic_cast()` Operator" section.

The `name()` Member Function

The member function `name()` returns a string that identifies the type name of the operand to `typeid`. The output of `typeid().name()` is implementation dependent.

Listing 9.2 demonstrates the use of the `name()` function.

LISTING 9.2. THE NAME() FUNCTION

```
#include <typeinfo.h>
#include <iostream.h>

class Window //polymorphic class type
```

continues

LISTING 9.2. CONTINUED

```cpp
{
public:
virtual void show() {};
//...
};

class Button : public Window
{/*...*/};

int f()
{
Button b;
Button* pb;
pb=&b;

if (typeid(*pb)==typeid(Button))
cout<<"Name is " <<typeid(*pb).name()<<endl;

if (typeid(*pb)!=typeid(Window))
cout<<typeid(*pb).name()<<" is not same as "<<typeid(Window).name()<<endl;

typedef int (*PF)();

PF pf=f;

cout<<"Type of PF="<<typeid(PF).name()<<endl;
cout<<"Type of pf="<<typeid(pf).name()<<endl;

int v;
int& rv=v;

cout<<"Type of v="<<typeid(v).name()<<endl;
cout<<"Type of rv="<<typeid(rv).name()<<endl;

cout<<"Type of result of typeid()="<<
typeid(typeid(rv)).name()<<endl;

return 0;
}
int main()
{
    f();
}
```

When I ran this program on Microsoft Visual C++ 5, it produced the following output:

```
Name is class Button
class Button is not same as class Window
Type of PF=int (__cdecl*)(void)
```

```
Type of pf=int (__cdecl*)(void)
Type of v=int
Type of rv=int
Type of result of typeid()=class type_info
```

Apart from showing the use of `name()`, this program also shows the use of the comparison operators to compare the types of two objects (`*pb` and `Button`). Here is another way the comparison could have been made:

```
if (!strcmp(typeid(*pb).name(),"class Button"))
//...
```

However, this approach may not work on all compilers because the output of `typeid().name()` is implementation dependent. When this example was compiled on a GNU C++ compiler, it produced the following output:

```
Name is 6Button
6Button is not same as 6Window
Type of PF=PFv_i
Type of pf=PFv_i
Type of v=i
Type of rv=i
Type of result of typeid()=19__builtin_type_info
```

As mentioned earlier, `typeid()` provides runtime type information only if the `typeid()` operand is a *dereferenced pointer* to a polymorphic type. Here is an example:

```
#include <iostream.h>
#include <typeinfo.h>

class Window
{
public:
virtual void show() //to make base polymorphic
{
    return;
}
};

class DialogBox:public Window
{
public:
};

Window* f()
{
    cout<<"in f()"<<endl;
    return (new DialogBox);
}

int main()
```

```
{
    cout<<typeid(f()).name()<<endl;
    cout<<typeid(*f()).name()<<endl;
    return 0;
}
```

This example produces the following output in Visual C++ 5:

```
class Window *
in f()
class DialogBox
```

Notice the output produced by this statement:

```
cout<<typeid(f()).name()<<endl;
```

This statement produces the static type information about the pointer that is returned by f() because the output of f() is not dereferenced here. As a result, the function f() does not run.

Now notice the output from this statement:

```
cout<<typeid(*f()).name()<<endl;
```

This statement produces the dynamic type information about the returned pointer f() because of dereferencing; it also runs the function f(). The function f() *must* run, or the dynamic type of the returned value from f() cannot be determined.

The before() Member Function

The member function before() is used to compare the *collation order* (not to be confused with the declaration order or the hierarchical order) of types. The output of the function is implementation dependent. Listing 9.3 uses the before() function.

LISTING 9.3. THE BEFORE() MEMBER FUNCTION

```
#include <iostream.h>
#include <typeinfo.h>
class Window //polymorphic class type
{
public:
virtual void show(){};
//...
};
class DialogBox:public Window
{
public:
virtual void show(){};
//...
};
```

```
template <class T,class U>
void f(T t,U u)
{
cout<<typeid(t).name()<<" before "<<
typeid(u).name()<<" : "<<
typeid(t).before(typeid(u))<<endl;
return;
}

void g(const Window& w1,const Window& w2)
{
cout<<typeid(w1).name()<<" before "<<
typeid(w2).name()<<" : "<<
typeid(w1).before(typeid(w2))<<endl;
return;
}

int main()
{
int i;
double d;
char* pc="C++";
f(d,i); //performed at compile-time
f(pc[0],pc); //performed at compile-time
Window* pw=new Window;
Window* pd=new DialogBox;
g(*pw,*pd); //performed at run-time
return 0;
}
```

This example produced the following output in Visual C++ 5:

```
double before int : 1
char before char * : 1
Window before DialogBox : 0
```

Although the identifier i is declared before the identifier d, and the class Window appears before the class DialogBox in the class hierarchy, the output of before() is different because this is how the implementation of Visual C++ 5 has defined the collation order of types. The before() function may not be very useful in day-to-day programming or the development of banking applications. However, it *can* be used as a comparison mechanism to define a map or hash table of types.

The typeid() Operator in Constructors and Destructors

You can invoke the typeid() operator during the construction or destruction of an object. If the operand of typeid() refers to the object under construction or destruction,

typeid() always yields the `type_info` that represents the class of the constructor or destructor. Consider this example:

```cpp
#include <iostream.h>
#include <typeinfo.h>

class Window
{
public:
Window()
{
cout<<typeid(*this).name()<<endl; //always yields Window
}
virtual void f()
{
cout<<typeid(*this).name()<<endl; //yields Window or
                                  //DialogBox
}
};

class DialogBox : public Window
{
public:
DialogBox(){}
};

int main()
{
DialogBox d;
d.f();
}
```

This code produces the following output in Visual C++ 5:

```
class Window
class DialogBox
```

Here, the function `f()` yields the dynamic type of the `this` pointer, whereas the constructor `Window()` yields the static type of the `this` pointer.

Misuses of `typeid()`

Although the `typeid()` operator is a useful feature, you should use it only when necessary. You should use compile-time–type checking when runtime-type checking is not really necessary because compile-time–type checking is more efficient. For example, when you are not dealing with polymorphic types, the application of `typeid()` is absolutely not required. Also, just because the language provides this feature, don't start overusing this feature to solve design problems related to virtual functions.

Listing 9.4 shows an example of one misuse of `typeid()`. The example shows how to *implement* virtual functions using `typeid()`; then we'll discuss why this is not a good design.

LISTING 9.4. MISUSING THE TYPEID() OPERATOR

```
#include <iostream.h>
#include <typeinfo.h>

class Window
{
public:
Window(){};
virtual ~Window(){};

void show(){}; //non-virtual
//...
};

class DialogBox:public Window
{
public:
DialogBox(){};
~DialogBox(){};

void show(){};
//...
};

void f(Window& w)
{
typedef DialogBox& RDIALOG;
if (typeid(w)==typeid(Window))
w.show();
else
if (typeid(w)==typeid(DialogBox))
RDIALOG(w).show();
}

int main()
{
Window* pw=new Window;
Window* pd=new DialogBox;

f(*pw); //invokes Window::show()
f(*pd); //invokes DialogBox::show()

delete pw;
delete pd;

return 0;
}
```

Listing 9.4 makes the function show() a virtual function through the use of typeid().
The global function f() takes a reference to the base type Window. At runtime, the reference w can refer to either a Window object or a DialogBox object. Within the function f(),
the actual type of w is *explicitly* determined using the typeid() operator and then the
correct function show() is invoked. Although this code works, it is against the very basic
objective of object-oriented programming: that a message can be dispatched to whatever
instance happens to be pointed at by a reference (or pointer). In true object-oriented programming, you do not have to resolve the type of an instance that is referred to by a reference (or a pointer). Another problem with this approach is that, as you add new classes
in the Window hierarchy, the function f() starts growing—it not only introduces many
maintenance problems, it also makes the program very difficult to understand.

Dynamic Typecasting of Objects

Nearly all safe type conversions are implicit in C++, and no explicit cast has to be written. However, you sometimes have to convert a value from one type to another; you may
have to do this when the compiler will not do it automatically because you are doing
something potentially dangerous or nonportable. Type conversions that you specify are
referred to as *casts* or *typecasts*. One example of an unsafe type conversion is the typecasting of a base object's pointer to a derived pointer. Such a cast is unsafe and unpredictable. Using such a pointer to invoke derived class methods produces catastrophic
results at runtime if the base pointer is actually not pointing to a derived object.
Therefore, C++ has a requirement for a mechanism that can perform runtime-type conversions between objects.

The dynamic_cast() Operator

C++ provides a special operator, dynamic_cast(), which is intended to remove some of
the problems and dangers inherent in typecasting between objects in a class hierarchy.
This operator navigates in a class hierarchy at runtime and can be safely used when other
kinds of typecasting are not appropriate. The dynamic_cast() operator provides a way to
determine at runtime whether a base-class reference (or pointer) refers to an object of a
specified derived class. It can be applied only when the base class is polymorphic (that
is, the base class must contain at least one virtual function).

The dynamic_cast() operator uses the following syntax:

```
dynamic_cast <Type>(Object)
```

The Type argument is the type being cast to; the Object argument is the object being cast
from.

Type must be a pointer or a reference to a defined class type. The argument Object must be an expression that resolves to a pointer or reference. If successful, dynamic_cast() converts Object to the desired type. If a pointer cast fails, the returned pointer is valued 0. If a reference cast fails, the bad_cast exception is thrown. Because it can throw an exception, the dynamic_cast() operator is much safer than the traditional cast; when a normal cast fails, it gives no indication of a failure—until, of course, you run your program and it manifests many faults.

The use of the operator dynamic_cast() is also called a *type-safe downcast.*

The conversion from a derived class pointer or reference to a base-class pointer or reference is resolved at compile time and results in a pointer or reference to the subobject of the base class. Such a conversion is called an *upcast.*

Listing 9.5 shows an example of applications that use dynamic_cast() to perform a downcast. The listing also shows a cross-hierarchical typecast using dynamic_cast().

LISTING 9.5. A TYPE-SAFE DOWNCAST USING DYNAMIC_CAST()

```
#include <typeinfo.h>
#include <iostream.h>

class Control //polymorphic class type.
{
public:
virtual void show() {};
//...
};

class Picture
{/*...*/};

class BitMap:public Control, public Picture
{/*...*/};

int f()
{
try
{
Control* pc=new BitMap;

//attempt downcasting
BitMap& rb=dynamic_cast<BitMap&>(*pc);
cout<< "The resulting reference's type:"<<typeid(rb).name()<<endl;

//attempt across-hierarchy casting
Picture& rp=dynamic_cast<Picture&>(*pc);
```

continues

9

LISTING 9.5. CONTINUED

```
cout<< "The resulting pointer's type:"<<typeid(rp).name()<<endl;
}

catch (const bad_cast&)
{
cout<<"dynamic_cast() failed"<<endl;
return 1;
}
return 0;
}

int main()
{
    f();
}
```

This program produces the following output in Visual C++ 5:

```
The resulting reference's type:class BitMap
The resulting pointer's type:class Picture
```

Here, pc pointer does, in fact, point to an object of type BitMap, and so the conversion from *pc to BitMap& is successful. The resultant reference rb refers to a complete object of type BitMap. Similarly, the conversion from *pc to Picture& is safe because Picture is a base class of BitMap. The resultant reference rp refers to a *subobject* of type Picture.

Using `dynamic_cast()`

With the dynamic_cast() operator, a program can determine at runtime which of the several known derived types a base-class reference or pointer refers to. This feature is very often used to make some runtime decisions during program execution. This feature can also be used to implement virtual functions in a hierarchy. For example, in a Window hierarchy, it is quite possible that a derived DialogBox object has the unique requirement of repainting its controls. Such a requirement is not shared by all derived Window objects. Therefore, it seems to be a good idea to avoid the virtual function repaintControls() in the base Window class. Instead, by applying dynamic_cast(), a Window pointer can be cast to a DialogBox pointer, and the function repaintControls() can be invoked. If the object is not a DialogBox or of a class derived from DialogBox, the cast returns a 0 value, and the program can decide not to call the function repaintControls().

Listing 9.6 shows an example of how the dynamic_cast() operator can determine at runtime which of the several known derived types a base-class reference or pointer refers to.

LISTING 9.6. USING DYNAMIC_CAST() TO DETERMINE THE ACTUAL TYPE OF A BASE-CLASS POINTER

```
#include <iostream.h>
#include <typeinfo.h>

class Window //polymorphic class type.
{
public:
virtual void show()
{/*...*/}
//...
};

class DialogBox:public Window
{
public:
virtual void repaintControls()
{
cout<<typeid(*this).name()<<endl;
}
};

class PrintDialog:public DialogBox
{/*...*/};

void f(Window* pw)
{
DialogBox* pd=dynamic_cast<DialogBox*>(pw);

if (pd)
pd->repaintControls();
else
cout<<"unwanted object type"<<endl;
}

int main()
{
    f(new Window);
    f(new DialogBox);
    f(new PrintDialog);

    return 0;
}
```

This program produces the following output:

```
unwanted object type
DialogBox
PrintDialog
```

In this example, the function `f()` is invoked three times. In the first invocation, the pointer `pw` points to an object of type `Window`. In this case, because `pw` does not actually point to a `DialogBox` or a class derived from `DialogBox`, `dynamic_cast()` fails and returns `0`. In the second and the third invocations of `f()`, however, `pw` actually points to a `DialogBox` and a `PrintDialog` (respectively). In these cases, `dynamic_cast()` succeeds, and the program invokes the virtual function `repaintControls()`.

Using `dynamic_cast()` with Virtual Base Classes

An object of a virtual base class cannot be converted into its derived class object—if you try to do this, you get a compile-time error because the compiler does not have all the necessary information to perform the conversion. The `dynamic_cast()` operator, however, solves this problem because it performs the conversion at runtime. Consider this example:

```
class Control //polymorphic class type.
{
virtual void show();
//...
};
class BitMap:public virtual Control
{/*...*/};
int main()
{
Control* pc=new BitMap;
BitMap* pb1=(BitMap*)pc; //error
BitMap* pb2=dynamic_cast<BitMap*>(pc); //ok
//...
}
```

In this example, `dynamic_cast()` is applied on the `Control` pointer `pc` to typecast it to the `BitMap` pointer. Of course, this works only if an unambiguous conversion exists from `Control` to `BitMap`.

The following statement fails to compile because `Control` is a virtual base class of the class `BitMap`:

```
BitMap* pb1=(BitMap*)pc; //error
```

Using `dynamic_cast()` in Constructors and Destructors

The `dynamic_cast()` operator can be used during construction or destruction. If the operand of the `dynamic_cast()` is the object under construction or destruction, `dynamic_cast()` cannot perform downcasting. Listing 9.7 shows an example of using `dynamic_cast()` in a constructor.

LISTING 9.7. USING DYNAMIC_CAST() IN A CONSTRUCTOR

```cpp
#include <iostream.h>
#include <typeinfo.h>

class base
{
public:
    base();
    virtual void f();
};

class derived : public base
{
public:
    derived(){}
};

base::base()
{
    try
    {
        dynamic_cast<derived&>(*this); //fails
    }
    catch(const bad_cast&)
    {
        cout<<"bad_cast in base::base()"<<endl;
    }
}

void base::f()
{
    try
    {
        dynamic_cast<derived&>(*this);
        cout<<"successful dynamic_cast in base::f()"<<endl;
    }
    catch(const bad_cast&)
    {
        cout<<"bad_cast in base::f()"<<endl;
    }
}

int main()
{
    derived d;
    d.f();
}
```

This program produces the following output:

```
bad_cast in base::base()
successful dynamic_cast in base::f()
```

During the construction of the object d in main(), the base subobject is first constructed using the default constructor base::base(). Therefore, during the construction of base, the information about the derived object is not available within base::base() at runtime. As a result, the call dynamic_cast() fails in the constructor. On the other hand, within the function base::f(), the dynamic_cast() call succeeds because the derived object d is completely constructed at that point.

The typeid() Versus the dynamic_cast Operator

The dynamic_cast() and typeid() operators are quite similar and are used in many similar situations. Together, they provide runtime object manipulation. Still, they have a few differences:

- The dynamic_cast() operator does not work with nonclass types; typeid() does work with nonclass types.

- To use the dynamic_cast() operator, the specified class must be polymorphic— that is, it must have at least one virtual member function. With the typeid() operator, the operand does not have to be a polymorphic type.

- The typeid() operator can only tell you the type of an object. The dynamic_cast() operator can tell you that an object is of a specified class or of a class derived from the specified class.

Other Cast Operators

The following sections describe three typecast operators that make no runtime check and are not restricted to base and derived classes in the same polymorphic class hierarchy. Although the focus of this chapter is the runtime manipulation of objects, the following discussion is important if you are to have a complete view of typecasting operators in C++.

The static_cast() Operator

The static_cast() operator is used for user-defined, standard, or implicit type conversions. Unlike dynamic_cast(), the static_cast() operator is used in the context of the compile-time type of an object. Its syntax is similar to that of dynamic_cast:

```
static_cast<Type>(Object);
```

In this expression, both `Type` and `Object` must be fully known at compile time. If a type can be converted to another type by some conversion method already provided by the language, making such a conversion by using `static_cast()` achieves exactly the same thing.

Here is a self-explanatory example:

```
void f()
{
    char ch;
    int i=8;
    float f=8.16;
    double d;
    ch=static_cast<char>(i); //int to char
    d=static_cast<double>(f); /float to double
    i=static_cast<unsigned char>(ch); //char to unsigned char
    return;
}
```

Here is another example that uses classes instead of C++ built-in types:

```
class Base1
{/*...*/};
class Base2
{/*...*/};
class DerivedClass:public Base1, public Base2
{/*...*/};
int h()
{
    Base1* pb1=new DerivedClass;
    DerivedClass* pd=static_cast<DerivedClass*>(pb1);
    if (pd)
    {
        cout <<"The resulting pointer's type:["<<
        typeid(pd).name()<<"]"endl;
    }
    return 0;
}
```

The preceding example produces this output:

```
The resulting pointer's type:[DerivedClass *]
```

Please note these four important points about the previous example:

- Because the `pb1` pointer actually points to an object of type `DerivedClass`, the cast works correctly.

- Because the base class `Base1` is not a virtual base class for `DerivedClass`, the operator `static_cast()` is successfully applied.

9

MANIPULATING
OBJECT TYPES AT
RUNTIME

- Because the base class `Base1` is not a polymorphic base class, the operator `static_cast()` can be safely applied.

- Unambiguous conversion exists from `Base1` to `DerivedClass`.

The `reinterpret_cast()` Operator

The `reinterpret_cast()` operator provides an alternative to nonportable and potentially unsafe uses of the old-style casts. The operator provides a conversion between pointers to other pointer types and numbers to pointers and *vice versa*. Here is its syntax:

```
reinterpret_cast<Type>(Object);
```

In this expression, `Type` can be a pointer, reference, arithmetic type, pointer to function, or pointer to member. The operator `reinterpret_cast()` works if an implicit conversion from `Object` to `Type` exists; otherwise, it generates a compile-time error. The operator does not change the scattered-bit pattern at the machine level. It may stretch out or truncate the size of the pattern, and of course, the meaning will change. The result of `reinterpret_cast()` is unpredictable, and it is often implementation dependent. For example, using `reinterpret_cast()`, a pointer can be explicitly converted to any integral type large enough to hold it. The mapping function is implementation defined. You should know what you are doing when you use `reinterpret_cast()`—just as you should when you use old-style casts.

The following example explains how to use the `reinterpret_cast()` operator:

```
#include <iostream.h>

void func(void* pv)
{
    //cast back from pointer type to integral type
    int value3=reinterpret_cast<int>(pv);        //works well
    cout<<"Value of value3:"<<value3<<endl;
    //...
}
int main()
{
    //cast from an integral type to pointer type

    int value1=8;
    double value2=13.169;

    func(reinterpret_cast<void*>(value1));
    func(reinterpret_cast<void*>(&value2));
}
```

When compiled using Visual C++ 5, this program produces the following results:

```
Value of value3:8
Value of value3:1245044
```

In the previous example, to use the converted value (`value1`), you must first convert it back to the original type (`int`) in the function `func()`. The second line of the output shows the unpredictable result as a result of invoking `reinterpret_cast()`.

When to Use the `dynamic_cast()`, `static_cast()`, or `reinterpret_cast()` Operator

When casting between polymorphic classes of the same hierarchy, always use the `dynamic_cast()` operator.

In other cases, you must use `static_cast()` or `reinterpret_cast()`. As long as the compiler does not give any error, use `static_cast()`; otherwise, it may be necessary to apply `reinterpret_cast()` to change the bit interpretation. Do not overuse `reinterpret_cast()` and `static_cast()`—use them only when you really need them. Remember: Simply because these operations are supported by your C++ compiler does not mean that their applications will always produce safe and predictable results.

The `const_cast()` Operator

The three cast operators discussed in the previous sections maintain and respect the const-ness of the object being converted to. In other words, these operators are not intended for casting away the const-ness of an object. The `const_cast()` operator is used to add or remove the const (and volatile) modifier from a type. Here is the syntax of the `const_cast()` operator:

```
const_cast<Type>(Object);
```

In this expression, `Type` and `Object` must be of the same type except for their const and volatile modifiers. The cast is resolved at compile time. The result is of type `Type`.

A pointer (or reference) to const can be converted to a non-const pointer (or reference) using `const_cast()`. If the operation is successful, the resulting pointer refers to a non-const object that is identical to the operand in all other respects. The `const_cast()` operator performs similar typecasts on the volatile modifier: It casts a pointer (or reference) to a volatile object into a non-volatile object without otherwise changing the type of the object. Listing 9.8 shows an example of this.

LISTING 9.8. CASTING AWAY THE CONST-NESS OF AN OBJECT USING CONST_CAST()

```
#include <iostream.h>
#include <typeinfo.h>

class myClass
{ public:
myClass(int v):_val(v),_count(0){};
~myClass()
{
cout<<"_val="<<_val<<endl;
cout<<"_count="<<_count<<endl;
}
void f() const;
private:
int _val,_count;
};
void myClass::f() const
{
//_count++; //error: hence commented
const_cast<myClass*>(this)->_count++; //ok
}
int main()
{
myClass m(8);
m.f();
m.f();
m.f();
return 0;
}
```

This code produces the following output:

```
_val=8
_count=3
```

Remember that when a member function is declared as const, the compiler flags as an error any attempt to change data in the parent object from within that function. Hence, within the member function f(), you cannot directly modify the member count. In the example, within this function, the operator const_cast() was applied on the const object this to cast it to a non-const object of the same type (myType*). It allowed the const function f() to modify the data member _count[*].

New Versus Old Typecasting

Certainly, the new typecast operators—dynamic_cast(), static_cast(), reinterpret_cast(), and const_cast()—need more text to write and read, but this was

---

[*] Such a thing is also possible using the mutable keyword with _count.

intentional. You must replace the old-style C++ typecasts with the new operators. Recall that C++ provides two types of old-style typecasts:

```
(Type)expression; //C style of type-cast
Type(expression); //functional notation type-cast
```

Although C++ still supports (and will continue to support) the old-style casts, you are encouraged to use typecast operators in your new programs. It is easy to make a mistake in an old-style cast—such as accidentally casting away const, or casting to an unrelated pointer type instead of within a hierarchy. Furthermore, an old-style cast may originally work but may become faulty (but still compile without error) when types are modified. The compiler won't help you find these errors. And old-style typecasts are painful to review and locate in a program. Here is an example to show why new-style casts are better and safer than the old-style casts:

```
class A
{};

class B
{
public:
    virtual void f(){}
};

class C : private B
{};

int main()
{
    A* pa=new A;

    B* pb1=(B*)pa; //no compile-time error
    B* pb2=static_cast<B*>(pa); //compile-time error

    C* pc=new C;

    B* pb3=(B*)pc; //no compile-time error

    B& pb4=dynamic_cast<B&>(*pc); //compile-time error
}
```

In this example, the following statement will successfully compile, even though it has a typecast from class A to an unrelated class B:

```
B* pb1=(B*)pa;    //no compile-time error
```

Such a typecast can be really unsafe at runtime. Such a mistake is also not easy to spot when you read the code.

Similarly, this line does not fail even though the program is trying to gain access to the private base B of the class C:

```
B* pb3=(B*)pc;     //no compile-time error
```

As you can see, such wrong casts are caught at compile time when you apply the new-style typecast operators.

Summary

The implicit application of upcasting a derived pointer to a base class is one of the most-used features of C++. However, you may sometimes find yourself in a situation in which you feel that you could have written an effective program if (at runtime) you knew the exact type of the object pointed to by the base pointer. RTTI provides this information. RTTI has proved to be a very favorable feature for many programmers. In fact, most of the commercial libraries have implemented some form of virtual function-based RTTI. Although RTTI is a big utility, it can be easily misused by both novice and expert programmers. Replacing virtual functions with either the typeid() or dynamic_cast() operator is one of the most general and fashionable misuses of RTTI. Like most features in C++, RTTI does not have any mechanism to safeguard itself from misuse, and if you want to determinedly misuse it, you can.

Tuning Application Performance

IN THIS CHAPTER

There is a difference of opinion among developers concerning application tuning. Some believe that tuning is not necessary given the power of today's machines. This group also believes that the compiler should be performing all obvious optimizations. The rest of us believe in designing for performance. When we implement a design, we choose optimal algorithms and use the performance features of the language because we can't predict the configuration of all our potential users and because the compiler can't always know when it's appropriate to optimize.

This chapter discusses inline functions, implementation code in header files, virtual functions and virtual base classes, runtime type information, and temporary objects. The chapter especially focuses on the runtime cost associated with each of these elements.

Inline Functions Outside Class Definitions

The `inline` keyword suggests that the compiler should expand a function body whenever it encounters a call to that function. This expansion reduces the overhead of a function call because there is no call to a function. Notice that I say "suggests"; it may not be feasible or practical for the compiler to inline a function. I discuss some of the reasons why a compiler might not inline a function later in this chapter.

Accepted style dictates that you should provide inline member function definitions outside the class declaration. Doing so keeps the class declaration uncluttered and easier to read. It is not necessary to apply the `inline` keyword to the member function's declaration; however, be sure to apply the keyword to the member function's definition. The following code snippet demonstrates the style:

```
class Object {
    public:
        inline void f( ) ; // not in the class declaration!
} ;
```

This example brings up a point concerning the placement of inline member function definitions. Where do you put them? Well, a compiler can inline a function only if it has seen its definition. The most logical place to put the definition is within the header file that contains the class definition. I put inline function definitions in (separate) inline header files. They are not actually header files *per se*; they are really implementation files given a `.cpp`, `.icc`, or `.i` extension. You can use any extension you want; just be sure that you use a standard extension name. These inline header files are then included at the end of the header file containing the class declaration. This is good style; following this practice separates interface from implementation. Doing so also eases maintenance. If you choose not to use inline header files, put the inline member functions after the class declaration. Again, this approach provides a clean separation of the class declaration from its implementation. A simple example follows:

```
// in file: Object.h
class Object {
    public:
        void f( ) ;
} ;
...
#include "object.i"

// in file: Object.i
inline void Object::f( )
{
    ....
}
```

To expand on this example, I also use macros to turn inlining on and off. In my header file, I insert the following:

```
// in file: Object.h
class Object {
    public:
        void f( ) ;
} ;
...
#ifdef DO_INLINE
#include "object.i"
#endif
```

Then all I have to do is throw a `-d DO_INLINE` switch to my compiler to get the features of the inline functions. Of course, the drawback is that I have to recompile all the code that needs the inline member functions. Unfortunately, there is no way around a recompile. If you build your application with inlining enabled and later decide to remove inlining (or vice versa), you have to recompile.

Developers have told me that inlining is just a fancy method of macro substitution. This is incorrect because an inline function follows the same rules concerning scope and type checking that noninline functions follow. Be aware that inline functions have internal linkage wherever the function call occurs.

There are some disadvantages to inlining. First of all, inlining may increase the size of an application. If the compiler decides to inline a function, the function body is expanded wherever the function is called. If the function is called 200 times, there are 200 occurrences of the function's body scattered throughout the application. This may actually cause your program to run *slower* than if you had not inlined the function.

Another drawback concerns application maintenance. Whenever the body of a function is modified, any translation units that call the function must be recompiled.

How do you decide whether a function should be inlined? Here are some general rules of thumb:

- When the function body is small.
- When the function is called numerous times.
- When the performance cost of the statements within the function's body is minimal.

You might argue the second bulleted point; I can empathize with you. In some instances, a compiler will inline a function that has a large body of code. If this function is called many times, your program may become rather bloated. In this scenario, the rule of thumb does not apply. So why did I include this bulleted point? As explained later in this chapter, it is possible that the total amount of inline code will be less than the amount of code for a function call. If you are unsure whether an inline function contributes to code bloat, see the following Note.

> **NOTE**
>
> To determine the effect of the resultant code size, build your application with inline functions enabled. Record the size of the application. Then rebuild the application with inline functions disabled. Compare the results to determine the effect of inlining.

Accessor and mutator member functions are prime candidates for inlining: they are small, normally called numerous times within an application's run, and consist of one to two simple statements. An *accessor* is used to return the value of an internal attribute within a class; these attributes should be declared with private visibility. A *mutator* function is used to set a value (passed as an argument) for a specific attribute within a class, as shown in the following code:

```
long Object::getID( ) const // accessor
{
    return( idNumber ) ;
}
void Object::setID(const long valueIn) // mutator
{
    idNumber = valueIn ;
}
```

To inline these member functions, you specify the inline keyword:

```
inline long Object::getID( ) const
{
    return( idNumber ) ;
}
inline void Object::setID(const long valueIn)
{
    idNumber = valueIn ;
}
```

Some functions, when inlined, may produce less code. To call a function, the compiler must produce code to prepare for the function call, set up the stack frame, make the call to the function, perform stack cleanup, and then return. For functions that implement simple functionality, such as returning the value of a variable, the actual function code can be considerably less than the code required to call the function.

When the `inline` keyword is applied to the member function's declaration, it is only an announcement to the compiler. If a body does not exist for the function, the compiler cannot determine whether the member function can be inlined. So applying the `inline` keyword to the declaration is useless information to the compiler. Also, applying the `inline` keyword to the declaration implies a specific implementation to users of the class. Again, the `inline` keyword should be applied only to the member function's definition. The following example shows that you should not apply the `inline` keyword to the declaration but to the definition.

```
// object.h
class Object {
    public:      // compiler doesn't know what to do yet.
        inline void setID( const long valueIn ) ;
} ;
```

Apply the `inline` keyword to the definition; now the compiler can see the body and decide whether to inline or not. And if the compiler does decide to inline, it now has the function body to use for insertion:

```
inline void setID( const long valueIn )
{
    idNumber = valueIn ;
}
```

Defining a member function at its declaration implies inlining. The `inline` keyword is not required when you are defining a member function within a class.

> **NOTE**
>
> Do not define a member function within the class declaration. Doing so clutters the class and makes maintenance more difficult.

10

TUNING
APPLICATION
PERFORMANCE

The following example demonstrates how a class might appear if you were to define the member functions within the class declaration. Just imagine that you have been elected to maintain this source code! The following is the example:

```
// object.h
class Object {
    public:
        Object( ) :
            idNumber(0L),
            name( new char[100] ;
            { /* empty */ }
        Object( const Object &rhs ) :
            IdNumber(0L),
            name( new char[strlen(rhs.name)+1] )
            {
                strcpy( name, rhs.name ) ;
            }       const Object& operator=( const Object &rhs )
            {   if( this != &rhs )
                {
                    delete [ ] name ;
                    name = new char[ strlen(rhs.name)+1] ;
                    strcpy( name, rhs.name ) ;
                    id = rhs.id ;
                }
                return *this ;
            }
            ~Object( )
            { if( name )
                    delete [ ] name ;
            }
        void setID(const long valIn)
            {idNumber = valueIn;};
        long Object::getID( ) const
            { return( idNumber ) ; };
        long Object::name( const char *name )
            { if( this.name )
                    delete [ ] this.name ;
                this.name = new char[ strlen(name)+1 ];
                strcpy( this.name, name };
            }
        long Object::name( ) const
            { return( idNumber ) ; };
    private:
        long idNumber;
        char *name ;
} ;
```

I mentioned earlier that a compiler might not honor the inline hint. The reasons a compiler would not inline a function are not always clear cut. Here are a number of situations in which a compiler will not honor the inline request:

- Functions that contain looping constructs such as `for`, `while`, and `do...while`.
- Functions that are recursive.
- If the compiler has not yet seen the function's definition.
- If the compiler has deemed the function too complex.

A note concerning the last item: Each compiler vendor implements complexity measurements in different ways, so it's difficult to know when a compiler will decide when a function is too complex to inline. In addition, it is in bad taste to inline virtual member functions because virtual functions are dynamically bound. In other words, their addresses must be known. There are also vendor-specific reasons not to inline; refer to your vendor's compiler documentation.

You should be aware of an interesting side effect of inlining. Suppose that you have a member function that the compiler has decided not to inline because of its size. Some compilers can create an *outline inline function*. These are also referred to as *static inline functions*. What in the world are these, you ask? Well, in every file that has a call to the function, the compiler creates the function's body with static linkage. This produces a version of the function in every translation unit. Be careful—your executable could, and probably will, become painfully large if the compiler chooses to outline inline. The situation can really become unbearable if the compiler decides to outline inline more than one function! Unfortunately, there is no rule of thumb to determine whether a member function is too large to inline; the compiler makes this decision.

NOTE

If you suspect that a function to be inlined is too large, check to see what the compiler is producing. Isolate the function in a separate file, if possible, and check the assembly code the compiler creates. By examining the assembly code, you can discover whether or not the compiler has inlined the function. If examining the assembly code is not possible, build the application with the function inlined. Then create a version of the application that does not inline the function and compare the sizes of the resultant applications.

HOW ABOUT USING MACROS INSTEAD OF INLINING?

Macros have disadvantages. One thing to note about macros is that they perform text substitution and nothing more. A macro does not evaluate the

continues

arguments provided to it; the arguments are merely "plugged in" at the point of insertion. More important, macros are not type safe and can be invisible within a debugger. Consider this example:

```
#define DOUBLE_IT(a) (a * a)
//If we do this:
int i = 5 ;
int j = DOUBLE_IT(i) ;
//the preprocessor will expand it to this:
int j = (5 * 5);
```

No surprises here. Now, consider this example:

```
int j = DOUBLE_IT(10 + 10) ;
//the preprocessor will expand the macro to this:
int j = (10+10 * 10+10) ;
```

This is not what we want. Here's another statement that can provide interesting results:

```
int j = DOUBLE_IT(++i) ;
```

This statement expands into this:

```
int j = (++i * ++i) ;
```

Again, this is not what we want. If we use an inline function in these two situations, the results would have been what we expected.

Use macros only for simple substitution. Better yet, use const instead of #define.

Avoid Revealing Implementation Code in Distributed Header Files

One of the basic }philosophies concerning (proper) object-oriented programming is hiding the implementation. You should never reveal how you implement the functionality of your classes. Class declarations should only reside within header files, not implementation files. Class declarations should reveal only member function declarations. You should hide the definition of your member functions in implementation files (.cpp, .cxx, or whatever extension is required); you should never expose implementation code in your header files.

Another reason you should not implement code in header files relates to code maintenance. It is much more difficult to maintain application source code when some of the code is found in header files. This problem is compounded when multiple developers are working on an application. Some developers may implement code in header files at every opportunity, other developers may never put code in header files, and others may do it "when it feels right." Hopefully, your team has a coding standards document to prevent this type of inconsistency. If you don't have one, you and your team members should sit down and draft onc.

> **NOTE**
>
> Never reveal implementation code in distributed header files.

Implementation code} in header files can introduce a performance penalty. If you put implementation code in header files, you will experience extended compile times and may discover that multiple versions of classes and functions exist across multiple translation units. Keeping the implementation separate from the interface allows you to change the implementation without having to recompile the whole system.

Avoid declaring static variables and composite types in header files. If you have a header file that declares some integer as static, then any translation unit that includes that header file will contain its own copy of that int. If there are many translation units and many static variable definitions within a header file, the size of your application can grow larger than you anticipate. The linker, of course, allows this to happen because the definitions are unique to each translation unit. If you removed the static keyword from those same data definitions, you would receive errors for} multiply defined variables.

In the previous paragraph, I use the term *static variables*. In C++, there are static global (or external) variables and static class members. A *static global variable* is declared outside any class or function and has visibility to all functions from its definition within the translation unit. A *static class member* is a member of a class that has static linkage. There exists only one copy of a static class member for all instances of a class. All instances of the class share this single static copy. This is in contrast to a *class instance member*; there exists an instance member for every instance of a class.

Analyzing the Cost of Virtual Functions and Virtual Base Classes

I get into many discussions concerning the "cost" of virtual functions and virtual base classes. One question I usually hear is this: "How much will I pay for calling virtual functions and using virtual base classes?" This is a good question and deserves an answer. But first, I want to review with you some of the basics of virtual functions and virtual base classes.

Virtual Functions

Let's define what a virtual function is so that we're on the same page. A *virtual function* is a member function that has the `virtual` keyword applied to it. Notice that I say *member function* because we can't apply the `virtual` keyword to nonclass functions. We apply the `virtual` keyword to the member function's declaration, not to the definition. With that said, here's an example:

```
class Object {
    public:
        virtual void f( ) ;
} ;
```

The corresponding definition is this:

```
void Object::f( ) {  ...  } ;
```

That's all we have to do to declare a virtual function. You do not have to do anything special to define a virtual function. Simply code the functionality required as you would any other function. It is important to think about the default functionality a base class virtual function provides to derived classes. A surprise to many developers is that the `virtual` keyword does not have to be applied to any derived class function's declaration. The compiler knows that the member function in a derived class is virtual *if it is virtual in the base class*, because the signature is the same as it is in the base class. This holds true all the way down the inheritance hierarchy. The following code snippet demonstrates the truth that virtualness is inherited by derived classes:

```
class Object {
    public:
        virtual void f( ) ;
} ;
class Derived : public Object {
    public:
        void f( ) ;
} ;
```

In this example, `Derived::f()` is automatically virtual. As far as coding style goes, I always show the `virtual` keyword; it is important to be explicit about every member function's use so that clients of the derived class understand its use.

You use the `virtual` keyword when you anticipate overriding member functions in a derived class. However, it is not always clear whether you will override a member function in a derived class. This is something that has to be hashed out when designing your classes. With enough forethought, you will know when any member functions have to be virtual. I will discuss the cost of using virtual methods later in this section.

By the way, this brings up a point concerning the declaration of a virtual destructor. You apply the `virtual` keyword to a destructor when you will be deriving from that base class or if the class has at least one virtual function. If you're unsure of what your class will be derived from, declare the destructor `virtual`. If you do not declare a destructor `virtual` when there is inheritance, the wrong destructor may be called. The following example shows that only `Object`'s destructor is called—which is not what you want:

```
class Object {
    public:
        ~Object( ) ;
} ;
class Derived : public Object {
    public:
        ~Derived( ) ;
} ;
//…
Object *thing = new Derived ;
delete thing ;
//…
```

This example demonstrates *polymorphic* (dynamic binding) behavior at runtime. The term *dynamic binding*, or *late binding*, is used because the function to be called is not resolved until runtime. *Early binding*, on the other hand, refers to the fact that the compiler can resolve the proper function to be called at compile time. With early binding, the compiler generates the proper code to perform a function call directly.

How does the runtime mechanism determine the correct virtual function to invoke? The determination is made based on the type of the object, not the reference to it. On the other hand, if a derived class contains a member function that overrides a base class function, and they are not virtual, then the reference determines the function called. The code in Listing 10.1 demonstrates this behavior.

LISTING 10.1. VIRTUAL AND NONVIRTUAL FUNCTION CALLS

```
#include <iostream>
class Base {
    public:
        virtual void vf( ) { std::cout << "Base::vf" << std::endl ; }
        void nvf( ) { std::cout << "Base::nvf" << std::endl ; }
} ;
class Derived : public Base {
    public:
        void vf( )  { std::cout << "Derived::vf" << std::endl ; }
        void nvf( ) { std::cout << "Derived::nvf" << std::endl ; }
} ;
int main( )
```

10

**TUNING
APPLICATION
PERFORMANCE**

continues

LISTING 10.1. CONTINUED

```
{
    Base aBase ;
    Derived aDerived ;

    Base *basePtrToDerived = &aDerived ;
    basePtrToDerived->vf( ) ;
    basePtrToDerived->nvf( ) ;

    return 0 ;
}
```

When you run the program in Listing 10.1, the following is the generated output:

```
Derived::vf
Base::nvf
```

Even though we are using a pointer of type `Base`, the actual object we are pointing to is of type `Derived`. So, how does the virtual mechanism work? Answering this question leads us back to the original question at the beginning of this section: "How much do I pay for calling virtual functions?"

The virtual mechanism is implemented using a *virtual function table*, abbreviated as *VTBL*, and a *virtual function pointer*, abbreviated as *VPTR*. There's nothing magic about these two elements. I'm sure you have implemented similar constructs. For every class that contains a virtual function, a single VTBL is created and maintained. The VTBL is an array of pointers, each pointer pointing to the implementation of each virtual function declared in the class. Although I say that the VTBL is an array, it may in fact be implemented as a linked list or some other specialized algorithm. The important thing to realize is that a pointer exists in the VTBL for every virtual function. Keep in mind that the pointer can point to a virtual function definition for the current class, if it exists, or to a virtual function definition of a base class. We will discuss this in more detail later in this chapter.

The VPTR is a hidden pointer found in every class. The VPTR's sole job is to point to the VTBL; specifically, it points to the first pointer entry in the VTBL. Most implementations use the first entry to hold a pointer to the `type_info` object of the class. For more information about the `type_info` class and runtime type information, refer to "RTTI Trade-Offs," later in this chapter. Whenever the compiler discovers a class with a virtual function declaration, it creates this hidden pointer along with the rest of the class's structure. There is only one VPTR no matter how many virtual functions exist for the class. The VTBL and VPTR do not exist for a class that does not have any virtual functions.

Let's think about the space and time cost associated with virtual functions. For every class that declares a virtual function, a VTBL exists. For every derived class containing virtual functions, a VTBL exists. This process continues as you add more levels of inheritance. Remember, too, that each instantiated object contains a VPTR that points to the VTBL. In the VTBL, a pointer exists for every virtual function of the class. The more virtual functions you declare in a class, the larger the VTBL. If the pointers are, say, four bytes, the size of the VTBL can add up quickly. And don't forget about the VPTR; it adds four bytes to every instance of the class. A concrete example follows:

```
class Base
{
    public:
        virtual void vfuncOne( ) { } ;
        virtual void vfuncTwo( ) { } ;
        virtual void vfuncThree( ) { } ;
    private:
        int value ;
} ;
class Derived : public Base
{
    public:
        virtual void vfuncOne( ) { } ;
        virtual void vfuncTwo( ) { } ;
        // vfuncThree is not overridden
    private:
        int value ;
} ;
```

In this example, there is a VTBL for `Base` and one for `Derived`, for a total of two VTBLs. The VTBLs for `Base` and `Derived` allocate space to hold three pointers each, or 12 additional bytes. You might be saying, "Yes, but `vfuncThree` was not overridden in `Derived`." That's true, but the pointer is still there and it points to `Base`'s `vfuncThree`. Notice that each class has only one attribute declared and that each function body is empty. Assume that you instantiate one object for each class at runtime; this adds eight additional bytes (for the VPTRs) for the two objects. The space penalty here could be significant if, for example, you are building an embedded system or other space-critical application. In the end, the benefits of using the virtual mechanism should outweigh the space penalty. Figure 10.1 shows a graphical representation of these two classes.

Keep in mind that pointer entries do not exist in the VTBL for nonvirtual functions. Constructors do not have an entry in the VTBL either. Remember, if a virtual function is not overridden in the derived class, then the function pointer will point to the virtual function in the base class.

FIGURE 10.1.

A graphical depiction of the virtual table and pointer.

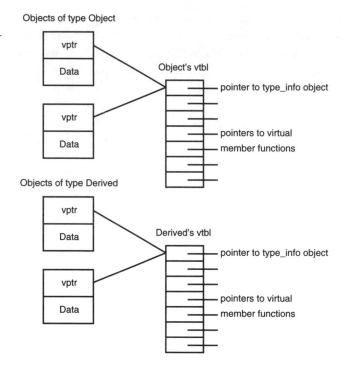

Virtual Base Classes

Let's explore the world of virtual base classes. When dealing with multiple inheritance, virtual base classes become an important part of the programming landscape. You should have a basic understanding of how they work if you are to implement them properly. You also need an understanding of some of the side effects of virtual base classes.

Virtual base classes are declared using the `virtual` keyword. The keyword is applied to the derived class declaration, just before the base class name. The benefit of using virtual base classes shines only if you create a class that inherits from two base classes that share a common base class. Following is an example that demonstrates the declaration:

```
class Base {
    public:
    ...
} ;
class Derived : public virtual Base {
    public:
    ...
} ;
```

This example implies that we are using singly rooted inheritance; it doesn't make any sense to use virtual base classes with this type of inheritance. The main reason you don't want to implement virtual inheritance for singly rooted inheritance is because of the run-time penalty associated with virtual inheritance. I am only demonstrating a declaration, not implying an implementation.

One reason for using virtual base classes is to alleviate the extraneous copies of a base class found when using multiple inheritance (and not using virtual base classes). In other words, if you are using multiple inheritance and don't use virtual base classes, you will get extra copies of the base class in your derived classes. As mentioned earlier, this applies only if you create a class that inherits from more than one derived class that have a common base class. Conversely, if you use virtual base classes, the derived classes will share a copy of the base class. Here is an example:

```
class Base {
    ...
    protected:
        int value ;
} ;
class OneDerived : public Base {
    ...
} ;
class TwoDerived : public Base {
    ...
} ;
class UltimatelyDerived : public OneDerived, public TwoDerived {
    public:
        int getValue( ) { return( value ) ; }
} ;
```

The class `UltimatelyDerived` publicly derives from both `OneDerived` and `TwoDerived`. What this means is that there will be a copy of class `Base` in both `OneDerived` and `TwoDerived` because class `Base` is not declared as a virtual base class.

Ambiguity sets in at class `UltimatelyDerived` with respect to the attribute `value` found in class `Base`. The member function in `UltimatelyDerived` named `getValue` returns the contents of `value`. Which copy of `value` will it use? The copy found in `OneDerived` or the one found in `TwoDerived`? The compiler will become confused and issue an error. You can resolve the ambiguity by explicitly specifying the copy of `value` you want by using the scope resolution operator:

```
int getValue( ) const { return( OneDerived::value ) ; }
```

This explicit qualification solves the ambiguity problem and quiets your compiler, but does not solve the problem of multiple copies of a base class. You must continually engage the scope resolution operator to resolve the ambiguity. Excessive use of the scope

10

TUNING
APPLICATION
PERFORMANCE

resolution operator can be unappealing to the eyes and can also confuse developers who inherit your code.

If you employ virtual inheritance, the compiler guarantees that there is only one copy of the base class. This exclusive base class copy is shared by any derived classes. Let's take a look at an example that demonstrates virtual inheritance:

```
class Base {
    ...
    protected:
        int value ;
} ;
class OneDerived : public virtual Base {
    public:
        void callMe( ) ;
} ;
class TwoDerived : public virtual Base {
    public:
        void callMe( ) ;
} ;
class UltimatelyDerived : public OneDerived, public TwoDerived {
    public:
        int getValue( ) { return( value ) ; }
} ;
```

The compiler creates a single copy of class Base to be shared by both OneDerived and TwoDerived. Doing this solves the ambiguity issue relating to value, but a new issue surfaces. Notice that the public member function callMe() is found in both OneDerived and TwoDerived. Again, the compiler is unable to determine the correct version of callMe() to invoke. You have to use the scope resolution operator to disambiguate the function call.

A basic design issue is involved in declaring callMe() in both OneDerived and TwoDerived. If the functionality provided by callMe() could be shared, then the declaration and implementation should be moved to Base. The other way to solve this issue is to declare and define callMe() in the UltimatelyDerived class. This approach hides the versions of callMe() in both OneDerived and TwoDerived. As you have seen, virtual base classes do not solve all your multiple inheritance problems.

Let's investigate some of the penalties experienced using virtual inheritance. First, let's take a look at the size cost for the following classes. Note that we are not using virtual inheritance.

```
class Base
{
    public:
        long value[ 100 ] ;
} ;
```

```
class OneDerived : public  Base  { /* nothing */ } ;
class TwoDerived : public  Base { /* nothing */ } ;
class UltimatelyDerived :
    public OneDerived, public TwoDerived  { /* nothing */ } ;

#include <iostream>
int main()
{
   Base b ;
   OneDerived one ;
   TwoDerived two ;
   UltimatelyDerived ultimate ;

   std::cout << "value =" << sizeof(b.value) << std::endl
       << "pointer =" << sizeof(Base*) << std::endl
       << "Base =" << sizeof(b) << std::endl
       << "One  =" << sizeof(one) << std::endl
       << "Two  =" << sizeof(two) << std::endl
       << "Ultimate =" << sizeof(ultimate) << std::endl ;
   return 0 ;
}
```

The output of this program is as follows:

```
value =400
pointer =4
Base =400
One  =400
Two  =400
Ultimate =800
```

This output should not be a surprise. The size of `Base` is four bytes; because `OneDerived` and `TwoDerived` inherit from `Base`, their size is also four bytes. `UltimatelyDerived` is eight bytes because it gets two copies of `Base`. Let's add virtual inheritance to the picture and see what happens. The code stays the same except for the following two lines of code:

```
class OneDerived : public virtual Base  { /* nothing */ } ;
class TwoDerived : public virtual Base { /* nothing */ } ;
```

Look at the output from the revised program:

```
value=400
pointer =4
Base =400
One  =404
Two  =404
Ultimate =408
```

You can see that there are four extra bytes in both `OneDerived` and `TwoDerived`. What are these extra bytes for? The extra bytes are there because `OneDerived` and `TwoDerived` contain a pointer that points to the single copy of Base. Remember that classes which virtually inherit from a base class are expressing a willingness to share the base class's data. The real eye-opener is the reduction in size for the object UltimatelyDerived! Using virtual inheritance has effectively trimmed the size of the object in half because we have eliminated an extra object. Although the cost of using the virtual inheritance mechanism is trivial (considering the extra pointers), the size of objects at runtime can be a significant burden.

One thing that I have not discussed is the mixing of virtual and nonvirtual inheritance. Let's modify our two lines of code again to reflect this consideration:

```
class OneDerived : public Base  {          /* nothing */ } ;
class TwoDerived : public virtual Base { /* nothing */ } ;
```

What is happening here is that OneDerived will have its own copy of Base, and TwoDerived will point to a shared copy of Base. When we run this program, the output is as follows:

```
value=4
pointer =4
Base =4
One  =4
Two  =8
Ultimate =12
```

Notice that OneDerived is now only four bytes in size. This confirms the fact that any class that virtually inherits contains a pointer.

Armed with this knowledge of virtual functions and virtual base classes, you can properly analyze the costs of using these facilities. Similarly, you should understand what the compiler is doing behind the scenes to properly implement these features.

RTTI Trade-Offs

Runtime Type Identification (RTTI) can be useful for specific programming situations, but RTTI can also lead to inefficient runtime behavior. More importantly, RTTI undermines polymorphism and reflects (potentially) poor design. The name itself declares the runtime nature of the RTTI facilities. Developers coming from other languages such as Smalltalk or Pascal (among others) may be tempted to use RTTI extensively. I urge you to keep RTTI coding activity to a minimum. If at all possible, eliminate the use of RTTI completely; use virtual functions instead of RTTI.

As the name suggests, RTTI is used to retrieve information about an object at runtime. The runtime identification mechanism is implemented with respect to polymorphic types. This implies that a class must contain at least one virtual function. For a discussion of virtual functions, virtual tables, and virtual base classes, refer to the preceding section, "Analyzing the Cost of Virtual Functions and Virtual Base Classes."

Information about a class is stored in an object of type `type_info`. A pointer to the `type_info` object is stored as an entry in the virtual table. The pointer entry is usually found in the first slot of the table. Because the `type_info` object exists as a separate entity, the size of the virtual table is increased by the size of a pointer.

The `type_info` object can reveal information about an object's name, its equality or inequality compared to other objects, and the collating sequence of an object. The `type_info` class has the following structure:

```
class type_info {
public:
    virtual ~type_info();
    bool operator==(const type_info&) const;
    bool operator!=(const type_info&) const;
    bool before(const type_info&) const;
    const char* name() const;
private:
    type_info(const type_info&); // prevent copying
    type_info & operator=(const type_info&) ; // prevent assignment
    ...
};
```

The `before` member function is used to reveal a collating sequence for an object. This collating sequence does not reveal information about the inheritance hierarchy, so you should not use it to explore relationships among objects. The collating sequence is also implementation defined, so don't count on the results being the same between vendor products.

Obtaining the name of an object might be useful for debugging activities. The `name` attribute is stored as a NULL-terminated string and is returned by the name member function.

You can use the `operator==` and `operator!=` member functions to determine equality or inequality of two `type_info` objects.

The `typeid` operator is used to return a `const` reference to a `type_info` object. The argument to `typeid` is either a type name or an expression. An expression can be a reference or a pointer of some type. If the expression is a reference or pointer, the `type_info` reference reveals the actual type referred to, not the type of the reference (or pointer). The `typeid` operator throws a `bad_typeid` exception if the value of the expression is zero. Please note that you must dereference the pointer to reveal the actual object pointed to. Here's an example of how RTTI might be used:

10

TUNING
APPLICATION
PERFORMANCE

```
void walk( const Animal &animal )
{
    if( typeid( animal ) == typeid( Tiger ) )
        // walk like a Tiger
    else if( typeid( animal ) == typeid( Monkey ) )
        // walk like a Monkey
    else if( typeid( animal ) == typeid( Elephant ) )
        // walk like an Elephant
    ...
}
```

As mentioned earlier, this code will look familiar to people who use Smalltalk or Pascal. I frown on this use of RTTI—and you should, too. Virtual functions are a more elegant solution to this type of runtime logic.

I can name another compelling reason why you should avoid the RTTI mechanism: code maintenance. Consider what would be required if you added another `Animal` type to your hierarchy. You would have to visit all your RTTI logic, make the appropriate enhancements, and then recompile the whole affair. The performance and readability penalty is also high with all the `if..else` statements to step through. It is my belief that you and your users will get tired of this kind of maintenance.

RTTI provides for type-safe downcasting for polymorphic types. The behavior is undefined for downcasting nonpolymorphic objects. Actually, you will most likely get the static type information for the object passed to `typeid`. Here is an example of code that uses a nonpolymorphic class hierarchy:

```
Animal *pa = new Tiger ;
const typeid &theType = typeid( *pa ) ;
if( theType == typeid( Animal ) ) // line 3
    cout << "It's only an Animal!" ;
else if( theType == typeid( Tiger ) )
    cout << "It's a Tiger, run!" ; // never executes!
```

The `if` statement in the third line always resolves to `true`.

The `typeid` operator works for built-in types of the language. I have not seen a real benefit for its use, but you can do it, nonetheless. In the following example, all the `if` statements will execute their respective statements:

```
char aChar = 'c' ;
if( typeid( aChar ) == typeid( char ) )
    cout << "It's a char!" ;
if( typeid( &aChar ) == typeid( char * ) )
    cout << "It's a char pointer!" ;
if( typeid( 'c' ) == typeid( char ) )
    cout << "Guess what, another char!" ;
```

You may be familiar with the `dynamic_cast` operator. The `dynamic_cast` operator determines whether or not a downcast is safe. Consider the following example; assume that class `Animal` and its derived classes are polymorphic:

```
Animal *pa = new Tiger ;
Tiger *pt = dynamic_cast< Tiger *>( pa ) ;
if( pt ) // pt will be cast to a Tiger
    cout << "There's a Tiger in the house!";
else
    cout << "Whew, no Tigers in here";
```

The argument provided to `dynamic_cast` within the angle brackets is the type to which you are trying to cast. The argument within the parentheses is the object from which you are trying to cast. If the cast is successful, you get the type requested. If the cast is unsuccessful, the `NULL` pointer is returned. Again, I prefer the use of virtual functions to downcasting with `dynamic_cast`. With virtual functions, you don't need to test whether a downcast is safe or not—the call always resolves to some virtual function in the hierarchy.

Use the RTTI mechanism sparingly. It is important for you to know the features of RTTI so that you can employ them properly. Understand the trade-offs of RTTI and know when it's proper to use virtual functions, virtual base classes, and RTTI. Realize the costs associated with each feature and use each when it makes sense.

Managing Memory for Temporary Objects

The compiler can surprise you in many ways. A surprise that every programmer experiences is that compilers tend to create temporaries. You may not even be aware that the compiler has created a temporary. Two of the most common situations are when a function has to return an object and when an object is passed to a function. We will explore some of the other reasons why a compiler creates temporaries.

One characteristic of a temporary is that it cannot be seen by the naked eye. You can't always see the temporary by looking at your code. You can, however, conceptually see a temporary if you understand how a compiler creates one. A temporary is never visible in code. Temporaries are considered unnamed objects; in other words, you never explicitly give them a name. The compiler generates a name for a temporary behind the scenes. You, of course, do not have to worry about them because the compiler takes care of everything. Temporary objects are not created on the heap—unless, of course, you have coded a constructor that dynamically allocates memory. You must also watch out for allocating memory within operator functions. One final thing I want to clear up before moving on is that I'm not talking about temporary *variables* you create within a function or code block. With all this said, let's create an `Integer` class and some working code:

```
class Integer {
  public:
    Integer( ) ;
    Integer( const Integer & ) ;
    Integer( int valueIn ) ;
    Integer( int valueIn, int addedValue ) ;
    Integer operator+( const Integer &lhs, const Integer &rhs ) ;
    void operator=( const Integer & ) ;
    ...
} ;
...
Integer value = 2 ; // first line (working code)
for( int i = 0; i < 100; i++ )
    value = value + 2 ;
```

The last three lines of code look harmless, wouldn't you say? The first line constructs an `Integer` and uses the assignment operator to place the value 2 into the object. First, however, the compiler must convert the constant '2' to an `Integer` object. The compiler does this by using the constructor that takes an integer argument. You can reduce the compiler's workload by doing this instead:

```
Integer value(2) ;
```

With that out of the way, let's take a look at the loop. The loop's expression is where the real bottleneck is. Let's take this expression apart, piece by piece, to see what is happening. First of all, there is a constant expression on the right side of `operator+`. The compiler has to construct a temporary and initialize it with the constant value '2'. The compiler has to do this because `operator+` requires an `Integer` object for its argument. The compiler uses the constructor that takes an integer argument, just as it did in the first line of code. Next, the compiler generates code to return an `Integer` object and uses the copy constructor to put the result into the object `value`. Finally, `operator=` is used to assign the result to the object `value`. You must realize that the compiler not only creates temporaries, it also has to destroy them. This continual construction and destruction can rob your application of valuable time and space.

I mentioned that a compiler would create a temporary if a member function returns by value. `Integer`'s `operator+` demonstrates this effect. Because the temporary is an unnamed object, the compiler can create and destroy an `Integer` object. The compiler does this even if you ignore the function's return value. Let's take a look at an example:

```
Integer calculate( int valueOne, int valueTwo ) ;
...
calculate( 5, 10 ) ;
```

The compiler will still create a temporary even though the return is ignored. There's not much you can do to get around this problem. Designing for efficiency is the key to reducing the occurrence of temporaries. I said *reduce*, not *eliminate*. There will be situations that are just out of your control. Let's look at one way you can battle the creation of temporaries. I will use `Integer`'s `operator+` to demonstrate the named return value optimization. Let's look at a potential implementation:

```
Integer Integer::operator+( const Integer &lhs, const Integer &rhs )
{
  Integer temp = lhs.value( ) + rhs.value( ) ;
  return temp ;
}
```

This code can be viewed as a very typical implementation. A local `Integer` object is instantiated to hold the result of the addition and then it is used in the `return` statement. If the `Integer` were replaced with, say, a native `int` type, the resultant source code would indeed look very natural. Of course, the code generated by the compiler would be insignificant. Unfortunately, the code generated for `Integer::operator+` is quite different. You need a way to reduce the runtime expense of creating the temporary. The way you do this is to use an explicit constructor of the class. The `operator+` member will then look like this:

```
Integer Integer::operator+( const Integer &lhs, const Integer &rhs )
{
    return Integer( lhs.value( ), rhs.value( ) ) ;
}
```

I'm sure you are thinking that this code will still generate a temporary object for the return. The difference in using the named constructor is that the compiler is free to perform some magic. It is allowed the freedom to optimize the temporary out of existence—something you definitely want the compiler to do. Having this knowledge gives you more control over the creation of temporaries. (In this case, I should be saying the *elimination*, rather than *creation*, of a temporary.) In a nutshell, the compiler actually builds the object to be returned in place. Your compiler vendor may or may not implement the named return value optimization; refer to the documentation for details.

Now that you have an understanding about temporary objects, you should keep a watchful eye on code that passes data to functions. You should also reexamine code that returns objects; the compiler will most likely create a temporary unless you have employed the *named return value optimization* technique. Consider this point: If you can provide a more efficient implementation, your compiler will thank you and, in turn, will produce code that is more efficient.

10

TUNING APPLICATION PERFORMANCE

Summary

This chapter has examined inline functions, virtual functions, virtual base classes, RTTI, and temporary objects. You should come away knowing the costs associated with each of these constructs. It is also important to know what the compiler is doing behind the scenes.

The `inline` keyword is only a hint to the compiler. You know some of the reasons why a compiler might not inline a function. You have also uncovered some side effects of inlining.

You have discovered the effects of revealing implementation code in header files. Think about the way your implementation code is organized and how you can improve on it.

In this chapter, you have seen the effects of using (and not using) virtual functions and virtual base classes. You have seen the effects of virtual functions on the VTBL. You also know how virtual base classes can eliminate multiple copies of a base class when using multiple inheritance.

RTTI is a feature available for specific programming situations, but you should not used it to replace the virtual mechanism. Remember that RTTI undermines polymorphism and reflects poor design.

Temporary objects can reach up and bite you if you are unfamiliar with these hidden beasts. Know when the compiler silently creates temporaries and what you can do to prevent their creation. Find out whether your compiler supports the named return value optimization feature; if this feature is supported, use it whenever you can.

Manipulating Data

IN THIS PART

Recursion and Recursive Data Structures

Recursion is a subject that seems to strike fear in the hearts of many software developers. It refers to things that are defined in terms of themselves, to code calling itself, and to objects pointing to images of themselves—these definitions seem frightening. They smack of infinity and paradox. But you need not fear, because we will slay this deadly beast with one simple phrase—*Forget about it*!

You won't, of course, forget about recursion altogether, you just won't think about the code as recursive while you are writing it. This is the big secret to recursion: Don't think about it as some infinite paradox and get wrapped up in the layers of self-reference; just think about one layer at a time. Then, when the time is appropriate, you'll look at the recursive aspects of your structure or function. We will apply this principle to a set of examples, from recursion in a function to recursive structures, and we will see that we can simplify the recursion process if we don't think about it—well, if we don't think about it too much. We will also talk about some different issues in recursion, such as tail and indirect recursion. Finally, we will discuss some of the special problems that come up when you try to debug recursive functions.

What Is Recursion?

Recursion is when a thing refers to itself or to an image just like itself. For a function, recursion means that the function calls itself. For an object, recursion is when the object refers to things like itself by means of a pointer or a reference. Often, recursive structures and recursive functions go hand in hand: The best way to do many of the common operations on recursive structures is to use a recursive function. We will look at some of these operations later in this chapter.

Fibonacci Numbers: A Recursive Definition

The classic example of recursion is the definition of Fibonacci numbers. The Nth Fibonacci number is defined as the sum of the (N-1)th Fibonacci number plus the (N-2)th Fibonacci number. The exception is that if N is less than or equal to 2, the Nth Fibonacci number is defined to be 1. In a mathematical notation, it looks like this:

```
Fibonacci (N)  =
    if (N <= 2)  : 1
    Otherwise    :  Fibonacci (N-1) + Fibonacci (N-2)
```

This seems very tricky, because for any value of N greater than 2, you don't know what the Fibonacci number is, except in terms of two other numbers. These other numbers you have to calculate using this same process, and when you try to do one of those, you are back where you were, and then you lose your place, and so on.

But, fortunately, we have computers! They are great at this sort of thing, and they don't mind the tedium of doing the same calculation steps over and over again. Let's look at this definition converted into C++ code, as shown in Listing 11.1.

LISTING 11.1. RECURSIVE FIBONACCI CALCULATION

```cpp
#include "iostream.h"

long fib(long n)
{
    if (n <= 2)
        return 1;
    else
        return fib(n-1) + fib(n-2);
}

int main()
{
    long N;
    cout << "Which Fibonacci number do you want?" << endl;
    cin >> N;
    cout << "Fibonacci (" << N << ") is " << fib(N) << "\n\n";

    return 0;
}
```

The following shows a sample execution, where the text in **bold** was typed by the user:

```
Which Fibonacci number do you want?
14
Fibonacci (14) is 377

Which Fibonacci number do you want?
40
Fibonacci (40) is 102334155
```

NOTE

For the program in Listing 11.1, it is not recommended that you enter any number larger than 40 because the required processing time grows exponentially. Calculating Fibonacci number 40 takes my computer 10 seconds. Calculating Fibonacci number 41 takes almost twice as long—and you continue to (almost) double the processing time with each increment.

As we look at the function `fib()`, we see that it is just like the mathematical definition of the operation. It seems a little scary, though, that the function is calling itself. How will it know what to return? The computer takes care of this by making a new copy of the parameter n for each call into the function.

Instead of the function calling itself, just imagine that you had been assigned the task of writing the following function: It should accept a single parameter—call it n. If n is less than or equal to 2, return 1. If n is greater than 2, return the sum `sqrt(n-1)` + `sqrt(n-2)`, where `sqrt()` is the square root function. You wouldn't have any problem with this—it wouldn't even occur to you to worry about what is going on inside that `sqrt` function. It is just a function provided by the math library, and you trust that it does its thing.

Writing a recursive function is exactly the same. When you have to make a recursive call, *forget about it*! Don't concern yourself with the fact that you are making a call into this same, half-written function that you are working on. Just trust that the function will do its thing. When you are done, and the function is fully debugged, your trust will be rewarded.

Stopping the Recursion

There is one extra requirement when writing a recursive function. At some point, it had better stop recursing or it will have the same effect as an infinite loop—at least, until you run out of stack space. (The stack is a special memory area where the computer keeps track of its position in each level of the recursion. More on the stack later in this chapter.) To make sure that the recursion always stops, you must fulfill two requirements. First, there must be some path through the function that returns without making any recursive call. The conditions that invoke this path are called the *termination conditions*. The second requirement for guaranteeing that the recursion will stop is that you should be getting closer, somehow, to the termination conditions on each recursion. As long as there is some way that the function stops recursing and that every recursion moves you closer to the termination conditions, then there is no risk that recursion will go on infinitely.

In the Fibonacci example, when the parameter is less than or equal to 2, the function simply returns 1 without making any more calls. Therefore, (n <= 2) is the termination condition. If n is greater than 2, then every recursive call that we make passes in a parameter that is smaller than the current n. In other words, each recursion moves us closer to the termination condition. Because we have met the two requirements, we can be confident that the Fibonacci recursion will eventually terminate.

Recursion and Recursive Data Structures

CHAPTER 11

435

11

RECURSION AND
RECURSIVE DATA
STRUCTURES

Recursive Structures

A recursive structure is one that points to a thing just like itself. The directory hierarchy on your computer is a good example: Every directory contains a list of files, and one special type of file is a directory entry. A class diagram would look something like the one in Figure 11.1.

FIGURE 11.1.

A file and directory class diagram.

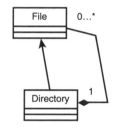

This is Universal Modeling Language notation for two classes, `File` and `Directory`. The arrow shows that `Directory` is a child class of `File`, an *is-a* relationship. The line with the diamond shows a one-to-many relationship between `Directory` and `File` (the diamond signifies aggregation or ownership). In other words, each `Directory` owns zero or more `Files` and every `File` is owned by exactly one `Directory`. Because a `Directory` *is-a* `File`, `Directorys` can also own other `Directorys` without any special work. It is this recursive nature that allows us to build up a hierarchy of directories based on two very simple classes.

Listing 11.2 shows us these two classes in C++. This listing is not a complete program—yet. First, let's look at the minimum we need to show these classes, and then we will put a complete program around the classes.

LISTING 11.2. FILE AND DIRECTORY CLASSES

```
#include <iostream>
#include <list>
#include <string>
using namespace std;

class File
{
public:
    File(const string & name) : m_name(name) {}
    ~File() {}

    const string & getName() const { return m_name; }
    void setName(const string & name) { m_name = name; }
```

```
private:
    string m_name;
};

class Directory : public File
{
public:
    Directory(const string & name) : File(name) {}
    ~Directory();
    void AddFile(File * fp) {m_FileList.push_back(fp);}
private:
    list<File *> m_FileList;
    typedef list<File *>::iterator FileIter;
};

Directory::~Directory()
{
    while (!m_FileList.empty())
    {
        delete m_FileList.front();
        m_FileList.pop_front();
    }
}
```

The first four lines set us up to use the standard template library versions of iostream, list, and string.

The class File is declared. Its only salient feature is its name, which is a string.

The class Directory is declared to inherit publicly from File—an *is-a* relationship. Its *responsibility* is to contain a list of files. Of course, a real directory would have a number of methods for inserting, removing, searching, and other operations that have to do with managing its responsibility. For brevity, we are only offering an Add() operation that adds new files to the end of its list.

Because the Directory *owns* the list of files, it is required to delete them when it is done. This is done explicitly in the Directory destructor.

We could now write a bit of code to put together an entire hierarchy of these objects, with directories that contain lots of files, including other directories. You could read in the file hierarchy off of your disk and put all that in these structures, giving yourself a map of your directory hierarchy in an interconnected set of these File and Directory objects.

Traversing a Recursive Structure with a Recursive Function

In this section, we will continue the `Directory` and `File` example and write a recursive function that traverses the entire directory tree and displays the name of every file. We will also talk about passing information through the levels of recursion.

Sometimes, when you are working with a recursive function, you want to know what level of recursion you are on. There are several reasons you might want this information: The termination condition may be that you simply go ten levels deep and no further. Perhaps you are displaying information and want to indent each level of recursion another tab stop. The simple way to obtain this information is to pass it along as a parameter to the function, increasing it by 1 each time you recurse. For the `Directory` and `File` example, we will just print out the level on each line.

Another issue that often arises with recursion is that you have some information that you want to accumulate through the different levels of recursion. If you are writing a function to evaluate the moves in a chess game, for example, you want to keep track of the moves you have made to get to your current position. In the directory/file hierarchy, we will accumulate the full pathname for a file by concatenating the names of the directories as we move, recursively, through the directory hierarchy. Listing 11.3 shows how to do this.

LISTING 11.3. A RECURSIVE WALK THROUGH A DIRECTORY TREE

```cpp
#include <iostream>
#include <list>
#include <string>
using namespace std;

class File
{
public:
    File(const string & name) : m_name(name) {}
    ~File() {}

    const string & getName() const { return m_name; }
    void setName(const string & name) { m_name = name; }
    virtual void Display(ostream & os,
                         int level = 1,
                         const string & prefix = "");
private:
    string m_name;
};
```

continues

LISTING 11.3. CONTINUED

```cpp
class Directory : public File
{
public:
    Directory(const string & name) : File(name) {}
    ~Directory();

    virtual void Display(ostream & os,
                         int level = 1,
                         const string & prefix = "");
    void AddFile(File * fp) {m_FileList.push_back(fp);}
private:
    list<File *> m_FileList;
    typedef list<File *>::iterator FileIter;
};

// To display a File, output prefix & name and newline
void File::Display(ostream & os, int level, const string & prefix)
{
    os << level << ".  " << prefix << m_name << endl;
}

// To display a Directory, output name and newline, then
// Display all of my contained Files using recursive call
void Directory::Display(ostream & os, int level, const string & prefix)
{
    File::Display(os, level, prefix);
    string newPrefix = prefix + getName() + ":";
    for (FileIter iter = m_FileList.begin();
                  iter != m_FileList.end();
                  iter++)
        (*iter)->Display(os, level + 1, newPrefix);
}

Directory::~Directory()
{
    while (!m_FileList.empty())
    {
        delete m_FileList.front();
        m_FileList.pop_front();
    }
}

int main()
{
    Directory * dir = new Directory("TheDir");
    dir->AddFile(new File("File 1"));
    dir->AddFile(new File("File 2"));

    Directory *subdir = new Directory("SubDir 1");
```

Recursion and Recursive Data Structures

CHAPTER 11

439

11

RECURSION AND
RECURSIVE DATA
STRUCTURES

```
        dir->AddFile(subdir);
        subdir->AddFile(new File("Sub File 1"));
        subdir->AddFile(new File("Sub File 2"));

        Directory *subdir2 = new Directory("SubDir 2");
        dir->AddFile(subdir2);
        subdir2->AddFile(new File("Sub File 4"));
        subdir2->AddFile(new File("Sub File 5"));
        subdir2->AddFile(new File("Sub File 6"));

        Directory *subsubdir = new Directory("SubSubDir 1");
        subdir->AddFile(subsubdir);
        subsubdir->AddFile(new File("Sub Sub File 1"));
        subsubdir->AddFile(new File("Sub Sub File 2"));
        subsubdir->AddFile(new File("Sub Sub File 3"));

        subdir->AddFile(new File("Sub File 3"));

        dir->AddFile(new File("File 3"));
        dir->AddFile(new File("File 4"));

        dir->Display(cout);
        delete dir;
        return 0;
}
```

Here is the output for Listing 11.3:

```
1.   TheDir
2.   TheDir:File 1
2.   TheDir:File 2
2.   TheDir:SubDir 1
3.   TheDir:SubDir 1:Sub File 1
3.   TheDir:SubDir 1:Sub File 2
3.   TheDir:SubDir 1:SubSubDir 1
4.   TheDir:SubDir 1:SubSubDir 1:Sub Sub File 1
4.   TheDir:SubDir 1:SubSubDir 1:Sub Sub File 2
4.   TheDir:SubDir 1:SubSubDir 1:Sub Sub File 3
3.   TheDir:SubDir 1:Sub File 3
2.   TheDir:SubDir 2
3.   TheDir:SubDir 2:Sub File 4
3.   TheDir:SubDir 2:Sub File 5
3.   TheDir:SubDir 2:Sub File 6
2.   TheDir:File 3
2.   TheDir:File 4
```

Here you have the two classes you are familiar with from earlier in the chapter, with a
Display() method added. Because it is a virtual method, we can walk through a list of
File pointers, calling Display() on each one, and know that the correct Display()
function will be called. We have declared the Display() function to accept three

parameters: the output stream, the recursion level, and a filename prefix. As we will see, this prefix is the accumulated set of names of the directories through which we "recursed" on our way to this function call. Do not think about these names recursively, however. Just assume that the function you are writing gets the proper value passed in and is expected to pass along the proper value when the time comes.

In the function `File::Display()`, all that is necessary to display a normal file is to output the recursion number, the prefix, and the filename.

On the other hand, the function `Directory::Display()` is more complicated. Displaying a directory means to display it as if it were a file, and then to call `Display()` on all the files that this directory contains. It is true that, for the contained files that are really directories, this function calls itself. But remember our first principle of writing recursive functions: Do not think about this task in multiple levels at once; this is just a simple `Directory()` function that does some operation on all its contained files, and we are just going to trust that the operation works.

Look at the one-line body of the `for` loop inside `Directory::Display()`. (The expression (`*iter`) here returns the *current* item in the list, according to the position defined by the iterator. It returns a `File *` because the list is defined to be a `list<File *>`.) The `for` loop is the recursion step. The first parameter is simple enough: It is just passing on the proper `ostream` to which the output should go. The second parameter is the recursion level, which we increase by 1 as we pass it to the next level down. When the function we are calling recurses, it increments the value for `level` again, but we don't need to worry about that. All we have to think about is that the next recursion level will be 1 more than the current level.

The last parameter is the prefix. We know that what was passed in to us was our prefix— the accumulated list of directory names that it took to get here. Again, don't worry about how that was built, just trust that it is correct. Now, to pass a correct prefix to all our contained files, we have to construct a new prefix that will have all the directories so far, plus the current name. This is how the prefixes were accumulated correctly: Each level received a correct prefix and passed on another that also was correct.

The only step that is missing is to make sure that the very first level of recursion starts with the correct value. We do this by including default values for the function parameters that contain the correct values for the first level. In this case, correct values for the first level are `level = 1` and `prefix` is a blank string, as we can see in the declaration of the `Display()` function in both the `File` class and the `Directory` class.

One last test before we run this program. Have we fulfilled the requirements for recursion to terminate? The first requirement is that there is a path through the recursive function that does not recurse. This is a little tricky because if we look at

`Directory::Display()`, there does not appear to be such a path. However, there are actually *two* ways we can sidestep the recursive call. First, if the `Directory` does not contain any files, the body of the `for` loop is skipped because the test portion of the `for` statement fails right away. The second way recursion can be avoided is by remembering that this is really only one instance of a virtual function; if all the contained files are really files and none of them are directories, then no additional recursion will occur.

The second requirement for recursion to terminate is that we always get closer to the termination conditions. We can assume that the directory hierarchy has a finite depth, and we can make sure that there are no instances of a directory containing itself, either directly or indirectly. With these two caveats, we know that, with each recursion step, we are always moving closer to a directory that contains only files and not other directories.

Finally, we are ready to build a little directory structure—which is done in `main()`—and to call `Display()` on the top level. The output follows the program.

This takes a bit of studying to really see what has happened, but the bottom line is that every `Directory` displayed all its `Files` in order. Whenever a `Directory` was the thing being displayed, the process for its parent was kept on hold until the `Directory` had finished displaying all its children. You can see the recursion level as it increments up to 4 and then returns to 3 and then to 2. It is not decremented anywhere in the code. When the level drops, this means that one level of the recursion has finished and has executed the `return()` statement. The version of `level` that held the larger value was thrown away when the function returned. It might be valuable to trace through this code with a debugger to see each function as it is called and how the calling function resumes when the called function returns.

Recursion Versus Iteration and Tail Recursion

It is generally true that any recursive function can be rewritten as an iterative operation. In some cases, this is quite easy, but in other cases, rewriting the function is difficult. When the very last operation of a recursive function is the recursive call, this is called *tail recursion*. It is always very easy to replace tail recursion with iteration—compilers often do so without our knowledge! In this section, we will look at a recursive way to think about a linked list and see how that kind of recursion is easily replaced with iteration.

A linked list is generally thought of as a collection of `Nodes`, where each `Node` contains one element and a pointer to the next `Node`. However, there is a recursive way to think about a linked list. Think instead that a linked list consists of a `Node` that contains a single element and a pointer to another linked list. (Readers familiar with LISP and its car/cdr functions should see a parallel here.)

This recursive way of thinking about a linked list considers each list to contain another list. Although the first model has Nodes pointing to other Nodes, you might, at first, be inclined to consider it recursive. It is not, however, because the Nodes are not considered to *contain* the other Nodes, they just refer to them.

This different way of thinking of linked lists means that you do not bother to make a separate class that represents the entire list. Every Node represents an entire list, which is made up of the Node's datum plus all the data contained in the Node's sublist. None of the operations involve any sort of looping or walking the list because we always think of a list as only two entities: the Node we are working with and its contained sublist. The only variation within any process is deciding whether the Node we are on has a sublist or just a NULL.

To simplify the code in this example, Listing 11.3 creates a linked list for which the datum for each Node is just a string.

LISTING 11.4. SIMPLIFYING THE CODE WITH A LINKED LIST

```
#include <iostream>
#include <list>
#include <string>
using namespace std;

class LLNode
{
public:
    LLNode(const string & data = "", LLNode * subList = NULL)
        : myData(data), mySubList(subList) {}
    ~LLNode() {delete mySubList;}

    const string & GetFirstData() const {return myData;}

    void SortedInsert(const string & data);
    bool isInList(const string & data) const;
    int Count() const;
    void Display(ostream & os) const;
    void ReverseDisplay(ostream & os) const;
private:
    string myData;
    LLNode * mySubList;
};

void LLNode::SortedInsert(const string & data)
{
    if (NULL == mySubList  || data <= mySubList->GetFirstData())
```

```cpp
            mySubList = new LLNode(data, mySubList);
        else
            mySubList->SortedInsert(data);
}

bool LLNode::isInList(const string & data) const
{
    if (data == myData)
        return true;
    else if (NULL == mySubList)
        return false;
    else
        return mySubList->isInList(data);
}

int LLNode::Count() const
{
    if (NULL == mySubList)
        return 0;
    else
        return 1 + mySubList->Count();
}

void LLNode::Display(ostream & os) const
{
    if ("" != myData)
        os << myData << endl;
    if (NULL != mySubList)
        mySubList->Display(os);
}

void LLNode::ReverseDisplay(ostream & os) const
{
    if (NULL != mySubList)
        mySubList->ReverseDisplay(os);
    if ("" != myData)
        os << myData << endl;
}

typedef LLNode SortedStringList;
int main()
{
    SortedStringList theList;
    theList.SortedInsert("Fred");
    theList.SortedInsert("Barney");
    theList.SortedInsert("Wilma");
    theList.SortedInsert("Betty");

    cout << "Display!  Count is " << theList.Count() << endl;
```

continues

LISTING 11.4. CONTINUED

```
    theList.Display(cout);

    cout << "\nReverse Display!  Count is " << theList.Count() << endl;
    theList.ReverseDisplay(cout);

    return 0;
}
```

The following is the output from the code in Listing 11.4:

```
Display!  Count is 4
Barney
Betty
Fred
Wilma

Reverse Display!  Count is 4
Wilma
Fred
Betty
Barney
```

Let's look at the function `SortedInsert()`. As we write this function, we don't want to think about recursion at all. The purpose of the function is to accept a string and insert it somewhere within the list that the `Node` represents. Because we are actively forgetting about recursion, we have only one decision to make about where to insert this new data: Either it belongs between the `Node` and its sublist, or it should be inserted somewhere deep in the sublist, and we don't care where. The first line in this function says, "If the `Node` doesn't have a sublist or this data belongs before the sublist it does have, insert the data immediately after the `Node`." If the data does not belong before the sublist, then it must belong somewhere inside the sublist. At this point, we just let the sublist deal with it, and we trust that the sublist will do the right thing.

Now that the function is written, we have to think about recursion a bit. First, are we satisfied that there is a path through this function where no recursion occurs? Yes—if the test is `true`. Second, do we always get closer to this termination condition? Yes—because we know that we will always reach a `Node` that has no sublist. Finally, does the recursion start off properly? Hmmm, there is an issue if the insertion should take place before the first `Node`. So let's assume that the first `Node` in every complete list is a blank `Node` that does not contain any data. This guarantees that there is never a chance that new data should be inserted before the first `Node`. When a client wants to create one of these linked lists, the client creates a single `Node` without data, and that `Node` will play this role.

Recursion and Recursive Data Structures

CHAPTER 11

445

11

RECURSION AND
RECURSIVE DATA
STRUCTURES

Note that when we do insert a new `Node`, we are actually creating an entirely new sublist. The new `Node` has data and a sublist (our old one), which makes it a complete list, fully qualified to participate as a sublist.

Now look at the two `Display()` functions and the simple difference between them. The first tests are just to skip the false `Node`, which we added to simplify the insert process. Study these functions and remember to think of them not as displaying a list of `Node` data, but instead as displaying the `Node`'s data and then telling the `Node`'s sublist to display itself.

Tail Recursion

Listing 11.3 contains a good example of tail recursion in the `LLNode::Display()` function (although not the `ReverseDisplay()` function). In this function, the recursive call is the very last operation before the function returns. This is an example of tail recursion. Tail recursion is important to people who develop compilers because all tail recursion can be trivially replaced by iteration. This substitution is generally a noticeable optimization because you save the processing time of putting arguments on the stack and making the function call. The reason compilers can confidently make this optimization is because there is no chance that the function will need its variables anymore. There is no need to make new copies of all the local variables if you are sure that they won't be needed.

Here is the C++ equivalent of the code an optimizing compiler would make for the `LLNode::Display()` function:

```
void LLNode::Display(ostream & os) const
{
    const LLNode * p = this;
TailRecursionLabel1:
    if ("" != p->myData)
        os << p->myData << endl;
    if (NULL != p->mySubList)
        {
        p = p->mySubList;
        goto TailRecursionLabel1;
        }
}
```

> **NOTE**
>
> Please don't send me email messages about the `goto` statement. I originally had a `do..while` loop with a `break`, but the preceding example is much closer to what the compiler would really create. The compiled version of any significant piece of code has what amounts to hundreds of `goto`s.

When should you think about tail recursion? Probably never—unless you work for a company that makes compilers. When I wrote the Count() function, I purposely wrote the function the way I did so that the compiler would optimize it for me. But it probably would have done so anyway. However, if you casually drop the phrase *tail recursion* into conversation at work, you will really come off as a mega-geek, which is probably the most use to which you can put this knowledge.

Indirect Recursion

Indirect recursion is where a function does not actually call itself, but it calls a different function that may then call the first function. In the File/Directory example from earlier in this chapter, we could create a DisplayChildren() method for the Directory class. Then we could change Directory::Display() to a call to File::Display() and a call to DisplayChildren(). This would now be an example of indirect recursion.

Listing 11.4 shows the new class declaration and its two methods. You can see that Display() does not call itself, but it does call DisplayChildren(). DisplayChildren() does not call itself, but it does call Display(). This is an example of indirect recursion. Note that this is not a complete listing; it shows just the classes.

LISTING 11.5. THE FILE AND DIRECTORY CLASSES USING INDIRECT RECURSION

```
class Directory : public File
{
public:
    Directory(const string & name) : File(name) {}
    ~Directory();

    virtual void Display(ostream & os,
                         int level = 1,
                         const string & prefix = "");
    void DisplayChildren(ostream & os, int level,
                         const string & prefix);
    void AddFile(File * fp) {m_FileList.push_back(fp);}
private:
    list<File *> m_FileList;
    typedef list<File *>::iterator FileIter;
};

// To display a Directory, output name and newline, then
// Display all of my contained Files using recursive call
void Directory::Display(ostream & os, int level, const string & prefix)
{
    File::Display(os, level, prefix);
    string newPrefix = prefix + getName() + ":";
    DisplayChildren(os, level, newPrefix);
```

Recursion and Recursive Data Structures

CHAPTER 11

447

11

RECURSION AND
RECURSIVE DATA
STRUCTURES

```
}

void Directory::DisplayChildren(ostream & os,
                    int level, const string & prefix)
{
    for (FileIter iter = m_FileList.begin();
                iter != m_FileList.end();
                iter++)
        (*iter)->Display(os, level + 1, prefix);
}
```

Recursion and the Stack

In the discussion of the Fibonacci function, it was noted that the computer has no trouble keeping track of where it is with each level of recursion, and that it makes new copies of all of the variables for each recursive level. The way the computer does this is by using the stack. The *stack* is a block of memory allocated by the compiler for exactly the purpose of keeping its place in a function when the function makes a call to any other function. Much like a stack of plates, you can add a new plate only to the top of the stack; you can take only the top plate off the top of the stack. There is no way to insert or remove from anywhere else in the stack.

When you make a function call, the computer saves on the stack (on the top, of course) four things, which are listed here. Note that this process is true for all function calls, not just those that are recursive:

1. *(still in your function)* The parameters you are passing to the function.

2. *(as it travels to the other function)* The code location to return to when the called function is completed.

3. *(inside the called function)* Your "base pointer" so that it will be able to restore it when it is done. It then sets the base pointer to the current stack location, for its own use. The base pointer is how it finds both the parameters you passed in and the local variables for which it is about to allocate space on the stack.

4. *(inside the called function)* Space for any local variables the function needs.

Of course, your function went through these same steps when it was called. In your function, every time you access one of the parameters you passed in or one of the automatic variables you declared as local to your function, the function pulls these values out of memory at a location defined by the base pointer—plus or minus some known amount. When a function returns, it undoes all these steps, in reverse order: The function deallocates the space for local variables, restores the base pointer of the caller, and returns to the code address saved (popping that address off the stack at the same time). Finally, the function deallocates the space for the parameters that were passed in.

When a function calls itself, this process doesn't change. In fact, the compiler does not even know the difference. But we can see that this process supports the effect we want. Each time our recursive function calls itself, new copies of the parameters are saved on the stack, the return address is saved if we are in the middle of evaluating an expression (as in the Fibonacci function), and the new recursion allocates its own space for all the local variables. In the function `Directory::Display()`, for example, the variable `newPrefix` is allocated fresh each time the function is called. This arrangement does not interfere with other versions of that variable that are still alive inside earlier recursions of the function.

Now we can consider the effects of infinite recursion—that is, recursion for which the author did not properly confirm the termination requirements. Every time you recurse, some amount of stack space is used. Even if you created a recursive function with no parameters and no local variables, you cannot get around the need to save the base pointer and the return address. If your function never stops recursing, it will grow the stack until the memory allocated for the stack is used up. Typically, the stack space is adjacent to the global memory that will be tromped on in the computer's desperate attempt to save base pointers and return addresses. Eventually, your computer will write over something critical or it will have a memory fault. In either case, your program will halt (or maybe your whole computer will halt). Because this is rarely the desired result, you should check your termination requirements carefully.

It is possible to have a similar result even with the termination requirements carefully implemented. You can halt the program or the computer if the proper recursion requires more stack space than you have allocated. If you have large variables that have to be allocated inside each level of recursion, you might consider doing so on the heap and just storing a pointer as a local variable. If you do want to calculate your memory requirements, remember that you only have to worry about the maximum depth of recursion, not the total number of times the recursive function is called. For example, consider the `Directory/File` example, with the recursive function `Directory::Display()`. Although this function is called for every `Directory` that exists, we never have both `SubDir 1` and `SubDir 3` stored on the stack at the same time. We are completely done with `SubDir 1` and all its children—and we have freed up all the stack space that they used—long before we have anything to do with `SubDir 3`.

Debugging Recursive Functions

We have now become adept at forgetting about the recursion when we are writing recursive functions and structures. Unfortunately, when we are debugging, we become all too aware of recursion because it is tricky to set a breakpoint inside the function without setting one inside the function that it calls. You cannot even single-step over the function call because the debugger secretly sets a temporary breakpoint when you step over a call. This breakpoint will be triggered somewhere deep inside the recursion, and you will be totally confused.

There are a couple of techniques for getting around these problems. The first is to tack on an extra parameter in your recursive function so that you always know where you are. You can even make conditional breakpoints (if your debugger supports them) that require you to be at a certain line *and* require the value of level to be some known quantity.

Another technique for getting around problems with breakpoints is to create a complete clone of your recursive function, which is the function the outside world calls. This function is safe to trace through, as you safely hop over the not-really-recursive calls. Of course, if you try this approach, you have to be careful to keep the two functions *true* clones, and you have to get rid of the extra function when you are done debugging.

Summary

Recursion has long been a source of fear and wonder for many aspiring software developers. However, if you start by *forgetting* about the recursion while you are writing the class or function, development is easier. Although you do have to go back and check the requirements that the recursion will terminate, and you have to take a little care in debugging, overall, recursion is nothing to fear.

CHAPTER 12

Designing Efficient Sorting Methods

Sorting is one of the most important functions performed in many applications. This chapter considers several strategies you can use for the purpose of sorting data and also compares the amount of work involved in each of these methods. As you read through the chapter, you will realize that the efficiency of the particular method depends on several factors such as implementation of the code and the actual data being sorted. Before you decide to use any sort method, you should test it against various types of input—and especially against some sample of the data that you will be sorting.

When you sort a given set of data (records), you do so with a *key value* contained in each record. This key value can be just one item of the record or it can be built using several items of the record. As far as the sorting process is concerned, however, the entire record is represented by the key value for that record. A sort eventually reorders the records based on their key values. Sorts can therefore be used to improve the performance of searching methods.

The dependence of the sort's efficiency on the input data will become clear as we look at different implementations. For a particular implementation of a sort method, the worst case and the best case are determined by the nature of the input data. For example, for some sort methods the amount of work done for forward-sorted records is linear, but the same method does work on the order of n2 for reverse-sorted records.

Analyzing the Performance of Algorithms

Unlike benchmarks, the performance of algorithms such as those for sorting and searching are not measured in terms of execution time because these algorithms are data dependent. Such data-driven algorithms are expressed in terms of the size of the input using the symbol O. This notation is referred to as the *Big-O notation*. Depending on the type of algorithm, the work done (and therefore the algorithm's performance) is determined by different characteristics. For example, for sorting algorithms such as a bubble sort, the number of comparisons done to place elements in their proper places is very important. As the algorithm attempts to sort the set of N elements, it performs a number of comparisons and swaps the elements if they are not in the desired order. For a bubble sort, the performance is given as `O((n² - n)/2)`. While sorting the list of N elements, the sort traverses the list once for each element in the list; at the end of each traversal, one element is placed in its correct location and is not considered for future traversals.

The search for a better-performing algorithm equates to the search for an algorithm that has a better equation represented by Big-O. Algorithms that perform worse than n2 are considered to be unusable; you should strive for `O(n)`. It should be understood that the degree of n (the data input size) is more important than the constant that precedes n.

In other words, you can say that O(n) is not much better than O(3n) but is much better than O(n²). You can easily see this truth by using specific values for n. A computer that performs an operation in 1 nanosecond can take over 90 years to complete an algorithm with a Big-O equation of O(n³), but that same computer can take only a couple hours to complete an algorithm with a Big-O equation of O(15,000,000n). As a result, Big-O notation does not consider the constants; it considers only the degree. Therefore, the performance of O(n) is comparable to the performance of O(4n).

Comparing the Average, Worst, and Best Cases

You should be very careful not to get caught up with the Big-O notation. Keep in mind that the performance is *data* dependent and not just *data-size* dependent. This means that your algorithm may have one order with certain types of data input and a different order with other types of data input. You should always understand the algorithm by looking at how it behaves *on an average*—under the best-case and also under the worst-case scenario. These various scenarios are based on the type of data that causes it to perform more or less work to get the desired result. Do not be surprised if you encounter an algorithm that performs very well on average but has a worst-case behavior so bad that you choose another algorithm that performs poorly on average simply because its worst-case behavior is not so bad. Table 12.1 shows how two algorithms compare for different values for n.

TABLE 12.1. COMPARING NLOGN WITH N²

Data Items (N)	Average Case: nlogn	Worse Case: n²
8	24	64
64	384	4096
2048	22528	4194304

NOTE

Best-case performance is generally not analyzed because it does not forecast potential dangers in an algorithm. However, you should still look at the best-case scenario because the best case can give you insight into the algorithm that enables you to manipulate the implementation to your advantage. For example, in the bubble sort method, if the data input is presorted (the best case), the bubble sort performs in O(n); however, on average, the bubble sort performs in O(n²). It is quite possible that the data is known in advance; if you know the data that the algorithm will process, you can choose the algorithm for which that data represents the best case.

Optimizing algorithms means that you should try to reduce the time it takes to perform the algorithm's most frequent operations. For sorting algorithms, optimization means minimizing the time it takes to perform comparisons and swapping. You can do this by performing these operations in memory and not on disk. You can see that the implementation of the code plays a major part in the optimization of the algorithm. However, the overall behavior of the algorithm does not change with implementation. In other words, no matter how you code the performance of a bubble sort, on average the algorithm performs in $O(n^2)$.

The Big-O notation gives us a way to compare algorithms, provided that all aspects are equal. It must be understood that Big-O is significant for sufficiently large values of n because, for small values of n, the constants (that Big-O ignores) can become an important part of the sort method's efficiency. For example, if $A_1(n) = 20n$ and $A_2(n) = 3000n$, they are both $O(n)$—but in reality, A_2 is 150 times faster than A_1. It can therefore be concluded that, all things being equal, an $O(n)$ algorithm always outperforms an $O(n^2)$ algorithm.

The Stability of Sorts

A sort is considered to be *stable* if it maintains any preexisting ordering of the records it is sorting. Suppose that you want to sort all the employees in a company by their department_code. The employees are already sorted by their employee_no. A stable sort by department_code would maintain the preexisting sort by employee_no. Stability of sort methods is possible in simple techniques, but as you look at more sophisticated sort methods, you will realize that it is very difficult to maintain stability. For this example, you can convert an unstable sort into a stable sort by using a composite key that contains both the employee_no and the department_code. However, this composite key may not be desired under certain circumstances.

Using Additional Storage During Sorting

Another factor that becomes significant when deciding among sort methods is the space requirement. Some sort methods require a trivial amount of temporary space; others require twice as much space as the size of the input. Recursive methods make use of stack space; you should implement the code carefully to minimize the use of additional space.

In addition to the temporary space requirement, the size of the input can sometimes force you to choose an external sorting method. Internal sorting occurs when the input can be loaded in main memory all at the same time. In contrast, if the input is too large for the main memory, you end up using the mass storage media for a portion of the input. In external sorts, the input is split into chunks that can be loaded into the main memory.

The chunks are sorted individually and then merged together. It is beyond the scope of this chapter to discuss external sorts in detail. However, we will discuss the merge sort method, which will give you some idea of how and when external sorts are used.

The Bubble Sort

The bubble sort is one of the simplest sort methods you can use. This method works well for simple data structures or if the data set to be sorted is more or less already sorted. The bubble sort is very inefficient for a general data set. In the bubble sort algorithm, successive sweeps are made through the records to be sorted. During each sweep, the algorithm compares the key to the data elements and swaps the elements if they are not in the desired order. Swapping occurs only among consecutive elements of the data structure. As a result, only one element is placed in its sorted place after each sweep. The sorted elements are not needed for comparison in successive sweeps. Here is the pseudocode for bubble sorting an array of n elements in ascending order:

```
For iteration = 0 to (n-1)
Begin
    For I = 0 to (n -1 - iteration)
    Begin
        if array[i] > array[i+1] then
            swap array[i] and array[i+1]
    end
end
```

A C++ implementation of this algorithm is shown in Listing 12.1.

LISTING 12.1. BUBBLE SORT IMPLEMENTATION

```cpp
// Program: bubble_sort.cpp
// Author: Megh Thakkar
// Purpose: Sort an array of n elements in ascending order
// using the bubble sort method

#include <stdio.h>
#include <string.h>
#include <stdlib.h>
#include <iostream.h>

class sort {
private:
        int *X;         //List of data elements
        int n;          //Number of elements in the list
    public:
        sort (int size) { X = new int[n=size]; }
```

continues

LISTING 12.1. CONTINUED

```cpp
                ~sort( ) { delete [ ]X; }
                void load_list (int input[ ] );
                void show_list (char *title);
                void bubble_sort( int input[ ]);
};

void sort::load_list(int input[ ])
{
    for (int i = 0; i < n; i++)
        X[i] = input[i];
}

void sort::show_list( char *title)
{
        cout << "\n" << title;
    for (int i = 0; i < n; i++)
                cout << " " << X[i];
        cout << "\n";
}

void sort::bubble_sort( int input[ ])
{
    int swapped = 1;
    char *title;
    load_list(input);
    show_list("List to be sorted in ascending order using bubble sort");

// The FOR loop is executed once for each element in the array.
// At the end of each iteration, one element will be "bubbled" to
// its correct position and is not considered for further iterations
// of the loop.
    for ( int i = 0; i < n && swapped == 1; i++)
    {
// If at the end of an iteration there was no swapping done
// then it indicates that the list is sorted as desired and
// there is no need to do more iterations.
        swapped = 0;
                for (int j = 0; j < n-(i+1) ; j++)
// if X[j] > X[j+1] then it indicates that they are out of order.
// Therefore swap them.
        if   ( X[j] > X[j+1] )
        {
            int temp;
            temp = X[j];
            X[j] = X[j+1];
            X[j+1] = temp;
            swapped = 1;
        }
```

```
    }
    show_list("List sorted in ascending order using bubble sort");
}

//main( ) : Test driver for bubble sort
void main(void)
{
// Create a new object which has the method "bubble_sort"
        sort sort_obj(5);
    static int unsorted_list[] = {54,6,26,73,1};
sort_obj.bubble_sort(unsorted_list);
}
```

As Listing 12.1 shows, the maximum number of swaps occurs when the list is sorted in the reverse order of the desired sorting order. In other words, maximum swaps occur if you want to sort the list in ascending order but the list is currently sorted in descending order.

Analysis of the Bubble Sort

The bubble sort has several characteristics:

- After each iteration, only one data element is placed in its proper sorted position.
- The bubble sort depends on the comparing and swapping of *consecutive* data elements.
- In each execution of the inner loop, there are at most (n-iteration-1) number of swaps.
- The worst-case scenario is when the data elements are reverse ordered.
- The best-case scenario is when the data elements are *almost* sorted in the correct order.
- The bubble sort has a simple implementation.

The Insertion Sort

The insertion sort is a very simple sorting method that uses the data elements as keys for comparison. The algorithm first orders A[0] and A[1] by inserting A[1] in front of A[0] if A[0] > A[1]. Using this ordered list, the rest of the data elements are iteratively inserted in the ordered list, one at a time. After the kth iteration, A[k] is inserted in its correct sorted position and A[0] through A[k] are sorted. The pseudocode for this method is as follows:

```
For done = 0 to n-1
begin
```

```
      temp = array[done]
      for I = done - 1 to 0
      begin
          while ( array[i] > temp ) {
            array[i+1] = array[i]
            I++;
          }
      end
      array[i+1] = temp
end
```

A C++ implementation of the insertion sort algorithm is shown in Listing 12.2.

LISTING 12.2. INSERTION SORT IMPLEMENTATION

```cpp
// Program: insertion_sort.cpp
// Author: Megh Thakkar
// Purpose: Sort an array of n elements in ascending order
// using the insertion sort method
#include <stdio.h>
#include <string.h>
#include <stdlib.h>
#include <iostream.h>

class sort {
    private:
        int *X;            //List of data elements
        int n;             //Number of data elements
        int scan_no;
    public:
        sort (int size) { X = new int[n=size]; }
        ~sort( ) { delete [ ]X; }
        void load_list (int input[ ] );
        void show_list (char *title);
        void insertion_sort( int input[ ]);
};

void sort::load_list(int input[ ])
{
    for (int i = 0; i < n; i++){
        X[i] = input[i];


    }
}

void sort::show_list( char *title)
{
        cout << "\n" << title;
    for (int i = 0; i < n; i++)
            cout << " " << X[i];
        cout << "\n";
```

```
}

void sort::insertion_sort( int input[ ])
{

    char *title;
// The array S is used for storing the elements as they get sorted.
        int S[100];
        load_list(input);
    show_list("List to be sorted in the ascending order using insertion
➥sort");

        S[0] = X[0];

//Each iteration of the FOR loop compares X[i] with the elements
//in the sorted list S, in order to find its place in the array S.
        for (int i = 1; i < n ; i++)
    {
                int temp = X[i];
                int j = i-1;

                while (( S[j] > temp ) && ( j >= 0))
                            {
                        S[j+1] = S[j];
                        j—;
                            }

            S[j+1] = temp;

        }

//The method "show_list" uses the private array X. Therefore, we copy the
// sorted array S to X , so that it can be printed.
        for (int m = 0; m < n; m++)
                X[m] = S[m];

    show_list("List sorted in ascending order using insertion sort");
}

void main(void)
{
    sort sort_obj(5);
    static int unsorted_list[] = {54,6,26,73,1};
    sort_obj.insertion_sort(unsorted_list);
}
```

Notice how a "hole" is created in the sorted portion of the list. The "hole" is created by copying the data to the `temp` location and by copying `S[j]` to `S[j+1]` if `S[j] > temp`. This hole moves backward through the sorted data elements until the correct spot for the new element is found. At this point, the `while` loop ends and inserts the element from the temporary space into the correct position.

Analysis of the Insertion Sort

The insertion sort has several characteristics:

- After each iteration, only one data element is placed in its proper sorted position.

- The insertion sort uses fewer swaps than the bubble sort. This can easily be seen because the bubble sort method always "bubbles" the largest element to the top; the insertion sort moves the "hole" through already sorted elements and can generally traverse only half of the sorted elements before it finds the spot for the new insertion.

- The worst-case scenario is when the data elements are reverse ordered.

- The best-case scenario is when the data elements are *almost* sorted in the correct order.

- The insertion sort has a simple implementation.

A very important design consideration for an insertion sort is the choice of scan direction through the sorted records. In other words, do you scan first-to-last or vice-versa through the sorted records? This decision is very important; the correct answer depends on the actual data you want to sort. To understand the importance of the scan direction, suppose that the list is sorted in reverse order {5,4,3,2,1}. If you decide to scan last-to-first through the sorted records, you can see that, with every iteration, the next element to insert is lower than the already sorted elements, and the sort takes fewer comparisons than if you had scanned in the first-to-last direction. On the other hand, if the list was almost sorted, a first-to-last scan direction would be faster and would require fewer comparisons than a last-to-first scan direction.

The Selection Sort

The selection sort algorithm is based on using the data elements as keys for comparison such that, at the end of each scan, only one data element is placed in its desired sorted position. This algorithm is simple but very inefficient because it does not consider partial or fully sorted lists. In other words, if you have a partially or fully presorted list, the selection sort does the same number of comparisons as it would on a completely random list and does not use any intelligence (unlike the bubble sort) to improve the performance. As a result, the selection sort method does not really lend itself to a best-case scenario. For a list of n data elements, the selection sort always does (n-1) iterations.

The pseudocode for the selection sort algorithm is shown here:

For j = 0 to (n-1), do the following steps:

1. For the elements X[j+1] through X[n-1], perform key comparisons and find the lowest element; we'll call that element X[lower].

2. Swap X[lower] with X[j]. X[lower] is now in its sorted position.

At the end of the loop, the list is sorted.

A C++ implementation of the selection sort is shown in Listing 12.3.

LISTING 12.3. SELECTION SORT IMPLEMENTATION

```cpp
// Program: selection_sort.cpp
// Author: Megh Thakkar
// Purpose: Sort an array of n elements in ascending order
//          using the selection sort method
#include <stdio.h>
#include <string.h>
#include <stdlib.h>
#include <iostream.h>

class sort {
    private:
        int *X;             //List of data elements
        int n;              //Number of elements in the list
    public:
        sort (int size) { X = new int[n=size]; }
        ~sort( ) { delete [ ]X; }
        void load_list (int input[ ] );
        void show_list (char *title);
        void selection_sort( int input[ ]);
};

void sort::load_list(int input[ ])
{
    for (int i = 0; i < n; i++)
        X[i] = input[i];
}

void sort::show_list( char *title)
{
        cout << "\n" << title;
    for (int i = 0; i < n; i++)
                cout << " " << X[i];
        cout << "\n";
}
```

continues

LISTING 12.3. CONTINUED

```
void sort::selection_sort( int input[ ])
{
    char *title;
    load_list(input);
    show_list("List to be sorted in the ascending order using selection
sort");

// Using the FOR loop, iteratively find the lowest element in the list
// and then move it to its correct position.
    for ( int j = 0; j < (n-1); j++)
    {
// For each iteration, start with the lowest element as the element
// at index j.
            int lowest = j;
            for ( int k = j+1; k < n ; k++)
                    {
                if (X[k] < X[lowest])
                  lowest = k;
                    }

//Once an element lower than the lowest known thus far is found, swap
them.
                    int temp;
                    temp = X[j];
                    X[j] = X[lowest];
                    X[lowest] = temp;

    }

    show_list("List sorted in the ascending order using selection sort");
}

//main( ) : Test driver for selection sort
void main(void)
{
    sort sort_obj (5);
    static int unsorted_list[] = {54,6,26,73,1};
    sort_obj.selection_sort(unsorted_list);
}
```

Analysis of the Selection Sort

From Listing 12.3, you can see that for the outer loop iteration j, the inner loop does at most (n-j) number of comparisons and the outer loop is executed (n-1) times. The total number of comparisons for the selection sort can be calculated like this:

(n-1) + (n-2) + (n-3) +...+ [n-(n-1)] = n(n-1)/2 = $n^2/2 - n/2 = O(n^2)$.

Thus, this is the worst-case scenario. In fact, the best-case scenario also takes the same number of comparisons because it does not consider any partial sorting that might exist in the input.

The Quick Sort

The quick sort is the most efficient internal sort algorithm. Its performance is largely influenced by the choice of the pivot. The quick sort makes use of three strategies:

1. Split the array into small subarrays

2. Sort the subarrays

3. Merge the sorted subarrays

A quick sort can be implemented in several ways, but the goal of each approach is to select a data element and place it in its proper position (which is referred to as the *pivot*) so that all the elements on the left side of the pivot are less than (or come before) the pivot and all the elements on the right side of the pivot are greater than (or come after) the pivot. The choice of the pivot and the method used to split the array has a big influence on the overall performance of the implementation. We will focus on a recursive implementation of the quick sort. The pseudocode for this implementation is as follows:

1. Select a data element and position it as a pivot so that it divides the array into a left subarray and a right subarray as just described.

2. Apply a quick sort to the left subarray.

3. Apply a quick sort to the right subarray.

The choice of the pivot is crucial. The following strategy can be used as an efficient split method:

1. Choose the first data element's key as the pivot. In other words, Pivot = X[first].

2. Initialize two search pointers, I and j, such that I = first (the lowermost index of the subarray) and j = last (the uppermost index of the subarray).

3. Using the search pointer I, search from the left for a data element greater than or equal to the pivot. This can be done by using the following pseudocode:
   ```
   While A[i] <= Pivot and I < last,
   continue incrementing I by 1
   otherwise stop incrementing I
   ```

4. Using the search pointer j, search from the right for a data element less than or equal to the pivot. This can be done by using the following pseudocode:

12
DESIGNING EFFICIENT SORTING METHODS

```
          While A[j] >= Pivot and j > first
          continue decrementing j by 1
          Otherwise stop incrementing j
```

5. If I < j, swap A[i] and A[j].

6. Repeat steps 2 through 4 until I > j.

7. Swap the pivot with A[j].

At the end of step 7, the pivot will be positioned as desired. This process is implemented in C++ using the code shown in Listing 12.4.

LISTING 12.4. QUICK SORT IMPLEMENTATION

```cpp
// Program: quick_sort.cpp
// Author: Megh Thakkar
// Purpose: Sort an array of n elements in ascending order
//          using the quick sort method
#include <stdio.h>
#include <string.h>
#include <stdlib.h>
#include <iostream.h>

class sort {
    private:
        int *X;            //List of data elements
        int n;             //Number of elements in the list
    public:
        sort (int size) { X = new int[n=size]; }
        ~sort( ) { delete [ ]X; }
        void load_list (int input[ ] );
        void show_list (char *title);
        void quick_sort( int first, int last);
};

void sort::load_list(int input[ ])
{
    for (int i = 0; i < n; i++)
        X[i] = input[i];
}

void sort::show_list( char *title)
{
        cout << "\n" << title;
    for (int i = 0; i < n; i++)
                cout << " " << X[i];
        cout << "\n";
}

void sort::quick_sort( int first, int last)
{
```

Designing Efficient Sorting Methods

CHAPTER 12

465

12

DESIGNING
EFFICIENT SORTING
METHODS

```
//"temp" variable is temporary space used during swapping
        int temp;
    if (first < last)
    {
//Start with the pivot as the first element in the list
        int pivot = X[first];
//The variable "i" is used for scanning from the left.
        int i = first;
//The variable "j" is used for scanning from the right.
        int j = last;
        while (i < j)
        {
// Search the list for a data element that is greater than or equal to
// the chosen pivot element. Search from the left.
            while (X[i] <= pivot && i < last)
                i += 1;
// Search the list for a data element that is less than or equal to
// the chosen pivot element. Search from the right.
            while (X[j] >= pivot && j > first)
                j -= 1;
            if (i < j) //swap(X[i],X[j])
                    {
                            temp = X[i];
                            X[i] = X[j];
                            X[j] = temp;
                    }

        }
                //swap(X[j],X[first])
                temp = X[first];
                X[first] = X[j];
                X[j] = temp;

//Recursively apply quick sort on the two splits
        quick_sort(first, j-1);
        quick_sort(j+1, last);
    }
}

//main( ) : Test driver for quick sort
void main(void)
{
    sort sort_obj (5);
    static int unsorted_list[] = {54,6,26,73,1};
        sort_obj.load_list(unsorted_list);
        sort_obj.show_list("List to be sorted in ascending order using
➡quick sort");
    sort_obj.quick_sort(0,4);
        sort_obj.show_list("List sorted in ascending order using quick
➡sort");
}
```

Analysis of the Quick Sort

The quick sort method should be one of the first you consider for internal sorts. With this algorithm, the split phase is complex and the merge phase is simple. In the best case, the work done is on the order of nlog2n; in the worst case, the work is equivalent to a selection sort, resulting in $O(n^2)$. The choice of the pivot is very important for the performance of the quick sort.

The Merge Sort

The merge sort is a very efficient method for external sorting when the data elements to be sorted do not fit in the available memory and you have to use a disk to perform the sort. The merge sort uses the same strategy as the quick sort:

1. Split the file into smaller files.
2. Sort the smaller files.
3. Merge the sorted files.

In the quick sort, the split is the complicated step and the merge is the simple step; in the merge sort, the split step is simple and the merge step is more involved. There are several versions of the merge sort, based on the strategy used for the split and merge phases. We will focus on the merge sort using the iterative method. Here are the steps involved in this method:

1. Open the file to be sorted (to_sort) in read/write mode; also open two temporary files for writing.
2. *Split Phase:* Copy elements of the to_sort file one at a time alternately to the temporary files.
3. *Merge Phase:* Compare each element from the two temporary files and write the lesser of the two elements first, followed by the greater, back to the to_sort file.
4. *Split Phase:* Copy the elements from to_sort two at a time alternately to the temporary files.
5. *Merge Phase:* Compare each group of two elements from the temporary files and write the lesser of the two element groups first, followed by the greater group, back to the to_sort file.
6. Repeat the split and merge phases with the group size 2I for I = 2,3,4,...log2n. The result is a sorted to_sort file.

Figure 12.1 shows how the merge sort works.

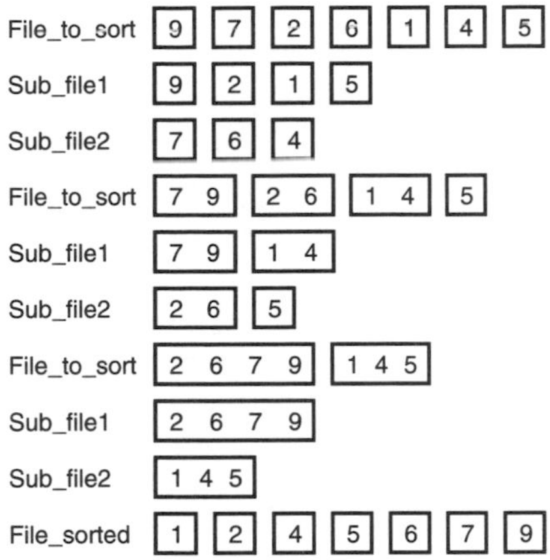

FIGURE 12.1.

The merge sort.

A C++ implementation of a merge sort is shown in Listing 12.5.

LISTING 12.5. MERGE SORT IMPLEMENTATION

```
//Program: merge_sort.cpp
//Author: Megh Thakkar
//Purpose: Sort a file containing data elements using merge sort
#include  <stdio.h>
#include  <stdlib.h>
#include <iostream.h>

#define   MIN(x,y)  ( (x <= y) ? x : y )

enum      STATUS  {UNSORTED, SORTED, DATA_AVAILABLE,
                   END_OF_FILE};

void open_for_split(FILE *sorted_file, FILE *sub_file1,FILE *sub_file2){

        rewind (sorted_file);
    fclose (sub_file1);
    fclose (sub_file2);

    remove ("subfile1.fil");
    remove ("subfile2.fil");

    sub_file1 = fopen ("subfile1.fil", "w+");
    sub_file2 = fopen ("subfile2.fil", "w+");
}

void open_for_merge(FILE *sorted_file, FILE *sub_file1,FILE *sub_file2){

    fclose (sorted_file);
```

continues

LISTING 12.5. CONTINUED

```c
    remove ("result.fil");

    sorted_file = fopen ("result.fil", "w+");
    rewind (sub_file1);
    rewind (sub_file2);
}

void close_files(FILE *sorted_file, FILE *sub_file1,FILE *sub_file2){

  fclose (sorted_file);
  fclose (sub_file1 );
  fclose (sub_file2 );

  remove ("subfile1.fil");
  remove ("subfile2.fil");
}

void Merge_Sort (char *sorted_file_name)
{
  FILE        *sorted_file, *sub_file1, *sub_file2;
  enum STATUS  status = UNSORTED, status_file1, status_file2;
  int    data_read, read_from_file1, read_from_file2, last_considered = 0;
  int         curr_file = 1;

  sorted_file = fopen (sorted_file_name, "r+");
  sub_file1   = fopen ("subfile1.fil", "w+");
  sub_file2   = fopen ("subfile2.fil", "w+");

  if (sorted_file == NULL || sub_file1 == NULL || sub_file2 == NULL){
     cout<< "\nSorry. Files cannot be opened\n";
     exit (-1);
        }

  while (status == UNSORTED) {
          open_for_split( sorted_file, sub_file1, sub_file2);

        //Split the file into sub_file1 and sub_file2.
        //The if statement checks for any preexisting ordering
        //of data elements and tries to use it to speed up
        //the sort process.
    while (fscanf (sorted_file, "%d", &data_read) != EOF) {
      if (data_read < last_considered) {
        if (curr_file == 1)
                    fprintf (sub_file2, "%d ", data_read);
        else
                    fprintf (sub_file1, "%d ", data_read);
      }
      else{
         if (curr_file == 1)
```

```
                    fprintf (sub_file1, "%d ", data_read);
                else
                    fprintf (sub_file2, "%d ", data_read);
                }
                    last_considered = data_read;

        }

            open_for_merge( sorted_file, sub_file1, sub_file2);

        status_file1 = DATA_AVAILABLE;
        status_file2 = DATA_AVAILABLE;

        if (fscanf (sub_file1, "%d", &read_from_file1) == EOF) {
            status   = SORTED;
            status_file1 = END_OF_FILE;
        }

        if (fscanf (sub_file2, "%d", &read_from_file2) == EOF) {
            status   = SORTED;
            status_file2 = END_OF_FILE;
        }

        last_considered = MIN (read_from_file1, read_from_file2);

        while (status_file1 != END_OF_FILE &&
               status_file2 != END_OF_FILE) {
            if (read_from_file1 <= read_from_file2 && read_from_file1 >=
        ➥last_considered) {
                // Write values from sub_file1
                fprintf (sorted_file, "%d ", read_from_file1);
                last_considered = read_from_file1;
                if (fscanf (sub_file1, "%d", &read_from_file1) == EOF)
                    status_file1 = END_OF_FILE;
            }
            else if (read_from_file2 <= read_from_file1 && read_from_file2 >=
        ➥last_considered) {
                // Write values from sub_file2
                fprintf (sorted_file, "%d ", read_from_file2);
                last_considered = read_from_file2;
                if (fscanf (sub_file2, "%d", &read_from_file2) == EOF)
                    status_file2 = END_OF_FILE;
            }
            else if (read_from_file1 >= last_considered) {
                // Write values from sub_file1
                fprintf (sorted_file, "%d ", read_from_file1);
                last_considered = read_from_file1;
                if (fscanf (sub_file1, "%d", &read_from_file1) == EOF)
                    status_file1 = END_OF_FILE;
            }
```

12

DESIGNING
EFFICIENT SORTING
METHODS

continues

LISTING 12.5. CONTINUED

```
      else if (read_from_file2 >= last_considered) {
        // Write values from sub_file2
        fprintf (sorted_file, "%d ", read_from_file2);
        last_considered = read_from_file2;
        if (fscanf (sub_file2, "%d", &read_from_file2) == EOF)
          status_file2 = END_OF_FILE;
      }
      else
        last_considered = MIN (read_from_file1, read_from_file2);
    }

  while (status_file1 != END_OF_FILE) {
      //Now the rest of sub_file1 can be written
      fprintf (sorted_file, "%d ", read_from_file1);
      if (fscanf (sub_file1, "%d", &read_from_file1) == EOF)
        status_file1 = END_OF_FILE;
  }
  while (status_file2 != END_OF_FILE) {
      //Now the rest of sub_file2 can be written
      fprintf (sorted_file, "%d ", read_from_file2);
      if (fscanf (sub_file2, "%d", &read_from_file2) == EOF)
        status_file2 = END_OF_FILE;
  }
  }

  close_files( sorted_file, sub_file1, sub_file2);
}

void main(void)
{

  cout << "Sorting filename : tosort.fil" << "\n\n\n";
  Merge_Sort ("result.fil");
  cout << "File has been sorted. Please see filename: result.fil" <<
➥ "\n\n\n";
}
```

Analysis of the Merge Sort

The merge sort is an example of the divide-and-conquer strategy. In this method, the split phase is simple: it simply halves the list. The merge phase is more complex. In each scan, the merge sort passes over the entire file and thus performs $O(n)$ comparisons. In the first scan, the merge sort considers only one list. In the second scan, the algorithm splits the list into halves and then sorts and merges them. In the kth scan, the algorithm splits the list into sublists, which are 2^k-1 in number. You can easily see that because we are basically halving the list, we have at the most $\log_2 n$ sublists for a list with n elements. In the worst case, the merge sort has a performance on the order of $n\log^2 n$—much better than most of the other methods.

The Shell Sort

The shell sort is a variation of the insertion sort. The insertion sort has the limitation that it compares consecutive data elements only—and as a result, a swap moves an element only one space. Elements far away from their correct location require many passes through the sort to properly place them. The shell sort allows "jumps" in sorting order to occur. To permit this, the records are subdivided into interleaved groups, and each group is sorted using an insertion sort. The subdivision is performed using an increment value (say h) to begin with; the increment value divides the original array into h subarrays. These subarrays are then sorted using an insertion or bubble sort. This step is referred to as an *h-sort*. The h-sort process is repeated using diminishing values for h until the last value of h is 1. During the last scan, the list is almost sorted, and the insertion sort during the final scan can complete the process in linear time, resulting in a sorted list. The shell sort is therefore also referred to as the *diminishing increment sort*.

The selection of an appropriate sequence of values for h is very important. A lot of research has been done regarding the choice of values for h without a clear mandate about how to make this choice. In the C++ implementation in Listing 12.6, we use the following strategy to choose the values for h. The following is a strategy that has been found to work well:

1. Let $h_1 = 1$ and n equal the number or elements to sort.
2. Let $h_{s+1} = 3 * h_s + 1$, stopping when h > n/9.

LISTING 12.6. SHELL SORT IMPLEMENTATION

```
// Program: shell_sort.cpp
// Author: Megh Thakkar
// Purpose: Sort an array of n elements in ascending order
//          using the shell sort method
#include <stdio.h>
#include <string.h>
#include <stdlib.h>
#include <iostream.h>

class sort {
    private:
        int *X;          //List of data elements
        int n;           //Number of data elements in the list
    public:
```

continues

12

DESIGNING
EFFICIENT SORTING
METHODS

LISTING 12.6. CONTINUED

```cpp
            sort (int size) { X = new int[n=size]; }
            ~sort( ) { delete [ ]X; }
            void load_list (int input[ ] );
            void show_list (char *title);
            void shell_sort( int input[ ]);
};

void sort::load_list(int input[ ])
{
    for (int i = 0; i < n; i++)
        X[i] = input[i];
}

void sort::show_list( char *title)
{
        cout << "\n" << title;
    for (int i = 0; i < n; i++)
                cout << " " << X[i];
        cout << "\n";
}

void sort::shell_sort( int input[ ])
{
    int i,h;
    int temp;
//Load the input list in the private array
    load_list(input);
    show_list("List to be sorted: ");
//Implementing the shell_sort algorithm
    for (h = 1; h <= n/9; h = 3*h + 1)
        ;
//Use diminishing values for "h"--the step.
    for ( ; h > 0; h /=3)
    {

        for (i = h ; i < n ; i++)
        {
            int j;
            temp = X[i];
            for ( j = i-h ; j >=0 ; j -= h )
            {
            if (temp < X[j])
            {
                X[j+h] = X[j];
            }
            else
                break;
            }
        X[j+h] = temp;
```

```
        }
    }

    show_list("List sorted using shell sort: ");
}

//main( ) : Test driver for shell sort
void main(void)
{
// Create a new object of the class "sort"
    sort sort_obj(10);
// List to be sorted
    static int unsorted_list[] = {54,6,26,73,1,43,51,83,5,28};
//Call the method shell_sort
    sort_obj.shell_sort(unsorted_list);

}
```

Analysis of the Shell Sort

A lot of research has been done about the shell sort, and it has shown that the worst-case performance is in the range of $n^{1.25}$ to $1.6n^{1.25}$. The efficiency of this method is largely influenced by the choice of the sequence of values for h. As mentioned earlier, there is no ideal formula for choosing this sequence, but well-chosen sequences have shown the performance of the shell sort to be on the order of $n(\log_2 n)^2$. The shell sort is pretty much insensitive to the input data, and so it performs worse than the bubble sort and insertion sort when the input data is almost sorted. However, for random data sets, the shell sort should be among your top considerations.

The Heap Sort

The heap sort does its job by looking at the array as a binary tree with certain characteristics. It basically rearranges the data elements in a tree so that the value at each node is greater than or equal to the values of its children. Keep in mind that the nodes in the heap are not sorted. However, the condition that any given parent node has a larger data element than all its child nodes ensures that the largest data element is at the top of the heap. If you then remove this top data element and swap it with the end of the array, the element is in its proper sorted position. The heap condition can now be reinforced: search through the remaining data elements to find the largest element among them. By repeating this procedure, you eventually sort the array.

A C++ implementation of a heap sort is shown in Listing 12.7.

LISTING 12.7. HEAP SORT IMPLEMENTATION

```cpp
//Program: heap_sort.cpp
//Author: Megh Thakkar
//Purpose: Sort an Array of data elements using heap sort method.

#include  <iostream.h>

class Heap {
  private:
    int  *X;
    int  heap_size;
  public:
    Heap (int n);
    ~Heap ()     { delete [] X; }
    void establish_heap_property (int root, int limit);
    void construct_heap (void);
    void heap_sort (int input[]);
    void show_list (char *title);
        void load_list(int input[]);
};

Heap::Heap (int n)
{
    X = new int [n + 1];
    heap_size = n;
}

void Heap::load_list(int input[ ])
{
    for (int i = 1; i <= 10; i++)
        X[i] = input[i-1];
}

void  Heap::establish_heap_property (int root, int limit)
{

    int  done = 0;
    int  biggest = X[root];
    int  j = 2 * root;
    while ((j <= limit) && (done == 0)) {
//Find which is the maximum among the left and right children
        if ((j < limit) && (X[j] < X[j + 1]))
            j++;
//Compare the maximum child found with biggest.
//If biggest is the maximum then we have established the heap property and
➥exit.
        if (biggest >= X[j])
            done= 1;
        else {
            X[j/2] = X[j];
```

```
            j = 2 * j;
        }
    }
    X[j/2] = biggest;
}

void  Heap::construct_heap (void)
{
    for (int i = heap_size/2; i > 0; i--)
        establish_heap_property (i, heap_size);

}

void  Heap::heap_sort (int input[])
{

    construct_heap ();

    for (int i = (heap_size - 1); i > 0; i--) {
        //Swap X[i+1] and X[1]
        int temp     = X[i + 1];
        X[i + 1] = X[1];
        X[1] = temp;
        //  Place the root in the sorted position
        input[i] = X[i + 1];
        establish_heap_property (1, i);
    }
    input[0] = X[1];
}

void  Heap::show_list (char *title)
{
//Based on whether the sorting is complete or not, different parts of
//the array are shown.
    cout << "\n" << title;
    for (int i = 1; i <= heap_size; i++)
        cout << "   " << X[i];
        cout << "\n";
}

void  main (void)
{

    Heap  heap_obj(10);
    //  Array of data elements to be sorted
    static  int input[] = {1,9,24,2,59,31,99,74,3,66};
    int sz = 10;

    cout << "List to be sorted: ";
```

continues

LISTING 12.7. CONTINUED

```
        for (int k = 0; k < sz; k++)
            cout << input[k] << " ";
        cout <<"\n\n\n";
        heap_obj.load_list(input);
    heap_obj.heap_sort (input);
    heap_obj.show_list ("List sorted using Heap sort: ");
}
```

Analysis of the Heap Sort

The heap sort method relies quite heavily on the `build_max_heap()` function. This function is used to build the heap and place the maximum value at the top so that it can be removed from consideration. The work done by this function is $O(n)$. An efficient implementation of this method can result in work that is $O(n\log_2 n)$.

Choosing a Sort Method

This chapter has discussed several algorithms for implementing a sort. Each of these algorithms represents a compromise of some kind because the best-case and worst-case scenarios for each depends on the actual data to be sorted. However, some algorithms are generally better than others because they minimize the number of comparisons, the number of swaps, or the number of scans. In general, if you have a small number of records to sort (say, less than a thousand), you can choose any of the advanced sort methods (such as the quick sort, heap sort, or shell sort) because, as shown in Table 12.2, the Big-O performance equation for the heap sort and quick sort are $O(n\log_2 n)$ and the shell sort is $O(n^{1.25})$. There is no significant difference between these performance statistics for small values of n.

You should also keep in mind that the actual implementation of a particular sort method determines the efficiency of that method. Table 12.3 compares the characteristics of different sort techniques. For example, for an insertion sort, the best-case scenario (presorted records) can easily become the worst-case scenario if you have a poor implementation (you scan last-to-first instead of first-to-last). The heap sort and shell sort have the advantage that they do not really depend on the input and are not affected by a true worst-case scenario. A clever implementation of the quick sort can often be much faster than any of the other advanced sort methods.

TABLE 12.2. COMPARING SORT METHODS

Sort Method	Worst Case	Best Case
Bubble sort	O(n2)	O(n)
Insertion sort	O(n2)	O(n)
Selection sort	O(n2)	O(n2)
Heap sort	O(nlog2n)	O(nlog2n)
Merge sort	O(nlog2n)	O(nlog2n)
Quick sort	O(n2)	O(nlog2n)
Shell sort	O(n(log2n)2)	

From Table 12.2, we can conclude that for a large number of data elements (a large n), the growth of $\log^2 n$ is smaller than n^2. As a result, sorting methods such as the heap sort, merge sort, and quick sort are very efficient. On the other hand, for a small number of data elements (a small n), sort methods such as the bubble sort, insertion sort, and selection sorts are efficient, as Table 12.3 shows.

TABLE 12.3. COMPARING THE CHARACTERISTICS OF SORT METHODS

Sort Method	Advantage	Disadvantage
Insertion sort	Code is simple	Comparisons are O(n2) on average
	Stable sort	
	In-place sorting of arrays	
	Comparisons are O(n) in the best case	
Heap sort	In-place sorting of arrays	Unstable sort
	Always O(nlogn) and relatively fast	Complex sort
Quick sort	On an average, this is the fastest	Complex code
		Worst-case performance is very bad
		Additional stack space required is O(logn)
		Unstable sort

continues

Table 12.3. Comparing the Characteristics of Sort Methods

Sort Method	Advantage	Disadvantage
Selection sort	Code is simple	Comparisons are $O(n^2)$ on average
	Stable sort	
	In-place sorting of arrays	
	Swapping is $O(n)$	
Shell sort	Simple code	Unstable sort
	In-place sorting of arrays	Heap sort and quick sort are better than the shell sort in most cases
	Worst-case behavior is better than others $O(n^{1.5})$	

Generating Test Data

Before you decide to use a particular sort implementation, you should check it against a variety of inputs to make sure that your implementation functions optimally under all conditions. You should at least check the implementation against forward-ordered, reverse-ordered, increasing-decreasing, and duplicate data records. In addition, you should also use a sample of the data you are expecting to sort.

The code in Listing 12.8 can be used to generate different types of test data.

Listing 12.8. Generating Test Data for the Sort Methods

```
// Program: test_data.cpp
// Author: Megh Thakkar
// Purpose: Generate data in forward, reverse, random and duplicate order
//          This data can be used for testing the various sort methods.
#include <stdio.h>
#include <stdlib.h>
#include <ctype.h>
#include <string.h>
#include <iostream.h>

class test_data {
    private:
        int *X;          //List of data elements
        int n;           //Number of elements in the list
    public:
        test_data (int size) { X = new int[n=size]; }
        ~test_data( ) { delete [ ]X; }
// Display the results using the method "show_list"
```

```
            void show_list (char *title);
// Generate data in the forward order using the method "forward_ord"
            void forward_ord( int n);
// Generate data in the reverse order using the method "reverse_ord"
            void reverse_ord( int n);
// Generate data in the duplicate order using the method "duplicate_ord"
            void duplicate_ord( int n);
// Generate data in the random order using the method "random_ord"
            void random_ord( int n);
};

void test_data::show_list( char *title)
{
        cout << "\n" << title;
    for (int i = 0; i < n; i++)
        cout << " " << X[i];
        cout << "\n";
}

void test_data::forward_ord(int n)
{
    int  i, step, first, last;

    first = 0;
    last = n;
    step = 1;
    for ( i = first; i < last; i +=step )
        X[i] = i;

    show_list("Test data generated in the forward order: ");
}

void test_data::reverse_ord(int n)
{
    int  i, step, first, last;

    first = n;
    last = 0;
    step = 1;
    for ( i = first; i > last; i -=step )
        X[n-i] = i;

    show_list("Test data generated in the reverse order: ");
}

void test_data::duplicate_ord(int n)
{
    int  i, step, first, last;

    first = 0;
```

continues

LISTING 12.8. CONTINUED

```cpp
        last = n;
        step = 1;
        for ( i = first; i < last; i +=step )
            X[i] = abs( rand( ) ) % 2;

        show_list("Test data generated in the forward order: ");
    }

    void test_data::random_ord(int n)
    {
        int  i, step, first, last;

        first = 0;
        last = n;
        step = 1;
        for ( i = first; i < last; i +=step )
            X[i] = abs( rand( ) ) ;

        show_list("Test data generated in the forward order: ");
    }

    //main( ) : Test driver for generating test data
    void main(void)
    {
        int n;

        cout  <<  "\n Enter the number of data elements you want to generate:
    ➥";
        cin  >>  n;

        cout << "\n We will generate numbers in the following orders: \n"
            <<              " (1) Forward-ordered\n"
            <<              " (2) Reverse-ordered\n"
            <<              " (3) Duplicate records\n"
            <<              " (4) Random ordered records\n";

    // Create an object to store the generated data
        test_data test_obj(n);

        test_obj.forward_ord(n);

        test_obj.reverse_ord(n);

        test_obj.duplicate_ord(n);

        test_obj.random_ord(n);

    }
```

Summary

This chapter enables you to choose the best sorting method for your needs. The key point to remember is that the efficiency of any sorting method strongly depends on the implementation of the method and the actual data the method is sorting. The best way to choose the right sorting method for your needs is to test each method against various types of input—in particular, against a sample of the kind of data you intend to sort.

12

DESIGNING
EFFICIENT SORTING
METHODS

Search Algorithms in C++

CHAPTER 13

Searching is the process of finding data in a set of data elements that fits a certain criteria. For various applications, efficient search techniques are the key to whether or not an application's performance is acceptable.

The ultimate goal of any technique you use for searching is the same: find the information requested. However, several factors, such as the implementation and the logic that the technique relies on, determine whether or not a particular search technique can be used for a given situation. You should consider several criteria when comparing search techniques:

- **Time to set up:** Several techniques require a substantial amount of time to set up the search environment before they can begin to really search for information. If you are planning to search through a small amount of data, the setup time becomes a big factor in which technique you choose.

- **Time to search:** The search time is basically the time it takes to run the search algorithm. Most of the search algorithms are of the order of O(n) where n is the number of data elements through which you are trying to search. This linear time is generally comprised of the setup time (x) and the search time (y). In other words, total time = x + y; the goal should be to minimize the x and y. In the preceding equation, the setup time is equivalent to x, and the search time y is equivalent to O(n). As n increases, the setup time generally becomes insignificant in the calculation of the total time.

- **Need to backtrack:** Some search algorithms do a simple linear scan through the data elements; others go back and forth through the data. You must consider this criteria when selecting a search algorithm.

Linear Searches

Linear searches are the simplest type of searches because they simply scan through the set of data elements and compare the elements to the data it is searching for until a match is obtained. Linear searches are therefore simple to implement but are not necessarily efficient. There is no time needed to set up and they may backtrack. Suppose that you want to search an unsorted array X consisting of N integers for a particular data item specified by search_item (S). The pseudocode to achieve this can be as follows:

```
Set i = 0
Compare X[i] with S. If there is a match return i otherwise increment i by
➥1.
Repeat step 2 and scan the array until either there is a match or
you have scanned the entire array and there is no match.
```

A C++ implementation of this algorithm is shown in Listing 13.1.

LISTING 13.1. C++ IMPLEMENTATION OF A LINEAR SEARCH METHOD

```
//Program: linear_search.cpp
//Author: Megh Thakkar
//Purpose: Search an unsorted array of N integers
//for an integer S.
#include <stdio.h>
#include <string.h>
#include <stdlib.h>
#include <iostream.h>

class Search {
    private:
        int *X;            //List of data elements
        int N;             //Number of data elements
    public:
        Search (int size) { X = new int[N=size]; }
        ~Search( ) { delete [ ]X; }
        void load_list (int input[ ] );
        void show_list (char *title);
        int  linear_search( int S);
};

void Search::load_list(int input[ ])
{
    for (int i = 0; i < N; i++)
        X[i] = input[i];
}

void Search::show_list( char *title)
{
    cout << "\n" << title;
    for (int i = 0; i < N; i++)
        cout << " " << X[i];
    cout << "\n";
}

int Search::linear_search( int S)
{
    for ( int j = 0; j < N; j++)
    {    if  (X[j] == S)
        // Match found.
        //Return j
            return(j);
    }
    return(-1);
}

//main( ) : Test driver for linear search
void main(void)
```

13

SEARCH
ALGORITHMS IN
C++

continues

LISTING 13.1. CONTINUED

```
{
    int search_key;
    Search search_obj (10);
    static int list_to_search[] = {54, 6,26,73,1,100,36,41,2,83};

     cout << "\n"
<< "C++ Implementation of Linear search"
<< " \n";

    search_obj.load_list(list_to_search);

    cout  <<   "\n" << "Enter the key to search:     ";
    cin  >>   search_key;

    search_obj.show_list("Searching the following list: ");
    cout << "\n\n\n";

    int result = search_obj.linear_search(search_key);
    if (result != -1)
        cout << "\n" << "Search Result: "
<< "X[" << result << "] = "
<< search_key;
    else
        cout << "\n" << "Search Result: "
<< search_key
<< " is not found in the list \n";

    cout << "\n\n\n";

}
```

Analysis of the Linear Search

The algorithm presented in Listing 13.1 is linear because, in the worst case, it will do n comparisons; therefore, the work done is on the order of $O(n)$. In addition, the best case is when the first comparison gives you the match. The average case is $O(n/2) = O(n)$.

Searching a Sorted Array

If the array that you are trying to search is already sorted, you can improve the performance of the search by using a divide-and-conquer strategy called a *binary search* (see Listing 13.2).

The pseudocode for the binary search is as follows:

```
Split the array into two halves. The split is done at the middle.
Compare the search_key with the X[middle].
```

If they match then the search is over.
If search_key > X[middle] then the search_key is in the upper half of the
➥array;
Therefore repeat the above steps to the upper half;
Otherwise, the search key is in the lower half of the array
And you should repeat the above steps to the lower half of the array.

LISTING 13.2. C++ IMPLEMENTATION OF A BINARY SEARCH FOR A SORTED ARRAY

```
//Program: binary_search.cpp
//Author: Megh Thakkar
//Purpose: Search a sorted array of N element
//for a given search_key
#include <stdio.h>
#include <string.h>
#include <stdlib.h>
#include <iostream.h>

class Search {
    private:
        int *X;            //List of data elements
        int N;             //Number of elements

    public:
        Search (int size) { X = new int[N=size]; }
        ~Search( ) { delete [ ]X; }
        void load_list (int input[ ] );
        void show_list (char *title);
        int binary_search( int S);
};

void Search::load_list(int input[ ])
{
    for (int i = 0; i < N; i++)
        X[i] = input[i];
}

void Search::show_list( char *title)
{
    cout << "\n" << title;
    for (int i = 0; i < N; i++)
        cout << " " << X[i];
    cout << "\n";
}

int Search::binary_search( int S)
{
    int head;
    int tail;
```

continues

13

LISTING 13.2. CONTINUED

```
    int middle;
    int bmiddle; //The element before the middle element
    int amiddle; //The element after the middle element

    head = 0;
    tail = N;

    if ( (S < X[0]) || S > X[N-1])
        //search_key is out of bounds,
//therefore there is no need to search the list.
        return(-1);

    while (head < tail)
    {
        middle = ((head + tail)/2) + 1;
        bmiddle = middle - 1;
        amiddle = middle + 1;
        if (S == X[middle] || S == X[bmiddle] || S == X[amiddle])
        //This comparison with not just
//the middle element but also the
        //elements before and after it is
//found to be more efficient
        //than a simple comparison with middle element.
        {
            if (S == X[middle]) return(middle);
            if (S == X[bmiddle]) return(bmiddle);
            if (S == X[amiddle]) return(amiddle);
        }
        else if (S > X[middle])
            //Search key (if exists) should be
//in the upper half of the list,
            //therefore eliminate the lower half.
            head = middle + 1;
        else
            //Search key (if exists) should be
//in the lower half of the list,
            //therefore eliminate the upper half.
            tail = middle - 1;
    }
    return (-1);

}

//main( ) : Test driver for binary search
void main(void)
{

    int search_key;
```

```
    Search search_obj (10);
    static int  sorted_list[] = {2,5,10,31,45,48,52,58,66,82};

     cout << "\n"
<< "C++ Implementation of Binary search" << " \n";

    search_obj.load_list(sorted_list);

    cout  <<  "\n" << "Enter the key to search:   ";
    cin  >>  search_key;

    search_obj.show_list("Searching the following sorted list: ");
    cout << "\n\n\n";

    int result = search_obj.binary_search(search_key);

    if ( result != -1)
        cout << "\n" << "Search Result: "
<< "X[" << result << "] = " << search_key;
    else
        cout << "\n" << "Search Result: "
<< search_key
<< " is not found in the list \n";

    cout << "\n\n\n";

}
```

The binary search is different from a regular linear search because it uses the divide-and-conquer strategy to eliminate portions of the sorted array that do not have to be searched. The binary search uses the knowledge that the array is presorted; with every comparison, the algorithm divides the array into two parts: one that can be eliminated from future scans and the other that must be searched further.

Pattern Matching

Pattern matching is a common operation performed on strings. Pattern matching can be defined as finding an occurrence of pattern of length B in a text of length A. Algorithms used for pattern matching can be easily extended to finding all the occurrences of a given pattern in the text because once a match is found, you can continue scanning the text to find the next match starting from the position directly after the beginning of the match. In such pattern matching problems, the pattern basically acts as the search key.

The Brute-Force Algorithm

When I think of pattern matching, the first algorithm that comes to mind is the brute-force method. This is the simplest search algorithm; it is not necessarily the most efficient, and it is also not very creative. The brute-force method scans the entire text to see whether the specified string exists. The following pseudocode describes this technique and finds the first occurrence of the string s in the text t:

```
int brutesearch(char *s, char *t)
{
    int i, j, m, n;
    i = 0;
    j = 0;
    m = strlen(s);
    n = strlen(t);

    while ( j < m && i < n)
    {
        if ( t[i] != s[j] )
        {
            i -= j-1;
            j = -1;
        }
        i++;
        j++;
    }
    if (j == m)
        return (i - m);
    else
        return i;
}
```

Explanation of the Brute-Force Algorithm

In the pseudocode just presented, the pointer i points to the characters in the text; the pointer j points to the characters in the pattern to be searched. These pointers are initialized to point to the beginning of the text and the pattern. The variables m and n are used to store the length of the two strings. The two pointers are incremented as long as they point to characters that match and as long as the ends of the strings have not been reached. If the algorithm encounters mismatching characters, the pointers are reset such that j points to the beginning of the pattern and the pointer i is reset back to one position to the right of what was the first character matched in the text. This is so that it can consider the rest of the text again for a possible match. If the end of the pattern is reached—indicated by (j == m)—the match is obtained and the pattern starts at t[i-m]. On the other hand, if the end of the text is reached without the pattern being matched—indicated by (j < m && i = n)—the result is that there is no match.

Analysis of the Brute-Force Algorithm

In the worst-case scenario, all the characters in the pattern (m) are checked against the text for all the possible match positions (n-m+1). This results in work of the order of `O(m(n-m+1)) = O(mn)`.

Pattern Representations

Patterns can be represented as symbols tied together with the following fundamental operations:

- **Concatenation:** Two symbols are considered to be concatenated if they are adjacent to each other. A match exists if and only if the two symbols are also adjacent in the text. For example, AB means A followed by B in the pattern.

- **OR:** An OR is represented by a plus sign (+). If two symbols have an OR between them, they are treated as alternatives—in other words A+B means either A or B can exist at that position.

- **Closure:** A closure is represented by an asterisk (*); if a character is followed by a closure, it means that there are zero or more occurrences of that character.

The following are some examples:

- (ABC)* means that there are alternating patterns of ABC. In other words, the pattern can be ABCABCABCABC. This is seen from the closure representation, which indicates that the pattern ABC keeps recurring.

- A(B+C)D means that the valid patterns are ABD or ACD. This is seen from the usage of the OR notation, which indicates that the pattern is A followed by B OR C and then followed by D.

Pattern matching searches can be simplified by algorithms that implement the construction of a finite-state machine that can locate the keywords (keywords are used to refer to the possible patterns being searched).

Constructing Finite-State Machines

The pattern to be searched can be used to construct a finite-state machine. Such finite-state machines are graphically represented as a network of nodes in which each node represents a particular state. The nodes are connected to other nodes as determined by the pattern. The input character that causes the transition is indicated on the link between the nodes. The construction and use of finite-state machines can be understood through the following examples. We will first consider how the fundamental operations can be represented, and then we will see how the entire pattern can be constructed by building partial machines, which can be combined to form larger machines:

- Recognize one character—A. This can be represented by a two-state machine. There is an initial state and the final state, which is derived when the character A is encountered (see Figure 13.1).

FIGURE 13.1.

A two-state machine.

- Concatenate two machines—M1 and M2. This can be done by merging the final state of the first with the initial state of the second (see Figure 13.2).

FIGURE 13.2.

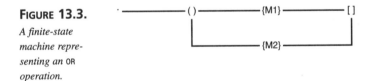

A finite-state machine representing concatenation.

- Perform an OR operation between two machines—M1 and M2. The OR operation is depicted by introducing a new null state as the initial state of both machines and the final state of one machine is also the final state of the second machine (see Figure 13.3).

FIGURE 13.3.

A finite-state machine representing an OR operation.

- Perform a closure operation. This is represented by having the final state loop back to the initial state (see Figure 13.4).

FIGURE 13.4.

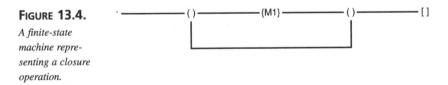

A finite-state machine representing a closure operation.

NOTE

In Figures 13.1 through 13.4, the following are true:

- ( ) represents the initial state.

- [] represents the final state.
- (X) represents a transition when the character X is encountered.
- {M} represents a finite-state machine.

By successively applying these rules, you should be able to construct finite-state machines for any pattern.

Let us construct a finite-state machine for the following pattern: A(BC+DE)F (see Figure 13.5).

FIGURE 13.5.

A finite-state machine representing A(BC+DE)F.

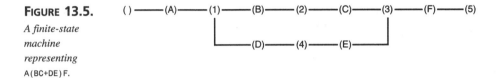

Transitions not defined by the diagram in Figure 13.5 go to a state known as FAIL_STATE. You can also create a transition table based on this diagram as shown in Table 13.1

Table 13.1. *Transition State Table for* A(BC+DE)F

State	0	1	2	3	4	5
Character read	A		C	F	E	
Next1_state	1	2	3	5	3	0
Next2_state	1	4	3	5	3	0

The way to interpret the transition table is such that if the machine is in state X and you read character Y, the machine goes into the state specified by Next1_state or Next2_state.

From the transition table, you can see that this is a nondeterministic machine because when it is in state 1, it can go to state 2 or to state 4 based on the character read. In other words, it has more than one FAIL_STATE for state 1.

There can be a result function that looks up successful matches determined by reaching the final state in the finite-state machine.

Finite-state machines can be deterministic or they can be nondeterministic. *Deterministic* machines are those in which the transition from a given state can be determined easily simply based on the next input character. On the other hand, *nondeterministic* machines are generally represented with the OR or closure operations because a simple comparison with one character cannot determine if the pattern matching fails at that step or not.

The pseudocode to implement such finite-state machines can be as described here:

```
State = 0;
While ((c = getchar( ) ) != EOF )
{
    if  (transition(state,c) IS NOT NULL)
        state = transition(state,c);
    if  (result(state) IS NOT NULL)
        //Match found
        printf("Match found.");

}
```

This pseudocode uses several functions: The `transition(state,c)` function looks up the transition table to see whether a transition is possible based on the current state and the next character read. The `result(state)` function looks to see whether the current state indicates that there is a match. The function `result(state)` checks to see whether the current state indicates a pattern match and the consequent end of the algorithm. This code is very generic; the actual implementation determines the performance of the search.

Graph Algorithms

A graph can be used to represent several situations you may face in day-to-day life. For example, you may be planning to travel from Orlando to San Francisco. The question can be *What is the airline route that will take you from Orlando to San Francisco in the shortest amount of time?* You can also ask *which is the cheapest route?* Another example is job scheduling when you have a number of tasks to perform and there are dependencies between the tasks such that one or more must be completed before another task can be started. The finite-state machines discussed earlier can also be considered examples of graphs.

Let us look at some simple definitions that can be used in association with graphs:

- **Graph:** A *graph* is a collection of nodes and connections between nodes.
- **Nodes:** *Nodes* are objects that can have names and other properties associated with them.

- **Link (or edge):** A *link* (also referred to as an *edge*) is a connection between two nodes.

- **Path:** A *path* from node A to node B is the list of nodes traversed when you move from node A to node B. For example, in Figure 13.6, ABCD and ACD are two paths from node A to node D.

FIGURE 13.6.

A graphical representation of the problem to determine paths between nodes.

- **Connected graph:** A graph is said to be *connected* if there is a path from one node to any other node in the graph.

- **Simple path:** A path between two nodes is *simple* if there is no node that is repeated. In other words, no node is visited more than once.

- **Cycle:** A *cycle* is a simple path with the additional characteristic that the first and the last node are the same.

- **Tree:** A graph that has no cycles is called a *tree*.

- **Binary tree:** A *binary tree* is a tree in which each node is connected to only three other nodes. One of these nodes is the parent of that node and the other two are the child nodes.

A tree can be easily converted to a cycle by adding just one more connection to it (the connection you add completes the loop). The following are known facts for a graph:

- A tree with N nodes has exactly N-1 connections.

- A graph with N nodes but fewer than N-1 connections cannot be connected.

- A graph with N nodes and more than N-1 connections must have a cycle.

- A graph with N nodes and N-1 connections is not necessarily a tree.

- A graph with N nodes can have connections that can range from 0 to N(N-1)/2.

- *Sparse graphs* are graphs with very few connections.

- *Dense graphs* are graphs with lots of connections.

- *Complete graphs* are those that have N(N-1)/2 connections.

- *Undirected graphs* are those in which the connections between nodes are bidirectional.

- *Directed graphs* are those in which the connections between nodes are one way.

- *Weighted graphs* are those in which weights are assigned to the connections between nodes. These weights can represent the cost to go from node A to node B.

- Two nodes are said to be *adjacent*, or *neighbors*, if there exists a connection (link) between them. The link or edge is said to be *incident* with the nodes A and B.

- The *degree* of a node A is the number of nodes incident with it.

- A node is considered to be *isolated* if its degree is zero.

Algorithms that operate on graphs have to be careful not to visit the same node more than once because this will improve their efficiency. Two methods that are widely used to perform graph traversals are the depth-first and the breadth-first searches.

Depth-First Search

The depth-first search is also referred to as *backtracking*, which will become clear from the manner in which the method works. Consider an undirected graph that starts its traversal from node A. Suppose that the degree of node A is d. This means that the nodes adjacent to node A are A_i, where $i = 1,2,3,...,d$. The key to this technique is to mark the nodes that have been visited. The depth-first search starts by visiting node A and then visits any unvisited adjacent node of node A, say A_1. The rest of the adjacent nodes are stored in a stack so that they can be visited later. All the adjacent nodes of each of the adjacent nodes of node A_1 are visited, and then the depth-first search backs up and visits the remaining unvisited adjacent nodes of A_i (where $i = 2,3,...,d$). This process continues until all the nodes in the graph are visited. The depth-first search is an example of an exhaustive search because it searches each and every node in the graph to determine the best answer to the problem.

The depth-first search can be implemented recursively as well as nonrecursively. Keep in mind that the depth-first search basically goes down the graph until it reaches a dead end or a leaf that has no more unvisited adjacent nodes; then it backtracks to visit the other child nodes (adjacent nodes) of the parent.

The following C++ code excerpt shows the recursive depth-first search:

```
void Depth_first_search(int n )
{
    int i;
    const int TRUE = 1;
    const int FALSE = 0;
    int *checked;
    struct node
        {int nodeid; struct node *adj; };

    for ( i = 0; i <= n; i++) checked[i] = FALSE;
    for ( i = 0; i <= n; i++)
```

```
        if (checked[i] == FALSE) check(i);
}

void check (int A)
{
    checked[A] = TRUE;

    For all adjacent vertices Ai ( i = 1,2,3,.....,d) of node A
        {
            if (Ai is not yet checked)
            check(Ai);
        }
}
```

The depth-first search method can also be shown graphically (see Figure 13.7).

FIGURE 13.7.

An illustration of a depth-first search.

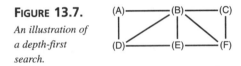

In Figure 13.7, the depth-first search starts with node A. Node A is checked and printed. Node A has nodes B and D as its adjacent nodes, so either of these nodes can then be checked. Suppose that node B is chosen; node B is then checked and printed. The depth-first search leaves the other adjacent nodes of node A (in this case, node D) for later checking. Node B has nodes A, C, D, E, and F as its adjacent nodes. Node A has already been checked, so let's say that the search chooses node C. Node C is checked and printed. Node C has nodes B and F as adjacent nodes. Because node B has already been checked, the depth-first search next checks node F. Node E will then be checked and finally node D will be checked. Thus the order in which the nodes are checked will be ABCFED.

The path produced by a depth-first search is not unique. A totally different path would be obtained if the search chooses a different adjacent node.

Breadth-First Search

The breadth-first search is an alternative method of traversing graphs. It is also an exhaustive search method, meaning that it also checks all the nodes. Unlike the depth-first search, the breadth-first search method checks all the adjacent nodes A_i (where $i = 1,2,3,...,d$) of a given node A before it checks the adjacent nodes of any of the nodes A_i. This method also marks the nodes already checked so that they are not rechecked.

This is the pseudocode for a breadth-first search:

```
Create an object "Queue_obj" that can act as a queue.
Initialize this queue object to be empty
```

```
Initialize the array checked[ ] such that all the elements are FALSE.
Suppose that you start with nodeid A. Set checked[A] = TRUE.
Add the nodeid A to the start of the queue.
Do the following steps while the queue object is not empty:
    Set current_node = head(queue_obj).
    Check all the nodes adjacent to the current_node that have not
        already been checked.
    Add all the nodes adjacent to the current_node to the queue so
        that their adjacent nodes can be checked later.
Deallocate the queue_obj
```

This method can be shown using the same diagram used to understand the depth-first search method (refer to Figure 13.7). Again, let's start with node A. Once node A is checked, we will check all its adjacent nodes (in this case, nodes B and D). Then we can check the nodes adjacent to node B or node D. Let's choose node D. Nodes adjacent to node D (in this case, node E) are checked; finally, the nodes adjacent to node B are checked and the resultant search path can be shown as ADBEFC.

As both the pseudocode and the figure show, even in this case, the search is not unique; it depends on the next node chosen during the traversal.

Comparing Depth-First and Breadth-First Searches

Depth-first search methods are easy to implement and can arrive at a good solution very quickly. The disadvantage of these methods is that you may spend a lot of time going on paths that may be a waste. The simplest alternative to the depth-first search is the breadth-first search strategy. The breadth-first search is guaranteed to find a solution (if one exists) with the best path, provided that the number of branches is finite. In order to understand this, assume that there is a path with a length p from the source to the destination. The breadth-first search searches all the nodes at level 1, then it searches all the nodes at level 2, and so on. Eventually, it checks all the nodes at level p. Thus the path it finds is not just *a* path, it is also the *best* path.

The breadth-first search has two disadvantages:

- It requires a lot of memory because the number of nodes increases exponentially as it checks each level.

- If the shortest path is very long, the search will involve checking a lot of levels, which will take more time than the depth-first search because the breadth-first search will check all the nodes at a given level before going to the next level.

The depth-first search is better than the breadth-first search for situations in which there are a lot of paths that lead from the source to the destination, but each of these paths is very long.

Best-First Search

The best-first search method is a clever algorithm that combines the depth-first search and the breadth-first search techniques into one method. The best-first search uses the best of both algorithms and is known as the best-first method because it attempts to explore the path that looks the most promising. The algorithm can be explained with the following steps:

1. Find the next nodes possible from the current node.

2. Apply a heuristic function to each of these next nodes. A *heuristic function* is basically a user-defined function that performs a calculation on the input to produce an output value that indicates the importance of that node. For example, "What are the chances of finding a solution if you are at that node?"

3. Choose the next node that has the best chance (per the heuristic function) to reach the solution faster.

4. If a solution is reached, you can quit; otherwise, you store the rest of the nodes for consideration later.

5. Set `current_node` = `best_next_node` and repeat steps 1 through 4 until a solution is found.

> **NOTE**
>
> A heuristic function is basically a user-defined function that performs a calculation on the input to produce an output value that indicates the importance of that node. For example, "What are the chances of winning if you are at that node?" or "What are the chances of finding a solution from that node?"

The best-first algorithm does a little bit of depth-first searching until it reaches a node that is not very promising and then it looks at the rest of the nodes and performs a breadth-first search. It chooses the best-chance node and then performs a depth-first search using that node until it reaches a solution or until the path is no longer better than the remaining nodes. This approach eventually leads to a solution with less effort than what is expended with either the depth-first or the breadth-first search.

Consider the graph in Figure 13.8. Initially, there is only one node (node A) but it is expanded to give four possibilities. *Expanding a node* simply means looking at the possible next nodes that can be visited from this node. The heuristic function is applied to these nodes; node C is selected as the best-chance node. Node C is expanded to give two possibilities, and the heuristic function is applied to them. It is seen that node E is not promising compared to node B. Therefore, node B is expanded and the heuristic function is applied to its successors. This process continues until we reach a solution.

FIGURE 13.8.

An example to illustrate the best-first search.

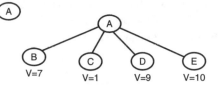

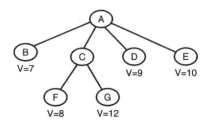

Implementing Graph Objects

We have already seen that the graph consists of a set of nodes, links between those nodes, and the cost associated with the links. There are several ways to implement such structures:

- An adjacency matrix
- An array of pointers to singly or doubly linked lists of adjacent nodes
- A linked list of pointers to singly or doubly linked lists of adjacent nodes
- An array of pointers to singly or doubly linked lists of links
- A linked list of pointers to singly or doubly linked lists of links

Of these implementations, the adjacency matrix is the most commonly used structure; it is generally represented as a two-dimensional array. Dijkstra (1960) proposed a method that can be used to find the shortest path between a start node and all other nodes. Dijkstra's algorithm provides a general method to solve the shortest path problem. It is an example of a greedy algorithm. *Greedy algorithms* solve a problem in stages; at each stage, the algorithm tries to do what seems to be the best action at that stage. At each stage, Dijkstra's algorithm selects a node that has the smallest distance among the nodes not yet visited and declares that the shortest path from the starting node to that node is known. The remainder of a stage consists of updating the values of the shortest path known so far. Refer to Listing 13.3 for an example of a C++ implementation of

Dijkstra's shortest path algorithm. The adjacency matrix can be used to represent all kinds of graphs: undirected, directed, weighted, unweighted, sparse, dense, and so on.

For a connected graph, the adjacency matrix `adj_mtx[][]` can be such that the following is true:

```
adj_mtx[i][j] = cij if node Ai is adjacent to node Aj
              = 0 if node Ai is not adjacent to node Aj
```

The following should be noted:

- For unweighted graphs, c_{ij} = 1, but for weighted graphs, c_{ij} represents the cost to traverse from node A_i to node A_j.

- For undirected graphs, the adjacency matrix is symmetric; for directed graphs, the adjacency matrix may or may not be symmetric.

LISTING 13.3. DIJKSTRA'S SHORTEST PATH ALGORITHM

```cpp
//Program: dsp.cpp
//Author: Megh Thakkar

//Purpose: C++ implementation of a weighted digraph object
//         and Dijkstra's shortest path algorithm.
#include <stdio.h>
#include <string.h>
#include <stdlib.h>
#include <iostream.h>

class graph {
    private:
        int adj_matrix[100][100];
//stores the cost input by the users
        int shortest_path_matrix[100][100];
//stores the shortest path between nodes

    public:
        graph (int size) { }
        ~graph( ) { }
        void setup_matrix(int num_nodes);
int find_cost_of_shortest_path(int source, int destination);
        void init_adj_matrix(int num_nodes);
        void init_shortest_path_matrix(int num_nodes);
        void load_adj_matrix(int num_nodes);
        void load_shortest_path_matrix( int num_nodes);
};

int graph::find_cost_of_shortest_path(int source, int destination)
{
```

13

SEARCH ALGORITHMS IN C++

continues

LISTING 13.3. CONTINUED

```
        int result;

    //shortest_path_matrix already contains the computed
    //shortest_path between the various nodes.

        result = shortest_path_matrix[source][destination];

        return(result);
}

void graph::setup_matrix(int num_nodes)
{
    init_adj_matrix(num_nodes);
//initialize the adjacency matrix to zero
    load_adj_matrix(num_nodes);
    init_shortest_path_matrix(num_nodes);
    load_shortest_path_matrix(num_nodes);
}

void graph::init_adj_matrix(int num_nodes)
{
    int i, j;
    for ( i = 1; i <= num_nodes; i++)
        for ( j = 1; j <= num_nodes; j++)
            adj_matrix[i][j] = 0;
}

void graph::init_shortest_path_matrix(int num_nodes)
{
//The shortest path matrix is initialized
//to the adjacency matrix
    int i, j;
    for ( i = 1; i <= num_nodes; i++)
        for ( j = 1; j <= num_nodes; j++)
            shortest_path_matrix[i][j] = adj_matrix[i][j];

}

void graph::load_adj_matrix(int num_nodes)
{
    int i, j;
    int cost;
    char direct[1];
    const int LARGE_COST = 999999;

    for ( i = 1; i <= num_nodes; i++)
    {
        for ( j = 1; j <= num_nodes; j++)
        {
```

```
//The adjacency matrix is loaded by input from the users
        cout << "Is there a direct path from Node "
<< i << " to Node " << j << "? : ";
        cin >> direct;

        if ( ( direct[0] == 'y' ) || (direct[0] == 'Y'))
            {
          cout << "Enter the cost of the path from Node "
 << i << " to Node " << j << " : ";
            cin >> cost;

            cout << "\n";

            adj_matrix[i][j] = cost;
            }
          else
            adj_matrix[i][j] = LARGE_COST;
// very large cost
        }
    }

}

void graph::load_shortest_path_matrix( int num_nodes)
{
    int i, j, k;
    const int LARGE_COST = 999999;

    for ( j = 1; j <= num_nodes; j++)
    {
        for ( i = 1; i <= num_nodes; i++)
        {
            for (k = 1; k <= num_nodes; k++)
            {
            if ( (shortest_path_matrix[j, k] > 0 ) )
                {
//If there is an indirect path between two nodes that is
//shorter than the path found so far then
//the indirect path becomes
//the shortest path between the two nodes.
    if  ( (shortest_path_matrix[j][k] == LARGE_COST) ||
                (shortest_path_matrix[i][j] +
shortest_path_matrix[j][k]
                < shortest_path_matrix[i][k]))
            shortest_path_matrix[i][k] = shortest_path_matrix[i][j]
                + shortest_path_matrix[j][k];
        }

        }
```

continues

LISTING 13.3. CONTINUED

```cpp
        }
    }
}

void main(void)
{
    int num_nodes;
    int source;
    int destination;
    int scost;

cout << "Enter the number of nodes in the graph (less than 100):  ";
    cin >> num_nodes;

    if ( num_nodes > 100 )
    {
        cout << " Sorry. This program has a limitation of only 100 nodes
➥";
        cout << "\n\n\n";
        exit (-1);
    }

    graph graph_obj(num_nodes);
    graph_obj.setup_matrix(num_nodes);

    cout << " Enter the node id of the source node: ";
    cin >> source;
    if (source > num_nodes)
    {
        cout << " Invalid source! ";

        cout << "\n\n\n";

    }

    cout << " Enter the node id of the destination node: ";
    cin >> destination;
    if (destination > num_nodes)
    {
        cout << " Invalid destination! ";

        cout << "\n\n\n";

    }

    scost = graph_obj.find_cost_of_shortest_path(source, destination);

    cout << "Shortest path between Node " << source
         << " and Node " << destination
```

```
        << " has a cost of " << scost;

    cout << "\n\n\n";

}
```

Representation of Tic-Tac-Toe

The game of tic-tac-toe can be represented as a structure containing a nine-element vector that represents the board positions. Also, we should store a list of board positions that are possible from a given board position and an evaluation value that shows the likelihood of an eventual win.

The algorithm basically consists of looking at the possible next moves and deciding which of these is the best position to be in. The next best move is determined as follows:

1. If the next move results in a win, then it is the best move.

2. If none of the next moves results in a win, then for each of your next moves, consider all the possible moves that the opponent can make. Keep in mind that the goal of the opponent is to make a move such that it minimizes your likelihood of winning. Thus the rating of our next move is as good as the worst rating of all its child nodes.

3. The best node (that is, the best next move) for us is thus the node with the highest rating.

This procedure is called the *minimax procedure* because at alternative levels of the tree, the goal is to maximize and then minimize the chance of winning.

Applying Alpha-Beta Cutoffs

The minimax procedure is an example of a depth-first search because it explores one path as deep as possible and then the evaluation function is applied to the last node in the path. This is then passed up one level at a time. Depth-first procedures such as these can be improved on by using techniques such as branch-and-bound described earlier. The efficiency of depth-first searches are possible because you can abandon the search of paths that are clearly worse than the best-known path so far. At the same time, it is very important to understand that the order in which paths are analyzed can have a big impact on the overall performance of such techniques. This is because if you start with the worst path first, it defeats the purpose of these techniques.

This search technique can best be described by examples that use minimax procedures such as the tic-tac-toe game.

Alpha-beta pruning requires the maintenance of two threshold values: alpha and beta. The *alpha value* is the lower bound on the value that a maximizing node may be assigned. The *beta value* is the upper bound on the value that a minimizing node may be assigned.

Look at the example in Figure 13.9. To search the tree, suppose that we apply a depth-first search: The entire subtree headed by node B is searched and the result of applying the evaluation function indicates that at node D we have a value of 6, and at node E we have a value of 9. Thus we are guaranteed that at node A the score is at least 6. This becomes the alpha value at node A and it can be used to eliminate certain portions of the entire tree from being searched. After examining node K, we realize that its evaluation is a value of 0. Thus node I will have a maximum value of 0. We do not need to explore any more subtrees of node I because we won't go to node I from node C; moving to node B can give us a value of 6. Now suppose that the node J gives a value of 10. Thus, node C will have a maximum value of 10. This becomes its beta value.

Let's see how the beta value is used. Keep in mind that the beta value is the upper bound for minimizing nodes. Suppose that the value at node M is 15, which is greater than the beta value of node C. In simple language, if we choose node G from node C, then we will have a value of 15, which is greater than 10 (the value at node F). However, the purpose of node C is to minimize, and so there is no point in choosing node G (which will at least have node M's value because the purpose of node G is to maximize). The overall result is that we can abandon searching all the subtrees of node G. In very large tree structures, this kind of elimination using alpha-beta cutoffs can lead to significant reductions in search paths and improve overall performance.

FIGURE 13.9.

An example illustrating alpha-beta cutoffs.

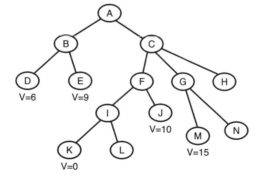

When using alpha-beta pruning, at maximizing levels, a path is abandoned if it becomes clear that its value is less than the alpha value of the parent node; at minimizing levels, a path is abandoned if it becomes clear that its value is more than the beta value of the parent node.

As already mentioned, the effectiveness of alpha-beta pruning depends on the order in which the paths are traversed. It can be proven that if a perfect ordering of nodes exists, the number of terminal nodes visited when using alpha-beta pruning and searching depth d is approximately twice the number of terminal nodes visited without using alpha-beta pruning and searching to a depth of d/2.

A further modification to the alpha-beta pruning called *futility cutoff* can provide significant improvement in performance. The idea behind futility cutoff is that we can abandon additional paths if the expected improvement is minimal compared to the best path obtained from the paths already explored. The logic is that we can spend more time exploring other parts of the tree in the hopes of getting a better path.

The Traveling Salesman Problem

Search techniques are not complete without mentioning the traveling salesman problem. This kind of problem involves searching through an extremely large number of potential solutions to find the answer to the question. Such search problems pretty much blow away the linear search we use for other types of problems because problems such as the traveling salesman would require an enormous amount of time to complete with linear search methods.

> **Definition of the problem:** Given a set of N cities, find the shortest route that connects them all without visiting any city more than once.

A lot of research has been done on problems of this nature; currently, there is no efficient way to solve these problems using exhaustive searches because you have to search through a large number of tours, each of which can be very long based on the value of N.

If you assume that the salesman can travel only between certain pairs of cities, the problem can be represented by a graph. The problem is then to find a cycle. There are several ways to tackle this problem, but none are very efficient. The first method is to apply an exhaustive search. This can be achieved by applying a modification of the depth-first search method such that instead of simply marking the nodes visited, we must unmark them if we realize that the path ends with a dead end. In other words, a depth-first search is performed, and the nodes that are checked are marked (so that they are not checked again) for the current path. If the current path leads to a dead end, we know that we have to backtrack and try another route. This backtracking requires that we unmark the nodes previously visited in our path. We then try another branch. This exhaustive search can take a very long time, particularly if the graph is complete.

A variety of techniques can be used to reduce the number of paths followed. These techniques rely on applying some tests at the nodes with the goal of eliminating certain branches because they are not worth pursuing. Backtracking is applied in various forms in such techniques.

When trying to find a simple cycle in such problems, you can eliminate certain alternatives by realizing that cycles are *symmetric*, meaning that there will be two paths that represent the same route. This can be detected by enforcing a restriction that three nodes should appear in a particular order. In other words, nodes A, B, and C should be such that node B comes after node A but before node C. By doing this, you check node C only if node B has been checked already.

Problems that involve finding the path with the least cost can be made more efficient by realizing that you do not have to continue on a path if the cost of the partial path found so far is greater than the lowest-cost path already known. It would be more efficient if we check the child nodes for a given node in increasing order of cost so that we can find the low-cost solutions first. By applying backtracking and sophisticated pruning techniques, we can get very efficient search results.

External Searching

Searching is a very important and frequently used operation in relation to disk drives. Files are stored on the disks, and you need a very efficient way to get to them. In most of the applications that require disk I/O, disk speed is the component that is the slowest, and we therefore have to minimize this time as much as possible.

Indexed Sequential Access

The basic methods of searching can be extended to disks. However, the sequential access methods we have discussed in this chapter are not very efficient. Linear search techniques simply scan through the keys until a match is found or the end of the list is reached. Improvements can be made by using an index to keep track of which keys belong to which pages on the disk. The first page of each disk can be its *index* page. You can further improve this approach by using a *master index* such that the master index page contains information about which keys are placed on which disks. For example, the master key can indicate that the keys on disk 1 are less than D, keys on disk 2 are between E and K, and so on. This master index can be small enough to be placed in memory, making it very fast to get to the record by using just two searches—once through the master index to find the disk that contains the key, and once through the index page on the disk to find where on the disk the record is kept. This method combines indexing techniques with sequential access of keys and is therefore known as the *indexed sequential access*. This method has the disadvantage that if there are a lot of updates to the index (by means of adding and removing records), then index maintenance can take up a lot of time.

Binary Trees

Binary trees can be used to improve the index scans by placing the keys in a tree structure such that keys in the left subtree of any node come before the node; keys in the right subtree of any node come after the node. There are three traversal methods that can be used with the `binary_tree` object: preorder, in-order, and postorder. Although the scans can be improved by following any traversal method, the in-order traversal is particularly efficient. The pseudocode for each of these methods follows. The main difference between these methods is in the order in which the nodes are checked with the search key. The following pseudocodes show how the preorder, in-order, and post-order traversals work.

Preorder traversal method:

```
preorder_traversal(node parent)
{
    check parent node;
    preorder_traversal(parent→left child);
    preorder_traversal(parent→right child);
}
```

In-order traversal method:

```
inorder_traversal(node parent)
{
    inorder_traversal(parent→left child);
    check parent node;
    inorder_traversal(parent→right child);
}
```

Postorder traversal method:

```
postorder_traversal(node parent)
{
    postorder_traversal(parent→left child);
    postorder_traversal(parent→right child);
    check parent node;

}
```

The binary tree search method is more flexible than the indexed sequential search because new nodes can easily find a spot in the tree. Likewise, nodes can be easily removed while maintaining the tree structure.

2-3-4 Trees

2-3-4 trees are referred to by several names such as *2-4 trees* and *symmetric binary B-trees*. In a B-tree, the nodes (which are the memory structures) are usually large enough

to at least store one block read from the disk. *2-4 trees*, on the other hand, can be used to store one, two, or at the most three elements per node. 2-4 trees are basically B-trees of a smaller order; they can be used to provide a more efficient search technique than is available with a binary tree. In 2-4 trees, there are three locations in which you can store the elements and four locations in which you can store the pointers. On an average, it has been shown that only two-thirds of the space is used in these nodes. Keep in mind that the main reason for using 2-4 trees is to improve the search performance in main memory—and it is very important to save space in main memory. The solution to this dilemma is to transform 2-4 trees to binary trees (refer to Figure 13.10) such that each node can store only one data element. By doing this, you save space and at the same time achieve good performance because you can still use the same search techniques you would have used with a 2-4 tree. Another important characteristic in such transformations is the use of two types of links:

- A type of link to represent the normal parent-child associations between nodes
- A type of link that associates keys that belong to the same node in the 2-4 tree

These types of links are referred to by several names such as *horizontal/vertical pointers* and *red-and-black pointers*.

From Figure 13.10, several distinctions between horizontal/vertical and the red-black trees become clear:

- Red-black trees are better for representing the binary tree form; horizontal/vertical trees are better at retaining the 2-4 tree structure.
- Horizontal/vertical trees are better suited for representing B-trees of any order.

No matter which representation you choose, you will have to somehow distinguish between the two types of links. You can do this easily by using a flag in the representation of the link.

The implementation of the horizontal/vertical trees and red-black trees are much different compared to a binary tree. However, the search technique used by them is the same: If the search key matches the current node, then stop. Otherwise, go to the left subtree if the search key is greater than the node element; go to the right subtree if the search tree is smaller than the node element.

The biggest factor when using implementations such as red-black trees is the maintenance involved in keeping the tree intact. For example, for horizontal/vertical tree implementation, the following things are true at all times:

- The path from the root to any leaf should contain the same number of vertical links.
- Two consecutive horizontal links are not allowed on any path from the root.

FIGURE 13.10.

Transforming 2-3-4 trees to horizontal/vertical and red-black trees.

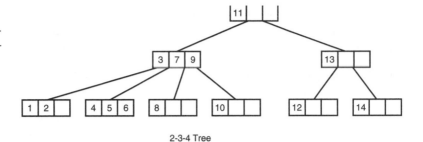

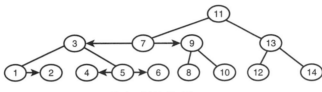

2-3-4 Tree

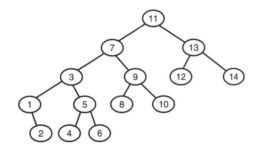

Horizontal-Vertical Tree

Red-Black Tree

These facts lead to the difficulty in the maintenance of these trees because inserting a key inserts a node and a link; you must decide whether the link is to be a horizontal or a vertical link. Likewise, deleting a key result in a node merging. Usually, node splitting is found to be a good technique when working with these trees.

Summary

Searching is a fundamental task involved in many applications. Normally, information is divided into records that are identified by means of keys. Searching generally involves not only finding the key but also accessing the information in the records. Several algorithms that can be used to solve problems require searching; the particular algorithm that will be effective depends on the representation of the data. The Big-O notation can be used to determine the amount of work involved in search algorithms.

13

SEARCH ALGORITHMS IN C++

In general, search algorithms involve scanning through the data set. This process can be improved by using some knowledge of the manner in which the data is represented. This is done in the binary search technique, which uses the knowledge that the data is presorted.

Pattern matching problems can be represented as finite-state machines. This chapter discussed the construction of such machines using the pattern to be searched.

A lot of real-world problems are represented naturally using a graph; several classical algorithms such as Dijkstra's algorithm have been developed to solve problems that can be represented by graphs. An ideal search technique is yet to be developed, so we can always be creative with our implementation of a search technique to minimize the complexity of the problem at hand.

Hashing and Parsing Techniques

Searching Versus Hashing

The different *search techniques* discussed in Chapter 13, "Search Algorithms in C++," made use of key comparison as the main approach to finding a desired element. In a sequential search, the table that contains the data elements is searched using key comparison to determine whether the search key is contained in the table. In a binary search, key comparison is used to split the table into halves and to determine whether the search key is found in either half of the table. In addition, the search direction is determined by the result of the key comparison.

On the other hand, *hashing* is a technique that uses the value of the search key to identify its position in the table without key comparisons. Hashing uses an arbitrary mapping function to determine the storage location of any given data element and to provide a roughly uniform distribution of data elements in the storage space allocated for performing the hash.

In an ideal scenario, the position is determined by applying a hashing function on the search key; the work done is $O(1)$ regardless of the actual number of data elements. In reality, however, the hash techniques are an approximation of this calculation and lead to "conflicts" such that the same hash function applied to two or more different search keys can lead to the same position. Therefore, it is very important to be able to perform conflict resolution.

Hash techniques greatly depend on the choice of the hash function. The purpose is to find a hash function h which, when applied to a search key K, will transform the key into an index in the table that contains the set of data elements. The goal is to create a perfect hash function that will not create conflicts. You can create a perfect hash function if the table contains at least as many positions as the number of data elements. However, we do not always know the number of data elements ahead of time, and we may also not have enough space to store all the data elements. Sophisticated hash functions can avoid collisions but can also take a lot of time to complete; therefore, we need to use a space-time tradeoff when using hashing.

For many applications, hashing is a preferred technique compared to the binary tree searches described in Chapter 13. Hashing is relatively cheap to implement (in terms of runtime speed and the space used) and it also provides very fast search times—especially if enough space is available to store a large hash table. On the other hand, binary searches have several advantages:

- Binary searches are dynamic and do not depend on previous knowledge of the number of data elements.

- The worst-case performance of a binary search is tolerable. When hashing, the worst case occurs when all the keys hash to the same slot; conflict resolution then becomes a nightmare.

- Binary searches can make use of advanced operations such as sorting.

Hash Functions

The hash function is an important part of the hashing technique. This function is used to transform the keys into table addresses. The hash function we choose should be easy to compute and should be able to transform the keys (usually integers or strings) into integers in the range 0 to TR-1 (where TR is the number of records that can fit in the table).

Because most of the commonly used hash functions are based on arithmetic operations, we should convert the keys to numbers on which arithmetic operations can be performed. Let's look at some hash functions that can be easily computed:

- **Division:** If you don't know much about the characteristics of the key, the division method is the best hash function. Suppose that TR represents the number of records in the table and that K is the search key; then h(K) = K mod TR. This function works best if TR is a prime number. If TR is not a prime number, you can use h(K) = (K mod p) mod TR, where p is a prime number greater than TR. It is important that the hash function returns a value that is less than TR; the modulo ensures that this is true. For keys that represent strings, the number K is obtained by looking at the binary representations of the string characters and converting them to decimal. Keep in mind that this method can still result in collisions.

- **Folding:** All of the several variations of the folding method rely on some manner of splitting the key into subkeys and then performing some arithmetic operation on the subkeys. Suppose that the phone numbers of people are the keys to be hashed. Each phone number can be split into five parts, the parts can be added, and the modulo applied to the result. For example, phone number (407) 555-1212 can be split into these five parts: 40, 75, 55, 12, 12. The result of adding these numbers is 194. The hash result is 194 mod TR. The different variations in the "folding" technique just described vary based on the manner in which the key is split and the type of operations performed on the subkeys. For a string, you can split it into substrings and then apply the XOR operation on the substrings, as in this example: h("xyzw") = "xy" XOR "zw".

- **Mid-Square:** In several instances, the mid-square technique is found to be very efficient. First, we use some folding technique and then square the result. The mid-part of the result is then extracted to form the table address. In the previous phone number example, we have a folding result of 194. We then square that result:

$(194)^2$ = 37636. For a table with 1,000 records, we can use 763 as the table address. Thus, h(407-555-1212) = 763.

Now you are familiar with the basic methods for creating a hash function. As you might guess, collision resolution is going to take a lot of effort during the implementation of these methods.

Collision Resolution

Perfect hash functions are difficult to implement under practical circumstances. Hash tables must be able to handle collisions that occur when the hash function is applied to two different data elements and the same result is returned. Several alternatives to resolving this problem are discussed in the following sections.

Linear Rehashing

Linear rehashing is the simplest form of conflict resolution. When a conflict is detected, the algorithm traverses the table until an empty slot is detected and then places the element in that slot. When the element is to be searched, the hash function points it to a location in the table and a conflict is detected (indicated by a no_match). The table is then traversed until one of the following happens:

- The element is found.
- The entire table is scanned.
- An empty slot is found in the table, indicating that the element is not found.

When you are stepping through the table, it is not necessary to single step—in fact, it is better if you step through multiple records. The choice of the step size should be a prime number and not a divisor of the table size to ensure that all the records will be traversed. The idea behind not using single stepping is to avoid any congestion caused by conflicts in the same general area of the table.

Linear rehashing has the following disadvantages:

- Elements cannot be deleted from the table. If you start deleting elements from the table, you should make the slots invalid, otherwise you may reach an empty slot and assume that the element to be searched is absent. Suppose that you have the following elements that all hash to the same position in the table: Mike, Michael, and Mikhael. If you delete Michael and do not invalidate the slot, you will have an empty slot. If you then search for Mikhael, the search may end at the slot, assuming that Mikhael does not exist. When the search encounters invalid slots, the search should continue.

- Performance is bad at times because the technique scans the rest of the table from the point of collision and hence encounters records that are definitely not a match.

Nonlinear Rehashing

Linear rehashing does a sequential scan from the point of collision to an empty slot. Nonlinear rehashing, on the other hand, rehashes the search key to determine a new value. If another conflict is detected, the method rehashes and keeps going until an empty slot is found. If the table is almost full, you may have to perform the hashing exercise several times—which can quickly make this an expensive hashing technique. A variation of this approach is called *double hashing*. This technique specifically addresses the problem of clustering. Using this technique, we apply a fixed "step" to the scan sequence instead of scanning every record. The "step" is obtained by applying a second hash function. The choice of the second hash function is important because an inappropriate value may prevent the program from running properly. The following restrictions on the second hash function can lead to a good implementation. Assume that h2 = hash2(K) and that there are TR slots in the table.

- h2 should not be zero, otherwise we will have a program that runs indefinitely.
- h2 and TR should be prime numbers so that all the records will be scanned and we will avoid clustering.
- The hash functions used should be different.

An example of a simple secondary hashing function is h2(K)= 16 ñ (K mod 16).

It is important to keep in mind that double hashing can sometimes make more comparisons than linear rehashing, but double hashing gives you a smaller cluster size. In general, however, on sparse tables, double rehashing uses fewer probes compared to the linear method.

Now consider the example of a simple hash function that reads a string of the form "mmddyyyy" and converts it into a position in a table with 360 slots. Listing 14.1 presents an implementation of a hash function that can result in collision.

LISTING 14.1. A SIMPLE HASH FUNCTION THAT CAN RESULT IN COLLISION

```
// hash_date.cpp
// This program accepts the string "mmddyyyy". The hash
// function uses only the "mm" and "dd"
// component of the string to compute the slot location.
// Note that the year is not considered at all.
// In other words, leap year etc. is not treated in any
```

continues

LISTING 14.1. CONTINUED

```
// special way. Also, this simple hash function considers each
// month to be 30 days long.
// Note: This function can result in conflicts.

int hash_date( char *datestring)
{
    int mm, dd;

    datestring[4] = '\0';
    dd = atoi (datestring + 2);
    datestring[2] = '\0';
    mm = atoi (datestring);

    if (mm < 1 || mm > 12 || dd > 30 )
    {
        cout << "Error in input string. ";
        return(-1);
    }

    return( mm*30 + dd);
}
```

The output of the function in Listing 14.1 should be taken with modulo TR to get values in the range 0 through TR-1. This function presents you a simple technique that shows how hashing can be done, but it does not resolve the problem of conflicts.

Load Factor (Alpha)

Load factor is a concept that greatly affects the performance of a hashing technique. The load factor is calculated by taking the number of elements (n) inserted into the table divided by the number of slots available in the hash table:

Alpha = n / TR

A load factor of 1.0 indicates that the number of elements inserted is equal to the number of available slots. Both the linear and nonlinear rehashing techniques discussed earlier in this chapter perform well under the following situations:

- If the load factor is low
- If deletions are not common

As the load factor increases, the cost of rehashing increases, and the cost of scanning the hash table quickly becomes very large. A real test of a hashing technique is its performance under high load factors. The chaining technique discussed in the next section performs very well under high load factors.

Chaining

The chaining technique basically looks at the hash table as an array of pointers to linked lists. Each slot in the hash table is either empty or simply consists of a pointer to a linked list. You resolve collisions by adding the elements that hash to the same slot to the linked list to which that slot points. At the same time, deletions are easy: You simply delete elements from the linked list. Use Table 14.1 to compare the chaining and rehashing techniques.

TABLE 14.1. COMPARING REHASHING AND CHAINING

Feature	*Rehashing*	*Chaining*
Number of entries in the hash table	Limited to the number of available slots	Limited to the available memory
Deletions are easy	No	Yes
Easy to code or implement	Yes	No
Uses linked lists	No	Yes
Collisions are possible	Yes	Yes (But resolves them very efficiently)
Performance under high load factors	Poor	Good
Uses extra space	No	Yes

Ordering the linked lists can further reduce the search time. Ordering prevents the exhaustive searching of the entire list. Chaining has several drawbacks:

- It requires additional space for the pointers.
- The cost to search can sometimes be high because of the need to dereference pointers instead of directly accessing the data used in the rehashing techniques.

But because memory is currently cheap and CPUs are fast, these drawbacks of chaining are not very significant.

A variation of chaining, called *coalesced chaining*, combines the best of both techniques. In this method, when a collision is encountered, the first available position is found for the new key and the slot position of this new key is stored along with the key that is already in the table. In other words, a pointer is created to point to another slot in the table. In C++, this technique can be implemented such that each position is a structure with two fields: one containing the key and the other field containing the next key position. You can use -2 to indicate that the next position is available for a given slot and use

-1 to indicate that you have reached the end of the chain. This method suffers from the limitation that you may get an overflow condition when the table is filled. However, you can make use of an overflow area to take care of additional space as needed.

Bucket Addressing

The bucket addressing technique is similar to chaining in that collision resolution is performed by using additional space. However, instead of using linked lists, we make use of buckets. A *bucket* can be defined as a block of space that can be used to store multiple elements that hash to the same position. In this method, you must give the buckets a fixed size; the choice of this size can sometimes be tricky. Collisions are still possible because you may fill a bucket completely—in which case the key must be stored somewhere. This storage location can be an available bucket or an overflow area. A variation can be used to eliminate the need for buckets with fixed size: You can allow each bucket to contain a pointer to a dynamically allocated array.

There are several things to keep in mind to obtain the best from a hashing technique:

- Try to keep the load factor between 0.2 and 0.7. This means that, if necessary, you should use large hash tables. Under certain types of input data conditions, large hash tables may not be easy to manipulate.

- The number of slots (TR) in the hash table should be a prime number. This allows you to be creative with the hash functions.

- Limit the hash function to only one division operation (which is preferably a modulo with the table size).

- Test the hash algorithm against some sample data and also against an extreme set of data. This approach tends to break the uniform distribution of data that hashing techniques strive to achieve.

- Accept collisions as a fact of life and prepare to resolve them, preferably using chaining. Note that using very large tables does not avoid collisions if rehashing is used.

Table 14.2 shows the prime numbers you can choose based on some common table sizes you might encounter.

TABLE 14.2. PRIME NUMBERS FOR USE WITH COMMON TABLE SIZES

Table Size	Prime Numbers That Can Be Used
100	97
250	241
500	499

Table Size	Prime Numbers That Can Be Used
1000	997
1500	1499
2000	1999
5000	4999
8000	7999
10000	9973

Hashing Character Strings

Although you may encounter applications for which the keys are numeric, it is also very common to have keys that are character strings (such as names, addresses, and keywords in a text). One approach to hashing with strings is to add up the ASCII values of the characters and apply modulo TR (where TR is the number of slots in the hash table). The following code snippet shows a simple and inefficient hash function that takes the key and the number of slots TR as input values and returns the bucket address as the result:

```c
int smpl_hash( char * key, int TR)
{
    int bucket = 0;
    while (*key) bucket += *key++;
    bucket = bucket % TR;
    return bucket;
}
```

It is very difficult to find a general-purpose hash function that performs well for all types of character strings, but the following ElfHash() function is very efficient. This function is part of the UNIX System V Release 4 and is used to hash character strings for ELF (Executable and Linking Format) files.

```c
unsigned long ElfHash(const unsigned char *key)
{
    unsigned long h = 0;
    while (*key){
        h = (h << 4) +  *key++;
        unsigned long g = h & 0xF0000000L;
        if (g) h ^= g >> 24;
        h &= ~g;
    }
    return h;
}
```

14

You should perform modulo TR on the result of this function. This function works very well for general cases and can be used to uniformly distribute the keys among the buckets.

Table 14.3 compares the hashing performance for the various techniques. Hashing uses the same performance measure as searching: the Big-O notation. The numbers in Table 14.3 represent the key comparisons

TABLE 14.3. COMPARING COLLISION RESOLUTION TECHNIQUES

Number of Key Entries	*Linear Hashing*	*Rehashing*	*Simple Chaining*	*Coalesced Chaining*
100	43	35	15	24
250	51	44	32	36
500	842	186	134	182
750	1983	641	299	504
1000	531	962	4971	64,594

Open Addressing

The technique of open addressing works best if you have a fairly good idea of the number of entries you are going to expect. Each bucket stores only one entry, and a hash function is applied on a key to determine its position in the table. If the bucket is empty, the key is copied to that bucket; otherwise, there is a collision and one of several strategies (discussed later in this chapter) is used to determine the location. Each of the strategies basically makes use of a predetermined sequence in which the table is probed until an empty bucket is found; then the entry is inserted. If you do not find an empty bucket, the table is full. This description implies that the probe sequence should eventually scan the entire table. Keep in mind that the same probe sequence is used when searching (instead of inserting) for a key. The search continues until either a match is found or an empty bucket is found, in which case the key does not exist in the table.

The open addressing method has two main problems:

- It is difficult to determine when you have encountered an empty bucket. In general, each bucket uses some kind of a flag to show whether or not it is empty.

- It is difficult to choose the best probe sequence. This is probably the most important decision because you need to make sure that the sequence can scan the entire table, if needed, and can also minimize clustering and collisions.

Suppose that the probe sequence is p_0, p_1, p_2, ... p_{s-1}. We can have p_0 as the result of the hash function, and the sequence can be a permutation of the numbers from 0 to $s-1$.

Linear Probing

The linear probing technique uses the following probe sequence: p_0, $p_0 + 1$, $p_0 + 2$, ... $p_0 + $ TR-1, taken modulo TR. The use of the modulo causes a wraparound to the beginning of the table when the end of the table is reached. The following equations can be used to easily represent this sequence:

```
p0 = hash(key) and
pi = (p0 + i) modulo TR
```

In these equations, p_i is the ith probe.

Example: Let's use linear probing to insert the following phone numbers into a hash table: 8881234, 8882345, 8883456, 8884321, 8885432, and 8886543. We will use the hash function hash(key) = key modulo 11 and insert the keys in a hash table of size 11. Here are the steps you follow in this hashing exercise:

1. hash(8881234) = 8881234 modulo 11 = 10

2. hash(8882345) = 8882345 modulo 11 = 10 (conflict)

    This conflict is resolved using the following probe sequence:

    ```
    p1 = (p0 + 1) mod 11
            = 11 mod 11
            = 0
    ```

3. hash(8883456) = 8883456 modulo 11 = 10 (conflict)

    This conflict is resolved using the following probe sequence:

    ```
    p1 = (p0 + 1) mod 11
       = 11 mod 11
       = 0 (conflict)
    ```

    This conflict is resolved using the following probe sequence:

    ```
    p2 = (p0 + 2) mod 11
            = 12 mod 11
            = 1
    ```

4. hash(8884321) = 8884321 modulo 11 = 6

5. hash(8885432) = 8885432 modulo 11 = 6 (conflict)

    This conflict is resolved using the following probe sequence:

    ```
    p1 = (p0 + 1) mod 11
            = 7 mod 11
            = 7
    ```

14

HASHING AND
PARSING
TECHNIQUES

6. `hash(8886543)` = `8886543 modulo 11` = `6 (conflict)`

This conflict is resolved using the following probe sequence:

$$p_1 = (p_0 + 1)\ \text{mod}\ 11$$
$$= 7\ \text{mod}\ 11$$
$$= 7$$

This conflict is resolved using the following probe sequence:

$$p_2 = (p_0 + 2)\ \text{mod}\ 11$$
$$= 8\ \text{mod}\ 11$$
$$= 8$$

Here is the resulting hash table with the phone numbers inserted:

Index	Value
0	8882345
1	8883456
2	
3	
4	
5	
6	8884321
7	8885432
8	8886543
9	
10	8881234

Any kind of probing causes further collisions, but the situation is worse for linear probing. In linear probing, the entries tend to be clustered, and the larger the cluster, the greater the chance of a collision. Clustering caused by linear probing is called *primary clustering*.

The average number of probes needed for a successful search (a match is found) and an unsuccessful search (an empty slot is found during insertion of the data element in the hash table) is given by the following equations:

`S(alpha)` = `1/2 + 1/2(1/(1-alpha))`,

`U(alpha)` = `1/2 + 1/2(1/(1-alpha))2`

In these equations, `alpha` is the load factor.

These formulas approximate the average number of trials for successful and unsuccessful searches. The formulas were developed by Donald Knuth and are described in detail in his book, *The Art of Computer Programming*.

As the table fills up, both the types of searches—S(alpha) and U(alpha)—take longer. When the table is almost full, the number of probes is on the order of O(TR). The searching done by hashing depends on the load factor and not necessarily on the number of entries.

Quadratic Probing

The performance problem encountered by linear probing is caused by the cluster buildup that occurs as a result of the probing sequence. *Quadratic probing* uses a different sequence to avoid primary clustering. The probes used can be represented as follows:

p$_0$ = hash(key) and
p$_i$ = (p$_0$ + i^2) mod TR

In these equations, p$_i$ is the ith probe and TR is the number of entries in the table.

Quadratic probing skips more buckets compared to linear probing and thereby causes less clustering. However, all the keys that map to the same bucket end up using the same probe sequence. This results in a condition called *secondary clustering*. The biggest drawback of quadratic probing is that after about half the number of buckets are scanned, the sequence starts repeating. As a result, you may miss empty buckets. A variation of quadratic probing can be used to improve the situation:

p$_0$ = hash(key) and
p$_i$ = (p$_0$ + i^2) mod TR

Uniform probing is a theoretical probe sequence that is basically random and in which each bucket has an equal probability of being selected. In this form of probing, there is no clustering, neither primary or secondary. The average number of probes for such a sequence can be given by the following equations:

S(alpha) = 1/alpha*l$_n$(1/(1-alpha)) and

U(alpha) = 1/(1-alpha)

In these equations, alpha is the load factor.

These formulas approximate the average number of trials for successful and unsuccessful searches. The formulas are developed by Donald Knuth and are described in detail in his book, *The Art of Computer Programming*.

There is no practical method to simulate such a sequence. However, double-hash probing comes very close to achieving this result.

Double-Hash Probing

Double hashing uses two hash functions such that the first hash function is applied to the key; if there is a collision, the second hash function is applied and its result is used as an offset to find the new bucket. The following equations can be used:

p_0 = hash1(key),

offset = hash2(key) and

p_i = (p_i-1 + c) mod TR

In these equations, TR is the number of buckets.

A full table scan can be guaranteed by making c relatively prime to TR.

It is very important to make sure that hash1 and hash2 are independent of each other. If a collision results from hash1, hash2 should not result in another collision.

In his book, *Mathematics for the Analysis of Algorithms*, Donald Knuth suggests a set of functions that do an excellent job in avoiding collisions:

hash1(key) = key mod TR,

hash2(key) = key mod (TR-2)

The randomization can further be increased by choosing TR such that TR and TR-x are both prime.

Example: Let's use the double-hashing technique on the same set of phone numbers described earlier:

8881234, 8882345, 8883456, 8884321, 8885432, 8886543

We will use these hash functions and insert the keys in a hash table of size 11:

hash1(key) = key modulo 11,

hash2(key) = key modulo 7

Here are the steps to perform this technique:

1. hash1(8881234) = 8881234 modulo 11 = 10
2. hash1(8882345) = 8882345 modulo 11 = 10 (conflict)
   This conflict is resolved using the following sequence:
   hash2(8882345) = 8882345 modulo 7 = 3
3. hash1(8883456) = 8883456 modulo 11 = 10 (conflict)
   This conflict is resolved using the following sequence:
   hash2(8883456) = 8883456 modulo 7 = 1

4. `hash1(8884321) = 8884321 modulo 11 = 6`

5. `hash1(8885432) = 8885432 modulo 11 = 6 (conflict)`

    This conflict is resolved using the following sequence:

    `hash2(8885432) = 8885432 modulo 7 = 3 (conflict)`

    We can now use linear probing to step further; the next empty bucket equals 4.

6. `hash1(8886543) = 8886543 modulo 11 = 6 (conflict)`

    This conflict is resolved using the following sequence:

    `hash2(8886543) = 8886543 modulo 7 = 1 (conflict)`

    Using linear probing, we get the next empty bucket equals 2.

Here is the resulting hash table with the phone numbers inserted:

Index	Value
0	
1	8883456
2	8886543
3	8882345
4	8885432
5	
6	8884321
7	
8	
9	
10	8881234

Thus you can see that the double-hashing technique does not eliminate collisions or clustering, but it does minimize them.

Listing 14.2 through Listing 14.6 show an implementation of a linked list and its routines: `previous_node()`, `current_node()`, `insert()`, and `remove()`.

LISTING 14.2. LINKED LIST CLASS DEFINITION

```
=============================================================

//The linked_list class can be defined as follows.
template <class Etype>
class linked_list
```

continues

LISTING 14.2. CONTINUED

```
{
    protected:
        struct node
        {
            Etype data;
            node *next;

            //Node constructor
            node( Etype D = 0, node *n = NULL):
                data(D), next(n) { }
        };

        node *list_head;
        void delete_list( );

        linked_lists( linked_list & value);

    public:
        linked_list( ) : list_head ( new node ) { }
        virtual ~linked_list( ) {delete_list( ); }

        virtual Etype * find_previous_node( const Etype & key);
        virtual int remove( const Etype & key);
        virtual Etype * find_node( const Etype & key);
        virtual int insert( const Etype & key);

};
```

LISTING 14.3. ROUTINE TO FIND THE NODE THAT COMES BEFORE THE NODE CONTAINING key

```
=============================================================
//This routine searches the linked list for the element
//"key" and returns the pointer to the node that comes
//just before the node that contains the "key". A header
//node is assumed for the linked list.

template <class Etype>
Etype *
linked_list<Etype>::
find_previous_node( const Etype & key)
{
    node *p;
    p = list_head;

    while ( p->next != NULL) {
        if (p->next->data == key )
        {
```

```
            return p;
        }
    p = p->next;
    }
    return p->next;
};
```

LISTING 14.4. ROUTINE TO DELETE THE NODE CONTAINING key

```
=============================================================

//This routine searches the linked list for the element
//"key" and then deletes the node that contains it.
//It makes use of the routine "find_previous_node".
//A header node is assumed for the linked list.

template <class Etype>
int
linked_list<Etype>::
remove( const Etype & key)
{
    node *to_delete, *previous_node;

    previous_node =  find_previous_node( key ) ;
    if (previous_node != NULL)
    {
        to_delete = previous_node->next;
        previous_node->next = to_delete->next;
        delete to_delete;
        return 1;
    }
    return 0;
};
```

LISTING 14.5. ROUTINE TO FIND THE NODE CONTAINING key

```
=============================================================
//This routine searches the linked list for the element
//"key" and returns the pointer to the node that contains
// the "key". A header node is assumed for the linked list.

template <class Etype>
node *
linked_list<Etype>::
find_node( const Etype & key)
{
    node *p;
```

continues

14

LISTING 14.5. CONTINUED

```
    p = list_head;

    while ( p->next != NULL) {
        if (p->next->data == key )
        {
            return p->next;
        }
    p = p->next;
    }
    return p->next;
};
```

LISTING 14.6. ROUTINE TO INSERT key IN A LINKED LIST

```
==============================================================
//This routine inserts the "key" at the head of the linked list.
//A header node is assumed for the linked list.

template <class Etype>
int
linked_list<Etype>::
insert( const Etype & key)
{
    node *p;
    node *i = new node( key, list_head->next);

    if ( i == NULL ){
        cout << "Error. Out of space";
        return 0;
    }

    p = list_head;
    p->next = i;
    return 1;


};
```

Listing 14.7 through Listing 14.11 provide the definition of an open_hash table and the implementation of its routines to insert, search, and remove keys.

LISTING 14.7. THE open_hash TABLE CLASS DEFINITION

```
==============================================================
//The class "open_hash_table" can be defined as follows.
template <class Element_Type>
class open_hash_table
{
```

```
    private:
        unsigned int table_size;
        linked_list<Element_Type> *lists;

        open_hash_table( open_hash_table & value);

    public:
        open_hash_table( unsigned int sz = 11);
        ~open_hash_table( ) { delete [ ] lists; }

        int search_key( const Element_Type * key );
        void remove( const Element_Type & key );
        void insert( const Element_Type & key );
};
```

LISTING 14.8. ROUTINE TO INITIALIZE THE open_hash CLASS

```
============================================================
//This routine initializes the open_hash_table.
template <class Element_Type>
open_hash_table<Element_Type>::
open_hash_table( unsigned int sz )
{
    table_size = sz;
    lists = new linked_lists<Element_Type> [table_size];
    if ( lists == NULL)
        cout << "Error. Out of space";
};
```

LISTING 14.9. ROUTINE TO SEARCH FOR key IN THE open_hash TABLE

```
============================================================
//This routine can be used to search for a key in the open
//hash table.
//It returns the "bucket" that contains the key.
//It makes use of the linked_list class and its public routines.

template <class Element_Type>
int
open_hash_table<Element_Type>::
search_key( const Element_Type * key )
{
    unsigned int hash_value = hash( key, table_size );

    if ( lists[hash_value].find_node(key))
    {
        bucket = hash_value;
```

continues

LISTING 14.9. CONTINUED

```
        return bucket;
    }
    return 0;
};
```

LISTING 14.10. ROUTINE TO REMOVE THE SPECIFIED key FROM THE open_hash TABLE

```
==============================================================
//This routine can be used to remove the specified key from
//the open hash table.
//It makes use of the linked_list class and its public
//routines.
template <class Element_Type>
void
open_hash_table<Element_Type>::
remove( const Element_Type & key )
{
    unsigned int hash_value = hash( key, table_size );

    lists[hash_value].remove(key);

};
```

LISTING 14.11. ROUTINE TO INSERT THE SPECIFIED key INTO THE open_hash TABLE

```
==============================================================
//This routine can be used to insert the specified key into
//the open hash table.
//It makes use of the linked_list class and its public
//routines.
template <class Element_Type>
void
open_hash_table<Element_Type>::
insert( const Element_Type & key )
{
    node *p;
    unsigned int hash_value = hash( key, table_size );

    //Duplicates are not allowed.
    p = lists[hash_value].find_node(key);
    if (p == NULL )
        lists[hash_value].insert(key);
    else
        cout << "Sorry. Key already exists";

};
```

Parsing

Parsing is a generic operation that identifies legal expressions and breaks them up into a form suitable for further processing. Parsing has applications in many different fields such as computer science (where it can be used by compilers to convert a high-level language to a lower-level language), interpreting human language, and so on. The main goal of parsing is to check the validity of an expression and make more sense out of it. The term "grammar" is commonly used in programming languages to identify legal expressions.

There are two approaches commonly used during parsing (see Table 14.4 for a comparison of these two methods):

- **Top-down approach:** This method looks at the program first, and recursively identifies parts that are eventually matched to the input expression.

- **Bottom-up approach:** This method looks at the input expression and combines the pieces of the expression to make a legal program from it.

TABLE 14.4. COMPARING PARSING APPROACHES

Feature	Top-Down Approach	Bottom-Up Approach
Approach	Break the bigger components into more manageable smaller parts.	Combines the small parts to form a bigger component.
Implementation	Easy	Difficult
Efficiency	Poor	Good
Implementation technique	Recursive	Iterative

Let's use a data structure called `stack` to understand parsing in more detail. This data structure will contain only two operations: `push()` (place an element at the top of the stack) and `pop()` (remove an element from the top of the stack). The C++ implementation of the `stack` class is shown in Listing 14.12.

LISTING 14.12. IMPLEMENTATION OF THE `stack` CLASS AND ITS ROUTINES

```
class stack
{
    private:
        char *stack_store;
```

continues

14

HASHING AND
PARSING
TECHNIQUES

LISTING 14.12. CONTINUED

```
//"top" is a pointer to the top of the stack
        int top;
    public:
        stack( int max_size=1000);
        ~stack( )  (delete stack_store;);
void push(char data);
        char pop( );

}

stack::stack( int max_size )
{
    stack_store = new char[max];
    top = 0;
}

stack::push( char data )
{
    stack[top++] = data;
}
char stack::pop( )
{
    return stack[--top];
}
```

Parsing Numeric Expressions

Numeric expressions are generally represented by the *infix notation*, in which the operator is placed between the operands and parentheses are used where necessary to indicate the order in which the operators are applied to the expressions. Numeric expressions are best computed using a *postfix notation* (also called *reverse polish notation*), in which the operator is placed after its two operands and parentheses are not required. The stack implementation shown in Listing 14.12 is ideal for calculating such numeric expressions. Table 14.5 gives some examples of numeric expression in the infix format and their postfix equivalents.

TABLE 14.5. CONVERTING INFIX EXPRESSIONS TO POSTFIX EQUIVALENTS

Infix Representation	Postfix Representation
5 + 4	5 4 +
6 * (7 + 4)	6 7 4 + *
(7 + 8) * (2 - 9) + 1	7 8 + 2 9 - * 1 +
2 * ((3 + 1) * 6)	2 3 1 + 6 * *

The algorithm used with stacks and postfix expressions is given here:

1. Scan the expression left to right.

2. If you encounter an operand, push it to the top of the stack.

3. If you encounter an operator, pop the top two stack elements and perform the operation on them; push the result back on top of the stack.

Listing 14.13 provides an implementation of numeric parsing using the `stack` class.

LISTING 14.13. IMPLEMENTATION OF NUMERIC PARSING

```
char c;
stack num_stack(100);
int sum;
int oper1, oper2;

while ( cin.get(c)  )
{
    sum = 0;
    while ( c == ' ' ) cin.get(c);

    if (c == '+' )
    {
        oper1 = num_stack.pop( );
        oper2 = num_stack.pop( );
        sum = oper1 + oper2;
    };

    if (c == '*' )
    {
        oper1 = num_stack.pop( );
        oper2 = num_stack.pop( );
        sum = oper1 * oper2;
    };

    if (c == '-' )
    {
        oper1 = num_stack.pop( );
        oper2 = num_stack.pop( );
        sum = oper2 - oper1;
    };

    if (c == '/' )
    {
        oper1 = num_stack.pop( );
        oper2 = num_stack.pop( );
        sum = oper2 / oper1;
    };
```

14

HASHING AND
PARSING
TECHNIQUES

continues

LISTING 14.13. CONTINUED

```
    while (c >='0' && c<= '9')
    {
        sum = 10*sum + (c-'0');
        cin.get(c);
    };

    num_stack.push(sum);
};

cout  << "The result of the expression is " & sum ;
```

Parsing String Expressions

String parsing can be more involved than numeric parsing and can be represented by using a parse tree. You can construct a *parse tree* for an expression by using the following simple recursive rule: Make the operator the root; the tree corresponding to the left operand (expression) is the left child, and the tree corresponding to the right operand (expression) is the right child. This simple rule results in a binary parse tree. Figure 14.1 shows the parse tree for the expression A*((B+C) + D).

FIGURE 14.1.

Parse tree for the expression
A*((B+C) + D).

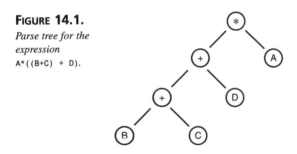

Parse trees can also be created for more complicated expressions, such as the expression of the English language. Such string parsing requires sophisticated techniques, the details of which are beyond the scope of this book. The `stack` object we used for numeric parsing can also be used for string parsing; the difference is that instead of pushing the intermediate results on the stack, we save the intermediate expression trees on the stack. Listing 14.14 shows the implementation for A*((B+C) + D). First, we convert this expression to its postfix equivalent: A B C + D + *. The reason we use postfix equivalent expressions is so that they can be easily implemented with the `stack` object.

LISTING 14.14. IMPLEMENTATION FOR A*((B+C) + D) USING THE `stack` CLASS

```
struct node
{
```

```
    char data;
    struct node *left, *right;
};
stack string_stack(100);
char c;
struct node *x, *dummy;

dummy = new node;
dummy->left = dummy;
dummy->right = dummy;

while (cin.get(c))
{
    while ( c==' ' ) cin.get(c);
    x = new node;
    x->data = c;
    x->left = dummy;
    x->right = dummy;
    if ( c == '+' || c== '*' )
    {
        x->right = stack.pop( );
        x->left = stack.pop( );
    }
    stack.push(x);
}
```

Context-Free Grammar and Parsing

A context-free grammar is often used to define legal constructs. It can be used to determine whether a given string of characters is valid in a language. The language can be a programming language or a natural language (such as English). For example, the following can be used as the context-free grammar that defines the set of all legal regular expressions:

```
<expression> ::= <term> | <term> + <expression>
<term> ::= <factor> | <factor> <term>
<factor> ::= (<expression>) | c | (<expression>)* | c*
```

Each line in the grammar description is called a *production rule*, or a *replacement rule*. The production or replacement rule contains the following:

- Terminal symbols such as (,), +, and *, which are used in the language.

- Non-terminal symbols such as <expression>, <term>, and <factor>, which are used in the grammar.

- The special symbol "c" that represents a letter or a digit.

- Meta-symbols such as ::= (which stands for "is a") and | (which stands for "or"), which are used in the grammar.

You can use a parse tree to describe a string expression using these production rules. You can use parsing to determine whether or not a given string can be derived using the production rules. If the string cannot be derived, then the string is illegal in the language being represented by the grammar.

An example of such a parse tree for the expression A*B+AC is shown in Figure 14.2.

FIGURE 14.2.

*The parse tree for the expression A*B+AC.*

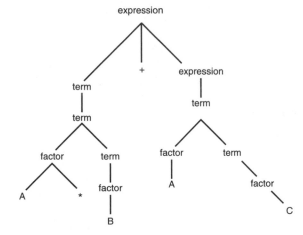

Using Top-Down Parsing to Validate Regular Expressions

The top-down parsing technique uses recursion to recognize strings. This technique uses a procedure to represent each of the production rules specified in the grammar such that nonterminal symbols on the left side of the rule becomes the name of the procedure, and nonterminal symbols on the right side of the rule become recursive calls. Terminal symbols are used to scan the string in the process of deriving a parse tree. Refer to Sedgewick's book, *An Introduction to the Analysis of Algorithms*, for details about how compilers can be generated for such regular expressions.

The regular expression being parsed can be represented in the array p; the index i can represent the character currently being analyzed. The idea is to start with i = 0; if, after going through the code that implements the parser, we reach i = strlen(p), the string is legal in the language. The code should be able to perform error handling as well as prevent infinite loops caused by improper recursion.

The following pseudocode shows how this can be implemented:

```
for(i=0;i<strlen(p);i++){
        //Code to implement the parser goes here.
        }
```

Summary

Choosing the best hashing technique for a particular application can be a very difficult decision. However, when memory is not an issue, you will find that all the various hashing techniques discussed in this chapter work with relatively similar performance. As a general rule, I suggest that if you are aware of the size of the key set, you should use the double-hashing technique. On the other hand, if you do not know the size of the key set, you should use the chaining method. Keep in mind that you should also consider the load factor, which is an important part of the hashing technique. For large load factors, the technique you use is really tested; you should also carefully consider the size of the links that are involved in the open addressing method.

In general, hashing is better than a binary search because hashing is simpler to implement and can usually provide a fast and almost constant search time (assuming that you have enough memory to store a large hash table). Binary searches can be useful if memory is an issue or the size of the key set is not known because they can give you predictable worst-case performance.

Parsing techniques are commonly used by compilers to interpret a given input and convert it into another form that can be interpreted by the machine. Parsing can make use of top-down or bottom-up approaches; the choice of parsing approach usually depends on the grammar being parsed. Numeric expressions are usually parsed using their postfix representation; string parsing is usually performed by using a parse tree to represent the expression being parsed. Parsing is widely used in artificial intelligence for language interpretation. By using the production rules and the grammar for a particular language, you can create parse trees for expressions.

Object Persistence and Encryption

PART

IV

IN THIS PART

Object Persistence

CHAPTER 15

C++ is in the business of manipulating objects in memory. At times, however, you will want these objects to be stored to disk and then restored to memory at a later time. Storing objects to disk allows you to manipulate a larger number of objects than can be housed in memory at any one time; it also enables you to shut down your program and resume its operation later.

Your compiler vendor provides ofstream objects that implement basic file manipulation. Your program can create an fstream object and then use it to open your files and to read data in and out. However, fstream objects know nothing about your data. They are terrific for reading in a stream of characters, but your objects are often more complex than that.

As you can imagine, it is your job to teach your classes how to stream to disk. There are a number of ways to do this.

The first question you must answer is whether your files will store mixed types of objects. If it is possible that you will have to read a record without knowing what type of object it is, then you will have to store more information in the file than you would if every record in that file were known to be of the same type.

The second question is whether you are storing data of a fixed length. If you know that the next object to be read is 20 bytes, for example, you have an easier task than if you don't know how big the object is. In the latter case, the length must be stored with the object.

Listing 15.1 demonstrates a very simple program that opens a file, stores some text to it, closes the file, and then reopens it and reads the text.

LISTING 15.1. A SIMPLE READ/WRITE PROGRAM

```
#include <fstream.h>
void main()
{
    char fileName[80];
    char buffer[255];
    cout << "File name: ";
    cin >> fileName;

    ofstream fout(fileName);  // open for writing

    fout << "This line written directly to the file...\n";

    cout << "Enter text for the file: ";

    cin.ignore(1,'\n');  // eat the new line after the file name
    cin.getline(buffer,255);  // get the user's input

    fout << buffer << "\n";    // and write it to the file
```

```
    fout.close();               // close the file, ready for reopen

    ifstream fin(fileName);     // reopen for reading
    cout << "Here's the contents of the file:\n";

    char ch;
    while (fin.get(ch))
    cout << ch;

    cout << "\n***End of file contents.***\n";

    fin.close();                // always pays to be tidy
}
```

This small program neatly shows the fundamentals of writing text out to a file. You create a filename, open an `ofstream` object with that name, and write to it using `fout`. This is very similar to writing to standard output using `cout`. You can also read from this file using `fin`, in a way that is directly analogous to `cin`.

Creating Storable Objects

Writing *objects*, rather than built-in types such as characters, is a bit more complicated than writing text. The object-oriented solution to this dilemma is to teach the objects to write themselves to disk and to read themselves *from* disk. To do this, you must designate your class as *storable*, a task we'll accomplish through inheritance.

Note that storable is not a built-in C++ construct; it is a capability you will add to your program by creating an abstract base type `Storable` and then implementing the necessary methods in your storable subclasses. Because the storable base class is fairly simple, you may often choose to make your storable objects multiply inherit—both from their "natural" base class and from the storable base class.

`Storable` is an abstraction, and so we'll designate one of its methods as pure virtual:

```
class Storable  // Abstract Data type
    {
    public:
        Storable() {}
        Storable(Reader&){}
        virtual void Write(Writer&)=0;
    private:
    };
```

Classes derived from `Storable` must implement the `Write()` method, which takes a `Writer` as a parameter. `Storable` objects can be created from disk by passing in a `Reader`. Here are the declarations of `Reader` and `Writer`:

15

OBJECT
PERSISTENCE

```
class Writer
    {
    public:
       Writer(char *fileName):fout(fileName,ios::binary){};
       ~Writer() {fout.close();}
       virtual Writer& operator<<(int&);
       virtual Writer& operator<<(char*);

    private:
          ofstream fout;
    };

    class Reader
    {
    public:
       virtual Reader& operator>>(int&);
       virtual Reader& operator>>(char*&);

       Reader(char *fileName):fin(fileName,ios::binary){}
       ~Reader(){fin.close();}

    private:
       ifstream fin;
    };
```

The job of `Reader` and `Writer` is to encapsulate the responsibility of reading and writing primitive data (such as integers, character strings, and so on) to permanent storage. Here we've implemented only the `int` and `char*` storage mechanisms. You can imagine adding `double`, `float`, and others.

To see how these classes are used, we need some objects to store to disk and read back from disk. We'll start by creating a `Note` class, which will derive from class `Storable`, as shown in Listing 15.2. The `Note` class stores some text, the length of that text, and a couple other pieces of information. For now, we'll just have it store two integers (`reserved1` and `reserved2`) to represent these additional values. In a commercial application, these variables might store the creation date or other relevant data.

LISTING 15.2. NOTE.H

```
class Note : public Storable
{
 public:
    Note(const String& text):
    itsText(text), reserved1(0L), reserved2(0L)
      {}

    Note(const char* text):
    itsText(text), reserved1(0L), reserved2(0L)
```

```
      {}

   Note::Note(Reader& rdr)  :itsText(rdr)
   {
     rdr >> reserved1;
     rdr >> reserved2;
   }

   ~Note(){}

   const String& GetText()const { return itsText; }

   //…

  void Write(Writer& wrtr)
  {
     itsText.Write(wrtr);
     wrtr << reserved1;
     wrtr << reserved2;
  }
private:
   String itsText;
   int reserved1;
   int reserved2;
};
```

The text that Note stores (itsText) is of type String. This is a user-defined type that manages character strings. The Note class delegates responsibility for the creation of reserved1 and reserved2 to the Reader, which we will pass into the constructor. The Reader is responsible for reserved1 and reserved2 because they are primitive data types (integers). The Note class asks the String object to construct itself, however, because it is a user-defined type. To do so, the Note class passes the Reader object to the String's constructor in the Note's initialization:

```
Note::Note(Reader& rdr)  :itsText(rdr)
```

Because Note is derived from class Storable, it has a constructor that takes a Reader object, and it must override the Write() method. Here again, the Note class delegates to itsText the responsibility to write the String (passing in the Writer object) but it delegates to the Writer object the responsibility to write out the two integers.

Once again, the rule is that primitive (built-in) types such as integers and characters are managed by the Reader and the Writer, but user-defined types such as String must read and write their own data.

15

OBJECT PERSISTENCE

To see how String accomplishes this, we must examine it in a bit more detail. String is a flexible utility class you would write yourself if the STL or your favorite library didn't provide one. The implementation shown in Listing 15.3 is rudimentary, but is sufficient for the following examples.

LISTING 15.3. STRING.H

```
class String : public Storable
    {
    public:

            // constructors
            String();
            String(const char *);
            String (const char *, int length);
            String (const String&);
            String(istream& iff);
            String(Reader&);
            ~String();

            // helpers and manipulators
            int    GetLength() const { return itsLen; }
            bool IsEmpty() const { return (bool) (itsLen == 0); }
            void Clear();                   // set string to 0 length

            // accessors
            char operator[](int offset) const;
            char& operator[](int offset);
            const char * GetString()const  { return itsCString; }

            // casting operators
             operator const char* () const { return itsCString; }
             operator char* () { return itsCString;}

            // operators
            const String& operator=(const String&);
            const String& operator=(const char *);

            void operator+=(const String&);
            void operator+=(char);
            void operator+=(const char*);

            bool operator<(const String& rhs)const;
            bool operator>(const String& rhs)const;
            bool operator<=(const String& rhs)const;
            bool operator>=(const String& rhs)const;
            bool operator==(const String& rhs)const;
            bool operator!=(const String& rhs)const;
```

```
           // friend functions
           String operator+(const String&);
           String operator+(const char*);
           String operator+(char);

           void Display()const { cout << itsCString << " "; }
           friend ostream& operator<< (ostream&, const String&);
           ostream& operator() (ostream&);
             void Write(Writer&);

     private:
           // returns 0 if same, -1 if this is less than argument,
           // 1 if this is greater than argument
           int StringCompare(const String&) const;
           char * itsCString;
           int itsLen;
     };
```

The implementation of this class includes the constructor taking a Reader, and also an override of the Write() method taking a Writer:

```
String::String(Reader& rdr)
    {
        rdr>>itsLen;
        rdr>>itsCString;
    }

void String::Write(Writer& wrtr)
    {
       wrtr<<itsLen;
       wrtr<<itsCString;
    }
```

Note how String manages its own reading and writing. It delegates its primitive data to the Reader and the Writer. Had String contained other user-defined objects, it would have asked *them* to read and write themselves; and they in turn would have passed *their* primitive types to Reader and Writer.

This makes sense; all user-defined types consist of some mix of other user-defined types and primitive data. Sooner or later, it all comes down to the built-in types, and Reader and Writer are equipped to deal with that. Each user-defined type has to know only its own composition; its responsibility consists only of proper delegation to other user-defined types or to the Reader and Writer objects.

Equipped with these methods, we're ready to walk our way through a driver test program, as shown in Listing 15.4.

15

OBJECT PERSISTENCE

LISTING 15.4. DRIVER PROGRAM FOR READER AND WRITER

```cpp
#include "note.h"   // see listing 15.2
#include <fstream.h>

// NOT a member function!
void operator<<(Writer& wrtr, Note& note)
{
    note.Write(wrtr);
}

const int howMany = 5;

int main()
{
    char fileName[80];
    char buffer[255];     // for user input
    cout << "File name: ";
    cin >> fileName;
    cin.ignore(1,'\n');   // eat the new line after the file name
    Writer * writer = new Writer(fileName);
    Note* theNote;

    for (long i = 0; i<howMany; i++)
    {
        cout << "Please enter a word: " ;
        cin.getline(buffer,255);
        theNote = new Note(buffer);
        (*writer) << *theNote;    // write it to the file
        delete theNote;
    }
    delete writer;

    Reader * reader = new Reader(fileName);

    cout << "Here are the contents of the file:\n";

    for (i = 0; i<howMany; i++)
    {
        theNote = new Note(*reader); // Create from the file
        cout << theNote->GetText()<< endl;
        delete theNote;
    }

    cout << "\n***End of file contents.***\n";
    delete reader;
    return 0;
}
```

The first thing we see is a globally defined operator<< that takes a Writer object and a Note. This allows us to mimic the cout format (you need the parentheses because of operator precedence):

```
(*writer) << *theNote;   // and write it to the file
```

This simple driver program begins by prompting the user for a filename. A Writer object is then created using that filename. The constructor of Writer uses the filename to initialize an fout object, passing in the filename it was given:

```
Writer(char *fileName):fout(fileName,ios::binary){};
```

We enter a loop and prompt the user for words. Each word is used to create a new Note object:

```
Note(const char* text):
    itsText(text), reserved1(0L), reserved2(0L)
      {}
```

The text is initialized with the word supplied by the user, and the integer variables reserved1 and reserved2 are initialized to zero. The Writer is then handed the Note to write to the file:

```
(*writer) << *theNote;
```

Stepping *into* this function takes you into the global function we defined earlier:

```
void operator<<(Writer& wrtr, Note& note)
{
    note.Write(wrtr);
}
```

This code invokes Note's Write() method. Stepping into Note's Write() method, we find that the Note is in fact delegating the task of writing out its text to the String class, and the Note class is delegating to the Writer object the responsibility to write out the integers. No one writes out the text length because we have no need to store this information for the Note; we'll simply call strlen() when the note is rebuilt—as we'll see in a moment.

```
void Write(Writer& wrtr)
    {
        itsText.Write(wrtr);
        wrtr << reserved1;
        wrtr << reserved2;
    }
```

Stepping into itsText.Write(wrtr) shows that the String delegates to the Writer the responsibility of writing out the length and contents of the text. This is a critical point: The string knows *what* to write, and the Writer knows how to write it:

```
void String::Write(Writer& wrtr)
    {
        wrtr<<itsLen;
        wrtr<<itsCString;
    }
```

The reason Note didn't do this itself is that it should not know what to write: that is an internal detail of the String class. All Note needed to know was that String was user-defined and that, therefore, String would know what to do to write itself.

Continuing with the Note's Write() method, after telling the String to write itself, the method tells the Writer object to write out the value of reserved1:

```
void Write(Writer& wrtr)
    {
        itsText.Write(wrtr);
        wrtr << reserved1;
        wrtr << reserved2;
    }
```

This call invokes Writer:: operator<<(int&):

```
Writer& Writer::operator<<(int& data)
        {
            fout.write((char*)&data,szInt);
            return *this;
        }
```

After the text and the two reserved fields are written, the Note has been stored. After all the words are written, we no longer need the Writer object, so it is deleted. Time passes, and we now want to read the Notes stored on disk. A Reader object is created and we enter a loop in which we re-create the five Notes from storage—at least for long enough for them to tell us their contents.

The Reader is initialized with the same filename as the Writer, and the Note's constructor is called, taking the Reader as a parameter:

```
        theNote = new Note(*reader);
```

The constructor of the Note reverses the process by which the Note was written. Note the initialization of itsText; this takes place before the body of the constructor runs:

```
Note::Note(Reader& rdr) :itsText(rdr)
    {
        rdr >> reserved1;
        rdr >> reserved2;
    }
```

This initialization invokes the String's constructor, which takes a Reader as a parameter:

```
String::String(Reader& rdr)
    {
        rdr>>itsLen;
        rdr>>itsCString;
    }
```

The string reads its length first:

```
rdr>>itsLen;
```

This action invokes Reader's operator >>, passing in itsLen by reference. The value is filled with the value stored on disk:

```
Reader& Reader::operator>>(int& data)
    {
        fin.read((char*)&data,szInt);
        return *this;
    }
```

It then does the same thing to get the string:

```
Reader& Reader::operator>>(char *& data)
    {
        int len;
        fin.read((char*) &len,szInt);
        data = new char[len+1];
        fin.read(data,len);
        data[len]='\0';
        return *this;
    }
```

Note that the Reader does *not* use the length stored by the String object. The length of the stored string is actually on the disk. When this string was written out by Writer, the length was recorded in the first four bytes; the String keeps this information redundantly as an optimization for use in other methods:

```
Writer& Writer::operator<<(char * data)
    {
        int len = strlen(data);
        fout.write((char*)&len,szInt);      // write the length
        fout.write(data,len);              // now write the data
        return *this;
    }
```

The Note's constructor continues by asking the Reader to restore the reserved1 field:

```
rdr >> reserved1;
```

This again invokes operator>>, which simply reads four bytes into this variable:

```
Reader& Reader::operator>>(int& data)
    {
        fin.read((char*)&data,szInt);
        return *this;
    }
```

The same is done for reserved2. Finally, the Note is displayed, and the Reader is destroyed.

After Reader and Writer are fully developed to support all the built-in types, it becomes a simple matter to implement serialization for your classes. Just do the following:

1. Derive from Storable.
2. Implement a constructor that takes a Reader and a Write() method.
3. Delegate to the Reader or Writer responsibilities for primitive types.
4. Delegate to contained Storable objects responsibility for reading and writing themselves.

Manipulation of Files

Although reading and writing to disk works quite well for many tasks, you sometimes need finer control of your files. To examine these issues, I'll create a B-tree which I'll use to keep Notes in order and to store them to disk both in a data file and in an index.

What Is a B-Tree?

The B-tree was invented in 1972 by R. Bayer and E. McCreight, and was designed from the start to create shallow trees for fast disk access.

Shallow trees have few "levels"; you have to seek through them fewer times, and therefore they run quickly. Because seeks often require going to disk for the information you need, the performance increase with a shallow tree rather than a deeper tree can be substantial. B-trees are a powerful solution to the problem of disk-based storage; virtually every commercial database system has used variations on a B-tree for years.

A B-tree consists of *pages*. Each page has a set of indices. Each index consists of a key value and a pointer. The pointer in an index can point either to another page or to the data you are storing in the tree.

Thus, every page has indices that point to other pages or to data. If the index points to another page, the page is called a *node page*; if the index points to data, the page is called a *leaf page*. The maximum number of indices on a page is the page's *order*.

Every page, therefore, has a maximum of *order* child pages. It is a rule of B-trees that no pages, other than the top page and the leaf pages, ever have fewer than `order/2` indices. A leaf page can have one fewer than that (`order/2-1`).

New indices are always added to leaf pages. This fact is critical: ***You never add an index to a node page***. Node pages are created by the B-tree when an existing page "splits."

Here's how it works: Assume that you are creating a B-tree of *order* 4 (to pick a number), to store words. To simplify the example, the index's key will be the word itself (that is, we won't distinguish between keys and data).

For this example, I'll build up a tree with the words "Four score and seven years ago, our fathers brought forth on this continent..." When the tree is created, its root pointer, `myRoot`, points to nothing, as shown in Figure 15.1.

FIGURE 15.1.

An empty B-tree.

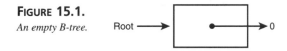

The first word, `Four`, is added to a new page, as shown in Figure 15.2. This new page is a leaf page, and the index, `Four`, points to the actual data.

FIGURE 15.2.

A leaf page.

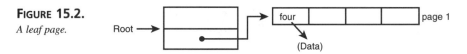

Words are added to the page until *order* words, in this case four words, at which time the page is full (see Figure 15.3).

FIGURE 15.3.

A full-leaf page.

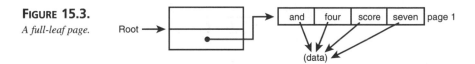

When it is time to enter the word `years`, the page must split to make room. The algorithm follows:

1. Split the page in half.
2. Add the new word in its appropriate position (in this case, alphabetical).
3. If the new word is smaller than the first word, and thus will be added in the first position, adjust the pointer.

4. Return a pointer to the new page.

5. If the root detects that a new top page is required, create it.

6. Add an entry in the new top page to point to what the root points to.

7. Add an entry in the new top page for the return value from step 4.

8. Point the root to the new top page.

In the case shown in Figure 15.4, the word years is to be added. To do this, the page must split. The new page is returned, and the root pointer recognizes that a new top page is needed. The new page is populated with an index pointing to the entry that myRoot used to point to (and), and a second entry is made pointing to the new page. myRoot then is pointed to this new node page.

FIGURE 15.4.

Splitting the page.

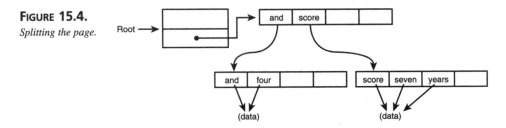

The next word to be added is ago. Because this is earlier than and, it is added before and on the leaf page, and the node page is "fixed up" to point to this earlier index, as shown in Figure 15.5.

FIGURE 15.5.

Fixing up the node.

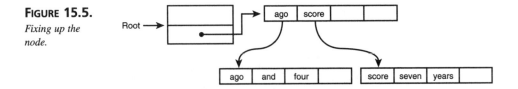

When a page node is filled, as shown in Figure 15.6, it splits, as shown in Figure 15.7, and the new pointer is added to the node pointer. This continues until the node page is full, as shown in Figure 15.8.

FIGURE 15.6.
Getting ready to split a page.

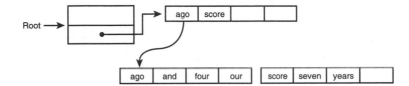

FIGURE 15.7.
After the page splits.

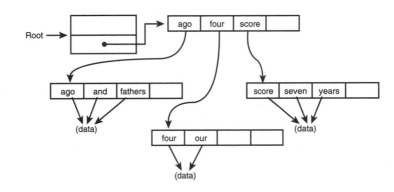

FIGURE 15.8.
The tree when the node page is full.

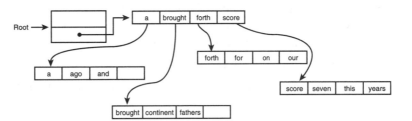

Adding the next word, new, to this tree presents a problem. The first page will have to split, and when it does, it will pass an entry to its parent node. That node, however, is full, so it too will have to split. When it does, the root pointer must recognize that a new node is required (see Figure 15.9).

FIGURE 15.9.
A third tier.

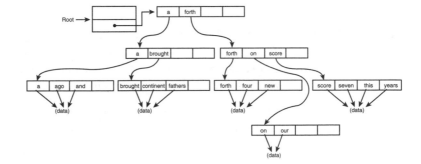

Writing It To Disk

The entire purpose of a B-tree is to store data on a disk. Somehow, the B-tree has to store the pages, the indices, and the data on disk. One task is to cache the pages; they'll be big, and you don't want them all in memory at the same time.

Let's take a short digression to talk about building a database in the real world. In all likelihood, here's how you will program your next database: You will pick up the phone, dial an 800 number to a mail-order house with a name like Programmer Credit-Card Heaven, and ask for the fastest, most reliable database system they have that meets your specifications.

You'll write the front end in MFC or ASP or some other whiz-bang technology, and you'll wire your application to your database using COM, perhaps wrapped under ODBC, ADO, or another technology.

Only in the rarest of circumstances will you actually "roll your own" database from scratch. Understanding how such a beast works, however, will deepen your understanding of how to use it well.

For our purposes, we'll build a small Personal Information Manager (PIM) that will let you create Notes (strings of characters) and store them in the database. Days later, you can query the database for a string and find every Note that contains that string. These Notes will be of variable length. We'll store each Note with a date, a length, and a set of characters representing the data.

The Notes will be stored sequentially, with each Note beginning right after the preceding Note in the file.

> **NOTE**
>
> For this simplified version, the Notes are just character strings. In a more complex implementation, you may want to use a class Note to store these strings and other state information.

The word index file (WORD.IDX) will consist of pages of indexes, leading ultimately to a leaf page with the index for the word found. This record still won't point to the data. After all, a single word may be in many Notes. We'll create an index file that will contain a linked list of pointers to records in the database itself.

All of this is based on a PIM I created for a now out-of-print book *Teach Yourself More C++ in 21 Days*. I've brought that code up to date and modified it for this book to keep the focus on persistence. That PIM was called ROBIN (after my first daughter); I'll name this one RACHEL (after my second).

Here's how it works: The user requests a search on the word THE. The WORD.IDX file, which is a disk-based B-tree, is searched. Node-page index entries lead to other node-page entries until a leaf page is found. The number recorded there is an offset into RACHEL.IDX. Each record in RACHEL.IDX points to a record in RACHEL.DB, and also points to the next entry in RACHEL.IDX (or to NULL when there are no more entries).

Caching

Rather than reading each page into memory each time it is needed and then tossing it away, it is far faster and more efficient if you can keep a few pages cached in memory. The index, however, doesn't want to keep track of whether the page it is pointing to is in memory (in which case, a pointer is needed) or is on disk.

Keeping track of where the pages are located (in memory or on disk) would require the index to understand far too much about how pages are stored to disk. All the index should know is that it points to page number 5, for example.

We need a disk manager. The node-page index hands the disk manager an offset and gets back a pointer to the requested page. It is the disk manager's job to decide whether the page is already in memory or must be picked up off the disk.

In the simplest case, the disk manager would keep an array of pages. When the array was full, it would toss out a page and bring in another. But which page should be tossed? It is far more efficient to toss out a page that is rarely used than to toss out a page that is used all the time. After all, tossing out a page that is used all the time just means that the page will be loaded back in soon, defeating your purpose of trying to minimize disk reads.

The answer is a least recently used (LRU) queue. A *recently used queue* is the queue that was used most recently; a *least recently used queue* contains the pages you have gone the longest without needing. The idea is that if you haven't needed it for a while, you probably will not need it any time soon.

Determining How Big Each Page Should Be

The goal is quick reads and writes. It turns out that most personal computers are fastest if they can read a block of data that is a multiple of 2 (no surprise!). The ideal size is determined by the sector size of your disk. Because this size varies, you will want the program to get this size from a configuration file, but for now I'll use 512, a reasonable guess.

Each index record has to be a divisor of the order so that an even number fits on each page. The index will be 16 bytes: 4 bytes of pointer (now offset) and 11 bytes of data, with a final NULL byte terminating the string. There are 32 sets of 16 bytes in a 512-byte page, so each page will hold 32 index objects. The order of the B-tree is therefore 32. A 32-order tree can hold 1,024 words in two levels, 32,768 words in three levels, and 33,554,432 words in five levels. Most searches probably can be accomplished in just a few disk reads, which is ideal.

Determining How Many Pages Can Be in Memory at Once

The algorithm you use to determine how many pages can be in memory at once is recursive, starting at the top node and working its way down through the tree. Because each page has room for 32 indexes, the average case is that at any time, half of these will be in use: 16 indexes per page.

10 levels of pages with 16 indexes per page provide access to a trillion keys. 10 pages, however, takes up only 2KB of memory. (16 bytes per index times 16 indices per page, times 10 pages, equals 2,560 bytes, or 2KB.)

This is the power of B-trees in a nutshell: By holding 2KB of pages in memory at any time, B-trees give you access to a trillion keys!

Swapping to Disk

The fastest way to swap to disk is to do a single `memcpy()`. C++ gains from its lineage in C the capability to hack memory when required so that all the indexes on a page can be loaded from disk in a single memory move.

When the `Page` object is in memory, you want to deal with it as if it consisted of four `int` objects and an array of `Index` objects. When getting the `Page` object off the disk, you want to deal with it as a block of 512 bytes. To do this, you make a union between a character array of 512 bytes and the other variables.

Because you cannot put an array of objects that have constructors into a union, you instead create an array of characters of the size of your array of `Index` objects. We'll then use a pointer to that array, casting it to the types needed. This is an effective hack to move objects into and out of memory. It sacrifices type safety for speed. Giving up type-safety puts you at risk of writing unreliable code, so be careful and make sure you know what you are doing.

Implementing the B-Tree

That's the theory. But implementation is sometimes a bit more complicated. In this case, we bring to bear a lot of solid object-oriented technique and one wicked hack.

With a program this complex, you really need two things: the complete source code and, after you've had a chance to get acquainted with the code's layout, you need to walk through the code in the debugger.

Rather than making this code "industrial strength," I've stripped it down to the bare bones required to show how the code works—and more important, how object persistence works.

The principal object is the BTree, as shown in Listing 15.5.

LISTING 15.5. BTree DECLARATION

```
class BTree
{
public:
    // constructors and destructor
    BTree();
    ~BTree();

    // utility functions
    void AddKey(char* data, int offset);
    bool Insert(char*);
    void PrintTree();
    int Find(char* data);

    // page methods
    Page* GetPage(int page)
    { return theDiskManager.GetPage(page); }
    int NewPage(Index& pIndex, bool IsLeaf)
    { return theDiskManager.NewPage(pIndex,false); }

    static int myAlNum(char ch);
    // public static member!
    static  IDXManager theDiskManager;
    static WNJFile    theWNJFile;
    static DataFile theDataFile;
    static bool GetWord(char*, char*, int&);
    static void GetStats();
    static int NodeIndexCtr;
    static int LeafIndexCtr;
    static int NodePageCtr;
    static int LeafPageCtr;
    static int NodeIndexPerPage[Order+1];
    static int LeafIndexPerPage[Order+1];

private:
    int myRoot;
};
```

The BTree's job is to act as an entry point into the tree and to keep some tree statistics. The work is done by the page and the index, as shown in Listing 15.6.

LISTING 15.6 PAGE DECLARATION

```
class Page
{
public:
 // constructors and destructor
    Page();
    Page(char*);
    Page(Index&,bool);
    Page(Index*, int, bool, int);
    ~Page(){}

    // insertion and search operations
    int Insert(Index&, bool findOnly = false);
    int Find(Index& idx) { return Insert(idx,true); }
    int InsertLeaf(Index&);
    int FindLeaf(Index&,bool findOnly);
    int InsertNode(Index&,bool findOnly = false);
    void Push(Index&,int offset=0, bool=true);

    // accessors
    Index GetFirstIndex() { return myKeys[0]; }
    bool GetIsLeaf() const { return myVars.IsLeaf; }
    int GetCount() const { return myVars.myCount; }
    void SetCount(int cnt) { myVars.myCount=cnt; }
    time_t GetTime() { return myTime; }
    bool GetLocked() { return myVars.IsLocked; }
    void SetLocked (bool state) { myVars.IsLocked = state; }

    // page manipulation
    int GetPageNumber() const { return myVars.myPageNumber; }
    Page* GetPage(int page)
    { return BTree::theDiskManager.GetPage(page); }
    int NewPage(Index& rIndex, bool IsLeaf)
    { return BTree::theDiskManager.NewPage(rIndex,false); }

    int NewPage(Index* arr, int off,bool isL, int cnt)
    { return   BTree::theDiskManager.NewPage(arr,off,isL, cnt); }

    // utility functions
    void Nullify(int offset);
    void Print();
    fstream& Write(fstream&);
    void ReCount();

    static int GetgPageNumber(){ return gPage; }
    static void SetgPageNumber(int pg) { gPage = pg; }

private:
    Index * const myKeys; // will point to myVars.mk
    union
```

```
   {
   char myBlock[PageSize];    // a page from disk
   struct
   {
      int myCount;
      bool IsLeaf;
      int myPageNumber;
      bool IsLocked;
      char mk[Order*sizeof(Index)];   // array of indexes
   }myVars;
};

   // memory only
   static int gPage;
   time_t myTime; // for lifo queue
};
```

There are a few constructors for `Page`; we'll see these at work as we step through the example. `Insert()`, `Find()`, and so forth are used for putting indices into pages and finding them later. Note that `GetPage()` is inline; it simply delegates to `DiskManager`. This makes for fast reads and good clean encapsulation of the work of caching pages in memory and retrieving them from disk.

Examine the `private` section closely. We have a union between a character array and the `myVars` structure. `myVars` consists of a count variable, a flag (indicating whether this is a leaf), a page number, a locked flag, and an array of indices. Indices are user-defined objects whose constructors take a parameter. When you create an array of user-defined objects, however, each object must be created using the default constructor.

What are we to do? We want to read these indices into the page all at one go, and we can't use the default constructor. We must trick the compiler into believing that we are not loading an array of indices at all—that we are just loading a character array. Note that `mk` is thus declared to be an array of characters. The array size is `Order` (32) times the size of an `Index` (16). No indices here, honest.

We also declare a *pointer* to an index: `myKeys`. No problem, a pointer is just fine; no constructor is called for the pointer.

The wicked hack comes in the `Page`'s constructor. We initialize that pointer (`myKeys`) to point to the first byte of `mk`. To do that, we must cast `myVars.mk` to a pointer to `Index`:

```
Page::Page(Index& index, bool bLeaf):
      myKeys((Index*)myVars.mk)
   {
```

Hey, presto! we have a pointer to an array of indices, and as you know, a pointer can be used *exactly* like an array. This allows us to write this later:

```
myKeys[i].PrintKey();
```

This is a classic example of trading away type safety for performance. You don't do it often, but it is nice when you need it. Try *that* in Java!

Listing 15.7 shows the declaration of the Index class.

LISTING 15.7. THE DECLARATION OF THE Index CLASS

```cpp
class Index
{
public:
    // constructors & destructor
    Index();
    Index(char *);
    Index (char*, int);
    Index(Index&);
    ~Index(){}

    // accessors
    const char * GetData() const  { return myData; }
    void SetData(const Index& rhs)
    { strcpy(myData,rhs.GetData()); }
    void SetData(const char * rhs)
    { strcpy(myData,rhs); }
    int GetPointer()const { return myPointer; }
    void SetPointer (int pg) { myPointer = pg; }

    // utility functions
    void PrintKey();
    void PrintPage();
    int Insert(Index& ref,bool findOnly = false);

    // overloaded operators
    int operator==(const Index& rhs);

    int operator < (const Index& rhs)
    {return strcmp(myData,rhs.GetData())<0;}

    int operator <= (const Index& rhs)
    {return strcmp(myData,rhs.GetData())<=0;}

    int operator > (const Index& rhs)
    {return strcmp(myData,rhs.GetData())>0;}

    int operator >= (const Index& rhs)
    {return strcmp(myData,rhs.GetData())>=0;}

public:
    int myPointer;
    char myData[SizeItem - SizePointer];
};
```

Note that you can compare two indices, and what you get is a comparison of the data to which they correspond. This allows us to keep the objects in order. A more generalized approach is to keep not an array of characters as the data, but rather a paramaterized type. Further, it would be better to delegate the responsibility of the comparison to the data object itself. I've not done that here to keep this example a bit simpler.

Note also}; that SizeItem is a constant set to 16. (Refer to the section "Determining How Big Each Page Should Be" to review why each item is 16 bytes.) We subtract from that the size of the pointer (allowing for the size of the member variable myPointer) so that the Index remains at the size of SizeItem. That is, with the two member variables, myPointer and myData, the}; Index is the size of SizeItem: 16.

There are three additional classes in this program: DataFile, DiskManager, and WNJFile. The DataFile class represents the actual database of Notes. Each Note is added sequentially to a disk file and its offset is recorded:

```
class DataFile
{
public:
    // constructors & destructor
    DataFile();
    ~DataFile(){}

    // management of files
    void Close();
    void Create();
    void GetRecord(int, char*, int&, time_t&);

    int Insert(char *);

private:
    fstream myFile;
};
```

The DiskManager class is responsible for managing the pages in memory: caching the most recently used, storing the remaining pages to disk, and retrieving them as needed:

```
class DiskManager
{
public:
    // constructors & destructor
    DiskManager();
    ~DiskManager(){}

    // management of files
    void Close(int);
    int Create();
```

```
    // Page manipulation
    Page* GetPage(int);
    void SetPage(Page*);
    void Insert(Page * newPage);
    void Save(Page* pg);
    int NewPage(Index&, bool);
    int NewPage(Index *array, int offset, bool leaf, int count);

private:
    Page* myPages[MaxPages];
    fstream myFile;
    int myCount;
};
```

Finally, the WNJFile (Word Node Join) class is responsible for mapping Words (keys) to Notes (data). This allows us to find *every* note with a given word in it rather than just the first Note that contains the given word:

```
class WNJFile
{
public:
    // constructors & destructor
    WNJFile();
    ~WNJFile(){}

    // management of files
    void Close();
    void Create();
    int* Find(int NextWNJ);
    int Insert(int, int);
    int Append(int);

private:
    static int myCount;
    fstream myFile;
    union
    {
      int myints[5];
      char  myArray[5*szInt];
    };
};
```

Here you see the array of five integers as discussed earlier. The first four represent offsets into the data file, the fifth (if used) is an offset back into WNJFile for the next array.

The following listings show the complete code for this example, which we'll walk through in some detail. Listing 15.8 shows BTree.hpp, the only header file for the entire program. It contains the declaration of all the classes as well as the constant values used in the program.

LISTING 15.8. FROM THE HEADER FILE BTree.hpp

```
#ifndef BTREE_HPP                    // inclusion guards
#define BTREE_HPP

#include <time.h>
#include <string.h>
#include <fstream.h>

const int SIZE_TIME =      4;
const int SIZE_INT =       4;
const int Order =         31;      // 31 indexes and 1 header
const int dataLen =       11;      // length of a key
const int MaxPages =      20;      // more than we need
const int SizeItem =      16;      //dataLen, plus the null, plus the
SizePointer
const int SizePointer =   SIZE_INT;    // size of offset
const int PageSize =      (Order+1) * SizeItem;
const int N_DATA_SETS = 5;
const int DATA_SET_POINTER_OFFSET = N_DATA_SETS-1;
const int N_ITEMS_IN_HEADER = 2;
const int MAX_ARRAY_SIZE = 256;

// forward declarations
class Page;
class Index;

class DataFile
{
public:
    // constructors & destructor
    DataFile();
    ~DataFile(){}

    // management of files
    void Close();
    void Create();
    void GetRecord(int, char*, int&, time_t&);

    int Insert(char *);

private:
    fstream myFile;
};

class WNJFile
{
public:
```

continues

LISTING 15.8. CONTINUED

```cpp
    // constructors & destructor
    WNJFile();
    ~WNJFile(){}

    // management of files
    void Close();
    void Create();
    int* Find(int NextWNJ);
    int Insert(int, int);
    int Append(int);

private:
    static int myCount;
    fstream myFile;
    union
    {
      int myints[5];
      char  myArray[5*SIZE_INT];
    };
};

// DiskManager - in memory keeps track of what pages are
// already in memory and swaps to disk as required
class DiskManager
{
public:
    // constructors & destructor
    DiskManager();
    ~DiskManager(){}

    // management of files
    void Close(int);
    int Create();

    // Page manipulation
    Page* GetPage(int);
    void SetPage(Page*);
    void Insert(Page * newPage);
    void Save(Page* pg);
    int NewPage(Index&, bool);
    int NewPage(Index *array, int offset, bool leaf, int count);

private:
    Page* myPages[MaxPages];
    fstream myFile;
    int myCount;
};
```

```
// the BTree itself - has a pointer to first page
class BTree
{
public:
    // constructors and destructor
    BTree();
    ~BTree();

    // utility functions
    void AddKey(char* data, int offset);
    bool Insert(char*);
    void PrintTree();
    int Find(char* data);

    // page methods
    Page* GetPage(int page)
    { return theDiskManager.GetPage(page); }
    int NewPage(Index& pIndex, bool IsLeaf)
    { return theDiskManager.NewPage(pIndex,false); }

    static int myAlNum(char ch);
    // public static member!
    static  DiskManager theDiskManager;
    static WNJFile    theWNJFile;
    static DataFile theDataFile;
    static bool GetWord(char*, char*, int&);
    static void GetStats();
    static int NodeIndexCtr;
    static int LeafIndexCtr;
    static int NodePageCtr;
    static int LeafPageCtr;
    static int NodeIndexPerPage[Order+1];
    static int LeafIndexPerPage[Order+1];

private:
    int myRoot;
};

// index objects point to pages or real data
class Index
{
public:
    // constructors & destructor
    Index();
    Index(char *);
    Index (char*, int);
    Index(Index&);
    ~Index(){}
```

continues

15

OBJECT PERSISTENCE

LISTING 15.8. CONTINUED

```cpp
    // accessors
    const char * GetData() const  { return myData; }
    void SetData(const Index& rhs)
    { strcpy(myData,rhs.GetData()); }
    void SetData(const char * rhs)
    { strcpy(myData,rhs); }
    int GetPointer()const { return myPointer; }
    void SetPointer (int pg) { myPointer = pg; }

    // utility functions
    void PrintKey();
    void PrintPage();
    int Insert(Index& ref,bool findOnly = false);

    // overloaded operators
    int operator==(const Index& rhs);

    int operator < (const Index& rhs)
    {return strcmp(myData,rhs.GetData())<0;}

    int operator <= (const Index& rhs)
    {return strcmp(myData,rhs.GetData())<=0;}

    int operator > (const Index& rhs)
    {return strcmp(myData,rhs.GetData())>0;}

    int operator >= (const Index& rhs)
    {return strcmp(myData,rhs.GetData())>=0;}

public:
    int myPointer;
    char myData[SizeItem - SizePointer];
};

// pages - consist of header and array of indexes
class Page
{
public:
 // constructors and destructor
    Page();
    Page(char*);
    Page(Index&,bool);
    Page(Index*, int, bool, int);
    ~Page(){}

    // insertion and search operations
    int Insert(Index&, bool findOnly = false);
    int Find(Index& idx) { return Insert(idx,true); }
    int InsertLeaf(Index&);
    int FindLeaf(Index&,bool findOnly);
```

```
    int InsertNode(Index&,bool findOnly = false);
    void Push(Index&,int offset=0, bool=true);

    // accessors
    Index GetFirstIndex() { return myKeys[0]; }
    bool GetIsLeaf() const { return myVars.IsLeaf; }
    int GetCount() const { return myVars.myCount; }
    void SetCount(int cnt) { myVars.myCount=cnt; }
    time_t GetTime() { return myTime; }
    bool GetLocked() { return myVars.IsLocked; }
    void SetLocked (bool state) { myVars.IsLocked = state; }

    // page manipulation
    int GetPageNumber() const { return myVars.myPageNumber; }
    Page* GetPage(int page)
    { return BTree::theDiskManager.GetPage(page); }
    int NewPage(Index& rIndex, bool IsLeaf)
    { return BTree::theDiskManager.NewPage(rIndex,false); }

    int NewPage(Index* arr, int off,bool isL, int cnt)
    { return    BTree::theDiskManager.NewPage(arr,off,isL, cnt); }

    // utility functions
    void Nullify(int offset);
    void Print();
    fstream& Write(fstream&);
    void ReCount();

    static int GetgPageNumber(){ return gPage; }
    static void SetgPageNumber(int pg) { gPage = pg; }
private:
    Index * const myKeys; // will point to myVars.mk
    union
    {
    char myBlock[PageSize];    // a page from disk
    struct
    {
        int myCount;
        bool IsLeaf;
        int myPageNumber;
        bool IsLocked;
        char mk[Order*sizeof(Index)];   // array of indexes
    }myVars;
  };

    // memory only
    static int gPage;
    time_t myTime; // for lifo queue
};

#endif
```

The driver program and ancillary global functions are in `Persist.cpp`, as shown in Listing 15.9.

LISTING 15.9. `Persist.cpp`

```cpp
#include "btree.hpp"
#include <Windows.h>
#include <iostream.h>
#include <stdlib.h>

// static definitions
DiskManager BTree::theDiskManager;
DataFile BTree::theDataFile;
WNJFile BTree::theWNJFile;

int WNJFile::myCount =      0L;
int Page::gPage =           1;
int BTree::NodeIndexCtr =   0;
int BTree::LeafIndexCtr =   0;
int BTree::NodePageCtr =    0;
int BTree::LeafPageCtr =    0;
int BTree::NodeIndexPerPage[Order+1];
int BTree::LeafIndexPerPage[Order+1];

// prototypes
void parseCommandLines(char *buffer,int argc,char **argv);
void ShowMenu(long*);
void DoFind(char*, BTree&);
void ParseFile(BTree&);

// driver program
int main()
{
    BTree myTree;

    for (int i = 0; i < Order +1; i++)
    {
        BTree::NodeIndexPerPage[i] = 0;
        BTree::LeafIndexPerPage[i] = 0;
    }

    char buffer[PageSize+1];

    bool fQuit = false;

    while ( !fQuit )
    {
        cout << "?: ";
        cin.getline(buffer,PageSize);
```

```
            if ( buffer[0] == '·' )
            {
                switch (buffer[1])
                {
                  case '?':
                     DoFind(buffer+2,myTree);
                     break;

                  case '!':
                       myTree.PrintTree();
                       break;

                  case 'F':
                  case 'f':
                       ParseFile(myTree);
                       break;
                  case '0':
                     fQuit = true;
                     break;
                }
            }
            else
            {
                if ( myTree.Insert(buffer) )
                  cout << "Inserted.\n";
                buffer[0] = '\0';
            }
        }
        return 0;
}

// having found matches, show the menu of choices
// each entry is numbered and dated
void ShowMenu(int *list)
{
  int j=0;
  char buffer[PageSize+1];
  time_t theTime;
  int len;
  char listBuff[256];
  struct tm * ts;
  int dispSize;

  while (list[j] && j < 20)
  {
     BTree::theDataFile.GetRecord(list[j],buffer,len, theTime);
  dispSize = __min(len,32);
     strncpy(listBuff,buffer,dispSize);
     if (dispSize == 32)
        {
        listBuff[29] = '.';
```

continues

15

OBJECT
PERSISTENCE

LISTING 15.9. CONTINUED

```
            listBuff[30] = '.';
            listBuff[31] = '.';
            }
        listBuff[dispSize]='\0';
        ts = localtime(&theTime);
        cout << "[" << (j+1) << "] ";
        cout << ts->tm_mon << "/";
        cout << ts->tm_mday << "/";
        cout << ts->tm_year << " ";
        cout <<  listBuff << endl;
        j++;
    }
}


// handle -? command
// find matches, show the menu, request choice
// display record and redisplay menu
void DoFind(char * searchString, BTree& myTree)
{

    // create an array of total set of WNJ
    // offsets. This will be used to display
    // choices and to find actual text
    int  list[PageSize];

    // initialize the array to all zeros
    for (int i = 0; i<PageSize; i++)
    list[i] = 0;

    int k = 0;

    char * p1 = searchString;
    while (p1[0] == ' ')
        p1++;

    int offset = myTree.Find(p1);
    if (offset)
    {
        // get the array of offsets from WNJFile
        int *found  =  BTree::theWNJFile.Find(offset);
        int j = 0;

        // add any you don't already have
        for (;k < PageSize && found[j];j++,k++)
        {
            for (int l = 0; l < k; l++)
            {
                if (list[l] == found[j])
```

```
                    continue;
            }
            list[k] = found [j];
        }
        delete [] found;
    }

    cout << "\n";

    if (!list[0])
    {
        cout << "Nothing found.\n";
        return;
    }

    ShowMenu(list);

    int choice;
    char buffer[PageSize];
    int len;
    time_t theTime;

    for (;;)
    {
        cout << "Choice (0 to stop): " ;
        cin >> choice;
        cin.ignore(PageSize,'\n');
        if ( choice < 1 )
            break;

        BTree::theDataFile.GetRecord(list[choice-1],buffer,len, theTime);
        cout << "\n>> ";
        cout << buffer;
        cout << "\n\n";
        ShowMenu(list);
    }
}

// open a file and create a new note for each line
// index every word in the line
void ParseFile( BTree& myTree)
{

    char fileName[256];
    cout << "FileName: ";
    cin.getline(fileName,PageSize);

    char buffer[PageSize];
    char theString[PageSize];
```

continues

15

OBJECT
PERSISTENCE

LISTING 15.9. CONTINUED

```
ifstream theFile(fileName,ios::in );
if (!theFile)
{
    cout << "Error opening input file " << fileName << endl;
    return;
}

int offset = 0;
for (;;)
{
    theFile.read(theString,PageSize);
    int len = theFile.gcount();
    if (!len)
        break;
    theString[len]='\0';
    char *p1, *p2, *p0;
    p0 = p1 = p2 = theString;

    while (p1[0] && (p1[0] == '\n' || p1[0] == '\r'))
        p1++;

    p2 = p1;

    while (p2[0] && p2[0] != '\n' && p2[0] != '\r')
        p2++;

    int bufferLen = p2 - p1;
    int totalLen = p2 - p0;

    if (!bufferLen)
        continue;

    // lstrcpyn(buffer,p1,bufferLen);
    strncpy(buffer,p1,bufferLen);
    buffer[bufferLen]='\0';

    // for (int i = 0; i< PageSize; i++)
        cout << "\r";
    cout << "Parsing " << buffer;
    myTree.Insert(buffer);
    offset += totalLen;
    theFile.clear();
    theFile.seekg(offset,ios::beg);
}
cout << "\n\nCompleted parsing " << fileName << endl;
}
```

Listings 15.10 through 15.15 give the implementation files for the various classes.

LISTING 15.10. BTree.cpp

```cpp
#include "btree.hpp"
#include <ctype.h>
#include <stdlib.h>

// construct the tree
// initialize myRoot pointer to nothing
// either create or read the index file
BTree::BTree():myRoot(0)
{
    myRoot = theDiskManager.Create();
    theDataFile.Create();
    theWNJFile.Create();
}

// write out the index file
BTree::~BTree()
{
    theDiskManager.Close(myRoot);
    theDataFile.Close();
    theWNJFile.Close();
}

// find an existing record
int BTree::Find(char * str)
{
    Index index(str);
    if (!myRoot)
        return 0L;
    else
        return GetPage(myRoot)->Find(index);
}
bool BTree::Insert(char* buffer)
{

    if (strlen(buffer) < 3)
        return false;

    char *buff = buffer;
    char word[PageSize];
    int wordOffset = 0;
    int offset;

    if (GetWord(buff,word,wordOffset))
    {
        offset = theDataFile.Insert(buffer);
        AddKey(word,offset);
    }
```

continues

15

OBJECT PERSISTENCE

LISTING 15.10. CONTINUED

```cpp
    while (GetWord(buff,word,wordOffset))
    {
        AddKey(word,offset);
    }

    return true;

}

void BTree::AddKey(char * str, int offset )
{

    if (strlen(str) < 3)
        return;

    int retVal =0;

    // create an index where the str is in upper case
    // and the offset is recorded in Index.myPointer
Index index(str,offset);
    if (!myRoot)
    {
        myRoot = theDiskManager.NewPage (index,true);
    }
    else
    {
        Page * pPage = GetPage(myRoot);
        retVal = pPage->Insert(index);
        if (retVal) // our root split
        {
         // create a pointer to the old top
            pPage = GetPage(myRoot);
            Index index(pPage->GetFirstIndex());
            index.SetPointer(myRoot);

            // make the new page & insert the index
            int PageNumber = NewPage(index,false);

            pPage = GetPage(PageNumber);

            //get a pointer to the new (sibling) page
            Page * pRetValPage = GetPage(retVal);
            Index Sib(pRetValPage->GetFirstIndex());
            Sib.SetPointer(retVal);

            // put it into the page
            pPage->InsertLeaf(Sib);
```

```cpp
            // reset myRoot to point to the new top
            myRoot = PageNumber;
        }
    }
}

void BTree::PrintTree()
{

    NodePageCtr  =    0;
    LeafPageCtr  =    0;
    NodeIndexCtr =    0;
    LeafIndexCtr =    0;
    for (int i = 0; i < Order + 1; i++)
    {
        NodeIndexPerPage[i] = 0;
        LeafIndexPerPage[i] = 0;
    }

    GetPage(myRoot)->Print();

    cout << "\n\nStats:" << endl;
    cout << "Node pages:   " << NodePageCtr << endl;
    cout << "Leaf pages:   " << LeafPageCtr << endl;
    cout << "Node indexes: " << NodeIndexCtr << endl;
    cout << "Total leaves: " << LeafIndexCtr << endl;
    for (i = 0; i < Order + 1; i++)
    {
        if (NodeIndexPerPage[i])
        {
            cout << "Pages with " << i << " nodes:  ";
            cout << NodeIndexPerPage[i] << endl;
        }
        if (LeafIndexPerPage[i])
        {
            cout << "Pages with " << i << " leaves: ";
            cout << LeafIndexPerPage[i] << endl;
        }
    }

}

bool BTree::GetWord(char* string, char* word, int& wordOffset)
{

    int i;
    if (!string[wordOffset])
        return false;

    char *p1, *p2;
    p1 = p2 = string+wordOffset;
```

continues

LISTING 15.10. CONTINUED

```
        // eat leading spaces
        for ( i = 0; i<(int)strlen(p1) && !BTree::myAlNum(p1[0]); i++)
            p1++;

        // see if you have a word
        if (!BTree::myAlNum(p1[0]))
            return false;

        p2 = p1; // point to start of word

        // march p2 to end of word
        while (BTree::myAlNum(p2[0]))
            p2++;

        int len = int (p2 - p1);
        int pgSize = PageSize;
    #if defined(_MSVC_16BIT) || defined(_MSVC_32BIT)
        {
            len = __min(len,(int)PageSize);
        }
    #else
        {
            len = __min(len,(int)PageSize);
        }
    #endif

        strncpy (word,p1,len);
        word[len]='\0';

        for (i = int(p2-string);
                i<(int)strlen(string) && !BTree::myAlNum(p2[0]);
                i++)
            p2++;

        wordOffset = int(p2-string);

        return true;
    }

    int BTree::myAlNum(char ch)
    {
        return isalnum(ch) ||
        ch == '-' ||
        ch == '\'' ||
        ch == '(' ||
        ch == ')';
    }
```

LISTING 15.11. Index.cpp

```cpp
#include "btree.hpp"
#include <ctype.h>

Index::Index(char* str):myPointer(1)
{
   strncpy(myData,str,dataLen);
   myData[dataLen]='\0';
   for (size_t i = 0; i < strlen(myData); i++)
      myData[i] = toupper(myData[i]);
}

Index::Index(char* str, int ptr):myPointer(ptr)
{

   strncpy(myData,str,dataLen);
   myData[dataLen]='\0';
   for (size_t i = 0; i< strlen(myData); i++)
      myData[i] = toupper(myData[i]);

}

Index::Index(Index& rhs):
   myPointer(rhs.GetPointer())
{
  strcpy(myData, rhs.GetData());
  for (size_t i = 0; i< strlen(myData); i++)
      myData[i] = toupper(myData[i]);

}

Index::Index():myPointer(0)
{
   myData[0]='\0';
}

void Index::PrintKey()
{
   cout << "  " << myData;
}

void Index::PrintPage()
{
   cout <<  myData << ": " ;
   BTree::theDiskManager.GetPage(myPointer)->Print();
}

int Index::Insert(Index& ref, bool findOnly)
{
```

continues

LISTING 15.11. CONTINUED

```
    return BTree::theDiskManager.GetPage(myPointer)->Insert(ref,findOnly);
}

int Index::operator==(const Index& rhs)
{
    return (strcmp(myData,rhs.GetData()) == 0); // case insensitive
}
```

LISTING 15.12. Datafile.cpp

```cpp
#include "btree.hpp"
#include <assert.h>

// on construction, try to open the file if it exists
DataFile::DataFile():
    myFile("RACHEL.DAT",
    ios::binary ¦ ios::in ¦ ios::out ¦ ios::nocreate ¦ ios::app)
{
}

 void DataFile::Create()
 {
    if (!myFile) // nocreate failed, first creation
    {

        // open the file, create it this time
        myFile.clear();

        myFile.open
            ("RACHEL.DAT",ios::binary ¦ ios::in ¦ ios::out ¦ ios::app);

        char Header[SIZE_INT];
        int MagicNumber = 1234; // a number we can check for
        memcpy(Header,&MagicNumber,SIZE_INT);
        myFile.clear();
        myFile.flush();
        myFile.seekp(0);
        myFile.write(Header,SIZE_INT);
        return;
    }

    // we did open the file, it already existed
    // get the numbers we need
    int MagicNumber;
    myFile.seekg(0);
    myFile.read((char *) &MagicNumber,SIZE_INT);

    // check the magic number. If it is wrong the file is
```

```
      // corrupt or this isn't the index file
      if (MagicNumber != 1234)
      {
            // change to an exception!!
            cout << "DataFile Magic number failed!";
      }
      return;
}

// write out the numbers we'll need next time
void DataFile::Close()
{
   myFile.close();
}

int DataFile::Insert(char * newNote)
{
   int len = strlen(newNote);
   int fullLen = len + SIZE_INT + SIZE_TIME;

   time_t theTime;
   theTime = time(NULL);

   char buffer[PageSize];
   memcpy(buffer,&len,SIZE_INT);
   memcpy(buffer+SIZE_INT,&theTime,SIZE_TIME);
   memcpy(buffer+SIZE_INT+SIZE_TIME,newNote,len);

   myFile.clear();
   myFile.flush();
   myFile.seekp(0,ios::end);
   int offset = (int) myFile.tellp();
   myFile.write(buffer,fullLen);
   myFile.flush();
   return offset;
}

void DataFile::GetRecord(int offset, char* buffer, int& len, time_t&
      theTime)
{
   char tmpBuff[PageSize];
   myFile.flush();
   myFile.clear();
   myFile.seekg(offset);
   myFile.read(tmpBuff,PageSize);
   memcpy(&len,tmpBuff,SIZE_INT);
   memcpy(&theTime,tmpBuff+SIZE_INT,SIZE_TIME);
   strncpy(buffer,tmpBuff+SIZE_INT+SIZE_TIME,len);
   buffer[len] = '\0';
}
```

LISTING 15.13. Page.cpp

```cpp
#include "btree.hpp"
#include <assert.h>

// constructors

// default constructor
Page::Page()
{
}

// create a page from a buffer read in from disk
Page::Page(char *buffer):
 myKeys((Index*)myVars.mk)
{
    assert(sizeof(myBlock) == PageSize);
    assert(sizeof(myVars) == PageSize);
    memcpy(&myBlock,buffer,PageSize);
    SetLocked(false);
    myTime = time(NULL);
}

// create a Page from the first index
Page::Page(Index& index, bool bLeaf):
    myKeys((Index*)myVars.mk)
{

    myVars.myCount=1;
    myVars.IsLeaf = bLeaf;
    SetLocked(false);
    // if this is a leaf, this is the first
    // index on the first page, set its pointer
    // based on creating a new wnj. otherwise
    // you are here creating a new node, do not
    // set the pointer, it is already set.
    if (bLeaf)
    {
        int indexPointer = index.GetPointer();
        int appendResult = BTree::theWNJFile.Append(indexPointer);
        index.SetPointer(appendResult);
    }
    myKeys[0]=index;
    myVars.myPageNumber = gPage++;
    myTime = time(NULL);
}

// create a page by splitting another page
Page::Page(Index *array, int offset, bool bLeaf,int count):
 myKeys((Index*)myVars.mk)
{
    myVars.IsLeaf = bLeaf;
```

```
    myVars.myCount = 0;
    for (int i=0, j = offset; j<Order && i < count; i++, j++)
    {
        myKeys[i]= array[j];
        myVars.myCount++;
    }
    myVars.myPageNumber = gPage++;
    SetLocked(false);
    myTime = time(NULL);
}

void Page::Nullify(int offset)
{
    for (int i = offset; i<Order; i++)
    {
        myKeys[i].SetPointer(0);
        myVars.myCount—;
    }
}

// decide whether I'm a leaf or a node
// and pass this index to the right
// function. If findOnly is true, don't insert
// just return the page number (for now)
int Page::Insert(Index& rIndex, bool findOnly)
{
    int result;
    if (myVars.IsLeaf)
    {
        SetLocked(true);
        result = FindLeaf(rIndex,findOnly);
        SetLocked(false);
        return result;
    }
    else
    {
        SetLocked(true);
        result = InsertNode(rIndex,findOnly);
        SetLocked(false);
        return result;
    }
}

// find the right page for this index
int Page::InsertNode(Index& rIndex, bool findOnly)
{
    int retVal =0;
    bool inserted = false;
    int i,j;
```

continues

LISTING 15.13. CONTINUED

```
assert(myVars.myCount>0); // nodes have at least 1
assert(myKeys[0].GetPointer()); // must be valid

// does it go before my first entry?
if (rIndex < myKeys[0])
{
    if (findOnly)
    return 0L; // not found

    myKeys[0].SetData(rIndex);
    retVal=myKeys[0].Insert(rIndex);
    inserted = true;
}

// does it go after my last?
if (!inserted)
for (i = myVars.myCount-1; i>=0; i—)
{
    assert(myKeys[i].GetPointer());
    if (rIndex >= myKeys[i])
    {
        retVal=myKeys[i].Insert(rIndex,findOnly);
        inserted = true;
        break;
    }
}

// find where it does go
if (!inserted)
for (j = 0; j<i && j+1 < myVars.myCount; j++)
{
    assert(myKeys[j+1].GetPointer());
    if (rIndex < myKeys[j+1])
    {
        retVal=myKeys[j].Insert(rIndex,findOnly);
        inserted = true;
        break;
    }
}

assert(inserted);  // change to exception if not!

// if you had to split
if (retVal && !findOnly) // got back a pointer to a new page
{
    Index * pIndex = new Index(GetPage(retVal)->GetFirstIndex());
    pIndex->SetPointer(retVal);
    retVal = InsertLeaf(*pIndex);
```

```
    }
    return retVal;
}

// called if current page is a leaf
int Page::FindLeaf(Index& rIndex, bool findOnly)
{
    int result = 0;

    // no duplicates!
    for (int i=0; i < myVars.myCount; i++)
        if (rIndex == myKeys[i])
        {
            if (findOnly)                  // return first WNJ
                //return BTree::theWNJFile.Find(myKeys[i].GetPointer());
                return myKeys[i].GetPointer();
            else
                return BTree::theWNJFile.Insert(
            rIndex.GetPointer(),
            myKeys[i].GetPointer());
        }

    if (findOnly)            // not found
        return result;

    // this index item does not yet exist
    // before you push it into the index
    // push an entry into the wnj.idx
    // and set the index to point to that entry
    rIndex.SetPointer(BTree::theWNJFile.Append(rIndex.GetPointer()));
    return InsertLeaf(rIndex);
}

int Page::InsertLeaf(Index& rIndex)
{
    int result = 0;
    if (myVars.myCount < Order)
        Push(rIndex);
    else        // overflow the page
    {
        // make sibling
        int NewPg =
         NewPage(myKeys,Order/2,myVars.IsLeaf,myVars.myCount);
        Page* Sibling = GetPage(NewPg);
        Nullify(Order/2);                       // nullify my right half

        // does it fit in this side?
        if (myVars.myCount>Order/2-1 && rIndex <= myKeys[Order/2-1])
            Push(rIndex);
```

continues

LISTING 15.13. CONTINUED

```cpp
        else  // push it into the new sibling
            Sibling->Push(rIndex);

        result = NewPg; // we split, pass it up
    }
    return result;
}


    // put the new index into this page (in order)
void Page::Push(Index& rIndex,int offset,bool first)
{
    bool inserted = false;
    assert(myVars.myCount < Order);
    for (int i=offset; i<Order && i<myVars.myCount; i++)
    {
        assert(myKeys[i].GetPointer());
        if (rIndex <= myKeys[i])
        {
            Push(myKeys[i],offset+1,false);
            myKeys[i]=rIndex;
            inserted = true;
            break;
        }
    }
    if (!inserted)
        myKeys[myVars.myCount] = rIndex;

    if (first)
        myVars.myCount++;
}

void Page::Print()
{
    if (!myVars.IsLeaf)
    {
        BTree::NodePageCtr++;
        BTree::NodeIndexPerPage[myVars.myCount]++;
        BTree::NodeIndexCtr+=myVars.myCount;
    }
    else
    {
        BTree::LeafPageCtr++;
        BTree::LeafIndexPerPage[myVars.myCount]++;
        BTree::LeafIndexCtr+=myVars.myCount;
    }

    for (int i = 0; i<Order && i < myVars.myCount; i++)
    {
```

```
            assert(myKeys[i].GetPointer());
            if (myVars.IsLeaf)
            {
                cout << "\nPage " << myVars.myPageNumber << ": ";
                myKeys[i].PrintKey();
            }
            else
            {
                cout << "\nPage " << myVars.myPageNumber << ": ";
                myKeys[i].PrintPage();
            }
        }
    }
}

// write out the entire page as a block
fstream& Page::Write(fstream& file)
{
    char buffer[PageSize];
    memcpy(buffer,&myBlock,PageSize);
    file.flush();
    file.clear();
    file.seekp(myVars.myPageNumber*PageSize);
    file.write(buffer,PageSize);
    return file;
}
```

LISTING 15.14. WNJ.cpp

```
#include "btree.hpp"
#include <assert.h>

// on construction, try to open the file if it exists
    WNJFile::WNJFile():
    myFile("RACHELWNJ.IDX",
    ios::binary | ios::in | ios::out | ios::nocreate)
{
    for (int i = 0; i<5; i++)
        myints[i]=0L;
}

void WNJFile::Create()
{
    char Header[2*SIZE_INT];
    int MagicNumber=0; // a number we can check for
    int zero = 0;

    if (!myFile) // nocreate failed, first creation
    {
```

continues

Listing 15.14. CONTINUED

```cpp
        // open the file, create it this time
        myFile.clear();
        myFile.open("RACHELWNJ.IDX",
            ios::binary | ios::in | ios::out);

        MagicNumber = 1234;
        memcpy(Header,&MagicNumber,SIZE_INT);
        memcpy(Header+SIZE_INT,&zero,SIZE_INT);
        myFile.seekp(0);
        myFile.write(Header,2*SIZE_INT);
        myFile.flush();
        return;
    }

    // we did open the file, it already existed
    // get the numbers we need

    myFile.seekg(0);
    myFile.read(Header,2*SIZE_INT);
    memcpy(&MagicNumber,Header,SIZE_INT);
    memcpy(&myCount,Header+SIZE_INT,SIZE_INT);

    // check the magic number. If it is wrong the file is
    // corrupt or this isn't the index file
    if (MagicNumber != 1234)
    {
        // change to an exception!!
        cout << "WNJ Magic number failed!";
        cout << "Magic number: " << MagicNumber;
        cout << "\nmyCount: " << myCount << endl;
    }
  return;
}

// write out the numbers we'll need next time
void WNJFile::Close()
{
   myFile.seekg(SIZE_INT);
   myFile.write((char*)&myCount,SIZE_INT);
   myFile.close();
}

int WNJFile::Append(int DataOffset)
{

    int newPos = (N_ITEMS_IN_HEADER*SIZE_INT) // initial header
        + myCount++ * (N_DATA_SETS*SIZE_INT); // how many sets
    int offsets[N_DATA_SETS];
```

```
    offsets[0] = DataOffset;
    for (int i = 1; i<N_DATA_SETS; i++)
        offsets[i]=0;
    myFile.seekg(newPos);
    myFile.write((char*)offsets,N_DATA_SETS*SIZE_INT);

    return newPos;
}

int WNJFile::Insert(int DataOffset,int WNJOffset)
{
    int ints[5];
    myFile.seekg(WNJOffset);
    myFile.read((char*)ints,5*SIZE_INT);

    int offset=WNJOffset;

    while (ints[4])
    {
        offset = ints[4];
        myFile.clear();
        myFile.flush();
        myFile.seekg(ints[4]);
        myFile.read((char*)ints,5*SIZE_INT);
    }
    if (ints[3]) // full!
    {
        ints[4] = Append(DataOffset);
        myFile.clear();
        myFile.flush();
        myFile.seekg(offset);
        myFile.write((char*)ints,5*SIZE_INT);
    }
    else
    {
        for (int i = 0; i<4; i++)
        {
            if (ints[i] == 0)
            {
                ints[i] = DataOffset;
                myFile.clear();
                myFile.flush();
                myFile.seekg(offset);
                myFile.write((char*)ints,5*SIZE_INT);
                break;
            }
        }
    }
    return 0;
```

continues

15

OBJECT PERSISTENCE

LISTING 15.14. CONTINUED

```cpp
}

int* WNJFile::Find(int NextWNJ)
{
    int ints[N_DATA_SETS];
    int * results = new int[MAX_ARRAY_SIZE];

    int i = 0, j=0;

    while (j<256)
        results[j++] = 0;

    j = 0;

    myFile.seekg(NextWNJ);
    myFile.read((char*)ints,N_DATA_SETS*SIZE_INT);

    while (j < MAX_ARRAY_SIZE)
    {
        if (ints[i])
        {
            if (i == N_DATA_SETS-1)
            {
                myFile.seekg(ints[DATA_SET_POINTER_OFFSET]);
                myFile.read((char*)ints,N_DATA_SETS*SIZE_INT);
                i = 0;
                continue;
            }
        results[j++] = ints[i++];
        }
        else
            break;
    }
    return results;
}
```

LISTING 15.15. DiskManager.cpp

```cpp
#include "btree.hpp"
#include <assert.h>

// on construction, try to open the file if it exists
DiskManager::DiskManager():
 myFile("RACHEL.IDX",ios::binary | ios::in | ios::out | ios::nocreate)
{
    // initialize the pointers to null
    for (int i = 0; i< MaxPages; i++)
    myPages[i] = 0;
    myCount = 0;
```

```
    }

// called by btree constructor
// if we opened the file, read in the numbers we need
// otherwise create the file
int DiskManager::Create()
{
    if (!myFile) // nocreate failed, first creation
    {
        // open the file, create it this time
        myFile.open("RACHEL.IDX",ios::binary ¦ ios::in ¦ ios::out);

        char Header[PageSize];
        int MagicNumber = 1234; // a number we can check for
        memcpy(Header,&MagicNumber,SIZE_INT);
        int NextPage = 1;
        memcpy(Header+SIZE_INT,&NextPage,SIZE_INT);
        memcpy(Header+(2*SIZE_INT),&NextPage,SIZE_INT);
        Page::SetgPageNumber(NextPage);
        char title[]="RACHEL.IDX. Ver 1.01";
        memcpy(Header+(3*SIZE_INT),title,strlen(title));
        myFile.flush();
        myFile.clear();
        myFile.seekp(0);
        myFile.write(Header,PageSize);
        return 0;
    }

    // we did open the file, it already existed
    // get the numbers we need
    int MagicNumber;
    myFile.seekg(0);
    myFile.read((char *) &MagicNumber,SIZE_INT);

    // check the magic number. If it is wrong the file is
    // corrupt or this isn't the index file
    if (MagicNumber != 1234)
    {
        // change to an exception!!
        cout << "Index Magic number failed!";
        return 0;
    }

    int NextPage;
    myFile.seekg(SIZE_INT);
    myFile.read((char*) &NextPage,SIZE_INT);
    Page::SetgPageNumber(NextPage);
    int FirstPage;
    myFile.seekg(2*SIZE_INT);
```

continues

LISTING 15.15. CONTINUED

```cpp
    myFile.read((char*) &FirstPage,SIZE_INT);
    const int room =  PageSize - (3*SIZE_INT);
    char buffer[room];
    myFile.read(buffer,room);
    buffer[20]='\0';
    // cout << buffer << endl;
    // read in all the pages
    for (int i = 1; i < NextPage; i++)
    {
        myFile.seekg(i * PageSize);
        char buffer[PageSize];
        myFile.read( buffer, PageSize);
        Page * pg = new Page(buffer);
        Insert(pg);
    }

    return FirstPage;
}

// write out the numbers we'll need next time
void DiskManager::Close(int theRoot)
{

    for (int i = 0; i< MaxPages; i++)
        if (myPages[i])
            Save(myPages[i]);
    int NextPage = Page::GetgPageNumber();
    if (!myFile)
        cout << "Error opening myFile!" << endl;
    myFile.flush();
    myFile.clear();
    myFile.seekp(SIZE_INT);
    myFile.write ( (char *) &NextPage,SIZE_INT);
    myFile.seekp(2*SIZE_INT);
    myFile.write((char*) &theRoot,SIZE_INT);
    myFile.close();
}

// wrapper function
int DiskManager::NewPage(Index& index, bool bLeaf)
{
    Page * newPage = new Page(index, bLeaf);
    Insert(newPage);
    Save(newPage);
    return newPage->GetPageNumber();
}

int DiskManager::NewPage(
Index *array,
```

```
    int offset,
    bool leaf,
    int count)
{
    Page * newPage = new Page(array, offset, leaf,count);
    Insert(newPage);
    Save(newPage);
    return newPage->GetPageNumber();
}

void DiskManager::Insert(Page * newPage)
{
    // add new page into array of page managers
    if (myCount < MaxPages)
    {
        assert(!myPages[myCount]);
        myPages[myCount++] = newPage;
    }
    else   // no room, time to page out to disk
    {
        int lowest = -1;

        for (int i = 0; i< MaxPages; i++)
        {
            if (myPages[i]->GetLocked() == false )
            lowest = i;
        }
        if (lowest == -1)
            assert(lowest != -1);

        for (i = 0; i< MaxPages; i++)
            if (myPages[i]->GetTime() < myPages[lowest]->GetTime() &&
            myPages[i]->GetLocked() == false)
                lowest = i;
        assert(myPages[lowest]);
        Save(myPages[lowest]);
        delete myPages[lowest];
        myPages[lowest] = newPage;
    }
}

// tell the page to write itself out
void DiskManager::Save(Page* pg)
{
    pg->Write(myFile);
}

// see if the page is in memory, if so return it
// otherwise get it from disk
```

15

OBJECT PERSISTENCE

continues

LISTING 15.15. CONTINUED

```cpp
// note: this won't scale, with lots of page managers
// you'd need a more efficient search. 10 levels of page
// managers, with 31 indexes per page gives you room for
// 800 trillion words. Even if each page is only 1/2 full
// on average, 10 levels of depth would represent 64 million
// keys alone, not to mention the actual records.

Page * DiskManager::GetPage(int target)
{
    for (int i = 0; i< MaxPages; i++)
    {
        if (myPages[i]->GetPageNumber() == target)
        return  myPages[i];
    }
    myFile.seekg(target * PageSize);
    char buffer[PageSize];
    myFile.read( buffer, PageSize);
    Page * pg = new Page(buffer);
    Insert(pg);
    return pg;
}
```

How It Works

The best way to see how this program works is to walk through an example of using it. First, we'll create a text file with the previous three paragraphs, called test.txt. Next, we run the program.

At the ? prompt, we enter We hold these truths to be self-evident that all men are created equal. After this is accepted, enter I regret that I have but one life to give to my country.

Now it is time to give the program the test file we created. At the prompt, enter -f and, when prompted for the filename, enter test.txt:

```
?: We hold these truths to be self-evident that all men are created equal
Inserted.
?: I regret that I have but one life to give for my country
Inserted.
?: -f
FileName: test.txt
Parsing Here you see the array of 5 integers as discussed earlier. The
first fou
Parsing the fifth <if used> is an offset back into the WNJFile for the
next arra
Parsing For demonstration purposes I've created a simple driver program
which di
```

```
Parsing and accepts input. Any text added is turned into a Note and stored
in th
Parsing characters or greater is indexed. If the user types a dash as the
first
Parsing <?>, bang <!> or the letter "f" the system treats it as a flag and
takes
Parsing a search, a bang forces a report of the structure of the tree and
the le
Parsing read into the system. When a file is read in, each line is treated
as a
Parsing extending this so that the user has the option that a file is
considered
Parsing imagine any number of improvements, starting with a more
reasonable user
Parsing _e_

Completed parsing test.txt
?:
```

It is time to see if it worked. Are the strings captured? Was the index built? One way to test this is to search for the word that:

```
?: -? that
[1] 7/6/98 We hold these truths to be se…
[2] 7/6/98 I regret that I have but one …
[3] 7/6/98 a search, a bang forces a rep…
[4] 7/6/98 extending this so that the us…
[5] 7/6/98 extending this so that the us…
Choice <0 to stop>: 1

>> We hold these truths to be self-evident that all men are created equal

[1] 7/6/98 We hold these truths to be se…
[2] 7/6/98 I regret that I have but one …
[3] 7/6/98 a search, a bang forces a rep…
[4] 7/6/98 extending this so that the us…
[5] 7/6/98 extending this so that the us…
Choice <0 to stop>: 2
>> I regret that I have but one life to give for my country
[1] 7/6/98 We hold these truths to be se…
[2] 7/6/98 I regret that I have but one …
[3] 7/6/98 a search, a bang forces a rep…
[4] 7/6/98 extending this so that the us…
[5] 7/6/98 extending this so that the us…
Choice <0 to stop>:
```

Clearly, the program worked quite well. We found five Notes with the word that, and we can examine them one by one. Let's take a look at the structure of the database itself:

```
Page 2:   PROGRAM
Page 2:   PURPOSES
```

15

```
Page 2:   QUESTION
Page 2:   READ
Page 2:   REASONABLE
Page 3: REGRET
Page 4:   REGRET
Page 4:   REPORT
Page 4:   REPRESENT
Page 4:   SEARCH
Page 4:   SEE
Page 4:   SELF-EVIDENT
Page 4:   SIMPLE
Page 4:   SINGLE
Page 4:   SPECIAL
Page 4:   STARTING
Page 4:   STORED
Page 4:   STRUCTURE
Page 4:   SYSTEM
Page 4:   TAKES
Page 4:   TEXT
Page 4:   THAT
Page 4:   THE
Page 3:   THESE:
Page 6:   THESE
Page 6:   THIS
Page 6:   THREE
Page 6:   TREATED
Page 6:   TREATS
Page 6:   TREE
Page 6:   TRUTHS
Page 6:   TURNED
Page 6:   TYPES
Page 6:   USED>
Page 6:   USER
Page 6:   WANTS
Page 6:   WHEN
Page 6:   WITH
Page 6:   WNJFILE
Page 6:   WORD
Page 6:   YOU

Stats:
Node pages:   1
Leaf pages:   5
Node indexes: 5
Total leaves: 109
Pages with 5 nodes:   1
Pages with 17 leaves: 1
Pages with 18 leaves: 1
Pages with 21 leaves: 1
Pages with 22 leaves: 1
Pages with 31 leaves: 1
?:
```

Much of the structure scrolls off the screen, but we can see that page 2 has a number of indexed words and page 3 has a node entry with REGRET, which points to page 4. Page 4 has 17 entries beginning (as we should expect) with the word Regret. Page 3 also points to page 6 with the word These, and page 6 has 18 entries beginning with THESE.

The statistics that follow are interesting. There is only one node page (must be page 3) and there are five leaf pages (thus, the final page is page 6, which is what we see indicated). There are five node indices, which is consistent. Together, those five nodes hold 109 leaves distributed as follows: one page has 17 leaves, one has 18, one has 21, another has 22, and the last has 31.

Thus we have only two levels. The top level (page 3) is a node pointing to five leaf pages (pages 1, 2, 4, 5, and 6). Those five leaf pages contain all 109 keys. Remember the rule: The pages must have order/2 or more entries. This is order 31, so can expect to see 15 or more entries on each page—and we do. The one exception is the top node, and that makes sense because it is created as soon as the first page splits.

Let's walk through the code to see how this all works.

Walking the Code

For demonstration purposes, I've created a simple driver program that displays a question mark to the user and accepts input. Any text added is turned into a Note and stored in the database. Each word of three characters or greater is indexed. Not indexing one- and two-letter words avoids storing such ubiquitous words as *of*, *or*, *and*, and so forth. You can imagine a more sophisticated mechanism whereby the user can establish "stop words" which the system will ignore.

If the user types a dash (-) as the first character followed by a question mark (?), bang (!), or the letter f, the system treats the entry as a flag and takes special action. A question mark initiates a search, a bang forces a report of the structure of the tree, and the letter f indicates that the user wants a file read into the system. When a file is read in, each line is treated as an individual Note. You can imagine extending this functionality so that the user has the option that a file is considered a single, large Note. In fact, you can imagine any number of improvements, starting with a more reasonable user interface.

Again, this program is for demonstration purposes and is not intended as a full-fledged Personal Information Manager.

The program begins with main():

```
int main()
{
   BTree myTree;

   for (int i = 0; i < Order +1; i++)
```

```cpp
{
   BTree::NodeIndexPerPage[i] = 0;
   BTree::LeafIndexPerPage[i] = 0;
}

char buffer[PageSize+1];

bool fQuit = false;

while ( !fQuit )
{
    cout << "?: ";
    cin.getline(buffer,PageSize);

    if ( buffer[0] == '-' )
    {
        switch (buffer[1])
        {
          case '?':
             DoFind(buffer+2,myTree);
             break;

          case '!':
                myTree.PrintTree();
                break;

          case 'F':
          case 'f':
                ParseFile(myTree);
                break;
          case '0':
             fQuit = true;
             break;
        }
    }
    else
    {
        if ( myTree.Insert(buffer) )
          cout << "Inserted.\n";
        buffer[0] = '\0';
    }
}
    return 0;
}
```

The main() function creates the tree and then prompts the user for input. If the user inputs a flag, the appropriate (global) method is called (doFind() or ParseTree()). If the flag is -!, the tree is told to print itself (thus printing the statistics).

The first line to execute is this one:

```
BTree myTree;
```

This of course invokes the BTree constructor:

```
BTree::BTree():myRoot(0)
{
    myRoot = theDiskManager.Create();
    theDataFile.Create();
    theWNJFile.Create();
}
```

The myRoot member (an integer) is initialized to zero and is then assigned the value returned from calling Create() on theDiskManager. Remember that theDiskManager, theWNJFile, and theDataFile are all static. This is a simple (although not robust) implementation of the Singleton design pattern. If I were creating this program for commercial use, I'd actually make these variables private and control their lifetime creation and destruction a bit more carefully. Again, to keep this simple, I just expose them as public members.

Stepping into theDiskManager.Create(), we see that the first test is whether or not the DiskManager's file is open. Because this is the first time we're in the code, the file is not yet open, and so we open the file and ready it for use. The first PageSize characters are of a specific format that we now set up:

- A four-byte "magic number" used to verify that the file is correct
- Four bytes for the "next page" (which we'll initialize to 1)
- Four bytes for the "first page" (which, again, we'll initialize to 1)
- An identifying string (which we'll initialize to RACHEL.IDX. Ver 1.01)

This is written out and the function returns with the value zero, which is assigned to BTree::myRoot:

```
int DiskManager::Create()
    {
        if (!myFile) // nocreate failed, first creation
        {
            // open the file, create it this time
            myFile.open("RACHEL.IDX",ios::binary | ios::in | ios::out);

            char Header[PageSize];
            int MagicNumber = 1234; // a number we can check for
            memcpy(Header,&MagicNumber,SIZE_INT);
            int NextPage = 1;
            memcpy(Header+SIZE_INT,&NextPage,SIZE_INT);
            memcpy(Header+(2*SIZE_INT),&NextPage,SIZE_INT);
```

15

```
                    Page::SetgPageNumber(NextPage);
                    char title[]="RACHEL.IDX. Ver 1.01";
                    memcpy(Header+(3*SIZE_INT),title,strlen(title));
                    myFile.flush();
                    myFile.clear();
                    myFile.seekp(0);
                    myFile.write(Header,PageSize);
                    return 0;
            }
        //…
}
```

We then enter theDataFile's Create() method. Again, because this is the first time through the code, we prep the file—this time by creating only a magic number (no other header information) and writing it out:

```
void DataFile::Create()
{
    if (!myFile) // nocreate failed, first creation
    {

        // open the file, create it this time
        myFile.clear();

        myFile.open
            ("RACHEL.DAT",ios::binary ¦ ios::in ¦ ios::out ¦ ios::app);

        char Header[SIZE_INT];
        int MagicNumber = 1234; // a number we can check for
        memcpy(Header,&MagicNumber,SIZE_INT);
        myFile.clear();
        myFile.flush();
        myFile.seekp(0);
        myFile.write(Header,SIZE_INT);
        return;
    }
    // …
}
```

We then do the same thing with WNJFile.

Returning to main(), we initialize all of BTree's counters to zero and set up a few local variables:

```
for (int i = 0; i < Order +1; i++)
    {
        BTree::NodeIndexPerPage[i] = 0;
        BTree::LeafIndexPerPage[i] = 0;
    }
    char buffer[PageSize+1];
    bool fQuit = false;
```

We are now ready to enter the prompt loop. Remember, the first time through the code, the user enters text, so the flags are skipped; we jump to the following bit of code:

```
if ( myTree.Insert(buffer) )
   cout << "Inserted.\n";
```

Stepping into `Insert()`, we first check to ensure that the buffer we're inserting is at least three characters. We then iterate through the buffer extracting words. The entire buffer is inserted into the data file, and each word is added to the index as a key:

```
bool BTree::Insert(char* buffer)
{

    if (strlen(buffer) < 3)
       return false;

    char *buff = buffer;
    char word[PageSize];
    int wordOffset = 0;
    int offset;

    if (GetWord(buff,word,wordOffset))
    {
       offset = theDataFile.Insert(buffer);
       AddKey(word,offset);
    }

    while (GetWord(buff,word,wordOffset))
    {
       AddKey(word,offset);
    }

    return true;

}
```

`GetWord()` is a private (utility) method that takes a character array (buffer) and the offset into that buffer and fills the character array word with the next word.

Let's step into `theDataFile.Insert(buffer)` to see how the text is added to the data file:

```
int DataFile::Insert(char * newNote)
 {
    int len = strlen(newNote);
    int fullLen = len + SIZE_INT + SIZE_TIME;

    time_t theTime;
    theTime = time(NULL);
```

```
        char buffer[PageSize];
        memcpy(buffer,&len,SIZE_INT);
        memcpy(buffer+SIZE_INT,&theTime,SIZE_TIME);
        memcpy(buffer+SIZE_INT+SIZE_TIME,newNote,len);

        myFile.clear();
        myFile.flush();
        myFile.seekp(0,ios::end);
        int offset = (int) myFile.tellp();
        myFile.write(buffer,fullLen);
        myFile.flush();
        return offset;
    }
```

This code is quite straightforward. The length is set as the length of the Note itself plus enough room to hold the length and the current time. A buffer is created, prepended with the length and the time, and then the Note is added. The Note is written to the end of the file, and the offset is returned.

Let's return to BTree::Insert() and follow the addition of the key:

```
void BTree::AddKey(char * str, int offset )
{

    if (strlen(str) < 3)
        return;

    int retVal =0;
```

Once again, we ensure that the key is at least three letters.

The return value is initialized to zero. Continuing on, the string (the contents of the Note) and the offset are passed to the constructor of Index to create a new Index object:

```
        Index index(str,offset);
```

This takes us into the constructor of Index, where the string is stashed away as the Index's data, and the offset is used to initialize the Index's myPointer member. Remember that this is the offset into the Data file. Ultimately, this is not what we want to store, but it gets us started.

Let's review: What we want to store is the index into the WNJFile, which in turn will point to the offset into the data file. We'll see how that works in a moment. Note also that the key is converted into all uppercase, which allows us to implement a case-insensitive search.

> **NOTE**
>
> An alternative, and perhaps more flexible, approach to storing keys is to store the keys in their original format and just compare keys against user input in all uppercase if we are asking for a case-insensitive search:
>
> ```
> Index::Index(char* str, int ptr):myPointer(ptr)
>     {
>
>         strncpy(myData,str,dataLen);
>         myData[dataLen]='\0';
>         for (size_t i = 0; i< strlen(myData); i++)
>             myData[i] = toupper(myData[i]);
>
>
>     }
> ```

Returning to `BTree::AddKey()`, the next step is to examine `myRoot`:

```
if (!myRoot)
{
    myRoot = theDiskManager.NewPage (index,true);
}
```

We initialized `myRoot` to zero, and so we enter the `if` statement:

```
        myRoot = theDiskManager.NewPage (index,true);
```

This statement invokes the `NewPage()` method of `DiskManager`, passing in the `Index` we just created and the flag `true`. The flag indicates that this new page will indeed be a leaf (this method is also called when creating a node). Here is the `NewPage()` method at work:

```
int DiskManager::NewPage(Index& index, bool bLeaf)
    {
        Page * newPage = new Page(index, bLeaf);
        Insert(newPage);
        Save(newPage);
        return newPage->GetPageNumber();
    }
```

A new page is created, marked as a leaf, inserted into the `DiskManager`'s array of pages, and saved to disk. The new page's page number is returned to the `BTree`, and the member variable `BTree::myRoot` is assigned that value.

15

OBJECT PERSISTENCE

Let's examine the three steps of creating a new page, inserting it, and saving it. The first step is creating a new page:

```
Page::Page(Index& index, bool bLeaf):
    myKeys((Index*)myVars.mk)
{
    myVars.myCount=1;
    myVars.IsLeaf = bLeaf;
    SetLocked(false);
    // if this is a leaf, this is the first
    // index on the first page, set its pointer
    // based on creating a new wnj. otherwise
    // you are here creating a new node, do not
    // set the pointer, it is already set.
    if (bLeaf)
    {
        int indexPointer = index.GetPointer();
        int appendResult = BTree::theWNJFile.Append(indexPointer);
        index.SetPointer(appendResult);
    }
    myKeys[0]=index;
    myVars.myPageNumber = gPage++;
    myTime = time(NULL);
}
```

The page constructor begins with the initialization of the myKeys variable as discussed earlier. A few member variables are initialized (for example, the page is set as a leaf or as a node, depending on the value of bLeaf) and the page is unlocked.

Remember that this is the constructor. We know there are no indices in this page yet. If this is a leaf, then we want to insert a record into the WNJFile, but if this is not a leaf, we need not do so. Assuming that it is a leaf, we first extract from this index the pointer it is holding (you will remember that the index is the offset into the data file). We then pass that pointer into the WNJFile::Append() method, and we take the result of that action and stash it back in the Index's pointer. Thus, the Index no longer points to the data file (the WNJFile record does); instead, the Index points to the appropriate entry in the WNJ (which you remember is the Word-Node-Join).

Let's step into the WNJFile::Append() method briefly to see how it does its magic:

```
int WNJFile::Append(int DataOffset)
{
    int newPos = (N_ITEMS_IN_HEADER*SIZE_INT) // initial header
        + myCount++ * (N_DATA_SETS*SIZE_INT); // how many sets
    int offsets[N_DATA_SETS];
    offsets[0] = DataOffset;
    for (int i = 1; i<N_DATA_SETS; i++)
        offsets[i]=0;
```

```
    myFile.seekg(newPos);
    myFile.write((char*)offsets,N_DATA_SETS*SIZE_INT);

    return newPos;
}
```

The variable newPos is initialized to point to the new offset into WNJFile. First, room for two integers is set aside for the header. Then room for data sets is also set aside. (A data set is five integers.) The first four integers point to records in the data file, the fifth points to a new data set in the WNJFile. Because myCount is initially zero, this equates to 8 bytes (just enough for the header).

A variable, offsets, is created to hold a new data set and is initialized with the data offset for this Index. The rest of the data set is set to all zeros. Finally, the data set is written to disk, and the newPos value is returned to Page's constructor, in which it is assigned to the Index.

Returning to DiskManager::NewPage(), the next step is inserting the newly created page into the DiskManager's array of pages:

```
void DiskManager::Insert(Page * newPage)
    {

        // add new page into array of page managers
        if (myCount < MaxPages)
        {
            assert(!myPages[myCount]);
            myPages[myCount++] = newPage;
        }
        else  // no room, time to page out to disk
        {
            int lowest = -1;

            for (int i = 0; i< MaxPages; i++)
            {
                if (myPages[i]->GetLocked() == false )
                    lowest = i;
            }
            if (lowest == -1)
                assert(lowest != -1);

            for (i = 0; i< MaxPages; i++)
                if (myPages[i]->GetTime() < myPages[lowest]->GetTime() &&
                        myPages[i]->GetLocked() == false)

                    lowest = i;

            assert(myPages[lowest]);
            Save(myPages[lowest]);
```

```
                    delete myPages[lowest];
                    myPages[lowest] = newPage;

            }
        }
```

The new page is inserted into the `DiskManager`'s array of pages if there is room in memory. Otherwise, the least recently used page is removed if it is not locked.

Finally, step three: The page is saved to disk:

```
void DiskManager::Save(Page* pg)
{
    pg->Write(myFile);
}
```

When the next key is added, `BTree::AddKey()` will not find its root value at zero—it will be pointing to the page already created:

```
    if (!myRoot)
    {
        myRoot = theDiskManager.NewPage (index,true);
    }
    else
    {
        Page * pPage = GetPage(myRoot);
        retVal = pPage->Insert(index);
        if (retVal) // our root split
        {
            // …
        }
    }
```

The root page is extracted by calling `GetPage()`, and that page is instructed to insert the new index. `BTree::GetPage()` delegates responsibility for obtaining the page to the `DiskManager`:

```
    { return theDiskManager.GetPage(page); }
```

The `DiskManager` probably has the page in memory; if it does not, it brings it off the disk and stashes it away in its array of pages.

> **NOTE**
>
> A word on nomenclature. The object we're calling an `Index` should, by all rights, be called a *key*—the files that hold the keys and associates them with data should be called the `Index`. However, pages call the keys indices, and that creates endless naming confusion.

Continuing with the `BTree::AddKey()` method, the `Index` is added to the page by calling
`Page::Insert()` and passing in the new `Index`. `Page::Insert()` takes two parameters,
the second defaults to `false`, which indicates that we are not searching for records with
the key passed in, but rather we are adding the key to the index:

```
int Page::Insert(Index& rIndex, bool findOnly)
    {
        int result;
        if (myVars.IsLeaf)
        {
            SetLocked(true);
            result = FindLeaf(rIndex,findOnly);
            SetLocked(false);
            return result;
        }
        else
        {
            SetLocked(true);
            result = InsertNode(rIndex,findOnly);
            SetLocked(false);
            return result;
        }
    }
```

The page determines whether it is a leaf or a node by examining its `myVars` variable. If
the page is a leaf, the index being added points to data. The page is locked (so that it
won't page out of memory!), and `FindLeaf()` is invoked, passing in the index and the
flag indicating that this is not a query but an insert:

```
int Page::FindLeaf(Index& rIndex, bool findOnly)
    {
        int result = 0;

        // no duplicates!
        for (int i=0; i < myVars.myCount; i++)
            if (rIndex == myKeys[i])
            {
                if (findOnly)                // return first WNJ
                    //return BTree::theWNJFile.Find(myKeys[i].
➥GetPointer());
                    return myKeys[i].GetPointer();
                else
                    return BTree::theWNJFile.Insert(
                            rIndex.GetPointer(),
                                myKeys[i].GetPointer());
            }

        if (findOnly)            // not found
            return result;
```

```
            // this index item does not yet exist
            // before you push it into the index
            // push an entry into the wnj.idx
            // and set the index to point to that entry
            rIndex.SetPointer(BTree::theWNJFile.Append(rIndex.GetPointer()));
            return InsertLeaf(rIndex);
    }
```

We check through the indices already in the page to see whether this key already exists. If so, we return the result of adding this offset into the WNJFile, making another connection between this key and the data file.

Having proven that this key is not yet in the Index, we insert it:

```
rIndex.SetPointer(BTree::theWNJFile.Append(rIndex.GetPointer()));
```

This is the same mechanism we reviewed earlier: Get the Index's pointer (which points to the data) and pass it into WNJFile::Append(). Take the return value and set the Index's pointer to that value. This time, we've combined all three steps into a single line of code.

We need now only add the modified index (with the new pointer into the WNJFile) into this page by calling InsertLeaf(), passing in the Index and returning the resulting value:

```
int Page::InsertLeaf(Index& rIndex)
{
```

In Page::InsertLeaf(), we begin by checking to see whether the page is full. If not, we push this Index into the page:

```
    if (myVars.myCount < Order)
        Push(rIndex);
```

If the page *is* full, we must split the page:

```
    else        // overflow the page
    {
        int NewPg =
         NewPage(myKeys,Order/2,myVars.IsLeaf,myVars.myCount);
        Page* Sibling = GetPage(NewPg);
        Nullify(Order/2);
        if (myVars.myCount>Order/2-1 && rIndex <= myKeys[Order/2-1])
            Push(rIndex);
        else
            Sibling->Push(rIndex);
        result = NewPg;
    }
```

Briefly, if we must split the page, we take the right half of the page and put it into a new page and return the result, which is the page number of the new page. Otherwise, we return zero, indicating no split.

In this particular case, we have not yet filled the page, so we'll push the new index:

```
void Page::Push(Index& rIndex,int offset,bool first)
{
    bool inserted = false;
    assert(myVars.myCount < Order);
    for (int i=offset; i<Order && i<myVars.myCount; i++)
    {
        assert(myKeys[i].GetPointer());
        if (rIndex <= myKeys[i])
        {
            Push(myKeys[i],offset+1,false);
            myKeys[i]=rIndex;
            inserted = true;
            break;
        }
    }
    if (!inserted)
        myKeys[myVars.myCount] = rIndex;

    if (first)
        myVars.myCount++;
}
```

We step through the keys, finding the right position for the new one. If we must insert it, we push the one next to it, iterating through what amounts to an insertion sort. Note the recursion in this routine: As we insert, we may have to *push* the next item in the index. When it all sorts itself out, the new Index is inserted, and the other items in the page have been shifted over.

Because we made sure that we had room before beginning (or we split the page if we did not have room), the amount of recursion is limited to, at most, order-1 iterations.

Because we did not split the page, zero is passed up the chain to the BTree, indicating that no page was split and no adjustment must be made. Let's see what happens, later, when we *do* split the page. Back in BTree::AddKey(), the return value from Page::Insert() will be nonzero. This nonzero result indicates that the root page has split, creating our first node page:

```
        if (retVal) // our root split
        {
            pPage = GetPage(myRoot);
            Index index(pPage->GetFirstIndex());
            index.SetPointer(myRoot);
```

```
int PageNumber = NewPage(index,false);
pPage = GetPage(PageNumber);

Page * pRetValPage = GetPage(retVal);
Index Sib(pRetValPage->GetFirstIndex());
Sib.SetPointer(retVal);
pPage->InsertLeaf(Sib);

myRoot = PageNumber;
}
```

The first task is to create a new Index object and point it to the old root page:

```
pPage = GetPage(myRoot);
Index index(pPage->GetFirstIndex());
index.SetPointer(myRoot);
```

This is a bit tricky. Step one is to get the page pointed to by the current root. Step two is to ask that page for its firstIndex:

```
Index GetFirstIndex() { return myKeys[0]; }
```

Step three is to invoke the copy constructor on Index, passing in that Index just obtained:

```
Index::Index(Index& rhs):
    myPointer(rhs.GetPointer())
{
    strcpy(myData, rhs.GetData());
    for (size_t i = 0; i< strlen(myData); i++)
        myData[i] = toupper(myData[i]);

}
```

The new index is initialized with the same data and pointer, but we then set its pointer to point to the old root page. Thus, we now have turned the root page into a node page and we have an index pointing to it.

Next, we create a new page, and pass in that index and get back the page number for the new page. We use that page number to get a pointer to the new page:

```
int PageNumber = NewPage(index,false);
pPage = GetPage(PageNumber);
```

We then get a pointer to the page indicated by the return value (that is, the newly split page). We create an index to point to that newly created page, which we call Sib, and we set our newly created index to point to the newly created page:

```
Page * pRetValPage = GetPage(retVal);
Index Sib(pRetValPage->GetFirstIndex());
Sib.SetPointer(retVal);
```

This new index (`Sib`) is now inserted into the new (root) page we created:

```
pPage->InsertLeaf(Sib);
```

We then assign `myRoot` to the `PageNumber` of the new root.

Let's review: Before we split the page, our B-tree looked as shown in Figure 15.10.

FIGURE 15.10.
Before splitting the page.

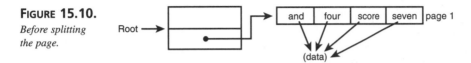

The root page was a leaf, and all the indices pointed to data. After the split, our tree looked as shown in Figure 15.11.

FIGURE 15.11.
After splitting the page.

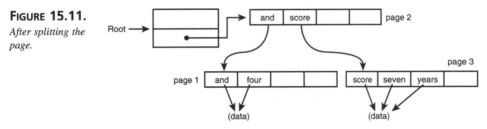

A new page (page 2) has been created, and it has two new indices. The first points to the old page 1, and the second points to the newly created page 3. How is data added now?

The call to `BTree::AddKey()` proceeds in the usual way, and it in turn calls `Page::Insert()` on the root. The root page, now recognizing that it is a node (rather than a leaf) page, calls `InsertNode()` passing in the new `Index`:

```
int Page::InsertNode(Index& rIndex, bool findOnly)
{
```

Once again, the `retVal` (return value) is set to zero, and a local flag, `inserted`, is initialized to `false`. The first test is whether the new index ought to go before the very first entry in the node. If so, we set the data of the first key (`myKeys[0]`) to point to the new data from the `Index`, and we insert the `Index` into the page pointed to by `myKeys[0]`:

```
if (rIndex < myKeys[0])
{
    if (findOnly)
    return 0L; // not found
```

```
        myKeys[0].SetData(rIndex);
        retVal=myKeys[0].Insert(rIndex);
        inserted = true;
    }
```

If the new index isn't inserted before the first key, we look for where in the array to insert it, and insert it into the correct page:

```
if (!inserted)
for (i = myVars.myCount-1; i>=0; i--)
{
    assert(myKeys[i].GetPointer());
    if (rIndex >= myKeys[i])
    {
        retVal=myKeys[i].Insert(rIndex,findOnly);
        inserted = true;
        break;
    }
}
```

In each case, we get back a return value from the Insert request, so that we can tell whether a page split. If that value is nonzero, the insertion caused a split and we must create an index to manage the new page and insert it into *this* page. Again, this may cause *this* page to split, so the return value from this insertion is passed back to the BTree:

```
if (retVal && !findOnly) // got back a pointer to a new page
{
    Index * pIndex = new Index(GetPage(retVal)->GetFirstIndex());
    pIndex->SetPointer(retVal);
    retVal = InsertLeaf(*pIndex);
}
```

Here is the entire InsertNode() method:

```
int Page::InsertNode(Index& rIndex, bool findOnly)
{
    int retVal =0;
    bool inserted = false;
    int i,j;

    assert(myVars.myCount>0); // nodes have at least 1
    assert(myKeys[0].GetPointer()); // must be valid

    // does it go before my first entry?
    if (rIndex < myKeys[0])
    {
        if (findOnly)
        return 0L; // not found

        myKeys[0].SetData(rIndex);
```

```
        retVal=myKeys[0].Insert(rIndex);
        inserted = true;
    }

    // does it go after my last?
    if (!inserted)
    for (i = myVars.myCount-1; i>=0; i--)
    {
        assert(myKeys[i].GetPointer());
        if (rIndex >= myKeys[i])
        {
            retVal=myKeys[i].Insert(rIndex,findOnly);
            inserted = true;
            break;
        }
    }

    // find where it does go
    if (!inserted)
    for (j = 0; j<i && j+1 < myVars.myCount; j++)
    {
        assert(myKeys[j+1].GetPointer());
        if (rIndex < myKeys[j+1])
        {
            retVal=myKeys[j].Insert(rIndex,findOnly);
            inserted = true;
            break;
        }
    }

    assert(inserted);   // change to exception if not!

    // if you had to split
    if (retVal && !findOnly) // got back a pointer to a new page
    {
        Index * pIndex = new Index(GetPage(retVal)->GetFirstIndex());
        pIndex->SetPointer(retVal);
        retVal = InsertLeaf(*pIndex);
    }
    return retVal;
}
```

Searching

The entire point of putting the Notes into the database is to be able to find them later. The goal, with this pseudo-application, is to be able to search by any of the keywords and find every Note that contains that word.

15

OBJECT
PERSISTENCE

Suppose that you entered these phrases:

> We hold these truths to be self-evident that all men are created equal
>
> If we can send one man to the moon why can't we send all of them
>
> Now is the time for all good men to come to the aid of their country
>
> Ask not what your country can do for you ask what you can do for your country

Now suppose that you search for *man* by entering -? man. You will receive the following output:

```
?: -?man

[1] 7/7/98 If we can send one man to the...
Choice <0 to stop>: 1

>> If we can send one man to the moon why can't we send all of them
```

Only one of these phrases has the word *man*. If we search for the word *men*, we find that two notes have the word *men*:

```
?: -?men

[1] 7/7/98 We hold these truths to be se…
[2] 7/7/98 Now is the time for all good …
Choice <0 to stop>: 2

>> Now is the time for all good mean to come to the aid of their country

[1] 7/7/98 We hold these truths to be se…
[2] 7/7/98 Now is the time for all good …
Choice <0 to stop>: 1

>> We hold these truths to be self-evident that all men are created equal

[1] 7/7/98 We hold these truths to be se…
[2] 7/7/98 Now is the time for all good …
Choice <0 to stop>:
```

The menu displays the first 32 characters of each note; if you choose one of them, you will see the entire note. Let's walk through this second search step by step.

When main() detects the dash (–) as the first character and the ? as the second character, it invokes DoFind(), passing in the buffer containing the search string (in this case, men) and the BTree itself. The string is parsed to remove leading spaces and then is passed to myTree::Find():

```
void DoFind(char * searchString, BTree& myTree)
{
```

```
int  list[PageSize];
for (int i = 0; i<PageSize; i++)
list[i] = 0;
int k = 0;
char * p1 = searchString;
while (p1[0] == ' ')
    p1++;

int offset = myTree.Find(p1);
```

`BTree::Find()` is very simple. If a page is assigned to the root (and thus if we are storing any keys at all), it creates an index from the buffer and calls `Find()` on the root page, passing along the newly created index:

```
int BTree::Find(char * str)
{
    Index index(str);
    if (!myRoot)
        return 0L;
    else
        return GetPage(myRoot)->Find(index);
}
```

`GetPage()`, of course, just returns the page. `Page::Find()` is an inline function that calls `Insert()`, passing in the Boolean flag `true`, indicating that it isn't a true insert, but rather a find:

```
int Find(Index& idx) { return Insert(idx,true); }
```

This code reuse is elegant, but the naming convention is perhaps poor. When you call `Insert()` with the second parameter set to `true`, you are not inserting at all, you are simply finding.

`Page::Insert()` is as it ever was: It determines whether the page is a leaf or a node and calls either `InsertLeaf()` or `InsertNode()`, respectively. In any case, it also passes along the flag indicating that we are finding, not inserting. The same logic used previously to detect "duplicate" keys is used here to find the offset into the `WNJFile` for this key.

As you would expect, what is returned, ultimately, is an offset into the `WNJFile`. This value is passed all the way up the stack back to `DoFind()`. The value is then used to call into `WNJFile::Find()`:

```
int offset = myTree.Find(p1);
if (offset)
{
    int *found  =  BTree::theWNJFile.Find(offset);
```

`WNJFile::Find()` chases through its arrays of offsets into the data file. For each data set, it builds up an array of results. When and if it hits the fifth element in its data set, it uses that as an offset back into its own file to get more:

```
int* WNJFile::Find(int NextWNJ)
    {
        int ints[N_DATA_SETS];
        int * results = new int[MAX_ARRAY_SIZE];

        int i = 0, j=0;

        while (j<256)
            results[j++] = 0;

        j = 0;

        myFile.seekg(NextWNJ);
        myFile.read((char*)ints,N_DATA_SETS*SIZE_INT);

        while (j < MAX_ARRAY_SIZE)
        {
            if (ints[i])
            {
                if (i == N_DATA_SETS-1)
                {
                    myFile.seekg(ints[DATA_SET_POINTER_OFFSET]);
                    myFile.read((char*)ints,N_DATA_SETS*SIZE_INT);
                    i = 0;
                    continue;
                }
                results[j++] = ints[i++];
            }
            else
                break;
        }
        return results;
    }
```

The list of matching Notes is then displayed and the user can read the entire note by choosing the appropriate entry from the list.

There are more details, but you've seen the essential code. Persistence, in this case, is more detailed than in the simpler "write the object to disk" example, but the fundamental principal of delegation of responsibility remains constant.

Fortunately, for commercial applications, most of these details would remain hidden. First, if you were going to use a data structure such as a B-tree, you would almost certainly look first to the Standard Template Library. Why reinvent your own when you can use readily available, fully tested code that has been generalized for virtually any data?

More important, if you were going to write software using a database, you would almost certainly use one of the many highly optimized commercial packages available. The point of this exercise was less to prepare you to write complex data structures than to examine some of the details of manipulating large objects onto and off of the disk and translating objects on the heap into objects on disk, and back again.

Summary

This chapter reviewed a few object-oriented approaches to storing data on disk. What is consistent among these disparate approaches is that storage is encapsulated in the responsible objects and that we are careful to make the details of object location (in memory or on disk) invisible to the clients of our objects.

In a well-designed object storage system, it is possible to work with the objects as if they are guaranteed to be in memory. With advanced component systems such as CORBA and COM, not only is it invisible whether the object is in memory or on disk, but the actual storage location is invisible as well. This is known as *location transparency*, and is covered in coming chapters.

CHAPTER 16

Relational Databases and Persistence

The overwhelming majority of commercial software applications use relational databases (RDBs) for object persistence. RDBs are a robust and mature technology, while object databases are still in their infancy. Further, the majority of business applications contain legacy code and design; the company already has its data in an RDB, and other company systems must continue to use that data.

These truths present us with a challenge because mapping objects to relations is not always straightforward. Although there are a number of solutions to this problem, most of the time, you will simply allow your application frameworks to do the mapping for you.

This chapter begins with a review of the fundamentals of relational database management and goes on to discuss how your C++ program can interact with relational databases. The chapter examines the Microsoft Foundation Classes support for databases.

Basic Concepts of Relational Databases

The essence of a relational database is quite simple: Your data is organized in tables. Each table consists of records (rows) and fields (columns), as shown in Figure 16.1.

FIGURE 16.1.

Relational database tables are organized into records and fields.

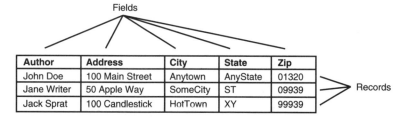

Author	Address	City	State	Zip
John Doe	100 Main Street	Anytown	AnyState	01320
Jane Writer	50 Apple Way	SomeCity	ST	09939
Jack Sprat	100 Candlestick	HotTown	XY	99939

The power of relational databases comes when you create two tables and "relate" them one to the other. You create that relationship by ensuring that there is a shared, unique identifier in each record. For example, if one table contains a list of every author who writes for your publishing company, and a second table contains a list of every book your company publishes, you can relate these two tables by author. One very powerful way to do so is to give each author a unique `authorID` and to add that `authorID` field to the Titles table.

In Figure 16.2, we see that each author has a unique ID. This ID also appears in the Titles table, relating the two tables and allowing us to see that both *What A Wonderful Program* and *Another Wonderful Program* were written by author 102. Author 102 is Jane Writer, who lives at 50 Apple Way in SomeCity, ST.

Relational Databases and Persistence

CHAPTER 16

623

16

RELATIONAL
DATABASES AND
PERSISTENCE

FIGURE 16.2.

Each author has a unique ID.

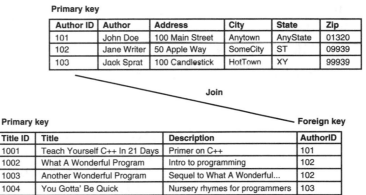

Primary key

Author ID	Author	Address	City	State	Zip
101	John Doe	100 Main Street	Anytown	AnyState	01320
102	Jane Writer	50 Apple Way	SomeCity	ST	09939
103	Jack Sprat	100 Candlestick	HotTown	XY	99939

Join

Primary key

Foreign key

Title ID	Title	Description	AuthorID
1001	Teach Yourself C++ In 21 Days	Primer on C++	101
1002	What A Wonderful Program	Intro to programming	102
1003	Another Wonderful Program	Sequel to What A Wonderful...	102
1004	You Gotta' Be Quick	Nursery rhymes for programmers	103

The `AuthorID` field uniquely identifies each author in the Author table and so is that table's *primary* key. When that key appears in the Titles table, it creates a relationship between the tables and is thus a *foreign* key in the Titles table. A foreign key is just a key that serves as a primary key in some other table.

This is a powerful idea to which we will return shortly. These tables, as you can imagine, can get pretty large. Searching for a particular author or title can be time consuming. To speed searching, columns can be *indexed*. When you create an index, the system creates a second file, sorted by whatever value you are indexing. This second file provides a pointer back into the original file. Typically, this pointer is just the offset of the record into the file, measured in the number of records or bytes.

A table is always indexed on its primary key. You can also index on any other field to speed up searching for a record based on information in that field. For example, in addition to indexing on `AuthorID` (the primary key), you may want to index on the author's name. If you Laos index on the author's name, you can zip through the Author Name index, find the record you are looking for, and then use the offset to jump to that record in your data file:

AuthorID (Primary Key)	Author	Address	City	State	Zip
101	John Doe	100 Main Street	Anytown	AnyState	01320
102	Jane Writer	50 Apple Way	SomeCity	ST	09939
103	Jack Sprat	100 Candlestick	HotTown	XY	99939
104	Jesse Liberty	1 Fake Street	Boston	MA	01297
105	Ernest Hemming	50 Famous Dr.	NY	NY	11209

Author	Offset
John Doe	0
Ernest Hemming	4
Jesse Liberty	3
Jack Sprat	2
Jane Writer	1

The use of indices works well because the index itself can be searched very quickly using a binary search (as described in Chapter 13, "Search Algorithms in C++"). As your data file grows, the number of required searches grows very slowly. For a file containing n records, you need, on average, to search only $log_2(n)$ records. If, on the other hand, you looked at every record in the original database, you'd have to examine an average of n/2 records.

With a database of 65,536 (n) records, brute-force searching would average 32,768 searches (n/2), but a binary search would average only 16 searches ($log_2(n)$)! Also consider that the 32,768 searches must each read in the entire data block, while the 16 searches read in the much smaller index records. There is no comparison in performance; indices are very efficient.

Of course, nothing is free. The cost of using indices is felt at the time you add records to the database. Each record must be indexed, and that takes time. In addition, each index takes up disk space and memory. In this, as in everything, this is true: TANSTAAFL (There Ain't No Such Thing As A Free Lunch).

After the data is found in the index file, the pointer is used. The pointer is just an offset into the data file. The operating system provides *very* fast access when you *seek* directly to an offset into a file.

Architecture of a Relational Database

Databases can be understood at three levels. First is the application's view of the data, including application-specific semantics and constraints. At this level, we are not talking about data modeling at all. We are talking about objects, entities, business rules, and so forth.

The next level is the level of entity-relationship modeling. It is only from this perspective that we think about tables, rows, columns, and indexes. At this level, we are concerned with understanding how the relationships among the various objects in the domain translate to tables and their interrelationships.

Relational Databases and Persistence

CHAPTER 16

625

16

RELATIONAL
DATABASES AND
PERSISTENCE

The most fundamental level, of course, is the *physical*, or *internal*, level, which maps to files on the disk. You almost never worry about databases at this level unless you are, in fact, creating your own database technology. It is at this level that you consider the size of the records in the file, data access blocks, disk access methods, and so forth.

Any given database has three users:

- The end user, who thinks only about objects and business rules.
- The programmer, who is responsible for developing the applications used by the end users and who thinks about objects and business rules, but also thinks about entity-relationship modeling.
- The database administrator (DBA), who defines the physical components and must also understand the entity relationships. The DBA also knows how to optimize for maximum performance.

Restrictions and Considerations

Relational databases work best when a few simple rules are followed:

- Duplicate rows are not allowed.
- Primary keys must be unique within any given table.
- The value of each field is atomic—that is, each field represents a single, indivisible bit of information. (The implications of this rule are that, in a relational database, you cannot store a list within a single field.)

Within any given relational database, there are three types of tables:

- **Entity table:** This table contains application-specific data meaningful to the end user.
- **Relationship table:** This table represents relationships between tables and is of no interest to (and is invisible to) the end user.
- **Virtual table:** This table is used to present a "view" of the database to an application.

SQL: Defining and Querying the Database

The industry standard for querying relational databases is the Structured Query Language (SQL). Unfortunately, as often happens, there are a number of extensions to SQL which, although they make SQL more powerful for individual database products, also undermine this lingua-franca of database access.

SQL is also a data definition language (DDL) and can be used to create databases and to define the structure of tables. SQL also provides the data manipulation language (DML) used to query the data. DDL statements are used to create the tables, views, keys, and constraints that define the database. DML statements are used to query the database, select records, and sort the results.

Data definition includes the name of the table and each of the fields, the contents and rules and restrictions for each field such as its type, length, whether it can be NULL and so forth. The DDL is also used to define keys and to establish referential integrity. (*Referential integrity* means that each of the various tables in a database are consistent *with one another* in their representation of the state of objects.)

When you query the database, what you get back is a set of rows in a table or a view. This is called your *answer set*. The view is a *virtual database*, which looks to the user like a standalone database, but actually represents a subset of the real database based on the results of the query. An iterator, called a *cursor*, is used to iterate through the answer set.

The normal way to search the database is with a SELECT statement:

```
SELECT AuthorID, Author, City FROM Author WHERE AuthorID > 101 AND Zip
➥AuthorID < 104
```

This SQL statement requests that the database return the AuthorID, the Author, and the City from the Author table for every record where the AuthorID is greater than 101 and also less than 104. Presumably, this would return two records: AuthorID 102 and 103 (assuming that no two records can have duplicate AuthorID values).

Normalization

One of the goals of the database designer is to eliminate duplication among the tables in a database. Duplication is expensive: It takes more disk space to store information twice, and it takes longer to search larger records. Duplication is also a risk to referential integrity: If you keep data twice, it is possible for the copies of the data to be out of synch with each other.

The process of eliminating duplication is called *normalization*.

Database theorists have defined several *normal forms* for relational databases. A normal form defines how much duplication has been eliminated; each successive normal form is more restrictive than the previous one. For example, the third normal form is more restrictive (that is, it allows less duplication) than the second form.

Relational Databases and Persistence

CHAPTER 16

627

16

RELATIONAL
DATABASES AND
PERSISTENCE

The first normal form (1NF) dictates that each field (often called an *attribute*) stores only one value (as opposed to a list of values). The second normal form (2NF) adds the requirement that each row (record) in the database must be unique. This criteria is usually achieved by creating a unique ID for each row called an *identity column*, or an *identity field*. If you have no other value on which to index, you may make the identity column the primary key, but that is not required. The identity column is created only to ensure uniqueness.

The third normal form (3NF) is the most popular compromise between too little normalization and too much normalization. In 3NF, you remove all redundant information in your tables except for the fields used as foreign keys.

There are a fourth and fifth normal form, but they are not commonly used because they are too difficult to implement and they impose significant performance penalties. In fact, some databases are intentionally *denormalized*, that is, some redundancy is added to the tables to enhance performance. Kids, don't try this at home; these people are trained professionals.

Joins

Normalizing a database limits what you can find in a simple query unless you *join* two or more tables together. Joining multiple tables creates a single "virtual table." It is as if the two tables were one larger table with duplicate values. This gives you the best of both worlds: You can search efficiently and still store the data efficiently.

There are various ways to join tables. The first and most common is the *natural join*, also called the *equi-join*. You perform an equi-join on two tables that have a common column. The join is accomplished using the SQL WHERE clause:

```
SELECT TableA.Title, TableB.Author FROM TableA, TableB
   WHERE TableA.AuthorID = TableB.AuthorID
```

The WHERE clause creates the equi-join. Note that the FROM clause lists the two tables to be joined. If you leave out the equi-join clause and join the tables by listing two or more in the FROM clause, you are creating a *cross-join*.

A variant on an equi-join is a *theta-join*. A theta-join is like an equi-join except that rather than equating the two columns, you use another relational operator.

You can generalize these statements into *inner-join* statements by explicitly naming the table columns to match. Note that with an inner-join, you do not have to compare the same columns in the two tables. Thus you can write the following query:

```
SELECT TableA.Title
FROM TableA inner join TableB ON TableA.AuthorID = TableB.AuthorID
AND TableB.State = ST
```

If there is an inner-join, you can guess that there is also an *outer-join*. An outer-join examines two tables and returns the records of one table where there is a matching record in the second table. This is a way to say, "Show me all the records in Table A; also show me all the records in Table B that have matches in Table A."

Outer-joins are "handed"—that is, they can be either left-handed or right-handed. A left-handed outer-join looks like this:

```
SELECT * FROM TableA left outer join TableB ON TableA.AuthorID =
TableB.AuthorID
```

This statement returns every record from Table A (the left table) and all the records in Table B that match the criteria.

Persisting to a Relational Database

A classic dilemma when creating an object-oriented program is how to map your objects to the columns and tables of a relational database. Typically, each member variable in the object corresponds to a field (column) in the database.

After you design this map, you have a few choices: You can teach your classes how to write themselves to the RDB (either by hand or using a tool that creates the persistence code), or you can use an application framework to get the work done.

Before examining what a framework can do for you, it is helpful to understand the task. Let's discuss what it would take to write the code yourself if you didn't use an application framework.

Assume that you are going to write your attributes (member variables) into fields. You start by deciding how to map the object's state to a row in one or more tables. You must decide how to represent an object's primitive data, and thus you must map the C++ data types such as `int` and `char` to the data types intrinsic to your chosen database. Note that the code you write will not necessarily be portable among databases. You may want to add an abstraction layer so that you can choose a new database without breaking the design of the objects. Tools are available that can read your header files and produce the necessary DDL.

You must then define the methods that create the database tables and keep them up to date. You then create the queries needed to manipulate the data, and you must create the

Relational Databases and Persistence

CHAPTER 16

629

16

RELATIONAL
DATABASES AND
PERSISTENCE

API to the database itself (the API is typically provided by the database manufacturer, but it does not support the concept of objects).

Each object and all its data members must be transformed to and from tables. The data members include not only primitive data (such as int and char) but also aggregated objects and base objects. In addition, objects on the heap must be swizzled out of and back into memory.

Swizzling with Object Identifiers

One of the difficult tasks in mapping objects to a relational database is what to do about objects stored on the heap. To understand how to solve this problem, we must examine how an object names another object in memory. For example, if I create a book order, how do I tell that book order about an author? Typically, I do so using pointers; one of the book order's member variables will be a pointer to an author:

```
class BookOrder
{
public:
    // . . .
private:
   Author * pAuthor;
};
```

When we map this to an RDB, we map the pointer to an Object Identifier (OID). The OID uniquely identifies an object and can be used to "swizzle" that object to and from disk. *Swizzling* is the process of chasing the pointer, getting the object, writing it to a table or reading it from a table, and calling the new operator to create the object in memory.

OIDs are often stored as numbers or short character arrays. Ideally, each OID is unique—if it is not unique across the world, it must be unique within one instance of the program. With a client/server application, the OID must be unique across the network; if that network is the Internet, the OID must be globally unique. Microsoft offers globally unique identifiers (GUIDS), which are covered in Chapter 21, "COM."

Using Blobs

The process of reading and writing data can be unacceptably slow, especially because each data member must be transformed to match the requirements of the database.

The alternative is to store the entire object as a binary stream of bytes. Key values can be stored as attributes in columns, but the bulk of the data is treated as a *blob*—that is, it has no semantic meaning. When you need the data, you use the key to access it and then you reconstitute the object in memory.

The advantage of storing much of the object as a stream of bytes is that you do less mapping between objects and tables. The disadvantage is that the semantics of the object (and even the identity of many of the attributes) are lost in the database.

If you are going to use a blob, the important decision to make is what data to throw in the blob and what data to use as keys. Remember that once the data is in the blob, it is invisible until it is brought out—and that can be done only by using the key values you explicitly hold out. Using blobs rather than mapping each attribute can enhance performance, but it can also dramatically increase the cost of design changes.

Hiding the Details

Unless you are developing a general application framework for resale, you typically avoid these issues by using a standard interface to the database provided by your vendor. It is important to understand the various levels of abstraction so that you can make the appropriate choices:

- Storing your objects directly
- Using your database's API
- Using ODBC (or something like it)
- Using MFC (or something like it)

Which is to say, you can write your own code to get your objects into or out of the database, or you can take advantage of the vendor-specific API to help you with the task. Going up a level of abstraction, you can use Microsoft's Open Database Connectivity (ODBC) technology, which is designed to create a uniform API to all databases that support SQL. Up an additional level of abstraction is Microsoft's Data Object (DAO) model, which provides an object-oriented front end to ODBC. Finally, we come to the Microsoft Foundation Class (MFC) library, which provides a high-level object abstraction of either ODBC or DAO.

Storing Objects Directly

Storing objects directly is the true programmer's favorite option. In this approach, we eschew wimpy commercial databases and the hundreds of developer-years they've spent getting it right: We write our own. We create our own indices and our own data files, and we write directly to the disk. Great fun—and totally insane for any reasonable commercial application.

If this option intrigues you, be sure to read Chapter 15, "Object Persistence."

Relational Databases and Persistence

CHAPTER 16

631

16

RELATIONAL
DATABASES AND
PERSISTENCE

Using Your Database's API

Using your database's API is a somewhat more realistic approach. In this method, you write directly to the API provided by the database vendor. The problem with this approach is that it is not the least bit encapsulated. We lock ourselves into a single database API, and if we want to change databases, we have to redo all that work. In addition, these APIs are most often C interfaces, not C++ interfaces, and we spend a fair amount of time writing C++ wrappers for the code.

Accessing ODBC Data Sources

Open Database Connectivity (ODBC) is a procedural C-style API that allows applications to access data in any database for which the end user has an ODBC driver. As a result, ODBC allows Windows applications to connect to different environments on multiple platforms.

ODBC has the following components:

- **ODBC API.** A library of function calls, error codes, and standard Structured Query Language (SQL) that can be used to access databases.

- **ODBC Driver Manager.** A dynamic link library (ODBC32.DLL) that loads ODBC database drivers that provide an API to the database.

- **ODBC Database Drivers.** One or more DLLs that process ODBC function calls to specific DBMSs.

- **ODBC Cursor Library.** A dynamic link library (ODBCCR32.DLL) that provides support for cursors (virtual views into the database). The cursor library sits between the ODBC driver manager and the drivers.

- **ODBC Administrator.** A tool that can be used to configure data sources. These data sources are used by the application to connect to the database.

You can write C++ applications to connect to any data source for which there is an ODBC driver. These data sources can include the following:

- Relational databases such as Oracle and Microsoft SQL Server
- Indexed Sequential Access Method (ISAM) databases
- Microsoft Excel spreadsheets
- Text files

A data source consists of several components that completely describe the data being accessed. These components include the following items:

- A specific set of data

- Connection information required to access the data

- Location of the data source

Data sources must be configured using the ODBC administrator. The complete set of functionality available depends on the ODBC driver installed and its capabilities.

The ODBC administrator tool is used to manage the data sources. It keeps the information about the data sources and their connection in the Windows Registry. Using the ODBC administrator, you can do the following:

- Add and delete ODBC drivers

- Add, modify, and delete data sources

The ODBC Cursor Model

Most DBMSes provide a simple method for retrieving data from a query. Rows are returned to the application one at a time until the last row in the set is returned. There is no provision to go back to a row without reexecuting the query. On the other hand, interactive applications usually allow the user to go back and forth through the set of data using the arrow keys or the Page Up and Page down keys. A *cursor* is a mechanism that allows individual rows returned from a query to be processed one at a time; the cursor points to the current row in the recordset. A cursor that provides the ability to scroll back and forth through the result set is called a *scrollable cursor*. A cursor that allows the modification and deletion of the fetched data is called a *scrollable, updateable cursor*. Concurrency control is important when using cursors (just like it is when working with transactions).

ODBC provides three types of cursors:

- **Static cursors:** In a static cursor, the membership, ordering, and values of the result set are fixed when the cursor is opened. These items remain fixed until the cursor is closed. This type of cursor is most useful for read-only applications. The static cursor provides a very consistent view of the data. The biggest disadvantage of this model is that the changes made by other transactions after the cursor is opened are not visible to this cursor.

- **Keyset-driven cursors:** In a keyset-driven cursor, the membership and ordering of the result set is fixed when the cursor is opened but the values can change.

- **Dynamic cursors:** In a dynamic cursor, all the committed changes made by anyone—as well as the uncommitted changes made by the cursor owner—are visible to the cursor owner. The membership and ordering of the result set can be affected by updates made by anyone:

Cursor Type	Accuracy	Consistency	Concurrency
Static	Low	High	Medium
Keyset-driven	Medium	Medium	Medium
Dynamic	High	Low	High

Concurrency Control Using ODBC

Locking (or *pessimistic concurrency control*) and *optimistic concurrency control* are the two primary methods for managing concurrency. The optimistic approach is used when the application is optimistic that no other transaction will update the data before the data is committed. On the other hand, locking is used to ensure that other transactions cannot make changes while the current transaction is holding the records in exclusive mode.

In ODBC, the application can specify the type of concurrency control by passing one of the following options to SQLSetStmtOption:

- SQL_CONCUR_READ_ONLY: This option indicates read-only access and that no updates will be attempted.

- SQL_CONCUR_LOCK: This option indicates that locking has to be used to prevent other transactions from modifying the records.

- SQL_CONCUR_ROWVER and SQL_CONCUR_VALUES: These options indicate that optimistic concurrency control is to be used.

Scrolling

Using ODBC, you can fetch rows from the recordset using SQLFetch (retrieve rows from forward-only cursors one at a time) or SQLExtendedFetch (retrieve rows from scrollable cursors; a multiple-row fetch is possible). The following operations are available with SQLExtendedFetch for scrolling operations:

- SQL_FETCH_NEXT: Fetch the next rowset

- SQL_FETCH_PRIOR: Fetch the previous rowset

- SQL_FETCH_FIRST: Fetch the first rowset

- SQL_FETCH_LAST: Fetch the last rowset

- SQL_FETCH_RELATIVE: Fetch the rowset that is n rows from the current rowset (n can be positive or negative)

- SQL_FETCH_ABSOLUTE: Fetch the rowset beginning with the nth row in the result set

Application programmers can make use of scrollable cursors without writing their own cursor code by using the ODBC cursor library. The driver manager calls the cursor library, and the cursor library calls the driver. The cursor library is enabled when the application calls `SQLSetConnectOption` with the `SQL_ODBC_CURSORS` option. This option allows the applications to make use of the scrollable cursor functions defined in ODBC Conformance Level 2 (`SQLExtendedFetch`, `SQLSetPos`, and the cursor options in `SQLSetStmtOption`).

Using MFC

All the details of ODBC are managed for you when you use an application framework. In a framework, you get an object-oriented wrapper around not only the database API but also around the ODBC layer. Your application can focus on its own internal business logic. The best way to see how this works is to study an example. Although you may never use the MFC, the lessons learned here should apply—at least at the highest level of abstraction—to whatever framework library you do use.

The dilemma, as always, is how complex to make the example. Too simple and it is a toy that doesn't relate to reality; too complex and it is too difficult to follow. I tend to believe in fairly simple examples, which can then be built on and generalized after the principles are understood.

We'll start with the analysis: What are we trying to model? I want a program to help me keep track of books I read. I want to know who wrote the book, when I read it, what topic it falls under, and so forth.

Because this example exists to demonstrate the database, I'll focus only on the tables for now. (Generally, I try to avoid data-driven design, preferring to use case-driven design as described in Chapter 1, "Object-Oriented Analysis and Design.")

The Book table tracks information about a particular book; its preliminary fields are shown in Figure 16.3.

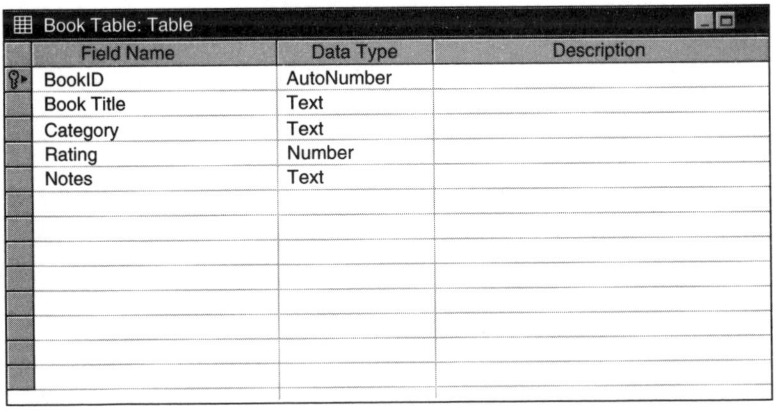

FIGURE 16.3.

The Book table.

Field Name	Data Type	Description
BookID	AutoNumber	
Book Title	Text	
Category	Text	
Rating	Number	
Notes	Text	

Relational Databases and Persistence

CHAPTER 16

635

16

**RELATIONAL
DATABASES AND
PERSISTENCE**

I'll also need an Author table, and I'll create a many-to-many relationship between book and author by creating a `AuthorBookJoin` table, as shown in Figure 16.4.

FIGURE 16.4.

*The
AuthorBookJoin
table.*

	Field Name	Data Type	
🔑►	AuthorID	AutoNumber	
	Author Name	Text	
	Author Notes	Text	

▦ AuthorTable: Table

	Field Name	Data Type	Description
🔑►	ID	AutoNumber	
	AuthorID	Number	
	BookID	Number	

▦ AuthorBookJoin: Table

Next, I'll add some sample data to get us started (see Figure 16.5).

FIGURE 16.5.

Sample data.

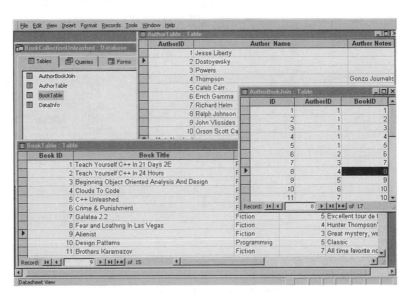

Note that each of these tables was created in a single Access database I've named `BookCollectionUnleashed.mdb`. I'll also have to create a data source that points to that collection, which I can do using the ODBC32 utility in the Windows NT Control Panel.

ODBC32 offers a variety of DataSource (DSN) connections. A User DSN is available to a single user, and a System DSN is available to everyone on your system. If you need to share a DSN among more than one computer, you can use a File DSN. I'll create a System DSN pointing to my newly created `.mdb` file, and I'll name it `BookCollectionUnleashed`.

It is now time to fire up Microsoft Visual C++ and create a new project. When we do so, we are immediately asked whether we want this application to be a Single Document Interface (SDI), a Multi-Document Interface (MDI), or dialog based. If we select either SDI or MDI, we have the option of asking for database support—and if so, we can add a database view.

If we ask for a database view, we are asked to point to the ODBC source and are then asked which tables we want to include in this view, as shown in Figure 16.6.

FIGURE 16.6.

Choosing a table.

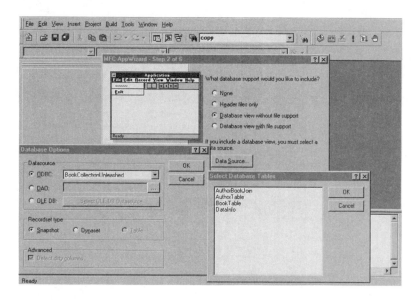

The wizard can create only a single view, but you are free to add additional record views as you develop the application. We'll create our primary view on the Book table because this is a good way to demonstrate what the wizard-generated record view can do. In a commercial application, you may choose the Header Files Only option if you want more control over all your views and would rather create them yourself.

After the wizard has gathered the information it needs, you are presented with a review of your classes, as shown in Figure 16.7.

FIGURE 16.7.

The wizard-generated review of classes.

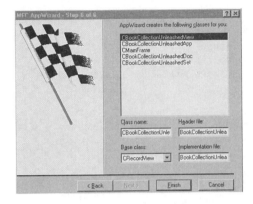

Note that the view class is a `CRecordView`, as we expected. Building this application provides you with the fundamentals, but the MFC expects you to create a dialog object for this view that will display the contents of the table. Thus, the preliminary dialog box, shown in Figure 16.8, is rather spartan.

FIGURE 16.8.

The preliminary dialog box for the sample application.

We'll add a few controls to display the contents of the fields we care about, as shown in Figure 16.9.

FIGURE 16.9.

Displaying fields.

Next, we need to hook these controls up to the contents of the database. To do this, we turn to the `DoDataExchange` code for our `RecordView`. The Application Wizard-supplied code looks like this:

```
void CBookCollectionUnleashedView::DoDataExchange(CDataExchange* pDX)
{
    CRecordView::DoDataExchange(pDX);
    //{{AFX_DATA_MAP(CBookCollectionUnleashedView)
        // NOTE: the ClassWizard will add DDX and DDV calls here
    //}}AFX_DATA_MAP
}
```

First, we'll ask the Class Wizard to create member variables for each of the dialog controls, as shown in Figure 16.10.

FIGURE 16.10.

Creating member variables.

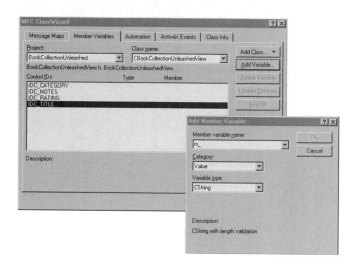

This causes the Class Wizard to create the following data exchange code:

```
void CBookCollectionUnleashedView::DoDataExchange(CDataExchange* pDX)
{
    CRecordView::DoDataExchange(pDX);
    //{{AFX_DATA_MAP(CBookCollectionUnleashedView)
    DDX_Text(pDX, IDC_CATEGORY, m_Category);
    DDX_Text(pDX, IDC_NOTES, m_Notes);
    DDX_Text(pDX, IDC_RATING, m_Rating);
    DDX_Text(pDX, IDC_TITLE, m_Title);
    //}}AFX_DATA_MAP
}
```

Unfortunately, this is still not quite what we want. Rather than putting the contents of the controls into the local variables, we want to talk directly to the database. We can fix this glitch by changing the `DDX_Text` calls to calls to `DDX_FieldText`. We make this change by hand, editing the code generated by the wizard. The `DDX_FieldText` macro takes four parameters: The first two are the same parameters used by `DDX_Text` and are followed by the member variable of the `CRecordSet` attached to the view, and the `CRecordSet` itself. First, I'll show you what it looks like, and then we'll discuss the mysterious `CRecordSet`:

```
void CBookCollectionUnleashedView::DoDataExchange(CDataExchange* pDX)
{
    CRecordView::DoDataExchange(pDX);
    //{{AFX_DATA_MAP(CBookCollectionUnleashedView)
    DDX_FieldText(pDX, IDC_CATEGORY, m_pSet->m_Category, m_pSet);
    DDX_FieldText(pDX, IDC_NOTES, m_pSet->m_Notes, m_pSet);
    DDX_FieldText(pDX, IDC_RATING, m_pSet->m_Rating, m_pSet);
    DDX_FieldText(pDX, IDC_TITLE, m_pSet->m_Book_Title, m_pSet);
    //}}AFX_DATA_MAP
}
```

Rebuilding and running this code creates an application that does, in fact, read directly from the database, as shown in Figure 16.11.

FIGURE 16.11.

The application reads from the database.

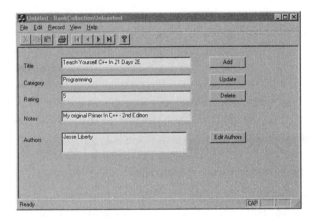

Clearly, the application works, but how? The magic is in the data member of your `CRecordView` class: `m_pSet`. This member is a pointer to a `CBookCollectionUnleashedSet` object. Both the type and the member variable were created and added by the Application Wizard.

So what is a `CBookCollectionUnleashedSet`? This type was created by the Application Wizard, and it derives from `CRecordSet`:

```
class CBookCollectionUnleashedSet : public CRecordset
{
public:
    CBookCollectionUnleashedSet(CDatabase* pDatabase = NULL);
```

```
        DECLARE_DYNAMIC(CBookCollectionUnleashedSet)

// Field/Param Data
    //{{AFX_FIELD(CBookCollectionUnleashedSet, CRecordset)
    long        m_Book_ID;
    CString     m_Book_Title;
    CString     m_Category;
    long        m_Rating;
    CString     m_Notes;
    //}}AFX_FIELD

// Overrides
    // ClassWizard generated virtual function overrides
    //{{AFX_VIRTUAL(CBookCollectionUnleashedSet)
    public:
    virtual CString GetDefaultConnect();    // Default connection string
    virtual CString GetDefaultSQL();         // default SQL for Recordset
    virtual void DoFieldExchange(CFieldExchange* pFX);    // RFX support
    //}}AFX_VIRTUAL

// Implementation
#ifdef _DEBUG
    virtual void AssertValid() const;
    virtual void Dump(CDumpContext& dc) const;
#endif

};
```

A `CRecordSet` is, essentially, an iterator over your table. It has one member variable for each column in your selected table, and you can use the recordset to interact with that data. We'll examine `CRecordSet` objects in some detail as we go forward, but for the moment we're just accepting the magic provided by the wizards: As we ask for each record, the `RecordSet` fetches it from the database.

This is fine as far as it goes. We would, however, like to be able to see the author (or authors!) for our books. This request is a bit tricky to implement, however, because we don't keep the name of the author (or even the author's ID) in the Book table. (Remember that we tie the Book table to the Author table with entries in the BookAuthorJoin table.)

Here's what we want to do: Each time we read a book record, we want to use the `m_book_ID` to find every matching record in the BookAuthorJoin table. For each record found, we want to look up the author name in the Author table, and then we want to display that name.

This is easier to code than you might think. The first thing to do is to create a `CRecordSet` class for each of the two tables:

```
class AuthorRecordSet : public CRecordSet
{
public:
    AuthorRecordSet(CDatabase* pDatabase = NULL);
    DECLARE_DYNAMIC(AuthorRecordSet)

// Field/Param Data
    //{{AFX_FIELD(AuthorRecordSet, CRecordSet)
    long    m_AuthorID;
    CString    m_Author__Name;
    CString    m_Author_Notes;
    //}}AFX_FIELD

// Overrides
    // ClassWizard generated virtual function overrides
    //{{AFX_VIRTUAL(AuthorRecordSet)
    public:
    virtual CString GetDefaultConnect();    // Default connection string
    virtual CString GetDefaultSQL();    // Default SQL for Recordset
    virtual void DoFieldExchange(CFieldExchange* pFX);  // RFX support
    //}}AFX_VIRTUAL

// Implementation
#ifdef _DEBUG
    virtual void AssertValid() const;
    virtual void Dump(CDumpContext& dc) const;
#endif
};

class BookAuthorRecordSet : public CRecordset
{
public:
    BookAuthorRecordSet(CDatabase* pDatabase = NULL);
    DECLARE_DYNAMIC(BookAuthorRecordSet)

// Field/Param Data
    //{{AFX_FIELD(BookAuthorRecordSet, CRecordset)
    long    m_ID;
    long    m_AuthorID;
    long    m_BookID;
    //}}AFX_FIELD

// Overrides
    // ClassWizard generated virtual function overrides
    //{{AFX_VIRTUAL(BookAuthorRecordSet)
    public:
    virtual CString GetDefaultConnect();    // Default connection string
    virtual CString GetDefaultSQL();    // Default SQL for Recordset
    virtual void DoFieldExchange(CFieldExchange* pFX);  // RFX support
    //}}AFX_VIRTUAL
```

```
// Implementation
#ifdef _DEBUG
    virtual void AssertValid() const;
    virtual void Dump(CDumpContext& dc) const;
#endif
};
```

What I show here is the code generated by the Class Wizard. Note that each class has a member variable which corresponds to a column in one of the tables.

The next step is to create a control that displays the author names. For simplicity, we'll use a list box. I'll ask the Class Wizard to create a member variable for that control so that I can call AddString directly on the control. Finally, I'll create a member method of the view to update the author list, and I'll call that method each time I update the other controls:

```
void CBookCollectionUnleashedView::DoDataExchange(CDataExchange* pDX)
{
    CRecordView::DoDataExchange(pDX);
    //{{AFX_DATA_MAP(CBookCollectionUnleashedView)
    DDX_Control(pDX, IDC_Authors, m_Author_Control);
    DDX_FieldText(pDX, IDC_CATEGORY, m_pSet->m_Category, m_pSet);
    DDX_FieldText(pDX, IDC_NOTES, m_pSet->m_Notes, m_pSet);
    DDX_FieldText(pDX, IDC_RATING, m_pSet->m_Rating, m_pSet);
    DDX_FieldText(pDX, IDC_TITLE, m_pSet->m_Book_Title, m_pSet);
    //}}AFX_DATA_MAP

    UpdateAuthor(m_pSet->m_Book_ID);
}

bool CBookCollectionUnleashedView::UpdateAuthor(int id)
{
    AuthorRecordSet ars;
    BookAuthorRecordSet bars;
    CString bookAuthorSQL;
    CString authorSQL;
    CString display;
    int pos;

    m_Author_Control.ResetContent();

    bookAuthorSQL.Format("BookID = %d",id);
    bars.m_strFilter = bookAuthorSQL;
    bars.Open();

    while ( ! bars.IsEOF() )
    {
        authorSQL.Format("AuthorID = %d",bars.m_AuthorID);
        ars.m_strFilter = authorSQL;
        if ( ars.IsOpen() )
```

```
            ars.Requery();
        else
            ars.Open();
        display = ars.m_Author__Name;
        pos - m_Author_Control.AddString(display);

        bars.MoveNext();
    }
    return true;

}
```

The essence of `UpdateAuthor` is that we pass in the ID of the currently selected book, which we get from the `CBookCollectionUnleashedSet` attached to our `RecordView`. After we're in `UpdateAuthor`, we tell the list box to reset itself (`m_Author_Control.ResetContent();`) and set up to query the database for records in the AuthorBookJoin table that match this `BookID`.

Let's walk through this code step by step:

1. Set up a search string that will become the `WHERE` clause in the SQL `SELECT` statement:

   ```
   bookAuthorSQL.Format("BookID = %d",id);
   bars.m_strFilter = bookAuthorSQL;
   ```

   I do this in two stages. First, I create the `Cstring`, and then I assign that string to the member variable `m_strFilter` of the `CRecordSet` object. This causes the `CRecordSet` object to return a recordset of matching records each time I open or requery that object. (Note how this is accomplished: The `CRecordSet` adds a `WHERE` clause to its query and inserts whatever string is in `m_strFilter`.)

2. Open the recordset:

   ```
   bars.Open();
   ```

3. Iterate through the records:

   ```
   while ( ! bars.IsEOF() )
   {
       //. . .
       bars.MoveNext();
   }
   ```

The idiom here is to keep iterating until you hit the end of the `RecordSet` (signified by `IsEOF` returning `true`).

Each time through the iteration, I must extract the `authorID` from the AuthorBookJoin record and use that ID to find the matching record in the Author table. Again, I create a `CString` with the `WHERE` clause for my search, and then assign that string to the `m_strFilter` variable of the *author* recordset. I then query against the recordset, which returns the single record that matches that author, and I extract that string and add it to the list box. Here's what it looks like:

```
authorSQL.Format("AuthorID = %d",bars.m_AuthorID);
ars.m_strFilter = authorSQL;
if ( ars.IsOpen() )
    ars.Requery();
else
    ars.Open();
display = ars.m_Author__Name;
pos = m_Author_Control.AddString(display);
```

When this is done, we can display the author names in context in each record, as shown in Figure 16.12.

FIGURE 16.12.

Displaying author names.

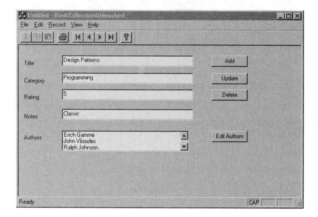

Editing

Try changing the rating or category of one of the books. Hey! Presto! The database is updated when you switch from one record to the next. This bit of magic is accomplished for you in the DoDataExchange() method of the view, which is automatically called when you switch records.

DoDataExchange() is invoked by CWnd::UpdateData, which takes a parameter bSaveAndValidate, a Boolean that defaults to true. When you move from one record to the next, the old record is updated, and the values in the dialog controls are written back into the database using the DDX_FieldText mechanism.

Immediate Updates

But what if you want the update to take effect immediately? Let's add an Update button that updates the current record in place. The code is fairly simple: Have Class Wizard

create a handler, and then all we have do is get the data from the control into the
CRecordSet variables and update the database:

```
void CBookCollectionUnleashedView::OnBookUpdate()
{
    m_pSet->Edit();
    UpdateData();
    m_pSet->Update();
    AfxMessageBox("Updated",MB_ICONEXCLAMATION | MB_OK);
}
```

In this example, I prepare the RecordSet by calling Edit(). Then I update the
CRecordSet variables from the dialog box by calling UpdateData(); finally, I update the
actual database from the CRecordSet by calling Update().

Updating the Authors

Unfortunately, the editing approach just outlined will not work for the author field
because it is a collection. For that field, you must do a bit of work yourself. When
UpdateData() calls DoDataExchange(), it passes in a CDataExchange object. One member of the CDataExchange object is m_bSaveAndValidate, the flag that indicates the
"direction" of the update (if the flag is false, we initialize controls from the database; if
the flag is true, we write from the controls to the database).

We can pass this information to the UpdateAuthor() method, but it won't help very
much in this particular application because the list box itself is read-only. To accomplish
an edit of the list of authors, we have to update the BookAuthorJoin table, a nontrivial
edit.

What might we want to do? We might want to add an author, in which case we can add
an author already in the Author table, or we might want to update *that* table. Further, we
might want to edit the list of authors in this list from the BookAuthorJoin table.

Setting aside the tricky user-interface considerations, we must keep clear what we are
trying to accomplish and write the code accordingly. This is, as they say, left as an exercise for the reader.

Adding Records

If I want to add a new book to our system, I have to create a new record. To begin, let's
add an Add Book button and have the Class Wizard wire up a handler method. Then let's
create a new dialog box to manage the input, as shown in Figure 16.13.

The user fills in the fields and clicks OK (to ensure I don't have empty fields, I dim the
OK button until the fields are populated). I then extract the data from the fields, create a
new record, and insert it into the database, as shown in Listing 16.1.

FIGURE 16.13.

Handling input.

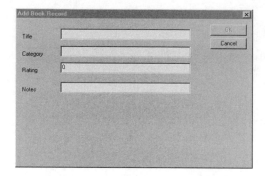

LISTING 16.1. OnBookAdd

```
void CBookCollectionUnleashedView::OnBookAdd()
{
    CAddBookDialog dlg;
    if ( dlg.DoModal() == IDOK )
    {
        CBookCollectionUnleashedSet book;
        ASSERT ( ! book.IsOpen() );

        try
        {
            book.Open();
            ASSERT ( book.CanAppend() );
            book.AddNew();
            book.m_Book_Title = dlg.m_Title;
            book.m_Category = dlg.m_Category;
            book.m_Notes = dlg.m_Notes;
            book.m_Rating = dlg.m_Rating;
            book.Update();
            book.Close();
        }

        catch(CDBException * e)
        {
            CString s;
            s.Format("DB Error in OnBookAdd: %d",e->m_nRetCode);
            AfxMessageBox("s",MB_ICONSTOP ¦ MB_OK );
        }

        catch(...)
        {
            CString s2;
            s2.Format("Unknown Error in OnBookAdd!");
            AfxMessageBox("s2",MB_ICONSTOP  ¦ MB_OK );
        }
    }
```

Relational Databases and Persistence

CHAPTER 16

647

16

RELATIONAL
DATABASES AND
PERSISTENCE

```
    else
        AfxMessageBox("No Record Added",MB_ICONEXCLAMATION ¦ MB_OK );
}
```

A local instance of `CAddBookDialog` is created on the stack:

```
    CAddBookDialog dlg;
```

I then launch it in modal mode and test the return value. If the user clicks Cancel, the `if` statement fails and the `AfxMessageBox` is displayed by the `else` clause:

```
    if ( dlg.DoModal() == IDOK )
```

If, on the other hand, the user clicks OK, it is time to add the new record. I create an instance of `CBookCollectionUnleashedSet` and open it:

```
        CBookCollectionUnleashedSet book;
            //. . .
        book.Open();
```

I then ready it for the new record with a call to `AddNew()`, which sets the `RecordSet` to a new, blank record:

```
        book.AddNew();
```

I populate this new record's fields from the controls in the dialog box:

```
        book.m_Book_Title = dlg.m_Title;
        book.m_Category = dlg.m_Category;
        book.m_Notes = dlg.m_Notes;
        book.m_Rating = dlg.m_Rating;
```

Then I update the new recordset, thereby adding the record to the database:

```
        book.Update();
```

Finally, I close the `RecordSet` because I'm done with it:

```
        book.Close();
```

Note that I do all of this inside a `try` block so that I can catch any `CDBExceptions` thrown by the ODBC system. This approach aids in debugging.

Next Steps

There are any number of improvements to be made to this application. Most are, again, left as exercises for the reader because they build on the skills already demonstrated. You might start by allowing the user to add new authors and to assign authors to your new books. You have all the tools you need to whip this sample application into shape, but there are a few issues remaining.

SQL Statements

At times, you'll want to issue direct SQL statements, without mediation by a CRecordSet object. You can do so by calling ExecuteSQL() on any CDatabase object.

A typical use of this technique is to call a paramaterized stored procedure:

```
CString sqlCmd;
sqlCmd.Format("exec usp_SomeProcedure \'%s\', \'%s\', %ld, \'%s\',
➥\'%s\'",
    String1,
    String2,
    String3,
    String4,
    String5);
try
{
    CDatabase * pDB = new CDatabase;
    pDB->OpenEx("DSN=MySystemDSN");
    pDB->ExecuteSQL( sqlCmd );
        // …
```

In this code, we create a CString, which invokes a stored procedure. Then we create a CDatabase object, use it to open the database by passing in the name of the DSN, and then we invoke ExecuteSQL(), passing in the CString.

Setting Database Characteristics

While we have that CDatabase object, we can in fact set the LoginTimeout and the QueryTimeout to regulate how quickly we must get a response from the database before failing:

```
pDB->SetLoginTimeout(loginTimeOut);
pDB->SetQueryTimeout(queryTimeOut);
```

Summary

This chapter reviewed the fundamentals of relational database technology and showed how relational databases can be used to store objects. The mapping between a relational database and your objects can be handled at various levels of abstraction. Many vendors provide standardized technology (for example, ODBC) to help you create an interface layer between your object model and the relational database itself.

Creating iterators on tables within a database and mapping fields in a database to member variables in your objects can be much simpler if your Application Frameworks Library provides supporting classes. MFC, by far the most popular library of this kind, provides two critical classes for working with databases by way of ODBC: CDatabase and CRecordSet. This chapter reviewed the use of these classes when working with relational databases.

Object Persistence Using Relational Databases

In This Chapter

Since their advent more than a decade ago, relational databases have been the database of choice for most corporations. Applications were written in some third-generation language (3GL) such as C++ to access the data stored in the RDBMS through SQL or some other application development tool. Relational databases are very good for storing application data, but they fail to capture the application logic. As a result, the front-end application has to contain the logic—which often leads to problems when one tries to match the application model with the data model. An *object relational DBMS* stores not only the data but also the logic. It achieves this by using objects to capture the attributes and the functionality associated with particular entities.

As market conditions become more and more competitive, corporations are under constant pressure to build efficient applications that are easy to maintain as well as cost effective. There is also a need for the applications to closely match particular business models and processes. Applications can be written to simulate the status and procedures of different stages of a real-world situation such as an assembly line in a manufacturing business. It is very common to build such applications and use objects to represent different entities of the assembly line. Such systems demand a lot from the applications they use. The cost of design, development, deployment, and support of these applications should be minimized.

Another factor that has to be given serious consideration is the type of data being used in the database. The explosion of the Internet and the World Wide Web has increased the complexity of the data in use. Hypertext, image, and audio data is used commonly in addition to the traditional scalar data.

Object-based technology can meet most of these demands. Databases should also be able to handle such objects—and at the same time, retain the scalability, robustness, and ease of use of relational database technology. Such object-relational databases must be able to store and manipulate complex structured data using object types as well as unstructured data such as images, audio, and video. And because most of the current application base consists of relational database applications, you should be able to smoothly mix the object technology with the existing relational technology.

Oracle8 is an example of a popular object-relational database. It provides an objects option that allows you to create and manipulate object types, in addition to the built-in types provided by Oracle. The object types give you the flexibility to model real-world entities along with the operations that can be performed on those entities. The Objects option also allows the data stored to be accessible from 3GL environments. Oracle8 has features such as client-side caching of objects and single-round-trip retrieval of related objects, which improves the performance of object-based applications. Other object-relational databases include IBM'S DB2 and Sybase System 10.

Traditional relational database applications can benefit from the object modeling and the multimedia capabilities provided by object-relational databases. You can write applications in C++ that can benefit from such object-relational databases.

Objects in Oracle8

In Oracle8, the type system has been extended to support not only objects but also collections of objects. Several key features are available in Oracle8 that can be used for the object-relational paradigm:

- The OBJECT type supports the definition of a structured object.
- The REF type supports object referenceability.
- The LOB type supports the definition of large and unstructured objects.
- The TABLE type supports unordered collections of objects.
- The VARRAY type supports ordered collections of objects. VARRAY is short for *variable-size array*.
- Extensions have been provided to SQL, DDL, and DML to facilitate the creation, retrieval, and modification of objects and collections.

Object Types

An *object type* is a user-defined type that can be used to model a real-world entity. Object types have the following features:

- One or more attributes. An *attribute* is basically a characteristic of the entity being defined. The attribute can be scalar (number, char, and so on), object type, collection (nested table or variable-size array), REF (reference to an instance of object type) or a LOB (large object) type.
- Zero or more methods. Methods are used to specify the application logic associated with the actions that can be performed on the entity. The methods can be written in PL/SQL, in a 3GL such as C++, or in Oracle8 using Java. Several methods are associated with objects, such as the *constructor* (used to instantiate and create object instances) and the *destructor* (used to clean out the object when it is removed from the system). These methods are generated by Oracle for you.
- Object types can be used as the data type of a column.
- It is possible to create tables of object types in which the rows of the table are populated using the object type.
- Instances of user-defined types are stored natively in the database and can be manipulated using SQL and DML extensions.

- The database features available to relational data (such as indexes and triggers) are also available to the object types.

The following examples show how to create a simple object type using SQL (for details on the syntax of the CREATE TYPE command, please refer to the Oracle SQL Language manual).

The following SQL command from SQL*PLUS creates the object type header:

```
create type complex as object (
    real_part real,
    im_part real,
    member function addcomplex (x complex) return complex
    );
/
```

The following SQL command from SQL*PLUS creates the object type body:

```
create type body complex as
    member function addcomplex (x complex) return complex is
    begin
    return complex (real_part + x.real_part, im_part+ x.im_part);
    end addcomplex;
end;
/
```

Object References

Object references are used to uniquely identify and locate objects. For every object stored in a reference table, a unique identifier is generated by the system for that object.

REFs in Columns

You can declare a column of a table or an attribute of an object type to be declared as a REF type. This column can contain references to objects of the declared object type regardless of the object table in which the object is stored. However, it is possible to scope a REF type column such that it contains references only to objects from a specified object table.

There are a few differences between REFs and foreign key columns:

- REFs provide navigational access to the referenced object.
- You can have "dangling" references, which means that the reference value stored in the columns can be a reference to nonexistent objects.

The following example creates the ACCOUNTS table with a reference to the CUSTOMERS table:

```
/* Create an object type */

CREATE TYPE customer_type AS OBJECT
    (cust_no        CHAR(5),
     accounts       account_array);
/

/* Create a table using the object type */

CREATE TABLE customers OF customer_type;

Create type ACCOUNTS as object
(
    ACCTNO number,
    ACCTYPE char(4),
    BALANCE number,
    CUST ref CUSTOMERS
);
```

> **NOTE**
>
> References can be generated only for objects stored in an object table.

The REF Operator

By using the REF operator, you can obtain a reference to an object in an object table. The following statement shows how to insert an object into an object table and also obtain a reference to the object. In the following example, assume that Person is an object table:

```
/* Declare a variable as a reference to an object table*/
DECLARE reftojane REF Person;

/* The REF operator returns a reference to the 'pref' table */
/* and this reference is stored in the variable 'reftojane' */

BEGIN
    INSERT INTO people pref
    VALUES (Person('Jane','Doe','02-FEB-1965'))
    RETURNING REF(pref) INTO reftojane;
END;
```

Once the reference to an object is obtained, you can use it in several ways:

- To pin the object in the cache.
- To operate on the object using the Oracle Call Interface (OCI).
- In the predicate of a SELECT or UPDATE statement.

The DEREF Operator

The DEREF operator can be used to obtain the object from the object reference. The following statement shows how the DEREF operator can be used to obtain an operator and assign it to a column:

```
UPDATE employees
SET personal = DEREF(reftojane)
WHERE empid = 21145;
```

Collections

A *collection* is an ordered group of elements of the same data type. A collection has the following characteristics:

- A unique subscript is used to determine the position of elements in the collection.

- Collections are similar to arrays; however, collections can have only one dimension and must be integer indexed. The integer values can be up to 4GB.

- Object types can make use of collections as their attributes.

- Oracle8 provides two types of collections: nested tables (which are unbounded and do not retain the order in which elements are added to the collection) and variable-size arrays (which are bounded and preserve the ordering of elements).

The following example uses SQL commands to show how nested tables can be used:

```
/* Create an object type for "projects" */

CREATE OR REPLACE TYPE  project_type  as OBJECT
    (projno         NUMBER(5),
    projname        CHAR(30),
    projlocation    CHAR(30));
/

/* Create a table of projects using the object type */

CREATE TABLE orl_projects OF project_type;

/* Insert records into the object table */

INSERT INTO orl_projects
VALUES (111, 'venus','orlando');
INSERT INTO orl_projects
VALUES (112, 'saturn','miami');

/* Create type for use as nested table */

CREATE TYPE project_table AS TABLE OF project_type;
/
```

```
/* Create a table that uses the nested table */

CREATE TABLE employees
    (empno       NUMBER(5),
     empname     CHAR(20),
     empprojs    project_table)
NESTED TABLE empprojs STORE AS nested_proj_table;

/* Insert into the object table */

INSERT INTO employees
VALUES (12345, 'MIKE',
    project_table(project_type(55555,'honda','orlando'),
                          project_type(66666,'toyota','miami'))));
```

The following example shows how to create a VARRAY using SQL commands:

```
/* Create an object type */

CREATE TYPE account_type as OBJECT
    (account_no      INT,
     account_type    CHAR(2),
     balance         DEC(10,2));
/

/* Create a VARRAY using the object type */

CREATE TYPE account_array AS VARRAY(10) OF account_type;
/

/* Create an object type */

CREATE TYPE customer_type AS OBJECT
    (cust_no        CHAR(5),
     accounts       account_array);
/

/* Create a table using the object type */

CREATE TABLE customers OF customer_type;

/* Insert into the object table */

INSERT INTO customers
VALUES (55555, account_array(account_type(11,'C',1000.00),
                          account_type(22,'S', 2000.00)));
```

Using External Procedures Developed in C++

Because Oracle8 allows you to call DLL functions and procedures from PL/SQL code, you can have objects with methods that are implemented as external C++ routines. Using external procedures developed in C++ allows you to benefit from the efficiency of a 3GL language; you can also make use of Win32 APIs.

You must perform the following two steps before calling external procedures from PL/SQL:

1. Register the DLL's location with Oracle8's data dictionary.

   ```
   Create or replace library external_lib as 'e:/datacartridge/debug/
                          cartridge.dll';
   ```

2. Declare the prototype of the C++ routine in the Oracle8 data dictionary.

Let's look at an example that makes use of an object type having methods implemented as external C++ procedures:

```
Create or replace package data_package as
    function ext_func (data CLOB) return binary_integer;
end;
/
create or replace package body data_package as
    function ext_func (data CLOB) return binary_integer is external
        name "c_func"
        library external_lib
        language C
        with context
        parameters (
            context,
            data OCILOBLOCATOR
        );
end;
/
create or replace type ext_objtype as object (
    data          CLOB,
    member function    ext_objtype_func return binary_integer
);
/
Create or replace type body ext_objtype is
    member function ext_objtype_func return binary_integer is
    begin
        return data_package.ext_func(data);
    end;
end;
/
```

The function prototype of the external function can be as follows:

```
#Include <oci.h>
#define DLLEXPORT __declspec(dllexport) __cdecl
int DLLEXPORT c_func (OCIExtProcContext *ctx, OCILobLocator *lobl);
int c_func (OCIExtProcContext *ctx, OCILobLocator *lobl)
{
    /*Place function code here */
    return 0;
}
```

The external callout can be tested using PL/SQL:

```
declare
    i binary_integer;
    x ext_objtype;
begin
    x := ext_objtype(EMPTY_CLOB());
    i := x.ext_objtype_func();
    DBMS_OUTPUT.PUT_LINE('ext_objtype_func() returned ' || i);
end;
```

If a process loads a DLL without symbolic debugging information, you can generally use Visual C++'s symbolic debugger to set breakpoints and troubleshoot the problem. When you implement object methods as external procedures using C++, the listener spawns the procedure on demand; therefore, you cannot debug the procedure using traditional techniques. The DebugBreak() Win32 API call can be placed at the beginning of an external procedure to debug it in such situations.

Consider an object called DataStore. This object can store a set of data in an Oracle8 character LOB (called a CLOB). You can perform several manipulations on the stored data, such as minimum, maximum, data regression, and so on. These are the major steps involved in such an implementation:

1. Create an object type to represent the DataStore. The attributes and methods of this object should represent the data stored and the functionality of the object. We will declare the methods as external because the kind of processing required is best performed using a 3GL such as C++:

```
create or replace type DataStore as object (
            pid     integer,
            name    varchar2(10),
            date_created date,
            value   clob,
            member function DataMinimum return integer,
            member function DataMaximum return integer,
            map member function DataToInt return integer,
            pragma  restrict_references(DataMinimum, WNDS, WNPS),
            pragma  restrict_references(DataMaximum, WNDS, WNPS));
```

2. Declare a package that will be used to hold all the external procedures:

```
create or replace package DataStore_package as
            function datastore_findmin (data IN clob) return integer;
            function datastore_findmax (data IN clob) return integer;
            pragma restrict_references (datastore_findmin, WNDS,
            ➥WNPS);
            pragma restrict_references (datastore_findmax, WNDS,
            ➥WNPS);
        end;
```

To call a packaged function from SQL expressions, you must code the pragma
RESTRICT_REFERENCES in the package specification (not in the package body
because the body of the packaged function is hidden). The pragma tells the
PL/SQL compiler to deny the packaged function read/write access to database
tables, packaged variables, or both. In the preceding example, the following are
true:

- WNDS means "Writes no database state" (that is, it does not change database
  tables).

- WNPS means "Writes not packaged state" (that is, it does not change packaged
  variables).

3. Implement the body of object type DataStore (note that the following package
   body is for illustration purposes and depends on the implementation of the functions findmin and findmax; it will not compile as shown:)

```
create or replace type body DataStore is
        member function DataMinimum return integer is
            x integer := DataStore_package.datastore_findmin(data);
            begin return x ; end;
        member function DataMaximum return integer is
            y integer := DataStore_package.datastore_findmax(data);
            begin return y ; end;
        map member function DataToInt return integer is
            z integer := id;
            begin return z; end;
        end;
    /
```

4. Provide a PL/SQL name to the library that contains the implementation of the
   external procedure:

```
create or replace library datastore_lib as '<directory_of_library> /
            libdatastore.so'
```

5. Declare the body of the package and define the associations between the package
   functions and the 3GL functions in the library:

```
Create or replace package body DataStore_package as
            function datastore_findmin(data clob) return integer is
            external name "c_minimum" library datastore_lib language
```

```
                    c with context; function datastore_findmax(data clob)
                    return integer is external name "c_maximum" library
                    datastore_lib language c with context;
             end;
```

6. Use C++ to implement the external procedures. The external procedure reads the CLOB argument passed to it and uses its as a LOB locator while calling the database:

```
#Include <oci.h>
int c_minimum (OCIExtProcContext *ctx,  OCILobLocator  *lobl)   {
        ub1 bufp[MAXBUFLEN];
        sword  retval;
        init_handles (ctx);
        retval = OCILobRead(...., lobl, bufp, ....);
        return (process_min(bufp));
}

#Include <oci.h>
int c_maximum (OCIExtProcContext *ctx,  OCILobLocator  *lobl)   {
        ub1 bufp[MAXBUFLEN];
        sword  retval;
        init_handles (ctx);
        retval = OCILobRead(...., lobl, bufp, ....);
        return (process_max(bufp));
}
```

To test the developed DataStore object, follow these steps:

1. Create a database table that can be used to store instances of the object DataStore:

   ```
   create table DataStore_table of DataStore;
   ```

2. Populate DataStore_table with a row:

   ```
   Insert into DataStore_table values (1, 'test1', to_date('03-28-1998',
   'MM-DD-YYYY'), EMPTY_CLOB() );

   commit;
   ```

3. Use an OCI program that uses the OCI routine OCILobWrite() to load the CLOB attribute of the DataStore object.

4. Compile the external procedures (the c_minimum and c_maximum routines) and put them into the library.

5. Invoke the object methods using PL/SQL routines:

   ```
   Select d.DataMimimum(), d.DataMaximum() from DataStore_table d;
   ```

Mapping UML Diagrams to an Object-Relational Database

To understand how UML diagrams can be mapped to an object-relational database, let's use a sample application, shown in Figure 17.1, that represents a simple banking system containing the entities CUSTOMERS, ACCOUNTS, and ADDRESS. The relationship between the entities can be described as follows:

CUSTOMERS : ACCOUNTS = one : many

ACCOUNTS : ADDRESS = one : one

CUSTOMERS : ADDRESS = one : one

FIGURE 17.1.

A simple banking application design.

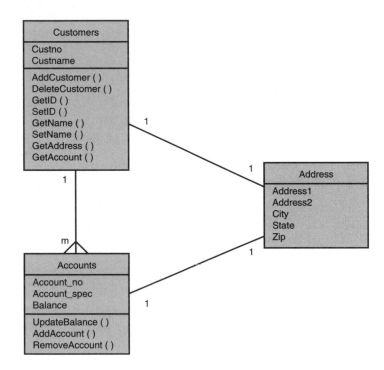

The UML specification for this scenario goes through the following stages:

- **Database design.** This stage is used to define how the UML specification will be represented using the object types.

- **C++ generation.** This stage is used to generate the header and source files for the set of types specified during database design.

- **Server generation.** This stage is used to generate the DDL that will be used to implement the database design on the server.

We will use Oracle8 to illustrate the procedure for the sample application.

Database Design

Each type defined in the UML is mapped to an Oracle8 data type. This type can then be used in defining the tables; the associations between the types are implemented in Oracle8 using the REF type. However, because ADDRESS is modeled by strong aggregation, its type is embedded. You identify the mapping of a type to multiple table implementations by using a *zone identifier* (an Object Database Designer—ODD—specific type used during C++ class generation):

```
create type address_type as object (
    address1        varchar2(100),
    address2        varchar2(100),
    city            varchar2(40),
    state           char(2),
    zip             varchar2(10));
/

create type account_type as object
(
    account_no      NUMBER(10),
    account_spec    CHAR(5),
    balance         DECIMAL(10,2),
    customer        REF customer_type,
    address         address_type
) ;
/
```

C++ Generation

Object Database Designer (ODD) is a new product derived from the Designer/2000 product set. It allows C++ programs to efficiently access Oracle8 databases. This product can be used in all the stages of object-relational database design, creation, and access. ODD has several key features:

- ODD implements abstract type modeling using UML.

- ODD transforms the abstract type model to database design.

- Oracle8 database schema modeling can be used to define physical Oracle8 objects.

- SQL generation can be used to translate the object-relational database designs to SQL DDL.

- The C++ generator creates C++ class definitions and implements the UML objects. The complexities and details of accessing the database are hidden from the user. As a result, the generated C++ classes can be treated as usual without worrying about the details of accessing the database.

The Development Process

The Designer/2000 C++ object layer generator allows C++ programmers to use Oracle as a persistent store. In addition, it provides a transparent way to use the store. The following definitions must be created:

- An entity relationship model to represent the persistent classes
- A relational schema that represents the persistent store
- Mapping between the preceding two components

Using these definitions, the server generator and the C++ object layer generator components of Designer/2000 create the following client and server components:

- C++ native classes with public methods for persistency
- C++ object layer library code to process the client/server transparently
- Oracle database definitions to store the object instances

Figure 17.2 shows the object database designer components that can be used for C++ generation. The programmer can control the C++ generation process by partitioning the source code between the source files on a class-by-class basis.

FIGURE 17.2.

Object Database Designer components.

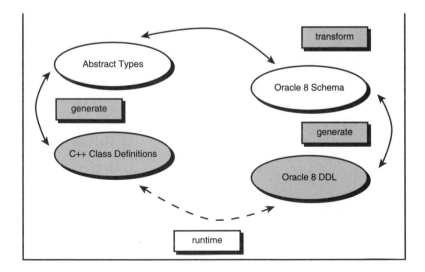

C++ Generation

The following steps describe how to generate C++ classes using the C++ generator:

1. Start the C++ Object Layer Generator.

2. Load a class set.

3. Correct any errors in the model.

4. Select the generation target.

5. Identify the classes to be generated.

6. Ensure that the source files into which the generated classes and global code will be placed have been specified.

7. Change any of the default generation options, if necessary, on the Options tab.

8. Select the Generate tab.

9. If code is to be generated to the application model class definition or implementation files, select the appropriate check boxes.

10. If new code sections are to be generated, select the Generate Classes check box.

11. If existing code sections are to be updated, select the Regenerate Classes check box.

12. Select the Generate button.

The C++ API consists of the generated classes and the runtime C++ class library. The C++ runtime library provides C++ class encapsulation for the database functions such as database connection, transaction, and statement classes. This API maps Oracle8 object references as "smart" pointers; the C++ class mapping is provided for different Oracle8 data types such as these:

- Strings
- Numbers
- Dates
- Collections
- LOBs
- Object references

The following class definitions are generated for a single UML type:

- A class for the actual type
- A smart pointer class
- A collection class
- An iterator class

Following is an example of a class that would be generated for a UML type `Customers`:

```
Class COLCustomers : public OLDBObject
{
public:
COLCustomers();
~COLCustomers();

static COLCustomersRef Create(COLLIFETIME life = COLLIFETIME ::
Persistent,
             OLZONEID id = OLZONEID:;Default);
static void Query(OLZONEID id,  COLCustomersRefSet &Set, OLString
&Predicate);

// Attribute Access
OLNumber &GetID() const;
void SetID(const OLNumber &ID);

OLString &GetName() const;
void SetName(const OLString &Name);

COLAccountsRefSet &GetAccount() const;
COLAddressRef &GetAddress() const;

// Methods
bool AddAccount ( COLAccountsRef &Accounts);
bool RemoveAccount(COLAccountsRef &Accounts);
private:

// Attributes
OLNumber m_ID;
OLString m_Name;

// Associations
COLAccountsRefSet m_Accounts;
COLAddressRef m_Address;
};
```

Server Generation

The sever-generation stage consists of the SQL DDL generation that is used to implement the database design on a server.

Initialization

Before any interaction with C++ objects can occur, the application must initialize the C++ runtime library and provide a database connection that is identified by a generated zone ID. The C++ runtime library contains several important components:

- A context manager to manage connections
- Meta-data to configure the runtime settings such as memory usage, locking policy, and so on.
- A cache for managing persistent C++ object instances.

The following code segment shows how the C++ runtime context can be initialized and a database connection created for a particular zone:

```
COLContext::Initialize();
COLDatabaseConnection *db = new COLDatabaseConnection(OLZONEID::Default);
if (db->Connect(OLZONEID::Default, "scott/tiger@ORCL") != true)
{
    // Error! Connection was not successful.
}
```

Querying an Object

A C++ object can be instantiated from persistent storage by a user application that performs a query with a predicate to identify the required object. In the following example, the predicate is part of a SQL WHERE clause that selects the set of REFs to customers with an ID of 25. The user application gets a root object by using the Query() method. The following code segment illustrates this:

```
COLCustomersRefSet Custrs;
COLCustomers::Query(OLZONEID::Default, custrs, "ID = 25");
```

Iterating Collections

It is necessary to construct iterators for the collections so that the individual objects that belong to the collections can be manipulated. Dereferencing an iterator provides a C++ REF to the generated object. The following code segment shows how iterators can be created for a collection of customers that are retrieved using the Query() method on Customers:

```
for (COLCustomersIter iter(custrs); iter; iter++)
{
    COLCustomersRef   Customers = *iter;
    OLString   name = customers->GetName();
}
```

Navigating Through Associations

Associations between the generated C++ classes are represented by using a REF or by embedding a SET, depending on the cardinality of the association. These REFs and SETs can be used to navigate the associations between the classes. The C++ runtime library must make sure that the Accounts object has already been instantiated from persistent storage; otherwise, the REF is not valid. Similarly, the SET of objects is instantiated only from persistent storage when the SET is iterated and dereferenced. The following code segment shows how the associations are navigated. It gets a REF to a Customer from an Account object:

```
COLAccountsRef  Accounts = *iter;
COLCustomersRef  Customers = Accounts->GetCustomer();
```

Modifying Persistent Objects

Three types of modifications can be performed on persistent objects:

- Create
- Update
- Delete

After modification, the user application must make sure that it marks the C++ object as modified. C++ classes can be generated with or without get or set methods for each attribute; therefore, it is not possible for the C++ runtime library to determine whether an object is modified unless the application informs the library of the modifications made. The following code segment shows how an address can be modified and the object marked as modified:

```
COLAddressRef  address = Customers->GetAddress();
address->SetStreet1("Wisconsin Avenue.");
address->MarkModified();
```

After the current transaction is complete, the object is written to persistent storage.

> **NOTE**
>
> When objects are created, they are automatically marked as created.

Deleting a persistent object also requires special considerations. Although you can use the C++ delete operator to remove the object from memory, this operator does not destroy the object from persistent storage. Again, the user application must specifically mark the object as destroyed so that it can be deleted from persistent storage.

The following code segment shows how an Account can be marked as destroyed:

```
COLAccountsRef    Accounts  =  *iter;
Accounts->Destroy();
```

The following code segment shows how a new Customer object can be created using the default zone:

```
COLCustomersRef   Customer = new COLCustomers(COLLIFETIME::Persistent,
       OLZONEID::Default);
```

Working with Transactions

The set of changes made to the C++ objects are grouped together into a *transaction*. These changes associated with the current transaction are processed when the transaction commits. The C++ runtime library supports *nested transactions*: You can have an outer transaction that opens inner transactions to perform specific tasks. Synchronization between the transactions is achieved by using persistent storage. In other words, when an inner transaction is opened, all the changes made up to that point are placed in persistent storage; in case the inner transaction aborts, the changes can be undone by using the information in the persistent storage. The user application can make use of the transaction object to begin, commit, or roll back a transaction. The following code segment shows how a transaction can be created and a save point created to use persistent storage:

```
COLTransaction   trans(OLZONEID::Default);
trans.Begin();
```

When the transaction commits, all the changes in that transaction are committed:

```
trans.Commit();
```

> **NOTE**
>
> If the preceding sample transaction represents an outer transaction, any changes in the inner transactions become persistent.

Locking

In a multiuser environment, the application being used must be able to provide concurrency control. Concurrency control is achieved by using locking. Object locking can be done at several levels:

- In the scope of the C++ runtime context as follows:

  ```
  COLContext::SetLockMode(COLLockMode::Default);
  ```

- On demand (for example, by refreshing the object). The following code segment gets the current value of the object from persistent storage and then locks it:

  ```
  COLCustomersRef   Customers = *iter;
  Customers->Refresh(true);
  ```

  When finished with the object, the application should release the lock. The lock can be released by committing the transaction.

It is important to realize that the `Refresh()` method protects the integrity and consistency of the database. If the object is not locked, any in-memory object can become out of synch with persistent storage.

The SQL Interface

SQL operations can be performed against the database connection using the SQL interface provided by the C++ runtime library. The following code segment shows how the interface can be used to provide a C++ encapsulation of the Oracle Call Interface (OCI):

```
Unsigned long rows = 0;
CCRDBCursor statement;
CCRDBVariable  var(EVType:: CT_REF);
statement.SetConnection(db->GetConnection());
statement.SetStatement("select ref(cust_tab) from cust_tab");
statement.AddVariable(&var);
statement.Bind(true);
statement.Execute(&rows);
```

This code creates an Oracle cursor object, sets a SQL SELECT statement, binds a variable, and then executes the statement.

The CURSOR Interface for Nested Tables

Oracle8 provides a new construct CURSOR(SELECT ...) that can be used to construct a result set from a nested table. Using this feature, you can fetch and manipulate data from a nested table into client-side host variables. Listing 17.1 shows how to use result-set cursors to print the information of all the accounts for a particular customer.

LISTING 17.1. USING CURSORS TO MANIPULATE NESTED TABLES

```
Select_customer_accounts() {
    account_type      *account_p;
    account_type_ref    *account_ref_p;
    sql_cursor    account_cur;
    char   accountname[20];
    int custid;

    EXEC SQL DECLARE custaccount_cur CURSOR FOR
        SELECT c.id, CURSOR(SELECT * FROM TABLE(c.accounts))
        FROM customers c;

    EXEC SQL OPEN custaccount_cur;

    EXEC SQL ALLOCATE :account_cur;
    EXEC SQL ALLOCATE :account_ref_p;
```

```
while(1){

EXEC SQL FETCH custaccount_cur INTO :custid, :account_cur;
cout << "Customer ID :   " << custid << " has the following accounts :
                                        \n \n";

while(1){
    EXEC SQL FETCH :account_cur INTO :account_ref_p;
    EXEC SQL OBJECT DEREF :account_ref_p INTO :account_p;
    EXEC SQL OBJECT GET name FROM :account_p INTO :accountname;
    cout << accountname << "\n";
}
}
EXEC SQL CLOSE custaccount_cur;
EXEC SQL CLOSE :account_cur;
EXEC SQL FREE :account_cur;
EXEC SQL FREE :account_ref_p;
}
```

The function select_customer_accounts() is used to print the accounts for all the customers using the nested table attribute accounts in the object customers. Listing 17.1 also uses two loops: one to open the cursor custaccount_cur and retrieve each customer object and another to loop through the accounts for this particular customer. The construct CURSOR (SELECT * FROM TABLE(c.accounts)) defines a result-set cursor for the accounts; the cursor custaccount_cur is used to retrieve the result-set cursor.

Accessing the Attributes of Objects

The object attributes cannot be manipulated by using native C++ functions and assignments because they are represented using opaque OCI8 types. Pro C/C++ provides a mechanism to convert OCIString to C char and OCINumber to C int, float, and double types. For example, the following statement can be used to set the balance of an account to a new value:

EXEC SQL OBJECT SET balance OF :account_p TO :new_balance;

> **NOTE**
>
> Pro C/C++ is an application development environment provided by Oracle. It uses the C/C++ and Oracle Call-Level Interface (OCI) to connect to Oracle databases.

Transaction Control Statements

Several statements can be used to control transactions. Committing and rolling back transactions can be handled by using the EXEC SQL COMMIT and the EXEC SQL ROLLBACK statements:

- EXEC SQL COMMIT

  This statement makes the changes caused by associative INSERT, UPDATE, and DELETE statements persistent in the database. In addition, the changes to objects that were navigationally created, updated, and deleted are flushed to the server. This statement notifies the object cache that its objects are not used anymore and releases them by unmarking them.

- EXEC SQL ROLLBACK

  This statement cancels the changes caused by associative INSERT, UPDATE, and DELETE statements. It notifies the object cache that its objects are not used anymore and releases them by unmarking them.

Case Study: Purchase Order System

Let's consider an example of a Purchase Order System that converts an entity-relationship model to an object-relational design.

System Description

The Purchase Order System contains several important entities. Customers can place orders and the purchase order for each customer is a collection of such orders.

Relational Model

The relational model can be used to represent such a system using four tables:

- customers: This table contains information specific to customers such as their address.
- purchase_order: This table contains information about particular purchase orders.
- line_items: This table contains details about a particular purchase order.
- stock: This table contains details about specific stock items that can be purchased by customers by placing purchase orders.

Relationship Between Tables

A customer can place many orders; this is indicated by placing a foreign key attribute in the purchase_order table that references the customers table. Each purchase order can have many line items that describe specific orders; this is indicated by placing a foreign key attribute in the line_items table that references the purchase_order table. The line_items table also refers to the stock table for information of the stocked items:

```
Create table customers (
    custno         number,
    custname       varchar2(50),
    address1       varchar2(100),
    address2       varchar2(100),
    city           varchar2(40),
    state          char(2),
    zip            varchar2(10),
    phone1         varchar2(20),
    phone2         varchar2(20),
    primary key    (custno));

create table purchase_order (
    pono           number,
    custno         number references customers(custno),
    orderdate      date,
    shiptoaddress1    varchar2(100),
    shiptoaddress2    varchar2(100),
    shiptocity     varchar2(40),
    shiptostate    char(2),
    shiptozip      varchar2(10),
    primary key      (pono));

create table stocks (
    stockno        number,
    stockname      varchar2(100),
    price          number,
    primary key    (stockno));

create table line_items (
    lineitemno     number,
    pono           number references  purchase_order(pono),
    stockno        number references  stocks(stockno),
    quantity       number,
    primary key    (pono,lineitemno));
```

custno	custname	address1	address2	city	state	zip	phone1	phone2
1	John Doe	2 Foothill Dr.	NULL	Orlando	FL	32817	407-555-1296	NULL
2	Mike Jordan	36 College Park Avenue	NULL	R. Shores	CA	95054	415-555-7620	NULL

pono	custno	orderdate	shiptoaddress1	shiptoaddress2	shipcity	shipstate	shipzip
101	1	sysdate	18 Madison St.	NULL	NY	NY	92312
102	2	sysdate	5 Church St.	NULL	Miami	FL	39815

stockno	stockname	price
1001	Intel Pentium	2100.00
1002	NC-workstation	220.50
1003	Sun Ultra	6900.00

lineitemno	pono	stockno	quantity
01	101	1001	25
02	101	1002	50
01	102	1002	20
02	102	1003	5

Although you can write applications using a 3GL like C++, the preceding model would require performing several complex joins to obtain the desired result. However, this system can be simplified using an object-based approach, as shown in the following code:

> **NOTE**
>
> This case study shows how to convert an entity-relationship model into an object-relational design. The actual objects are created using SQL. Although applications can be written using C++ in either the relational or object-relational approach, the object-relational approach simplifies the writing of such applications.

```
create type stocks_t as object (
    stockno         number,
    stockname       varchar2(100),
    price           number);
/
create type address_t as object (
    address1        varchar2(100),
    address2        varchar2(100),
    city            varchar2(40),
    state           char(2),
    zip             varchar2(10));
/

create type phone_t as varray(10) of varchar2(20);
/
```

```
create or replace type customer_t as object (
    custno          number,
    custname        varchar2(50),
    address         address_t,
    phone_list      phonc_t,
    po_list         po_reflist_t,
    member function add_po(poref REF purchase_order_t) return
➥po_reflist_t);
/

create type line_item_t as object (
    lineitemno      number,
    stockref        ref  stocks_t,
    quantity        number);
/

create type line_item_list_t as table  of  line_item_t;
/

create or replace type purchase_order_t as object (
    pono            number,
    custref         ref customers_t,
    orderdate       date,
    line_item_list      line_item_list_t,
    shipto_addr  address_t);
/

create type po_ref_list as table of REF purchase_order_t;
/
```

Object-Oriented Databases

For most corporate developers, a large portion of our daily life is dedicated to providing our customers with the best tools to gather, retrieve, and analyze their data. Data management is usually the center of IT strategic planning and development. It is almost impossible to find a business that does not have some form of database system.

This chapter starts with an introduction to Object-Oriented Databases and the Object Database Management System (ODBMS). In this chapter, we develop a simple application using the Object Data Management Group (ODMG, formerly Object Database Management Group) standard C++ interface to object databases. This chapter concludes with discussions about some of the ODBMS design and implementation issues.

Overview of ODBMS

An Object Database Management System (ODBMS) provides several key features:

- **Persistence:** Data is stored in a nonvolatile medium and is consistent among different applications and sessions.
- **Transaction:** Data integrity is maintained because a set of operations in a transaction is executed as an atomic unit.
- **Concurrency:** Data can be accessed by multiple applications simultaneously. Locking mechanisms are employed to ensure that data does not become corrupt or inconsistent as it is accessed by different applications at the same time.
- **Query:** Data can be queried using one or more query languages. The most popular query language for relational databases is the Structured Query Language (SQL).
- **Others:** Other features include recovery, fault tolerance, and data replication.

Relational Database Management Systems (RDBMS) currently dominate the database marketplace because of their reliability and maturity. In an RDBMS, data is organized into tables that model the entities of an application. Each table contains a set of records, or rows, that represent the instances of the entity. Columns in a table correspond to the attributes of the entity. Each column has a type defined by the RDBMS.

A table has a *primary key* that uniquely identifies each record. For instance, an invoice can be identified by an invoice number such that no two invoices have the same invoice number. Therefore, invoice numbers are the primary key of an invoice table. A primary key does not have to be contained in a single column. For example, if no student has the same surname and first name as any other student in the same school, the *combination* of a student's surname and first name uniquely identifies the student.

Relationships among entities are represented with the concept of *foreign keys*. If each invoice must be issued to a customer, we can define the customer number column of the invoice table as a foreign key to the customer table.

Data in an RDBMS is usually accessed using SQL queries or other vendor-defined methods. Applications are often written in programming languages that are independent of the RDBMS. This approach allows a single RDBMS to be accessed by applications written in different programming languages such as C++ and COBOL. Applications must provide the mapping between their language data types and the database data types. For example, to map a C++ class Person to a table, the application may map each member variable to a column in the table:

```
class Person
{
    string  mSurname;
    string  mFirstName;
    int     mAge;
}
```

Although it is still in its early development stage, the ODBMS provides the following advantages over the RDBMS:

- **Tight integration to object-oriented programming languages.** An ODBMS provides an interface between the database and the programming language. This relationship enables application developers to create and access objects in a database from within the native programming language.

- **Flexible data type definitions.** An ODBMS supports the creation and manipulation of user-defined data types. The ODBMS is capable of directly storing instances of application object types (classes) defined in a native programming language.

- **Automatic networks of objects maintenance.** An ODBMS supports the storage, retrieval, and navigation of networks of objects. Each object in a network is related to one or more other objects. A relationship can be one-to-one, one-to-many, or many-to-many using database-assigned object identifiers.

Each ODBMS vendor provides an ODBMS implementation that serves its target market best. This arrangement provides close modeling of application domains to the database implementation; it also enables the customers to design better applications that can take full advantage of an ODBMS. A side effect of having different implementations is, of course, that a user is tied to a particular vendor. Porting applications from one ODBMS implementation to another is extremely difficult, if possible at all. Customers worry about being locked into a proprietary implementation of a particular product. Because ODBMS vendors are relatively small and consequently vulnerable to market changes, relying on a particular product is obviously not the best investment. Clearly, without a standard, the market acceptance of ODBMS would remain poor.

18

OBJECT-ORIENTED DATABASES

The ODMG Standard

In recognition of the need for an ODBMS standard, the Object Database Management Group (ODMG) was formed in 1991 to define and promote a standard for object storage. Its members currently include many major object database vendors and other interested parties. The ODMG standard defines database bindings for three of the most popular object-oriented programming languages: C++, Java, and Smalltalk. Using the ODMG language bindings, developers can incorporate into applications the ability to manipulate persistent objects in native language syntax.

In the following sections, we implement a very simple invoicing program that allows us to manage a stock of inventory and create invoices. We start with a normal C++ application without any data persistence; then we improve it by adding the ability to store and retrieve data from an object database using the ODMG standard C++ binding.

A C++ Invoicing Application

Listings 18.1 through 18.6 show the complete code for a trivial invoicing application. In this application, I make three variations in the conventional coding practice. First, all members of classes in this example are declared `public` so that the code is easier to follow. In real-world applications, member variables are usually declared `private`, and a set of functions are implemented to access them. Second, the application uses compiler-generated copy constructors and assignment operators because there is no need to provide our own in this sample application. It is also always a good practice to define those functions explicitly. The last deviation from standard coding practice is that there is very little error-handling code. The sample application is admittedly less than robust without comprehensive error-handling capabilities. The only reason I used these less conventional coding methods in this example is to reduce the amount of code to better demonstrate the core functionality of the program.

The application is divided into six listings so that we can keep the discussion of each component close to the code. To compile the application, we must add all the files into a project. Let's take a look at the `Product` class shown in Listing 18.1.

LISTING 18.1. A TRIVIAL INVOICING APPLICATION: THE PRODUCT CLASS

```
//===============================================================
// Product.h - Product class definition
//===============================================================

#ifndef __Product_H
#define __Product_H
```

```cpp
#include <iostream>
#include <string>
using namespace std;

class Product
{
public:
    // Constructors and destructor
    Product();
    Product(const string& newID, const string& newName, const int
➡newPrice);
    virtual ~Product();

    // Member variables
    string    mID;
    string    mName;
    int       mPrice;

    // Overloaded insertion operator
    friend ostream& operator<<(ostream& os, const Product* const
➡aProduct);
};

#endif

//==============================================================
// Product.cpp - Product class implementation
//==============================================================

#include "Product.h"

// Constructors and destructor
Product::Product()
: mID(""), mName(""), mPrice(0)
{}

Product::Product(const string& newID, const string& newName, const int
➡newPrice)
: mID(newID), mName(newName), mPrice(newPrice)
{}

Product::~Product()
{}

// Overloaded insertion operator
ostream& operator<<(ostream& os, const Product* const aProduct)
{
    os << aProduct->mID << "\t" << aProduct->mName << "\t" << aProduct-
➡>mPrice;
    return os;
}
```

The `Product` class is relatively simple. The string class defined in the standard library is used to store product ID and name values. Compared to the C-style null-terminated character strings, the C++ string class is much easier to use and is more powerful. The string class is defined in header file `<string>` in `namespace std` and provides a set of functions to manipulate character strings.

Two constructors are defined. A default constructor simply initializes all member variables to blank or 0. The second constructor is used to create a product with its member variables initialized to values passed as function parameters. The default constructor is not explicitly used in our application. It is provided so that we can create a list of products; the C++ standard containers require the element type to have a default constructor. You learn more about this when we look at the product map class.

An overloaded insertion operator is defined to take a pointer to a product object as a parameter and to print member variables of the product object. I decided to pass product objects using pointers because this will help in the discussion of some of the ODMG features later.

An invoice typically consists of a header and a list of items. Each item specifies the product sold and the quantity ordered. The `InvoiceItem` class is shown in Listing 18.2.

LISTING 18.2. A TRIVIAL INVOICING APPLICATION: THE `InvoiceItem` CLASS

```
//===============================================================
// InvoiceItem.h - Invoice item class definition
//===============================================================

#ifndef __InvoiceItem_H
#define __InvoiceItem_H

#include <iostream>
using namespace std;

#include "Product.h"

class Invoice;
class InvoiceItem
{
public:
    // Constructors and destructor
    InvoiceItem();
    InvoiceItem(Product* pProduct, const int newQuantity);
    virtual ~InvoiceItem();

    // Member variables
    Invoice*    mpInvoice;    // Pointer to the associated invoice object
```

```
    Product*      mpProduct;     // Pointer to the product object
    int           mQuantity;     // Quantity sold

    // Other member functions
    // Get the total amount of the item
    int             GetTotal()     const;

    // Overloaded insertion operator
    friend ostream& operator<<(ostream& os, const InvoiceItem&
➥anInvoiceItem);
};

#endif

//================================================================
// InvoiceItem.cpp - Invoice item class implementation
//================================================================

#include "InvoiceItem.h"

// Constructors and destructor
InvoiceItem::InvoiceItem()
: mpProduct(0), mQuantity(0)
{}

InvoiceItem::InvoiceItem(Product* pProduct, const int newQuantity)
: mpProduct(pProduct), mQuantity(newQuantity)
{}

// Destructor
// Do not delete the product object
InvoiceItem::~InvoiceItem()
{}

// Get item total amount
int    InvoiceItem::GetTotal()    const
{
    return mpProduct->mPrice * mQuantity;
}

// Overloaded insertion operator
ostream& operator<<(ostream& os, const InvoiceItem& anInvoiceItem)
{
    os << anInvoiceItem.mpProduct << "\t" << anInvoiceItem.mQuantity <<
➥"\t"
        << anInvoiceItem.GetTotal();
    return os;
}
```

The `InvoiceItem` class has three member variables. The first is a pointer to its parent `Invoice` object, which we will discuss later. The second is a pointer to a product, and the third is the sale quantity. We could actually store the product object instead of a pointer—both methods are valid. The advantage of storing a pointer is that it allows us to reference a product in a product list, and it establishes a relationship between an invoice item and a product. If we decide to change the product's name, the invoice item will automatically have the updated product name. This helps us maintain data integrity.

Storing the object, on the other hand, does not maintain the relationship between the product sold and a list of available products. Therefore, any changes to the product do not affect the invoice item.

> **NOTE**
>
> It is often desirable to create a snapshot of product information at the time the invoice is created and to store this snapshot with the invoice. If we later reprint the invoice, we will have exactly the same product information as at the time of sale. In this example, however, we are more interested in maintaining the relationship between an invoice item and a product.

A default constructor is also defined explicitly (although it is not used in the project). This constructor becomes useful if we need to create a list of empty invoice items (the C++ standard container list calls its member's default constructor to allocate memory). The destructor does nothing more than the standard cleanup; we do not want to delete the related product object when the invoice item is deleted.

A member function `GetTotal()` is provided to calculate the total value of the item. We could create a member variable to store this value, but doing so would be redundant. It could also cause data inconsistency when the price of a product changes.

An invoice item can be printed using the overloaded insertion operator. This operator prints information about the sold product, the sale quantity, and the total value.

With the `InvoiceItem` class fully defined, we can turn our attention to the `Invoice` class. Listing 18.3 shows the `Invoice` class definition and implementation.

LISTING 18.3. A TRIVIAL INVOICING APPLICATION: THE `INVOICE` CLASS

```
//==============================================================
// Invoice.h - Invoice class definition
//==============================================================

#ifndef __Invoice_H
```

```
#define __Invoice_H

#include <iostream>
#include <string>
#include <list>
using namespace std;

#include "InvoiceItem.h"

typedef list<InvoiceItem *>               InvoiceItemList;
typedef InvoiceItemList::const_iterator   IIL_CItor;
typedef InvoiceItemList::iterator         IIL_Itor;

class Invoice
{
public:
    // Constructors and destructor
    Invoice();
    Invoice(const long mID, const string& newDate);
    virtual ~Invoice();

    // Member variables
    long            mID;        // Invoice ID
    string          mDate;      // Invoice date
    InvoiceItemList mItems;     // A list of pointers to invoice items

    void AddItem(InvoiceItem* pItem);    // Add an item to item list
    int  GetTotal()     const;           // Invoice total amount

    // Overloaded insertion operator
    friend ostream& operator<<(ostream& os, const Invoice& anInvoice);
};

#endif

//================================================================
// Invoice.cpp - Invoice class implementation
//================================================================

#include "Invoice.h"

// Constructors and destructor
Invoice::Invoice()
: mID(0), mDate("")
{}

Invoice::Invoice(const long newID, const string& newDate)
: mID(newID), mDate(newDate)
{}

Invoice::~Invoice()
```

18

OBJECT-ORIENTED
DATABASES

continues

LISTING 18.3. CONTINUED

```cpp
{
    // Delete all invoiced items
    for (IIL_Itor i = mItems.begin(); i != mItems.end(); ++i)
        delete *i;
}

// Add an item to item list
void Invoice::AddItem(InvoiceItem* pItem)
{
    mItems.push_back(pItem);    // Use standard list push_back() function
    pItem->mpInvoice = this;    // Associate the item to the current
➥invoice
}

// Get total invoice amount
int Invoice::GetTotal()      const
{
    int intTotal = 0;

    // Iterate through the item list and calculate the total
    for (IIL_CItor i = mItems.begin(); i != mItems.end(); ++i)
        intTotal += (*i)->GetTotal();

    return intTotal;
}

// Overloaded insertion operator
ostream& operator<<(ostream& os, const Invoice& anInvoice)
{
    // Print invoice header
    os << "Invoice: " << anInvoice.mID << "\n"
       << "Date    : " << anInvoice.mDate << "\n";

    // Print all invoice items
    for (IIL_CItor ci = anInvoice.mItems.begin();
                   ci != anInvoice.mItems.end(); ++ci)
        os << **ci << "\n";

    // And the total amount
    os << "Total: " << anInvoice.GetTotal() << "\n";

    return os;
}
```

An invoice has an invoice number, or an ID, that uniquely identifies the invoice. Other member variables are the date when the invoice is created and a list of items. There are two possible ways to associate items to invoices: We could store the actual item objects, or we could store pointers to externally stored item objects. In terms of class relationship, there is not much difference between these options because invoice items cannot exist without an associated invoice. In practice, storing items externally makes it easy to construct queries. For example, if we want a stock movement report, we can search all invoice items to get a list of all invoice items related to a particular product. In this example, we store a list of pointers to items in an invoice and let the item objects reside externally.

When an invoice is created, an empty invoice item list is constructed using the default constructor of the standard list class. When an invoice is deleted, all items are destroyed by the invoice's destructor because items cannot exist without an invoice.

The AddItem() member function simply adds a pointer to an invoice item to the item list. This action associates an item to an invoice. It also sets the mpInvoice member variable of an item to point to the invoice. The GetTotal() member function simply adds up the sale amount of all items and returns the result. The overloaded insertion operator prints the invoice ID, date, and all items.

Now all the fundamental classes for our invoicing application are defined. Our application, however, is more than just a collection of unrelated products and invoices. It must organize them in such a way that those objects are easily accessible. For example, when we create an invoice, we need to know whether a product exists and where to find it. This can be achieved by creating a list of all available products. It is also desirable that a product can be accessed by its ID. Listing 18.4 defines a product list.

LISTING 18.4. A TRIVIAL INVOICING APPLICATION: THE PRODUCT MAP

```
//===========================================================
// ProductMap.h - Product map class definition
//        This class encapsulates the product list and associated
//        functions.
//===========================================================

#ifndef __ProductMap_H
#define __ProductMap_H

#include <iostream>
#include <string>
#include <map>
using namespace std;

#include "Product.h"

typedef map<string, Product *>          ProductPtrMap;
typedef ProductPtrMap::const_iterator   PPM_CItor;
typedef ProductPtrMap::iterator         PPM_Itor;
```

continues

LISTING 18.4. CONTINUED

```cpp
class ProductMap
{
public:
    // Constructor and Destructor
    ProductMap();
    virtual ~ProductMap();

    // Member functions
    void        Add();                  // Add products to the list
➥interactively
    void        Edit();             // Edit products
    void        Delete();           // Delete products
    Product* Find(const string& id);    // Find a product with a given ID
    bool        IsEmpty()    const;     // Check if the map is empty

    ProductPtrMap    mProducts;     // A map of pointers to products

    // Overloaded insertion operator
    friend ostream& operator<<(ostream& os, const ProductMap&
➥aProductMap);
};

#endif

//=============================================================
// ProductMap.cpp - Product map class implementation
//=============================================================

#include <iostream>
using namespace std;

#include "ProductMap.h"

// Constructor
ProductMap::ProductMap()
{
    // Fill list with products
    mProducts["OS-WinNT4"] = new Product("OS-WinNT4", "Windows NT 4.0",
➥500);
    mProducts["OS-Linux"]  = new Product("OS-Linux", "Linux", 20);
    mProducts["OS-MacOS8"] = new Product("OS-MacOS8", "MacOS 8.0", 300);
    mProducts["OS-Win98"]  = new Product("OS-Win98", "Windows 98", 89);
}

// Destructor
ProductMap::~ProductMap()
{
    // Delete all products pointed to by the map elements
    for (PPM_Itor i = mProducts.begin(); i != mProducts.end(); ++i)
```

```
            delete i->second;
}

// Add products to the list interactively
void ProductMap::Add()
{
    string        strID;
    string        strName;
    int           intPrice;

    cout << "Add Products:\n";
    while(1)
    {
        cout << "ID (Type 0 to finish): ";
        getline(cin, strID);
        if (strID == "0")     break;

        cout << "Name                 : ";
        getline(cin, strName);
        cout << "Price                : ";
        cin  >> intPrice;
        cin.ignore();

        mProducts[strID] = new Product(strID, strName, intPrice);
        cout << "Product added to the list\n\n";
    }
}

// Edit Products
void ProductMap::Edit()
{
    PPM_Itor    i;
    string      strID;
    string      strName;
    int         intPrice;

    // Use the standard map class find() function to find a product
    // and edit it if found
    cout << "Edit Products:\n";
    while(1)
    {
        cout << "ID (Type 0 to finish): ";
        getline(cin, strID);
        if (strID == "0")     break;
        i = mProducts.find(strID);

        if (i != mProducts.end())
        {
            cout << "Editing product: " << i->second << "\n";
            cout << "New name : ";
            getline(cin, strName);
```

18

OBJECT-ORIENTED
DATABASES

continues

LISTING 18.4. CONTINUED

```
//          cout << "New price: ";
            cin  >> intPrice;
            cin.ignore();

            i->second->mName = strName;
            i->second->mPrice = intPrice;

            cout << "Product modified: " << i->second << "\n";
        }
        else
            cout << "Product not found!\n";
    }
}

// Delete Products
void ProductMap::Delete()
{
    string         strID;

    // Use the standard map class find() function to find a product
    // and edit it if found
    cout << "Delete Products:\n";
    while(1)
    {
        cout << "ID (Type 0 to finish): ";
        getline(cin, strID);
        if (strID == "0")    break;

        if (mProducts.find(strID) != mProducts.end())
        {
            mProducts.erase(strID);
            cout << "Product deleted\n";
        }
        else
            cout << "Product not found!\n";
    }
}

// Find a product with a given ID
// Input : Product ID
// Output: if found, a pointer to the product
//         otherwise 0
Product* ProductMap::Find(const string& id)
{
    // Use the standard map class find() function to find a product
    // and return a pointer to it
    PPM_CItor ci = mProducts.find(id);
    if (ci != mProducts.end())
        return ci->second;
```

```
        else
            return 0;
}

// Check if the map is empty
bool ProductMap::IsEmpty()    const
{
    return mProducts.empty();
}

// Overloaded insertion operator
ostream& operator<<(ostream& os, const ProductMap& aProductMap)
{
    // Iterate through the map and print all products pointed to by
    // the elements in the map
    os << "Product Listing:\n";
    for (PPM_CItor ci = aProductMap.mProducts.begin();
                    ci != aProductMap.mProducts.end(); ++ci)
        os << ci->second << "\n";
    return os;
}
```

The C++ standard container map allows for the direct access of objects by their key values and is perfect for our product list. So we use it to hold pointers to available products. A pointer to a product can be accessed using the ID of the product. When the map is destroyed, all product objects are deleted. Our product map extends the standard map by providing a set of functions required in our application to maintain products.

The default constructor populates the product map with four products. The Add() function allows us to add products to the map interactively. The Edit() and Delete() functions can be used to modify product objects in the map and to remove product objects from the map, respectively. We can use the Find() function to get a pointer to a product with a given ID. The IsEmpty() function simply returns a Boolean value indicating whether or not there is a product in the map. At last, the overloaded insertion operator prints all products in the map.

Now let's define an invoice list so that invoices can be accessed. Listing 18.5 shows the invoice list for our application.

LISTING 18.5. A TRIVIAL INVOICING APPLICATION: THE INVOICELIST CLASS

```
//================================================================
// InvoiceList.h - Invoice list class definition
//          This class encapsulates the invoice list and associated
//          functions.
//================================================================
```

continues

LISTING 18.5. CONTINUED

```cpp
#ifndef __InvoiceList_H
#define __InvoiceList_H

#include <iostream>
#include <list>
using namespace std;

#include "Invoice.h"
#include "ProductMap.h"

typedef list<Invoice *>                   InvoicePtrList;
typedef InvoicePtrList::const_iterator    IPL_CItor;
typedef InvoicePtrList::iterator          IPL_Itor;

class InvoiceList
{
public:
    // Destructor
    virtual ~InvoiceList();

    // Enter invoices interactively.  A reference to a product map
    // is passed to link the invoice items with products.
    void Add(ProductMap& PMap);

    // Invoice list implemented with a standard list
    InvoicePtrList    mInvoices;

    // Overloaded insertion operator
    friend ostream& operator<<(ostream& os, const InvoiceList&
anInvoiceList);

private:
    // Enter items to an invoice interactively, a reference to a product
➥map
    // is passed to verify the invoice items.
    void AddItems(ProductMap& PMap, Invoice* pInvoice);
};

#endif

//================================================================
// InvoiceList.cpp - Invoice list class implementation
//================================================================

#include <iostream>
using namespace std;

#include "InvoiceList.h"
```

```
// Destructor
InvoiceList::~InvoiceList()
{
    // Delete all invoices pointed to by elements in the list
    for (IPL_Itor i = mInvoices.begin(); i != mInvoices.end(); ++i)
        delete *i;
}

// Enter invoices interactively
void InvoiceList::Add(ProductMap& PMap)
{
    if (PMap.IsEmpty())
    {
        cerr << "No product available, "
             << "please enter products and try again!" << endl;
        return;
    }

    Invoice*    pInvoice;
    Long        lngID;
    string      strDate;

    cout << "Add Invoices:\n";
    while(1)
    {
        cout << "ID (Type 0 to finish): ";
        cin  >> lngID;
        cin.ignore();
        if (lngID == 0)          break;

        cout << "Date                : ";
        getline(cin, strDate);

        pInvoice = new Invoice(lngID, strDate);
        mInvoices.push_back(pInvoice);

        AddItems(PMap, pInvoice);
        cout << "Invoice added to the list\n\n";
    }
}

// Enter items to an invoice interactively
// Input : PMap - A list (implemented as a map) of available products
//         pInvoice - Pointer to the invoice
void InvoiceList::AddItems(ProductMap& PMap, Invoice* pInvoice)
{
    InvoiceItem*    pItem;
    Product*        pProduct;
    string          strProductID;
    int             intQty;
```

continues

LISTING 18.5. CONTINUED

```
    cout << "Add Invoice Items:\n";
    while(1)
    {
        do
        {
            cout << "Product ID (Type 0 to finish): ";
            getline(cin, strProductID);
            if (strProductID == "0")         return;
        } while ((pProduct = PMap.Find(strProductID)) == 0);

        cout << "Quantity                       : ";
        cin  >> intQty;
        cin.ignore();

        pItem = new InvoiceItem(pProduct, intQty);
        pInvoice->AddItem(pItem);
        cout << "Item added\n";
    }
}

// Overloaded insertion operator
ostream& operator<<(ostream& os, const InvoiceList& anInvoiceList)
{
    // Print all invoices pointed to by the elements in the list
    os << "Invoice Listing:\n";
    for (IPL_CItor ci = anInvoiceList.mInvoices.begin();
                    ci != anInvoiceList.mInvoices.end(); ++ci)
        os << **ci << "\n";
    return os;
}
```

Normally, we want to be able to enter new invoices, modify existing ones, and search for invoices by their IDs. They are almost identical to the corresponding functions in the Product map. To simplify this example, I will only implement the invoice creation function. The C++ standard container list is therefore chosen to store the invoice list.

The Add() function allows us to enter invoices and add them to the invoice list. It takes a reference to the Product map so that we can link invoice items to product objects. The overloaded insertion operator prints all invoices in the list. The destructor takes care of the deletion of all invoice objects.

So far, we have implemented almost all the features of our fairly small application. The last task is to create a driver program to link them together. Listing 18.6 shows the main function of our application.

LISTING 18.6. A TRIVIAL INVOICING APPLICATION: THE MAIN PROGRAM

```cpp
//==============================================================
// main.cpp - The driver program for the application
//==============================================================

#include <iostream>
using namespace std;

#include "ProductMap.h"
#include "InvoiceList.h"

int main()
{
    int            intChoice = 0;
    ProductMap     Products;    // Construct an empty product map
    InvoiceList    Invoices;    // Construct an empty invoice list

    do
    {
        cout << "\nA Trival Invoice Entry Program\n\n";
        cout << "  1. Enter invoices\n";
        cout << "  2. Print invoice list\n";
        cout << "  3. Add products\n";
        cout << "  4. Edit product\n";
        cout << "  5. Delete products\n";
        cout << "  6. Print product list\n";
        cout << "  9. Exit\n\n";
        cout << "Enter your choice: ";
        cin  >> intChoice;
        cin.ignore();
        cout << endl;

        switch(intChoice)
        {
        case 1:    Invoices.Add(Products);        break;
        case 2:    cout << Invoices << endl;      break;
        case 3:    Products.Add();                break;
        case 4:    Products.Edit();               break;
        case 5:    Products.Delete();             break;
        case 6:    cout << Products << endl;      break;
        case 9:    cout << "Bye!\n\n";            break;
        default:   cout << "Please select 1, 2, 3, 4, 5, 6 or 9.\n";
        }
    } while (intChoice != 9);

    return 0;
}
```

The `main()` function simply presents a menu so that we can perform various operations. Let's take a test drive.

```
A Trival Invoice Entry Program

    1. Enter invoices
    2. Print invoice list
    3. Add products
    4. Edit product
    5. Delete products
    6. Print product list
    9. Exit

Enter your choice: 3

Add Products:
ID (Type 0 to finish): Compiler-MSVC5
Name                   : Microsoft Visual C++ 5.0
Price                  : 500
Product added to the list

ID (Type 0 to finish): Compiler-BCB
Name                   : Borland C++ Builder
Price                  : 520
Product added to the list

ID (Type 0 to finish): 0

A Trival Invoice Entry Program

    1. Enter invoices
    2. Print invoice list
    3. Add products
    4. Edit product
    5. Delete products
    6. Print product list
    9. Exit

Enter your choice: 6

Product Listing:
Compiler-BCB    Borland C++ Builder     520
Compiler-MSVC5  Microsoft Visual C++ 5.0          500
OS-Linux        Linux    20
OS-MacOS8       MacOS 8.0          300
OS-Win98        Windows 98         89
OS-WinNT4       Windows NT 4.0   500

A Trival Invoice Entry Program

    1. Enter invoices
```

```
    2. Print invoice list
    3. Add products
    4. Edit product
    5. Delete products
    6. Print product list
    9. Exit

Enter your choice: 4

Edit Products:
ID (Type 0 to finish): Compiler-BCB
Editing product: Compiler-BCB   Borland C++ Builder    520
New name : Borland C++ Builder 3.0
New price: 550
Product modified: Compiler-BCB  Borland C++ Builder 3.0 550
ID (Type 0 to finish): 0

A Trival Invoice Entry Program

    1. Enter invoices
    2. Print invoice list
    3. Add products
    4. Edit product
    5. Delete products
    6. Print product list
    9. Exit

Enter your choice: 5

Delete Products:
ID (Type 0 to finish): Compiler-BCB
Product deleted
ID (Type 0 to finish): 0

A Trival Invoice Entry Program

    1. Enter invoices
    2. Print invoice list
    3. Add products
    4. Edit product
    5. Delete products
    6. Print product list
    9. Exit

Enter your choice: 6

Product Listing:
Compiler-MSVC5  Microsoft Visual C++ 5.0          500
OS-Linux        Linux    20
OS-MacOS8       MacOS 8.0        300
OS-Win98        Windows 98       89
```

```
OS-WinNT4        Windows NT 4.0  500


A Trival Invoice Entry Program

    1. Enter invoices
    2. Print invoice list
    3. Add products
    4. Edit product
    5. Delete products
    6. Print product list
    9. Exit

Enter your choice: 1

Add Invoices:
ID (Type 0 to finish): 1
Date               : 07/24/98
Add Invoice Items:
Product ID (Type 0 to finish): OS-Linux
Quantity               : 1
Item added
Product ID (Type 0 to finish): OS-MacOS8
Quantity               : 10
Item added
Product ID (Type 0 to finish): OS-Win98
Quantity               : 6
Item added
Product ID (Type 0 to finish): 0
Invoice added to the list

ID (Type 0 to finish): 2
Date               : 07/25/98
Add Invoice Items:
Product ID (Type 0 to finish): OS-WinNT4
Quantity               : 2
Item added
Product ID (Type 0 to finish): OS-Win98
Quantity               : 50
Item added
Product ID (Type 0 to finish): Compiler-MSVC5
Quantity               : 5
Item added
Product ID (Type 0 to finish): OS-MacOS8
Quantity               : 3
Item added
Product ID (Type 0 to finish): 0
Invoice added to the list

ID (Type 0 to finish): 0
```

```
A Trival Invoice Entry Program

  1. Enter invoices
  2. Print invoice list
  3. Add products
  4. Edit product
  5. Delete products
  6. Print product list
  9. Exit

Enter your choice: 2

Invoice Listing:
Invoice: 1
Date    : 07/24/98
OS-Linux        Linux    20      1       20
OS-MacOS8       MacOS 8.0        300     10      3000
OS-Win98        Windows 98       89      6       534
Total: 3554

Invoice: 2
Date    : 07/25/98
OS-WinNT4       Windows NT 4.0   500     2       1000
OS-Win98        Windows 98       89      50      4450
Compiler-MSVC5  Microsoft Visual C++ 5.0        500     5       2500
OS-MacOS8       MacOS 8.0        300     3       900
Total: 8850

A Trival Invoice Entry Program

  1. Enter invoices
  2. Print invoice list
  3. Add products
  4. Edit product
  5. Delete products
  6. Print product list
  9. Exit

Enter your choice: 9

Bye!
```

First, we added two compilers to our product map. Next, we modified a product and then deleted it. After checking our product map, we created two invoices and displayed our invoice list.

Our little application does all we want except one thing: All products and invoices are destroyed when the program exits. It would be of little use if that is all our application can do. We need to add the ability to store data persistently to this application.

18

OBJECT-ORIENTED
DATABASES

Data Persistence

To make an object persistent, we need to derive it from the d_Object class:

```
class MyClass : public d_Object
{}
```

ODMG provides a subset of C++ primitive types, as shown in Table 18.1.

TABLE 18.1. ODMG PRIMITIVE TYPES

ODMG Type	*Size*	*Description*
d_Char	8 bits	ASCII character
d_Boolean	Implementation defined	Either d_True or d_False
d_Short	16 bits	Signed short integer
d_UShort	16 bits	Unsigned short integer
d_Long	32 bits	Signed long integer
d_ULong	32 bits	Unsigned long integer
d_Float	32 bit	IEEE Standard 754-1985; single-precision floating-point number
d_Double	32 bit	IEEE Standard 754-1985; double-precision floating-point number

Notice that the C++ int and unsigned int types are not mapped to ODMG because the C++ integer sizes vary among different operating systems and machines.

Let's start by modifying our Product class to make it persistent. Listing 18.7 shows a persistent Product class.

> **NOTE**
>
> The remaining listings in this chapter show an application using the ODMG standard C++ binding. They cannot be compiled with only a C++ compiler. If you want to test this application, you must obtain an ODBMS that supports the ODMG standard; you must also make implementation-specific modifications to the listings.

LISTING 18.7. PERSISTENT PRODUCT CLASS DEFINITION

```cpp
//================================================================
// Product.h -  Persistent Product class definition
//================================================================

#ifndef __Product_H
#define __Product_H

#include <iostream.h>
#include <odmg.h>          // ODMG header file
#include <d_String.h>      // ODMG d_String header file

class Product : public d_Object
{
public:
    // Constructors and destructor
    Product();
    Product(const d_String& newID,
            const d_String& newName,
            const d_Long newPrice);
    virtual ~Product();

    // Member variables
    d_String    mID;        // product ID
    d_String    mName;      // product name
    d_UShort    mPrice;     // product price

    // Overloaded insertion operator
    friend ostream& operator<<(ostream& os, const Product* const
➥aProduct);
};

#endif
```

First, we no longer use the namespace std because ODMG does not yet support the concept of the C++ namespace. The Product class is now derived from the ODMG d_Object class. To use the ODMG-specific features, we must include an odmg.h file supplied by vendors.

> **NOTE**
>
> The names of the ODMG header files are not specified in the standard and vary among ODBMS implementations.

In the original Product class (refer to Listing 18.1), the mID and mName member variables
were defined as C++ standard strings. ODMG does not yet directly support the use of
C++ strings. Instead, it defines a d_String class that serves the purpose of storing vari-
able-length character strings in a database. The reason for this is historical: When the
ODMG standard was first defined, there was no standard C++ library. We will define
those member variables as d_Strings. To use the d_String class, we must include the
d_String.h header. The mPrice member variable is also changed to be the ODMG
d_UShort type.

Database Schemas and Schema Capture Tools

To store objects in a database, we must create a description of the persistent classes so
that the database knows how to store those objects. This description is called a *schema*. A
database creates a data dictionary from a schema. Various data access tools—such as
form generators, query optimizers, and report writers—communicate with the database
using the schema.

A normal C++ compiler does not know anything about object databases. It cannot create
a database schema, nor can it generate code for accessing objects in a database. In the
ODMG standard, the C++ header file for a persistent-capable class must be processed
by a schema capture tool. Figure 18.1 shows a complete application compilation and
linking procedure.

A schema caption tool parses the C++ class definitions and generates a schema for the
database. In addition, the tool also generates enhanced C++ header and source files
that help C++ compilers understand database operations. These files can be compiled
by a normal C++ compiler. Class implementation source files must include (using
#include) the enhanced C++ header files instead of the original header files. A linker
then links all object files and database vendor-supplied libraries to create an application executable file.

FIGURE 18.1.

The application generation procedure.

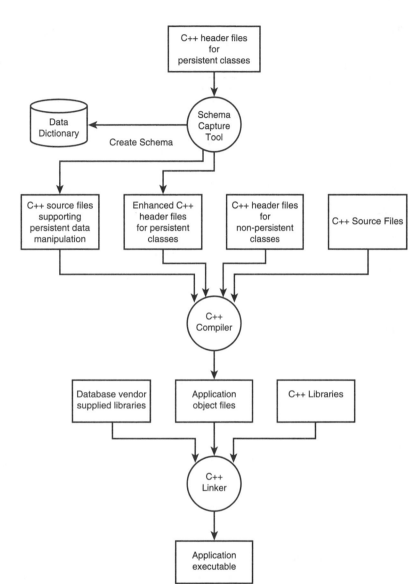

The Product class implementation is modified as shown in Listing 18.8.

LISTING 18.8. THE PERSISTENT PRODUCT CLASS IMPLEMENTATION

```cpp
//==============================================================
// ProductSrc.cpp - Persistent Product class implementation
//==============================================================

#include <odmg.h>            // ODMG header file
#include "Product.hxx"

// Constructors and destructor
Product::Product()
: mID(""), mName(""), mPrice(0)
{}

Product::Product(const d_String& newID,
                 const d_String& newName,
                 const d_Long newPrice)
: mID(newID), mName(newName), mPrice(newPrice)
{}

Product::~Product()
{}

// Overloaded insertion operator
ostream& operator<<(ostream& os, const Product* const aProduct)
{
    os << (const char *)aProduct->mID << "\t"
       << (const char *)aProduct->mName << "\t" << aProduct->mPrice;
    return os;
}
```

Recall that the schema processor is likely to generate implementation-dependent new Product header and implementation files. We rename our Product class implementation source file from Product.cpp to ProductSrc.cpp because the schema processor may generate a Product.cpp file that defines various support functions for the Product class. We also include a generated class header file that might be named Product.hxx by the schema processor. The default constructor and destructor remain unchanged. Because d_String variables can be initialized with a C++ character array, we can initialize mID and mName to an empty string "". Although the default constructor for d_String also initializes an instance to NULL, I would rather do it explicitly. This is mainly a matter of personal preference; in my experience with RDBMS, NULL is not the same as an empty string. The user-defined constructor now takes d_String and d_UShort parameters and calls the d_String's copy constructor to initialize mID and mName.

The overloaded insertion operator << is changed to cast mID and mName to const char * before printing them. We do this because the d_String class does not support the C++ standard iostream interface.

Before turning our attention to the Invoice and InvoiceItem classes, let's first look at three concepts: collections, iterators, and relationships.

Collections

A *collection* is a set of objects of the same type. The C++ Standard Library provides several container classes to manage collections. The ODMG standard also defines a set of collection classes. ODMG does not use the C++ standard containers for two reasons: First, the C++ standard containers are C++ specific; ODMG is designed to also support Java and Smalltalk. Second, when ODMG released its ODMG-93 specification, the C++ standard committee had not yet approved the STL specification.

Since the adoption of the STL and the Standard C++ Library specification, the ODMG C++ interface has been enhanced to provide support for the Standard C++ Library. The ODMG iterator class implements the C++ standard constant bidirectional iterator. The ODMG collection classes now support the C++ standard container begin() and end() operations. The C++ standard algorithms can also be used with the ODMG collections.

The ODMG collections are derived from an abstract base class d_Collection<T>. This base class defines a set of common collection operations, as summarized in Table 18.2.

TABLE 18.2. THE ODMG d_COLLECTION CLASS OPERATIONS

Function	*Descriptions*
Collection Operations	
d_Collection();	Creates a collection with no elements.
d_Collection(const d_Collection<T>& c);	Creates a collection and copies all elements from collection c using T's copy constructor.
d_Collection<T>&operator= (const d_Collection<T>& c); d_Collection<T>&assign_from (const d_Collection<T>& c);	Removes all existing elements using T's destructor and copies all elements from collection c using T's copy constructor. The assign_from() function is usually used to copy elements from a collection of a different type, such as copying elements from a list to a set.
~d_Collection();	Removes all existing elements using T's destructor.

TABLE 18.2. CONTINUED

Function	Descriptions
Element Operations	
`unsigned long cardinality() const;`	Returns the number of elements in a collection.
`d_Boolean is_empty() const;`	Returns whether or not the collection is empty.
`d_Boolean is_ordered() const;`	Returns whether or not the collection is ordered.
`d_Boolean allow_duplicates() const;`	Returns whether or not the elements can have the same values.
`d_Boolean contains_element` `(const T& v) const;`	Returns whether or not one or more elements have the value v.
`d_Boolean insert_element` `(const T& v) const;`	Inserts an element. Returns d_True if the insertion is successful and d_False otherwise. Use this operation to insert an element in a set that already contains the value v.
`void remove_element(const T& v);` `void remove_all(const T& v);`	Removes the first or all elements of value v.
`void remove_all();`	Removes all elements.
Iteration	
`d_Iterator<T> create_iterator()` `const;d_Iterator<T> begin() const;`	Returns an iterator pointing to the first element. The begin() function is compatible to the C++ standard const bidirectional iterators.
`d_Iterator<T> end() const;`	Returns an iterator pointing to the last element.
Equality	

`friend d_Booleanoperator==`
`(const d_Collection<T>& c1,`
`        const d_Collection`
`<T>& c2);`
	c1 and c2 are equal if they have the same cardinality and each element in c1 is equal to an element in c2. c1 and c2 can be different types of collections.

`friend d_Boolean operator!=`
`(const d_Collection<T>& c1,`
`        const d_Collection`
`<T>& c2);`
	Returns !(c1 == c2).

ODMG provides five collections, as shown in Table 18.3.

TABLE 18.3. ODMG COLLECTIONS

Collection	Description
d_Varray<T>	A variable-length array (similar to the C++ standard container vector).
d_List<T>	An ordered collection of elements that may have duplicate values (similar to the C++ standard container list—but d_List<T> also sorted).
d_Set<T>	An unordered collection of elements that have no duplicate values (similar to the C++ standard container set).
d_Bag<T>	An unordered collection of elements that may have duplicate values (similar to the C++ standard container multiset).
d_Dictionary<Key, Value>	An unordered collection of key, value pairs. Values can be accessed through key values (similar to the C++ standard container multimap).

In addition, ODMG supports a subset of C++ standard containers as shown in Table 18.4.

TABLE 18.4. ODMG-SUPPORTED C++ STANDARD CONTAINERS

C++ Name	ODMG Name
vector<T>	d_vector<T>
list<T>	d_list<T>
map<Key, Value>	d_map<Key, Value>
multimap<Key, Value>	d_multimap<Key, Value>
set<T>	d_set<T>
multiset<T>	d_multiset<T>

The C++ allocator template argument is not supported because the database is responsible for memory management. In fact, applications must never attempt to allocate memory for the containers.

18

OBJECT-ORIENTED
DATABASES

The `Invoice` class in our application contains an unordered collection of items. If we assume that no two items in an invoice can be identical, we can define the item collection as a d_Set:

```
d_Set<InvoiceItem> mItems;
```

Iterators

The ODMG standard provides a `d_Iterator` class that can be used to iterate over collections. As mentioned earlier in this chapter, the `d_Iterator` class implements a C++ standard constant bidirectional iterator. The overloaded dereference operator `*` is defined to return a copy of the referenced element. We can use a `d_Iterator` to access elements in a collection in the same way as we use a C++ iterator:

```
d_Set<T> aSet;
for (d_Iterator<T> i = aSet.begin(); i != aSet.end(); ++i)
{
    cout << *i;          // *i returns a copy of the referenced element
    *i = someValue;
}
```

Relationships

Another important concept in ODBMS is *relationship*. A relationship represents associations among objects. The number of classes in a relationship is called its *degree*. The most common type of relationship is the binary relationship that models the association between two classes.

Unidirectional Relationships

A binary relationship can be either unidirectional or bidirectional. A *unidirectional* relationship models a one-way traversal between two objects. In the invoicing application, for example, an invoice item must relate to a product, but a product does not have to relate to an invoice item. We can traverse from an invoice item to a product, but we do not have to find an invoice item from a product.

The ODMG standard defines a `d_Ref<T>` template class that stores a reference to a persistent object of type `T`. Each persistent object is assigned an immutable object identifier that cannot be changed by an application. When a `d_Ref<T>` instance is stored in the database, it contains the object identifier of the referenced object. When it is loaded again, it references the same object again if the referenced object is already loaded in memory. If the referenced object is not in memory, the object is retrieved from the database. An ODMG implementation handles this process automatically.

> **NOTE**
>
> The ODMG standard also defines a d_Ref_Any class. It is a reference to any persistent object. The d_Ref_Any class may be vaguely considered as the C++ void * and d_Ref<T> is like the C++ T *.

The overloaded operator ->() of the d_Ref class behaves exactly the same as its counterpart for a normal pointer. Suppose that we define a variable like this:

```
d_Ref<Product> rProduct;
```

We can access the mPrice member of a product referenced by rProduct using the following statement:

```
rProduct->mPrice.
```

The d_Ref class also overloads the operator *() to dereference a reference, just as we do with pointers. So *rProduct evaluates to the product object referenced by rProduct. A member function ptr() of the d_Ref class returns the referenced object's address, or a C++ pointer to the object, in the application's memory.

The copy constructor of the d_Ref class performs a shallow copy: It copies only the reference, not the referenced object. We can use this fact to work around the limitation of the d_Iterator class. Because a d_Iterator is a constant iterator, we cannot directly modify its elements. A workaround is to store a set of references to objects in a collection:

```
d_Set<d_Ref<T> > aRefSet;
for (d_Iterator<d_Ref<T> > i = aRefSet.begin(); i != aRefSet.end(); ++i)
{
    cout << *i;         // *i returns a copy of reference to an object of
➥type T
    *i->aMember = someValue;
}
```

Bidirectional Relationships

A *bidirectional* relationship, on the other hand, models a two-way traversal between two objects. For instance, we have to be able to access all items of an invoice and vice versa.

The ODMG standard defines template classes that represent bidirectional relationships:

```
d_Rel_Ref<T, const char * Member>
```

This class represents a one-to-one relation to an object of type T. That is, there is only one object of type T in this relationship between the current class and class T. The second parameter, Member, is a character string containing the name of the member variable in type T that stores a reference to the current object. From the current object's perspective, the member variable Member in T is called the *inverse relationship*. A simple one-to-one bidirectional relationship is demonstrated in Listing 18.9.

LISTING 18.9. A SIMPLE ONE-TO-ONE BIDIRECTIONAL RELATIONSHIP

```
// A.h
class B;
extern const char _mRelVarB [];

class A : public d_Object
{
    d_Rel_Ref<B, _mRelVarB>    mA;
};

// B.h
class A;
extern const char _mRelVarA [];

class B : public d_Object
{
    d_Rel_Ref<A, _mRelVarA>    mB;
};

// C.cpp ñ some source file
const char _mRelVarA [] = "mA";
const char _mRelVarA [] = "mB";
```

You can also have one-to-many bidirectional relationships. For instance, an invoice item can have only one associated invoice but an invoice can have many items. ODMG defines two one-to-many relationship classes: d_Rel_Set and d_Rel_List. The d_Rel_Set class represents an unordered relationship and the d_Rel_List class represents an ordered relationship. The ODMG bidirectional relationship classes are shown in Table 18.4.

TABLE 18.4. ODMG BIDIRECTIONAL RELATIONSHIP CLASSES

Class	*Base Class*
d_Rel_Ref<T, const char* Member>	d_Ref<T>
d_Rel_Set<T, const char* Member>	d_Set<d_Ref<T>>
d_Rel_List<T, const char* Member>	d_List<d_Ref<T>>

As an example, the relationship between the `Invoice` and `InvoiceItem` classes in the invoicing application can be defined as in Listing 18.10.

LISTING 18.10. THE RELATIONSHIP BETWEEN THE INVOICE AND INVOICEITEM CLASSES

```
extern const char _mInvoice[], _mItems[];

class Invoice : public d_Object
{
    d_Rel_Set<InvoiceItem, _mInvoice>    mItems;
};

class InvoiceItem : public d_Object
{
    d_Rel_Ref<Invoice, _mItems>    mpInvoice;
};

// In some source file
const char _mInvoice[] = "mpInvoice";
const char _mItems[] = "mItems";
```

Now we take a look at the changes to be made to the `Invoice` and `InvoiceItem` classes. The two header files are merged and shown in one listing so that we can easily discuss the relationships between them. Listing 18.11 demonstrates the definition of the persistent `Invoice` and `InvoiceItem` classes.

LISTING 18.11. DEFINITION OF THE PERSISTENT INVOICE AND INVOICEITEM CLASSES

```
//==============================================================
// Invoice.h - Invoice class definition
//==============================================================

#ifndef __Invoice_H
#define __Invoice_H

#include <iostream.h>

// ODMG header files
#include <odmg.h>
#include <d_Date.h>
#include <d_Ref.h>
#include <d_RelRef.h>
#include <d_RelSet.h>
#include <d_Iterat.h>

class Product;
class InvoiceItem;
```

18

OBJECT-ORIENTED
DATABASES

continues

LISTING 18.11. CONTINUED

```cpp
extern const char _mInvoice[], _mItems[];    // defined in source files

typedef d_Rel_Set<InvoiceItem, _mInvoice>    InvoiceItemList;
typedef d_Iterator<d_Ref<InvoiceItem> >        IIL_CItor;

class Invoice : public d_Object
{
public:
    // Constructors and destructor
    Invoice();
    Invoice(const d_ULong mID);
    virtual ~Invoice();

    // Member variables
    d_ULong            mID;        // Invoice ID
    d_Date             mDate;      // Invoice date
    InvoiceItemList    mItems;     // A list of references to invoice
items

    void    AddItem(d_Ref<InvoiceItem> pItem);    // Add an item to item
list
    d_ULong    GetTotal()    const;               // Invoice total amount

    // Overloaded insertion operator
    friend ostream& operator<<(ostream& os, const Invoice& anInvoice);
};

class InvoiceItem : public d_Object
{
public:
    // Constructors and destructor
    InvoiceItem();
    InvoiceItem(d_Ref<Product> pProduct, const d_UShort newQuantity);
    virtual ~InvoiceItem();

    // Member variables
    // Reference to the associated invoice object
    d_Rel_Ref<Invoice, _mItems>    mpInvoice;
    d_Ref<Product>    mpProduct;       // Reference to the product object
    d_UShort                mQuantity;    // Quantity sold

    // Other member functions
    // Get the total amount of the item
    d_UShort    GetTotal()    const;

    // Overloaded insertion operator
    friend ostream& operator<<(ostream& os, const InvoiceItem&
►anInvoiceItem);
};

#endif
```

First, let's look at the InvoiceItem class. The sale quantity variable mQuantity is defined as a d_UShort so that it can be stored in the database. The mpProduct variable was originally defined as a pointer to a Product object Product*. In C++, a pointer stores the memory address of an object—which is fine as long as the current application remains in the memory. When the application is terminated and reloaded, however, the memory address of the object will be different. After the invoice item is stored in the database, the memory address becomes irrelevant. Storing such an address in a database is rather useless. The mpProduct variable is thus defined as follows:

```
d_Ref<Product> mpProduct;
```

Similarly, the one-to-many relationship between the Invoice class and the InvoiceItem class is represented with the d_Rel_Ref<Invoice, _mInvoice> mpInvoice; member in the InvoiceItem class and the d_Rel_Set<InvoiceItem, _mInvoice> mItems; member in the Invoice class.

The member variable mID in the Invoice class is now defined as a d_ULong so that it can be stored in the database. The member variable mDate is designed to store the invoice date. ODMG defines a d_Date class that represents a date with year, month, and day. It has a static member function current() that returns a d_Date object with the current system date. The default constructor of the d_Date class initializes an instance with the current system date. This is ideal for our Invoice class because it stores the date when the invoice is created.

> **NOTE**
>
> ODMG also provides a d_Time class that represents a specific time of day. It contains the hour, minute, and seconds. The default constructor sets an instance to the current time. Another class, d_TimeStamp, represents both the date and time. Last, a d_Interval class is provided to represent a duration of time.

The implementation of the Invoice class and the InvoiceItem class must also be changed. Listing 18.12 shows the modified InvoiceItem implementation file.

LISTING 18.12. THE PERSISTENT INVOICEITEM CLASS IMPLEMENTATION

```
//================================================================
// InvoiceItemSrc.cpp - Invoice item class implementation
//================================================================

#include <odmg.h>
#include "Product.hxx"
```

continues

18

OBJECT-ORIENTED
DATABASES

LISTING 18.12. CONTINUED

```
#include "Invoice.hxx"

// Member variable represents the relationship with Invoice
const char _mInvoice[] = "mpInvoice";

// Constructors and destructor
InvoiceItem::InvoiceItem()
: mpProduct(0), mQuantity(0)
{}

InvoiceItem::InvoiceItem(d_Ref<Product> pProduct, const d_UShort
➥newQuantity)
: mpProduct(pProduct), mQuantity(newQuantity)
{}

// Destructor
// Do not delete the product object
InvoiceItem::~InvoiceItem()
{}

// Get item total amount
d_UShort    InvoiceItem::GetTotal()      const
{
    return mpProduct->mPrice * mQuantity;
}

// Overloaded insertion operator
ostream& operator<<(ostream& os, const InvoiceItem& anInvoiceItem)
{
    os << anInvoiceItem.mpProduct.ptr() << "\t" << anInvoiceItem.mQuantity
➥<< "\t"
        << anInvoiceItem.GetTotal();
    return os;
}
```

Here we initialize _mInvoice with the name of the member variable mpInvoice. The overloaded constructor now initializes the mpProduct member variable with a reference to a product. The overloaded operator ->() of d_Ref class is used in the GetTotal() function to access the mPrice member of a product pointed to by mpProduct using mpProduct->mPrice. The overloaded insertion operator << uses the d_Ref<T>::ptr() function to obtain a pointer to a product.

Databases and Transactions

So far, we have been dealing with objects loaded in the application's memory. To access objects in a database, we must open a database. We can use the ODMG d_Database class to create a database object. A database can be opened as shown here:

```
d_Database db;
db.open("DB_Name");
// Database operations
db.close();
```

The open() function is defined as follows:

```
enum access_status { not_open, read_write, read_only, exclusive };
void open(const char* db_name, access_status access = read_write);
```

Opening a database in the exclusive mode prevents other processes from accessing that database. You use the exclusive mode when you have to perform certain database mainte-nance operations. The read-only mode does not allow any modification to objects in a database.

In database systems, a *transaction* is a set of operations performed to a database. All operations in a transaction must be performed for the transaction to be complete. If any of the operations within a single transaction fails, all other operations must not be exe-cuted. Operations that have been executed before the failure must be *rolled back* to ensure that data integrity is maintained. A classic example of this integrity requirement is a bank fund transfer system in which *both* the withdrawal from one account and the deposit to another must be successful if the transaction is to be successful. If the applica-tion fails to withdraw funds from one account, it must not make the deposit, and vice versa.

ODMG provides a d_Transaction class that performs a set of transaction operations such as starting a transaction and *committing a transaction* (finishing a successful trans-action). A typical transaction in ODMG is demonstrated in the following code fragment:

```
d_Transaction tx;      // create a transaction
tx.begin();            // start a transaction
DeleteObjects();       // operations on database objects
AddObjects();
tx.commit();           // commit a transaction
```

Operations in a transaction must be enclosed within the begin() and commit() state-ments. The commit() function performs both DeleteObjects() and AddObjects() oper-ations. If one of these operations fails, the other must not be performed; if one of these operations has been performed, it must be rolled back. The application can also issue an abort() command for certain conditions:

18

OBJECT-ORIENTED DATABASES

```
d_Transaction tx;      // create a transaction
try
{
    tx.begin();            // start a transaction
    DeleteObjects();       // operations on database objects
    AddObjects();
    tx.commit();           // commit a transaction
}
catch (SomeException)      // There is an error!
{
    tx.abort();            // abort the transaction.
}
```

In the preceding example, we use the C++ exception handling method, which is supported by the ODMG standard. The ODMG d_Error class is derived from the C++ exception
class. The get_kind() member function of the d_Error class returns the error code, and
the what() member function gives the description of the error.

It is time to get back to our invoicing application. Listing 18.13 shows the revised
Invoice class implementation.

LISTING 18.13. PERSISTENT INVOICE CLASS IMPLEMENTATION

```
//===============================================================
// InvoiceSrc.cpp - Invoice class implementation
//===============================================================

#include <odmg.h>       // ODMG header file
#include "Product.hxx"
#include "Invoice.hxx"

// Member variable represents the relationship with InvoiceItem
const char _mItems[] = "mItems";

// Constructors and destructor
Invoice::Invoice()
: mID(0)
{}

Invoice::Invoice(const d_ULong newID)
: mID(newID)
{}

Invoice::~Invoice()
{
    // Delete all invoiced items
    for (IIL_CItor i = mItems.begin(); i != mItems.end(); ++i)
        delete (*i).ptr();
}
```

```cpp
// Add an item to item list
void Invoice::AddItem(d_Ref<InvoiceItem> pItem)
{
    d_Transaction    tx;

    try
    {
        tx.begin();
        mItems.insert_element(pItem);
        tx.commit();
    }
    catch (d_Error derr)
    {
        tx.abort();
        cerr << "ODMG Error [" << derr.get_kind() << "] " << derr.what()
➡<< endl;
    }
}


// Get total invoice amount
d_ULong Invoice::GetTotal()    const
{
    int intTotal = 0;

    // Iterate through the item list and calculate the total
    for (IIL_CItor i = mItems.begin(); i != mItems.end(); ++i)
        intTotal += (*i)->GetTotal();

    return intTotal;
}


// Overloaded insertion operator
ostream& operator<<(ostream& os, const Invoice& anInvoice)
{
    // Print invoice header
    os << "Invoice: " << anInvoice.mID << "\n"
        << anInvoice.mDate.month() << "/"
        << anInvoice.mDate.day() << "/"
        << anInvoice.mDate.year() << "\n";

    // Print all invoice items
    for (IIL_CItor ci = anInvoice.mItems.begin();
                   ci != anInvoice.mItems.end(); ++ci)
        os << **ci << "\n";

    // And the total amount
    os << "Total: " << anInvoice.GetTotal() << "\n";

    return os;
}
```

18

OBJECT-ORIENTED
DATABASES

The mItems constant is initialized with the name of the member variable mItems. The default constructor no longer has to initialize the mDate member variable because that variable will be initiated with the current date by the dDate's default destructor. The destructor is modified to use a d_Iterator to iterate through the item collection and delete each item. We use the d_Ref<T>::ptr() function to obtain a pointer to an item and delete the referenced item.

The AddItem() function demonstrates a way of accessing objects in a database. If we attempt to add an item to an invoice that contains an identical item, a d_Error_NameNotUnique exception is thrown. If that happens, we abort the transaction and display an error message.

The GetTotal() function also uses a d_Iterator to go through the item list and calculate the total sale amount. This is almost identical to the original GetTotal() function, in which we used a C++ standard iterator to access each element in the list.

The overloaded insertion operator << implementation is also similar to the original version. The notable difference is in the way we print the mDate member. Because the d_Date class does not directly support the C++ iostream, we end up printing the year, month, and day value of mDate.

In the original version of our application, we created a Product map to hold pointers to available product objects. Because all products will now be stored in a database, such a map becomes redundant. Instead, we will create a class that encapsulates all operations on the product objects in a database. Listing 18.14 shows the product operation class.

LISTING 18.14. THE PRODUCT OPERATION CLASS

```
//===========================================================
// ProductOps.h - Product Operations class definition
//         This class encapsulates the operations on Product
//         objects in a database
//===========================================================

#ifndef __ProductOps_H
#define __ProductOps_H

#include "Product.hxx"

class ProductOps
{
public:
    // Constructor and Destructor
    ProductOps(d_Database* pDatabase);
    virtual ~ProductOps();
```

```
    // Member functions
    void    Add();              // Add products to the database
    void    Edit();             // Edit products in the database
    void    Delete();           // Delete products from the database
    int     IsEmpty()   const; // Check if there are products in the
database
    void    List();             // List all products in the database

    // Member Variables
    d_Database*    pDB;        // A pointer to the database
};

#endif

//================================================================
// ProductOps.cpp - Product Operation class implementation
//================================================================

#include <iostream.h>
#include <algorithm>
#include <odmg.h>
#include <d_Extent.h>

#include "InvApp.h"
#include "Product.hxx"
#include "ProductOps.h"

// Constructor
ProductOps::ProductOps(d_Database* pDatabase)
: pDB(pDatabase)
{}

// Destructor
ProductOps::~ProductOps()
{}

// Add products to the database
void ProductOps::Add()
{
    d_Transaction    tx;
    Product*         pProduct;
    char             strID[MAXLEN + 1];
    char             strName[MAXLEN + 1];
    unsigned short   ushortPrice;

    cout << "Add Products:\n";
    while(1)
    {
        cout << "ID (Type 0 to finish): ";
        cin.getline(strID, MAXLEN);
        if (strID[0] == '0')    break;
```

continues

LISTING 18.14. CONTINUED

```cpp
        cout << "Name                    : ";
        cin.getline(strName, MAXLEN);
        cout << "Price                   : ";
        cin  >> ushortPrice;
        cin.ignore();

        try
        {
            tx.begin();
            pProduct = new(pDB) Product(strID, strName, ushortPrice);
            pDB->set_object_name(pProduct, strID);
            tx.commit();
            cout << "Product " << pProduct << " added\n";
        }
        catch (d_Error derr)
        {
            tx.abort();
            if (derr.get_kind() == d_Error_NameNotUnique)
            {
                cerr << "Product already exists!" << endl;
                continue;
            }
            else
            {
                cerr << "ODMG Error [" << derr.get_kind() << "] "
                    << derr.what() << endl;
                return;
            }
        }
    }
}

// Edit Products
void ProductOps::Edit()
{
    d_Transaction    tx;
    d_Ref<Product>   pProduct;
    char             strID[MAXLEN + 1];
    char             strNewID[MAXLEN + 1];
    char             strName[MAXLEN + 1];
    unsigned short   ushortPrice;

    // Use the d_Database lookup_object() function to find a product
    // and edit it if found
    cout << "Edit Products:\n";
    while(1)
    {
        do
```

```
        {
            cout << "ID (Type 0 to finish): ";
            cin.getline(strID, MAXLEN);
            if (strID[0] == '0')    break;

            tx.begin();
            pProduct = pDB->lookup_object(strID);
            tx.commit();

            if (pProduct.is_null() == d_True)
                cerr << "Invalid product ID, please try again." << endl;
        } while (pProduct.is_null() == d_True)

        cout << "Editing product: " << pProduct.ptr() << "\n";
        cout << "New ID    : ";
        cin.getline(strNewID, MAXLEN);
        cout << "New name : ";
        cin.getline(strName, MAXLEN);
        cout << "New price: ";
        cin  >> ushortPrice;
        cin.ignore();

        try
        {
            tx.begin();
        pProduct->mID = strNewID;
        pProduct->mName = strName;
        pProduct->mPrice = ushortPrice;
        pDB->rename_object(strID, strNewID);
        tx.commit();

        cout << "Product modified: " << pProduct.ptr() << "\n";
    }
    catch (d_Error derr)
    {
        cerr << "ODMG Error [" << derr.get_kind() << "] " << derr.what()
➥<< endl;
    }
    }
}

// Delete Products
void ProductOps::Delete()
{
    d_Transaction      tx;
    d_Ref<Product>     pProduct;
    char               strID[MAXLEN + 1];

    // Use the d_Database lookup_object() function to find a product
    // and delete it if found
    cout << "Delete Products:\n";
```

18

OBJECT-ORIENTED
DATABASES

continues

LISTING 18.14. CONTINUED

```
    while(1)
    {
        cout << "ID (Type 0 to finish): ";
        cin.getline(strID, MAXLEN);
        if (strID[0] == '0')      break;

        tx.begin();
        pProduct = pDB->lookup_object(strID);
        tx.commit();

        if (pProduct.is_null() == d_False)
        {
            try
            {
                tx.begin();
                pProduct.delete_object();
                tx.commit();
                cout << "Product deleted\n";
            }
            catch (d_Error derr)
            {
                cerr << "ODMG Error [" << derr.get_kind() << "] "
                     << derr.what() << endl;
                return;
            }
        }
        else
            cerr << "Invalid product ID, please try again." << endl;
    }
}

// Check if there are any product objects in the database
int ProductOps::IsEmpty()      const
{
    d_Extent<Product>     ProductExtent(pDB);
    return     ProductExtent.is_empty();
}

void ProductOps::List()
{
    d_Extent<Product>          ProductExtent(pDB);
    d_Bag<d_Ref<Product> >     ProductBag;

    ProductExtent.query(ProductBag, "this->mID != \"\"");

    cout << "Product Listing:\n";

    // Method 1
    for (d_Iterator< d_Ref<Product> > i2 = ProductBag.begin();
```

```
                                        i2 != ProductBag.end(); ++i2)
        cout << (*i2).ptr() << "\n";

    // Method 2
    PrintPtr<d_Ref<Product> >    DoPrintPtr;
    std::for_each(ProductBag.begin(),ProductBag.end(), DoPrintPtr);
}
```

The `Find()` function is removed from the `Product` map class because the `d_Database`
class provides a member function `lookup_object()` to find an object using its object
name. All other functions are implemented. The only member variable is now a pointer
to a database. It is initialized to point to a currently opened database object. We do not
delete the database object in the destructor because it may be in use by other objects.

In the `Add()` function, we use a fixed-length character array to accept user input because
ODMG does not support the C++ standard string class. An arbitrary `MAXLEN` constant is
defined to specify the maximum string length. The following statement demonstrates
how a persistent object is created:

```
    pProduct = new(pDB) Product(strID, strName, ushortPrice);
```

ODMG defines the overloaded operator `new(d_Database *)` that takes a pointer to a
database. Objects created using this `new()` operator are stored in the database automatically. We also call the `set_object_name()` member function of `d_Database` to specify a
unique key value—the product ID in this case—for the product. This key value can be
used to access the product in the database, as we do in the `Edit()` function. The key
value must be unique among all objects, not just the `Product` objects, in the database. We
wrap these two operations in a transaction.

Because the key value, or the object name, must be unique, we must check whether that
object name already exists in a database. If it does, we throw an exception with an error
code `d_Error_NameNotUnique`. This exception is caught in the `catch` block that follows.
A database implementation can automatically abort the transaction in this situation, but it
is always a good idea to explicitly abort it. The `catch` block simply prints an error message if another exception is caught.

The `Edit()` function shows two useful `d_Database` functions. The first is the
`lookup_object()` function. It accepts a string containing the object name and returns a
`d_Ref_Any` reference to the found object. If there is no object with the name, a `NULL`
reference is returned. We can test the result using the `is_null()` function of the
`d_Ref_Any` class.

If a product's ID is modified, we must update the object name for that product. The
`d_Database::rename_object()` function is used to achieve this. The function takes two

18

OBJECT-ORIENTED DATABASES

arguments: the old name and the new name. Again, all operations that change the Product object are enclosed in a transaction.

As does the Edit() function, the Delete() function calls the lookup_object() function to retrieve a product from the database. It then calls the d_Ref<T>::delete_object() function to remove the object from the database and from the application memory.

The List() function queries all Product objects in a database. In ODMG, a set of all persistent instances of a class is said to be its *extent*. A d_Extent<T> template class is defined to provide access to all objects of type T in a database. It is essentially an unordered collection of references to those objects, similar to a d_Set<d_Ref<T>>. It is instantiated with the following syntax:

```
d_Extent<T>    TExtent(pDB);
```

In this syntax, pDB is a pointer to a database and TExtent is an instance of T's extent. The extent is updated automatically by the database so that new elements are added to or removed from the extent when they are added to or removed from the database. The synchronization process may have a certain impact on the performance of applications. Consequently, you should avoid keeping an instance of an extent for a long period of time.

Extents can be queried by invoking the query() member function. The first argument is a reference to a collection that will store the result of the query; the second argument is a string containing a predicate. In the List() function, we get all products with a predicate:

```
this->mID != "";
```

The ProductExtent.query() statement looks rather strange:

```
ProductExtent.query(ProductBag, "this->mID != \"\"");
```

Here, the escape character \ is used to prevent the compiler from interpreting the double quotation marks embedded in the predicate string.

The resulting collection can be iterated over as we see in method 1. Because the ODMG collections work with C++ standard algorithms, we can use the for_each algorithm to simplify the code. The function object PrintPtr<d_Ref<Product>> is defined in a header file InvApp.h, as shown in Listing 18.15.

LISTING 18.15. MISCELLANEOUS FUNCTIONS

```cpp
//==============================================================
// InvApp.h - Misc function objects and other declarations
//==============================================================

#include <iostream.h>
#include <functional>

// Print an object referenced by a d_Ref<T> or pointed to by a pointer T*
// argument
// The overloaded insertion operator<<(ostream&, T&) is used
template<class Ref >
class PrintRef : public std::unary_function<Ref, void>
{
public:
    void operator()(Ref& r)
    {
        cout << *r << "\n";
    }
};

// Print an object referenced by a d_Ref<T> argument
// The overloaded insertion operator<<(ostream&, T*) is used
template<class Ref>
class PrintPtr : public std::unary_function<Ref, void>
{
public:
    void operator()(Ref& r)
    {
        cout << r.ptr() << "\n";
    }
};

// Arbitrary string length
const unsigned MAXLEN = 30;
```

The PrintPtr function object takes a d_Ref<T> argument and prints the value using
T::operator<<(ostream&, T*). The PrintRef function object takes a d_Ref<T> or T*
argument and prints the value using T::operator<<(ostream&, T). It is used to list all
invoices in Listing 18.16. This file also defines a MAXLEN constant that is used to accept
the string inputs in Listings 18.14 and 18.16.

The original InvoiceList class has been renamed InvoiceOps and has been modified to
take advantage of object persistence. Listing 18.16 shows the InvoiceOps class.

LISTING 18.16. THE INVOICE OPERATION CLASS

```cpp
//================================================================
// InvoiceOps.h - Invoice Operations class definition
//          This class encapsulates the operations on Invoice
//          objects in a database
//================================================================

#ifndef __InvoiceOps_H
#define __InvoiceOps_H

#include <iostream.h>
#include <odmg.h>
#include "ProductOps.h"
#include "Invoice.hxx"

class InvoiceOps
{
public:
    // Constructor & Destructor
    InvoiceOps(d_Database* pDatabase);
    virtual ~InvoiceOps();

    void Add(ProductOps& POps);     // Create invoices
    void Delete();                  // Delete invoices
    void List();                    // Print invoice listing

    d_Database*     pDB;

private:
    // Enter items to an invoice interactively, a reference to a product
➥map
    // is passed to verify the product in invoice items.
    void AddItems(ProductOps& POps, Invoice* pInvoice);
};

#endif


//================================================================
// InvoiceOps.cpp - Invoice Operations class implementation
//================================================================

#include <iostream.h>
#include <algorithm>
#include <odmg.h>
#include <d_Extent.h>

#include "InvApp.h"
#include "Product.hxx"
#include "InvoiceOps.h"
#include "Invoice.hxx"
```

```
// Constructor
InvoiceOps::InvoiceOps(d_Database* pDatabase)
: pDB(pDatabase)
{}

// Destructor
InvoiceOps::~InvoiceOps()
{}

// Enter invoices
void InvoiceOps::Add(ProductOps& POps)
{
    if (POps.IsEmpty())
    {
        cerr << "No product available, "
            << "please enter products and try again!" << endl;
        return;
    }

    d_Transaction      tx;
    Invoice*           pInvoice;
    long               lngID;
    char               strID[MAXLEN + 1];

    cout << "Add Invoices:\n";
    while(1)
    {
        cout << "Invoice ID (Type 0 to finish): ";
        cin  >> lngID;
        cin.ignore();
        if (lngID == 0)          break;

        _ltoa(lngID, strID, 10);

        try
        {
            tx.begin();
            pInvoice = new(pDB) Invoice(lngID);
            pDB->set_object_name(pInvoice, strID);
            tx.commit();
            cout << "Invoice added to the list\n\n";
            AddItems(POps, pInvoice);
        }
        catch (d_Error derr)
        {
            tx.abort();
            if (derr.get_kind() == d_Error_NameNotUnique)
            {
                cerr << "Invoice already exists!" << endl;
                continue;
```

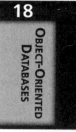

18

OBJECT-ORIENTED
DATABASES

continues

LISTING 18.16. CONTINUED

```
            }
            else
            {
                cerr << "ODMG Error [" << derr.get_kind() << "] "
                    << derr.what() << endl;
                return;
            }
        }
    }
}

// Delete invoices from the database
void InvoiceOps::Delete()
{
    d_Transaction      tx;
    d_Ref<Invoice>     pInvoice;
    long               lngID;
    char               strID[MAXLEN + 1];

    // Use the d_Database lookup_object() function to find an invoice
    // and delete it if found
    cout << "Delete Invoices:\n";
    while(1)
    {
        cout << "ID (Type 0 to finish): ";
        cin  >> lngID;
        if (lngID == 0)     break;

        _ltoa(lngID, strID, 10);

        tx.begin();
        pInvoice = pDB->lookup_object(strID);
        tx.commit();

        if (pInvoice.is_null() == d_False)
        {
            try
            {
                tx.begin();
                pInvoice.delete_object();
                tx.commit();
                cout << "Invoice deleted\n";
            }
            catch (d_Error derr)
            {
                cerr << "ODMG Error [" << derr.get_kind() << "] "
                    << derr.what() << endl;
                return;
            }
```

```
        }
        else
            cerr << "Invalid invoice ID, please try again." << endl;
    }
}

// Enter items to an invoice interactively
// Input : POps - A reference to a ProductOps object
//         pInvoice - Pointer to the invoice
void InvoiceOps::AddItems(ProductOps& POps, Invoice* pInvoice)
{
    d_Transaction      tx;
    InvoiceItem*       pItem;
    d_Ref<Product>     pProduct;
    char               strProductID[MAXLEN + 1];
    int                intQty;

    cout << "Add Invoice Items:\n";
    while(1)
    {
        do
        {
            cout << "Product ID (Type 0 to finish): ";
            cin.getline(strProductID, MAXLEN);
            if (strProductID[0] == '0')          return;

            tx.begin();
            pProduct = pDB->lookup_object(strProductID);
            tx.commit();

            if (pProduct.is_null() == d_True)
                cerr << "Sorry, wrong product ID.  Please try again." <<
➥endl;
        } while (pProduct.is_null() == d_True);

        cout << "Quantity                      : ";
        cin >> intQty;
        cin.ignore();

        try
        {
            tx.begin();
            pItem = new(pDB) InvoiceItem(pProduct, intQty);
            pItem->mpInvoice = pInvoice;
            pInvoice->mItems.insert_element_last(pItem);
            tx.commit();
            cout << "Item added\n";
        }
        catch (d_Error derr)
        {
            cerr << "ODMG Error [" << derr.get_kind() << "] "
```

continues

18

OBJECT-ORIENTED
DATABASES

LISTING **18.16.** CONTINUED

```
                    << derr.what() << endl;
            return;
        }
    }
}

// List all invoices in the database
void InvoiceOps::List()
{
    d_Extent<Invoice>          InvoiceExtent(pDB);
    d_Bag<d_Ref<Invoice> >     Invoices;
    InvoiceExtent.query(Invoices, "this->mID > 0");

    cout << "Invoice Listing:\n";

    PrintRef<d_Ref<Invoice> >    DoPrintRef;
    std::for_each(Invoices.begin(), Invoices.end(), DoPrintRef);
}
```

Most of the `InvoiceOps` functions are similar to their `ProductOps` counterparts. The constructor initializes the member variable `pDB` with a pointer to a database. The `Add()` function first checks to see whether there are any products in the database before adding invoices. The object name of an invoice is set to its ID. Because an object name must be a character string, we convert the ID from a long to a string using the `_ltoa()` function. Although it is not a C or C++ standard library function, almost all vendors provide a conversion function such as `_ltoa()`. (You can always write your own version if your compiler does not provide one.)

The `AddItem()` function demonstrates an important feature of ODMG databases. Recall that there is a bidirectional relationship between an invoice and an item. This relationship is automatically maintained by the database. All we have to do is specify the objects to be related. We can assign a reference to an `Invoice` object `pInvoice` to `pItem->mpInvoice` like this:

```
pItem->mpInvoice = pInvoice;
```

In this statement, we tell the database that this item relates to the invoice pointed to by `pInvoice`. The database automatically adds this item to the `pInvoice->mItems` set.

We can use the `d_Set<T>::insert_element_last()` function to add `pItem` to `pInvoice->mItems` set, as in this example:

```
pInvoice->mItems.insert_element_last(pItem);
```

In this statement, the database automatically assigns `pInvoice` to the `pItem->mpInvoice` member variable. This ensures that we will not have a broken relationship between invoices and items.

The `Delete()` function is almost identical to the `ProductOps::Delete()` function, except that we must first convert the invoice ID from a long to a character string. The `List()` function also uses the C++ standard algorithm `for_each` and the `PrintRef` function object defined in Listing 18.15 to print invoices in the database.

Now there is only one missing piece left: the `main()` function. It is shown in Listing 18.17.

LISTING 18.17. THE MAIN PROGRAM

```cpp
//================================================================
// main.cpp - The driver program for the application
//================================================================

#include <iostream.h>
#include <odmg.h>

#include "ProductOps.h"
#include "InvoiceOps.h"

const char    dbName[]    = "InvApp";

int main()
{
    d_Database*    db = new d_Database;
    try
    {
        db->open(dbName);
    }
    catch (d_Error derr)
    {
        cerr << "ODMG Error [" << derr.get_kind() << "] " << derr.what()
➥<< endl;
        return 1;
    }

    int            intChoice = 0;
    ProductOps    Products(db);
    InvoiceOps    Invoices(db);

    do
    {
        cout << "\nA Trival Invoice Entry Program\n\n";
        cout << "  1. Enter invoices\n";
        cout << "  2. Delete invoices\n";
        cout << "  3. Print invoice list\n";
        cout << "  4. Add products\n";
        cout << "  5. Edit product\n";
        cout << "  6. Delete products\n";
```

continues

18

LISTING 18.17. CONTINUED

```cpp
        cout << "  7. Print product list\n";
        cout << "  9. Exit\n\n";
        cout << "Enter your choice: ";
        cin  >> intChoice;
        cin.ignore();
        cout << endl;

        switch(intChoice)
        {
        case 1: Invoices.Add(Products);    break;
        case 2: Invoices.Delete();         break;
        case 3: Invoices.List();           break;
        case 4: Products.Add();            break;
        case 5: Products.Edit();           break;
        case 6: Products.Delete();         break;
        case 7: Products.List();           break;
        case 9: cout << "Bye!\n\n";        break;
        default:    cout << "Please select 1, 2, 3, 4, 5, 6, 7 or 9.\n";
        }
    } while (intChoice != 9);

    db->close();
    delete db;

    return 0;
}
```

The major change from the original version of the main program is that a database must be open before any operations can be performed. After finishing all operations, we close the database and delete the database object.

We have seen how a database application can be developed using the ODMG standard. Now let's consider some of the background issues related to ODBMS.

ODBMS Technical Issues

Several technical issues in the ODBMS design can affect the performance of certain databases. Vendors must investigate how their customers will be using the product and decide the best strategy for tackling these technical issues.

Client/Server Architecture

In a client/server environment, database server processes are responsible for data transfer between the data storage and the server cache. These processes also manage transaction processing and concurrent access to database objects. Depending on the ODBMS implementations, there may be one or more server processes. A server process can have multiple threads, and each can perform operations for one client process. This arrangement allows concurrent database access from many clients. Object representation in a server cache is generally identical to object representation when stored in a database: It is independent to the client application, which may be a C++ application running on a UNIX box or a Java application on a Windows NT workstation.

A client cache serves as a view to a database. Objects are represented in native client application format. For instance, a C++ application will see all objects—persistent or not—as native C++ objects. Object mapping between server cache and client cache is performed by an ODBMS automatically, transparent to the application software.

When a client application requires an object that is not in the client cache, it sends out a request to a server process. The server process may return the requested object along with others, depending on the data transfer granularity.

Data Storage and Object Clustering

Data is stored on pages in the storage media, usually hard disks. Each page is typically 2KB to 16KB in size. Disk managers usually read a block of pages of data at a time from the disk. When a page is loaded in memory or the application cache, subsequent reads and writes to objects on the same page are performed in the cache. If a group of objects is likely to be accessed together, storing them on the same page can save a large amount of disk access time and can greatly improve the application's performance. The technique for object grouping is called *object clustering*.

An ODBMS supports the storage and retrieval of networks of objects. In our simple invoicing application, an `Invoice` object, a set of `Item` objects, and related `Product` objects form a network of objects and are likely to be accessed at the same time. Thus, it makes sense to store them on the same page. There are two common models for object clustering.

The first is the *a priori* model. In this model, application developers decide what objects should be grouped. This decision is based on a developer's knowledge about the most likely object access patterns. The ODMG standard provides a method to specify the object grouping. When a new persistent object is created, we use an overloaded operator `new()`:

```
pProduct = new(pDB) Product(strID, strName, ushortPrice);
```

Another version of the overloaded operator `new()` accepts a reference to an object (`pProduct`) and places the new object next to `pProduct`:

```
pProduct1 = new(pProduct) Product(strID, strName, ushortPrice);
```

This approach requires only that the new object be placed *next to* the referenced object, not necessarily on the same page. It is up to the implementation to decide whether the objects should be on the same page.

A drawback of this approach is that the object access patterns are not constant; they may change over time. The access patterns may overlap as well. For example, a stock level analyzer may want to access invoices and related products, but a customer report may want to access invoices and customers. If we cannot place all objects related to an invoice on one page, which objects should be on the same page?

To overcome this weakness, the ODBMS can use another model: the *ex post* model. In this model, the database or the administrator makes the decision after carefully analyzing the access patterns statistics in real time. Objects can be reorganized according to the best clustering strategy. This model, however, has the drawback of having to reorganize objects in real time, which has significant impact on database performance.

Data Transfer Granularity

Objects in a database are loaded in the server cache. When the objects are processed by a client-side application, they must be transferred to the client cache. Technically, we can just transfer the object to be processed to the client because network throughput is limited. Unfortunately, applications often have to access a group of objects at a time. For example, to display an invoice, we need one `Invoice` object, several `InvoiceItem` objects, and several `Product` objects. If we transfer one object at a time, we invoke a number of network requests and responses. That transfer time will become slower as the number of involved objects increases.

A natural solution for this is that, in combination with object clustering, we can transfer a page at the time. After all, the entire page is already loaded in the server cache. A pleasant side effect is that the page may also hold the next object to be accessed. This approach can be very efficient when we need to perform an operation on a sequence of objects. For example, when printing product lists, we have a very good chance of getting the next product in the list on the same page.

Transferring objects by page, however, is not very efficient when we have to access only a small number of objects. For instance, if an application process is interested in only two objects—an invoice and a customer—transferring a page that contains 100 objects wastes a large chunk of network bandwidth.

A more clever approach is to transfer only required objects between the server cache and the client cache. This eliminates the unnecessary network round trips incurred with object transfer, and also reduces the use of the network bandwidth. This approach requires a more sophisticated negotiation process between the client and the server. The client must indicate the required objects and the server must be able to respond correctly. This approach, however, adds workload to the server process and can slow down the server access time.

Data Locking Granularity

Databases support concurrent access of the same objects by different applications. To prevent data corruption caused by two or more processes modifying the same objects, one process that wants to modify a particular object must *lock* it so that others cannot modify it. When the modification is done, the object is unlocked, and other processes can proceed to change it. There may be situations in which deadlocks arise. Assume that process A locks object X, and process B locks object Y. If A requests a lock on object Y before it releases the lock on object X, it must wait until B releases the lock. If, in the meantime, process B tries to lock object X, it must wait for process A to release the lock. Now processes A and B are in a deadlock: Neither of them can apply the second lock or release the first lock.

An ODBMS can lock a particular object, or it can lock the entire page that contains the object. Locking by object reduces the chance of deadlocks because fewer objects are being locked. Locking individual objects is more efficient when only a small number of objects are involved. When the number of objects to be updated increases, the application must apply for dozens or even hundreds of locks. Such a lock-application process can become lengthy. Locking individual objects does not take advantage of object clustering.

Locking by page, on the other hand, works well with good object clustering. If objects to be locked are located on the same page or pages, a few page locks can replace hundreds of object locks. However, locking by page has a higher chance of causing false deadlocks because it locks objects that do not have to be locked. This weakness, however, becomes less relevant when object clustering is implemented correctly; in a well-designed clustering situation, the unrelated objects will occupy only a small portion of the locked page.

18

OBJECT-ORIENTED DATABASES

Summary

This chapter introduced the concept of ODBMS and some of its technical issues. In the chapter, we demonstrated the ODMG standar d C++ binding features with a simple invoicing application. Compared to traditional DBMS, ODBMS has yet to live up to the high expectations put on the technology. Its market acceptance is moderate because MIS managers are generally reluctant to move mission-critical corporate data to a relatively young and evolving technology.

As the technology has matured, however, ODBMS vendors have greatly improved their products to offer almost all the features provided by traditional DBMS. In addition, current ODBMS products offer the ability to store complex object structure, the ease of development, and object-oriented programming language support. Many vendors have also started to comply with the ODMG standard, which will help encourage the industry adoption of ODBMS in the near future.

Protecting Applications Using Encryption

Encryption

CHAPTER 19

A Brief History of Encryption

Encryption is a way of protecting data against unauthorized use. Several techniques have been used throughout the years to protect data against enemies who would misuse the information. Thousands of years ago, the main use of using encryption was to protect data during war. David Kahn, in his impressive work, *The Codebreakers: The Comprehensive History of Secret Communication from Ancient Times to the Internet*, has traced the history of cryptography as far back as ancient Egypt, progressing through India, Mesopotamia, Babylon, World War I, World War II, and into modern times, where encryption has taken on new meaning.

The extensive use of telegraph and radio waves in modern times has increased the need to encrypt information because sophisticated techniques are available to intercept the information that flows in today's global environment. Military communication without the use of encryption is worthless. The biggest achievements in cryptography can be attributed to the work done by Alan Turing during World War II. Using the help of Alan Turing in Britain, the allies were able to use computers to break the Enigma code used by Germany during the war.

Since World War II, the National Security Agency (a branch of the Department of Defense) has become the center for cryptographic research and activity. The existence of this highly secret organization within the government was denied until recently and is jokingly referred to as "No Such Agency." The budget and activities of this agency are highly classified. It has been rumored that the NSA employs the largest number of mathematicians in the world and actively eavesdrops on phone conversations.

For years, the use of codes and ciphers was reserved to the NSA and military operations. Civilians had to be content with using envelopes and couriers to protect data. With the computer revolution and the explosion of the information age—and especially the Internet—the need for encryption in civilian use was recognized. The manner in which data was disseminated through electronic mail and the Internet, and the financial value attached to the information, fueled enough research for civilians to use encryption.

In the late 1960s, a cryptographic research group was set up by IBM chairman Thomas Watson, Jr. This group, led by Horst Feistel, developed a private key encryption method called Lucifer, which was used by Lloyd's of London to protect a cash-dispensing system. The success of Lucifer prompted IBM to make it available for commercial use. The team formed for this purpose was headed by Dr. Walter Tuchman and Dr. Carl Meyer, who tested the cipher and fixed the flaws they found in the method. By 1974, the cipher was ready and available on a silicon chip.

However, IBM was not the only company to make ciphers available commercially. Other companies made other codes available, but there were some problems associated with all these ciphers:

- They could not communicate with each other
- There was no way to determine their strength

The Role of the National Bureau of Standards

In 1968, the National Bureau of Standards (NBS)—which has since been renamed to the National Institute of Standards and Technology (NIST)—took on the task of researching the needs of civilians and the government in terms of computer security. It was determined that the United States needed a single and interoperable standard for encrypting data for the purposes of storing and transmitting unclassified information. It was decided that classified data was still in the jurisdiction of the NSA.

A request for proposals was published in the Federal Register by the NBS on May 15, 1973. There were several requirements for the algorithm, which included the following:

- The algorithm should provide a high level of security
- The algorithm should be public and peer reviewed
- The algorithm should be easy to understand
- The security of the algorithm should lie with the key and not with the algorithm
- The algorithm should be flexible enough to be easily adapted to a variety of applications
- The implementation of the algorithm should be cost effective
- The algorithm and the devices implementing it should be exportable
- The algorithm should be easy to validate
- The algorithm should perform efficiently in a reasonable amount of time

The initial submissions to this request were not encouraging because none of them satisfied all the requirements. Another request was made on August 27, 1974, in the Federal Register and there was one response: a version of the Lucifer algorithm that was weakened in some ways and strengthened in other ways by the NSA. This algorithm became the U.S. Data Encryption Standard (DES)

DES was created by the cooperative efforts of IBM and the NSA. Instead of the 128-bit keys used in the Lucifer algorithm, DES used 56-bit keys. Several changes were made to the algorithm as recommended by NSA, and finally the NBS published it on March 17, 1975, in the Federal Register. The algorithm was formally adopted for widespread use on

19

USING
ENCRYPTION

November 23, 1976. Federal Information Processing Standard (FIPS PUB 46) describes the algorithm.

On the surface, it appears that the security of DES is less than that of Lucifer. According to cryptography historian David Kahn, DES resulted from a compromise between two separate sides in the NSA: One side of the codemaking group wanted to make sure that any code they made public should be good; the other side of the codebreaking group wanted to make sure that any code made public should be such that the NSA should be able to break it when the code is used by foreign governments. The resultant algorithm was a weaker version that used 56-bit keys but strengthened the "S-boxes" that perform substitution.

At the 1993 Crypto Conference held at the University of California at Santa Barbara, a paper was presented by Michael Wiener of Bell Northern Research that described how a machine can be created to break the DES code. This machine makes use of a chip that tries 50 million DES keys per second. Using the brute-force approach, the average time it took to break a DES-encrypted message was 3.5 hours; the machine would cost $1 million.

Alternatives to DES were sought because of the weaknesses identified in DES. Still, DES remained in wide use until recently. Other variations of DES used longer keys, larger block sizes, and increased rounds of encryption (such as that approach used in Triple-DES). The government has recently proposed *Clipper* as an alternative to DES; however, this alternative is already under fire from several sides. Clipper is described later in this chapter.

Understanding Encryption

Encryption relies on a branch of mathematics called *cryptography* to protect information. The principles behind cryptography are simple. A practical encryption system consists of four parts:

- **Plaintext:** The message to be encrypted.
- **Ciphertext:** The message after it has been encrypted.
- **Encryption algorithm:** The mathematical function or algorithm used to encrypt the message.
- **Encryption key:** The number(s) or word(s) or phrase(s) used by the encryption algorithm.

The main goal of performing encryption is to create a ciphertext from plaintext such that it is impossible to convert the ciphertext back to the plaintext without using the encryption key.

Codes

Codes are the simplest encryption technique because they use a code table to encrypt information. Suppose that you want to send a secret message to a friend; you do not want the message to be intercepted or understood by someone eavesdropping. Also suppose that the message you want to convey to your friend could be one of four possibilities:

- Go out for dinner and movie
- Go out for dinner only
- Go out for movie only
- Stay home

You can use codes for these messages as shown in Table 19.1.

TABLE 19.1. USING CODES TO PERFORM ENCRYPTION

Code Word	Message
Mercury	Go out for dinner and movie
Venus	Go out for dinner only
Earth	Go out for movie only
Mars	Stay home

You can create two copies of this table and give one to your friend. Now, when you say the word *Earth*, your friend knows exactly what you mean. This method works well for a few occasions, but if used repeatedly, it becomes less effective: Someone eavesdropping won't take long to figure out the meaning of those words. (One variation of the code approach is to use multiple code tables and use different code tables on different occasions.) Another disadvantage of this method is that the number of messages you can send is limited to the size of the table.

Ciphers

Ciphers are an alternative to codes. Ciphers use a scrambling technique to scramble the letters in the message; the message can be deciphered by the receiver using the descrambling key. Ciphers eliminate the problem of having limited messages. The simplest technique for ciphering is to use *substitution ciphers*: In a substitution cipher, each letter of a message is substituted with a different letter. The *Caesar Cipher* is a very common substitution cipher technique; it simply shifts the alphabet three places to the right. Variations of this method can be done by shifting *n* places to the right. Suppose that we decide to shift the letters in a message five places, as shown in Figure 19.1.

FIGURE 19.1.

Using a five-place shift cipher.

A	B	C	D	E	F	G	H	I	J	K	L	M	N	O	P	Q
5	6	7	8	9	A	B	C	D	E	F	G	H	I	J	K	L

S	T	U	V	W	X	Y	Z	0	1	2	3	4	5	6	7	8
N	O	P	Q	R	S	T	U	V	W	X	Y	Z	0	1	2	3

The messages are now coded as follows:

```
MOVIES => HJQD9N
DINNER => 8DII9M
HOME => CJH9
```

The biggest problem with ciphers is that they are easy for an experienced cryptanalyst to crack. Given a few words, it can be easy to find some regularities in them. An implementation of the substitution cipher is shown in Listing 19.1.

LISTING 19.1. AN IMPLEMENTATION OF THE SUBSTITUTION CIPHER

```cpp
//Author: Megh Thakkar
//  A Simple implementation of a substitution cipher
//  Purpose: This cipher prompts the user
//  for the number of
// places to shift and then shifts the characters
// by that many
// places.

#include <stdio.h>
#include <iostream.h>

int main()
{
    int c;

    int sf_places;

cout << "\n Enter the number of places to "
    << "shift characters:    ";
    cin  >>  sf_places;

    while ((c = getchar()) !=EOF) {
        if ('a' <= c && c <= 'l' )
            c += sf_places;
        else if ('A' <= c && c <= 'L' )
            c += sf_places;
        else if ('m' <= c && c <= 'z' )
            c -= sf_places;
        else if ('M' <= c && c <= 'Z' )
```

```
            c -= sf_places;
        putchar(c);
    }
    return 0;
}
```

Listing 19.2 shows an implementation of the Caesar Cipher.

LISTING 19.2. AN IMPLEMENTATION OF THE CAESAR CIPHER

```
//   Author: Megh Thakkar
//   A Simple implementation of the Caesar Cipher
//   Usage:  caesar input_file output_file key
//      Purpose: This program takes a plaintext file
//               and encrypts it using the
//               Caesar Cipher.
// It can also be used to decipher a file that
//               been encrypted using the Caesar Cipher.

#include <iostream.h>
#include <stdio.h>
#include <ctype.h>
#define l2n(X) (toupper(X) - 'A')
#define n2l(X) ((X) + 'A')
#define ALPHABET_LEN 26

int main(int argc,char *argv[])
{
    char c;
    char *key;
    int z;
    int decrypt = 0;
    FILE *infile;
    FILE *outfile;

    infile  = fopen(argv[1], "rb");
    outfile = fopen(argv[2], "wb");
    key = argv[3];

    if (infile == NULL || outfile == NULL)
    {
    cout<< "\nSorry. Files cannot be opened\n";
    return -1;
    }

    cout << "\n Do you want to encrypt[0] or decrypt[1]: ";
    cin >> decrypt;
```

continues

LISTING 19.2. CONTINUED

```
    while ((z = getc(infile)) != EOF) {
c = (char)z;
        if (isalpha(c)) {
        c = l2n(c);
        if (! decrypt) {
        c = (c + l2n(*key)) % ALPHABET_LEN;
        }
        else
        {
        c = (c + ALPHABET_LEN - l2n(*key)) % ALPHABET_LEN;
        }
        c = n2l(c);
        }
    putc(c,outfile);
    }
    return(0);
}
```

Vernam Cipher

Vernam ciphers are also called *one-time pads*. You can use them to get the flexibility of ciphers and also retain the security of a code. Basically, this technique uses a set of code tables such that each table represents one particular part of the message. Essentially, it uses the words in one table to create a part of the message and then shuffles the words in the table to create a new table, which is then used to write another part of the message; the words in that second table are then shuffled again to write a third part of the message. The process continues in this way until the message is done. The only way to break this ciphertext is to use the exact same shuffle and the exact same number of words. Figure 19.2 shows a one-time pad.

FIGURE 19.2.

An example of a one-time pad.

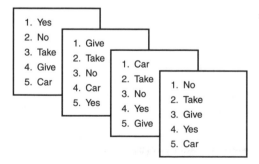

You can make use of a random number generator to determine how to shuffle the letters; shuffling is done for each letter. The one-time use of the code table before it is reshuffled gives it the necessary security. Each table can represent a paper in the one-time pad. In other words, only the one-time pad used to encrypt the message can be used to convert the ciphertext back to the plaintext.

Each page in the pad consists of a different set of codes. You can create part of the message using one page, create another part of the message using the second page, and so on. In other words, parts of the message are constructed using different "code tables"; to decrypt this message, you must use the code tables in the exact same sequence they were used to encrypt the message.

Listing 19.3 shows an implementation of a one-time pad.

LISTING 19.3. AN IMPLEMENTATION OF A ONE-TIME PAD

```
//Author: Megh Thakkar
//Implementation of one-time pad
//Usage: onetime input_file key_file output_file offset
//Description: It accepts three files as parameters.
//      It performs exclusive OR on the first two files and
//                 places the result in the third file.
//

#include <stdio.h>
#include <stdlib.h>
#include <iostream.h>

#define BUF_SZ 32768U

long offset = 0;     // Offset into key file.
FILE *infile = 0;
FILE *keyfile = 0;
FILE *outfile = 0;

size_t amt_read = BUF_SZ;
size_t amt_write = BUF_SZ;
size_t amt_key;

//amt_read, amt_write and amt_key are used during encryption
//to find the number of characters in use.

// Allocate disk buffers.
// b1 is used for input and output files
//while b2 is used for the key file

char * iobuf;
char * kbuf;

int i;     //Used for looping.
```

19

USING
ENCRYPTION

continues

LISTING 19.3. CONTINUED

```cpp
int main(int argc, char * argv[])
{
    if (argc != 5)
    {
     cout <<"\nUsage: onetime input_file "
<< "key_file output_file offset.";
        return -1;
    }

    offset = strtol(argv[4], NULL, 0);
    if (offset < 0)
    {
        cout << "\n " << argv[4]
<< " is not a valid value."
                << "\nOnly positive offset values"
 << "are allowed.\n";
        return -1;
    }

    // Open files.

    infile = fopen(argv[1], "rb");

    keyfile = fopen(argv[2], "rb");

    outfile= fopen(argv[3], "wb");

    if ((infile == NULL) || (keyfile == NULL)
|| (outfile == NULL))
    {
    cout << "\n Sorry. Unable to open files";

    }

    // Go to the specified offset position in the key file

    if (offset != 0)
    {
      if (fseek(keyfile, offset, SEEK_SET))
      {
        cout << "\nError: Unable to seek to "
<< "the offset value" << "\n";

    }
    }

    iobuf = new char[BUF_SZ];
    kbuf = new char[BUF_SZ];
```

```
        if ((iobuf == NULL) ¦¦ (kbuf == NULL))
        {
        cout << "Error.Insufficient memory\n";
        return -1;
        }

        //Perform the encryption.

        while (amt_write > 0)
        {

        amt_write = fread(iobuf, 1, amt_read, infile);
        amt_key = fread(kbuf, 1, amt_write, keyfile);
        if (amt_key < amt_write)
          {
            cout << "\nERROR:  Key length after "
<< "offset is too short";
            amt_write = amt_key;

          }

        for (i = 0; i < BUF_SZ; i++)
          iobuf[i] ^= kbuf[i];
        amt_key = fwrite(iobuf, 1, amt_write, outfile);
        }

        // Close files

        fclose(infile);
        fclose(keyfile);
        fclose(outfile);

    return 0;
}
```

Private Key Cryptography

The kind of cryptography used in earlier days and in the code and cipher techniques such as the Caesar Cipher and Vernam Cipher is called *private key* or *secret key* cryptography. The term *private key* is used because this technique implies that both the sender and the receiver of the message have a key that must be kept private. Private key cryptography makes use of the same key on both the sending and the receiving end and is therefore also referred to as *symmetric cryptography*.

Whenever you want to communicate with someone using these methods, you must give the cryptographic key to the person with whom you want to communicate. The process of exchanging the cryptographic key is referred to as *key distribution* and can be very difficult: The key is the secret to breaking the ciphertext; if there exists a really secure method of communicating the key, why isn't that method used to communicate the message in the first place? For many years, the key distribution method used by the United States government was to place the keys in a locked briefcase which was handcuffed to a courier. The courier would board an airplane and would be met at the destination country by an official from the U.S. embassy and taken to the embassy. The cuffs would be removed at the embassy, and the keys were then available to decipher diplomatic messages. The courier did not have a way to remove the cuffs or open the briefcase. If the bad guys caught the courier, the diplomats in the United States would know about it and would not use those particular keys to encrypt messages.

Private Key Algorithms

There are several popular private key algorithms. We will briefly describe just a few of them:

- **DES:** The Data Encryption Standard was adopted by the U.S. government in 1977 and as an ANSI standard in 1981. It makes use of 56-bit keys to encrypt the information.

- **Triple-DES:** This algorithm is a variation of DES; it uses the DES encryption algorithm three times with two different keys. This technique is currently used by financial institutions.

- **RC codes:** Rivest codes are named after MIT professor Ronald Rivest who is also the coinventor of the RSA public key encryption algorithm. These methods are proprietary algorithms that are distributed by RSA Data Security. The two most popular codes are RC2 (which is a block cipher method like DES) and RC4 (which is a stream cipher that produces a stream of pseudo-random numbers that are XORed with the information).

  These codes can be used with keys from 1 to 1,024 bits in length. There is no estimate of how secure these codes really are because they are proprietary.

- **IDEA:** In 1990, James L. Massey and Xuejia Lai developed and published the International Data Encryption Algorithm in Zurich, Switzerland. This technique uses a 128-bit key and seems to be very strong (although the exact nature of the security it provides is not known).

- **Skipjack:** This secret algorithm was developed by the National Security Agency for civilian purposes. It uses an 80-bit key. It is at the heart of the Clipper chip used by law enforcement agencies to perform legal wiretaps. The Clipper chip is not as secure as Skipjack.

There are several problems associated with private key encryption:

- As mentioned earlier, the biggest problem with private key encryption is the method of key distribution. Figure 19.3 shows that for secure communication among three people, you need three keys. Figure 19.4 shows that for similarly secure communication among four people, you need twice as many keys. If two more people join the secure loop, you need 15 keys. In general, for a secure loop involving *n* people, you need *n(n-1)/2* keys. This can be quite a large number of keys to manage for real-world situations such as those in financial institutions. The reason for such a large number of keys is that each pair of individuals involved in private key encryption shares a key.

- The second problem with private key encryption is the security involved in distributing the key itself.

FIGURE 19.3.

Private encryption with three people.

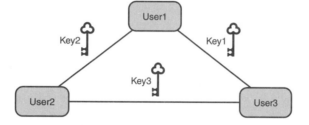

FIGURE 19.4.

Private encryption with four people.

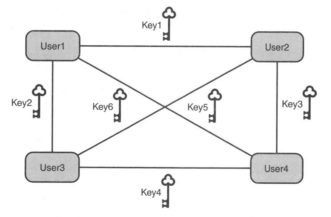

19

USING
ENCRYPTION

Mechanics of Secret Key Encryption

Most successful secret key encryption techniques use a simple set of functions and procedures to convert the plaintext into ciphertext. The concept of *block encryption* is very commonly used for this purpose; it involves the use of a block or a group of bytes for encryption purposes instead of a single byte or character. Each block can be operated on by any combination of several processes. The final ciphertext can be generated by applying the following processes during several iterations or rounds of encryption:

- **Substitution techniques:** Substitution techniques are very commonly used in encryption algorithms. As we have seen earlier, a knowledge of the language and the context of the message gives a hacker a lot of information about how to decipher the code. Therefore, block encryption is used instead of bit or character substitution. Security is obtained by having a one-to-one mapping between blocks of characters of plaintext and blocks of ciphertext of the same size—but the relationship between them is not easy to figure out. Substitution techniques usually use some simple strategy such as a lookup table or the XOR function.

- **Permutation:** You can rearrange the characters of a plaintext message to convert the message into an anagram that looks like a message with random characters. For example, most messages consist of 7-bit ASCII characters. By scrambling the bits to create a random set of bits, you can get the desired encryption. Permutation techniques are usually used in conjunction with other techniques such as substitution.

- **Encryption functions:** Exclusive OR is an example of an encryption function (as described in the following section). Other functions such as binary addition, multiplication, and modular arithmetic functions are also common.

Using Exclusive OR (XOR) to Perform Block Encryption

A very popular method for performing simple encryption is the XOR function. The Exclusive OR function is used to indicate that if there are two conditions (say conditionA and conditionB), then either conditionA is true or conditionB is true—but not both. The complete set of possibilities for two values being XORed and their result is as follows:

```
XOR(0,0) = 0
XOR(0,1) = 1
XOR(1,0) = 1
XOR(1,1) = 0
```

The best thing about the XOR function is that it can be used to reverse itself and can therefore be used for encryption purposes.

Suppose that we take the values A = 10101000 and B = 00111001. Therefore, C = XOR(A,B) = 10010001.

Now if we take B and XOR it with C, we will obtain A:

```
XOR(B,C) = XOR(00111001, 10010001) = 10101000 = A
```

Listing 19.4 shows how the XOR function can be implemented.

LISTING 19.4. AN IMPLEMENTATION OF THE XOR FUNCTION

```
//Author: Megh Thakkar
//   A Simple implementation of XOR function
//   Usage:  xor key input_file output_file
//   Purpose: This program takes a plaintext file
//         and performs XOR
// between each character of the file and the supplied key
//     and places the encrypted result in the "cipher" file.

#include <stdio.h>
#include <iostream.h>

int main(int argc, char *argv[])
{
    FILE *plain, *cipher;
    char *cp;
    int c;

    if ((cp = argv[1]) && *cp!='\0')
    {
        plain  = fopen(argv[2], "rb");
        cipher = fopen(argv[3], "wb");

        if (plain == NULL || cipher == NULL)
        {
        cout<< "\nSorry. Files cannot be opened\n";
        return -1;
        }

        while ((c = getc(plain)) != EOF)
        {
                if (*cp == '\0')
                    cp = argv[1];
                c ^= *cp++;
                putc(c, cipher);
        }
        fclose(cipher);
        fclose(plain);

    }
    return 0;
}
```

Using Substitution Boxes

A popular method of implementing a substitution function is to use a construct referred to as a *substitution box*, or an *S-box*. The S-box function takes some bit or set of bits as input and provides some other bit or set of bits as output. It makes use of a replacement table to perform the conversion.

> **Note**
>
> These reference tables can map more than one input to the same output. As a result of this truth, a hacker cannot take the output from an S-box and figure out which of the many inputs may have been used to generate the output.

Using Expansion Permutation

The expansion permutation takes a block of data and expands it into a set of overlapping groups; each group may be small compared to the original block. Suppose that we have a block of 24 bits; we can perform expansion permutation to convert it into a block of 36 bits as follows:

1. Break the 24 bits into six groups of four bits each.
2. To each group, add the bit that precedes it and the bit that follows it.

Now we have six groups with six bits each for a total of 36 bits.

The techniques in this and the preceding sections are just some of the commonly used methods in encryption algorithms. You can mix and match them to obtain an encryption algorithm. However, the security of encryption algorithms is not related to the usage of specific techniques or at least a certain number of these methods. The security of encryption algorithms is discussed in the section "Strong Algorithms" later in this chapter.

Using Encryption Rounds

Encryption algorithms become more complex and secure at the same time by using different encryption techniques one after the other. However, it is important to use different techniques in different rounds. For example, if you use substitution (or iteration) during the first round of encrypting plaintext, and use substitution again on the ciphertext in the second round (even if the substitution characters are different in the two rounds), the resultant ciphertext is no more secure than using just one round of substitution. In fact, even if you use a thousand rounds of substitution, the security is the same as using one round because there is always a one-to-one mapping between the plaintext and the final ciphertext. A much more secure encryption can be obtained by using one round of substitution followed by a second round of permutation. Popular encryption algorithms make use of 8 or 16 different rounds of encryption techniques.

Using Key Distribution Centers

One commonly used technique with private key encryptions is the Key Distribution Centers (KDC). Whenever userA wants to communicate with userB, userA calls the KDC, which generates a random and one-time usage session key. The generated key is encrypted and sent to the appropriate users who can then communicate with each other. The problem with this method is that the key used to encrypt the session keys is on file at the KDC. So anyone who has access to the files at the KDC can get the encryption keys. A recent Secret Service spy case involved an NSA agent, Ronald Pelton, who was selling cryptographic keys to the communists.

From the preceding discussion, it should be clear that private keys can become hard to manage for communication between civilians. The solution to this problem is the use of public encryption keys.

Public Key Cryptography

Public key cryptography is also referred to as *asymmetric cryptography* and is the result of a mathematical breakthrough that occurred in 1970. Unlike symmetric key methods that use a single key for encryption and decryption, asymmetric methods make use of two keys: a secret key and a public key. The public key is used to encrypt the message and the secret key is used to decrypt the message. The receiver has the secret key that should be protected. A mathematical process can be used to generate the two keys that are mathematically related. Refer to Figure 19.5 to understand how the different keys are used in public cryptography.

FIGURE 19.5.
Understanding public key cryptography and the use of public and secret keys.

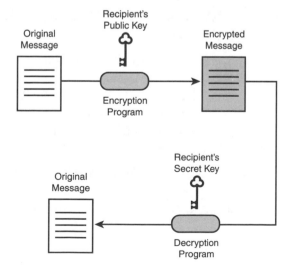

19

USING
ENCRYPTION

The goal of public key cryptography was to eliminate the biggest problem of private key cryptography of key distribution. Several techniques have been identified in the domain of public key cryptography over the years. These techniques are described in the following sections.

Ralph Merkle's Puzzle Technique

Ralph Merkle has published his work in *Communications of the ACM*, a premier computer science journal. He said that his work was "secure communication over insecure channels." The basis of his communication approach involves the use of puzzles. To understand this method, assume that John and Jane want to communicate with each other over a channel that is known to be insecure. John first creates a large number of encryption keys—say a million keys. John then places the keys in puzzles—one key per puzzle. Each puzzle takes a couple minutes to solve. John sends the puzzles to Jane, who chooses any one of the puzzles and its associated key. Using this key, Jane encrypts a message and sends it to John. John now figures out the key Jane chose based on his list of keys. Future communications between John and Jane occur using this key. An eavesdropper will be aware of the puzzles going back and forth but will take an extremely long time to figure out the exact key.

In simple words, John creates a very large number of keys and "envelopes" or hides the keys in some "cover"—one key in one envelope—and sends these envelopes to Jane. Jane randomly picks any envelope and therefore one key, encrypts a message using that key, and sends the message to John. John can figure out which key was chosen because John has all the keys. This key then becomes the key for future conversations.

Diffie-Hellman Multiuser Cryptographic Techniques

A paper called "Multiuser Cryptographic Techniques" was published in 1975 by Whitfield Diffie and Martin Hellman. Their cryptographic techniques used the concept commonly used now in public key cryptography. The basic idea of this strategy was that it should be possible to encrypt a message using one key and decrypt the message using another key. Several suggestions were made to Diffie and Hellman about how this could be achieved, including the following:

- Multiplying prime numbers, which can be done easily; but it is difficult to factor the corresponding result.

- Using a discrete exponentiation of numbers; the corresponding task of discrete logarithms is difficult.

Diffie and Hellman chose the second approach to conduct further research. The Diffie-Hellman exponential key exchange approach was published in their paper "New Directions in Cryptography" in *IEEE Transactions on Information Theory.*

The Diffie-Hellman approach is based on the following suggestion by John Gill, another Stanford colleague: Take the exponents of numbers and calculate the results modulo some prime number.

The method works as follows:

1. Both the active participants must first agree on two numbers, p and q. Numbers p and q can be publicly known.

2. Each participant must now choose a number, perform a mathematical operation that involves p, q, and the chosen number, and transmit the result to the other participant.

   Suppose that the first participant chooses M1 and the other participant chooses M2. The result of their separate mathematical operations are N1 and N2.

3. Using a second mathematical formula, both participants can now compute another number, K, such that K can be computed as a function of the numbers M1 and N2 or the numbers M2 and N1—but not the numbers N1 and N2. Future communications occur using the session key K.

The eavesdropper can have access to p, q, N1, and N2 but neither M1 nor M2. As a result, the eavesdropper cannot calculate K. Thus K can be used as a session key for a private key encryption algorithm such as DES.

This method is used for communication between two people and makes use of three keys: two secret keys (one for each person) and a session key determined by the two people during the course of the conversation. In other words, the conversation starts with the two people using their own keys; they exchange information to determine a session key which is then used for all future messages.

The RSA Technique

The RSA technique is one of the most powerful encryption methods known. It is used as the public key system in PGP (Pretty Good Privacy, a popular encryption method described later in this chapter). RSA makes use of any publicly available key to encrypt the information, but the decryption can be done only by the person who holds the matching secret key. RSA can also be used as a digital signature system.

The biggest problem with the Diffie-Hellman method is that the two participants must communicate actively. This may not be possible in email communication between two people who are not necessarily actively conversing.

19

USING
ENCRYPTION

In 1976, three professors in the computer science lab at MIT—Ronald Rivest, Adi Shamir, and Len Adelman—started working on the proposition made in the Diffie-Hellman paper, "New Directions in Cryptography," to find a practical multiuser cryptography system. After several months of research, they were about to conclude that such a public system was not possible. Then, in 1977, they realized a basic fact: It is very easy to multiply two prime numbers to get a large composite number, but it is difficult to take that composite number and find its prime number components. The outcome of this research is the technique simply referred to by the initials of its three inventors: RSA. This method is better than the Diffie-Hellman key exchange method because it does not rely on active participation between the person performing the encryption and the person performing the decryption.

To understand how RSA works, here's an example described in Bruce Schneier's book, *Applied Cryptography*. The steps to effectively use RSA are as follows:

1. Choose two very large prime numbers at random, say M and N.
2. Obtain Z (the encryption modulo) by multiplying M and N. In other words, Z = M*N.
3. Choose E (the encryption key), which is relatively prime to (M-1)*(N-1).
4. Publish Z and E as the RSA keys that others can use to encrypt the information.

Suppose that you choose M = 47 and N = 71. Therefore, Z = 47*71 = 3337. Now you have to choose E such that it is relatively prime to (M-1)*(N-1) = 46*70 = 3220. Suppose that you pick E = 79. The decryption key is now calculated using the extended Euclid algorithm and the prime numbers as follows:

D = 79-1 (mod 3220) = 1019

> **NOTE**
>
> This algorithm is in the PGP source code; it is not described here because it is beyond the scope of this book.

Now a user who wants to encrypt and send some information to us can use Z and E to encrypt the data. Suppose that someone wants to send us the number 688. To do so, they'd perform the following calculation:

688^{79} mod 3337 = 1570

We would receive the number 1570 and decrypt it as follows:

1570^{1019} mod 3337 = 688

The security of RSA depends on the following:

- The numbers M and N must be kept secret. This is obvious: If Z and E are already public and you also know M and N, it is not very difficult to figure out the decryption key D.

- It should be extremely difficult to factor Z. If Z can be easily factored, you can derive M and N from it, and then you can easily find out the decryption key.

- There should be no other mathematical techniques to derive the decryption key using Z and E.

Using Pretty Good Privacy (PGP)

Pretty Good Privacy (PGP) is a very popular encryption method that makes use of both public and private key cryptography. The latest version—PGP 3.x—uses the following steps to create a secure message-passing environment:

1. Create a random session key for each message.
2. Encrypt the message with the session key using the private key IDEA algorithm.
3. Encrypt the session key with the recipient's public key using the public key RSA algorithm.
4. Mail the encrypted message and the session key.

Table 19.2 presents a comparison between public and private key systems.

TABLE 19.2. COMPARING PRIVATE AND PUBLIC KEY ENCRYPTION METHODS

Public Key Systems	*Private Key Systems*
Can make the encryption key public	Cannot make th encryption key public
Only the recipient possesses the secret key	The secret key is with the sender and the recipient
Asymmetric encryption	Symmetric encryption
Can be used for digital signatures	Cannot be used for digital signatures
No need to exchange key before communication	Need to exchange key before communication

19

USING
ENCRYPTION

Choosing Prime Numbers in PGP

PGP uses the following technique to generate a prime number of n bits:

1. PGP first generates a random binary number that consists of two 1s followed by (n-2) random binary digits.

2. PGP uses a very efficient algorithm (referred to as a *fast sieving* algorithm) to determine whether the random number generated is a prime number.

3. If the algorithm determines that the random number generated is not a prime number, PGP tries the next odd number.

4. If the algorithm determines that the number might be prime, PGP prints a period (.) and uses Fermat's Little Theorem to check for primality. A minimum of 50 percent of all primes are ruled out in each pass through Fermat's algorithm. Each time this test succeeds, PGP prints an asterisk (*).

This information can be used to understand the output from PGP when you are trying to find a key pair. Suppose that you are trying to generate a 512-bit prime number and get the following printed output from PGP:

```
....................****............****
```

This output indicates that PGP found 20 different prime number candidates that passed through the sieve but were rejected by Fermat's algorithm. The four asterisks indicate that the first number to pass the first Fermat test passed all four tests. The next set of periods (.) indicates that the second prime number choice involved 12 different numbers that were rejected by Fermat's algorithm before a choice was finally derived.

The following code segment shows a simple implementation of the sieve algorithm that can be used to check whether or not a particular number r is a prime number:

```c
int primes[100];       // 'primes' is an array used to store
                       //   the prime numbers generated.
int total_primes = 0;  // 'total_primes' is used to store
                       //   the number of primes generated thus far
check_for_prime(int r)
{
    int i;
    int p = sqrt((double)r);

    for(i=0;i<total_primes;i++)
    {
        if (r % primes[i] == 0) return 0;
        if (primes[i] > p ) return 1;
    }
    return 1;
}
```

Using Random Numbers in Cryptography

Random numbers are commonly used in cryptographic algorithms to increase the security of the algorithms. PGP uses random numbers for different purposes:

- To determine the secret key
- To determine the session key used to encrypt each message
- To determine the key used in conventional cryptographic algorithms

Random numbers can be generated using a truly random natural process such as radioactive decay. Computers are equipped with random number functions that generate a sequence of numbers that are random in the sense that they are easy to predict. An expert hacker can have knowledge of the internal state of the machine and the starting number, and break such pseudo-random functions. PGP generates a random number by asking the user to type on the keyboard. It determines the time between successive keystrokes and builds a random number. Once a random number with a sufficient number of bits is generated, PGP asks the user to stop typing. This random number is used as a seed for the random number generator. A new seed is generated for each new public key being generated. The seed generation using keyboard speed is not really random; in fact, a flaw was discovered in the seed-generation routine of PGP 2.6. This flaw prevented the seed generation from being really random and became predictable to an experienced hacker. This flaw was fixed in PGP 2.6.1.

File Encryption Using PGP

The simplest use of PGP is to encrypt files and protect information on the computer against hackers. There are several reasons to encrypt files on your computer:

- If you are sharing your computer and the computer contains private information you do not want others to know.
- If you are storing confidential information on your computer that you may not want to be revealed publicly should your computer be lost or stolen.
- If you do not want sensitive information to be available to the public should your computer be sold or donated before you eliminated all the data.

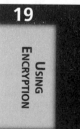

19

USING
ENCRYPTION

Encryption of a file can be done by using the `-c` option with PGP. Suppose that you want to encrypt the file called `secret`. You can enter the following:

```
c:> pgp -c secret
```

PGP responds to this command by prompting you for a pass phrase. It then encrypts the file to generate file `secret.pgp`.

The security of the file protected by PGP now depends entirely on the pass phrase and its safeguard. You can take several simple steps to secure this pass phrase:

- Do not write down the pass phrase.
- Do not store the pass phrase in a file that is stored on the computer.
- Do not choose a pass phrase that is easy to guess by others.
- Choose a pass phrase that you can remember easily.

The following kinds of information are easily guessed; you should ***not*** choose pass phrases that consist solely of these items:

- Your name
- Your spouse's name
- Your parent's name
- Your pet's name
- Your kid's name
- Your favorite cartoon character
- The name of the operating system you are using
- Your phone number
- Your license plate number
- Anyone's Social Security number
- Anyone's birthdate
- Your favorite movie
- Your favorite vacation spot
- Any of the preceding items spelled backwards
- Any of the preceding items followed by or preceded by a digit

After the file is encrypted, the next step you should take is to erase the original unencrypted file from the system. The standard delete commands available on most operating systems do not really eliminate the file; they simply remove the file link from the directory. As a result, the file can be undeleted. The -w option of PGP can be used to obtain a secure delete. The wiping process used by PGP overwrites the file with random data. Using random data instead of all 1s or all 0s makes it harder for hackers to retrieve plaintext. However, there *are* some cases in which simply wiping the file is not enough. For example, if you are using write-once media, wiping does not erase the old sectors. Also make sure that any backups of the plaintext (including program caches and automatic and user backups) are also somehow being wiped.

A file that is encrypted using PGP can be decrypted by using PGP with the name of the encrypted file as the only parameter:

```
C:> pgp secret.pgp
```

PGP reads the file, determines the encryption, and prompts for the pass phrase. When the pass phrase is provided. PGP decrypts the file and writes the decrypted information into a separate file.

The pass phrase used in PGP generates a 128-bit code using a hash function. PGP uses the IDEA algorithm with a 128-bit key to perform encryption.

Table 19.3 lists the standard file extensions used by PGP and their interpretations.

TABLE 19.3. FILE EXTENSIONS USED BY PGP

File Extension	Use
.txt	The plaintext file created using a text editor or a word processor.
.pgp	An encrypted file; it is a binary PGP file.
.asc	An ASCII-armored file. A file encrypted using the -a option of PGP has this extension.
.bin	The file created when the -kg (key generate) option of PGP is used. The file stores the seed for PGP's random number generator.

The DOS and UNIX versions of PGP make use of certain environment variables, which are described in Table 19.4

TABLE 19.4. ENVIRONMENT VARIABLES USED IN PGP

PGP Environment Variables	Use
PGPPASS	Stores the pass phrase. It is recommended that this variable not be used because storing the pass phrase in memory is probably the easiest way for a hacker to find it.
PGPPASSFD	Specifies a file descriptor from which your pass phrase should be read.
PGPPATH	Specifies the directory that contains the standard PGP files.
TMP	Specifies the directory in which PGP stores its temporary files. Be extra careful that others cannot access this directory or you open up an opportunity to break the pass phrase.
TZ	Indicates the time zone you are in.

19

USING
ENCRYPTION

With a DOS-based computer, you can set the environment variables using the SET command as follows:

```
c:> SET PGPPATH=c:\pgptemp
```

On a UNIX system, the setting of environment variables is determined by the shell being used. If you are using the Bourne or Korn shell, you set the environment variables as follows:

```
$ PGPPATH=/usr/temp; export PGPPATH
```

If you are using the C shell, you set the environment variables as follows:

```
% setenv PGPPATH /usr/temp
```

Limitations of Cryptography

You should understand several things in terms of the limitations involved in using cryptography to encrypt your messages:

- **Unencrypted information cannot be protected.** You may have access to the best encryption technique available, but if the data is still unencrypted on your machine, your data is at risk. A hacker who somehow gains physical access to your machine can get the information. Even if you delete the information, you should be aware that there are utilities to "unerase" and retrieve data that has not been properly removed.

- **Encryption keys must be protected.** The encryption keys are the solution to decrypting the ciphertext. If the keys are not secured properly, people can obtain the keys, and the whole point of encryption is moot.

- **Protect data against destructive attacks.** If the main purpose of a hacker is not to obtain the encryption keys but to prevent you from looking at the data, the hacker can destroy the encrypted file itself.

- **Beware of encryption programs with undesired hidden features.** Unless you write the encryption program yourself, there is no way to be completely sure of what else the encryption program may do in addition to performing the obvious task of encrypting the information. For example, it may place the secret key in the header of every file that is encrypted and also mail the encrypted file to the hacker.

- **Be careful of traitors.** You should make sure that the human beings involved in the key distribution process are completely trustworthy.

The effectiveness of an encryption method is determined by how well it defends against attacks. Good cryptographic methods are those that are resistant to brute-force attacks on the algorithm or the keys. In other words, a good cryptographic method makes use of very long keys and complicated algorithms that are extremely difficult to break. Even if a brute-force attack was applied, it would take millions of years before the code could be broken. On the other hand, *bogus cryptography* refers to the use of techniques that are easy to break. Bogus cryptography makes use of small keys or algorithms that are easy to crack. Crypt is a popular UNIX encryption utility that falls in the category of bogus cryptography. Another common technique used by bogus methods is the use of a password that is stored in a file; the file is not opened until the user types the particular password.

It is not easy to differentiate between good and bogus algorithms. A good hacker can usually find flaws in bogus methods in a reasonable amount of time. Until recently, the use of encryption was limited to government and major corporations, but at the present time, the use of personal computers, the Internet, e-commerce, and email to transfer information is so widespread that encryption techniques are very common in day-to-day use. Currently, a large number of systems for personal computers, mainframes, and even standalone systems such as telephones and fax machines are available—but they are not necessarily secure. Table 19.5 shows a comparison for a quick determination whether an algorithm is good or bogus.

TABLE 19.5. COMPARING STRONG AND BOGUS ALGORITHMS

Strong Algorithm	*Bogus Algorithm*
Uses long keys and a complex algorithm	Uses short keys and a simple algorithm
Difficult to break	Easy to break
Patented	Freely available
Based on encryption schemes that are published, analyzed, and thoroughly tested by experts	Based on unknown encryption schemes
Example: DES and IDEA	Example: CRYPT
Companies that provide these algorithms do not shy away from explaining what scheme they use	Companies that provide these algorithms are not comfortable explaining their encryption techniques

19

USING ENCRYPTION

In the entire encryption system, the weakest entity is the person holding the encryption key. This person must take every precaution to protect the key from getting into the wrong hands. Using a weak or bogus encryption algorithm is similar to using a cheap lock on a file cabinet. It depends how important the data is to you and how much someone can benefit from having the information. If you are trying to protect the data from people who do not possess much technical skill or who do not have any interest in your information, a weak algorithm may suffice. Otherwise, you should use the strongest algorithm you can afford.

Legal Restrictions on Cryptography

The U.S. government has placed two major restrictions on the use of cryptography in the United States of America:

- **U.S Patents:** The U.S. Patent and Trademark Office is increasingly being attacked for granting patents for products that are apparently not new. All the public key cryptography patents are now exclusively licensed to Public Key Partners (PKP). The penalties for patent infringement are the jurisdiction of civil courts.

  Most software programs such as Lotus Notes and many other Microsoft Windows programs come with a license for the RSA and Stanford public key encryption patents. The RSA algorithm was published even before its inventors filed for a patent; as a result, Japan and countries in Europe have been able to use most kinds of encryption without the trouble of negotiating licenses for patents from RSA or PKP.

- **Export controls:** You should not think about sending a copy of PGP to your friends who live outside the United States so that you can communicate with them without interception by the authorities. Doing so can make you subject to a heavy fine, or jail, or both. Export of cryptographic material is governed by Defense Trade Regulations (formerly known as International Traffic in Arms Regulation or ITAR).

  A program that implements encryption can be exported only after obtaining a license from the office of Defense Trade Controls (DTC). Before providing such a license, DTC—together with National Security Agency (NSA)—will evaluate the program. Part of the evaluation includes the determination of the encryption scheme. Generally, if a weak encryption is implemented, the export is allowed; otherwise, the request is denied.

  In 1992, an agreement was reached between the State Department and the Software Publishers Association (SPA) to allow the export of programs that implement RSA Data Security's RC2 and RC4 algorithm with a key size of 40 bits or less. Canada is a special case in the laws of exportation for cryptographic material. Canada has a liberal policy and allows any cryptographic software made in Canada to be exported without licensing. Current U.S. policy allows any cryptographic software to be exported to Canada without any license. However, as per Canada's Rule #500, software cannot be further exported to a third country.

Because of these strict requirements in U.S. policy, many companies are developing their software overseas and then importing it into the United States. An alternative to obtaining the privacy you need and avoiding the hassles of getting a license is to use PGP version 2.6, which is available easily in the United States, to communicate with PCP 2.6ui, which is available easily outside the United States.

Cryptographic Attacks

A hacker can use several techniques to "break the code" or decrypt a message you have encrypted without your authorization. Let's look at some of these methods.

Brute-Force Attack

A brute-force attack is also referred to as a *key search attack* because it involves trying every possible key until the code is broken. This method assumes that the hacker somehow knows when to detect that a key search is successful. The strategy is simple: Apply keys one after the other until you have success.

The brute-force method is inefficient and impractical because of the number of keys that may be possible. For example, if you consider an algorithm that uses 64-bit keys, the number of possible keys is 2^{64}. If you make use of a computer that tries a billion keys per second, it would still take that computer an exorbitant amount of time to break the code.

Cryptanalysis

The importance of cryptanalysis can be understood by realizing that key length is not the only consideration in determining the strength of an encryption method. You should also understand that knowledge of the key is not the only way to break the code. An expert hacker can make use of mathematics and computer skills to break most of the algorithms that claim to be unbreakable. There are two possible goals in making an attack:

- To decipher the ciphertext and find the plaintext.
- To find the encryption key.

The most basic types of cryptanalysis attacks rely on the knowledge of the language of the plaintext. In other words, the following information can help an attacker easily break the code:

19

USING
ENCRYPTION

- **Frequency of letters.** Common knowledge of the language used for plaintext can allow the attacker to make certain guesses in the deciphering process. For example, knowledge about the letters commonly used in the language (in English, the letters *a*, *e*, *s*, *o*, and *t* are used most commonly) and those not so commonly used (such as *x*, *q*, and *z*) can aid the attacker.

- **Letter affinity.** Some letters commonly occur next to each other (such as *io* and *ing*) while others rarely occur next to each other (such as *tp* and *iy*). This knowledge can be used for guessing the letters.

- **Length of the word.** In English, one-letter words are usually *I* or *A*. Also, there are a limited number of two-letter words.

- **Message context.** It can help the attacker to know the context of the message in terms of the sender, the recipient, the general content of the message, and the nature of the message.

The following attacks are quite commonly used:

- **Attack to find the encryption key after the plaintext is known.** This type of attack is quite common when breaking into encrypted email or a protected hard disk. Electronic mail has a standard header that the hacker can use as a basis for deciphering. Also, hard disks are used to store information at specific locations. In other words, the hacker can use common knowledge to figure out the rest of the encrypted information.

- **Attack to find the encryption key on a predetermined plaintext.** In this approach, the hacker can have the victim unknowingly encrypt certain information and then work on the ciphertext generated from the known data to find the encryption key. The hacker can then use the key to decrypt all messages that use the same encryption key.

- **Differential cryptanalysis.** This attack compares the results of encrypting several plaintexts that are very similar except for some minor variations.

Hacking a PGP-Encrypted File

Hackers can use several strategies to find the plaintext from a PGP-encrypted file. Several of these methods are based on the fact that PGP uses the IDEA algorithm:

- **Brute-force attacks against the IDEA key.** IDEA used by PGP makes use of a 128-bit key that leads to the possibility of several billion keys (specifically, 2^{128} keys). The hacker can try each of these keys one after the other (this approach can take a very long time before it is successful). As can be easily seen, this method is not the ideal method for breaking code.

- **Brute-force attacks against the pass phrase of PGP.** Instead of trying to figure out the encryption key, a hacker can attack the pass phrase that has been chosen to encrypt the file. The length of the pass phrase chosen becomes very important in determining the security of the pass phrase. I recommend using at least 12 characters and mixing uppercase, lowercase, digits, and special characters in the pass phrase.

- **Scanning the hard disk for an unencrypted copy of the encrypted file.** You can safeguard against this by wiping the plaintext file using PGP.

- **Booby-trapped PGP.** An experienced hacker may be able to booby-trap PGP so that it places a copy of each key or the unencrypted file in a hidden directory, encrypts the files with a pass phrase different than the one you have chosen, or does not encrypt the files at all and simply gives you the impression that the files are encrypted.

- **Kidnapping or threats.** The hacker may even decide to kidnap you and threaten you if the information is really critical. This kind of attack is something you really have to be careful about.

Digital Signatures

We have seen that public key encryption algorithms use a one-way function such that we can get encrypted data by passing the data through the function that uses the public key. We can get plaintext by running the encrypted data through the function that uses the private key. The entire process works in the reverse direction also: We can pass the plaintext through the function with the private key and create ciphertext; we can decrypt the ciphertext by passing it through the function that uses the public key.

A *digital signature* is a powerful feature provided by PGP that allows you to authenticate messages. There are several situations in which you may not want to encrypt the message but you do want to prevent the message from being changed. In other words, you want to assure others that you are the original author of a message short of them calling you up to verify the authenticity of a message they suspect someone else may have changed.

It should be understood that although the public key encrypts data in such a way that it cannot be interpreted by someone who does not have the proper key, digital signatures add data to the messages without adding any encryption to the message itself and without changing the message in any way. In other words, even if you do not verify the digital signature, you can still read the message. The only way to make sure that a digital signature actually certifies that the accompanying message is valid is to use the appropriate software and run through the process of verifying the message with the public key of the sender.

19

USING
ENCRYPTION

PGP creates a digital signature by processing the message with a message digest function to produce a 128-bit number. The message digest function is basically a mathematical function that converts all the information in a file into one large number. A PGP signature block is then created by signing this message with your private key. The PGP signature block is then placed at the end of the message. When a digitally signed message is received, PGP verifies the signature by extracting the message and running the same message digest function that was run on the original message. The public key of the sender is then used to decrypt the signature block. The two message digests are then compared to make sure that they match, thereby indicating that the message was not modified since the signature was placed in the message.

The only problem with digital signatures is that they can only tell you that a change was made. They cannot tell you the nature of the change or the amount data that was changed.

Two popular standards are currently in use for digital signatures: the Public Key Cryptography Standard (PKCS) and the Digital Signature Standard (DSS). These standards are described in the following sections.

The Public Key Cryptography Standard (PKCS)

RSA DSI developed a standard for digital signatures that uses the same public key encryption algorithm used for RSA public key encryption. The standard referred to as Public Key Cryptography Standard (PKCS) represents a set of standards for a variety of functions and a variety of data types. It standardizes the method of exchanging public keys and formatting encrypted data. The RSA digital signature standard is part of PKCS #1 and defines the manner in which encrypted data can be represented. The following steps are used to generate the digital signature:

1. A cryptographic hash function is applied to the data to be digitally signed.
2. The RSA public key encryption algorithm is used to encrypt the result of the cryptographic hash function.
3. The digital signature is obtained by placing the result of the hash function and the type of cryptographic hash that is used in the PKCS format.

The Digital Signature Standard (DSS)

In 1991, the NIST, in cooperation with the NSA, proposed the Digital Signature Algorithm (DSA) to be used with the Digital Signature Standard (DSS). This proposal was immediately followed by criticism that the NSA was involved in this process.

The NSA is against the wide use of strong cryptography because its functions would be seriously affected by strong algorithms. DSA has several drawbacks when compared to RSA:

- DSA is more complex than RSA.
- Public keys for DSA must be chosen with more care than those chosen for RSA.
- DSA is slower than RSA because it involves significant processing by both the signer and the verifier.

The DSA public key includes the following four values:

- A prime number p which is more than 512 bits but less than 1,024 bits in length.
- A 160-bit prime number q which is a factor of $(p-1)$.
- A value v calculated such that $v^q = 1 \mod p$. Note that v cannot equal 1.
- A value n calculated using the private key K such that $g^k = 1 \mod p$ and $K < q$.

Of these four values, p, q, and v can be made public; n cannot be public because it is based on the private key K.

The actual process of signing and verifying the message using DSA is much more complicated and involves the generation of another public/private key pair to be used one time only with the message. The actual process is beyond the scope of this book.

Nonrepudiation

Nonrepudiation is a term that refers to the quality of a digital signature. It provides a guarantee to the recipient that the digital signature is authentic, provided that the sender has safeguarded the private key and that the digital signature algorithm is reliable. Suppose that John ordered 1,000 shares of Company XYZ by sending a digitally signed message to his broker just before the market closed. The next day, the company announces that it will post a significant loss for the current quarter, and its stock opens lower by 20 percent. John cannot argue that he sent the order the previous day because he is the only one who holds the private key.

Commercial Cryptographic Products

Several commercially available products make use of a variety of encryption technologies. The following sections explore the different categories of such products to help you understand how they use encryption.

19

USING ENCRYPTION

Secure Web Clients

For quite some time now, the two popular Web clients or browsers in the market have been Microsoft Internet Explorer and Netscape Communicator/Navigator. Cryptographic security has been an important component of Web browsers since Netscape used Secure Sockets Layer (SSL) in its first version of Navigator in 1994. SSL provides secure encrypted communication channels between the browser and the server. In early 1997, Netscape included support for S/MIME (Secure MIME), which allows users to generate their own public key pairs, get certificates for that key pair from a certificate authority, and store the certificates in a browser. This key can then be used to digitally sign email or encrypt data using public key encryption. In September 1997, Microsoft followed suit by including support for S/MIME in its Internet Explorer 4.0 and its Outlook and Outlook Express email clients. S/MIME requires triple-DES encryption, which makes it a pretty secure environment. The explosion in the use of the Internet has made it important to consider other features in Web clients, including the following:

- Verification of users on each end of the Web communication channel
- Handling of *cookies* (user-specific information stored on the browser)
- Safety of downloaded software including ActiveX controls and Java applets

Microsoft Internet Explorer

Microsoft Internet Explorer is probably one of the best pieces of free software around. It can be downloaded from the Microsoft Web site at `www.microsoft.com`. It implements the following security features:

- Content protection options that allow users to put restrictions on the material accessed over the Internet. Inappropriate material can be prevented from being accessed by children.
- Certificate management tools can be used to keep track of user and site certificates.
- Allows access to security information for any Web page being browsed.
- Provides options to allow you to determine how the browser will interact with data coming from a variety of sources.

Certificate management options are also available in the Outlook and the Outlook Express email clients.

Netscape Communicator/Navigator

In early 1998, Netscape made a surprising announcement: It made its standard client available free to the public and also made its code freely available for other developers to improve on and add to. The Communicator Professional edition, which adds enterprise clients for calendaring, terminal emulation, and autoconfiguration is still sold for $29 per client. You can download the free client software from www.netscape.com. It implements the following security features:

- Allows access to security information for any Web page being browsed.
- Provides protection for browser certificates.
- Provides options for configuring encryption and other settings for SSL channels.
- Provides email security settings, including the option to choose the message to be encrypted and/or signed, to choose the certificate to use for digital signatures, and to configure S/MIME encryption options.
- Includes Java and JavaScript applets.
- Allows viewing and management of cryptographic modules used by the browser.
- Provides certificate management functions to manage user and site certificates.

Secure Email Clients

An email client is considered to be secure if it can handle the following tasks:

- Encrypt messages as well as attachments
- Digitally sign messages as well as attachments
- Decrypt encrypted messages with a private key
- Verify messages using the sender's public key

These functions require that the email client be able to manage the public and the private keys of the sender, as well as the public keys belonging to the recipient of the email message. Several secure email clients are commercially available, but the following three are the most popular.

Netscape Messenger

The Netscape Messenger bundled with the Communicator is a full-featured email and news client. The Communicator is a communications suite that includes email, a browser, a news reader, and conferencing—with other options to provide calendaring and legacy system terminal emulation. It is available for a variety of platforms including Windows 3.x, Windows 95, Windows NT, Linux, and others. It supports SNMP and POP, and is capable of sending and receiving S/MIME secured email.

Microsoft Outlook and Outlook Express

Microsoft provides Outlook 97 and Outlook Express, a pair of Internet-capable email clients bundled with the Internet Explorer. Outlook and Outlook Express are available for

19

USING
ENCRYPTION

Windows 95 and Windows NT, and there are plans to make them available for Windows 3.x and Macintosh clients. Outlook and Outlook Express support SNMP and POP and are capable of sending and receiving S/MIME secured email. Outlook 97 provides several advanced email features as well as functions for enterprise network users, including scheduling and task management features.

Qualcomm Eudora and Eudora Light

Eudora was the pioneer in email clients. It was introduced in 1990 when it supported the Post Office Protocol (POP). Eudora is now sold by Qualcomm, Inc., and a freeware version called Eudora Light is available at `www.eudora.com/eudoralight`. Eudora clients are available for Windows 3.x, Windows 95, Windows NT, Macintosh OS, and Macintosh Newton. In 1997, Qualcomm began shipping Eudora with a fully functional plug-in version of PGP for Personal Privacy 5.0, which allows the sending and receiving of PGP secured email.

Secure Desktop Products

The main focus of desktop security is to protect the information stored on the desktop. These products allow stored information to be accessed only by the person who owns it and by others who are given permission by the owner. Following are some of the most common features expected from secure desktop products:

- **File encryption and decryption.** Selected files can be encrypted or decrypted in place, allowing only authorized users to access the files after providing a pass phrase to decrypt the file. The product may require verification of the user at the time of system boot or every time the file is accessed.

- **Directory encryption and decryption.** Some desktop products allow certain directories to be designated as encrypted so that any file created or moved in that directory is automatically encrypted and can be accessed by a user only after authentication.

- **Pass phrase protection at boot time.** Some desktop products allow you to protect data by requiring a pass phrase before the boot can be completed successfully.

- **System lock.** Some desktop products allow locking of the system to protect against unauthorized use. This system lock can be implemented as a keyboard lock or as a pass phrase-protected screen saver.

- **Secure delete.** Files or directories deleted under the DOS or Windows operating systems are not really eliminated; their directory entries are simply removed. Various software commercially available allows the re-creation and salvage of deleted information. Although this can be good if you really want to recover lost data, it can be a problem if you really want to eliminate confidential information. Several desktop products allow the removal of data in such a way that not only are the directory entries removed, but the bits of each byte are set to a random value or to all 0s or 1s.

- **Support for public key cryptography and digital signatures is desirable**.
- **Access to data by a master entity.** Some desktop products protect data in such a way that some specified entity with a pass phrase and an ID can decrypt any data encrypted by any user of the product on a particular system or a set of systems.

RSA SecurPC v2.0

RSA Data Security, Inc. owns some of the most important cryptographic algorithm implementations currently in use. It publishes a personal desktop encryption product called SecurPC, which uses public key cryptography minimally. Although it does not use digital signatures, it provides the following important features:

- Secret key encryption of files and directories
- Ability to encrypt the file and store it as an executable such that it can be opened only by running the program and supplying a pass phrase
- Autoencrypt directories
- Bootup authentication
- Secure delete
- Access to data by a master entity
- Integration with Windows 95
- Hot-key system protection

Pretty Good Privacy (PGP) for Personal Privacy 5.0

PGP provides several important features in Personal Privacy version 5.0:

- Ability to encrypt and/or digitally sign data, email messages, and files
- Ability to decrypt and/or verify the digital signature of data, email messages, and files
- Support for Windows users
- Support for Macintosh users
- Use of PGPtray in applications (PGPtray allows users to perform cryptographic functions on data that resides in the system Clipboard; PGPtray can be used to prevent unencrypted data from being written to disk and to prevent decryption and verification of data in the Clipboard)

19

USING ENCRYPTION

Several important features that are not provided by PGP for Personal Privacy include:

- System lock
- Autoencrypting directories
- Secure delete

Symantec's Norton Your Eyes Only

Symantec's Norton Your Eyes Only is available for Windows 95 and provides personal desktop encryption. You can make use of an administrative add-on to allow the management of certificates. It makes use of public key encryption and digital signatures, provided that all the participants are using the product. Some of the key features of this product include:

- File and directory encryption
- Optional use of digital signatures
- Autoencryption of directories
- Secure delete
- Screen lock capabilities
- Boot lock capabilities
- Choice of various strong encryption algorithms

NSA's Clipper Chip

On April 16, 1993, the White House unveiled the super-secret encryption algorithm developed by NSA called the *Clipper chip*. The intention was to make this algorithm the public standard and to replace the aging DES algorithm. Clipper chip uses a classified algorithm called *Skipjack* and can be used to encode voice communications over digital telephones and fax machines. Data and email are handled by a PCMCIA card called a *Fortezza card*, which plugs into most laptop computers. Skipjack is an 80-bit encryption algorithm that is considered to be extremely secure. The only problem with Clipper chip is that the government has the keys to this algorithm. Therefore, it can crack any message encrypted using Clipper. Each Clipper chip uses two unique codes: a serial number and a master encryption key. These keys are tamper-proof and are destroyed when any attempt is made to reveal the code.

Clipper uses the Diffie-Hellman key exchange algorithm to exchange keys. Whenever you encrypt a message, Clipper takes a copy of the session key (used to decrypt the message) and encrypts it with the master encryption key. It sends the encrypted session key and the serial number along with the encrypted message.

The government has a plan called Escrowed Encryption Standard (EES), which has the purpose of creating two databases so that each holds the serial number of each Clipper chip and half of each master encryption key. Each half key is held by a different "escrow key"—specifically, one half is held by the National Institute for Standards and Technology (NIST) and the other half is held by the Automated Systems Division of the Department of the Treasury.

The Clipper code is very secure. When a law enforcement agency wants to perform a legal and authorized wiretap of a conversation encrypted with Clipper, the agency applies to each of the escrow agents. If the request is approved, the escrow agents send their respective keys to a black box that accepts the encrypted input and spits out the decrypted message. The keys have an associated expiration date after which the black box cannot use them to decrypt.

In 1994, Matthew Blaze of AT&T Bell Labs discovered a design flaw in Clipper's "back door" called the Law Enforcement Access Field (LEAF). Using LEAF, law enforcement agencies can obtain copies of the Clipper keys that can be used to read the encrypted data. LEAF is protected by a 16-bit checksum, and Blaze realized that if you can corrupt the key, the government agencies cannot unscramble the encrypted data.

Summary

Cryptography and encryption has long been the domain of government organizations and big businesses. The explosion in the use of computers, the Internet, and public key cryptography has made it possible for individuals to protect their data using a variety of encryption techniques. This chapter discussed the various strategies used by encryption algorithms and the most common methods an experienced hacker may use to break into the code and decipher the message. Several commercially available products (such as PGP for Personal Privacy and the Norton Your Eyes Only) can be used to encrypt your messages. Various types of security are provided in Internet browsers such as Netscape Navigator and Microsoft Internet Explorer.

We analyzed some commonly used techniques such as substitution; permutation, XOR, and other cryptographic functions were also discussed. No matter which technique you use, keep in mind that a desperate hacker can always decipher the message. You should take necessary precautions to protect your data. Those precautions range from proper choice of pass phrases to physically protecting your assets and yourself.

19

USING ENCRYPTION

Distributed Computing Topics

PART
V

IN THIS PART

CORBA

CHAPTER 20

In traditional network programming, the developer is responsible for message structure, error recovery, and runtime server management—not to mention scalability and failure recovery mechanisms. Managing software changes across languages and platforms can use up development resources, raise development costs, and extend project schedules. Over 800 of the software industry's top organizations came together to form the Object Management Group (OMG at `www.omg.org`) with the goal of defining an infrastructure for object computing.

The most prominent accomplishment of the OMG was the Common Object Request Broker Architecture (CORBA) specification. CORBA defines an object bus, enabling the integration and management of objects defined by C++, Java, Smalltalk, and "most" other object-oriented languages. Most of all, CORBA environments provide a robust network computing model.

This chapter presents a fast-paced examination of CORBA development. For the C++ programmer, CORBA enables objects to operate in a distributed manner. Calls made to a local C++ object are transparently routed to a remote object. The calling mechanism is virtually transparent, leaving the code clean and straightforward. The coding examples in this chapter bear out these benefits.

There are several roles for the CORBA developer:

- **Client developer:** The client developer works at the API level, making method calls to a local object. These objects are proxy objects that communicate to the server object to perform the necessary functionality.

- **Server developer:** The server developer is much like the C++ class developer, creating an interface for the object and packaging it correctly.

- **System architect:** The CORBA architect is the developer who creates the framework in which the objects exist and interoperate.

The following are some common CORBA terms that are used in this chapter:

- **Stub.** The proxy code generated by an IDL compiler that sends requests to an ORB. This is the C++ class that makes it appear as though the methods are executing locally.

- **Skeleton.** The server classes generated by the IDL compiler. You extend the skeleton through inheritance to provide the functionality needed on the server object.

- **BOA (Basic Object Adapter).** The interface your server object uses to connect the ORB.

- **ORB (Object Request Broker).** A pseudo object, assumed to be always available in both the client and server runtime environments. The ORB is typically a server application listening at a specific port, waiting to accept a TCP/IP socket connection. Client applications connect to the ORB, send request messages, and receive reply messages from the ORB.

- **Request.** A method call from the client stub to the server object, the request is a package of the method's arguments and return values.

- **Object.** The instance of an object, defined by an interface; resides under the control of an ORB.

- **IDL (Interface Definition Language).** A modified subset of C++ type and class definitions. The IDL typically has the same goals as a C++ utility class.

- **Marshaling.** The process of changing data from a language-dependent format to a language-independent format.

- **Service**. An interface defined by the CORBA specification, such as the naming service, Interface Repository, or ORB. A service is equivalent to an operating system API, providing access to a particular system service of CORBA.

Theory and Justification

It is helpful to think of CORBA as an integration toolkit: It eases the intricate details of network programming. There is no need to be intimidated by CORBA; as a C++ programmer, you already have the skills to use it effectively.

The skills needed for CORBA development are a subset of those you have gained in dealing with compilers, operating systems, and Internet server applications (HTTPD, daemons, mail servers, and so on). You can apply your object-oriented programming and design pattern skills to understanding and using the CORBA environment.

The following sections explain what constitutes a CORBA environment and how CORBA relates to your C++ programming.

The Minimal CORBA Environment

To execute methods on a remote object, you need the following elements:

- An ORB
- A server application
- A client application

> **NOTE**
>
> Many ORB vendors use the _bind() method to attach a client object to the server object. The _bind() method is a proprietary method that is not interoperable between different ORB vendors.
>
> For a discussion of ORB interoperability, see "The Naming Service and Interoperability," near the end of this chapter.

CORBA environments differ greatly depending on how the vendor decided to implement the ORB. The client and server may both have access to their own ORB interfaces. Whether these interfaces are several ORBs or are libraries compiled into each executable module depends on the vendor. It is only important that the environment have an ORB interface available. Figure 20.1 displays the interaction of the client, server, and ORB.

FIGURE 20.1.

The relationship between the CORBA client, server, and ORB.

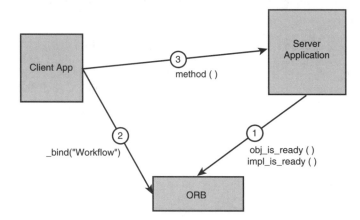

For interaction in CORBA, a client and server connect to each other through the CORBA *environment*. What constitutes the environment may be vendor specific, but the following three steps are necessary:

1. The server object registers itself with the CORBA environment.

2. The client asks the CORBA environment to bind a server object to the client object.

3. The client begins making method invocations on the client object; these invocations are redirected to the server object.

A Framework for Object Technology

Fully understanding object-oriented programming and design is important for the advanced developer. Because the OMG has already defined a framework definition, it is as if all CORBA developers are following the same coding and design standards. Many organizations have embraced CORBA for enterprise development. Part of the reason is because the framework of interfaces and services is defined by the CORBA specification. The overall distributed computing architecture is already there for the developer. The developer can reuse predefined interfaces to create new components.

CORBA allows developers to deliver object technology as a more complete package than was previously possible. The object interfaces missing from networks and operating systems are defined by CORBA. The awkward shoe-horning of objects typically required to integrate objects with procedural interfaces is therefore eliminated.

Migration to the object model is most prevalent in languages, operating systems, and databases. Objects have been retrofitted to Visual Basic, Lisp, Rexx, and even COBOL. Most operating systems have proprietary object frameworks attached to them. Object databases have attempted to bridge the object-relational gap with little success. CORBA allows the completion of this migration, object interaction.

The OMG acts as a mediator between vendors, defining the responsibilities of each, keeping constant vigil over the larger architectural issues such as portability and interoperability. To this end, the OMG has assigned committees to standardize interfaces to vertical domains such as finance and health care.

> **NOTE**
>
> As this book goes to press, the Open Group (www.opengroup.org) has devised a certification for CORBA implementations. Vendors who want to make interoperability claims now have an independent body to back up their claims.

IIOP: The Object Glue

The Internet Inter-ORB Protocol (IIOP) provides the network glue for objects. IIOP adds the layer for moving aggregate data types across TCP/IP. Data is sent and type checked across the socket connection. The IIOP also defines message structures for method call requests and error handling. As a transport protocol, IIOP is not only used by CORBA, but also by Java's RMI.

20

CORBA

How IIOP Moves Data

On the lowest level, IIOP makes socket calls. IIOP sends streams of encoded bytes across TCP/IP. The bytes are encoded, or marshaled, from their language-specific data structures into streams of raw bytes.

The data structures are comprised of arguments, return values, and message structures that make up the IDL definition for CORBA objects. If data from the socket isn't an IIOP data type, exceptions are thrown. Type safety has been instrumental in the success of C++; CORBA has reaped the same rewards.

Each message is a predefined structure, and both the client and server know the message format. There is also a dynamic invocation mechanism for CORBA, but this chapter is concerned with the static mechanism.

Figure 20.2 shows a layered diagram of how the different elements of CORBA relate to IIOP.

FIGURE 20.2.

CORBA's rela-
tionship to IIOP.

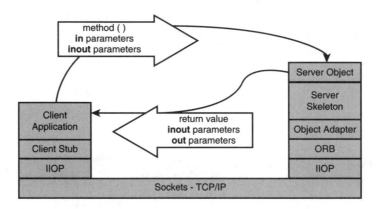

IIOP defines eight different message types:

- Request
- Reply
- Cancel Request
- Locate Request
- Locate Reply
- Close Connection
- Message Error
- Fragment

Most of these messages have a header and a body. Some of the message types have additional data appended to the end of the body.

Among the data in the message header are the message type and size of the message body that will follow. The header also indicates whether integers are encoded for Intel or Motorola. The encoding allows machine architectures to switch the bytes that make up the integers. If two machines use the same integer types, the machines do not translate the integers.

Only the client is allowed to send and cancel requests. Only the server is allowed to send responses and exceptions. The request message is a method invocation on an object. The body of the message has the method's input arguments appended. The response has the return value and any arguments containing output data appended to the message body.

The mechanism of IIOP is actually quite simple and quite versatile. Each individual type is encoded in a specific manner. If data is moving between a client and stub by the same vendor, it may not be using IIOP. Many vendors optimize communication when the client and server reside on the same machine, sending the data using interprocess communication.

A Component Model

Developers can use CORBA to build software components without being tied to a certain language, platform, or network. Other developers can use CORBA to integrate their applications with those same software components using the IDL for the component.

By implementing additional interfaces for an object, you create components that can be managed and manipulated. For example, if your object implements a transactional resource interface, transaction monitors, fault tolerant systems, and other services could interoperate with your object. An object that implements a transaction resource interface makes transactions with your object highly reliable; that object can be trusted to work within complex transactional systems.

IDL: The Binding Contract

In CORBA, the IDL represents the contract between the client and the server. The IDL is the agreement of functionality that a component should provide. Equivalent of the class declaration in C++, the IDL is the primary integration mechanism of CORBA.

The design pattern closest to a CORBA IDL is the Façade. In *Design Patterns*, the Façade pattern is described as providing "a unified user interface to a set of interfaces in a subsystem. Façade defines a higher-level interface that makes the subsystem easier to use."

20

CORBA

(Gamma: 185) The instantiation of a Façade interface object is typically a Singleton (Gamma: 127). Interfaces defined in the IDL have no such limitation.

Interface definition offers flexibility, reuse, and replacement of software components. Other benefits of the IDL include the following:

- A language-independent mechanism for defining methods and arguments.
- Exception handling in a consistent manner across different languages with the IDL.

Listing 20.1 is a real IDL sample used in a workflow application. We will use this example through the rest of the chapter.

LISTING 20.1. THE IDL FOR A WORKFLOW SYSTEM: `Workflow.IDL`

```
/* Workflow.IDL */
module Workflow
{

typedef string TaskId;
typedef string PersonId;

enum TaskStatusCode // TSC
{
    TSC_NOT_STARTED,
    TSC_IN_PROGRESS,
    TSC_ON_HOLD,
    TSC_FINSHED
};

struct Task
{
    TaskId                  id;
    TaskStatusCode          status;
    string                  description;
};

typedef sequence<Task> TaskList;

interface Workflow
{
    void createNewTask( in Task aTask );
    void updateTask( inout Task aTask );
    void updateTaskList( inout TaskList aList );

    void assignTask( in TaskId aTaskId,
                     in PersonId aPersonId );

    void getTask( in TaskId aTaskId, out Task aTask );
    void getTasksForPerson( in PersonId aPersonId,
```

```
        out TaskList aList );

    void taskStarted( in TaskId aTaskId );
    void taskOnHold( in TaskId aTaskId );
    void taskFinished( in TaskId aTaskId );

};// end of interface definition
};// end of module definition
```

The listing declares a `Workflow` interface, allowing the client developer to interact with a `Workflow` system. Details of the system are hidden from the client developer. This interface is almost self-documenting and allows the server developer to explicitly define the access to the underlying `Workflow` system.

Following are the elements of the IDL:

- **Structural:** `module`, `interface`
- **Simple Types:** `void`, `boolean`, `char`, `octet`, `string`, `unsigned short`, `short`, `unsigned long`, `long`, `float`, `double`, `enum`
- **Aggregate Types:** `typedef`, `struct`, `union`
- **Collections:** `sequence`, `array`
- **Argument Modifiers:** `in`, `out`, `inout`
- **Special Constructs:** `exception`, `attribute`
- **Directives:** `#include`, `#pragma`

The IDL Compared to a C++ Class Definition

The CORBA specification defines the mapping between IDL types and the types in various languages. C++ and Java developers have the most direct language mappings. Data types and definitions of IDL closely match the target language. The IDL should read like a C++ header file. The IDL even has the `#include` and `#pragma` directives.

The IDL defines types such as integers, decimal numbers, Boolean, and strings. There is only one type of container: the sequence. Many of the simple C++ types have CORBA equivalents. For example, `typedefs`, `enums`, and `structs` are equivalent to the C++ constructs of the same names. The `class` keyword is replaced by the `interface` keyword.

Method arguments have additional qualifiers, not familiar to C++ developers: `in`, `out`, and `inout`. These qualifiers indicate the intended direction of data: into or out of the method. The `in` qualifier is similar in meaning to `const`. The value of the argument is not expected to be modified by the method.

20

CORBA

For most interfaces, `typedefs`, `structs`, `enums`, and `interfaces` can be combined to implement many design patterns. However, for those who need additional features, the IDL provides attributes and exceptions.

Although object implementation data is not directly accessible from a client, the language mapping requires that the IDL compiler generate accessor methods for setting (`_set`) and retrieving (`_get`) the values for each attribute. The `readonly` attribute instructs the IDL compiler not to generate the `_set` method.

You may define a structure to hold exception data and then specify that a particular method will throw the specific exception. The client developer can catch the exception and handle the error condition using the predefined exception data. Structured exception handling simplifies source code and helps express what failures the client can expect.

Inheritance

For reuse and extension, few language constructs provide the flexibility of inheritance. Inheritance in the CORBA IDL is very similar to inheritance in C++, but without an access qualifier: Interface inheritance in the CORBA IDL is always public.

Inheritance can be used to enhance an existing interface. For example, if client applications are dependent on `Workflow` and need additional methods, you can inherit from `Workflow` and add the methods to the derived class. In this way, clients dependent on `Workflow`'s interface do not have to be changed; only the new client interfaces need to have their stubs regenerated. This approach allows runtime enhancement of a CORBA interface.

The Object Request Broker

The Object Request Broker (ORB) is a defined set of methods that has a vendor-specific implementation. The actual location of the ORB is not defined; it is assumed to be accessible to any object in the CORBA environment—both client and server objects. Brokering requests for method invocation is the ORB's main job. The ORB performs this task transparently and can encrypt, compress, or validate access rights of the calling ORB's request data.

> **CAUTION**
>
> Some ORBs are built from scratch; others may have been a full-blown application server or a Web server. ORB vendors sometimes get a little too much reuse

from their past development efforts. These ORBs may be very nonstandard or lack interoperability.

If the salesman starts pushing the application server end of the ORB, start asking about interoperability with other ORBs and conformance to IIOP.

The architecture of an ORB is similar to that of a socket server. The ORB listens to a port, waiting for a socket connection. When a client connects to the socket, the ORB takes the request and routes it to the server object.

> **Caution**
>
> The Portable Object Adapter (POA) is part of the CORBA 2.2 specification and ensures server-side portability. With the POA, you can be very specific about how you want your server objects treated. Specifically, the server object defines the options for instantiation and persistence it supports.

Object Lifetime

Objects in CORBA are persistent: It is assumed that an object will exist for all time. In C++, most objects are transient: They are created at runtime and destroyed when the application ends.

One method for handling objects is to create a server object factory to construct the object type you need. Creating a factory interface is useful in some circumstances, but doing so for every interface is tedious. ORB vendors may use a pseudo object to fake server object persistence. The pseudo object simplifies the client's view of the distributed environment, making it appear as though there is a single object, when in fact, there may be many objects.

To accomplish this effect, a single pseudo object is registered on the naming service or using the ORB's location mechanism. When a client wants an implementation of the object, it attempts to connect to the ORB containing the object. The ORB then creates the object and redirects the client to the new object.

To the client, it looks as though the object has always been there. For the server, however, the object is created and destroyed based on the connection of the client.

20

CORBA

Development Environments

Because CORBA is an open standard, implemented by several vendors, you have the opportunity to mix and match your development and runtime environment. This can work if you avoid the proprietary extensions provided by some vendors. However, as with any multiple-vendor situation, you should make certain that you get significant benefit from mixing vendors to justify the potential problems.

For example, you may generate your Java client stubs using VisiBroker and use Orbix for C++ client stubs and server skeletons. Your reason for using VisiBroker on the client side may be motivated by the existence of a VisiBroker ORB in every Netscape 4.x/5.x browser. This logic expedites the distribution of Java CORBA clients for your runtime environment.

In the runtime environment, you may use Netscape's Web server for HTTP, naming services, and LDAP Directory services, while using an Orbix runtime environment to bridge over to a Microsoft ActiveX control.

> **Note**
>
> If your organization has not standardized on a CORBA development environment, several vendors offer evaluation periods on their development tools (for example, Inprise and Iona). Others offer evaluation periods on only their ORB, minus the development environment (for example, ObjectSpace).
>
> Having just an ORB isn't necessarily useful unless you are testing for interoperability.

The two leading C++ CORBA development environments are Inprise's VisiBroker and Iona's Orbix. Both of these products are state of the art, providing all the tools you need to create solutions for even the most complex problems. These vendors are highly motivated to make your development successful. Many companies use these ORBs as the engine for application servers and more sophisticated development environments.

> **Caution**
>
> Watch out for public domain ORBs. CORBA development is not the best time to be without vendor support. If you are a veteran of the free stuff, look over the ORBs described at `research.iphil.net/Corba`. Don't forget to check licensing limitations for commercial development when using free ORBs.

Comparing CORBA Environments

Every development environment has problems, quirks, and a host of underdeveloped features. When going for feature-rich environments, it can be hard to tell which features are proprietary extensions to the CORBA specification. Lack of research may leave you married to a single proprietary solution.

ORB Interoperability

Interoperability has been a big problem with ORB vendors. Although the standardization on IIOP has helped, the ambiguity in the specification means that incompatibilities still exist. Most ORB vendors don't put a high priority on testing their ORBs against competing ORBs. If you have dealt with incompatibilities between C++ compilers' implementations of the C++ standard, you will understand that CORBA implementations have many of the same difficulties.

Following are some questions you should answer before you choose a specific ORB:

- **Are the language mappings all at the same CORBA specification level?** Vendors may be more interested in Java than C++, focusing their marketing and development on Java. This can often lead to the impression that the vendor has a CORBA 2.1 environment for C++ when, in fact, its Java environment is 2.1– compliant but its C++ environment is compatible with some earlier version.

- **Does your ORB interoperate with JavaIDL/Visigenics/Orbix?** If they don't interoperate (or haven't been tested for interoperability), the ORB may have some real issues. Demand proof of interoperability and know whether it will be maintained in the future.

- **What language compilers and versions of those compilers are required for your development environment?** C++ library linkage is still a problem, and as long as compiler vendors keep breaking their own code, you have to be careful to specify the details of your target development environment. Vendors should supply you with a list of compiler versions that are compatible.

- **What operating system version is required?** As with compiler vendor/versions, make sure that the ORB has been tested on the latest version of your OS. If it hasn't, you'll know that the vendor isn't interested in supporting the platform.

- **Do you have a proxy mechanism for firewalls and browsers?** Security mechanisms in firewalls and Web servers are rarely designed to handle IIOP. Make sure that the vendor has a solution for operating its ORBs in sophisticated, real-world networks. It's not so important that it produces the proxy, but that it has tested its product with one.

- **What level of IIOP do you support?** Most vendors should support IIOP 1.0 or 1.1. If they don't say or don't know, consider this a negative. Make sure that the vendor isn't using a proprietary interORB protocol. Some vendors who have converted their application servers to ORBs have this problem. If so, you may encounter sever interoperability problems down the road if you are snared by IIOP incompatibilities.

- **When will you support the CORBA 2.2/3.0 specification?** Make sure that your ORB vendor is still working on improving its ORBs and maintaining compatibility with the newer specifications. Vendors can overcommit resources to proprietary extensions, to the point that they neglect interoperability.

> **NOTE**
>
> The applications presented in this chapter are compatible with Inprise's VisiBroker for C++ and Borland's C++ compiler. If you use Iona's Orbix, the generated files will have different names, but the sample code should be fairly compatible.
>
> The details of CORBA and C++ development environments are not our concern at the moment: Our goal is a detailed conceptual understanding.
>
> Compile the applications in this chapter and refer to the vendor's documentation for setting up and running the CORBA environment.

Creating the C++ Client

The client application consists of ORB connection code and method invocations on a client proxy. The client proxy *is* a C++ class; it appears to the client developer as if the class is local, not remote.

The challenges in client development usually have to do with connecting to the naming service or the server ORB hosting the object. "Testing Strategies," later in this chapter, describes some of the methods for debugging connection problems.

Follow these steps to create the client application:

1. Obtain the IDL for the interface you will be accessing.
2. Generate the client stub code from the IDL.
3. Write the code to connect the client object to the ORB.
4. Using the label `Workflow`, create an instantiation of the client stub. The instantiated stub is your client object.

5. Now write the code to call methods against the client object.

Now that we have an overview, let's work through the details.

Generating the Stub

We will be using the `workflow.idl` shown in Listing 20.1, earlier in this chapter. In the VisiBroker environment, the command to generate the CORBA classes from an IDL template is as follows:

```
dos> idl2cpp -src_suffix cpp -no_tie workflow.idl
```

When this command is executed, four files are created:

- `workflow_c.hh`
- `workflow_c.cpp`
- `workflow_s.hh`
- `workflow_s.cpp`

The header and source files with the appended _c are for the client application; the files with the appended _s are for the server application. Concern yourself right now with the files generated for the client. The classes defined in these files make up the client stub. Be warned: The code is generated for performance, not readability.

To obtain the details of the C++ class interface, read the `workflow_c.hh` file. Open the file and search for the `bind()` method. Look for the methods directly after this method. For convenience, you can copy the following method declarations and move them into a comment in your client code:

```
/*
Methods:
virtual void taskStarted( const char* _aTaskId );
virtual void updateTask( Task& _aTask );
virtual void taskOnHold( const char* _aTaskId );
virtual void createNewTask( const Task& _aTask );

virtual void assignTask( const char* _aTaskId,
                         const char* _aPersonId);
virtual void taskFinished( const char* _aTaskId );
virtual void getTasksForPerson(
                const char* _aPersonId,
                TaskList*& _aList );

virtual void getTask( const char* _aTaskId,
                      Task*& _aTask );

virtual void updateTaskList( TaskList& _aList );

*/
```

These are the methods you will use to access the functionality of the server. The idl2cpp utility generates C++-specific mappings for each method, type, and argument.

Connecting to the ORB

Follow these steps to connect with the server object:

1. Initialize the local ORB.

2. Bind to the object.

Hope that wasn't too complicated. You do need an object name specified by the server developer. In this case, the server developer gave us the name Workflow Server. Here's what the code looks like:

```
CORBA::ORB_ptr broker = CORBA::ORB_init( argc, argv );
Workflow::Workflow_var workflow =
        Workflow::Workflow::_bind( "Workflow Server" );
```

The argc and argv are sent to the ORB to define options for the ORB. Don't worry about these; the server developer will tell you if you need any options specified.

Invoking Methods

Calls made on the client object workflow are redirected for execution by the server object. For example, to create a new workflow task you would use the following code:

```
Task task;
task.id          = "TASK123";
task.status      = TSC_NOT_STARTED;
task.description = "Create the server application";

workflow->createNewTask( task );
workflow->getTask( "TASK123", &task );

cout << "TASK123: " << task.description() << endl;
```

The description() method is called against the client object workflow. The functionality for adding a new task resides on the server object and is on the remote object.

In this code block, the distributed functionality is completely hidden. The server object can be running on the same computer as the client object, or the server object can be running on the local network or even across the Internet. The people who created the ORB have taken care of the network programming.

The Completed C++ Client Application

Listing 20.2 shows the complete client application.

LISTING 20.2. COMPLETED CLIENT APPLICATION: client.cpp

```cpp
/* client.cpp */
#include "workflow_c.hh"

#include <iostream.h>

int main( int argc, char* argv[] )
{
   try
   {
      CORBA::ORB_ptr broker =
          CORBA::ORB_init( argc, argv );

      Workflow::Workflow_var workflow =
          Workflow::Workflow::_bind( "Workflow Server" );

      Task task;
      task.id          = "TASK123";
      task.status      = TSC_NOT_STARTED;
      task.description = "Create the server application";

      workflow->createNewTask( task );
      workflow->getTask( "TASK123", &task );

      cout << task.id()          << ": "
          << task.description() << endl;
   }
   catch ( CORBA::SystemException& anException )
   {
      cout << "CORBA Exception: " << anException << endl;
      return 1;
   }

   return 0;
}
```

The client application builds up a Task structure and asks the server to create a task based on that structure. The client application then asks for the same task from the server. The expectation is that the Task returned from getTask() is the result of processing performed by the createNewTask() method. The server may have added or changed the data according to its needs. The task status may even have been modified, setting the task into a *started* state.

Creating the C++ Server

Now let's create the server side of our CORBA application. There eight steps involved in constructing the C++ server object:

20

CORBA

1. Create the IDL.

2. Generate the server skeleton.

3. Inherit your server class from the skeleton.

4. Initialize the connection to the ORB.

5. Create an instance of the server class and specify a label in the constructor.

6. Initialize a BOA.

7. Attach the server object to the BOA/ORB.

8. The server is now ready to accept method invocations from the client object.

Generating the Skeleton

We will be using the `workflow.idl` in Listing 20.1. In the VisiBroker environment, the command to generate the CORBA classes from an IDL template is as follows:

```
dos> idl2cpp -src_suffix cpp -no_tie workflow.idl
```

When this command is executed, four files are created:

- `workflow_c.hh`
- `workflow_c.xpp`
- `workflow_s.hh`
- `workflow_s.xpp`

The header and source file with the appended _c are for the client stub. The files with the appended _s are for the server skeleton.

The `-no_tie` option suppresses the generation of the TIE classes. TIE classes provide an alternative implementation model for server objects. TIE can be used in situations in which your server object has to inherit from a class other than the skeleton.

We will be using inheritance to implement the server object. The IDL compiler created a pure virtual method for each method specified in the interface for `Workflow`. Each of these methods must be implemented in the derived class.

Implementing the Server Methods

The IDL generator created the skeleton class `_sk_Workflow` with pure virtual methods for each method defined in the IDL interface.

We will now derive `Workflow` from `_sk_Workflow`, implementing the server object methods, as shown in Listings 20.3 and 20.4.

LISTING 20.3. SERVER CLASS DECLARATION: `Workflow.hpp`

```
// Workflow.hpp
class Workflow : public _sk_Workflow
{
    void taskStarted        ( const char* aTaskId );
    void updateTask         ( Workflow::Task& aTask );
    void taskOnHold         ( const char* aTaskId );
    void createNewTask      ( const Workflow::Task& aTask);
    void assignTask         ( const char* aTaskId,
                              const char* aPersonId );
    void taskFinished       ( const char* aTaskId );
    void getTasksForPerson  ( const char* aPersonId,
                              Workflow::TaskList*& aList );
    void getTask            ( const char* aTaskId,
                              Workflow::Task*& aTask );
    void updateTaskList     ( Workflow::TaskList& aList );
};
```

LISTING 20.4. SERVER METHOD DEFINITIONS: `Workflow.cpp`// `Workflow.cpp`

```
void Workflow::createNewTask( const Workflow::Task& aTask )
{
//    writeTaskToDatabase( aTask );
}

Workflow::getTask( const char* aTaskId,
                   Workflow::Task*& aTask )
{
//    readTaskFromDatabase( aTaskId, aTask );

    // Set value for testing
    aTask->setId( aTaskId );
    aTask->setDescription( "The method was called!" );
}
```

Connecting the Server Class

Connecting to the ORB is the same for the server object as it was for the client object. Think of the ORB as an ever-present interface:

```
CORBA::ORB_ptr broker = CORBA::ORB_init( argc, argv );
```

Loading the BOA into the ORB

The Basic Object Adapter (BOA) is a poorly defined interface that server objects use to connect to their ORBs. The CORBA 2.2 specification provides Portable Object Adapter

20

CORBA

(POA), an interface that is far superior to the BOA, and it should be portable between different ORB vendors.

For now, we will continue our implementation using the BOA defined by the CORBA 2.1 specification, and as implemented by VisiBroker.

Now we instantiate our server object with a label. This is the label the client will use to reference this server object:

```
Workflow::Workflow_ptr workflow =
        new WorkflowImpl( "Workflow Server" );
        Now connect the server object to the ORB:
CORBA::BOA_ptr adapter = broker->BOA_init( argc, argv );
adapter->obj_is_ready( workflow );
```

All that's left is to start receiving requests:

```
adapter->impl_is_ready();
```

The server application will now receive requests until it is shut down by the ORB (see Listings 20.5 and 20.6).

LISTING 20.5. THE COMPLETE C++ SERVER HEADER: Workflow.hpp

```
// Workflow.hpp
#include "workflow_s.hh"

class Workflow : public _sk_Workflow
{
    void taskStarted        ( const char* aTaskId );
    void updateTask         ( Workflow::Task& aTask );
    void taskOnHold         ( const char* aTaskId );
    void createNewTask      ( const Workflow::Task& aTask);
    void assignTask         ( const char* aTaskId,
                              const char* aPersonId );
    void taskFinished       ( const char* aTaskId );
    void getTasksForPerson  ( const char* aPersonId,
                              Workflow::TaskList*& aList );
    void getTask            ( const char* aTaskId,
                              Workflow::Task*& aTask );
    void updateTaskList     ( Workflow::TaskList& aList );
};
```

LISTING 20.6. THE COMPLETE C++ SERVER BODY: Workflow.cpp

```
// Workflow.cpp
#include "workflow.hpp"

void Workflow::taskStarted( const char* aTaskId )
```

```
{
}

void Workflow::updateTask( Workflow::Task& aTask )
{
}

void Workflow::taskOnHold( const char* aTaskId )
{
}

void Workflow::createNewTask( const Workflow::Task& aTask )
{
//    writeTaskToDatabase( aTask );
}

void Workflow::assignTask( const char* aTaskId,
                           const char* aPersonId )
{
}

void Workflow::taskFinished( const char* aTaskId )
{
}

void Workflow::getTasksForPerson( const char* aPersonId,
                       Workflow::TaskList*& aList )
{
}

Workflow::getTask( const char* aTaskId,
            Workflow::Task*& aTask )
{
//    readTaskFromDatabase( aTaskId, aTask );

    // Set value for testing
    aTask->setId( aTaskId );
    aTask->setDescription( "The method was called!" );
}

void Workflow::updateTaskList( Workflow::TaskList& aList )
{
}

/* server.cpp */
#include "workflow.hpp"

#include <iostream.h>
```

continues

20

CORBA

LISTING 20.6. CONTINUED

```cpp
int main( int argc, char* argv[] )
{
   try
   {
      CORBA::ORB_ptr broker =
                        CORBA::ORB_init( argc, argv );

      Workflow::Workflow_ptr workflow =
            new WorkflowImpl( "Workflow Server" );

      CORBA::BOA_ptr adapter =
                        broker->BOA_init( argc, argv );

      adapter->obj_is_ready( workflow );

      adapter->impl_is_ready();

   }
   catch ( CORBA::SystemException& anException )
   {
      cout << "CORBA Exception: " << anException << endl;
      return 1;
   }

   return 0;
}
```

A Java Client

The ability to integrate with other languages is one of the outstanding features of CORBA. With only an IDL definition, you can create a client application that will interface seamlessly to your server object.

The following sections show the Java equivalent of the C++ client presented in the preceding section. We will show only the differences in code generation, startup, and method invocation. Our goal is to familiarize you with alternative language bindings for CORBA.

Generating the Stub

We'll use `workflow.idl` to generate the client stubs in Java. Execute the following line:

```
dos> idl2java -no_tie workflow.idl
```

VisiBroker creates a `Workflow` directory with the following files:

- `PersonIdHelper.java`
- `PersonIdHolder.java`
- `Task.java`
- `TaskHelper.java`
- `TaskHolder.java`
- `TaskIdHelper.java`
- `TaskIdHolder.java`
- `TaskListHelper.java`
- `TaskListHolder.java`
- `TaskStatusCode.java`
- `TaskStatusCodeHelper.java`
- `TaskStatusCodeHolder.java`
- `Workflow.java`
- `WorkflowHelper.java`
- `WorkflowHolder.java`
- `WorkflowOperations.java`
- `_example_Workflow.java`
- `_sk_Workflow.java`
- `_st_Workflow.java`
- `_WorkflowImplBase.java`

These are the Java classes for both the client stub and the server skeleton. The server-specific files are _example_Workflow.java and _sk_Workflow.java. All other files are needed for the client application.

Startup and Method Invocation Code

Here is the Java equivalent of the C++ client startup and method invocation code for the Workflow client:

```
org.omg.CORBA.ORB broker =
        org.omg.CORBA.ORB.init( args, null );

Workflow.Workflow workflow =
      Workflow.WorkflowHelper.bind( "Workflow Server" );

Task task;
task.id          = "TASK123";
task.status      = TaskStatusCode._TSC_NOT_STARTED;
task.description = "Create the server application";

workflow.createNewTask( task );

TaskHolder taskHolder;
TaskIdHolder taskId( "TASK123" );
workflow.getTask( taskId, &taskHolder );
```

Aside from language-specific syntactical differences, the Java code is very similar to the C++ client code. Additional code is generated because Java lacks user-definable conversion operators and enums.

Testing Strategies

With objects executing method calls remotely, what could go wrong? Well, maybe less than you think. Because ORBs are used in mission-critical applications, they must be bulletproof. You may find that the added layer of CORBA objects lowers failure rates.

It may be impossible to simulate the environment in which an error occurred. In these cases, more traditional network programming tools can be used.

The following sections describe techniques that can help you debug your CORBA applications.

Tracing

Almost every ORB has a trace facility. Use it. Some tracing facilities use the Implementation Repository to store information; others use management consoles or flat files.

Get used to what tracing looks like when things are going fine. Then, when there's trouble, you can spot it quickly.

Monitor and Logging Services

Event logging is runtime tracing. Send events to logging interfaces and give your objects a heartbeat.

When things go wrong, users can supply you with the log and maybe even fix their own problems.

Exception Handling

IDL allows you to define structured, detailed exceptions. By using dynamic type discovery, logging tools can display data thrown in an exception.

For example, the following exception could be added to the Workflow example:

```
// Add to Workflow.IDL:
exception TaskAlreadyAssigned
{
   TaskId    assignedToId;
}
. . .
// Change the method in the Workflow.IDL
void assignTask( in TaskId aTaskId, in PersonId aPersonId ) raises
            (TaskAlreadyAssigned);
. . .
// Add to Workflow.cpp
try
{
   workflow->assignTask( "TASK123", "CHUCKPACE" );
}
catch ( TaskAlreadyAssigned& anException )
{
   cout << "TASK123 already assigned to: " << anException.assignedToId()
                                << endl;
}
```

This method provides details for the exception, and the IDL specifies the exception that the method might throw.

Remote Debugging

Some C++ compilers allow limited remote debugging of applications. In the past, these debuggers worked over serial connections. With the prominence of the Internet, these debuggers now run over TCP/IP.

20

CORBA

In the absence of remote debugging, you can use remote-control software under Windows, and, of course, Telnet or X Window under UNIX.

The Naming Service and Interoperability

CORBAServices is a specification of more than 13 services that you may need in creating CORBA applications. An IDL is defined for each of these services. The closest analogy is system services for an operating system. The naming service (NS) is the most commonly used service.

For most applications, a naming service is not needed. As application dependencies between different systems grow, however, the need for an organization tool also grows. The NS provides a way to assign names to objects and to organize those objects into federated hierarchies. This idea is similar to the file system directories defined across networks.

The naming service has a defined interface. The server object registers itself with the NS. The registration is the association of an object reference (IOR) and a name. The name is a sequence of naming contexts, similar to a directory's name in a file system.

The client object gives the NS a name, and the NS returns an IOR. The client then makes a connection to the ORB specified by the IOR. Method invocations on the server object are requested through the ORB.

Without the NS, the client needs the specific location of the server, which is similar to a URL. Moreover, when the location of the server object changes, the link is lost. The client can then no longer connect to the ORB.

As you can see, the NS is much like a directory of objects. The sequences naming an object are hierarchical, as they are in a directory structure. For simple environments, all the objects are identified by names on a single root level. As the architecture becomes more complex, the hierarchical element differentiates interfaces by breaking them down categorically.

Interoperable Object Reference (IOR)

Think of the IOR as equivalent to a reference in C++. The IOR contains the host IP address, port number, and an implementation-specific object key. The client uses this information to find and connect to the ORB listening on the host and the port specified in the IOR. After the client is connected to the ORB, it can start issuing requests across the connection, referencing the object key to target the request to the specific object.

An object reference can be turned into an ASCII string by calling the
`object_to_string()` method for any object. The CORBA specification defines the
structure of this string explicitly. The string can then be passed outside the CORBA environment, and an IOR can be re-created on a different machine using the object method
`string_to_object()`. This process is how ORBs from different vendors can interoperate.

IORs don't necessarily last forever. Because of the inadequacies and ambiguity in the
CORBA specification, the IOR is overworked.

CAUTION

IORs are used in nonstandard ways by different ORB vendors. Safeguard yourself by always asking the NS for the IOR, and use the IOR in a reasonable
amount of time.

After you make your connection to your target ORB, you shouldn't have any
problems. At that point, a socket connection has been made, and the object
should stay around until you destroy the client proxy stub class.

Finding the NS for the first time can be problematic. As of the CORBA 2.1 specification, there is no boot-strapping protocol for a client to find the first ORB.

Naming Contexts

In CORBA, *naming contexts* solve the name-clashing problems namespaces solve in
C++. Naming contexts are arranged in a hierarchy similar to file system directory structures or class hierarchies. A name context is a sequence of naming contexts that uniquely
identify a single object.

Figure 20.3 shows how names are constructed from the naming contexts. The semicolon-
separated name represents the name of the object. Where C++ namespaces safeguard
variables and class names, the CORBA naming contexts ensure the uniqueness of object
names.

Interoperability Issues

The `_bind()` method is VisiBroker's bootstrap mechanism that enables name resolution.
The `_bind()` method makes the client code nonportable, but very readable.

Universal bootstrapping should be included in the CORBA 3.0 specification. For different ORBs, you may have to replace `_bind()` with the vendor-specific mechanism for
name resolution.

20

CORBA

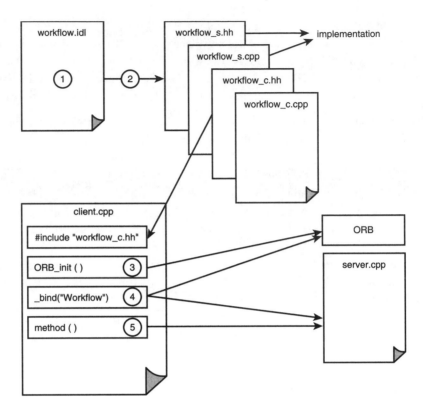

FIGURE 20.3.
Hierarchical nesting to prevent object-naming conflicts.

It is important to understand the three layers of possible boot-strapping:

- Using a proprietary method in a client object, such as _bind(). This method is used for small to mid-sized applications, where the client and server are on the same machine or LAN.

- Proprietary connection to the naming service, where the naming service and the ORB have a proprietary connection initiation mechanism. Here, the application is more complex and needs the Naming Service to find the server objects, which may be on the LAN or across the Internet.

- When the naming service is from a different vendor than the client object, stringification is needed. This is when the naming service writes out its *stringified IOR* (a string that can be reconstituted into an IOR) to a file system. The client then reads the string from the file system, reconstituting the IOR, and connecting to the first ORB.

Performance

Performance in a CORBA environment is unexpectedly fast. When I started CORBA development, I expected the slow speeds experienced under OLE/COM development.

The following sections describe areas in which you can make your applications more robust. Many of these areas are similar to those in C++ development—with a distributed computing twist.

ORB Memory Leaks

If an application runs in a spawned process, it is very difficult to spot a memory leak. The operating system acts as the garbage collector for the application. But when a memory leak occurs within a single process space, the application must perform its own garbage collection. Most C++ applications do not incorporate a garbage collection scheme. Therefore, C++ programmers must be highly sensitive to leaks in server applications in most CORBA environments. A simple leak that may be hidden in a CGI-spawned process can become a huge problem in an ORB. The cost on the CGI side typically shows up in process startup time and awkward architectures.

Granularity of Interface

Because the linkage mechanism of IIOP is sockets, data transfer tends to be much slower than it is in IPC or direct memory transfer. To offset this, you can consolidate the accessor methods into single method calls that set or get values from a passed structure.

> **NOTE**
>
> ORB vendors may optimize their ORBs using IPC or direct memory access when the client and server are on the same machine. Some ORBs even use faster transports than IIOP when their product is used on the client and the server.
>
> When the client and the server are different, a proxy ORB can be inserted over the slowest connection to speed up the ORB requests.
>
> Some implementations of TCP/IP use IPC when the client and server are on the same machine.

You can provide additional methods that perform batch processing for frequently called methods. To do this, create a structure with the arguments, return value, and exception information. Create a sequence of these structures and use the sequence as the argument to the batch version of the function.

20

CORBA

Avoid passing too much data around. If the server supplies the client with a list of data from a database table, and the user marks the rows for deletion, insertion, or update, transfer back only the rows you need to change.

Hardware efficiencies eliminate many granularity issues when the client and server are running on the same box.

Passing Object References

An IOR in CORBA is the equivalent of a reference in C++. The IOR can be passed as an argument into a method. The server object can then access that object to perform whatever operations it requires. This indirection involves overhead; don't overuse IORs in this way.

Summary

The CORBA specification and implementations are a major step in the evolution of software development. The developer can now focus on solving the architectural issues, not the integration issues.

Intermediate and novice developers can use the flexibility and ubiquity of CORBA to create the next generation of software systems. These systems will allow distributed computing environments to have the control and maintainability of older mainframe systems, as well as the flexibility of yesterday's client/server applications.

COM

CHAPTER 21

IN THIS CHAPTER

Object-oriented languages represent a significant step in the evolution of the software industry. This whole book focuses on the philosophy of building object-oriented projects with C++. As the software industry evolves, new requirements on the software tools are being imposed. It has come to the point at which individual languages do not suffice because of their nature—binary and interlanguage standards become necessary.

The problem with C++ (as well as any other object-oriented language) is that it provides an object paradigm on the source code level. The program is built using reusable classes in source form. It is possible to package classes in reusable binaries—dynamic link libraries (DLLs)—and publish only class headers. Unfortunately, this approach introduces more problems than it solves. Because there is no standard for how different C++ compilers implement many language features, the binary DLL becomes tightly coupled with the compiler used to generate it. The header should present all the implementation details (data and hidden methods) because the compiler needs to generate proper memory allocation of the class, including virtual tables. Another problem is the versioning of the code. Although the new version can allow older clients to use it, the newer clients are doomed to fail with the older version of the library. These problems force the vendors of software class libraries to use inefficient workarounds (for example, Microsoft's Foundation Classes library shipped with a different DLL name in every subsequent version), or to ship the library in source code.

To solve these problems, as well as to provide language independence, Microsoft created the Component Object Model (COM) specification—a binary standard for the deployment and use of binary software components.

Historically, COM was created to solve the needs of another Microsoft technology: Object Linking and Embedding (OLE). Later, its creators realized that they had created a very simple, powerful, and easily extensible architecture. Microsoft employed the COM technology in virtually all their products, even turning their operating systems into sets of components. This does not mean that COM benefits only Microsoft. In the standard versioning scheme, many source component vendors saw the perfect solution to their need to distribute binary libraries. A new concept was introduced: *componentware*.

The key to the evolutionary versioning presented by COM is the delayed runtime coupling between the components' binaries and their clients (don't confuse runtime coupling with definition coupling; the client still needs the definition header for the component at compile time for C++; other programming languages may need another definition). When a newer component is deployed, the older clients can still use it through its legacy functionality. The newer clients can use the newer functionality, too. If a newer client encounters the older version of the component, the client recognizes it in a standard way and can choose to degrade and work only through the older functionality.

The advent of COM in no way diminishes the usefulness of C++ as a programming language. In fact, because COM was developed with C++ concepts as a base, it is natural to write COM programs in C++. This chapter focuses on using and writing COM objects. It is divided into three sections: COM fundamentals, using COM objects, and writing COM objects. The COM fundamentals section describes the foundation of COM. Readers who have some familiarity with COM may want to skip this introduction. The other sections describe C++ techniques for using and writing COM objects. COM is too large a subject to be covered in just one chapter, however, so a "Further Reading" section has been provided at the end of the chapter.

COM Fundamentals

This part of the chapter provides a brief introduction to the concepts of COM. Readers who have basic familiarity with COM may want to skip to the section "Other COM Technologies" or to "Using COM Objects."

COM Architecture

The Component Object Model (COM) defines the following main entities:

- **Object:** This element relates most closely to a C++ class. Objects implement the functionality and contain the flesh of COM.

- **Interface:** This element provides a definition of some functionality common to many objects. Interfaces define the rules for interaction with the objects.

- **COM runtime:** This element contains a small set of routines for maintaining object services.

Every object implements one or more interfaces through which that object is accessible to the world. The interfaces that the object implements represent its functionality. The choice of implemented interfaces is the responsibility of the object designer.

Every object can choose to create another object as an output of a method call in one of its interfaces (the implementation of an interface method creates an object and returns a pointer to one of its interfaces through an output parameter). This process is part of the interface semantics. It is rarely useful to have one object manufacture another and then to have the second object produce another object of the first object's class. Most often, there is one directly createable object that, in turn, creates other objects. Those objects create other objects, and so on. The result is a tree of object classes, in which each parent class can produce objects of its descendants. The hierarchy of objects created by one root object and its descendants is called a *component*. Component is a vague term: It sometimes refers to a group of object hierarchies implemented in a single module (an executable or

DLL) that together encapsulate the necessary functionality to perform some task. The objects from different hierarchies are usually strongly interdependent (for example, one object is used extensively by another to accomplish its task).

One particular class of COM objects that can be created directly through the COM runtime is of special interest. It is the COM class, or *coclass*. As you'll see later in this chapter, this class is associated with another class of COM objects—class factories—that manufacture them. The class factory object has a method in one of its interfaces that produces an instance of the coclass and thus can be considered a language-independent construct analogous to the C++ new operator.

COM objects can be used by their clients in two distinct modes (which are transparent to the object and its client): *direct* or *marshaled*. When the object and its client reside in single execution context (called an *apartment*), the client uses direct pointers on the object interfaces. When the object and the client reside in different apartments, COM interposes itself between them and provides the necessary support for calling the interface methods and returning the results. Two objects provide the necessary support. The proxy resides in the client context and acts as the object for that particular interface (the client cannot differentiate between an object and its proxy). The stub resides in the context of the object and acts as the client of the object's interface. The connection between the objects uses protocols appropriate for the particular connection (Windows messages, RPC, or something else).

Interfaces

In COM, interfaces define the functionality that objects implement. They most closely relate to C++ classes that contain no data members and only pure virtual methods. This is the way COM interfaces are implemented in C++. The keyword interface used in code to describe an interface is replaced by struct in a C++ header: #define interface struct. All interface methods are declared as pure virtual methods in a C++ struct. Consider the following C++ definition of the interface ICar:

```
interface ICar
{
    void SetSpeed( long nSpeed );
};
```

This definition translates to this in COM:

```
struct ICar
{
    virtual void SetSpeed( long nSpeed ) = 0;
};
```

Because C++ structures make all their methods and members public, a simple preprocessor command suffices. If a class is used, the addition of the `public` keyword is necessary. The similarity between interfaces and C++ classes is intentional: It stems from the fact that virtually all C++ compilers generate the same virtual method table (VTBL)—in this particular case, the class containing only pure virtual methods—and the VTBL is the binary definition of the interface. To complete the picture, all methods should conform to the `stdcall` calling convention to achieve binary compatibility with other languages such as Pascal and Fortran (the preceding translation needs `__stdcall` after `void`—or some similar keyword, depending on the compiler).

Interfaces as C++ classes are subject to the following restrictions:

- They don't provide an implementation, only pure virtual methods.
- They cannot contain data members.
- They can be derived from other interfaces, but derivatives can add only new, pure virtual methods; only single inheritance is allowed.

The restriction about data members is crucial to the COM architecture. Data cannot be manipulated directly; instead, the client must conform to the exposed interfaces. This is necessary to preserve binary and language independence between the client and the object, and provides the foundation for execution context switching independence, as we will see later. The restriction about single inheritance is necessary because no standard exists for the binary layout of VTBLs of base classes when multiple inheritance is involved. With this restriction, the complications of virtual inheritance are avoided. In the discussion of `IUnknown`, later in this chapter, we'll see the COM solution to multiple inheritance.

Although VTBL is an excellent binary identity of the interface, there should be some means for source identity (that is, some way C++ or another language can name the interface in the source code). One approach is to use the interface's textual name as it is typed in the definition. Although this approach is great for C++ sources, it doesn't stand when looked at from the position of COM goals: It isn't binary form, it can't be understood by other languages, and it isn't unique (two developers can give their interfaces the same name). The solution comes in the form of a binary identifier called an *interface identifier* (IID). IIDs are variations of GUIDs or UUIDs—16-byte arrays that are guaranteed to be unique by the algorithm used for their generation. Globally Unique Identifier (GUID) is the name Microsoft gave to Universally Unique Identifiers (UUIDs)—entities defined by the Open Software Foundation Distributed Computing Environment (OSF DCE) consortium. The IID is the GUID assigned as the name of an interface. The COM function `CoCreateGuid()` generates a new GUID every time it's called. Of course, it is rarely necessary to call this function directly. Some tools such as Microsoft's `guidgen.exe` provide a user interface for allocating GUIDs. A GUID is needed only once—when you are designing the interface. We will see how to use the IID in the discussion about the `IUnknown` interface.

In the previous example, an interface was voluntarily described using C++-like syntax with a nonstandard keyword `interface`. In reality, interfaces are described in a language unsurprisingly called the Interface Definition Language (IDL). The IDL is part of OSF DCE Remote Procedure Call (RPC). The IDL is used to define the transparent definition of RPC calls over network transports and to generate appropriate network remoting code. Microsoft added some extensions for COM specifics. The result is that COM interfaces can be used remotely over RPC (this means between processes as well as between machines; this topic isn't explored any further in this chapter).

IDL syntax is similar to the syntax of C++ declarations with some additional annotations. The earlier example of the `ICar` interface definition written in IDL looks like this:

```
[object, uuid(C21D0200-2FB6-11d2-8952-444553540000)]
interface ICar
{
    void SetSpeed( [in] long nSpeed );
};
```

The keyword `object` indicates that this is a COM interface (as opposed to an RPC interface), `uuid()` gives the interface IID, `in` denotes an argument as an input parameter. Tools exist that take the IDL definition file describing an interface and produce a C/C++-compatible header file that should be used when implementing or using the interface. These tools also generate proxy/stub code for remoting the interface and a file that defines the IID (GUIDs are represented as structures and need to be allocated). Multiple interfaces can be defined in a single IDL file.

The way the sample interface is defined so far, it won't compile. If we run it through a Microsoft IDL compiler (MIDL), the result contains two errors. The first error stems from the fact that COM interfaces should derive from `IUnknown`, as discussed later in this chapter. The second error relates to the fact that all methods in COM interfaces should return `HRESULT`. Let's rewrite the sample so that MIDL accepts it:

```
import "unknwn.idl"

[object, uuid(C21D0200-2FB6-11d2-8952-444553540000)]
interface ICar : IUnknown
{
    HRESULT SetSpeed( [in] long nSpeed );
};
```

The resulting header file contains, among the other debris, the following C++ interface definition:

```
interface
DECLSPEC_UUID("C21D0200-2FB6-11d2-8952-444553540000")
ICar : public IUnknown
```

```
{
public:
   virtual HRESULT STDMETHODCALLTYPE
      SetSpeed( /* [in] */ long nSpeed ) = 0;
};
```

We include `public` just in case `interface` is defined as a class in the COM header.
`STDMETHODCALLTYPE` enforces the `stdcall` calling convention. `DECLSPEC_UUID` can be
safely ignored—it is a C++ extension introduced by Microsoft in Visual C++ 5.0.
`IUnknown` is publicly inherited because a base interface is part of VTBL and should be
visible. The resulting C++ class contains only pure virtual and publicly visible methods.

`HRESULT`s are 32-bit integers that describe the status of the method invocation. The name
implies that it will be read as a handle to a result—which isn't the case. (Historically,
`HRESULT` was intended to be a handle and the name was established; later it was found
that 32 bits suffice to describe the result itself.) COM enforces all methods to return
`HRESULT`s because it needs to report network failures to the caller in a uniform way.
`HRESULT` consists of the following bit fields:

SRRFFFFFFFFFFFFFFCCCCCCCCCCCCCCCC

S (1 bit)	Severity code: `SEVERITY_SUCCESS` or `SEVERITY_FAIL`
R (2 bits)	Reserved, should be zero
F (11 bits)	Facility
C (16 bits)	Status code

The status code itself occupies the first 16 bits of the `HRESULT`. Next comes facility,
which points out which subsystem returned the code. All custom codes are bound to
`FACILITY_ITF` (4), which means interface specific. The most important bit is the severity bit: `SEVERITY_SUCCESS` (0) means that the operation succeeded, `SEVERITY_FAIL` (1)
means that the operation failed. The two macros `FAILED(hr)` and `SUCCEEDED(hr)` test the
returned `HRESULT` `hr` for success or failure.

The symbolic names corresponding to defined `HRESULT`s also contain three parts in the
following order: facility, severity, and status code description. A few widely used
`HRESULT`s omit the facility part. Examples that do omit facility are
`CO_E_NOTINITIALIZED`, `DRAGDROP_S_DROP`, `E_OUTOFMEMORY`, `E_FAIL`, `S_OK`, and `S_FALSE`.
You should use standard `HRESULT`s where appropriate. `HRESULT`s should be used to report
exceptions because exceptions are not allowed to pass interface boundaries (they are
implementation specific in C++ or have completely different or no implementations in
other languages). Exceptions that pass beyond interface boundaries force RPC to return
`RPC_E_SERVERFAULT` (0x80010105) if the interface is remoted. If the object is in process,
an exception will probably crash the client.

Interfaces can be inherited. It seems natural because they are just C++ classes. However, things are quite different from C++ in this particular aspect. Because interfaces consist solely of pure virtual methods, a derived interface contains all the methods of its base interface. This means that the object that implements the derived interface must expose the base interface, too (it is implemented anyway). And if two or more interfaces are derived from some base interface and are all implemented on one object, the methods of the base interface can possibly have different implementations (sometimes this is desired, but mostly it is not because it confuses the object client). In short, it isn't advised to use interface inheritance except in special circumstances. COM offers a better way of achieving polymorphism—the `QueryInterface()` method of the `IUnknown` interface (discussed in the next section). Interface inheritance is necessary only if an interface cannot exist without implementing methods of its base interface. An example is `IUnknown`, which must be the base interface for all COM interfaces.

Listing 21.1 shows the IDL used in the samples throughout this chapter. Some details of this code become clear later in the chapter, in the discussion of type libraries.

LISTING 21.1. SAMPLE IDL FOR A CAR OBJECT AND ITS INTERFACES

```
import "unknwn.idl"

[
    object,
    uuid(C21D0200-2FB6-11d2-8952-444553540000),
    helpstring("Car driving")
]
interface ICar : IUnknown
{
    HRESULT SetSpeed( [in] long nSpeed );
};

[
    object,
    uuid(C21D0200-2FB6-11d2-8952-444553540000),
    helpstring("Engine control")
]
interface IEngine : IUnknown
{
    HRESULT Start();
    HRESULT Stop();
};

[
    uuid(310C97F4-3ABE-11d2-915E-52544C004D83),
    version(1.0),
    helpstring("Car library 1.0")
```

```
]
library YourLib
{
   importlib "stdole2.tlb"
   importlib "stdole32.tlb"

   [
      uuid(310C97D0-3ABE-11d2-915E-52544C004D83},
      helpstring("Car class")
   ]
   coclass Car
   {
      [default] interface ICar;
      interface IEngine;
   };
};
```

The `IUnknown` Interface

All COM interfaces must derive from `IUnknown`. Its definition is as follows:

```
[
   local,
   object,
   uuid(00000000-0000-0000-C000-000000000046),
   pointer_default(unique)
]
interface IUnknown
{
   HRESULT QueryInterface(
      [in] REFIID riid,
      [out, iid_is(riid)] void **ppvObject );
   ULONG AddRef( void );
   ULONG Release( void );
};
```

The keyword `local` means that the interface is not remotable (that is, no marshaling code should be generated by the IDL compiler). This seems strange because COM interfaces are generally remotable (that is, they can be called through execution context boundaries). `IUnknown` is remotable. Its remoting scheme relies on another interface (`IRemUnknown`) used internally, which allows certain call optimizations to be performed. `pointer_default(unique)` instructs marshaling code that `NULL` pointers can be returned on method invocations. `iid_is` instructs the marshaling code to treat the pointer as an interface pointer and names it with an IID. Here, IIDs come into play for the first time. `REFIID` is `IID&` and is the only non-C–compatible element used in interface methods. It exploits the fact that C++ compilers pass reference arguments as pointers. Armed with these additional considerations, let's explore the methods of the `IUnknown` interface.

QueryInterface() is used to ask the object whether it supports a particular interface named with its IID. The result is returned in the second parameter. Because QueryInterface() returns a general interface pointer, no type-safe definition is possible. However, it could at least return IUnknown **. The caller passes the address of the interface pointer of the type named by riid parameter (it should reference the correct VTBL for the returned interface). QueryInterface() should return S_OK when it succeeds or E_NOINTERFACE if that particular interface is not implemented on the object (in which case, the output parameter ppv should be filled with NULL). This behavior is similar to the C++ operator dynamic_cast (which has been taken as a model). QueryInterface() provides the client with a way to query the object for its functionality at runtime. Strong requirements are imposed on the behavior of QueryInterface(), as we'll see shortly.

AddRef()and Release() are used to manage the interface pointer lifetime by way of reference counting. When first obtained, every interface pointer has a reference of 1 (which is the first requirement for QueryInterface()—on success, it should call AddRef() on the returned interface pointer). When the client finishes using the interface, it should call Release() on the pointer. Every time an interface pointer is duplicated (stored in another variable or structure field or whatever), AddRef() should be called to increase its reference count. Before destroying the copy (such as when releasing a heap or when a local variable goes out of scope), Release() should be called. The implementation of Release() should check when the reference count reaches zero to free any resources required by the interface.

> **NOTE**
>
> Every interface on the object manages its own reference count. The actual implementation is free to use a single reference count for all interfaces on an object. Nevertheless, when all interfaces on an object reach zero reference count, the object destroys itself. (Of course, the reference count on any interface shouldn't drop below zero—or else the client is in error.)

Because all interfaces derive from IUnknown, all interfaces have QueryInterface() in their VTBLs. The objects usually populate VTBLs of all interfaces with a single implementation of QueryInterface()—although this is not mandatory. All implementations of QueryInterface() on an object should conform to the following rules (all referred interfaces are from one object):

- QueryInterface() for IUnknown always succeeds and always returns the same interface pointer, regardless of the interface on which it was called.

  IUnknown is the base interface for every other interface; usually, one interface is chosen to be returned and no special VTBL for IUnknown is designated. This rule ensures that IUnknown is unique for the object and can be used as the object's identity. When in doubt about whether two interfaces point to one object, you can use QueryInterface() for IUnknown on both interfaces and compare the resulting pointers.

- If QueryInterface() for IX succeeds once, it should succeed for the lifetime of the object, regardless of the interface on which it is used.

  This rule ensures the stability of the object's implementation and provides clients with a certain degree of trust so that they don't have to keep interface pointers once they get them: The client is guaranteed to receive the interface pointers when it needs them in the future. Of course, the client has to hold at least one interface pointer if it wants to keep the object alive.

- If QueryInterface() for IY succeeds on interface IX, then QueryInterface() for IX on IY should succeed, too.

  QueryInterface() for IX called on IX should always succeed.

  If QueryInterface() for IY succeeds on interface IX, and QueryInterface() for IZ succeeds on interface IY, then QueryInterface() for IX on interface IZ should succeed, too.

The preceding three rules ensure safety when navigating through the object interfaces and guarantee that all interfaces are reachable from everywhere.

Following is a simple implementation of QueryInterface() for an object that exposes two interfaces: IEngine and ICar through multiple inheritance:

```
STDMETHODIMP CCar::QueryInterface( REFIID riid, void **ppv )
{
   HRESULT hr = S_OK;

   // Note that IEngine is designated for IUnknown queries
   if ( IsEqualIID( riid, IID_IUnknown ) ) {
      *ppv = (void*)static_cast<IEngine*>( this );
   } else if ( IsEqualIID( riid, IID_IEngine ) ) {
      *ppv = (void*)static_cast<IEngine*>( this );
   } else if ( IsEqualIID( riid, IID_ICar ) ) {
      *ppv = (void*)static_cast<ICar*>( this );
   } else {
      hr = E_NOINTERFACE;
      *ppv = NULL;
   }
```

```
// Note that we call AddRef on the returned pointer
if ( SUCCEEDED( hr ) ) {
   reinterpret_cast<IUnknown*>( *ppv )->AddRef();
}

return hr;
}
```

Important issues are the `IUnknown` query handling and the final `AddRef()` call. The object designates the `IEngine` interface as its identity and returns it when queried for `IUnknown`. And before returning the interface pointer, `AddRef()` is called on the returned interface pointer. This is mandated by the rule that every interface maintains its own reference count.

> **NOTE**
>
> Implementations such as those I have presented are rarely used. When there are many interfaces exposed on the object, the code becomes large. The table-driven approach is preferred. However, this implementation serves as a good example.

COM Objects

So far, we've seen all the mechanics of using and navigating through interfaces on a single object, but not how the client gets its initial `IUnknown` pointer on the object.

There are four different ways of obtaining an initial interface pointer on an object:

- Through generic COM creation functions such as `CoGetClassObject()`, `CoCreateInstance()`, and so on.

- Through an interface method call on another object that returns the interface on a new object.

- When the client of an object passes an interface pointer of another object to the first object using an interface method call. Thus, the first object receives a pointer on the new object for internal use—the first object is the client.

- Through another API function that manufactures a specific object and returns one of its interfaces to the caller. An example is `CreateStreamOnHGlobal()`, which creates the standard OLE object representing a memory stream and returns its `IStream` interface.

The last method is rarely used. It was modern in the early days of OLE (which had the Win32 API background). The second method represents the object hierarchy navigation. The third method presents the objects with a way to communicate proactively with their clients and is briefly discussed in "Other COM Technologies," later in this chapter.

The first method is the most widely accepted way of distributing COM components. It works on coclasses. Every coclass has an associated object called a *class object* or *class factory*. Although not mandatory, this object exposes the interface IClassFactory:

```
[
   object,
   uuid(00000001-0000-0000-C000-000000000046),
   pointer_default(unique)
]
interface IClassFactory : IUnknown
{
   HRESULT CreateInstance(
      [in, unique] IUnknown *pUnkOuter,
      [in] REFIID riid,
      [out, iid_is(riid)] void **ppvObject );
   HRESULT LockServer( [in] BOOL bLock );
};
```

The LockServer() method is used to prevent the server that implements the objects of interest from unloading when no objects are alive. Thus creation requests issued later are serviced considerably more quickly. All calls to LockServer(TRUE) must be matched with the appropriate number of calls to LockServer(FALSE) (as is true with AddRef() and Release() for interfaces). The method of importance is CreateInstance().

CreateInstance() takes three parameters. The last two are the ones passed to QueryInterface() and enable the client to directly obtain a pointer for a specific inter-face, not just IUnknown. The first parameter is the new object's controlling IUnknown and is used in aggregation as we'll see shortly. For regular clients, it is always NULL. This method has an intimate knowledge of the object it should create. The returned interface pointer should be reference counted (AddRef() should be called).

The COM runtime has mechanisms for locating class factories, which aren't discussed here. The COM function that does this is CoGetClassObject():

```
STDAPI CoGetClassObject(
   REFCLSID      rclsid,
   DWORD         dwClsContext,
   COSERVERINFO *pServerInfo,
   REFIID        riid,
   void         **ppv );
```

The last two parameters are the ones passed to the QueryInterface() method of the class factory and represent the requested interface from the class factory itself (usually IClassFactory). pServerInfo is used to describe the machine and security context of the call. When on the same machine using default security, pServerInfo can be NULL. Through dwClsContext, the caller specifies how far it wants the object to be created.

Most important is the first parameter: REFCLSID is CLSID& and CLSID is GUID (it shows that we have encountered more GUIDs). Each coclass has a CLSID associated with it (each interface is named by IID). Thus, any two coclasses can be safely distinguished. Therefore, rclsid safely names the requested coclass. This is the CLSID of the coclass, which the class factory manufactures (class factories have no CLSIDs). If this function succeeds, the caller holds the pointer to the class factory of the coclass of interest and can create as many instances as desired (the interface is usually IClassFactory). When finished with the class factory, the client should call Release() as usual.

> **NOTE**
>
> COM objects can be activated in three different class contexts: in-process, local, and remote. The in-process (in-proc) context means that the object is created in the address space of the calling process. The object server resides in a DLL. Local and remote activations are referred to together as out-of-process (out-of-proc) activations. The object server resides in a separate executable, and the object is created in a different process. The two contexts differentiate whether the object server resides on the same machine or on another machine.

If the class factory exposes IClassFactory (which is recommended), the COM runtime provides a wrapper for creating a single instance of the coclass:

```
STDAPI CoCreateInstance(
    REFCLSID rclsid,
    IUnknown *pUnkOuter,
    DWORD    dwClsContext,
    REFIID   riid,
    void     **ppv );
```

This is a somewhat outdated function because it misses the COSERVERINFO* argument, but for our discussion, it suffices. rclsid and dwClsContext are passed to CoGetClassObject() to get the class factory of the object (the IID that is passed is IID_IClassFactory). If the class factory is obtained successfully, IClassFactory::CreateInstance() is called, passing the remaining three arguments, and the class factory is released. The output argument contains the requested interface pointer on success.

COM has all the characteristics necessary to be considered an object-oriented system: encapsulation, polymorphism, and reusability. The only feature dropped is the object implementation reuse (also called *implementation reusability*). To solve this problem, we use the technique called *aggregation*. Through aggregation, one object can directly expose the implementation of some interfaces of another object. Everything seems quite easy until we reach the requirements for IUnknown and they cannot be achieved. The problem is that when we get a direct pointer to the aggregated object, it doesn't know that it is being aggregated. It cannot return the interfaces on the aggregating object when the client asks through one of the interfaces of the aggregated object. The only solution is to make the object aware that it is being aggregated. Then it can react to QueryInterface() calls by delegating them to its controlling object IUnknown implementation. The coclass has two IUnknown implementations. The first implementation is used when the object is not aggregated and is returned by the class factory in case of aggregation (for example, when the aggregating pUnkOuter parameter of IClassFactory::CreateInstance() is not NULL, the requested IID should be IID_IUnknown). The second implementation is shared by all interfaces and delegates to the first implementation (if no aggregation takes place) or to the controlling IUnknown. It is very important to note that aggregation is allowed only if the client and the object reside in the same apartment (that is, if no proxies and stubs are involved). Another technique for binary reuse, called *containment*, can be applied in all cases. In containment, the outer object implements all desired interfaces; to do the job on certain interfaces, it simply delegates all calls to another object. It instantiates the object during its own creation and releases it on destruction. The contained object doesn't notice that it is being contained (it cannot do that).

Type Libraries

For C++ programs, the IDL compiler processes ID descriptions of the interfaces and generates a header file with native C++ definitions. The compiler also generates a file that stores the GUIDs for interfaces and coclasses. This is all well and good for C++; as far as the readers of this book are concerned, this is all that is needed. As you know, however, other languages don't understand native C++ headers and need another way to describe the interfaces and coclasses. The binary analog of a C++ header is called a *type library*.

A type library contains much richer information than a regular C++ header. The IDL contains as a subset another language (developed by Microsoft) called the Object Description Language (ODL). A discussion of the ODL is beyond the scope of this chapter. Suffice it to say that the IDL can contain a type library definition:

```
[
    uuid(98178CD0-3467-11d2-914B-52544C004D83),
    version(1.0),
    helpstring("This is type library")
]
library YourLib
```

```
{
    ...
};
```

Usually, coclasses are described in the type library:

```
[
    uuid(55712EB0-3468-11d2-914B-52544C004D83),
    helpstring("This is coclass")
]
coclass YourClass
{
    [default] interface IMain;
    interface ISecond;
};
```

In addition to the coclass, this definition pulls in the definition of the two interfaces IMain and ISecond. A type library can also contain type definitions, enumerators, C structures, unions, and so on.

A type library is generated by the IDL compiler or by a separate tool. The result is a binary file that can be distributed instead of the original IDL. The user then uses some deciphering tool to convert the type library into a language proprietary format. We'll address this topic later.

COM defines two interfaces for directly reading the contents of the type library: ITypeLib and ITypeInfo. Although it is unlikely that a regular C++ program will use a type library directly, it is possible to process it and generate the appropriate method calls for interfaces at runtime or to generate appropriate VTBLs for an object's outgoing interfaces (this topic is discussed briefly in the following section, "Other COM Technologies").

Other COM Technologies

The following sections review some technologies based on COM. The discussions are very general because these technologies are used widely in most of the COM applications. Many complete COM-based technologies are built on them.

Memory Management

When the client and the object are in the same apartment, the client calls interface methods using a direct pointer so that it can pass pointers safely. When the proxy and stub are involved, it is often necessary to marshal data pointed to by an argument between the client and the object to satisfy the object's expectation to receive real data at the location being pointed to. COM mandates that [in] parameters are maintained by the client. When the object has to return data in an [out] argument of an interface method, it allocates the data, and the client frees it. To preserve binary independence, some universal mechanism for memory management is necessary. This is the purpose of the IMalloc interface:

```
[
   local,
   object,
   uuid(00000002-0000-0000-C000-000000000046)
]
interface IMalloc : IUnknown
{
   void  *Alloc( [in] ULONG cb );
   void  *Realloc ( [in] void *pv, [in] ULONG cb );
   void  Free( [in] void *pv );
   ULONG GetSize( [in] void *pv );
   int   DidAlloc( void *pv );
   void  HeapMinimize();
};
```

The first three methods directly map to the C runtime functions `malloc()`, `realloc()`, and `free()`. `IMalloc` is implemented on the object, provided by COM using the `CoGetMalloc()` function. For the programmer's convenience, COM provides three wrapper functions to access the first three methods of `IMalloc`: `CoTaskMemAlloc()`, `CoTaskMemRealloc()`, and `CoTaskMemFree()`. Objects are mandated to allocate all returned data using `IMalloc`. This way, the data is freed by the stub; when it reaches the proxy, it is allocated again through `IMalloc` by the proxy itself. Then the client processes the returned data and frees its copy through `IMalloc`, too.

Connectable Objects

Objects can return results to the client on each method call. However, some objects may have to express some situations to their clients at certain times—independent of the client's intent of making interface calls. One possible solution is if the client passes an interface pointer to the object, the object holds the pointer (that is, it calls `AddRef()`) and uses it to fire its events when necessary. When the client doesn't want to listen any more, it stops listening to the events by invoking the same method and passing a `NULL` pointer, which effectively breaks the connection. The client object that implements the interface is called a *sink*. The interface is called the object's outgoing, or *source*, interface because the object doesn't implement it but uses it instead. The connection established between the client's sink and the object is called an *advisory connection*.

This approach has been used by the first event interface `IAdviseSink`. When using this approach, certain inconveniences arise. Only one client can receive the notifications—an satisfactory situation if the object is shared in multiple contexts. If the object fires several sets of events, multiple methods should be designated for passing the client's sinks. Because many objects may have to fire events, many interfaces will be sharing the same advisory method.

To solve these problems, two main and two helper interfaces have been defined:
IConnectionPoint serves the connections for a single outgoing interface on an object. It
isn't implemented on the main object (QueryInterface() doesn't see it), but instead
each connection point is implemented on a small separate object. To access the connection points, the object implements the interface IConnectionPointContainer:

```
[
    object,
    uuid(B196B286-BAB4-101A-B69C-00AA00341D07),
    pointer_default(unique)
]
interface IConnectionPoint : IUnknown
{
    HRESULT GetConnectionInterface( [out] IID * piid );
    HRESULT GetConnectionPointContainer(
        [out] IConnectionPointContainer ** ppCPC );
    HRESULT Advise(
        [in]  IUnknown *pUnkSink,
        [out] DWORD     *pdwCookie );
    HRESULT Unadvise( [in] DWORD dwCookie );
    HRESULT EnumConnections( [out] IEnumConnections **ppEnum );
}


[
    object,
    uuid(B196B284-BAB4-101A-B69C-00AA00341D07),
    pointer_default(unique)
]
interface IConnectionPointContainer : IUnknown
{
    HRESULT EnumConnectionPoints(
        [out] IEnumConnectionPoints ** ppEnum );
    HRESULT FindConnectionPoint(
        [in]  REFIID riid,
        [out] IConnectionPoint ** ppCP );
}
```

By using the methods in the IConnectionPointContainer interface, the client can enumerate the supported outgoing interfaces and attach the sinks for those connection points
that it recognizes, or it can ask directly for a specific outgoing interface. In both ways,
the client finishes with a pointer to IConnectionPoint on an object that recognizes a
particular source interface. By using the IConnectionPoint::Advise() method, the
client attaches its sink and receives a handle for this advisory connection called a *cookie*.
The cookie is used later in a call to IConnectionPoint::Unadvise() to terminate the
connection. There is a method to enumerate the sinks attached to the connection point.

Enumeration

The two interfaces used to enumerate connection points and connections on a particular connection point are part of a family of interfaces called *enumerators*. The common definition of an enumerator is as follows:

```
interface IEnumXXX
{
    HRESULT Next(
        [in]  ULONG nCount,
        [out, size_is(nCount), length_is(*pnFetched)] XXX *pXXX,
        [out] ULONG *pnFetched );
    HRESULT Skip( [in] ULONG nCount );
    HRESULT Reset();
    HRESULT Clone( [out] IEnumXXX **ppEnum );
};
```

This is not an existing interface. Instead, for every type you want to enumerate, you define a new interface, which has these four methods for the particular enumerated entity. The Next() method is used to fetch the next portion of items, Skip() skips portions of items, Reset() starts enumeration from the beginning, and Clone() creates a copy of the enumerator object. In the case of connection points, enumerated entities are interface pointers. They are received with an outstanding reference, so it's the client's responsibility to release every received pointer.

Structured Storage and Object Persistence

When a coclass is created by its class factory, the object is said to be in an uninitialized state. Some objects need no further initialization and can act happily in this state. Other objects require initialization from some previously stored state to become operational. These objects are called *persistent* objects. COM defines two ways to achieve object persistence: It provides a standard storage model called *structured storage*, and it defines a persistence model to be followed by those objects.

Structured storage is built on two interfaces: IStorage and IStream. The COM runtime includes a ready-made implementation for both of these interfaces in a traditional file and in system memory. Other implementations may be implemented too (for example, on database records and fields). A *storage* is a collection of streams or other substorage systems such as a directory in a traditional file system. A *stream* is a binary sequence and is analogous to a disk file. A stream is manipulated in a way nearly identical to an operating system file. The interfaces provide greater flexibility than a file system by defining transactioned operations and some other enhancements.

Objects conform to the COM persistence model by implementing one or more of the persistence interfaces: IPersistStorage, IPersistStream, IPersistStreamInit, or IPersistFile (other persistence interfaces exist, but these are the most fundamental). Every interface defines a specific persistence model. IPersistStorage defines storage-level persistence and offers the greatest flexibility of implementation but is the hardest to implement. The object is allowed to create streams and additional substorages. IPersistStream defines persistence in a single stream and is the easiest to implement. IPersistStreamInit is the same as IPersistStream but comes with an additional method for initializing empty objects. IPersistFile is used to initialize the object from the operating system file. All persistence interfaces derive from the interface IPersist, which has a single method to return the object's CLSID to the caller.

Automation

In the world of components, it becomes easier for the average user to perform some general application tasks by writing macros or scripts in some high-level language to achieve his or her specific goals. To facilitate this process, COM defines a standard for accessing COM object servers called *automation*. Automation defines another type of interface called a *dispatch interface* or a *dispinterface* (they are also sometimes referred to as *automation interfaces*). These interfaces are centered around objects implementing the interface IDispatch:

```
[
   object,
   uuid(00020400-0000-0000-C000-000000000046),
   pointer_default(unique)
]
interface IDidspatch : IUnknown
{
   HRESULT GetTypeInfoCount( [out] UINT *pctinfo );
   HRESULT GetTypeInfo(
      [in] UINT       iTInfo,
      [in] LCID       lcid,
      [out] ITypeInfo **ppTInfo );
   HRESULT GetIDsOfNames(
      [in] REFIID riid,
      [in, size_is(cNames)] LPOLESTR *rgszNames,
      [in] UINT    cNames,
      [in] LCID    lcid,
      [out, size_is(cNames)] DISPID *rgDispId );
   HRESULT Invoke(
      [in] DISPID           dispIdMember,
      [in] REFIID           riid,
      [in] LCID             lcid,
      [in] WORD             wFlags,
      [in, out] DISPPARAMS  *pDispParams,
```

```
        [out] VARIANT        *pVarResult,
        [out] EXCEPINFO      *pExcepInfo,
        [out] UINT           *puArgErr );
};
```

A dispinterface, unlike a COM interface, contains no VTBL layout representation. Instead, all methods are marked by integer identifiers called *dispatch IDs*, or *dispids*. In addition to methods, dispinterfaces bring the notion of *properties*—an abstraction for a C++ structure's data members. Each property is associated with get and put methods that retrieve and store its value, resulting in two different methods having the same dispid value in the dispinterface. Methods (including property accessors) are called in two stages. Given the textual names of the method and its parameters, the caller gets the corresponding dispid and similar IDs for parameter positions using IDispatch::GetIDsOfNames(). Then a call to IDispatch::Invoke() is made with all parameters passed in the pDispParams array. The whole process is a big pain. The result is returned in the output parameter pVarResult. The method call allows a dispatch exception to be thrown; this exception is reported by way of pExcepInfo (this is not a C++ exception—it is a standard mechanism to pass rich exception-like information). Implementing IDispatch is very difficult. A few functions exist to simplify the implementation using the type library definition of the dispinterface. To access dispinterface from C++, a wrapper class for IDispatch::Invoke() calls is necessity.

COM interfaces use the early binding scheme because the client binds to the interface VTBL at compile time. This process is also called VTBL binding. Dispinterfaces, on the other hand, offer a late binding scheme that has two variations. The client knows dispids in advance by way of the type library and omits calling IDispatch::GetIDsOfNames()—this approach is called early binding because the client binds to the dispids at compile time. If the client uses IDispatch::GetIDsOfNames() to discover dispids at runtime, the scheme is called late binding. Of course, VTBL binding is the most efficient scheme but is not supported by all programming languages; in fact, it is not supported by some widely distributed scripting languages (such as the JavaScript and VBScript used in WWW HTML pages). To make the interface both effective and widely accessible, a common scheme is designed. The dispinterface is implemented as a regular COM interface deriving from IDispatch. The implementation of the IDispatch portion just calls the appropriate methods in the VTBL part of the interface. These interfaces are called *dual interfaces*.

In automation, only a subset of all the types available in the IDL is supported. Most important, composite types such as structs, arrays, and strings are not supported. Instead, automation defines the new types BSTR, SAFEARRAY, and VARIANT. Structures are passed using an implementation of IDispatch on a separate object, which exposes all fields using get and put properties. BSTR is a string that contains its length just before the actual data pointer. SAFEARRAY is a multidimensional array that holds lower and upper bounds for each dimension. It is a fairly complex structure. VARIANT is structure that contains a discriminated union of all the types available in automation. All three types have special maintenance functions in the automation runtime.

The advantage of using automation types is that the runtime has a standard implementation of the IDispatch marshaler, which can also be used for other interfaces. The only requirement is that these interfaces use only automation types in their methods and include the keyword oleautomation in the interface description in the IDL file. Dual interfaces are marked with the keyword dual in the IDL, which implies oleautomation.

Using COM Objects in C++

Using COM objects in C++ is very simple. It is almost identical to using C++ classes through pointers. The differences come when dealing with the interface lifetime.

Using Raw Interfaces

Creating the object (which exposes the interface) comes first. There is a difference between interfaces and C++ classes. Each interface is implemented on some object. The object exposes other interfaces, too. To get another interface, the client makes a QueryInterface() call on its interface pointer to obtain a pointer to another interface on the same object. This approach is similar to the C++ operator dynamic_cast. Another difference is the destruction mechanism. Instead of using a delete operator, the client calls Release() to instruct the object to destroy itself (well, some C++ classes are designed in the same way). If the object finds that this was the last outstanding reference (on all of its interfaces), it destroys itself. Here is an example:

```
HRESULT hr;
ICar    *pCar;
IEngine *pEngine;

hr = CoIntialize( NULL );
assert( SUCCEEDED( hr ) );
hr = CoCreateInstance(
   CLSID_Car,
   NULL,
   CLSCTX_ALL,
   IID_ICar,
   (void**)&pCar );
if ( SUCCEEDED( hr ) ) {
   hr = pCar->QueryInterface( IID_IEngine, (void**)&pEngine );
   if ( SUCCEEDED( hr ) ) {
```

```
        pEngine->Start();
        Drive( pCar );
        pEngine->Stop();
        pEngine->Release();
    }
    pCar->Release();
}
CoUnitialize();
```

This code fragment initializes a COM library, creates the object Car (Car is a coclass), and obtains its ICar interface. It then asks for the IEngine interface. The code then starts the engine, calls some function to drive the car, and then stops the engine. Finally, both the IEngine and ICar interfaces are released, and the COM library is released. The second release leaves the object with no outstanding references on all of its interfaces, so the object destroys itself. All this is easy and doesn't need further explanation. For the sake of simplicity, the results returned by the method invocations are not checked. In real life, you should check these results. Even if the method is guaranteed not to fail, its marshaling code could fail for various reasons (including network failures).

More interesting is that the Drive() function, by the laws of COM, should call AddRef() on the received pointer and call Release() when it finishes. Clearly, this is unnecessary because the argument interface pointer's lifetime is equal to the lifetime of the function call and is nested in the lifetime of the calling context, which holds the reference on the interface. Therefore, for the duration of the function execution, the interface has a positive reference, and the object won't destroy itself. Because of this, an optimization can be made and the AddRef()/Release() pair can be omitted. In all cases in which it can be inferred from the programming logic that the variable that gets a copy of an interface has its lifetime nested in the lifetime of the original variable holding the interface reference (*lifetime* means from the initialization time until the final Release() is called through it), this optimization is allowed. If the original variable has a shorter lifetime, the copy contains an invalid pointer, and the optimization cannot be made. Usually, AddRef() and Release() have very simple implementations so that the optimization is rarely necessary except if the speed is of extreme importance. When passing a local interface pointer to other functions, it is safe to omit AddRef()/Release(). If the interface pointer is in a global variable and the process has a single thread of execution that uses that variable, it is safe, too.

Using Smart Pointers

The lifetime of any interface pointer must begin with AddRef()—either when received by some external function or method or when a local copy is made (then it is explicit). Its lifetime should finish by calling Release(). It's easy to forget to call AddRef() or

Release() or to call Release() more than once. The result is often disastrous and is very hard to debug and spot. To make life easier, it is better to hide these actions in an interface wrapper class. Such a class will automatically call AddRef() and Release() on the contained interface pointer at the appropriate times. The wrapper class will ultimately call Release() in its destructor.

A class in this category is the smart pointer class. A *smart pointer* behaves like an ordinary pointer for its user. About the only thing it does is to manage the lifetime of its contained interface pointer. Any method call available through the original pointer is available through the smart pointer. This is easily achieved by overriding the class operator ->. Because the smart pointer cannot distinguish invocations of AddRef() and Release() through the pointer, the programmer should follow some discipline and not call AddRef() and Release() directly through the contained pointer. Instead, the smart pointer should provide AddRef() and Release() methods to allow the programmer to explicitly control the lifetime of the contained pointer. Listing 21.2 gives an example of a smart pointer class.

LISTING 21.2. A SIMPLE SMART POINTER CLASS

```
template<class Itf>
class CSmartPtr
{
// Constructor and destructor
public:
   CSmartPtr() : m_pItf( null )
   {
   }

   CSmartPtr( Itf *pItf ) : m_pItf( null )
   {
      Store( pItf );
   }

   ~CSmartPtr()
   {
      // Release interface pointer if not null
      Release();
   }

// Extractors
public:
   // Get underlying pointer for method calls
   Itf* operator->()
   {
      assert( m_pItf != null );
      return m_pItf;
   }

   // Get address of underlying pointer
   Itf** operator&()
```

```
    {
        // Ensure previous pointer is released
        Release();
        return &m_pItf;
    }

// Assignment
public:
    Itf* operator=( Itf *pItf )
    {
        // Ensure previous pointer is released
        Release();
        // Save the new pointer
        Store( pItf );
        return m_pItf;
    }

// Content testing
public:
    bool operator!()
    {
        return ( m_pItf == null );
    }

    operator bool()
    {
        return ( m_pItf != null );
    }

// Implementation
protected:
    void Release()
    {
        if ( m_pItf != null ) {
            m_pItf->Release();
            m_pItf = null;
        }
    }

    void Store( Itf *pItf )
    {
        // Store new pointer
        m_pItf = pItf;
        // Call AddRef on the new pointer, check for null
        if ( m_pItf != null ) {
            m_pItf->AddRef();
        }
    }

// Implementation members
protected:
    Itf *m_pItf;
};
```

This is the simplest form of a smart pointer. It covers assignment from another pointer of the same type and getting the address of the contained pointer for assigning a raw pointer returned by a function or method. It covers the definition of a smart pointer as it handles AddRef() and Release() automatically. It also provides operator-> for accessing the methods in the contained pointer. It also includes operators for testing whether the class contains an interface pointer. Of course, it could easily contain a copy constructor, too.

The problem with the smart pointer shown in Listing 21.2 is that it always needs a QueryInterface() or CoCreateInstance() call (or some other means) to fill its value:

```
CSmartPtr<IMyInterface> pMyInterace;
HRESULT                 hr;
...
hr = pSomeInterface->QueryInterface(
    IID_IMyInterface,
    (void**)&pMyInterface );
```

A better smart pointer should also handle QueryInterface(). The problem is that QueryInterface() returns HRESULT in case of failure. The smart pointer should decide how to report this situation. An obvious solution is to throw an exception, but the problem is that the semantics of the operator = don't imply catastrophic failure. A better approach is to silently ignore the failure and leave the programmer to check each assignment using operator! or operator bool. Of course, the class should remember the last HRESULT so that the programmer can identify the reason for the failure. Listing 21.3 shows the proposed addition.

LISTING 21.3. ENHANCEMENTS TO THE SMART POINTER CLASS

```
...
/* at constructors */
CSmartPtr( IUnknown *pUnk ) : m_pItf( null ), m_hr( E_POINTER )
{
    StoreUnk( pUnk );
}
...
/* at extractors */
operator IUnknown*()
{
    return m_pItf;
}
/* at assignment */
Itf* operator=( IUnknown* pUnk )
{
    // Ensure previous pointer is released
    Release();
    // Save the new pointer
    StoreUnk( pUnk );
```

```
      return m_pItf;
   }
   ...
   /* at implementation */
   void StoreUnk( IUnknown *pUnk )
   {
      if ( pUnk != null ) {
         m_hr = pUnk->QueryInterface(
            IID_##Itf,
            (void**)&m_pItf );
      } else {
         m_hr = E_POINTER;
      }
   }
   ...
   /* at content testing */
   HRESULT GetLastError()
   {
      return m_hr;
   }
   ...
   /* at implementation members */
   HRESULT m_hr;
   ...
```

The other constructors should initialize the m_hr member; the other assignment operator should set it. Store() finishes with this line:

```
m_hr = ( m_pItf != null ) ? S_OK : E_POINTER;
```

For consistency, Release() should finish the if statement with this line:

```
m_hr = E_POINTER;
```

E_POINTER is dedicated to be the error when the contained pointer is NULL.

Note that this class template has problems when instantiated for the IUnknown interface. Two constructors and two assignment operators exist with the same parameters. To resolve this ambiguity, their AddRef() optimization should be sacrificed, and only the versions with IUnknown* as the parameter should remain. If the template will never be instantiated for IUnknown, however, this template is acceptable.

Using this improved smart pointer, the fragment presented in the discussion of raw interface pointers now looks like this:

```
HRESULT hr;
CSmartPtr<ICar>    pCar;
CSmartPtr<IEngine> pEngine;

hr = CoIntialize( NULL );
```

```
assert( SUCCEEDED( hr ) );
hr = CoCreateInstance(
   CLSID_Car,
   NULL,
   CLSCTX_ALL,
   IID_ICar,
   (void**)&pCar );
if ( (bool)pCar ) {
   pEngine = pCar; // QueryInterface here
   if ( (bool)pEngine ) {
      pEngine->Start();
      Drive( pCar );
      pEngine->Stop();
   }
}
CoUninitialize();
```

Note that the call to CoCreateInstance() has not changed. It is potentially unsafe because the IID can be misplaced. To avoid this problem, it's beneficial to include a new method—CreateInstance(), as shown in Listing 21.4.

LISTING 21.4. SMART POINTER HANDLING OBJECT CREATION

```
/* at assignment */
   HRESULT CreateInstance(
      REFCLSID rclsid,
      DWORD    dwClsContext = CLSCTX_ALL,
      IUnknown *pUnkOuter = NULL )
   {
      Release();
      m_hr = ::CoCreateInstance(
         rclsid,
         pUnkOuter,
         dwClsContext,
         IID_##Itf,
         (void**)&m_pItf );
      return m_hr;
   }
```

Using the CreateInstance() method, the sample code fragment simplifies further:

```
CSmartPtr<ICar>    pCar;
CSmartPtr<IEngine> pEngine;

hr = CoIntialize( NULL );
assert( SUCCEEDED( hr ) );
pCar.CreateInstance( CLSID_Car );
if ( (bool)pCar ) {
```

```
   pEngine = pCar; // QueryInterface here
   if ( (bool)pEngine ) {
      pEngine->Start();
      Drive( pCar );
      pEngine->Stop();
   }
}
CoUninitialize();
```

In this fragment, the syntax of the call to Drive() has changed—we are passing a smart pointer instead of the raw pointer it expects. Of course, the code can be rewritten to use smart pointers, too, but this isn't always possible (for example, if the code was written by a third party and we don't have the source). We could preserve the parameter by using Drive(*&pCar), but this looks ugly. The smart pointer can be nice enough to present a raw interface pointer extractor: operator Itf*(). Really nice smart pointers provide methods for dynamically attaching and detaching raw interface pointers.

Using Type Libraries

Smart pointers greatly simplify the maintenance of the lifetime of COM interface pointers. What they cannot solve is the necessity to continuously check the result of every interface call to the pointer. For simplicity, the code fragment discussed with smart pointers does not check the results returned by the interface method calls. In real programs, however, the results cannot be ignored.

When we discussed QueryInterface() assignment earlier, we noted that the assignment operator semantics don't allow exceptions. This was because the class should behave like a pointer, hence no exceptions. But if the whole class is organized to throw exceptions when errors occur, an exception at this place is desirable. Of course, we cannot make exceptions through smart pointers.

To achieve exception semantics, a full wrapper class around the pointer should be designed. Listing 21.5 defines a wrapper for the IEngine interface.

LISTING 21.5. A SIMPLE INTERFACE WRAPPER CLASS

```
class CEnginePtr
{
// Constructor and destructor
public:
   CEnginePtr() : m_pEngine( null ), m_hr( S_OK )
   {
   }

   CEnginePtr( IUnknown* pUnk ) :
```

LISTING 21.5. CONTINUED

```cpp
      m_pEngine( null ),
      m_hr( S_OK )
   {
      Store( pUnk );
   }

   ~CEnginePtr()
   {
      Release();
   }

// Extraction
   operator IEngine*()
   {
      CheckPointer();
      return m_pEngine;
   }

   operator IUnknown*()
   {
      CheckPointer();
      return m_pEngine;
   }

// Status information
public:
   HRESULT GetLastStatus()
   {
      return m_hr;
   }

// Assignment
public:
   void CreateInstance(
      REFCLSID rclsid,
      DWORD    dwClsContext = CLSCTX_ALL,
      IUnknown *pUnkOuter = NULL )
   {
      Release();
      CheckError( ::CoCreateInstance(
         rclsid,
         pUnkOuter,
         dwClsContext,
         IID_IEngine,
         (void**)&m_pEngine ) );
   }

   IEngine* operator=( IUnknown *pUnk )
   {
```

```
        // Ensure previous pointer is released
        Release();
        // Save the new pointer
        Store( pUnk );
        return m_pEngine;
    }

// Interface methods
public:
    void Start()
    {
        CheckPointer();
        CheckError( m_pEngine->Start() );
    }

    void Stop()
    {
        CheckPointer();
        CheckError( m_pEngine->Stop() );
    }

// Implementation
protected:
    void Store( IUnknown *pUnk )
    {
        Release();
        if ( pUnk != null ) {
            CheckError( pUnk->QueryInterface(
                IID_IEngine,
                (void**)&m_pEngine ) );
        } else {
            CheckError( E_POINTER );
        }
    }

    void Release()
    {
        if ( !IsEmpty() ) {
            m_pEngine->Release();
            m_pEngine = null;
            m_hr = S_OK;
        }
    }

    bool IsEmpty()
    {
        return ( m_pEngine == null );
    }

    void CheckPointer()
    {
```

continues

LISTING 21.5. CONTINUED

```
        if ( IsEmpty() ) {
            CheckError( E_POINTER );
        }
    }

    void CheckError( HRESULT hr )
    {
        m_hr = hr;
        if ( FAILED( hr ) ) {
            throw hr;
        }
    }

// Implementation members
protected:
    IEngine *m_pEngine;
    HRESULT m_hr;
};
```

Most of this code is similar to the implementation of a smart pointer with the semantic difference that it throws exceptions instead of providing a way to test for success or failure. The method `GetLastStatus()` is necessary to distinguish between multiple success codes because no exception is thrown. As you can see from the code, only a small part is specific to the interface. The rest is boilerplate and can be implemented in a template. The fragment that uses it will look as follows, assuming that a similar wrapper for `ICar` exists:

```
CCarPtr    CarPtr;
CEnginePtr EnginePtr;
HRESULT    hr;

hr = CoIntialize( NULL );
assert( SUCCEEDED( hr ) );
try {
    CarPtr.CreateInstance( CLSID_Car );
    EnginePtr = CarPtr; // QueryInterface here
    EnginePtr.Start();
    Drive( CarPtr );
    EnginePtr.Stop();
} catch ( HRESULT hr ) {
    ...
}
CoUninitialize();
```

Wrappers can be made by hand, but this is tedious work and is, of course, impractical. It would be better if some tool gets the description of the interface and produces the wrapper class. Because IDL files of interfaces defined by third parties aren't generally accessible, and because C++ headers don't contain sufficient information to describe all parameters, we should have some other way for the tool to discover the interface specifics. Here, type libraries come into play. Type libraries contain the IDL description of the interface in binary form so that they are smaller and better to distribute. Another benefit of type libraries is that they describe dispinterfaces so that you can also generate wrappers for them, which yields much greater benefit.

The following discussion is specific to the Visual C++ 5.0 compiler. It implements Microsoft's extension to the preprocessor, the `#import` directive:

```
#import <type_lib> no_namespace
```

`no_namespace` is used to suppress the generation of a separate namespace for the definitions in the type library. Several other options control the behavior of `#import`. When the preprocessor encounters `#import` in the source, it scans the referenced type library and generates two files with the extensions `tlh` and `tli` (these extensions stand for type library header and type library implementation). The former contains the header for the generated class; the latter contains the implementation of the wrapper methods. Any other details are beyond the scope of this discussion. Generated wrappers leverage an existing smart pointer template with exception semantics. All wrapping methods also generate exceptions on failure.

Writing COM Objects in C++

The following sections focus on writing COM objects. They don't cover the boilerplate code required to make a COM server fully operational. Several strategies for building COM objects are presented.

Multiple Inheritance

The IDL compiler generates interface definitions as C++ classes containing only pure virtual methods. It is natural to implement COM objects with C++ classes that inherit the definitions of the exposed interfaces, as shown in Listing 21.6.

LISTING 21.6. A DEFINITION OF A C++ CLASS IMPLEMENTING A COM OBJECT THROUGH MULTIPLE INHERITANCE FROM THE IMPLEMENTED INTERFACES

```
class CCar : public ICar, public IEngine
{
// Constructor and destructor
public:
   CCar();
   ~CCar();
```

continues

LISTING 21.6. CONTINUED

```cpp
// IUnknown methods
public:
    STDMETHOD( QueryInterface )( REFIID riid, void **ppv );
    STDMETHOD_( ULONG, AddRef )();
    STDMETHOD_( ULONG, Release )();

// ICar methods
public:
    STDMETHOD( SetSpeed )( long nSpeed );

// IEngine methods
public:
    STDMETHOD( Start )();
    STDMETHOD( Stop )();

// Implementation specific
protected:
    ULONG m_nRef;
    bool  m_bEngineStarted;
    long  m_nSpeed;
};
```

The macro STDMETHOD expands to the appropriate calling convention and specifies HRESULT as the return type. The STDMETHOD_ macro is similar to STDMETHOD and allows the interface designer to specify the explicit type of the return value. This is necessary only for some old interfaces (which are always local, that is, they cannot be marshaled) such as IUnknown, IMalloc, and so on. Similar macros exist for the method's implementation—STDMETHODIMP and STDMETHODIMP_(<type>). Listing 21.7 shows a sample implementation of the class.

LISTING 21.7. AN IMPLEMENTATION OF A C++ CLASS THAT IMPLEMENTS A COM OBJECT THROUGH MULTIPLE INHERITANCE FROM THE IMPLEMENTED INTERFACES

```cpp
CCar::CCar() :
    m_nRef( 0 ),
    m_bEngineStarted( false ),
    m_nSpeed( 0 )
{
}

CCar::~CCar()
{
}
```

```
STDMETHODIMP CCar::QueryInterface( REFIID riid, void **ppv );
{
    HRESULT hr = S_OK;

    // Note that IEngine is designated for IUnknown queries
    if ( IsEqualIID( riid, IID_IUnknown ) ) {
        *ppv = (void*)static_cast<IEngine*>( this );
    } else if ( IsEqualIID( riid, IID_IEngine ) ) {
        *ppv = (void*)static_cast<IEngine*>( this );
    } else if ( IsEqualIID( riid, IID_ICar ) ) {
        *ppv = (void*)static_cast<ICar*>( this );
    } else {
        hr = E_NOINTERFACE;
        *ppv = NULL;
    }

    // Note that we call AddRef on the returned pointer
    if ( SUCCEEDED( hr ) ) {
        reinterpret_cast<IUnknown*>( *ppv )->AddRef();
    }

    return hr;
}

STDMETHODIMP_(ULONG) CCar::AddRef()
{
    m_nRef++;
    return m_nRef;
}

STDMOETHODIMP_(ULONG) CCar::Release()
{
    m_nRef—;
    if ( m_nRef == 0 ) {
        delete this;
    }
    return m_nRef;
}

STDMETHODIMP CCar::SetSpeed( long nSpeed )
{
    HRESULT hr = S_OK;

    if ( m_bEngineStarted ) {
        if ( nSpeed >= 0 ) {
            m_nSpeed = nSpeed;
        } else {
            hr = E_INVALIDARG;
        }
    } else {
```

continues

LISTING 21.7. CONTINUED

```
      hr = CAR_E_POWER;
   }
   return hr;
}

STDMETHODIMP CCar::Start()
{
   HRESULT hr = S_OK;

   if ( !m_bEngineStarted ) {
      m_bEngineStarted = true;
      m_nSpeed = 0;
   } else {
      hr = CAR_E_POWER;
   }
   return hr;
}

STDMETHODIMP CCar::Stop()
{
   HRESULT hr = S_OK;

   if ( m_bEngineStarted ) {
      if ( m_nSpeed == 0 ) {
         m_bEngineStarted = false;
      } else {
         hr = CAR_E_SPEED;
      }
   } else {
      hr = CAR_E_POWER;
   }
   return hr;
}
```

When using multiple inheritance, all interfaces share a common reference count. Because the methods of the IUnknown portion of all interfaces are implemented in the class, all interfaces have a single implementation of these methods in their VTBLs. When all interfaces on the object are released, the object destroys itself. The implementation shown in Listing 21.7 is not thread safe. If multiple threads execute the AddRef() and Release() methods concurrently, race conditions exist and the object can be destroyed prematurely. It is easy to modify this implementation to make it thread safe, however.

A modification of the multiple inheritance approach is to implement interface-specific methods of all interfaces on separate classes and have the object class derive from the implementation classes. IUnknown methods should be implemented on the object class. This approach is necessary if two interfaces share methods with the same definition but need different implementations. The drawback of multiple inheritance is that per-interface reference counting is impossible. Fortunately, it is rarely needed.

Nested Classes

Another approach is to implement every interface in a separate class. These helper classes are usually defined inside the object class, which has member variables for each of them. The object class implements methods of IUnknown. The nested classes' implementation of IUnknown simply delegates to the object's implementation of IUnknown. Each interface is free to implement its own reference counting as well. Listing 21.8 shows the definition of our sample object using nested classes.

LISTING 21.8. A DEFINITION OF A C++ CLASS IMPLEMENTING A COM OBJECT THROUGH NESTED CLASSES

```
class CCar : public IUnknown
{
protected:
   // ICar implementation
   class XCar : public ICar
   {
   // Constructor and destructor
   public:
      XCar( CCar *pOwner ) : m_pOwner( pOwner )
      {
         assert( pOwner != null );
      }

      ~XCar()
      {
      }

   // IUnknown methods
   public:
      STDMETHOD( QueryInterface )( REFIID riid, void **ppv );
      STDMETHOD_( ULONG, AddRef )();
      STDMETHOD_( ULONG, Release )();

   // ICar methods
   public:
      STDMETHOD( SetSpeed )( long nSpeed );

   // Implementation
   protected:
      CCar *m_pOwner;
   };

   // IEngine implementation
   ...

// Constructor and destructor
```

continues

LISTING 21.8. CONTINUED

```cpp
public:
    CCar();
    ~CCar();

// IUnknown methods
public:
    STDMETHOD( QueryInterface )( REFIID riid, void **ppv );
    STDMETHOD_( ULONG, AddRef )();
    STDMETHOD_( ULONG, Release )();

// Nested classes
protected:
    XCar    m_ICar;
    XEngine m_IEngine;

// Implementation
protected:
    ULONG m_nRef;
    bool  m_bEngineStarted;
    long  m_nSpeed;
};
```

Each nested class holds a pointer to the main object instance and delegates IUnknown calls to it. Data common to multiple interfaces is located there, too. Our example is not well suited for nested implementation; it is presented only to explain how nested classes are managed. Implementation of ICar and IEngine methods is omitted. Listing 21.9 shows the implementation.

LISTING 21.9. IMPLEMENTATION OF A C++ CLASS IMPLEMENTING A COM OBJECT THROUGH NESTED CLASSES

```cpp
STDMETHODIMP CCar::XCar::QueryInterface(
    REFIID riid,
    void   **ppv )
{
    return m_pOwner->QueryInterface( riid, ppv );
}

STDMETHODIMP_(ULONG) CCar::XCar::AddRef()
{
    return m_pOwner->AddRef();
}

STDMETHODIMP_(ULONG) CCar::XCar::Release()
{
    return m_pOwner->Release();
}
```

```
CCar::CCar() :
   m_ICar( this ),
   m_IEngine( this ),
   m_nRef( 0 ),
   m_bEngineStarted( false ),
   m_nSpeed( 0 )
{
}

CCar::~CCar()
{
}

STDMETHODIMP CCar::QueryInterface( REFIID riid, void **ppv );
{
   HRESULT hr = S_OK;

   // Note that IEngine is designated for IUnknown queries
   if ( IsEqualIID( riid, IID_IUnknown ) ) {
      *ppv = (void*)static_cast<IUnknown*>( this );
   } else if ( IsEqualIID( riid, IID_IEngine ) ) {
      *ppv = (void*)static_cast<IEngine*>( &m_IEngine );
   } else if ( IsEqualIID( riid, IID_ICar ) ) {
      *ppv = (void*)static_cast<ICar*>( &m_ICar );
   } else {
      hr = E_NOINTERFACE;
      *ppv = NULL;
   }

   // Note that we call AddRef on the returned pointer
   if ( SUCCEEDED( hr ) ) {
      reinterpret_cast<IUnknown*>( *ppv )->AddRef();
   }

   return hr;
}

STDMETHODIMP_(ULONG) CCar::AddRef()
{
   m_nRef++;
   return m_nRef;
}

STDMOETHODIMP_(ULONG) CCar::Release()
{
   m_nRef—;
   if ( m_nRef == 0 ) {
      delete this;
   }
   return m_nRef;
}
```

The nested-class approach is similar to the modification of the multiple-inheritance approach with interface implementation base classes. The main difference is that nested classes implement IUnknown methods, while implementation classes don't. The nested classes' implementations of IUnknown methods delegate to the object's implementation of IUnknown. The object's implementation of QueryInterface() changes to seek interface implementations from member variables, while IUnknown has a separate implementation in the base class.

It is possible to combine this approach with multiple inheritance and to implement several interfaces on one nested class. Each group of interfaces on a nested class has a single implementation of IUnknown delegating to the main object, while using multiple inheritance for implementing the interfaces.

Using Tear-Off Classes

There are occasions when some interface on an object is rarely used but consumes a large amount of resources. It is preferable to avoid wasting those resources if the interface is never used. The implementation approaches seen so far cannot solve the problem of wasted resources because they allocate all the object resources when the object is created. The solution is a so-called *tear-off interface*. When the interface is requested for the first time, the implementation of QueryInterface() dynamically creates an instance of a class, which implements the interface. IUnknown members of the class delegate to the main object's IUnknown just as they do with nested classes. A separate count on the tear-off interface is maintained; when the interface is released for the last time, the tear-off class is in turn destroyed.

The implementation of tear-off classes is almost identical to that used for nested classes and isn't presented here. The difference is that instead of members, the object class holds pointers to tear-off classes and holds additional reference counts on each of them. Changed are QueryInterface() and Release(). Another approach is to let the tear-off class implement its own reference and to clear the object pointer as part of its deletion within its own Release()implementation.

Summary

This chapter presents the most essential of the important topics in the Microsoft COM technology. Many minor details are left out. The books listed in "Further Reading" can fill the gaps in your COM education and can present a consistent coverage of a broad range of COM technologies. This chapter focuses on the details of using and implementing COM objects. Even if you have known COM in advance, I hope you found something new in these pages.

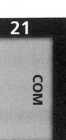

Further Reading

For an excellent introduction from C++ to COM, as well as full coverage of details of core COM, read *Essential COM*, by Don Box. Another good introduction to COM is *Inside COM*, by Dale Rogerson. For those who know the basics of COM, *COM/DCOM Unleashed*, published by Macmillan Publishing, will soon be available. The classic book on the matter is *Inside OLE*, by Kraig Brockschmidt. It details the specification of the first implementation of COM: object linking and embedding (OLE).

Java and C++

CHAPTER

22

It may seem somewhat inappropriate to include a chapter about Java in a book about C++, but it is actually a natural transition for the C++ programmer to learn the Java programming language. There are many similarities between Java and C++. Each language has its own unique advantages and limitations, and the C++ programmer who does the work of learning Java can use Java to complement his or her programming in C++. Many C++ programmers are interested in (and perhaps a bit afraid of) Java; this chapter shows how remarkably similar the two languages actually are and then points out their major differences so that C++ programmers can painlessly familiarize themselves with the important aspects of Java.

The Java programming language has made a significant impact on the computing industry. During Java's infancy, vendors and developers flocked to implement solutions using Java. Now that the hype has settled, the focus is returning back to C++. After reading this chapter, you will be well equipped to decide which tool to use in a given situation.

Similarities Between C++ and Java

We will progress through the similarities between the C++ and Java languages by discussing the basics and then moving on to the more advanced features of the Java language.

Comments

The Java programming language supports comment characters of C++: both the *block sequence* /* */ and the *single line* comment pair // characters are supported by Java.

In Java, comments have an added benefit. By using special character tokens in your source files and the javadoc utility program, you can produce documentation for your source files. A documenting comment must begin with the character sequence /** and must end with the sequence */. Special document keywords, preceded with the @ symbol, are used to specify comment sections. You can also imbed HTML tags within the document block. The following example demonstrates the document commenting feature:

```
/**
    * sleepMethod - sleeps a specified number of milliseconds
    * @param long millis - milliseconds to sleep
    * @return void
    * @exception IOException
    * @author: Some Java Developer
    * @version: 1.0
*/
public void sleepMethod( ) thows IOException
{
```

```
//...
}
```

You execute the javadoc utility program, specifying one or more source files to parse. The javadoc utility outputs HTML files containing documentation for the parsed source files. This documentation can then be viewed using a Web browser.

Data Types

Java divides data types into two distinct categories: primitive types and reference types. Java has no struct or union types—these are replaced by classes. More important to C++ programmers, *Java has no pointers*. All nonprimitive types are passed by reference; Java takes care of the garbage collection (cleaning up memory) for you.

Primitives Data Types

The eight primitive data types supported by Java are byte, boolean, char, short, int, long, float, and double. Table 22.1 lists the primitive data types and their respective sizes.

TABLE 22.1. JAVA DATA TYPES AND THEIR SIZES

Type	Size
byte	1 byte (signed 8-bit)
boolean	1 byte (signed 8-bit)
char	2 bytes Unicode (signed 16-bit Unicode)
short	2 bytes (signed 16-bit integer)
int	4 bytes (signed 32-bit integer)
long	8 bytes (signed 64-bit integer)
float	4 bytes (signed 32-bit integer)
double	8 bytes (signed 64-bit integer)

Each Java primitive data type is classified into one of two categories, either *numeric* or *Boolean*. The numeric category consists of the integral and floating-point types byte, short, int, long, char, float, and double. The Boolean category, of course, consists solely of the boolean data type. char is a special primitive type for character representation. Each Java data type maintains its size for every platform supported. This helps to maintain Java's platform independence. Note that Java does not support unsigned types.

The data types listed in Table 22.1 are considered native data types. Java also offers class types, specifically Integer, Long, and Character (note the capitalization). The native

types are smaller and more efficient than the class types, but are passed into and out of
methods by value rather than by reference.

The `char` Data Type

A character in Java is represented using two bytes and employs the international Unicode
scheme. Java therefore allows you to represent most of the international character sets.
Although the char data type provides support for various international character sets, you
cannot simply convert and display characters from, say, English to Japanese. The support
for Unicode must also be provided by the operating system.

The `boolean` Data Type

The boolean data type supported by Java is a true Boolean, not just an integral type. The
only two values that can be stored to and retrieved from a boolean are true and false.
The result of a conditional expression *must* be Boolean and not integral. The following
code snippet shows legal and illegal uses of the boolean type:

```
boolean result = false ;    // okay, default is false
int value = result ;        // wrong! Java doesn't allow this.
value = 1 ;                 // okay
result = value ;           // sorry, can't do this either!
```

You cannot coerce the conversion using an explicit cast, as in this example:

```
result = (boolean)value ;   // this will not work either.
```

The `byte` Data Type

Java's byte data type is comparable to the C++ char data type, but is not a direct
replacement. The Java byte is stored as an 8-bit signed integer and maintains a range of
values from –128 through 127. Some C++ programmers new to Java want to use an array
of byte to simulate C++ (and C) strings. Java does not support this use of byte; the Java
library provides a String class for this purpose.

Reference Data Types

The three types of references are class, interface, and array. A *reference* in Java is very
similar to a reference in C++: It is a variable that is bound to some object other than
itself.

Let's look at an example in C++:

```
int value = 5 ;
int & rv = value ;
```

In this example, rv actually refers to value. You can access the contents to which rv
refers, namely the contents of value.

Something similar occurs in Java. The following is an example of a reference in Java. (Some Java programmers refer to references as *handles*.)

```
String  str = new String( ) ;
System.out.println( "str is: " + str.length() + " characters long.");
```

In C++, the new operator returns a pointer. In Java, the new operator returns a *reference* to the object on the heap—and this is the only access you ever have to that object. You do not have to worry about freeing the memory—Java takes care of that for you. Also, this is the only way to create an object in Java; all objects are dynamically allocated, and you always use the reference to the object, rather than the object itself.

Operators

All the usual arithmetic, relational, and conditional operators are available in C++ are also found in Java. The + operator, in addition to providing arithmetic operations, is used for string concatenation.

You'll be happy to discover that the bitwise operators are also available. Java adds a new one to the mix: the (unsigned) *triple-right-shift*. The triple-right-shift, >>>, is a logical operator used to shift the bits of an integral value to the right. The supplied operand determines the number of bits to shift. When shifting the bits, zeros are inserted on the left side. The following example shows how to divide a number by 2 using the triple-right-shift operator:

```
import java.io.* ;
public class Test
{
    public static void main( String args[] )
    {
        int anInt = 10 ;
        System.out.println( "anInt before is:" + anInt ) ;
        anInt = anInt >>> 1 ;
        System.out.println( "anInt after  is:" + anInt ) ;
    }
}
```

The output from this application is shown here:

```
anInt before is: 10
anInt after  is: 5
```

In addition, all the C++ assignment operators are included in Java. And to be consistent, there exists the *triple-right-shift assignment* operator, >>>=. The following sample demonstrates its use:

```
import java.io.* ;
public class Test
{
    public static void main( String args[] )
    {
        int anInt = 10 ;
        System.out.println( "anInt before is:" + anInt ) ;
        anInt >>>= 1 ;
        System.out.println( "anInt after  is:" + anInt ) ;
    }
}
```

The output is as follows:

```
anInt before is: 10
anInt after  is: 5
```

Overloading arithmetic operators is not allowed in Java. Operator overloading can lead to nonsensical code if improperly implemented. There is one exception that the Java compiler will allow, and that is with the String class. The String class overloads the plus + operator for string concatenation. You do have the ability to simulate operator overloading using member functions to represent arithmetic operators.

Control Flow Statements

All the statements used to control the flow of a C++ application are also provided for in Java. For decision making, you have the if-else and switch-case statements; for looping, you have for, while, and do-while; for exception handling, there is try-catch-finally and throw; and finally, in the miscellaneous category, you have break, continue, label:, and return. Exception handling is discussed later in this chapter.

The keyword goto is reserved, but is not supported by the Java language. You should also be aware that the result of a control flow expression must be Boolean.

Differences Between C++ and Java

Now that we have briefly summarized some of the similarities between Java and C++, let's move on to some of the differences between the two languages.

Memory Management

The Java garbage collector automatically reclaims memory allocated for an object once all references to that object have been released. Take note that *all* references to an object must be redirected. When the garbage collector runs, it searches out all objects that are no longer being referred to and reclaims the memory.

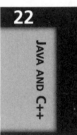

No Pointers

There are no pointers in Java. Because of this, some esoteric techniques are difficult, but programming without pointers with the built-in garbage collection of Java generally proves to be quicker and more robust than having to handle the memory management problems involved in using pointers in C++.

No Preprocessor

Java does not use `include` files, `#define` directives, or `typedefs` and so has no preprocessor.

No Destructor

Java uses the facilities of a garbage collector to reclaim memory consumed by objects that are no longer referenced. Although Java offers the `new` keyword to allocate objects at runtime, there is no corresponding `delete` keyword as is found in C++. Quite simply, all you need to do in Java is allocate an object with `new`; you do not have to worry about explicitly destroying the object.

Java does offer the `finalize()` method, but `finalize()` is not quite the same as a destructor. The garbage collector will call the `finalize()` method for an object that has been determined to be garbage (no longer required). You will never know when `finalize()` will run; that is not under your direct control.

Any resources managed by an object should be released at the point that object goes out of scope. If a class owns resources that will have to be released, you should define a member function to act as a destructor. You could call this member function `cleanup()` or some such name. This is rarely needed as the built-in garbage collection should be sufficient in most cases.

You should also get in the habit of setting a reference to an object to `NULL` when you are done with the object. This gives a hint to the garbage collector that you are finished with that particular object. This, of course, does not mean that the garbage collector will run and reclaim the object; there may be other references lingering about that refer to the same object. The following example demonstrates our intention of releasing some object:

```
InterestingObject yoohoo = new InterestingObject( ) ;
yoohoo.yodel( ) ;
yoohoo.cleanup( ) ;
yoohoo = null ;
```

You should be in the habit of performing this "closure" when working with objects. Doing so assists the garbage collector in reclaiming memory as quickly and efficiently as possible.

Access Specifiers

An *access specifier* allows you to control the visibility of member functions and attributes. Java offers the same access keywords C++ does, but with a twist: They are part of the declaration syntax. In other words, you explicitly specify the visibility of each individual class and class member. In C++, you specify access to members with block scope. In Java, you end up typing more, but you have finer control over the visibility (and placement) of individual members. To clarify access control, the following example demonstrates how visibility is specified in C++.

```
class Goofy
{
    public:
        Goofy ( ) ;
        ~Goofy( ) ;
        int getValue( ) ;
    protected:
        int negotiateValue( const int valueIn );
    private:
        bool verifyValue( const int valueIn ) ;
        int value ;
} ;
```

To contrast the preceding C++ example, here is the same declaration in Java:

```
public class Goofy
{
    public Goofy( ) { /* ... */ }
    public int getValue( ) { return value ; }
    protected int negotiateValue( int valueIn ) { return value ; }
    private boolean verifyValue( int valueIn ) { return true ; }
    private int value ;
    // … and so on and so forth
}
```

If you do not explicitly specify access, the member defaults to *package*. Package access specifies that the member is accessible to other classes within the same package.

> **NOTE**
>
> In version 1.0 of Java, there was a fifth access specifier: `private protected`. This specifier has been dropped from versions of Java after 1.0.

In addition to specifying access to each individual member, access is also specified for the class. There is no semicolon after the class's closing brace. In Java, member functions are always defined in the class declaration. Take note: This does not mean that Java will produce inline member functions.

Method Parameters

Another distinction between Java and C++ is that the `const` keyword is not applied to method parameters. The `const` keyword (or some variation of it) is not required in Java because Java uses pass-by-value for primitive type arguments to a method. This means that you cannot change the value of the object argument. Within the member function, you operate on a *copy* of the original object, not the actual object referred to by the argument. In Java, if you pass an object (nonprimitive), a reference is passed, not the object itself. You cannot change the reference passed in, but you can access the actual object's public methods and instance variables. The example in Listing 22.1 should clarify this for you.

LISTING 22.1. PASSING A PRIMITIVE PARAMETER IN JAVA

```java
import java.io.* ;
public class Goofy
{
    public Goofy( ) { /* ... */ }
    public void doubleArg( int value ) { value *= 2 ; }

    static public void main( String arg[] )
    {
        int theValue = 5 ;
        System.out.println("1. theValue is: " + theValue ) ;
        Goofy g = new Goofy( ) ;
        g.doubleArg( theValue ) ;
        System.out.println("2. theValue is: " + theValue ) ;
    }
}
```

The output of this application is as follows:

```
1. theValue is: 5
2. theValue is: 5
```

This code demonstrates that the member function `doubleArg()` merely gets a copy of, not a reference to, the original object `theValue`. If you pass a reference to the member function, you actually operate on the referenced-to object. The example in Listing 22.2 is a modification of the example in Listing 22.1 and demonstrates passing an object (nonprimitive).

LISTING 22.2. PASSING AN OBJECT PARAMETER IN JAVA

```java
import java.io.* ;
public class Int
{ // this class will need to be in it's own file
    public Int() { /* ... */ }
    public int intValue = 5 ;
}
public class Goofy
{
    public Goofy( ) { /* ... */ }
    public void doubleArg( Int value ) { value.intValue *= 2 ; }

    static public void main( String arg[] )
    {
        Int theValue = new Int( ) ;

        System.out.println("1. theValue is: " + theValue.intValue ) ;
        Goofy g = new Goofy( ) ;
        g.doubleArg( theValue ) ;
        System.out.println("2. theValue is: " + theValue.intValue ) ;
    }
}
```

The output from this application is shown here:

```
1. theValue is: 5
2. theValue is: 10
```

One last note in closing: Arrays are first-class objects in Java. In the previous example, if theValue was an array of int, then the member function doubleArg() would change the actual passed-to argument.

External Functions

In Java, every function *must* be a member of a class. There are no global functions.

Enumerations

In C++, the enum keyword is available to specify an entity that contains enumerated values. Java does not offer the enum keyword, but you can simulate enum by creating a class that only contains instance variables that are static final. By declaring the instance variables as static final, you are, in effect, defining the variables as constant. The following example demonstrates a simulated enum in Java:

```java
public class DrawingColor
{
    public static final int red = 1;
    public static final int yellow = 2;
```

```
    public static final int green  = 3;
}
//...
pen.color( DrawingColor.red ) ;
//...
```

There is a drawback to the C++ (and C) enum: Each member of an enum must have a unique name with respect to other enums and variables. Consider the previous example's equivalent declaration in C++. If you had an additional enum named WindowColor that contained member variables named red, yellow, and green, you would have a name clash. This sort of problem does not happen in Java.

Strings

In Java, there is no equivalent representation of a string as there is in C++. Strings in C++, of course, are represented as an array of char (terminated by the NULL character). In Java, the immutable String object is available to represent strings and is considered a first-class object. In Java, you can create quoted (literal) strings as you can in C++, but the compiler actually converts this representation to a String object. For example:

```
String str = "This is a quoted string" ;
```

The Java compiler creates a String object for the quoted string and then assigns it to str. String is immutable; you cannot modify the contents of a String object. If you require a mutable string, Java offers the StringBuffer class.

Although Java does not offer operator overloading, the String class does offer the + operator for the concatenation of Strings. Remember that String objects are immutable, so you cannot concatenate a String onto another String; the result of the concatenation must be a new String. The String class also offers the member function length() to obtain the length of a String object.

Arrays

Arrays in Java are considered first-class objects. You access the elements of a Java array in the same way you access the elements of a C++ array: You use array indexing. Java offers runtime array-bounds checking. Java arrays contain an instance variable named length that holds the number of elements (depending on the context) of the named array. The placement of the brackets can be on the left or right side of the array name.

In Java, you cannot specify the array dimension at the point of declaration as you can in C++. Arrays in Java must be allocated using new. Let's look at an example of declaring and using a Java array:

```
#1: int array1[]  ; // brackets on right
#2: int [] array2 ; // brackets on left, both are okay
#3: int array3[10] ; // ERROR, can't specify dimension!
#4: Object [] array3 = new Object[10] ;
#5: array1 = new int[10] ;
#6: array2 = new int[10] ;
#7: array1[1] = 5 ;
#8: array1[12] = 5 ; // ERROR, beyond boundaries
#9: for( int i = 0; i < array1.length; i++ )
#10:        array1[i] = i ;
```

The first two statements merely declare a reference to an int array; we have not yet defined the dimension of the two arrays. The third line produces a compile-time error. Line 4 allocates an array of 10 Objects, and array3 is the named reference to those objects. Lines 5 and 6 allocate 10 ints and bind them to the array names. An assignment happens on line 7: The value 5 is assigned to the second element of array1. Line 8 is interesting because, although the compiler allows the statement, you get a runtime diagnostic: java.lang.ArrayIndexOutOfBoundsException. Finally, line 9 uses the length member variable of array1 to determine the upper bound.

Object-Oriented Features of Java

Now that we have the basic similarities and differences between Java and C++ out of the way, let us begin to examine the more advanced features of the Java language. Among other topics, we will explore features such as inheritance, encapsulation, abstract base classes, and memory management. Let us begin by discussing the basic object-oriented element of Java, the class.

Classes

A class in Java maintains the same concept and functionality of a C++ class. A class in Java contains declarations—for example, variables and member functions. Let's begin with a simple example:

```
public class Goofy
{
    public Goofy() { /* ... */ }
    private bool interpret( ) { return true ; }
    public int value ;
    int noAccess ;
}
```

Three quick observations to note in this example: An access specifier is applied to the class and members of the class, functions are defined within the declaration of the class, and there is no trailing semicolon following the class's closing brace.

As mentioned previously, the four access specifiers available are `public`, `protected`, `private`, and `package`. Actually, you do not explicitly use `package`, but it is the default access if you do not specify one. A `package` in Java provides the same basic functionality as namespaces provide in C++.

The `static` keyword can be applied to a member of a class. The effect is the same as when `static` is used in C++. If the member is a class variable, there will be only one occurrence of the variable for all instances of the class, even if the number of class instances is zero. Member variables declared with the `transient` keyword applied are not subject to serialization. That is, transient variables cannot be stored to disk or to a database.

Class (static) and instance variables can be declared `final`. You use `final` to obtain the same effect as you get with `const` in C++. A `final` variable must be initialized at the point of declaration. You cannot change the value of a `final` variable. If the `final` variable is a reference to an object, you can operate on the object itself, but you cannot change the reference to refer to another object. The same holds true for `final` arrays because arrays are considered objects in Java.

Interface Classes

Java does not provide multiple inheritance, but it does provide *interfaces*, and a class can implement one or more interfaces. An interface defines an abstraction that can be implemented by other classes. This is similar to abstract data types in C++.

In an interface class, member functions are declared but are not defined, and all the instance variables in the interface are considered final. Like an abstract data type, you cannot instantiate an interface; you must create a new class that implements the interface.

The implementing class defines the methods declared in the interface. Here is a brief example for an `interface` class:

```
public interface Silly
{
    public void smile( long timeSpan ) ;
    public void laugh( ) ;
    public final long HowLong = 5000 ; // constant long
}
```

The previous example declares that `Silly` is an interface class. You cannot instantiate a `Silly` object, as in the following example:

```
// ...
Silly s = new Silly( ) ;
```

You must implement the interface class as in the following example:

```
public class Goofy implements Silly
{
    public void smile( long timeSpan ) { /* ... */ }
    public void laugh( ) { /* ... */ }
}
```

You must remember to implement the member functions found in the interface class. If you forget to implement just one member function, the derived class will also be considered abstract.

Now that `Goofy` has its member functions defined, you can instantiate objects of type `Goofy`. In addition, objects of type `Goofy` can access (read-only) the constant `HowLong`. Let's examine a fully functional application.

```
public class Goofy implements Silly
{
    public void smile( long timeSpan ) { /* ... */ }
    public void laugh( ) { /* ... */ }

    public static void main( String args[] )
    {
        Goofy g = new Goofy( ) ;
        g.smile( g.HowLong ) ;
    }
}
```

Use the `interface` class when you want to express a design as a class, but not provide an implementation for it.

Abstract Classes

Java also offers the `abstract` keyword to denote a class that presents an abstract interface. A class declared with the `abstract` keyword cannot be instantiated. To declare a class as abstract, you apply the `abstract` keyword before the `class` keyword, as in the following example:

```
abstract class Funny
{
    public void smile( long timeSpan ) { /* ... */ }
    abstract void laugh( ) ;
    public final long HowLong = 5000 ; // constant long
}
```

Within the abstract class, you can provide default implementations for the member functions of the class. This is in contrast to an `interface` class; you cannot provide a body for a member function declared within an `interface` class. If you inherit from an abstract class, it is not necessary for you to implement the member functions that are defined within the abstract class. You must, however, define any member functions declared with the `abstract` keyword. As with an `interface` class, you can define constant variables within an abstract class. To subclass an abstract class, you use the `extends` keyword. The following code declares `Joke` as a subclass of `Funny`:

```
public class Joke extends Funny
{
    public void laugh( ) { /* ... */ }

    public static void main( String args[] )
    {
        Joke f = new Joke( ) ;
        f.laugh( ) ;
        f.smile( f.HowLong ) ;
    }
}
```

Notice that I did not have to define the member function `smile()`. In the context of class `Joke`, I feel that the implementation of `smile()` within `Funny` is adequate. You can, however, override the member function defined within the abstract class. The following example demonstrates how to override a member function:

```
public class Hilarious extends Funny
{
    public void laugh( ) { /* ... */ }
    public void smile( long timeSpan ) { /* ... */ } // override

    public static void main( String args[] )
    {
        Hilarious f = new Hilarious ( ) ;
        f.laugh( ) ;
        f.smile( f.HowLong ) ;
    }
}
```

In the preceding example, I chose to override the member function `smile()` because I determined that `Funny` does not provide enough laughter for the `Hilarious` class. I know the question you're asking right now: "How can I call the superclass's member function?" Well, the answer lies with the `super` keyword. Here is the member function `smile()` (in `Hilarious`) redefined to call the `smile()` in `Funny`:

```
public void smile( long timeSpan )
{
    super.smile( super.HowLong ) ;
}
```

Notice that the keyword `super` is also applied to the argument `HowLong`. You are not required to do this; I applied the keyword to be explicit.

One difference between an `interface` class and an `abstract` class is that you can only singly inherit from an `abstract` class, whereas you can combine more than one `implement` class. To clarify this, the following example is valid:

```
public class Goofy implements Silly, Wacky
{
    //...
}
```

You can also take this a step further by inheriting from `Funny` and implementing `Silly` and `Wacky`. The following example demonstrates this feat of magic:

```
public class Goofy extends Funny implements Silly, Wacky
{
    //...
}
```

Use `abstract` when you want to express a design as a class (as with interface) and also to include some default functionality. This will provide a template for potential users looking for specific class functionality.

Member Initialization

In Java, member initialization is guaranteed for you. In C++, locally or dynamically allocated objects are not initialized automatically. Class references, if you do not initialize them, are defaulted to NULL. The primitive data types, if they exist for a class, are defaulted to zero. This default initialization also applies to member variables declared as `static` and `final`. Of course, you do have the option of explicitly initializing the instance variables.

Returning to the `Goofy` example, let's see how this is applied:

```
public class Goofy
{
    public void laugh( ) { /* ... */ }
    static final int value = 10 ;
    private boolean notLaughing ;
    private String name ;
}
```

In the preceding example, `value` does not have to be initialized outside the class as is required in C++. This follows the Java rule that everything must exist within a class. The `boolean` instance variable `notLaughing` is defaulted to `false`. The member variable `name` is declared as a reference to a `String` and is initialized to NULL.

The `this` Keyword

Java provides the keyword `this`, just as C++ does. In Java, `this` provides the same functionality as it does in C++: It allows you to access a member of the class with current scope. Note, however, that in Java, this is a *reference* to the object, not a pointer—and it does not have to be dereferenced. The following example shows a use of `this`:

```
public class Goofy
{
    public void laugh( boolean notLaughing )
    {
        this.notLaughing = notLaughing ;
    }
    static final int value = 10 ;
    private boolean notLaughing ;
    private String name ;
}
```

The `this` keyword is primarily used to explicitly identify a class member because of a name ambiguity. In the previous example, the argument `notLaughing` is the same name as an instance variable of the class. The `this` keyword is applied to resolve the member variable.

Constructors

The basic concepts of constructors in C++ also apply to Java. A constructor in Java has the same name as the class in which the constructor is defined. You can name overloaded constructors within a class just as you can in C++. The default constructor restriction found in C++ also applies in Java: If you define any constructor other than the default, you must also define the default constructor. If you do not define any constructor for a class, the compiler will synthesize a default constructor for you.

You have the option of applying an access specifier to a constructor. If you do not specify access, the default `package` is applied. Applying an access specifier allows you to determine the objects that can create instances of the specified class.

You can call a superclass constructor using the `super` keyword. Simply use the keyword `super` and apply any arguments that may be required. This, of course, works only if the superclass has a matching constructor. The following example demonstrates this concept:

```
public class Goofy extends Strange
{
    public void Goofy( )
    {
        super( "GoofBall" ) ; //apply identifying name
    }
    //...
}
```

One thing you have to remember about using super: It must be the first call within a constructor. If you do not explicitly call a base class constructor within a derived class, the default constructor is used to construct the base class portion.

The this keyword can be used (within a constructor) to call other constructors of a class. The syntax is the same as using super to call a base class constructor. As with super, if you use this to call a sibling constructor, this must be the first statement within the constructor. The following is an example of the this constructor call:

```
public class Goofy
{
    public Goofy( String name ) { /* ... */ }
    public Goofy( String name, boolean notLaughing )
    {
        this( name ) ; // let specific constructor do work
        //...
    }
    //...
}
```

Another difference between a Java and C++ constructor is that Java constructors do not have initializer list syntax. Initialization of a class instance variable is performed in one of three ways. You explicitly initialize the variable at the point of its declaration, you explicitly initialize the variable within a constructor's body, or the compiler implicitly initializes the variable for you:

```
public class Strange
{
    Strange( )
    {
        ival3 = 10 ;
    }
    private int ival1 = 10 ; // explicit
    private int ival2 ;      // guaranteed initialization
    private int ival3 ;      // done in constructor
}
```

The finalize() Method

Java offers a class method named finalize(). This method roughly correlates to a C++ destructor, except that finalize() is not as predictable as a C++ destructor. In C++, whenever the destructor is invoked, you know that the object will be destroyed and its memory will be reclaimed. You know that that will happen when the destructor is called, implicitly or explicitly. With Java, you never know when the finalize() method is called. The finalize() method is invoked when the garbage collector gets around to reclaiming the object. I said "gets around to"—that could mean "right now" or it could mean "a little later." In some programmatic instances, "a little later" is the wrong time.

It is not a good idea to release resources within the `finalize()` method because you can never be sure when `finalize()` will be called. If you feel that it is important to release resources that an object owns, you should implement a cleanup function. At the point you are finished with an object, simply call your cleanup function and then set the object to NULL. Setting the object reference to NULL gives a hint to the garbage collector that you are finished with this particular object. I say *hint* because the garbage collector is not obliged to collect the object at that point in time. You must always remember this fact. The following example demonstrates the idea of cleaning up an object after use.

```
Goofy g = new Goofy( ) ;
g.doSomething( ) ;
g.cleanup( ) ;
g = null ;
```

If you do define a `finalize()` method for your class, you must also be sure to call the `finalize()` method of the base class. It is unfortunate that Java does not take care of this for you, as C++ does with its destructors. What happens if you do not call the base class `finalize()` method? Quite simply, it is never called.

If your application gets to the point of exiting, the garbage collector will go around and collect any objects that have not been reclaimed.

Inheritance

At the core of Java inheritance is a singly rooted hierarchy. All classes within a Java hierarchy inherit from the root class `Object`. If you do not explicitly state a base class, your class is implicitly derived from `Object`.

Rather than using a colon as in C++, in Java you use the keyword `extends`.

There is no need to designate a specifier for inheritance in Java because there is no such thing as private inheritance. The following example shows how you declare a class to be derived from some other class:

```
public class Strange
{
    public void memberF( )
    //...
}
public class Goofy extends Strange
{
    private void memberF( ) // sorry, can't change access
    //...
}
```

In C++, member functions are dynamically invoked at runtime only if the `virtual` keyword has been applied to them. In Java, all member functions are dynamically dispatched at runtime. The `final` keyword can be applied to a member function to prevent that member function from being overridden in a subsequent derived class. In an earlier section in this chapter, I mentioned that the Java compiler does not necessarily inline functions. Applying the `final` keyword to a member function may be a case in which the compiler does inline a function. If nothing else, a `final` member function may be statically bound. The compiler is not obligated to honor the `final` hint; it is only a suggestion.

In Java, a base class reference can be used to refer to some derived class object. The operator `instanceof` can then be used to check whether some reference refers to some derived class object. The example that follows shows how to use `instanceof`:

```
Joke aJoke = new Joke( ) ;
Laughter funny = aJoke ;
//...
if( funny instanceof Joke )
{
    Joke j = (Joke)funny ;
    //...
}
```

An exception is generated at runtime for any illegal cast. The following shows a potential exception waiting to happen:

```
Window win = new Window( … ) ;
Joke j = (Joke)win ;
```

The rules for member inheritance are straightforward. Any instance variables declared in a superclass that are not redefined in the subclass are accessible by the subclass. For the subclass to access the instance variable, that instance variable must not be `private` in the superclass. Any member function declared in a superclass that is not overridden in the subclass is accessible by the subclass, provided that access for the base member function is not `private`.

Declaring an instance variable with the same name in a subclass hides the instance variable found in the superclass. The same applies to member functions. In a subclass, you can only call a member function in the immediate superclass.

You use the `super` keyword to call a member function of the superclass. Constructors, because they are not truly members of a class, cannot be inherited by a derived class. If a constructor is explicitly called in a subclass, it must be called using the `super` keyword. A constructor, if explicitly called within the same class as another constructor, must be invoked using the `this` keyword. The following example illustrates these rules:

```
public class Goofy
{
    Goofy( ) { /* ... */ }
```

```
    public  void publicFunc( ) { /* ... */ }
    private void privateFunc( ) { /* ... */ }
    public  int publicValue ;
    private int privateValue ;
}
public class Silly extends Goofy
{
    Silly( )
    {
        super( ) ;
    }
    Silly( String name )
    {
    }
    Silly( String name, int value )
    {
        this( name ) ;
    }
    public void publicFunc( )
    {
        super.publicFunc( ) ;
        //...
    }
    public  int publicValue ;
}
```

The member function `publicFunc()` in `Goofy` is overridden in the class `Silly`. The instance variable `publicValue` in `Silly` hides the instance variable with the same name in `Goofy`. The constructor within `Silly` that has two arguments (a `String` and an `int`) calls the constructor within `Silly` that has a single `String` argument. The default constructor in `Silly` calls the default constructor in the base class `Goofy`. You should remember that if you use either `super` or `this` to call a constructor or a superclass member function, it must be the first statement within the constructor or member function.

Multiple Inheritance

Java does not have multiple inheritance, but you can simulate multiple inheritance in Java by using interfaces. The following example shows a derived class that implements multiple interfaces:

```
interface Setup
{
    public void delivery( String text ) ;
    //...
}
interface  PunchLine
{
    public void pause( ) ;
```

```
//...
    public long timeToHesitate = 2000 ;
}
public class Joke implements Setup, PunchLine
{
    Joke( ) { /* ... */ }
    public void delivery( String text ) { /* ... */ }
    public void pause( ) { /* ... */ }
    //...
}
```

You can also extend a single base class, in addition to implementing from multiple inter-faces, as the following example shows:

```
public class Joke extends Laughter implements Setup, PunchLine
{
    Joke( ) { /* ... */ }
    public void delivery( String text ) { /* ... */ }
    public void pause( ) { /* ... */ }
    //...
}
```

Exception Handling

The Java exception handling mechanism is very similar to the one found in C++. Java adds a new keyword to the exception-handling arsenal: `finally`. The `finally` block is always executed after a `try` and all `catch` blocks have executed. Any object that is thrown in Java must be inherited from `Throwable`. Let's look at an example:

```
//...
public void func( ) throws IOException
{
    ImportantObject iObj = new ImportantResource( );
    try {
        iObj.method( ) ;
    }
    catch( ImportantObjectException e)  {
        // do any handling required
    }
    catch( Throwable e)  {
        // handle Throwable exception
    }
    finally  {
        iObj.cleanup( ) ; // my defined cleanup method
    }
}
```

If an exception is thrown within the `try` block, control is transferred to the appropriate `catch` block. After the `catch` statements have executed, control is then transferred to the `finally` block. This provides a mechanism to ensure a forceful cleanup; you can be assured that control will eventually enter the `finally` block.

One nice feature of Java exception handling is that a check is made at compile time for proper exception specifications. In C++, you do not discover improper exception usage until runtime. In addition, in Java, any derived class member functions that override a base class function must conform to the exception specifications of the base member function.

In C++, the ellipsis is used with a `catch` to denote a "catch any" clause. The following example demonstrates this concept:

```
try {
    //...
}
catch( ... ) {
    // handle all cases
}
```

In Java, you catch a `Throwable` object, as in the following example:

```
try {
    //...
}
catch( Throwable e )
//...
```

The `catch(Throwable)` can be used as a "catch all" (no pun intended).

Summary

This chapter provides an overview of the similarities and differences between C++ and Java, which are recapped here.

Java supports both the block and single-line comment style of C++. Java provides an additional benefit using the documenting comment. Using the `javadoc` utility program, you can create programmer documentation from the source code that has been documented with special tokenized keywords.

Java provides the primitive data types `byte`, `boolean`, `char`, `short`, `int`, `long`, `float`, and `double`. The size of these data types is consistent across all platforms that support Java. Java does not support `struct` or `union`; the `class` type replaces these types. Java does not have pointers, but does have reference types as does C++. Unlike C++, a reference in Java can be rebound to another object.

Java supports all the relational, arithmetic, and conditional operators as does C++, but adds the triple-right-shift operator >>>. All the assignment operators found in C++ are supported in Java; Java also adds the triple-right-shift assignment operator >>>=.

Member overloading in supported in Java, but operator overloading is not as it is in C++. The exception to this rule is the Java String class; the plus + operator is overloaded to support concatenation of Strings.

All flow-control statements and loops found in C++ are equally supported in Java. The keyword goto is reserved in Java, but is not currently supported.

Java uses the facilities of a garbage collector to automatically reclaim unused (or unreferenced) memory. Java does not have destructors as does C++. Java does support the new keyword for the creation of objects. The finalize() method is called by the garbage collector for objects that are being reclaimed; however, you never know when the garbage collector will call the finalize() method.

Java does not use include files, #define directives, or typedefs, so there is no pre-processor.

The access specifiers public, protected, and private are provided in Java as they are in C++. Java adds a default specifier, package, if no access is specified. The access specifier keywords are used when declaring a class and members of a class.

Primitive data types are passed by value in Java. Objects in Java are passed by reference.

Java does not support external (global) functions as does C++. All functions must be a member of some class in Java.

Java does not have the concept of enum as does C++, but the logic can be simulated using member variables as public static final.

The String object in Java is a first-class object and is immutable (that is, you cannot alter the contents). Java offers the StringBuffer class if you need to alter the contents of a string.

Arrays in Java are also first-class objects and include a length member that holds the number of elements in the array. Java also offers runtime array-bounds checking. Java supports class as does C++. A class in Java can have an access specifier applied to limit its accessibility. The static keyword, when applied to a member variable, has the same meaning in Java as it does in C++. The final keyword applied to a class variable has the same effect as const in C++.

Java does not support multiple inheritance, but it does provide implementation of multiple interfaces; an interface defines an abstraction, similar to abstract data types in

C++. Java also has the abstract keyword that is used to define a class that represents an abstract interface. The difference between interface and abstract is that within an interface class, you can provide default functionality for the member functions. Also, you can only singly inherit from an abstract class. Java uses a singly rooted inheritance hierarchy; the root class is called Object.

Member initialization is guaranteed in Java. Primitive data are defaulted to zero and references are defaulted to NULL.

The this keyword is supported as it is in C++, but in Java, this is a reference, not a pointer.

A constructor in Java has the same name as the class name and can be overloaded as it can be in C++. You can call the superclass constructor using the super keyword (it must be the first call). The this keyword can be used to call other constructors within a class; it must be the first call within a constructor.

The finalize() method is called by the garbage collector when an object is being reclaimed. The finalize() method is similar to a C++ destructor. You can never be sure when the finalize() method will be called.

Exception handling in Java is similar to the C++ mechanism. Java adds the finally keyword that defines a block of code that will always be executed after a try and all catch blocks have executed.

22

JAVA AND C++

INDEX

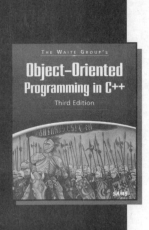

The Waite Group's Object-Oriented Programming in C++, Third Edition

This classic tutorial presents the sophisticated new features of the most current ANSI/ISO C++ standard as they apply to object-oriented programming. Learn the concepts of object-oriented programming, why they exist, and how to utilize them to create sophisticated and efficient object-oriented applications. *The Waite Group's Object-Oriented Programming in C++, Third Edition* assumes no C programming experience, but does expect the reader to be familiar with basic programming concepts. It is no longer enough to understand the syntax and features of the language. Programmers must also be familiar with how these features are put to use. Get up to speed quickly on the emerging new concepts of object-oriented design patterns (ways to handle recurrent problems), CRC modeling (deriving the necessary C++ classes starting from a real-world situation), and the new Universal Modeling Language (UML), which provides a systematic way to diagram the relationship between classes. Object-oriented programming is presented through the use of practical task-oriented examples and figures that help conceptualize and illustrate techniques and approaches, and questions and exercises to reinforce learning concepts. This book has been used widely in academic settings and provides special guidance to instructors on how to present and enhance object-oriented programming in C++ concepts and techniques.

- The third edition of *The Waite Group's Object-Oriented Programming in C++, Third Edition* will continue to build on the successful past performance of previous editions

- Go from simple programming examples straight to full-fledged object-oriented applications with quick real-world examples, conceptual illustrations, questions, and exercises

$34.99 U.S./$32.49 CAN   *1-57169-160-X*   *Sams*

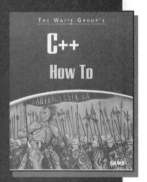

The Waite Group's C++ How-To

The Waite Group's C++ How-To presents a rich diversity of examples and techniques for pushing C++ to its limits and beyond. You locate information by task or function and then walk through a series of How-Tos to find the solution. No current C++ reference tool on the market offers this unique step-by-step approach and organization of C++ topics and categories. Receive answers to questions like "how do I use the C++ ASM keyword," "how do I write a simple Tee command," and "how do I overload the Array operator"? This book provides C++ programming solutions for categories and concepts, such as types and declarations, pointers, arrays and structures, expressions and statements, functions, namespaces and exceptions, source files and programs, classes, operator overloading, derived classes, templates, exception handling, class hierarchies, the Standard Template Library, and other programming concepts. Each How-To is graded by complexity level, with information on additional uses and enhancements to fit your needs exactly.

- The all-new definitive C++ problem-solving resource! Programmers can quickly and efficiently find specific solutions to real-world problems in *The Waite Group's C++ How-To*

- The quick, problem-answer design provides C++ programmers with all the tools they need to solve complex and everyday problems quickly

- Because every concept and example is graded by complexity, you can easily find practical information at you level, without having to wade through hundreds of pages of information you don't need

$39.99 U.S./$57.95 CAN   *1-57169-159-6*   *Sams*

Sams Teach Yourself C++ in 21 Days, Second Edition

Sams Teach Yourself C++ in 21 Days, Second Edition is a hands-on guide to learning object-oriented programming design and analysis. You'll gain a thorough understanding of all basic concepts, including program flow, memory management, and compiling and debugging. To better facilitate retention and promote learning, the book is structured in the form of a 21-day self-paced workshop. This book breaks down the concepts into easy-to-understand chapters, using many listings to illustrate not just code, but how to improve upon code. It's fully revised, updated, and ANSI-compliant.

- Teaches the basics of object-oriented programming with C++
- Completely revised to ANSI standards
- Can be used with any of the C++ compilers on the market

$29.99 U.S./ $42.95 CAN   *0-672-31070-8*   *Sams*

Add to Your C++ Library Today with the Best Books for Programming, Operating Systems, and New Technologies

To order, visit our Web site at www.mcp.com or fax us at

1-800-835-3202

ISBN	Quantity	Description of Item	Unit Cost	Total Cost
0-7897-1667-4		Using C++	$29.99	
0-672-31239-5		C++ Unleashed	$39.99	
1-57169-160-X		The Waite Group's Object-Oriented Programming in C++, 3E	$34.99	
1-57169-159-6		The Waite Group's C++ How-To	$39.99	
		Shipping and Handling: See information below.		
		TOTAL		

Shipping and Handling

Standard	$5.00
2nd Day	$10.00
Next Day	$17.50
International	$40.00

201 W. 103rd Street, Indianapolis, Indiana 46290   1-800-835-3202 — FAX

Book ISBN 0-672-31239-5

What's on the Disc

The companion CD-ROM contains all of the authors' source code and samples from the book and some third-party software products.

Windows NT 3.5.1 Installation Instructions

1. Insert the CD-ROM disc into your CD-ROM drive.
2. From File Manager or Program Manager, choose Run from the File menu.
3. Type `<drive>\START.EXE` and press Enter, where `<drive>` corresponds to the drive letter of your CD-ROM. For example, if your CD-ROM is drive D:, type `D:\START.EXE` and press Enter.
4. Follow the onscreen instructions to finish the installation.

Windows 95, Windows 98, and Windows NT 4 Installation Instructions

1. Insert the CD-ROM disc into your CD-ROM drive.
2. From the desktop, double-click the My Computer icon.
3. Double-click the icon representing your CD-ROM drive.
4. Double-click the START.EXE icon to run the installation program.
5. Follow the onscreen instructions to finish the installation.

> **NOTE**
>
> If Windows 95, Windows 98, or Windows NT 4 is installed on your computer, and you have the AutoPlay feature enabled, the START.EXE program starts automatically whenever you insert the disc into your CD-ROM drive.

UNIX Installation Instructions

Because there are many flavors of UNIX, we will not attempt to provide specific instructions for your version. Your UNIX administrator or the man pages will be your best source of information if you need help on a particular command in these instructions.

> **NOTE**
>
> Before mounting a CD-ROM on `<mountpoint>`, please make sure that `<mountpoint>` exists, or the mount command will fail. If your operating system is running a volume manager, mounting will occur automatically.

To install the book's source code, follow these steps:

1. Insert the CD-ROM disc into your CD-ROM drive.
2. Mount the CD-ROM onto your mount point. Typically, this is done by typing

```
mount [options] /dev/cdrom /<mountpoint>
```

3. Create a directory on your local file system, such as cppunl, by typing

```
mkdir /cppunl
```

4. Move into this directory by typing

```
cd /cppunl
```

5. Now you are ready to copy the source code. Copy all of the source code from the CD-ROM to your local file system by typing

```
cp -r /<mountpoint>/source/* .
```